The
American
Democracy

FIFTH EDITION

The American Democracy

★ ★ ★

Thomas E. Patterson

Bradlee Professor of Government and the Press
John F. Kennedy School of Government
Harvard University

Boston   Burr Ridge, IL   Dubuque, IA   Madison, WI   New York   San Francisco   St. Louis
Bangkok   Bogotá   Caracas   Kuala Lumpur   Lisbon   London   Madrid   Mexico City
Milan   Montreal   New Delhi   Santiago   Seoul   Singapore   Sydney   Taipei   Toronto

McGraw-Hill Higher Education

*A Division of The **McGraw-Hill** Companies*

THE AMERICAN DEMOCRACY, FIFTH EDITION

Published by McGraw-Hill, an imprint of The McGraw-Hill Companies, Inc., 1221 Avenue of the Americas, New York, NY 10020. Copyright © 2001, 1999 by The McGraw-Hill Companies, Inc. All rights reserved. Previous editions © 1997, 1996, 1994, 1993, 1990 by Thomas E. Patterson. All rights reserved. No part of this publication may be reproduced or distributed in any form or by any means, or stored in a database or retrieval system, without the prior written consent of The McGraw-Hill Companies, Inc., including, but not limited to, in any network or other electronic storage or transmission, or broadcast for distance learning.

Some ancillaries, including electronic and print components, may not be available to customers outside the United States.

This book is printed on acid-free paper.

2 3 4 5 6 7 8 9 0 DOW/DOW 0 9 8 7 6 5 4 3 2 1

ISBN 0–07–248501–9

Vice president and editor-in-chief: *Thalia Dorwick*
Editorial director: *Jane E. Vaicunas*
Sponsoring editor: *Monica Eckman*
Marketing manager: *Janise A. Fry*
Senior project manager: *Marilyn Rothenberger*
Media technology producer: *Lance Gerhart*
Production supervisor: *Enboge Chong*
Coordinator of freelance design: *Michelle D. Whitaker*
Freelance cover designer: *Jamie A. O'Neal*
Cover image: © *William S. Helsel/Tony Stone Images; Backcover image: EyeWire, Inc.*
Senior photo research coordinator: *Carrie K. Burger*
Photo research: *Feldman & Associates, Inc.*
Supplement producer: *Brenda A. Ernzen*
Compositor: *GAC—Indianapolis*
Typeface: *10/12 Palatino*
Printer: *R. R. Donnelley & Sons Company/Willard, OH*

The credits section for this book begins on page C-1 and is considered an extension of the copyright page.

Library of Congress Cataloging-in-Publication Data

Patterson, Thomas E.
    The American democracy / Thomas E. Patterson. — 5th ed.
       p.   cm.
    Includes bibliographical references and index.
    ISBN 0–07–232250–0
    1. United States—Politics and government. I. Title.

JK274 .P358   2001
320.473—dc21   00–032894
                                          CIP

www.mhhe.com

ABOUT THE AUTHOR

*T*homas E. Patterson is Benjamin Bradlee Professor of Government and the Press in the John F. Kennedy School of Government at Harvard University. He was previously a distinguished professor of political science in the Maxwell School of Citizenship at Syracuse University. Raised in a small Minnesota town near the Iowa and South Dakota borders, he was educated at South Dakota State University and the University of Minnesota, where he received his Ph.D. in 1971.

He is the author of six books and dozens of articles, which focus primarily on the media and elections. His book, *Out of Order* (1994), received national attention when President Clinton said every politician and journalist should be required to read it. An earlier book, *The Mass Media Election* (1980), received a *Choice* award as Outstanding Academic Book, 1980–1981. Another of Patterson's books, *The Unseeing Eye* (1976), was selected by the American Association for Public Opinion Research as one of the fifty most influential books of the past half century in the field of public opinion.

His current research includes the Vanishing Voter Project—a study of public involvement in the 2000 presidential election campaign. He is also conducting a five-country study of the news media's political role. His work has been funded by major grants from the National Science Foundation, the Markle Foundation, the Smith-Richardson Foundation, the Ford Foundation, and the Pew Charitable Trusts.

TO MY CHILDREN, ALEX AND LEIGH

CONTENTS IN BRIEF

CONTENTS

PART THREE   Governing Institutions   319

PART FOUR   Public Policy   490

18 Economic and Environmental Policy: Contributing to Prosperity   492

19 Welfare and Education Policy: Providing for Personal Security and Need   526

PART FIVE   State and Local Governments   587

APPENDIXES   624

Anyone who writes an introductory American government text faces the challenge of describing and explaining a vast amount of scholarship. One way is to pile fact upon fact and list upon list. It's a common enough approach but it turns politics into a pretty dry subject. Politics doesn't have to be dry, and it certainly doesn't have to be dull. Politics has all the elements of drama and the added feature of affecting the everyday lives of real people.

The late twentieth century has been a period of extraordinary change in America, which has raised new challenges to the practice of government. New people in the millions from Asia and Latin America have joined the American community, bringing with them cultural traditions that have made our society richer and fuller, but also more fragmented and contentious. Traditional institutions, from political parties to families, have weakened dramatically, straining the fabric of our politics but also creating the possibility of adaptive new arrangements. Minorities and women, long denied access to political and economic power, are seeking a fairer share, and sometimes getting it. America's workers and firms have built a highly productive economy but are now facing the risks and opportunities of the global marketplace. The cold war that dominated our attention in foreign policy for decades has been replaced by ethnic rivalries and localized conflicts that raise troubling new issues of world insecurity that, so far, have defied tidy solutions.

Scholars are striving to keep pace with these changes. Never before has scholarship been so closely tied to the real world. If much of what political scientists study is arcane, we have increasingly tried to connect our work and our thinking to the everyday realities of politics. The result is a fuller understanding of how American government operates. I have tried in this book to convey this advancement in knowledge in an accurate and interesting way.

Reaching Out to the Student

This is a narrative-based text. It is the opposite of a text that piles list upon list and divides its material into narrow compartments. A narrative text provides plenty of information, but it is always part of a larger discussion that is wrapped in "story" form.

Research indicates that the narrative style is a superior method for teaching students a "soft" science such as political science. They learn more readily because a narrative makes the subject more readable, more accessible, and more compelling. Studies also indicate that students can read attentively for a longer period of time when a text is narrative in form.

A narrative text weaves together theory, information, and examples in order to bring out key facts and ideas. The goal is to draw the students into the subject, give them a contextual understanding of major concepts and issues, and encourage them to think about the implications for themselves and society. To quicken this process, I begin each chapter by telling a story that addresses a basic issue. The chapter on civil liberties, for example, begins with the case of the Creighton family, whose home was raided in the middle of the night by gun-toting FBI agents who suspected they were harboring a relative who was suspected of bank robbery. The suspect was not found, and the Creightons, who were badly frightened by the intrusion, sued the FBI for wrongful search. Did the FBI have sufficient cause for a warrantless search? Or did the FBI violate the Creightons' constitutional rights? Where should society draw the line between its public safety needs and the rights of the individual? Such questions in the context of a real-life situation immediately plunge students into the chapter's subject and into the process of thinking about its importance.

This approach is part of a second pedagogical goal of this text: helping students to think critically. Critical thinking is, I believe, the most important skill that a student can acquire from a social science education. Students do not learn to think critically by engaging in rote memorization. They acquire the skill by reflecting on what they read, by resolving challenges to their customary ways of thinking, and by confronting difficult issues. To this end, each chapter contains "Critical Thinking" boxes that ask students to use the material in the chapter to resolve, at least in their own minds, difficult political issues. And throughout the book, I have attempted to structure the discussion in ways that ask students to think more deeply and systematically about politics. In the first chapter, for example, I discuss the inexact meanings, conflicting implications, and unfilled promise of Americans' most cherished ideals, including liberty and equality. The discussion includes the "Chinese Exclusion," a grotesque and not-well-known chapter in our history that should lead students to think what it means to be an American.

Finally, I have attempted in this book to present American government through the analytical lens of political science but in a way that captures the vivid world of real-life politics. I regularly reminded myself while writing this book that only a tiny percentage of introductory students are interested in an academic political science career. Most of them take the course because it is required or because they enjoy politics. I have sought to write a book that will kindle political interest in the first type of student and deepen interest in the second type, while also giving them the systematic knowledge that a science of politics can provide. I had a model in mind for the kind of book that could achieve these goals. It was V. O. Key's absorbing *Politics, Parties, and Pressure Groups,* which I had read many years earlier as an undergraduate student. The late Professor Key was a masterful scholar who had a deep love of politics and who gently chided colleagues whose interest in political science was confined to the "science" part.

Few scholars can match Key's brilliance, but most political scientists share his fascination with politics. The result of their combined efforts is a body of knowledge about American government that is both precise and politically astute. This scholarship gives the text its unifying core. Political scientists have identified several major tendencies in the American political system that are a basis for a systematic understanding of how it operates, namely:

- Enduring ideals that are the basis of Americans' political identity and culture and that are a source of many of their beliefs, aspirations, and conflicts
- Extreme fragmentation of governing authority that is based on an elaborate system of checks and balances, which serves to protect against abuses of political power but also makes it difficult for political majorities to assert power when confronting an entrenched or intense political minority
- Many competing groups which are a result of the nation's great size, population diversity, and economic complexity, and which, separately, have considerable power over narrow areas of public policy

- Strong emphasis on individual rights which is a consequence of the nation's political traditions and which results in substantial benefits to the individual and places substantial claims on the community
- Preference for the marketplace as a means of allocating resources, which has the effect of placing many economic issues beyond the reach of popular majorities

These tendencies are introduced in the first chapter and discussed frequently in subsequent chapters. If students forget many of the points made in this book, they may at least take away from the course a knowledge of the deep underpinnings of the American political system.

Changes for This Edition

The basic organization of *The American Democracy* is unchanged for this edition except for the final chapter. Some instructors who use the text regularly suggested that the coverage of state and local politics, which was in the appendix, be converted into a regular chapter. Their advice has been followed. The final chapter of this edition examines state and local government and, unlike the earlier appendix version, is a thorough treatment of the subject. In adding this chapter, I deleted the previous concluding chapter. It was very brief and mostly speculative—an attempt to peer into the future of American government. We discovered through a survey that most instructors did not include the chapter as an assigned reading and almost none regarded it as indispensable. I liked it, but that seemed an insufficient reason when balanced against the realization that students in one way or another pay the cost of every extra page a text contains.

Although the final chapter is the only major change from the last edition, all chapters have been thoroughly reviewed and updated to reflect the latest scholarship and the most recent political developments at home and abroad. The role of the Internet in American politics, for example, features more prominently in this edition than in previous ones. The Internet is also part of this text's instructional content. Each chapter includes one or more worldwide web icons (identified by a globe within which WWW appears). Each icon indicates the availability of relevant supplementary material (self-quizzes, simulations, and graphics) on the text's web site.

I have tried to illustrate many of the points in this book with developments that are a remembered part of students' lives. For most of them, Vietnam is ancient history, and the fall of the Berlin Wall is, at best, a distant memory. Students need to know about, and learn from, these events. But they sometimes learn more when asked to apply the discipline of political science to events they believe they already thoroughly know. Accordingly, this text strives to deepen their understanding of the significance of the 2000 presidential election campaign and other recent developments.

To encourage students to dig more deeply into today's issues, this edition of the text features a new box series entitled "Current Controversies." Each chapter includes a "Current Controversies" box that contains opposing opinions on the issue in question. Among the issues discussed in these boxes are Internet voting, media mergers, presidential fast-track trading authority, minority redistricting, school vouchers, and the role of soft money in election campaigns.

These boxes and the other boxed features in the text are based on the same instructional philosophy that guided earlier editions. The boxes are not mere fillers or diversions. They are not meant to entertain in the way that some texts use titillating or trivial material to distract a student's attention. These boxes are part of a broad pedagogical strategy of heightening students' interest in politics. Once interest is generated, students naturally want to learn more about a subject and derive enjoyment through studying it.

In addition to the "Current Controversies" and "Critical Thinking" boxes, each chapter has a "How the United States Compares" box and a "States in the Nation" box. The United States in many ways has the world's preeminent democracy, but it also has distinctive policies and practices. The American states, too, are quite different in their politics and policies, despite belonging to the same union. American students invariably gain a deeper understanding of their own communities when they recognize the ways in which their nation or state differs from others.

Ancillary Package

This text is accompanied by supplementary materials. Please contact your local McGraw-Hill representative or McGraw-Hill Customer Service (800-338-3987) for details concerning policies, prices, and availability, as some restrictions may apply.

FOR INSTRUCTORS

Instructor's Manual/Test Bank 0-07-303409-6 This revamped instructor's manual (IM) gives the instructor both an overview and an in-depth picture of each chapter of the text. The IM consists of Chapter Learning Objectives, a "Focus and Main Points" section, a Chapter Summary, a List of Major Concepts, a Comprehensive Lecture Outline, and a Complementary Lecture Topics section. The IM was prepared by Professor David Garrison of Collin County Community College.

The IM is followed by the Test Bank (TB) material for each chapter. The TB file contains over 1,700 questions. For most chapters, there are 60 multiple-choice questions, 20 true-false, and 5 essay/short answer questions. The answer key accompanies the questions on a chapter-by-chapter basis.

Computerized Test Bank (Windows) 0-07-303408-8 and (Macintosh) 0-07-303407-X In addition to the printed TB, the test questions are available in a computerized form that enables the user to edit, supplement, scramble, and print various versions of the questions.

Overhead Transparencies 0-07-303733-8 This supplement includes over fifty four-color overheads of graphs, tables, and charts from the fifth edition of *The American Democracy.*

Simulation Exercises This ancillary includes several simulations that the instructor can assign as class or individual exercises. Examples of the available simulations include election campaigns, public opinion polling, and legislative coalitions. The simulations are contained in a student CD-ROM that is described below.

NEW! Presentation Manager 0-07-303411-8 This new ancillary is an instructor's custom presentation tool and includes Power Point. The CD-ROM contains American Government Power Point slides, an electronic version of the Instructor's Manual, Computerized Test Bank, Image Bank for photos, and additional materials.

NEW! Video #1 of the "American Government Video Library" 0-07-303414-2 This supplement is the first video of a new library that McGraw-Hill is developing. The ten-minute video covers the timely issue of devolution within American federalism. The video was created and produced by the award-winning Baker-Losco Multimedia Company. Future videos will address other issues of American government.

Website *The American Democracy* website has been completely updated to reflect changes in the new edition. The website includes study guide questions and answers, interactive exercises, research links, simulations, the instructor's manual, and more. The Patterson website can be reached by following the links at McGraw-Hill's general web site (www.mhhe.com).

MHLA (McGraw-Hill Learning Architecture) Designed to manage the use of information over the Internet and campus Intranets using the World Wide Web, the MHLA is a complete solution for delivering educational content over networked environments. The Patterson MHLA successfully combines the following features: (1) course and class management, (2) content creation and management, (3) on-line quizzing and testing, (4) secure individualized access requiring only a standard web browser, and (5) gateway to other sites on the World Wide Web.

Pageout Pageout is an easy-to-use HTML tool designed specifically for faculty interested in developing their own web pages for the course. Pageout enables the instructor to create professional-quality web pages and requires no experience or knowledge of HTML programming. It is free to adopters of McGraw-Hill textbooks and learning materials.

FOR STUDENTS

Study Guide 0-07-303576-9 This revamped study guide is designed to assist the student in getting the most out of the text and introductory course. It is designed so the student can efficiently review material presented in the text, prepare effectively for tests, develop critical thinking skills, and more. Each chapter includes the following sections: Chapter Outline, Chapter Summary, Learning Objectives, Self-Test Section, and Answer Key. The study guide was prepared by Professor Mark Byrnes of Middle Tennessee State University.

NEW! Student CD-ROM 0-07-303732-X This new state-of-the-art student CD-ROM includes an Interactive Study Guide, Simulation Software, Video Clips, Document Library, and other material. These simulations include, for example, election campaigns, public opinion polling, and legislative coalitions and can be assigned as class or individual exercises.

Website The Patterson website includes study guide questions, interactive exercises, research links, simulations, and more. The site can be reached by following the links at McGraw-Hill's general website (www.mhhe.com).

Your Suggestions Are Invited

The American Democracy has now been in use in college classrooms for more than a decade. During that time, the text (including its concise version, *We the People*) has been adopted at more than five hundred colleges and universities. I am very grateful to all who have used it. I am particularly indebted to the many instructors and students over the years who have offered suggestions for strengthening each subsequent edition. The strengths and weaknesses of a text are best discovered in its use, and I hope you will share your thoughts with me. You can contact me at the John F. Kennedy School of Government, Harvard University, Cambridge, MA 02138 or by e-mail: thomas_patterson@harvard.edu

Thomas E. Patterson

PREFACE FOR THE STUDENT: A GUIDED TOUR

This book describes the American political system, which is one of the most interesting and intricate in the world. The discussion is comprehensive; there is a lot of information packed into the text. No student could possibly remember every tiny fact or observation that each chapter contains, but the main points of discussion are easily grasped if you make the effort.

The text has several features that will help you to understand the major points of discussion. Each chapter has, for example, an opening story that illustrates a central theme of the chapter. This story is followed by a brief summary of the chapter's main ideas.

The guided tour below describes the organization and special features of your text.

Thomas E. Patterson

OPENING ILLUSTRATION

A narration of a compelling event introduces the chapter's main ideas.

Senate majority Leader Trent Lott declared it a great day for those who believe that the answers to America's problems are more likely to be found in Albany, Sacramento, and Jackson than in Washington. Senator Daniel Patrick Moynihan, an outspoken critic of the legislation, called it "the most brutal act of social policy since Reconstruction." The Urban Institute estimated that within a decade the legislation would push more than a million children into poverty.[2]

At issue was the nation's program of assistance for poor families and whether the program would be directed by the national government or the states. Since the 1930s, the program had been run out of Washington as an entitlement policy, which meant that every American family who met the eligibility criteria was entitled to assistance. For many liberal Democrats, it was the cornerstone of the idea that no needy American family, wherever it resided, would be denied help. Individual states had some leeway in deciding the amount of support a needy family would receive each month, but all states had to participate in the program and contribute to its funding.

The new legislation ended this federal guarantee of cash assistance and replaced it with a system of cash grants to the states, which would assume responsibility for caring for welfare recipients and getting them into jobs. The legislation fulfilled the long-held desire of conservative Republicans to reduce welfare dependency and move welfare recipients into tax-paying jobs. It also met their goal of reducing the power of the federal government. Under the new program, states would have to support a needy family for five years but could deny benefits if, after two years, an able-bodied adult refused to accept a job or job training. And after five years, a state could unconditionally deny benefits to poor families.

The 1996 Welfare Reform Act is one of thousands of controversies during American history that have hinged on whether national or state authority should prevail. Americans possess what amounts to dual citizenship: they are citizens both of the United States and of the state where they reside. The American political system is a *federal system*, one in which constitutional authority is divided between a national government and state governments: each is assumed to derive its powers directly from the people and therefore to have sovereignty (final authority) over the policy responsibilities assigned to it. The federal system consists of nation *and* states, indivisible and yet separate.[3]

This chapter on American constitutionalism focuses on federalism. The nature of the relationship between the nation and the states was the most pressing issue when the Constitution was written in 1787, and this chapter describes how that issue helped shape the Constitution. The chapter's closing sections discuss

MAIN POINTS

The chapter's three or four main ideas are summarized in the opening pages.

★ *The American political culture centers on a set of core ideals—liberty, equality, self-government, individualism, diversity, and unity—that serve as the people's common bond.* These mythic principles have a substantial influence on what Americans will regard as reasonable and acceptable and on what they will try to achieve.

★ *Politics is the process that determines how a society will be governed.* The play of politics in the United States takes place in the context of democratic procedures, constitutionalism, and capitalism, and involves elements of majority, pluralist, and elite rule.

★ *Politics in the United States is characterized by a number of major patterns, including a highly fragmented governing system, a high degree of pluralism, an extraordinary emphasis on individual rights, and a pronounced separation of the political and economic spheres.*

Political Culture: The Core Principles of American Government

The people of every nation have a few great ideals that characterize their political life, but, as James Bryce observed, Americans are a special case.[3] Their ideals are the basis of their national identity. Other people take their identity from the common ancestry that led them gradually to gather under one flag. Thus, long before there was a France or a Japan, there were French and Japanese people, each a kinship group united through blood.[4] Even today, it is kinship that links them. There is no way to become Japanese, except to be born of Japanese parents. Not so for Americans. They are a multitude of immigrant peoples linked by a political tradition. The United States is a nation that was founded abruptly in 1776 on a set of principles that became its people's common bond.[5]

A strong bond of some kind was a necessity. Nationalities that warred constantly in Europe had to find a way to live together in the New World. Their search for common ground has been replayed many times during America's history. The United States is, and always has been, a nation of immigrants and _____ ter measure of respect and opportunity (see Fig-_____ people, brought together through allegiance to a _____ bits of mind, a customary way of thinking about _____ hat social scientists call **political culture**, a term _____ and deep-seated beliefs of a particular people.[6] _____ ure is said to include the following beliefs in ide-

_____ ividuals should be free to act and think as they choose, _____ nreasonably on the freedom and well-being of others. _____ e that the people are the ultimate source of governing _____ welfare is the only legitimate purpose of government. _____ uals have moral worth, are entitled to fair treatment _____ e equal opportunity for material gain and political

---

★ STATES IN THE NATION

DIRECT DEMOCRACY: THE INITIATIVE AND REFERENDUM

The Progressive movement's reforms included the initiative (which allows citizens through petition to place legislative measures on the ballot) and the referendum (which permits legislative bodies to submit proposals to the voters for approval or rejection). Not all states adopted these devices or have them today. The initiative and referendum are common in the Midwest and West, where the Progressive movement was strong. They are less prevalent in the Northeast, where the party machines were strong, and in the South, where political elites opposed reforms that would have enabled African Americans and poor whites to exercise more power.

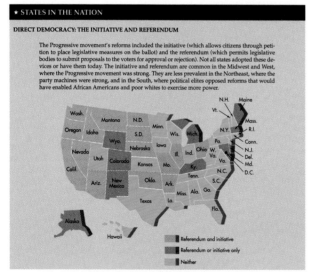

Referendum and initiative
Referendum or initiative only
Neither

SOURCE: Council of State Governments, *Book of the States*, 1998–1999 (Lexington, Ky.: Council of State Governments, 1999), 210.

Eventually, however, the Senate was persuaded to support an amendment by pressure from the Progressives and by revelations that corporate bribes had influenced the selection of several senators.

A second Progressive reform that affected national politics is the **primary election,** which gives rank-and-file voters the opportunity to select party nominees. Nearly all states in the early 1900s adopted the primary election as a means of choosing nominees for at least some federal and state offices. Before this change, nominees were chosen by party leaders.

The Progressive era spawned attacks on the Framers. A prominent criticism was the historian Charles S. Beard's *Economic Interpretation of the Constitution.*[23]

primary election A form of election in which voters choose a party's nominees for public office. In most states, eligibility to vote in a primary election is limited to voters who are registered members of the party.

"STATES IN THE NATION" BOXES

Each chapter has a box that compares the fifty states on some aspect of politics.

MAJOR CONCEPTS

The introduction of a major concept is signaled by **bold type** and accompanied by a concise definition. These concepts are also listed at the end of the chapter and are compiled in a glossary in the back of the text.

FIGURES AND TABLES

Each chapter has figures and tables that relate to points made in the discussion.

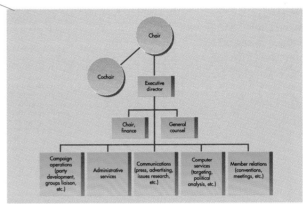

FIGURE 9-2 Organization Chart of the Republican National Committee.
Source: Used by permission of Republican National Committee, 2000.

staffs, state parties have used them to expand their activities, which range from polling to issues research to campaign management. (These activities are discussed in greater detail later in this chapter.)

State party organizations concentrate on statewide races, including those for ⋯ ces for the state legislature. ⋯ or local offices, and in most ⋯ primary contests.

⋯ much like those at the state ⋯ arty chairperson, and a sup-⋯ rters for the Republican and ⋯ .C. Although in theory the ⋯ her the Democratic National ⋯ Committee (RNC) has great ⋯) and the DNC (with more ⋯ liberative bodies. They meet ⋯ ned to setting organizational

CURRENT CONTROVERSIES

SHOULD SCHOOL VOUCHERS BECOME NATIONAL POLICY?

As the demand for quality schools has increased, some parents have sought an answer in a "school voucher" system. Each student would be entitled to a taxpayer-provided voucher of a few thousand dollars, which could be applied to admission at a public, private, or religious school of the student's choice. Advocates claim that the voucher system would create competition for students that would enhance performance levels across the entire school system. Opponents say that the voucher system would undermine the public schools not only by decreasing their funding but also by drawing the better students away from public into private schools. They also say that the voucher system is little more than a middle-class subsidy since, even with a voucher, poorer families cannot afford the price of private school tuition.

YES: Modern day choice proposals are aimed at helping children who are most in need. In Milwaukee and Cleveland decades of failure and lost years of learning prompted the pilot programs. . . . Parents now know that they have a guarantee: either the school their child attends will work, or they will be given an opportunity to enroll their child in one of their choice that does work. . . . [Just as] important, however, is that these programs work to instill institutional incentives for school improvement and they consider every child's education an uncompromising priority. . . . Some opponents call the concept of choice radical. They say the best children will leave failing schools, leaving the worst behind. But aren't they really saying that they know schools are already failing? Aren't they really saying that they are worried about bricks and mortar, and not about children?
— The Center for Education Reform

NO: Although supporters have tried, over the years, to present vouchers as a good way to "reform" public education, vouchers are quite simply and plainly a way to use public money to send children to private schools. They're a scheme to siphon off money from public schools rather than help them improve. . . . A particularly dishonest argument that voucher advocates use in selling "parental choice" is that all parents should have the right to choose a good private school for their children—"the way President and Mrs. Clinton did for Chelsea." The people using this argument conveniently forget to point out that good private schools generally have many more applicants than places, so it's the schools—not the parents—who do the choosing. And of course they don't mention that parents can't choose what they can't afford. As one New York City parent said about a private school voucher she won in a lottery, "You're supposed to be poor to get the scholarship, but you have to be rich to use it."
— American Federation of Teachers

"CURRENT CONTROVERSIES" BOXES

Each chapter has a box that introduces a current controversy and includes opposing opinions on the issue.

Since then, federal assistance to public schools and colleges has been an important part of their financing, albeit a small part relative to the overall amount that the nation spends on public education. Federal funds during the past two decades have been split almost equally between support for college and for public school education.

As education, particularly in the public schools, has become increasingly an issue of national debate, the pressures on Washington to play an even larger role have intensified. In 1989, George Bush declared he would be "the education president," saying that he would do more for education than any other president had done. Unlike his predecessor, Ronald Reagan, Bush did not threaten to abolish the Department of Education, which Congress had created in 1979. He urged it to coordinate federal education efforts and to help states and localities strengthen their programs. For himself, Bush took on the task of promoting school choice, urging states and localities to allow parents to make the decision about which school their children would attend.

"HOW THE UNITED STATES COMPARES" BOXES

Each chapter has a box that compares the United States with other countries in regard to a major political feature.

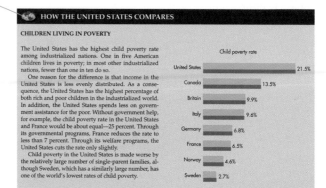

HOW THE UNITED STATES COMPARES

CHILDREN LIVING IN POVERTY

The United States has the highest child poverty rate among industrialized nations. One in five American children lives in poverty; in most other industrialized nations, fewer than one in ten do so.

One reason for the difference is that income in the United States is less evenly distributed. As a consequence, the United States has the highest percentage of both rich and poor children in the industrialized world. In addition, the United States spends less on government assistance for the poor. Without government help, for example, the child poverty rate in the United States and France would be about equal—25 percent. Through its governmental programs, France reduces the rate to less than 7 percent. Through its welfare programs, the United States cuts the rate only slightly.

Child poverty in the United States is made worse by the relatively large number of single-parent families, although Sweden, which has a similarly large number, has one of the world's lowest rates of child poverty.

Child poverty rate

United States	21.5%
Canada	13.5%
Britain	9.9%
Italy	9.6%
Germany	6.8%
France	6.5%
Norway	4.6%
Sweden	2.7%

Adapted from Timothy Smeeding, "Doing Poorly: The Real Income of American Children in a Comparative Perspective," Luxembourg Income Study Working Paper No. 127 (Syracuse: Maxwell School of Citizenship and Public Affairs, 1995), reprinted in *The State of America's Children Yearbook* (Children's Defense Fund, 1996). Used by permission.

level) has an annual income of about $12,000, which is well below the poverty line. Millions of Americans—mostly household workers, service workers, unskilled laborers, and farm workers—are in this position. The U.S. Bureau of Labor Statistics estimates that roughly 7 percent of Americans who work full time do not earn enough to lift their family above the poverty line.[7]

nd Policies of Social Welfare

generally been debated along partisan lines, a reflection of alitions and philosophies of the Republican and Democra- ies to labor, the poor, and minorities, the Democratic party all major federal welfare programs. The key House of Rep- the Social Security Act of 1935, for example, found 85 per- upporting it and 99 percent of Republicans against it.[8] ually came to accept the idea that the federal government has re but argued that the role should be kept as small as practi- the 1960s, Republican opposition to President Lyndon John- was substantial. His programs included federal initiatives in on, public housing, nutrition, and other areas traditionally and local government.[9] The Great Society programs were en- e they were supported by Johnson's fellow Democrats. More

securities, and worker safety. This multilateral trading system is coordinated by the World Trade Organization (WTO), which was established in 1995 as the successor to GATT. The WTO's member nations (roughly 130 in number) have basically committed themselves to an open trade policy buttressed by regulations that are designed to ensure fair play among the participants.

The WTO, however, is certain to be the target of intense criticism. Some Americans oppose, in principle, any international organization with the power to set policy that is binding on the United States. The WTO will be no different in this respect than the UN has been. The WTO will also be subject to more precise forms of pressure, as was evident when mass protests disrupted the 1999 WTO Conference in Seattle. To gain support among member nations, the WTO has focused on trade barriers and has shied from issues that are more contentious, such as a country's labor laws. The Seattle protests, which drew international activists as well as ones from the United States, were aimed at forcing the WTO to take environmental and labor practices (for example, child labor) into account in its trade agreements. It is generally conceded that the Seattle protests were but one round in what is sure to be a protracted struggle over the shape of global trade policy.

Access to Natural Resources

Although the United States is rich in natural resources, it is not self-sufficient. The major deficiency is oil; domestic production provides for only about half the nation's use.

Outside the United States, most of the world's oil is found in the Middle East, Latin America, and Russia. Access to this oil has occurred mainly through the marketplace, but U.S. military force has also been instrumental. In the Middle East, for example, U.S. oil companies controlled one-tenth of Middle Eastern oil reserves before World War II began. Just twenty years later, they controlled six-tenths.[26] This change was in part the result of the ability of U.S. firms after the war to furnish the capital to reopen oil fields damaged by the conflict and to open new fields. The United States also gained leverage through its support of reactionary regimes in Iran and other Middle Eastern countries, which responded by giving U.S. firms a larger role in their oil production.

The 1990–91 war in the Persian Gulf is a more recent example of how U.S. military force has served the nation's resource needs. Iraq's invasion of oil-rich Kuwait threatened western supplies, and its defeat quelled the threat.

In general, however, military power has increasingly become a less-effective means of preserving economic leverage. Economic interdependence has made military intervention mostly counterproductive. For example, when Iranian fundamentalists took over the U.S. embassy in Teheran in 1979, one of the reasons the United States refrained from attacking Iran's oil fields was that the action would have substantially reduced the Middle East's oil-producing capacity.

Relations with the Developing World

Political instability in the less developed countries, as in the case of Iraq's invasion of Kuwait, is disruptive to world markets. Less developed countries also offer marketplace opportunities. In order to progress, they need to acquire the

★ CRITICAL THINKING ★

WHAT'S YOUR OPINION?

Free Trade: Good or Bad?
Two of the most heated congressional debates in recent years were those on NAFTA and GATT. The debates pitted proponents of free trade against advocates of protectionism.

The free-trade faction argued that protectionism is ultimately self-defeating, that other nations will simply respond in kind. The free traders cautioned against the notion that the global economy is a zero-sum game, saying that the economic interests of all countries are furthered by an open trading system. They also argued that the United States has a competitive advantage because of its technological know-how and will be one of the big winners in a global free-trade system.

The protectionist faction argued that the United States is already a big loser in the international market, that its trade deficit far exceeds that of other countries. They also noted the loss of jobs and factories to overseas locations. They contended that U.S. firms should be protected from foreign competitors who gain an unfair advantage from their access to cheap labor and that the United States should first secure its own market, which would generate new jobs and income for Americans.

What is your position on the free-trade versus protectionist issue? What arguments, other than those above, would you make in support of your position?

"CRITICAL THINKING" BOXES

Boxes in the margins ask you to critically analyze and integrate material presented in the chapter.

SUMMARY

A short discussion, organized around the chapter's main points, summarizes each chapter's content.

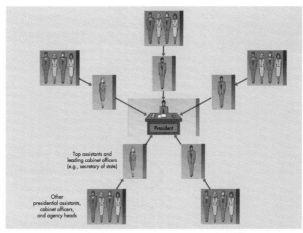

FIGURE 14-4 Managing the Presidency: The Hub-of-the-Wheel (Circular) Form of Organization
In the hub-of-the-wheel form of organization, the president is at the center of a circle composed of a fairly large number of top-level aides, each of whom has direct access to the president. Lower-level advisers have correspondingly closer access to the president than they do in the pyramidal form.

Top assistants and leading cabinet officers (e.g., secretary of state)

Other presidential assistants, cabinet officers, and agency heads

President

double-edged sword. Presidents today have greater responsibilities than their predecessors, and the increase in responsibilities expands their opportunities to exert power. At the same time, the range of these responsibilities is so broad that they must rely on staffers who may or may not act in the best interests of the president. The modern president's recurring problem is to find some way of making sure that aides serve the interests of the presidency above all others. The subject of presidential control of the executive branch will be discussed further in Chapter 16.

Summary

The presidency has become a much stronger office than the Framers envisioned. The Constitution grants the president substantial military, diplomatic, legislative, and executive powers, and in each case the president's authority has increased measurably. Underlying this change is the president's position as the one leader chosen by the whole nation. The public's support and expectations underlie presidential claims of broad authority.

National crises have contributed to the growth of presidential power. The public looks to the president during national emergencies, in part because Congress is poorly suited to the decisive and continuous action that emergencies require. Changing world and national conditions have also enhanced the presidency. These changes have placed new and greater demands on the federal government, demands that the president is in some ways better able to meet than Congress.

The nation has had four systems of presidential selection. The first centered on Congress and the Electoral College, the second on party conventions, the third on a convention system with some state primaries, and the current one on state primaries and open caucuses as the dominant method of choosing presidential nominees. Each succeeding system has been more "democratic" in that it was designed to give the public greater influence in the choice of the president and thus to make the selection more legitimate.

To gain nomination, a strong showing in the early primaries is necessary because news coverage and other resources flow toward winning candidates. This momentum is a critical factor in nominating races but normally

dency, the responsibilities of the modern presidency far exceed any president's personal capacities. To meet their obligations, presidents have surrounded themselves with large staffs of advisers, policy experts, and managers. These staff members enable the president to extend control over the executive branch while providing the information necessary for policymaking. All recent presidents have discovered, however, that their control of staff resources is incomplete and that some actions that others do on their behalf actually work against what they are trying to accomplish.

KEY TERMS

A list of the chapter's major concepts facilitates review.

SUGGESTED READINGS

Annotated references encourage further pursuit of some of the best works of political science, both classic studies and recent research.

Key Terms

cabinet
legitimacy (of election)
momentum
open party caucuses

stewardship theory
unit rule
Whig theory

Suggested Readings

Haskell, John. *Fundamentally Flawed: Understanding and Reforming Presidential Primaries.* Lanham, Md.: Rowman & Littlefield, 1996. An analysis that argues the presidential nominating process is flawed and requires major reform.
Kendall, Kathleen E. *Communication in the Presidential Primaries.* Westport, Conn.: Praeger, 2000. A look at communication in the 1912–2000 nominating campaigns.
Kraus, Sidney. *Televised Presidential Debates and Public Policy,* 2d ed. Mahwah, N.J.: Lawrence Erlbaum Publishers, 2000. An analysis by one of the leading presidential debates experts.

Patterson, Thomas E. *Out of Order.* New York: Vintage, 1994. A study of the news media's coverage of presidential campaigns.
Pfiffner, James P. *The Strategic Presidency: Hitting the Ground Running,* 2d ed. Chicago: Dorsey Press, 1996. An analysis of the way a newly elected president can convert electoral support into power in office.
Ponder, Daniel E. *Good Advice.* College Station: Texas A&M University Press, 2000. An examination of the role of information in White House policy making.
Walch, Timothy, ed. *At the President's Side: The Vice Presidency in the Twentieth Century.* Columbia: University of Missouri Press, 1997. An assessment of the vice presidency and its twentieth-century occupants.

ACKNOWLEDGMENTS

*E*arly in the writing of the first edition of *The American Democracy*, my editor and I concluded that it would be enormously helpful if a way could be found to bring into each chapter the judgment of those political scientists who teach the introductory course year in and year out. These instructors are most able to provide the required insight into improving the pedagogical value of an introductory text. This recognition led us to initiate what is still today the most thorough review process ever undertaken for an American government text. In addition to the chapter reviews of a select number of expert scholars, we sent each chapter to a dozen or so faculty members at U.S. colleges and universities of all types—public and private, large and small, four-year and two-year. These political scientists, 213 of them in all, had well over a thousand years of combined experience in the teaching of the introductory course and provided various constructive ideas. They will go unnamed here, but my debt to these scholars remains undiminished by time. Reviewers are the lifeblood of a text, and their contribution lasts far beyond the edition they help strengthen.

For the second, third, and fourth editions, we also sought suggestions from a large number of reviewers—eighty-nine in total. Their suggestions were detailed, lengthy, and extremely useful. It might be thought that the comprehensive nature of the first review process would have eliminated even the more minor defects. Nevertheless, these reviewers found some and, more than that, offered invaluable advice on the latest scholarship in their subfields within political science.

For this new edition, we again sought a wide range of advice. In fact, we asked reviewers for a more thorough assessment of the text than had been asked of previous reviewers. The reviewers for this edition concluded that an overall revision was not necessary. However, they offered a great many suggestions that have been adopted into this edition. I am grateful that they took so much time from their own work to improve mine. My thanks to:

Cecile Artiz, *Houston Community College-Southeast*

Evelyn Ballard, *Houston Community College*

James J. Best, *Kent State University*

Bob Bilodeau, *South Plains College*

Henry Bowers, *Henry Ford Community College*

Bill Bloomquist, *Indiana University-Purdue University at Indianapolis*

Robert C. Bradley, *Illinois State University*

Mark Byrnes, *Middle Tennessee State University*

Dolane Clark, *United States Air Force Academy*

J. Kevin Corder, *Western Michigan University*

William H. Coogan, *University of Southern Maine*

Kenneth Dautrich, *University of Connecticut*

Bruce Drury, *Lamar University*

Philip L. Fetzer, *California Polytechnic State University*

Susan P. Fino, *Wayne State University*

Robert K. Goidel, *Indiana State University*

David Garrison, *Collin County Community College*

Forest Greives, *University of Montana*

Donald A. Gross, *University of Kentucky*

Lori Cox Han, *Austin College*

W. Gary Howard, *University of West Florida*

Richard D. Hughes, *University of California-Sacramento*

Loch K. Johnson, *University of Georgia-Athens*

Carl Meecham, *SUNY Oneonta*

Nancy Marion, *University of Akron*

Charles McCloy, *Trident Technical College*

Paul R. Petterson, *Central Connecticut State University*

David F. Prindle, *University of Texas-Austin*

Steven Puro, *St. Louis University*

T. Ramakrishna Reddy-*Weber State University*

Todd Sheilds, *University of Arkansas*

Robert Sivey, *John Jay College*

Ann-Marie Syzmanski, *University of Oklahoma*

James Scott, *University of Nebraska-Kearney*

Mort Sipress, *University of Wisconsin-Eau Claire*

Barbara S. Stone, *California State University-Fullerton*

John E. Stetzinger, *Valencia Community College*

Beatrice Talpos, *Wayne County Community College*

Bedford Umez, *Lee College*

John H. Wilson, *Itawamba Community College*

Charles E. Walcott, *Virginia Tech University*

Finally, I want to acknowledge those at McGraw-Hill and Harvard University who contributed to the fifth edition. Monica Eckman, my editor, deserves a special thanks. Monica's enthusiasm for the text was a source of inspiration and a constant reminder of the importance of the revision process. Hannah Glover, the editorial assistant, provided the finest revision reviews that I have ever experienced. Marilyn Rothenberger also had a major impact. She carefully supervised the production of the fifth edition. Michelle Whitaker, Carrie Burger, Brenda Ernzen, and Enboge Chong also worked hard to make this edition a reality. At Harvard, I had the constant and valuable support of my faculty assistant, Melissa Ring. She flawlessly updated nearly all the tables and figures and provided the research materials that informed the text revisions.

Thomas E. Patterson

The American Democracy

PART ONE

Foundations

★　★　★

The United States has the world's oldest constitution still in force. France has had fourteen constitutions during the same period in which the United States has had one. The British statesman William Gladstone in 1878 declared the U.S. Constitution to be "the most wonderful work ever struck off at a given time by the brain and purpose of man."

A reason why this remarkable system has endured is that the United States was founded on a set of common ideals that continue to serve as Americans' bond. Chapter 1 describes these ideals and their lasting influence on the nation's politics.

Chapters 2 and 3 examine how the writers of the Constitution resolved fundamental issues—liberty, self-government, and union. A central theme of these chapters is that basic constitutional issues are never fully settled. They are recurring sources of debate, and each generation is forced to find new answers.

Constitutional government is also a matter of individual rights, of a system in which people have basic freedoms that are constitutionally protected from infringement by government. Although these rights are rooted in principle, they are achieved through politics. Chapter 4 discusses how civil liberties—for example, free speech—are protected both from and through political action. Chapter 5 examines the degree to which Americans' rights are affected by characteristics such as gender and race. ★

CHAPTER 1

The American Heritage: Seeking a More Perfect Union

★

One hears people say that it is inherent in the habits and nature of democracies to change feelings and thoughts at every moment. . . . But I have never seen anything like that happening in the great democracy on the other side of the ocean. What struck me most in the United States was the difficulty experienced in getting an idea, once conceived, out of the head of the majority.

—Alexis de Tocqueville[1]

★ ★ ★

*I*t was the closest presidential race in history. A small percentage of votes in a single state, Florida, were all that separated the winner from the loser. Who would be the next president? As the uncertainty mounted, Al Gore and George W. Bush sought to assure Americans that the nation and the presidency would avert a constitutional collapse. Their statements were at times deeply partisan but, sprinkled throughout, were allusions to time-honored American ideals: the will of the people, justice, fairness, rule by law.

The high-sounding ideals embedded in Bush and Gore's statements would have been familiar to any generation of Americans. The same ideals had been used to take America to war, to declare peace, to celebrate national holidays, to declare major policies, and to assert new rights. The same ideals expressed by Bush and Gore had punctuated the speeches of George Washington and Abraham Lincoln, Susan B. Anthony and Franklin D. Rossevelt, Dr. Martin Luther King and Ronald Reagn.

The ideals were also there at the nation's beginning, when they were put into words in the Declaration of Independence and the Constitution. Of course, the practical meaning of these words has changed greatly during the more than two centuries that the United States has been a sovereign nation. When the writers of the Constitution began the document with the words, "We, the People," they did not have all Americans equally in mind. Black slaves, women, and men without property did not have the same constitutional status as propertied white men.

Yet America's ideals have been remarkably enduring. Throughout their history Americans have embraced the same set of core values. They have quarreled over the meaning, practice, and fulfillment of these ideals, but they have never seriously questioned the principles themselves. As the historian Clinton Rossiter concluded, "There has been in a doctrinal sense, only one America."[2]

This book is about contemporary American politics, not U.S. history or culture. Yet American politics today cannot be understood apart from the nation's heritage. Government does not begin anew with each generation; it builds on the past. In the case of the United States, the most significant link between past and present lies in the nation's founding ideals. This chapter briefly examines the principles that have helped shape American politics since the country's earliest years.

The chapter also explains basic concepts, such as power and pluralism, that are important in the study of government and politics, and describes the underlying rules of the American governing system, such as constitutionalism and capitalism. The main points made in this chapter are the following:

★ *The American political culture centers on a set of core ideals—liberty, equality, self-government, individualism, diversity, and unity—that serve as the people's common bond.* These mythic principles have a substantial influence on what Americans will regard as reasonable and acceptable and on what they will try to achieve.

★ *Politics is the process that determines how a society will be governed.* The play of politics in the United States takes place in the context of democratic procedures, constitutionalism, and capitalism, and involves elements of majority, pluralist, and elite rule.

★ *Politics in the United States is characterized by a number of major patterns, including a highly fragmented governing system, a high degree of pluralism, an extraordinary emphasis on individual rights, and a pronounced separation of the political and economic spheres.*

Political Culture: The Core Principles of American Government

The people of every nation have a few great ideals that characterize their political life, but, as James Bryce observed, Americans are a special case.[3] Their ideals are the basis of their national identity. Other people take their identity from the common ancestry that led them gradually to gather under one flag. Thus, long before there was a France or a Japan, there were French and Japanese people, each a kinship group united through blood.[4] Even today, it is kinship that links them. There is no way to become Japanese, except to be born of Japanese parents. Not so for Americans. They are a multitude of immigrant peoples linked by a political tradition. The United States is a nation that was founded abruptly in 1776 on a set of principles that became its people's common bond.[5]

A strong bond of some kind was a necessity. Nationalities that warred constantly in Europe had to find a way to live together in the New World. Their search for common ground has been replayed many times during America's history. The United States is, and always has been, a nation of immigrants and of people struggling for a greater measure of respect and opportunity (see Figure 1-1). Yet they are also one people, brought together through allegiance to a set of commonly held ideals.

America's principles are habits of mind, a customary way of thinking about the world. They are part of what social scientists call **political culture,** a term that refers to the characteristic and deep-seated beliefs of a particular people.[6]

The American political culture is said to include the following beliefs in idealized form:

political culture The characteristic and deep-seated beliefs of a particular people.

- **Liberty** is the principle that individuals should be free to act and think as they choose, provided they do not infringe unreasonably on the freedom and well-being of others.
- **Self-government** is the principle that the people are the ultimate source of governing authority and that their general welfare is the only legitimate purpose of government.
- **Equality** holds that all individuals have moral worth, are entitled to fair treatment under the law, and should have equal opportunity for material gain and political influence.

U.S. politics is remarkable for its historical continuity, which is celebrated here in a ceremony at the Capitol in Washington, D.C.

- **Individualism** is a commitment to personal initiative, self-sufficiency, and material ac-
  cumulation. This principle upholds the superiority of a private-enterprise economic
  system and includes the idea of the individual as the foundation of society.
- **Diversity** holds that individual differences should be respected and that these differences are a source of strength and a legitimate basis of self-interest.
- **Unity** is the principle that Americans are one people and form an indivisible union.

These ideals, taken together, are sometimes called "the American Creed." In practice, they mean different things to different people, and it is not useful to provide more elaborate definitions of these values at this point in the book. Few observers would argue, however, with the proposition that *a defining character-istic of the American political system is its enduring and powerful set of cultural ideals.* The Frenchman Alexis de Tocqueville was among the first to see that the main tendencies of American politics cannot be explained without taking into account the country's core beliefs. "Habits of the heart" was de Tocqueville's description of Americans' ideals.[7]

THE POWER OF IDEALS

America's ideals have had a strong impact on its politics. Ideals serve to define the boundaries of action. They do not determine exactly what people will do, but they affect what people will regard as reasonable and desirable. If people believe, as Americans do, that politics exists to promote liberty and equality, they will attempt to realize these values through their political actions.

Why, for example, does the United States spend relatively less money on government programs for the poor and disadvantaged than do other fully in-dustrialized democracies, including Germany, France, Switzerland, the Nether-lands, Spain, Britain, Sweden, Italy, and Japan? Are Americans so much better off than these other people that they have less need for welfare programs? The answer is no. Of all these countries, the United States has in both relative and

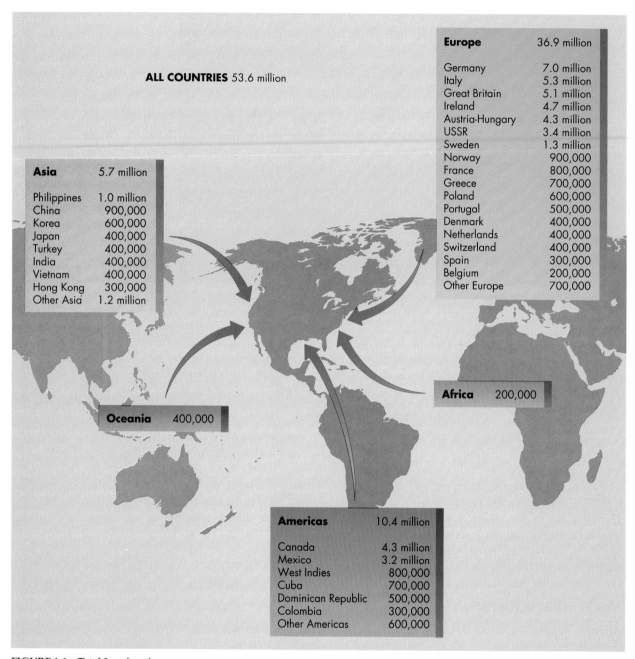

ALL COUNTRIES 53.6 million

Asia   5.7 million

Philippines	1.0 million
China	900,000
Korea	600,000
Japan	400,000
Turkey	400,000
India	400,000
Vietnam	400,000
Hong Kong	300,000
Other Asia	1.2 million

Europe   36.9 million

Germany	7.0 million
Italy	5.3 million
Great Britain	5.1 million
Ireland	4.7 million
Austria-Hungary	4.3 million
USSR	3.4 million
Sweden	1.3 million
Norway	900,000
France	800,000
Greece	700,000
Poland	600,000
Portugal	500,000
Denmark	400,000
Netherlands	400,000
Switzerland	400,000
Spain	300,000
Belgium	200,000
Other Europe	700,000

Africa   200,000

Oceania   400,000

Americas   10.4 million

Canada	4.3 million
Mexico	3.2 million
West Indies	800,000
Cuba	700,000
Dominican Republic	500,000
Colombia	300,000
Other Americas	600,000

FIGURE 1-1   Total Immigration to the United States, 1820–1990, by Continent and Country of Origin. *Source: U.S. Immigration and Naturalization Service.*

absolute terms the greatest number of hungry, homeless, and poor people. The reason the United States spends less on social welfare lies chiefly in the emphasis that American culture places on *individualism*. Americans have resisted giving government a larger social welfare role because of their deep-seated cultural belief that able-bodied individuals should take responsibility for themselves (see Figure 1-2).

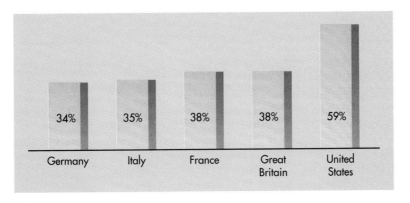

FIGURE 1-2 Opinions About the Source of Personal Success Americans are more likely than Europeans to believe that personal effort is the key to success. Figures are the percentage of respondents who agreed with the statement "In the long run, hard work usually brings a better life." *Source: World Values Surveys, 1990–1997.*

Of course, social welfare policy is not simply an issue of cultural differences. The welfare issue, like all other issues, is part of the rough and tumble of everyday politics everywhere. There are always powerful interests aligned on both sides of important issues. In the United States, the Republican party, business groups, antitax groups, and others have resisted the expansion of the government's social welfare role, while liberal Democrats, unions, minority groups, and others have from time to time argued for greater intervention. Nevertheless, Americans' belief in individualism, which has no exact equivalent in European society, has played a defining role in shaping U.S. welfare policy.

American *individualism* has its roots in the country's origins as a wilderness society. Land was plentiful, and there was no aristocracy to stifle the ambitions of ordinary people. The early Americans developed a pride in their hardy independence and from this experience grew the idea that people ought to make it on their own. It was a very different outlook than the one that prevailed in Europe, where one's place in life was determined by whether one was born into the tiny aristocracy, the small middle class, or the huge peasant mass. The European experience created a belief that one's place in society was largely beyond personal control, which, when democracy emerged centuries later, spawned the belief that government has a responsibility for the material well-being of the less fortunate. The enduring nature of these differences is evident in a Times Mirror Center survey of European and American opinions. When asked whether it is the responsibility of the government "to take care of very poor people who can't take care of themselves," only 23 percent of Americans said they completely agreed. The Germans were the closest to the Americans in their response to this question, but twice as many of them, 50 percent, claimed that the state was obliged to take care of the very poor. More than 60 percent of the British, French, and Italians held the same opinion. Americans do not necessarily have less sympathy for the poor; rather, they place more emphasis on personal responsibility than Europeans do.[8]

This belief includes an emphasis on equal opportunity. If individuals are to be entrusted with their own welfare, they must be given a fair chance to succeed on their own. Nowhere is this philosophy more evident than in the American education system. The United States spends more on education at all levels than nearly any other country. The nation's college system, for example, is open virtually to any high school graduate who wants to attend. This elaborate system

★ STATES IN THE NATION

PERCENTAGE OF ADULTS WITH COLLEGE DEGREES

Reflecting their culture beliefs of individualism and equality, Americans have developed the world's largest system of college education. Every state has at least eight colleges and universities within its boundaries and eleven states have more than 100. California with 322 colleges and New York with 320 are the highest ranking states by this measure. No European democracy has as many institutions of higher education as these two states. As a result of their cultural commitment to equal opportunity through education, many Americans have college degrees. On a state-by-state basis, the range is 16.2 percent in Arkansas to 34.0 percent in Colorado. The European average is less than 10 percent. American college graduates are concentrated in the urbanized and affluent states. Young people in these states can better afford the costs of college and are more likely to need a college degree for the work they seek.

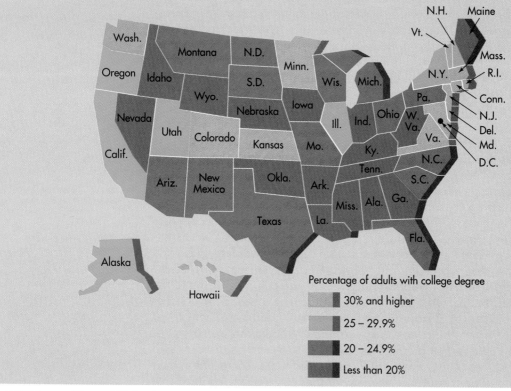

SOURCE: U.S. Bureau of Census, 1999. Based on percentage of adults twenty-five years of age or older with a college degree.

includes nearly three thousand two-year and four-year institutions. The democracies of Europe have nothing remotely comparable to this system. College in some of these countries is so restricted that barely a tenth of the young people attend. In contrast, a third of young Americans enter college. The difference is reflected in the number of citizens with college degrees (see box: States in the Nation). Even the American state that ranks lowest by this indicator—Arkansas

The old slave prison on Goree Island in Senegal was the last stopping place for many slaves before they were placed on ships and sent in chains to America.

with its 16.2 percent college graduates—has a higher percentage of residents with a bachelor's degree than the European average.

THE LIMITS OF IDEALS

Cultural beliefs originate in a country's political and social practices, but they are not perfect representatives of these practices. They are mythic ideas—symbolic positions taken by a people to justify and give meaning to their way of life.[9] Myths contain elements of truth, but they are far from the full truth.

High ideals do not come with a guarantee that a people will live up to them. The clearest proof of this failing in the American case is the human tragedy that began nearly four centuries ago and continues today. In 1619 the first black slaves were brought in chains to America. Slavery lasted 250 years. Slaves in the field worked from dawn to dark (from "can see, 'til can't"), whether in the heat of summer or the cold of winter. They could be bought and sold, and could be beaten, mutilated, and sexually abused with impunity. The Civil War changed the future of African Americans but did not ensure their equality. Slavery was followed by the Jim Crow era of legal segregation: black people in the South were forbidden by law to use the same schools, hospitals, restaurants, and restrooms as white people. Those blacks who got uppish with their white superiors endured beatings, firebombings, castrations, rapes, and worse—hundreds of African Americans were lynched by white vigilantes in the early 1900s. Today African Americans have equal rights under the law, but in fact they are far from equal. Compared with whites, blacks are three times as likely to live in poverty, twice as likely to be unable to find a job, twice as likely to die in infancy, seven times as likely to be sentenced to death if convicted of an interracial murder.[10] There have always been at least two Americas, one for whites and one for blacks.

Despite the lofty claim that "all men are created equal," equality has never been an American birthright. In 1882 Congress suspended Chinese immigration

www.mhhe.com/patterson5

Graphic

TABLE 1-1   Telling the American Story to Children   Americans' values and myths are reflected in their preferences in teaching children about the nation's history.

In teaching the American story to children, how important is the following theme?	Essential/Very Important	Somewhat Important	Somewhat Unimportant/ Very Unimportant/ Leave it out of the story
With hard work and perseverance, anyone can succeed in America.	83%	14%	4%
Our founders limited the power of government, so government would not intrude too much into the lives of its citizens.	74	19	8
America is the world's greatest melting pot in which people from different countries are united into one nation.	73	21	5
America's contribution is one of expanding freedom for more and more people.	71	22	6
Our nation betrayed its founding principles by cruel mistreatment of blacks and American Indians.	59	24	17
Our founders were part of a male-dominated culture that gave important roles to men while keeping women in the background.	38	28	35

Used by permission of the Survey of American Political Culture, James Davison Hunter and Carol Bowman, Directors, University of Virginia.

Cultural Beliefs as Myth and Reality
Cultural beliefs are mythical in that they are combinations of fact and wishful thinking. This mythical dimension can have far-reaching consequences. Consider the Harris poll in which two-thirds of white Americans said they believed that black Americans "get equal pay for equal work." The reality is otherwise: statistics indicate that, on average, blacks are paid less than whites in every job category. In your opinion, does the mythical aspect of belief in equality allow white Americans to deceive themselves about how well off black Americans are? If not, what else might account for the misperception? To what degree do such misconceptions lessen the concern of white Americans with racial equality? Conversely, how does equality as myth promote progress in racial relations?

on the assumption that the Chinese were an inferior people. Calvin Coolidge in 1923 asked Congress for a permanent ban on Chinese immigration, saying that people "who do not want to be partakers of the American spirit ought not to settle in America."[11] Not until 1965 was discrimination against the Chinese and other Asian peoples effectively eliminated from U.S. immigration laws.

The discrimination against the Chinese is not among the stories that Americans like to tell about themselves. Such lapses of historical memory can be found among all peoples, but the tendency to recast history is perhaps exaggerated in the case of Americans because their beliefs are so idealistic (see Table 1-1). How could a people that upholds the ideal of human equality have barred the Chinese, enslaved the blacks, stolen the Indians' lands, subordinated women, and interned the Japanese?

Cultural beliefs can even lull a people into a false sense of what they have accomplished. Some Americans think that by saying they believe in equality, they have achieved it. A Harris poll showed that two-thirds of white people believe that blacks "get equal pay for equal work." In fact, as U.S. Department of Labor statistics show, blacks in every occupational category are paid less than whites.

One reason America's ideals do not match reality is that they are general principles, not fixed rules of conduct. They derive from somewhat different experiences and philosophical traditions, and there are points at which they conflict. Equality and diversity, for instance, emphasize fairness and a full opportunity for all to partake of society's benefits, whereas liberty and individualism emphasize personal freedom and threats posed to it by political power. Conflict between these sets of beliefs is inevitable. Both are commendable, but the advancement of one set comes only at some cost to the other. One example is the issue of affirmative action. Proponents say that only through aggressive affirmative action programs will women and minorities receive the equal treatment in the job market to which they are entitled. Opponents say that aggressive affirmative action infringes unreasonably on the liberty of the employer

E PLURIBUS UNUM (EXCEPT THE CHINESE).

This Thomas Nast cartoon from 1882 mocks restrictions on Chinese immigration, reflecting the fact that Americans' cultural beliefs have always been somewhat mythical.

and the initiative of the work force. Each side can say that it has America's ideals on its side, and no resort to logic can persuade either side that the opposing viewpoint should prevail.

Despite their inexact meanings, conflicting implications, and unfulfilled promise, the ideals of Americans have had a strong impact on the nation's politics, and they still do. If racial, gender, ethnic, and other forms of intolerance constitute the sorriest chapter in the nation's history, the centuries-old struggle of Americans to create a more equal society is among the finest chapters. Few nations have battled so relentlessly against the insidious hatreds that stem from superficial human differences such as the color of one's skin. High ideals are more than mere abstractions. They are a source of human aspiration and, ultimately, of political and social change.

Politics: The Process of Deciding on Society's Goals

Cultural ideals help shape what people expect from politics and how they conduct their politics. However, politics is more than the pursuit of shared ideals; it is also about getting one's own way. Commenting on the competitive nature of politics, Harold Lasswell described politics as the struggle over "who gets what, when, and how."[12]

CONFLICT AND CONSENSUS

Political conflict is rooted in two general conditions of society. One is scarcity. Society's resources are finite, but people's appetites are not. There is not enough wealth in even the richest of countries to satisfy everyone's desires. Conflict over the distribution of resources is the inevitable result. This conflict is perhaps clearest on issues regarding how taxes will be spread among various income groups and who will be eligible for welfare benefits and how much aid those eligible will receive.

Differences in values are the other main source of political conflict. People see things in different ways. The right of abortion is freedom of choice to some and murder to others. People bring to politics a wide range of conflicting values—about abortion, about the environment, about the level of defense spending, about crime and punishment, about the poor, about the economy, about almost everything imaginable.

Politics in the United States is not the life-and-death struggle between opposing groups that typifies some countries, but there are many sources of contention. Perhaps no country has more competing interests than does the United States. Its settlement by people of many lands and religions, its enormous size and geographical diversity, and its economic complexity have made the United States a pluralistic nation. *This feature—competition for power among a great many interests of all kinds—is a major characteristic of American politics.*

It is a mistake to assume, however, that competition and conflict are the sum of politics. People must find agreeable ways of living together. Politics is not only a means of settling disputes; it is also a way of promoting collective interests. Politics is not solely about winners and losers; it is also about problem solving. Public safety and national defense are prime examples of people working together for an agreed-upon purpose. Public education is another. It reflects the older generation's willingness to tax itself for the benefit of the younger generation and ultimately for the benefit of society as a whole.

In sum, politics is a process that includes conflict and consensus, competition and cooperation. Accordingly, **politics** can be defined as, simply, the process through which a society makes its governing decisions.

politics The process through which society makes its governing decisions.

Politics includes conflict and consensus. Women have had to struggle to be treated as equals in the workplace, but their efforts have been supported by public opinion and public policies.

GOVERNMENT, POWER, AUTHORITY, AND POLICY

What is government? What is its purpose? It might be thought that the answer to these age-old questions is that government is a means by which people work together to solve their common problems. To be sure, government can serve the collective good. But it can also serve the naked interests of a few, as in the case of Stalin's Russia, Hitler's Germany, or Saddam Hussein's Iraq.

Government can be defined as consisting of the institutions, processes, and rules that are specifically designed to facilitate control of a particular area and its inhabitants.[13] There are only two things that all governments have in common. One is a capacity to raise revenues, usually in the form of taxation, to support governing activities. The other is coercion—the ability to compel inhabitants to abide by the government's rules. Without these capacities, a government would be unable to exercise control over the territory and inhabitants it claims to rule.

> **government** The institutions, processes, and rules that are specifically designed to facilitate control of a particular area and its inhabitants.

Those individuals who exercise this control are said to have **power,** a term that refers to the ability of persons or institutions to decide society's allocation of benefits and costs.[14] Power is perhaps the most basic concept of politics. Those who have sufficient power can decide how society will be governed. With so much at stake, it is not surprising that power is widely sought and often tightly held.

> **power** The ability of persons or institutions to control policy.

When power is exercised through the laws and institutions of government, the concept of authority applies. **Authority** can be defined as the recognized right of an individual, organization, or institution to make binding decisions. By this definition, government is not the only source of authority: parents have authority over their children; professors have authority over their students; firms have authority over their employees. However, government is a special case in that its authority is more encompassing in scope and more final in nature. Government's authority extends to all within its geographical boundaries. It can be used to redefine the authority of the parent, the professor, or the firm. Government's authority is also the most coercive. It includes the power to arrest and imprison, even to punish by death those who violate its rules.

> **authority** The recognized right of an individual or institution to exercise power.

Government needs coercive power to ensure that its laws will be obeyed. Without this power, lawlessness would prevail, as it does in Colombia, where drug lords control large areas of the country. But government power itself can be abused. In a perfect world, political power would be used in evenhanded ways for the benefit of all citizens. But the world is imperfect, and those with government power can use it for selfish ends, whether to enrich themselves or to deprive others of liberty. "Power tends to corrupt, and absolute power tends to corrupt absolutely," was how Lord Acton described the problem.

Although no governing system can ensure that power will be applied fairly, the U.S. system strengthens this prospect through an elaborate system of *checks and balances.* This system, which is designed to protect against abuses of power (see Chapter 2), includes the division of authority among the executive, legislative, and judicial branches of government. Each branch acts as a check on the power of the others and balances their power by exercising power of its own. Many other democratic countries have no comparable fragmentation of power. *Extreme fragmentation of governing authority is a major characteristic of the American political system. This fact, as will be seen in subsequent chapters, has profound implications for how politics is conducted, who wins out, and what policies result.*

HOW THE UNITED STATES COMPARES

AMERICANS AS A POLITICAL PEOPLE

By some standards, Americans are not a very political people. The United States ranks near the bottom, for example, in voter turnout. Barely half of Americans go to the polls in a presidential election, compared with 70 to 90 percent of adults in many democratic countries. Typically, in France, Italy, and Belgium turnout, for example, exceeds 80 percent.

In other ways, however, Americans are a highly political people. Americans have long believed in the exceptionalism of their political system. They have tended to believe that what works for them will also work for others and indeed that what works for Americans would be better for others than what they already have. In his book *World Politics and Personal Insecurity*, the political scientist Harold Lasswell wrote that "Americans who think about the problem of unifying the world tend to follow the precedent set in their own history." Presented after World War I with President Woodrow Wilson's plan for world peace based on American principles, the French premier Georges Clemenceau exclaimed, "This man Wilson with his Fourteen Points! The good Lord had only ten."

Given Americans' pride in their political system, it is not surprising that they attach great importance to political symbols. In Europe, national flags are not routinely displayed in public. In America, the flag is flown daily on government buildings and even on many private homes. The Pledge of Allegiance to the flag that is recited daily by American school children and the playing of the "Star-Spangled Banner" at public events have no equivalents in European nations.

The distinctiveness of Americans' beliefs was evident in a five-nation Times Mirror survey that asked respondents whether they agreed with the statement, "I am very patriotic." As the accompanying graph shows, Americans ranked at the top; nearly 90 percent claimed to be highly patriotic. The disparity between the United States and Europe was particularly apparent among young adults. In Europe, young adults were substantially less likely to say they were patriotic than were older people. In the United States, the proportion of eighteen- to twenty-four-year-olds who said they were patriotic, 82 percent, was nearly as high as in other age groups.

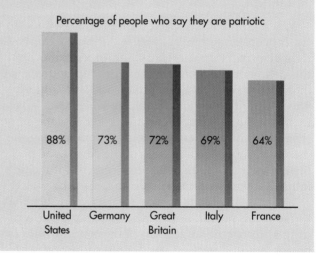

Percentage of people who say they are patriotic

United States 88% | Germany 73% | Great Britain 72% | Italy 69% | France 64%

policy Generally, any broad course of governmental action; more narrowly, a specific government program or initiative.

Governments exercise authority through policy. In its most general sense, **policy** refers to any broad course of action undertaken by government. U.S. policy toward Japan, for example, consists of a wide range of activities, from trade relations to diplomatic overtures. But policy is also used more narrowly to refer to specific programs or initiatives. The Head Start program for improving the educational prospects of poor children, for example, is a policy of government. The general view of policy is the more evocative, because it acknowledges that government exercises authority by not making decisions as well as by making them. In choosing not to decide, a government accepts the existing situation as well as the distribution of benefits and costs embedded in it.

THE RULES OF THE POLITICAL GAME

The play of politics takes place according to rules that the participants accept. The rules establish the process by which power is exercised, define the legitimate uses of power, and establish the basis for allocating costs and benefits among the participants. In the American case, the rules of the game of politics include democracy, constitutionalism, and capitalism.

Democracy

Democracy is a set of rules designed to promote *self-government*. Democracy comes from the Greek words *demos*, which means "the people," and *kratis*, meaning "to rule." In simple terms, **democracy** is a form of government in which the people govern, either directly or through elected representatives (see Chapter 2).

democracy A form of government in which the people govern, either directly or through elected representatives.

Democratic government is based on the idea of the consent of the governed, which in practice has come to mean majority rule. The principle of majority rule, in turn, is based on the notion that the view of the many should prevail over the opinion of the few. The principle also represents a form of *equality* in that the vote of each citizen counts equally, a principle expressed by the phrase "one person, one vote." In practice, democracy in America works primarily through elections. There are other, more direct forms of democracy, such as the town meeting and the initiative, but American democracy is mainly a representative system in which people's influence is based on their votes.

As Americans discovered during the 2000 campaign, even the one person, one vote principle is not inviolate. Al Gore received a half million more votes nationally than George W. Bush but lost the election through the electoral college. Each state has electoral votes equal in number to its representatives in Congress, and these votes are allocated to the candidate who wins its popular vote. The candidate with a majority of the electoral votes from all the states wins the presidency. Florida's electoral votes were decisive in the outcome of the 2000 election and, even in Florida, the one-person, one-vote principle did not hold completely. Thousands of Florida's ballots went uncounted because they could not be read by machine. After an effort to have them counted by hand failed, Gore conceded the election. Polls indicated that many Americans questioned the fairness of the election, but they accepted the outcome without violent protest. Bush's peaceful accession to the presidency is an indication of just how deeply Americans are committed to a system that operates by a set of rules rather than by force or dictate.

Constitutionalism

For many Americans, *democracy* has the same meaning as *liberty*—the freedom to think, talk, and act as one chooses. However, the terms are not synonymous. The concept of democracy implies that the will of the majority should prevail over the wishes of the minority, whereas the concept of liberty implies that the minority has rights and freedoms that cannot be taken away by the majority. The democratic model of government has long been accompanied by a fear of tyranny by the majority—the concern that a majority might ruthlessly impose its will on the minority. A more general concern about all government is the possibility of abuse of power. James Madison said that the possession of all power in the "same hands, whether of the many or the few, is the path to tyranny."[15]

Constitutionalism is a set of rules that restricts the lawful uses of power. In its original sense, constitutionalism in western society referred to a government based on laws and constitutional powers. **Constitutionalism** has since come to refer specifically to the idea that there are limits to the rightful power of government over citizens. In a constitutional system, officials govern according to law, and citizens have basic rights that government cannot take away or deny.[16] An example of constitutionalism in the United States is freedom of speech. Government is prohibited from interfering with the lawful exercise of free speech. No right is absolute, which means that some restrictions are permissible. For example, a person could be forcibly removed from the visitors' gallery overlooking the floor of the U.S. Senate for shouting at the lawmakers during debate. Nevertheless, free speech is broadly protected by the courts. During the Vietnam war, for example, there were thousands of demonstrations against U.S. policy without a single arrest and conviction for spoken words alone. In some instances protesters were harassed by officials or other citizens, but those who opposed the war had the opportunity to express their views publicly.

The constitutional tradition in America is at least as strong as the democratic tradition. In fact, *a major characteristic of the American political system is its extraordinary emphasis on individual rights.* Issues that in other democratic countries would be resolved through elections and in legislatures are, in the United States, worked out through court action as well. As Tocqueville noted, there is hardly a political issue in America that does not sooner or later become a judicial issue.[17] Abortion rights, nuclear power, busing, toxic waste disposal, and welfare services are among the scores of issues that in recent years have been played out in part as questions of rights to be settled through judicial action.

constitutionalism The idea that there are definable limits on the rightful power of a government over its citizens.

Free speech is a familiar aspect of constitutionalism. This anti-gun control rally took place in Austin, Texas.

This tradition reflects the strong influence of cultural beliefs about liberty, individualism, equality, and diversity. Through claims to rights, Americans find protection against majorities and governmental authority, assert their individuality, and strive for equality, both as individuals and as groups. (Constitutionalism is discussed further in Chapters 2–5.)

Capitalism

Just as democracy and constitutionalism are each a set of rules governing the process by which society's costs and benefits are allocated, so too is capitalism. Societies have adopted alternative ways of organizing their economies. One way is socialism, which assigns government a large role in the ownership of the means of production, in regulating economic decisions, and in providing for the economic security of the individual. Under the form of socialism practiced in democratic countries such as Sweden, the government does not attempt to manage the overall economy. In communist-style socialism, the government does take responsibility for overall management.

Capitalism is an alternative method for distributing economic costs and benefits. **Capitalism** holds that the government should interfere with the economy as little as possible. Free enterprise and *individualism* are the principles of capitalism. Firms are allowed to operate in a free and open marketplace, and individuals are expected to rely on their own initiative to establish their economic security.

As is the case with the rules of democracy and constitutionalism, the rules of capitalism are not neutral. If democracy responds to numbers and constitutionalism responds to individual rights, capitalism responds to wealth. Economic power is largely a function of accumulated wealth, whether in the hands of the individual or the firm. "Money talks" in a capitalist system, which means, among other things, that wealthier people will have by far the greater say in the distribution of costs and benefits through the economic system.

capitalism An economic system based on the idea that government should interfere with economic transactions as little as possible. Free enterprise and self-reliance are the collective and individual principles that underpin capitalism.

Capitalism, the organizing principle of the American economic system, emphasizes marketplace competition and self-initiative. In recent years, this competition has centered on the challenges posed by new technologies and global markets.

FIGURE 1-3   Average Amount of Income Taxes Paid by Citizens Americans pay less taxes than Europeans do. *Source: OECD, 1999. Percentages based on taxes paid by average worker with two children.*

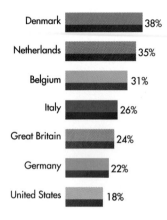

Denmark — 38%
Netherlands — 35%
Belgium — 31%
Italy — 26%
Great Britain — 24%
Germany — 22%
United States — 18%

The United States does not have a purely capitalist system, in that the government plays a role in regulating and stimulating the economy (see Chapter 18). The term *mixed economy* is used to define this hybrid form of economic system, with its combination of socialist and capitalist elements. The United States has more elements of the capitalist model and fewer elements of the socialist model than do the countries of Europe. Because of their strong tradition of *individualism*, Americans tend to restrict the scope of governmental action in the area of the economy. *A major characteristic of the American system is a relatively sharp distinction between what is political and therefore to be decided in the public arena, and what is economic and therefore to be settled in the private realm.*

For all practical purposes, this outlook places many kinds of choices, which in other countries are decided collectively, beyond the reach of political majorities in the United States. Although Americans complain that their taxes are too high, they actually pay few taxes compared with Europeans (see Figure 1-3). This situation testifies to the extent to which Americans believe that wealth is more properly allocated through the economic marketplace than through government policy.

The past decade has witnessed the triumph throughout most of the world of the capitalist, free-market economy. Its chief rival, Soviet-style communism with its system of central planning, collapsed from within. As the former Soviet Union and the eastern European countries within its orbit shifted toward market-based economic systems, they also moved toward a greater degree of democracy and constitutionalism in their political systems. These different forms of allocating costs and benefits in a society do not necessarily have to go together. However, as the American experience suggests, democracy, constitutionalism, and a free-market economy do reinforce one another in practice. Each is based on the free choices of free individuals.

Who Governs America?

The rules of the political game help decide who will exercise power and to what ends. The ultimate question about any political system is the issue of who governs. Is power widely shared and used for the benefit of the many? Or is power narrowly held and used to the advantage of the few? Although this entire book is in some respects an answer to these questions, it is useful here to consider what analysts have concluded about the American political system. Three broad theories predominate (see Table 1-2). None of them describes every aspect of American politics, but each has some validity.

RULE BY THE PEOPLE: MAJORITARIANISM

majoritarianism The idea that the majority prevails not only in elections but also in determining policy.

A basic principle of democracy, as discussed previously, is the idea of majority rule. **Majoritarianism** is the notion that the majority prevails not only in the counting of votes but also in the determination of public policy.

Majorities do sometimes rule in America. Their power is perhaps most evident in those states that offer voters the opportunity to decide directly on policy initiatives, which then become law if they receive a majority vote. The majority's influence is also felt indirectly through the decisions of elected

TABLE 1-2 Theories of Power: Who Governs America?   There are three theories of power in America, each of which must be taken into account in any full explanation of the nation's policies.

Theory	Description
Majoritarianism	Holds that numerical majorities determine issues of policy
Pluralism	Holds that policies are effectively decided through power wielded by special interests that dominate particular policy areas
Elitism	Holds that policy is controlled by a small number of well-positioned, highly influential individuals

representatives. When Congress in 1996 passed a welfare reform bill that included provisions requiring able-bodied welfare recipients to accept a job or job training after a two-year period or face a loss of their welfare benefits, it was acting in accord with the thinking of the majority of Americans, who believe that employable individuals should be self-reliant. A more systematic assessment of the power of majorities is provided by Benjamin Page and Robert Shapiro's study of the relationship between majority opinions and more than three hundred policy issues in the period from 1935 to 1979. On major issues particularly, they found that policy tended to change in the direction of change in majority opinion.[18]

Majorities do not always rule, however. There are many policy areas in which majority opinion is nonexistent or is ignored by policy makers. In these cases, other explanations of power and policy are necessary.

RULE BY GROUPS: PLURALISM

One of these explanations is provided by the theory of **pluralism,** which focuses on group activity and holds that many policies are effectively decided through power wielded by diverse (plural) interests.

Many policies are in fact more responsive to the interests of particular groups than to majority opinion. Agricultural subsidies, broadcast regulations, and corporate tax incentives are examples. In many cases, the general public has no real knowledge or opinion of issues that concern particular groups. For pluralists, the issue of whether interest-group politics serves the public good centers on whether it serves a *diversity* of interests. Pluralists contend that it is misleading to view society only in terms of majorities that may or may not form around given issues. They see society as primarily a collection of separate interests. Farmers, broadcasters, and multinational corporations have different needs and desires and, according to the pluralist view, should have a disproportionate say in policies directly affecting them. Thus, as long as many groups have influence in their own area of interest, government is responding to the interests of most Americans. Pluralists such as Robert Dahl have argued that this is in fact the way the American political system operates most of the time.[19]

Some critics argue that pluralists wrongly assume that nearly all of society's interests are able to compete effectively through group politics. They see a system

★ CRITICAL THINKING ★

WHAT'S YOUR OPINION?

Natural Advantages
In 1940, Senator Kenneth Wherry soberly exclaimed, "With God's help, we will lift Shanghai up and up, ever up, until it is just like Kansas City." Like many Americans before and since, Wherry assumed that our form of government could work as well nearly anywhere else in the world.

Some analysts believe that with the collapse of global communism the world has entered an age when democracy could be extended throughout most of the globe.

What's your opinion on the likelihood that democracy will take root in the countries of Asia, Africa, and the Middle East that currently have other forms of government? What conditions in these countries might foster or inhibit the process of democratization? You might ask yourself such questions as: Does democracy flourish only in relatively wealthy societies? Only in countries that do not have a tradition of authoritarian rule? Only in countries that are not threatened by hostile neighbors?

pluralism A theory of American politics that holds society's interests are substantially represented through the activities of groups.

The Federal Reserve Board of Governors is a government body that through its interest-rate policies exerts a substantial influence on the American economy. The Board meets in secrecy and is an example of the influence of political elites.

biased toward a small number of powerful groups. These critics are proponents of elite theory.

RULE BY A FEW: ELITISM

elitism The view that the United States is run essentially by a tiny elite (composed of wealthy or well-connected individuals) who control public policy through both direct and indirect means.

Elite theory offers a pessimistic view of the U.S. political system. **Elitism** holds that power in America is held by a small number of well-positioned, highly influential individuals who control policy for their own purposes. A leading proponent of elite theory was the sociologist C. Wright Mills, who argued that key policies are decided by an overlapping coalition of select leaders, including corporate executives, top military officers, and centrally placed public officials.[20] Other proponents of elite theory have defined the core group somewhat differently, but their contention is the same: America is essentially run, not by majorities or a plurality of groups, but by a small number of well-placed and privileged individuals.

Some theorists, including G. William Domhoff, hold a conspiratorial view of elites, contending that they consciously operate behind the scenes in order to manipulate government for their selfish purposes.[21] Other theorists argue that elite influence is a result of complexity. Nearly a century ago, Roberto Michels articulated an "iron law of oligarchy," concluding that power inevitably gravitates toward a few people at the top, even in societies and organizations that aim to be governed more democratically.[22]

Although some of the claims about a "power elite" are exaggerated, there is no question that certain policy areas are effectively controlled by a tiny circle of influential people. The nation's monetary policy, for example, is set by the decisions of the Federal Reserve Board, which meets in secrecy and is highly responsive to the concerns of bankers and financiers (see Chapter 18).

A PERSPECTIVE ON WHO GOVERNS

The perspective of this book is that each of these theories—majoritarianism, pluralism, and elitism—must be taken into account in any full explanation of

CURRENT CONTROVERSIES

SHOULD ENGLISH BE MADE AMERICA'S OFFICIAL LANGUAGE?

America's ideals are broad principles that include conflicting elements. The principle of diversity extols Americans' differences. The principle of unity proclaims that Americans are one people and one nation. These principles have clashed whenever newly arrived immigrants have been at issue. Should immigrants be allowed to maintain their distinctive characteristics? Or should their assimilation be accelerated? Which principle should govern—unity or diversity? The issue has emerged recently with the arrival of record numbers of Hispanic and Asian immigrants. A point of contention has been whether they should be required to use English as the first language in school and in the conduct of government-related business.

YES: We are one nation even though each of us may have ancestors who fought against each other in generations past. This has been made possible by our . . . common language. . . . The English language was both the language of opportunity and the language of unity. . . . Government multilingualism is divisive. . . . Michigan offers its driver test in 20 languages. There are 100 languages spoken in the Chicago school system. . . . Preserving national unity through making English this Nation's official language is . . . a critical issue. Look around the world. . . . Linguistic divisions swiftly lead to other divisions. . . . I submit that the time has indeed come for the English Language Amendment and I urge its adoption.

—U.S. Representative John Doolittle (R-Calif.)

NO: Whereas, several bills have been introduced in the U.S. Congress to make English the official language of the United States; and whereas, the issue often has a divisive effect on the public and does not meet with the inclusive spirit and vision of a democratic and diverse society; and whereas, the passage and implementation of such legislation could restrict the program options that local school systems have for limited English proficient children; therefore, let it be resolved that the Council of the Great City Schools opposes federal legislation that mandates that English is the official U.S. language; and . . . opposes such legislation that may appear in state legislatures and on state ballots.

—Council of the Great City Schools

politics and power in America. Some policies are decided by majority influence, whereas others reflect the influence of special interests and elites. The challenge is to distinguish the situations where each of these influence patterns predominates. Although subsequent chapters will attempt that task, a brief look ahead will provide an indication of what can be expected.

Although it is common in America to say that "the people govern," most citizens have only a limited appetite for politics. There are only a few issues at any moment that have the general public's attention and an even smaller number that it really cares about. If these are the issues where majority influence is most likely to occur, there is still the question of how popular influence works its way into public policy. The fact is, the lone individual is nearly powerless in a nation of 275 million people. Self-government requires institutions strong enough and effective enough to enable people to express a collective voice. Elections are one of these institutions. Another is political parties, which are organized to mobilize majorities behind particular candidates and issues. In the modern era, the mass media and opinion polls are other mechanisms through which popular opinion affects governmental decisions. And, of course, the public's views are also registered through the nation's two majoritarian institutions—Congress and the presidency. If these institutions are also responsive to group and elite influence, they are, through elections, a locus of majority sentiment.

Democracy—the idea of a government of, for, and by the people—is an organizing principle of the American political system. In practice, democracy—and its accompanying feature, majoritarianism—is most clearly evident in elections when Americans through their votes choose their representatives. Shown is a scene from the first televised general election debate of the 2000 race between presidential candidates Al Gore (left) and George W. Bush (right). In the center is debate moderator Jim Lehrer of the Public Broadcasting System (PBS).

The bureaucracy and the courts are relatively insulated from popular opinion. Elections and politicians come and go, but the bureaucrats who staff executive agencies and the judges who run the courts stay on and on. Government could not function without them, but in most instances, they are not instruments of the majority. Bureaucrats are more closely linked to narrower constituencies, such as farmers, broadcasters, or defense firms. These lobbying groups are also connected to Congress through its committees and subcommittees. In these arenas, a form of pluralist politics usually prevails. The courts are harder to characterize. They deal with individual cases but increasingly have also been a means by which groups try to influence broad issues of policy. Environmental and civil rights policies are among the areas in which groups through the court system have affected the way America is governed. Groups also play an increasingly large role in elections, mainly through the money they give to candidates for public office. If elections are primarily an arena of majority politics, they are also, and increasingly, a stage for group influence.

Elite influence is the most difficult of all to locate, which is a reason why analysts disagree on the degree to which elites affect policy. Elites have an uncommon degree of access to top officials, the media, and other sources of influence. What is less clear is the type of influence that this access provides. Do elites pursue their own agenda, or are their efforts tied to popular or group agendas? This book will identify instances of both patterns, but in general, the separate influence of elites is most pronounced in the areas of economic and foreign policy.

The Concept of a Political System and this Book's Organization

As the foregoing discussion suggests, American government is based on a great many related parts, including the voters, institutions, interest groups, and the political culture. It is useful in some respects to regard these components as con-

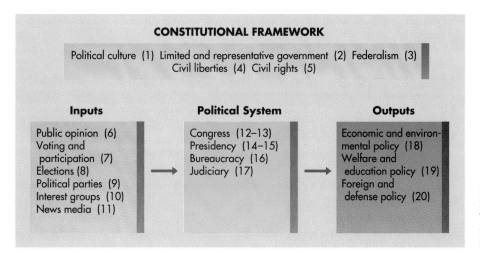

FIGURE 1-4 The American Political System
The book's chapters are organized within a political system's framework.

stituting a **political system.** The parts are separate but they connect with each other, affecting how each performs. The political scientist David Easton, who was a pioneer in this conception of politics, said that it makes little sense to study political relations piecemeal when they are, in reality, "interrelated."[23]

The complexity of government has kept political scientists from developing a dynamic explanatory model of the full political system, but the concept of politics as a system is useful for instructional purposes. The concept emphasizes the actual workings of government rather than its institutional structures alone. This approach characterizes this book, beginning with its organizational sequence.

As Figure 1-4 indicates, the political system operates against the backdrop of a constitutional framework that defines how power is to be obtained and exercised. This framework is the focus of Part One (Chapters 1–5), which examines the governmental structure and individual rights. *Inputs* are another part of the political system; these are the demands that people and groups place on government and the supports they provide for its institutions, leaders, and policies. These inputs are the subject of Part Two (Chapters 6–11), which examines public opinion, political participation, voting, political parties, interest groups, and the news media. Part Three (Chapters 12–17), examines the nation's elective and appointive institutions—Congress, the presidency, the courts, and the bureaucracy. Some of the discussion in Part Three is devoted simply to describing these institutions, but most of it explores their relationships and how their actions are affected by inputs and the constitutional framework. Part Four (Chapters 18–20) examines major areas of public policy: the economy and environment, social welfare and education, and foreign affairs and national defense. These are the system's *outputs:* its binding decisions on society. Part Five (Chapter 21) examines state and local governments. They play a vital political and policy role in the American governing system.

The chapters are collectively designed to convey a reliable body of knowledge that will enable the reader to think broadly and systematically about the nature of the American political system. To assist in this process, this chapter has identified five encompassing tendencies of American politics that will be examined more closely in later chapters. The United States has:

political system The various components of American government. The parts are separate, but they connect with each other, affecting how each performs.

- Enduring cultural ideals that are its people's common bond and a source of their political goals
- Extreme fragmentation of governing authority that is based on an elaborate system of checks and balances
- Many competing interests that are the result of the nation's great size, diverse population, and complex economic structure
- Strong emphasis on individual rights that is a consequence of the nation's political traditions
- Relatively sharp separation of the political and economic spheres that has the effect of placing many economic issues outside the reach of political majorities

www.mhhe.com/patterson5

Self-Quiz

Underlying this book's concern with the broad patterns of the American political system is a question that must be asked of any democracy: what is the relationship of the people to their government? The answer to this question is the foundation not only of a reasonable assessment of the state of American democracy but also of good citizenship. Responsible citizenship depends ultimately on an informed perspective, on a recognition of how difficult it is to govern effectively and yet how important it is to try. It cannot be said too often that the issue of governing is the most difficult issue facing any society. Nor can it be said too often that governing is a quest, not a resolved issue. The Constitution's opening phrase, "We, the People," is a call to Americans to join that quest. E. E. Schattschneider said it clearly: "In the course of centuries, there has come a great deal of agreement about what democracy is, but nobody has a monopoly on it and the last word has not been spoken."[24]

Summary

The United States is a nation that was formed on a set of ideals that include liberty, equality, self-government, individualism, diversity, and unity. These ideals were rooted in the country's European heritage, and early America's vast open lands and abundant natural resources influenced their growth. They became Americans' common bond and today are the basis of their political culture. Although they are mythic, inexact, and conflicting, these ideals have had a powerful effect on what generation after generation of Americans has tried to achieve politically for themselves and others.

Politics is the process by which it is determined whose values will prevail in society. The basis of politics is conflict over scarce resources and competing values. Those who have power win out in this conflict and are able to control governing authority and policy choices. In the case of the United States, no one faction controls all power and policy. Majorities govern on some issues, while groups and elites each govern on other issues.

The play of politics in the United States takes place through rules of the game that include democracy, constitutionalism, and capitalism. Democracy is rule by the people, which, in practice, refers to a representative system of government in which the people rule through their elected officials. Constitutionalism refers to rules that limit the rightful power of government over citizens. Capitalism is an economic system based on a free-market principle that allows the government only a limited role in determining how economic costs and benefits will be allocated.

Key Terms

authority
capitalism
constitutionalism
democracy

diversity
elitism
equality
government

individualism
liberty
majoritarianism
pluralism
policy
political culture

political system
politics
power
self-government
unity

Suggested Readings

Dahl, Robert. *On Democracy*. New Haven, Conn.: Yale University Press, 1998. A handbook on democracy by a leading advocate of pluralism.

DeLaet, Debra L. *U.S. Immigration Policy in an Age of Rights*. Westport, Conn.: Praeger Publishers, 2000. Analysis of the impact of civil rights action on the changes in U.S. immigration policy in recent decades.

Domhoff, G. William. *Who Rules America? Power and Politics in the Year 2000*. Mountain View, Calif.: Mayfield Publishing, 1998. A critical assessment of American government by a leading proponent of elite theory.

Ellis, Richard J. *American Political Cultures*. New York: Oxford University Press, 1996. An assessment of the American political culture that concludes that individualism and egalitarianism are the main dimensions.

Fischer, William, David Gerber, Jorge Guitart, and Maxine Seller. *Identity, Community, and Pluralism in American Life*. New York: Oxford University Press, 1996. Primary source readings on cultural diversity and pluralism in American life.

Lipset, Seymour Martin. *American Exceptionalism: A Double-Edged Sword*. New York: Norton, 1996. Argues that Americans' tendency to view society in idealized terms is a source of both alienation and progress.

McElroy, John Harmon. *American Beliefs: What Keeps a Big Country and a Diverse People United*. Chicago: I. R. Dee, 1999. An examination of the role of beliefs in Americans' political identity.

Norton, Anne. *Republic of Signs: Liberal Theory and American Popular Culture*. Chicago: University of Chicago Press, 1993. An insightful study of just how deeply American ideals have seeped into the country's symbols and language.

Salins, Peter D. *Assimilation, American Style*. New York: Basic Books, 1996. A study of immigration and its impact on American culture.

Schmidt, Ronald. *Language Policy and Identity Politics in the United States*. Philadelphia: Temple University Press, 2000. A critical assessment of language policy and its role in Americans' identity.

CHAPTER 2

Constitutional Democracy: Promoting Liberty and Self-Government

★

The people must be governed by a majority, with whom all power resides. But how is the sense of this majority to be obtained?

—Fisher Ames (1788)[1]

★ ★ ★

On the night of June 17, 1972, a security guard at the Watergate apartment-office complex in Washington, D.C., noticed that the latch on a basement door had been taped open. He called the police, who apprehended five burglars inside the National Democratic Party headquarters. As it turned out, the men had links to Republican President Richard Nixon's Committee to Re-elect the President.

Nixon called the incident "bizarre" and falsely denied that anyone on his staff had had anything to do with the break-in. Nixon knew that the truth could destroy his presidency. The Watergate break-in was just one incident in an orchestrated campaign of "dirty tricks" designed to ensure Nixon's reelection. Funded by illegal contributions and conducted through the CIA, IRS, FBI, Secret Service, and Nixon's own operatives (called the White House "plumbers"), the dirty-tricks campaign extended to wiretaps, tax audits, and burglaries of Nixon's political opponents (the "enemies list"), who included journalists and anti-war activists in addition to Democrats. Nixon understood that if his abuse of power became known, his impeachment and removal from office by Congress were distinct possibilities. He told his close aides, "I want you all to stonewall it, let them [the Watergate burglary defendants] plead the Fifth Amendment, cover up, or anything else."[2]

Although the Nixon White House managed for a time to hide the truth (in one ploy, the president's assistants asked the CIA to tell the FBI to stop the Watergate investigation on fictitious "national security" grounds), the facts of the dirty-tricks campaign gradually became known. In early 1974 the House Judiciary Committee began impeachment proceedings, helped along, ironically, by Nixon's own words. During Senate hearings, a White House assistant revealed that Nixon had tape-recorded all his telephone calls and personal conversations in the Oval Office. At first Nixon refused to release the tapes, but then made public what he claimed were "all the relevant" ones. The House Judiciary Committee demanded additional tapes, as did the special prosecutor who had been appointed to investigate criminal aspects of the Watergate affair. In late July the Supreme Court of the United States, which included four justices appointed by Nixon, unanimously ordered the president to supply sixty-four additional tapes. Two weeks later, on August 9, 1974, Richard Nixon, citing a loss of political support, resigned from office, the first president in U.S. history to do so.

Nixon's downfall was owed in no small measure to the handiwork, two centuries earlier, of the writers of the Constitution. They were well aware that power could never be entrusted to the goodwill of leaders. "If angels were to govern men," James Madison wrote in *Federalist* No. 51, "neither external nor internal controls on government would be necessary." Madison's point, of course, was that leaders are not angels and, as mere mortals, are subject to temptation and vice, including a lust for power—hence the Framers' insistence on constitutional checks on power, as when they gave Congress the authority to impeach a president and remove him from office.

The writers of the U.S. Constitution were intent on protecting *liberty* and therefore sought to restrict political power. Yet they also wanted a government that would allow the majority to rule. The first objective was **limited government**—a government that is subject to strict limits on its lawful uses of power. The second objective was **self-government**—a government that is subject to the will of the people as expressed through the preferences of a majority. Self-government requires that the voters' preferences find their way into public policy in a substantial and timely way. However, limited government requires restraints on the majority as a way of protecting the rights and interests of the minority. These considerations resulted in a constitution that has provision for majority rule but also has built-in restrictions on the exercise of majority power.

This chapter describes how the principles of self-government and limited government are embodied in the Constitution and explains the tension between them. The chapter also indicates how these principles have been modified in practice in the course of American history. The main points of this chapter are the following:

★ *America during the colonial period developed traditions of limited government and self-government.* These traditions were rooted in governing practices, philosophy, and cultural values.

★ *The Constitution provides for limited government mainly by defining lawful powers and by dividing those powers among competing institutions.* The Constitution, with its Bill of Rights, also prohibits government from infringing on individual rights. Judicial review is an additional safeguard of limited government.

limited government A government that is subject to strict limits on its lawful uses of powers, and hence on its ability to deprive people of their liberty.

self-government The principle that the people are the ultimate source and proper beneficiary of governing authority; in practice, a government based on majority rule.

The Senate Judiciary Committee holds hearings on allegations of illegal acts by President Richard Nixon. The congressional investigation led to Nixon's resignation.

★ *The Constitution in its original form provided for self-government mainly through indirect systems of popular election of representatives.* The Framers' theory of self-government was based on the notion that political power must be separated from immediate popular influences if sound policies are to result.

★ *The idea of popular government—in which the majority's desires have a more direct and immediate impact on governing officials—has gained strength since the nation's beginning.* Originally, the House of Representatives was the only institution subject to direct vote of the people. This mechanism has been extended to other institutions and, through primary elections, even to the nomination of candidates for public office.

Before the Constitution: The Colonial and Revolutionary Experiences

Early Americans' admiration for limited government was based partly on their English heritage. Other European nations of the eighteenth century implicitly acknowledged the divine right of their kings; England was an exception. British courts had developed a system of precedent known as "common law," which guaranteed trial by jury and due process of law as safeguards of life, liberty, and particularly property. These rights were defended by the courts and ordinarily respected by the king and Parliament. The king was also subject to control by Parliament, which gained supremacy over the Crown in the Glorious Revolution of 1689.

This tradition of limited government was evident in the American colonies. In each colony there was a right to trial by jury. There was also freedom of expression, although of a limited kind. Religious freedom, for example, was not granted by all the colonies. Nevertheless, religious oppression of the kind that was commonplace in Europe was rare. There was also a degree of self-government in all the colonies. Each had an elected assembly and, although the assemblies were usually controlled by wealthier interests, they acted as representative bodies and grew increasingly powerful as the number of settlers increased. There was also a "natural" liberty to be had in America. Europe's stifling aristocratic tradition could not be maintained in the New World, where a greater measure of personal freedom was as close as the next frontier.

"THE RIGHTS OF ENGLISHMEN"

The Revolutionary War was partly a rebellion against England's failure to respect its own tradition of limited government in the colonies. Many of the colonial charters had conferred on Americans "the rights of Englishmen," but British kings and ministers showed progressively less respect for this guarantee as time went on. The period after the French and Indian War (1755–1763) was a turning point in the relationship between the colonists and Britain. Until then the colonists had viewed themselves as loyal subjects of the Crown, and although there had been occasional disputes, few voices argued for independence. In fact, colonists had fought alongside British soldiers to drive the French out of Canada and the Western territories.

Life in colonial America was hard and sometimes dangerous. Colonial men often carried guns when traveling alone or with their families.

At the end of the French and Indian War, however, Britain imposed burdensome taxes on the colonists. The war with France, which had also been waged in Europe, had created a severe financial crisis for the British government, which looked to the increasingly prosperous colonies for relief. The colonies were not accustomed to paying taxes to the British. The practice was for Britain to raise its revenues from tariffs on imports and exports while the colonists kept any tax revenues they raised. But the British Parliament in 1765 levied a stamp tax on colonial newspapers and business documents, disrupting commerce and public communication. Because the colonists were not represented in the British Parliament that had imposed the tax, the colonial pamphleteer James Otis declared that the Stamp Act violated the fundamental rights of the colonists as "British subjects and men." "No taxation without representation" became a rallying cry for the colonists, who convened a special congress that declared that the only laws binding on the colonies were those enacted by a legislature "chosen therein by themselves."

Although Parliament backed down and repealed the Stamp Act, it then passed the Townshend Act, which imposed taxes on all paper, glass, lead, and tea entering the colonies. In *Letters from a Farmer in Pennsylvania* (1767), John Dickinson claimed that the Townshend duties were punitive and destructive of the goodwill between Britain and its colonies. When other colonists joined the protest, King George III sent additional British troops to America and interfered with colonial legislatures. These actions served only to arouse the colonists further. England then tried to placate the Americans by repealing the Townshend duties except for a nominal tea tax, which Britain retained in order to display its authority. The colonists viewed the tea tax as a petty insult, and in the Boston Tea Party of December 1773, a small band of patriots disguised as Indians boarded an English ship in Boston Harbor and dumped its cargo of tea overboard.

In 1774, the colonists met in Philadelphia at the First Continental Congress to define their demands of the British Crown: they called for free assembly, an end to the British military occupation, their own councils for the imposition of taxes, and trial by local juries. (British authorities had resorted to shipping "trouble-makers" back to London for trial.) King George III refused their petition, and in 1775, British troops and colonial minutemen clashed at Lexington and Concord. Eight colonists died on the Lexington green in what became known as "the shot heard 'round the world."

Within a year, sporadic acts of defiance had become a full-scale revolution. In a pamphlet called *Common Sense*, which sold 120,000 copies in its first three months, Thomas Paine claimed that all of Europe was rife with political oppression and that America was humanity's last hope of liberty. "Freedom has been hunted around the globe. . . . Receive the fugitive, and prepare in time an asylum for mankind."

THE DECLARATION OF INDEPENDENCE

Although grievances against Britain were the immediate cause of the Revolution, ideas about the proper form of government were also on the colonists' minds. A century earlier, the English philosopher John Locke (1632–1704) had written that government must be restrained in its powers if it is to serve the common good. In his *Two Treatises of Government* (1690), Locke advanced the liberal principle that people have **inalienable rights** (or **natural rights**), including those of life, liberty, and property. In Locke's view, such rights belonged to people in their natural state before governments were created. When people agreed to come together (or, in Locke's term, entered into a "social contract") in order to have the protection that only organized government could provide, their natural rights were neither taken from them by government nor surrendered by them to government. If the government protected their natural rights, they were obliged to obey it, but if the government failed to protect their rights, they could rightfully rebel against it.[3]

Locke's ideas inspired a generation of American leaders.[4] The notion that people had natural and inalienable rights was a central theme of Paine's *Common Sense,* as was his claim that oppression justified revolution. Thomas Jefferson declared that Locke "was one of the three greatest men that ever lived, without exception," and Jefferson paraphrased Locke's ideas in key passages of the Declaration of Independence:

> We hold these truths to be self-evident, that all men are created equal, that they are endowed by their Creator with certain unalienable rights, that among these are life, liberty and the pursuit of happiness.
>
> That to secure these rights, governments are instituted among men, deriving their just powers from the consent of the governed.
>
> That whenever any form of government becomes destructive of these ends, it is the right of the people to alter or to abolish it, and to institute a new government.

The Declaration was a call to revolution rather than a framework for a new form of government, but the ideas it contained—liberty, self-government, individual rights, lawful powers—were to become the basis, eleven years later, for the Constitution of the United States.

inalienable (natural) rights
Those rights that persons theoretically possessed in the state of nature, prior to the formation of governments. These rights, including those of life, liberty, and property, are considered inherent and, as such, are inalienable. Since government is established by people, government has the responsibility to preserve these rights.

Drafting the Declaration of Independence, a painting by J. L. Ferris. Benjamin Franklin, John Adams, and Thomas Jefferson (standing) drafted the historic document. Jefferson was the principal author; he inserted the inspirational words about liberty, equality, and self-government.

THE ARTICLES OF CONFEDERATION

The first government of the United States was based, not on the Constitution, but on the Articles of Confederation. The Articles were adopted during the Revolutionary War and created a very weak national government that was subordinate to the states. This arrangement stemmed from the colonial experience. The colonies had always been governed separately, and their people considered themselves Virginians, New Yorkers, or Pennsylvanians as much as they thought of themselves as Americans. They naturally preferred a government that was constitutionally derived from the states. Moreover, they were leery of a powerful central government. The American Revolution was sparked by grievances against the arbitrary policies of King George III, and Americans were in no mood to replace him with a strong national authority of their own making.

Under the Articles of Confederation, each state retained its "sovereignty, freedom and independence." There was a national Congress, but its members were appointed and paid by their respective state governments. Each of the thirteen states had one vote in Congress, and the agreement of nine states was required to pass legislation. Moreover, any state could block constitutional change: the Articles of Confederation could be amended only by unanimous approval of the states.

The American union held together during the Revolutionary War out of necessity: the states had either to cooperate or to surrender to the British. But once the war ended, the states felt free to go their separate ways. Several states sent representatives abroad to negotiate their own separate trade agreements with foreign nations. Others negotiated directly with the Indian tribes. New Hampshire,

This is a portion of Thomas Jefferson's handwritten draft of the Declaration of Independence, a formal expression of America's governing ideals.

with its eighteen-mile coastline, even established its own navy. In a melancholy letter to Thomas Jefferson, George Washington wondered whether the United States deserved to be called a nation.

Congress was expected to provide for the nation's defense and establish the basis for a general economy, but it lacked the power to achieve these goals. It was not allowed to interfere in the states' commerce policies, and the states were soon engaged in ruinous trade wars. Congress also lacked the power to tax and consequently had no money with which to build a navy and hire an army. Its plight was dramatically evident soon after the Revolutionary War when unpaid army units mutinied and marched on Congress, whose members fled in panic to another location.

SHAYS'S REBELLION: A NATION DISSOLVING

By 1784, the nation was unraveling. Congress was so weak that its members often did not bother to attend its sessions.[5] Finally, in late 1786, a revolt in western

Massachusetts prompted leading Americans to conclude that the country's government had to be changed. A ragtag army of two thousand farmers, armed with pitchforks, marched on county courthouses to prevent foreclosures on their land and cattle. Many of the farmers were veterans of the Revolutionary War; their leader, Daniel Shays, had been a captain in the Revolutionary army. They had been given assurances during the Revolution that their land, which lay fallow because they were away at war, would not be confiscated for reasons of unpaid debts and taxes.

Although many Americans, including Jefferson, sympathized with the farmers, Shays's Rebellion scared propertied interests, and they called on the governor of Massachusetts to put down the revolt. He asked Congress for help, but it had no army to send.[6] He finally raised enough money to hire a militia that put down the rebellion, but Shays's Rebellion made it clear that a strengthening of national authority was necessary if public order and the American union were to be preserved. At Virginia's urging, five states met at the Annapolis Convention in late 1786 to address the crisis. They did not reach agreement on a solution but

County courthouses in Massachusetts in 1786 were the scenes of brawls between angry farmers and those who supported the state's attempts to foreclose on their property because of unpaid debts. The violence of Shays's Rebellion convinced many political leaders that the central government needed to be more powerful.

urged Congress to authorize a constitutional convention of all the states that would be held the following spring in Philadelphia. Congress agreed to authorize a convention but placed a restriction on it: the delegates were to meet for "the sole and express purpose of revising the Articles of Confederation."

Negotiating Toward a Constitution

The delegates to the Philadelphia constitutional convention ignored the instructions of Congress. They drafted a plan for an entirely new form of government. Prominent delegates (among them George Washington, Benjamin Franklin, and James Madison) were determined from the outset to establish an American nation built on a strong central government.

The process of writing the Constitution was a contentious one. All the delegates were men of means: they were for the most part lawyers, large landowners, and merchants. They shared a commitment to the interests of the propertied class, but they also had their differences. The Constitution is sometimes portrayed as the work of intellectual geniuses who put politics aside to create a document that would endure the test of time. In reality, the Framers of the Constitution fought like any other group of politicians, each promoting the ideas and values in which he believed. What set the Framers apart was the nature of the times in which they lived. They had experienced the American Revolution and the problems of nation building. They had thought long about and worked hard at the problems of government, and the Philadelphia convention gave them a unique opportunity to apply the constitutional lessons they had learned.

THE GREAT COMPROMISE: A TWO-CHAMBER CONGRESS

Debate at the constitutional convention of 1787 began over a plan put forward by the Virginia delegation, which was dominated by strong nationalists. The **Virginia Plan** (also called the large-state plan) called for a two-chamber Congress that would have supreme authority in all areas "in which the separate states are incompetent," particularly defense and interstate trade. The Virginia Plan also provided that the states would have numerical representation in Congress in proportion to their populations or tax contributions. Either way, representatives of the small states would be greatly outnumbered. Small states such as Delaware and Rhode Island would be allowed only one representative in the lower chamber, while large states such as Massachusetts and Virginia would have more than a dozen.

Not surprisingly, the Virginia Plan was roundly condemned by delegates from the smaller states. They rallied around a counterproposal made by New Jersey's William Paterson. The **New Jersey Plan** (also called the small-state plan) called for a stronger national government with the power to tax and to regulate commerce among the states; in most other respects, however, the Articles would remain in effect. Congress would have a single chamber in which each state, large or small, would have a single vote.

The debate over the New Jersey and Virginia plans dragged on for weeks before the delegates reached what is now known as the **Great Compromise.** It provided for a bicameral (two-chamber) Congress: the House of Representatives

Virginia (large-state) Plan A constitutional proposal for a strong Congress with two chambers, both of which would be based on numerical representation, thus granting more power to the larger states.

New Jersey (small-state) Plan A constitutional proposal for a strengthened Congress but one in which each state would have a single vote, thus granting a small state the same legislative power as a large state.

Great Compromise The agreement at the constitutional convention to create a two-chamber Congress with the House apportioned by population and the Senate apportioned equally by state.

The Constitution was written in Philadelphia during the summer of 1787 in the East Room of the Old Pennsylvania State House, where the Declaration of Independence had been signed a decade earlier. George Washington presided over the Constitutional Convention but played a less active role in the debate than many of the delegates.

would be apportioned among the states on the basis of population and the Senate on the basis of an equal number of votes (two) for each state. The small states would never have agreed to join a union in which their vote was always weaker than that of large states,[7] a fact reflected in Article V of the Constitution: "No state, without its consent, shall be deprived of its equal suffrage in the Senate."

THE NORTH-SOUTH COMPROMISE: THE ISSUE OF SLAVERY

North-South Compromise The agreement over economic and slavery issues that enabled northern and southern states to settle differences that threatened to defeat the effort to draft a new constitution.

The separate interests of the states were also the basis for a second major agreement: the **North-South Compromise** over economic issues. The South had a slave-based agricultural economy, and its delegates feared that the North, which had a stronger manufacturing sector, would gain a numerical majority in Congress and then proceed to enact unfair tax policies. If Congress levied high import tariffs on finished goods from foreign nations in order to protect domestic manufacturers and placed heavy export tariffs on agricultural goods, the burden of financing the new government would fall mainly on the South. Its delegates also worried that northern representatives in Congress might tax or even bar the importation of slaves.

After extended debate, a compromise was reached. Congress was to be prohibited by the Constitution from taxing exports but could tax imports. In addition, Congress would be prohibited from passing laws to end the slave trade until 1808. The South also gained a constitutional provision requiring each state to return runaway slaves to their state of origin. A final bargain was the infamous "Three-fifths Compromise": for purposes of both taxation and representation in Congress, five slaves were to be considered the equivalent of three white people; in effect, a slave was to be counted as three-fifths of a human being.

Although the Philadelphia convention has been criticized for the compromise over slavery, the southern states' dependence on slavery was a formidable obstacle to union. Northern states had no economic use for forced labor and had few slaves, whereas southern states had based their economies on large slave populations (see Figure 2-1). John Rutledge of South Carolina asked during the convention debate whether the North regarded southerners as "fools." Southern

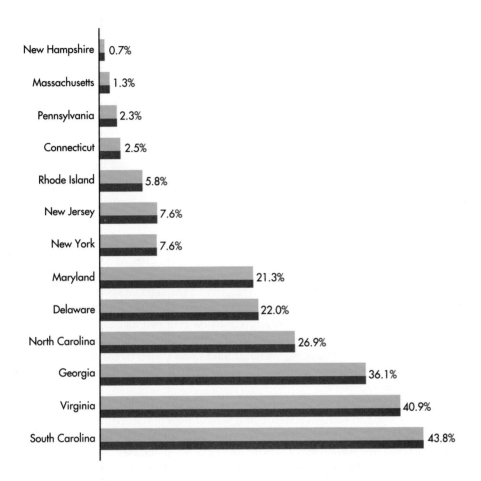

New Hampshire 0.7%
Massachusetts 1.3%
Pennsylvania 2.3%
Connecticut 2.5%
Rhode Island 5.8%
New Jersey 7.6%
New York 7.6%
Maryland 21.3%
Delaware 22.0%
North Carolina 26.9%
Georgia 36.1%
Virginia 40.9%
South Carolina 43.8%

FIGURE 2-1   African Americans as a Percentage of State Population, 1790. *Source: U.S. Bureau of the Census, 2000.*

delegates declared that they would bolt the convention and form their own union rather than join one that prohibited slavery.

A STRATEGY FOR RATIFICATION

The compromises over slavery and the structure of the Congress took up most of the four months that the convention was in session. Some major issues, such as the structure and powers of the federal judiciary, were decided without extensive debate. In the end, the delegates were not fully convinced that they had always made the best choices, but they were confident that the Constitution was a vast improvement on the Articles.

There remained a final issue, however: would those Americans not at the convention share the delegates' opinion of the Constitution? The delegates realized that ratification was not a sure thing. Congress had not authorized a wholesale restructuring of the federal government and had created a barrier to any such plan. In authorizing the Philadelphia convention, Congress had stated that any proposed change in the Articles would have to be "agreed to in Congress" and then "confirmed by [all of] the states." The delegates recognized that if they followed this procedure, which required unanimous agreement, the Constitution

James Madison is often called the "father of the Constitution" because he was instrumental in its writing and its ratification (through his contributions to the *Federalist Papers*). The portrait is by Gilbert Stuart.

Anti-Federalists   A term used to describe opponents of the Constitution during the debate over ratification.

Federalists   A term used to describe proponents of the Constitution during the debate over ratification.

had almost no chance of ratification. In a bold move, they established their own ratifying process. They instructed Congress to submit the document directly to the states, where it would become law after being approved by at least nine states in special ratifying conventions of popularly elected delegates. It was a masterful strategy: there was little hope that all thirteen state legislatures would approve the Constitution, but nine states through conventions might be persuaded to ratify it. And indeed, North Carolina and Rhode Island were steadfastly opposed to the new form of government and did not ratify the Constitution until the eleven other states ratified and declared that they would form a union without them, leaving them weak and isolated.

THE RATIFICATION DEBATE

The debate over ratification was a contentious one. The **Anti-Federalists** (as opponents of the Constitution were labeled) raised arguments that still echo in American politics. They claimed that the national government would be too powerful and would threaten the sovereignty of the separate states and the liberty of the people. Many Americans had an innate distrust of centralized power and worried that the people's liberty could be eclipsed as easily by a distant American government as it had been by the British king. The fact that the Constitution contained no bill of rights heightened this concern. Did its absence indicate that the central government would be free to define for itself what the people's rights would be?

The presidency was also a source of concern. No such office had existed under the Articles, and some worried that it would lead to the creation of an American monarchy. Even the motives of the men who wrote the Constitution came under attack. They were men of wealth and education and had acted in response to debtors' riots. Would the Constitution become a tool by which the wealthy ruled over those with little or no money? And who would bear the burden of additional taxation? For Americans struggling with local and state tax payments, the creation of yet another tax agency was hardly an attractive proposal.

Most Anti-Federalists acknowledged a need to strengthen national commerce and defense. What they opposed was the creation of a powerful national government as the mechanism. They favored a revised Articles, which in their opinion could accomplish these goals without the risk of establishing a government that could threaten their liberties, their livelihoods, and their local interests.

The **Federalists** (as the Constitution's supporters called themselves) responded with a persuasive case of their own. Their strongest arguments were set forth by James Madison and Alexander Hamilton, who, along with John Jay, wrote a series of essays during the New York ratification debate. The essays were published in a New York City newspaper under the pen name Publius and were entitled "The Federalist." (The essays are collectively referred to as *The Federalist Papers* and are widely acknowledged as a brilliant political treatise.) Madison and Hamilton argued that the government of the Constitution would correct the defects of the Articles; it would have the power necessary to forge a secure and prosperous union. At the same time, because of restrictions on its powers, the new government would endanger neither the states nor personal liberty. In *Federalist* Nos. 47, 48, 49, 50, and 51, for example, Madison explained how the separation of national institutions was designed to both empower and restrict the federal government. (The Federalist and Anti-Federalist arguments are discussed further in Chapter 3.)

Whether the ratification debate changed many minds is unknown. Historical evidence indicates, however, that a majority of ordinary Americans opposed the Constitution's ratification. But their voice in the state ratifying conventions was smaller than that of wealthier interests, which, in the main, supported the change. The pro-ratification forces were also bolstered by the widespread assumption that George Washington would become the first president. He was the most trusted and popular American leader, and historians believe that Washington's endorsement of the new government tipped the balance in favor of ratification.[8]

Delaware was the first state to ratify the Constitution, and Connecticut, Georgia, and New Jersey followed, an indication that the Great Compromise had satisfied several of the small states. In the early summer of 1788, New Hampshire became the ninth state to ratify. The Constitution was law. But neither Virginia nor New York had ratified, and a stable union without these two major states was almost unthinkable. They were as large in area as many European countries and conceivably could survive as independent nations. They nearly did choose a separate course. In both states, the Constitution barely passed, and then only after the Federalists promised to support a bill of rights designed to protect individual freedoms from the power of the central government.

www.mhhe.com/patterson5

Simulation

THE FRAMERS' GOALS

A **constitution** is the fundamental law that defines how a government will legitimately operate: how its leaders will be chosen, the institutions through which these leaders will work, the procedures they must follow in making policy, and the powers they can lawfully exercise. The Constitution that was written in Philadelphia in 1787 is exactly such a law. In theory, it is the highest law of the land: neither a popular majority nor a leader at the highest pinnacle of power stands above it. Its provisions define how power is to be acquired and can be used.

constitution The fundamental law that defines how a government will legitimately operate.

The Constitution reflected the Framers' vision of a proper government for the American people. Its provisions addressed four broad goals (see Table 2-1). One was the creation of a national government strong enough to meet the nation's

---

TABLE 2-1   Major Goals of the Framers of the Constitution

1. To establish a government strong enough to meet the nation's needs—an objective sought through substantial grants of power to the federal government in areas such as defense and commerce (see Chapter 3).

2. To establish a government that would not threaten the existence of the separate states—an objective sought through federalism (see Chapter 3) and through a Congress connected to the states through elections.

3. To establish a government that would not threaten liberty—an objective sought through an elaborate system of checks and balances.

4. To establish a government based on popular sovereignty—an objective sought through provisions for the direct and indirect election of public officials.

needs, particularly in the areas of defense and commerce. Another goal was to preserve the states as governing entities. The states already existed and had the loyalty of their people. Accordingly, the Framers established a system of government (*federalism*) in which power is divided between the national government and the states. Federalism is discussed at length in Chapter 3, which will also explain how the Constitution laid the foundation for a strong national government.

The Framers' other goals were to establish a national government that was restricted in its lawful uses of power (limited government) and that gave the people a voice in their governance (self-government). These two goals and how they were written into the Constitution are the focus of the rest of this chapter.

Providing for a Limited Government

A challenge facing the Framers of the Constitution was how to control the coercive force of government. Government's unique characteristic is that it alone can legally arrest, imprison, and even kill people who break its rules.[9] Force is not the only basis of effective government, but government must be able to use force or lawless elements would take over society. The dilemma is that government itself can destroy civilized society by using its force to brutalize and intimidate its opponents. "It is a melancholy reflection," James Madison wrote to Thomas Jefferson shortly after the Constitution's ratification, "that liberty should be equally exposed to danger whether the government has too much or too little power."[10]

The men who wrote the Constitution sought to establish a government strong enough to enforce national interests, including defense and commerce among the states (see Chapter 3), but not so strong as to destroy liberty. Limited government was built into the Constitution through both grants and restrictions of political power.

GRANTS AND DENIALS OF POWER

grants of power The method of limiting the U.S. government by confining its scope of authority to those powers expressly granted in the Constitution.

The Framers chose to limit the national government in part by confining its scope to constitutional **grants of power**. Congress's lawmaking powers are specifically listed in Article I, section 8, of the Constitution. Seventeen in number, these listed powers include, for example, the powers to tax, to establish an army and navy, to declare war, to regulate commerce among the states, to create a national currency, and to borrow money. Authority *not* granted to the government by the Constitution is in theory denied to it. In a period where other governments had unrestricted powers, this limitation was remarkable.

denials of power A constitutional means of limiting government by listing those powers that government is expressly prohibited from using.

The Framers also used **denials of power** as a means to limit government, prohibiting certain practices that European rulers had routinely used to intimidate their political opponents. The French king, for example, could imprison a subject indefinitely without charge or trial. The U.S. Constitution prohibits such action: individuals have the right to be brought before a court under a writ of habeas corpus for a judgment as to the legality of their confinement. The Constitution also forbids Congress and the states from passing *ex post facto* laws, under which citizens can be prosecuted for acts that were legal at the time they

This 1790s colored engraving by William Birch depicts a Philadelphia street scene. Philadelphia's role in the birth of the American nation is rivaled only by Boston's contribution.

were committed. Among its other denials of power, the Constitution prohibits religious tests as a qualification for office, and it forbids Congress and the states to enact bills of attainder (legislative trials).

As a further denial of power, the Framers made the Constitution difficult to amend. Those in authority would not be able to increase their lawful powers unless the change had broad and extraordinary support. An amendment could be proposed only by a two-thirds majority in both chambers of Congress or in a national constitutional convention called by the legislatures of two-thirds of the states. Such a proposal would then become part of the Constitution only if ratified by three-fourths of the state legislatures or by three-fourths of the states in a special national convention. (The Constitution has been amended only twenty-seven times during the nation's history; in each instance, the amendment was proposed by Congress and ratified by the state legislatures.)

USING POWER TO OFFSET POWER

Although the Framers believed that grants and denials of power could act as controls on government, they had no illusion that written words alone would restrain power. As a consequence, they sought to check power with power. The idea was to divide the authority of government, so that no single institution could exercise great power without the agreement of other institutions.[11]

The idea that a **separation of powers** was necessary to the preservation of liberty had been proposed decades earlier by the French theorist Montesquieu. His argument was widely accepted in America, and when the states drafted new constitutions after the start of the Revolutionary War, they built their

separation of powers The division of the powers of government among separate institutions or branches.

Constitutional Necessity
The Englishman James Bryce ranked America's written constitution as its greatest contribution to the practice of government. The Constitution offered a new model of government in which a written document defining the state's lawful powers was a higher authority than the actions of any political leader.

The Framers' commitment to constitutionalism grew out of their recognition that, although government must have coercive power in order to function properly, this same power can be used by unscrupulous leaders to repress their opponents.

Do you think these two considerations—the coercive power of government and the corruptibility of human nature—lead almost inevitably to a belief in limited government and to the use of a constitution as a means to control the uses of power?

separated institutions sharing power   The principle that, as a way to limit government, its powers should be divided among separate branches, each of which also shares in the power of the others as a means of checking and balancing them. The result is that no one branch can exercise power decisively without the support or acquiescence of the others.

checks and balances   The elaborate system of divided spheres of authority provided by the U.S. Constitution as a means of controlling the power of government. The separation of powers among the branches of the national government, federalism, and the different methods of selecting national officers are all part of this system.

governments around the concept of a separation of powers. Pennsylvania was an exception, and its experience only seemed to prove the necessity of separated powers. Unrestrained by an independent judiciary or executive, Pennsylvania's all-powerful legislature systematically deprived minority groups of their basic rights and freedoms: Quakers were disenfranchised for their religious beliefs, conscientious objectors to the Revolutionary War were prosecuted, and the right of trial by jury was eliminated.

In *Federalist* No. 10, Madison asked why governments often act according to the interests of overbearing majorities rather than according to principles of justice. He attributed the cause to "the mischiefs of faction." People, he argued, are divided into opposing religious, geographical, ethnic, economic, and other factions. These divisions are natural and desirable, in that free people have a right to their personal opinions and interests. Yet factions can themselves be a source of oppressive government. If a faction gains full power, it will use government to advance itself at the expense of all others. (*Federalist* No. 10 is widely regarded as the finest political essay ever written by an American. It is reprinted at the back of this book.)

Out of this concern came the Framers' special contribution to the doctrine of the separation of powers. They did not believe that it would be enough, as Montesquieu had suggested, to divide the government's authority strictly along institutional lines, granting all legislative power to the legislature, all judicial power to the courts, and all executive power to the presidency. This *total* separation would make it too easy for a single faction to exploit a particular kind of political power. A faction that controlled the legislature, for example, could enact laws ruinous to other interests. A better system of divided government would be one in which political power could be applied forcibly only when institutions agreed on its use. This system would require separated but *overlapping* powers. Since no one faction could easily gain control over all institutions, factions would have to work together, a process that would require each to moderate its demands and thus would serve many interests rather than one or a few.[12]

SEPARATED INSTITUTIONS SHARING POWER: CHECKS AND BALANCES

The Framers' concept of divided powers has been described by political scientist Richard Neustadt as the principle of **separated institutions sharing power**.[13] The separate branches are interlocked in such a way that an elaborate system of **checks and balances** is created (see Figure 2-2). No institution can act decisively without the support or acquiescence of the other institutions. Legislative, executive, and judicial powers in the American system are divided in such a way that they overlap; each of the three branches of government checks the others' powers and balances those powers with powers of its own. (As natural as this system now might seem to Americans, most democracies have a parliamentary system, where executive and legislative power are combined in a single institution rather than invested in separate ones. In a parliamentary system, the majority in the legislature selects the prime minister, who is both the legislature leader and the chief executive. See "How the United States Compares.")

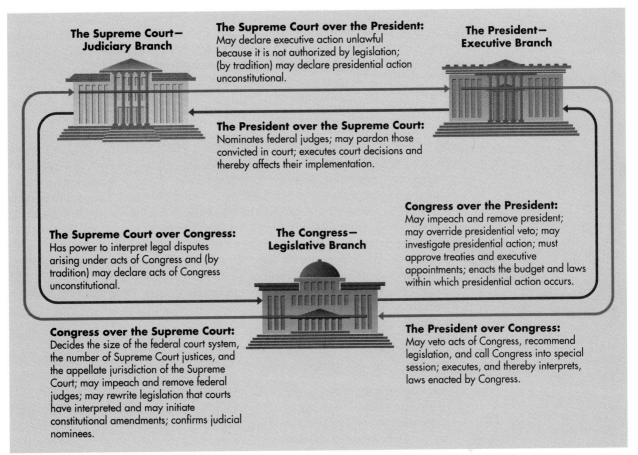

The Supreme Court—Judiciary Branch

The Supreme Court over the President: May declare executive action unlawful because it is not authorized by legislation; (by tradition) may declare presidential action unconstitutional.

The President—Executive Branch

The President over the Supreme Court: Nominates federal judges; may pardon those convicted in court; executes court decisions and thereby affects their implementation.

Congress over the President: May impeach and remove president; may override presidential veto; may investigate presidential action; must approve treaties and executive appointments; enacts the budget and laws within which presidential action occurs.

The Supreme Court over Congress: Has power to interpret legal disputes arising under acts of Congress and (by tradition) may declare acts of Congress unconstitutional.

The Congress—Legislative Branch

Congress over the Supreme Court: Decides the size of the federal court system, the number of Supreme Court justices, and the appellate jurisdiction of the Supreme Court; may impeach and remove federal judges; may rewrite legislation that courts have interpreted and may initiate constitutional amendments; confirms judicial nominees.

The President over Congress: May veto acts of Congress, recommend legislation, and call Congress into special session; executes, and thereby interprets, laws enacted by Congress.

FIGURE 2-2 The System of Checks and Balances
This elaborate system of divided spheres of authority was provided by the U.S. Constitution as a means of controlling the power of government. The separation of powers among the branches of the national government, federalism, and the different methods of selecting national officers are all part of this system.

Shared Legislative Powers

Under the Constitution, Congress has legislative authority, but that power is partly shared with the other branches and thus checked by them. The president can veto acts of Congress, recommend legislation, and call special sessions of Congress. The president also has the power to execute—and thereby to interpret—the laws made by Congress.

The Supreme Court has the power to interpret acts of Congress that are disputed in legal cases. By tradition, the Court also has the power of judicial review; it can declare laws of Congress void when it finds that they are not in accord with the Constitution.

Within Congress, there is a further check on legislative power: for legislation to be passed, a majority in each house of Congress is required. Thus the Senate and the House of Representatives can block each other from acting.

Shared Executive Powers

Executive power is vested in the president but is constrained by legislative and judicial checks. The president's power to make treaties and appoint high-ranking officials, for example, is subject to Senate approval. In practical terms,

Congress's greatest checks on executive action are its lawmaking and appropriations powers. The executive branch cannot act without laws that authorize its activities or without the money that pays for these programs.

The judiciary's major check on the presidency is its power to declare an action unlawful because it is not authorized by the legislation that the executive claims to be implementing.

Shared Judicial Powers

Judicial power rests with the Supreme Court and with lower federal courts, which are subject to checks by the other branches of the federal government. Congress is empowered to establish the size of the federal court system, to restrict the Supreme Court's appellate jurisdiction in some circumstances, and to impeach and remove federal judges from office. More important, Congress can rewrite legislation that the courts have misinterpreted and can initiate amendments when it disagrees with the courts' rulings on constitutional issues.

The president has the power to appoint federal judges with the consent of the Senate and to pardon persons convicted in the courts. The president is also responsible for executing court decisions, a function that provides opportunities to influence the way rulings are implemented.

THE BILL OF RIGHTS

Although the delegates to the Philadelphia convention discussed the possibility of placing a list of individual rights (such as freedom of speech and the right to a fair trial) in the Constitution, they ultimately decided that such a list was unnecessary because of the doctrine of expressed powers: government could not lawfully assume powers, such as the abridgment of human rights, that were not authorized by the Constitution. Moreover, the delegates concluded that a bill of rights was undesirable because government might feel free to disregard any right that was inadvertently left off the list or that emerged at some future time.

These considerations did not allay the fears of leading Americans who believed that no possible safeguard against tyrannical government should be omitted. "A bill of rights," Jefferson argued, "is what the people are entitled to against every government on earth, general or particular, and what no just government should refuse or rest on inference." Jefferson had included a bill of rights in the constitution he wrote for Virginia at the outbreak of the Revolutionary War, and all but four states had followed Virginia's example.

Opposition to the absence of a bill of rights in the federal constitution led to its addition. Madison himself introduced a series of amendments during the First Congress, ten of which were soon ratified by the states. These amendments, traditionally called the **Bill of Rights,** include such rights as free expression and due process for persons accused of crimes. (These rights, termed "civil liberties," are the subject of Chapter 4.)

Bill of Rights The first ten amendments to the Constitution. They include such rights as freedom of speech.

The Bill of Rights is a precise expression of the concept of limited government. In consenting to be governed, the people agree to accept the authority of government in certain areas but not in others; the people's constitutional rights cannot lawfully be denied by governing officials.

JUDICIAL REVIEW

The writers of the Constitution both empowered and limited government. But who was to decide whether the government was operating within its constitutional powers? The Framers did not specifically entrust this power to a particular branch of government, although they did grant the Supreme Court the authority to decide on "all cases arising under this Constitution."

Most delegates to the Philadelphia convention apparently assumed that the Supreme Court would have the power to decide whether a governmental institution has acted within its constitutional powers and, if not, to nullify its action. There was precedent for this form of judicial authority in several states, and a form of it had existed during the colonial period. It is also noteworthy that the power of the courts to declare laws null and void was discussed and accepted at the ratifying conventions of at least eight of the thirteen states.[14] Still, because the Constitution did not explicitly grant the judiciary this authority, it was a principle that had to be established in practice.

The opportunity arose with an incident that occurred after the election of 1800, in which John Adams lost his bid for a second presidential term after a bitter campaign against Jefferson. Between November 1800, when Jefferson was elected, and March 1801, when he was inaugurated, the Federalist-controlled Congress created fifty-nine additional lower-court judgeships, enabling Adams to appoint loyal Federalists to those positions before he left office. However, Adams's term expired before the secretary of state could deliver the judicial commissions to all the appointees. Without this formal authorization, an appointee could not take office. Knowing this, Jefferson told his secretary of state, James Madison, not to deliver them. William Marbury was one of those who did not receive his commission, and he asked the Supreme Court to issue a writ of *mandamus* (a court order that directs an official to take a specific action) requiring Madison to deliver it.

Marbury v. Madison (1803) became the foundation for judicial review by the federal courts. Chief Justice John Marshall wrote the *Marbury* opinion, which declared that Marbury had a legal right to his commission. The opinion also said, however, that the Supreme Court could not issue him a writ of *mandamus* because it lacked the constitutional authority to do so. Congress had granted the Court the power to issue such writs in an ordinary act of legislation—the Judiciary Act of 1789. Marshall pointed out that the Constitution prohibits any expansion of the Supreme Court's authority except through an amendment to the Constitution. That being the case, Marshall stated, the portion of the Judiciary Act that provided the authorization was constitutionally invalid.[15]

Marshall's decision was ingenious because it asserted the power of judicial review without creating the possibility of its rejection by either the executive or the legislative branch. In declaring that Marbury had a right to his commission, the Court in effect said that President Jefferson had failed in his constitutional duty to execute the laws faithfully. But since it did not order Jefferson to deliver the commission, he had no opportunity to refuse to comply with the Court's judgment. At the same time, the Court admonished Congress for passing legislation that exceeded its constitutional authority. And in the process of invalidating an act of Congress on constitutional grounds, the Court asserted its power of **judicial review**—that is, the power of the judiciary to decide whether

Thomas Jefferson admired the natural-rights philosophy of the English philosopher John Locke. Jefferson used some of Locke's phrases almost word for word in writing the Declaration of Independence and applied Locke's ideas when writing the Virginia bill of rights.

John Marshall forcefully expressed his nationalist views in important Supreme Court decisions during his thirty-four years as chief justice.

judicial review The power of courts to decide whether a governmental institution has acted within its constitutional powers and, if not, to declare its action null and void.

LIMITS ON GOVERNMENT IN THE U.S. CONSTITUTION

Grants of power: powers granted to the national government by the Constitution; powers not granted it are denied it unless they are necessary and proper to the carrying out of granted powers.

Separated institutions sharing power: the division of the national government's power among three branches, each of which is to act as a check on the powers of the other two.

Federalism: the division of political authority between the national government and the states, enabling the people to appeal to one authority if their rights and interests are not respected by the other authority.

Denials of power: powers expressly denied to the national and state governments by the Constitution.

Bill of Rights: the first ten amendments to the Constitution, which specify rights of citizens that the national government must respect.

Judicial review: the power of the courts to declare governmental action null and void when it is found to violate the Constitution.

Elections: the power of the voters to remove officials from office.

a government official or institution has acted within the limits of the Constitution and, if not, to declare its action null and void.

Providing for Self-Government

"We the People" is the opening line of the Constitution. It expresses the idea that, in the United States, the people will have the power to govern themselves. In a sense, there is no contradiction between this idea and the Constitution's provisions for limited government, since individual *liberty* is part of the process of *self-government*. In another sense, the contradiction is clear: restrictions on the power of the majority are a denial of its right to govern society as it chooses.

In its original form, the Constitution had only limited provisions for popular control through elections. The House of Representatives was the only institution that was subject to direct election by the voters. Popular voting for the President was widespread by the 1820s and direct election of senators began in 1914.

HOW THE UNITED STATES COMPARES

CHECKS AND BALANCES

All democracies place constitutional limits on the power of government. The concept of rule by law, for example, is characteristic of democratic governments but not of authoritarian regimes. Democracies differ, however, in the extent to which political power is restrained through constitutional mechanisms. The United States is an extreme case in that its government rests on an elaborate system of constitutional checks and balances. The system employs a separation of powers among the executive, legislative, and judicial branches. It also includes judicial review, the power of the courts to invalidate actions of the legislature or executive. These constitutional restrictions on power are not part of the governing structure of all democracies.

Most democracies, for example, have parliamentary systems, which invest both executive and legislative leadership in the office of prime minister. Britain is an example of this type of system. Parliament under the leadership of the prime minister is the supreme author-

ity in Britain. Its laws are not even subject to override by Britain's high court, which has no power to review the constitutionality of parliamentary acts.

Country	Separation of Executive and Legislative Powers?	Judicial Review?
Belgium	No	No
Canada	No	Yes
France	Yes	No
Germany	No	Yes
Great Britain	No	No
Israel	No	Yes
Italy	No	Yes
Japan	No	Yes
Mexico	In theory only	Yes
United States	Yes	Yes

The Framers believed that the people deserved and required a voice in their government, but they also feared popular government. They worried that the people would become inflamed by a passionate issue or fiery demagogue and act without due regard for the interests of the minority. To the Framers, the great risk of popular government was **tyranny of the majority**—the people acting as an irrational mob that tramples on the rights of others. Their fear was not without foundation. The history of democracies was filled with popular excesses, and there were even examples from the nation's brief history. In 1786, for example, debtors had gained control of Rhode Island's legislature and made paper money a legal means of paying debts, even though existing contracts called for payment in gold. Creditors were then hunted down and held captive in public places so that debtors could come and pay them in full with worthless paper money. A Boston newspaper wrote that Rhode Island should be renamed *Rogue* Island.

tyranny of the majority The potential of a majority to monopolize power for its own gain and to the detriment of minority rights and interests.

DEMOCRACY VERSUS REPUBLIC

No form of self-government could eliminate completely the threat to liberty of majority tyranny, but the Framers believed that the danger would be greatly diminished by properly structured institutions.[16] Madison summarized the Framers' intent when he said in *Federalist* No. 10 that the Constitution was "a republican remedy" for the excesses historically associated with "democratic"

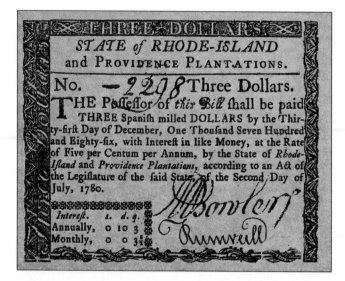

Rhode Island was nicknamed "Rogue Island" for its disregard of property rights. Shown here is the Rhode Island three dollar banknote, which came to be worth no more than the paper on which it was written and yet was used to pay off gold debts.

democracy A form of government in which the people rule, either directly or through elected representatives.

republic Historically, the form of government in which representative officials met to decide on policy issues. These representatives were expected to serve the public interest but were not subject to the people's immediate control. Today, the term *republic* is used interchangeably with *democracy.*

representative democracy A system in which the people participate in the decision-making process of government not directly but indirectly, through the election of officials to represent their interests.

trustees Elected representatives whose obligation is to act in accordance with their own consciences as to what policies are in the best interests of the public.

rule. Today the terms **democracy, republic,** and **representative democracy** are often used interchangeably to refer to a system of government in which ultimate political power rests with the majority through its capacity to choose representatives in free and open elections. To the writers of the Constitution, however, *democracy* and *republic* had different meanings. When the Framers complained about the risks of democracy, they were referring to *pure democracy,* in which popular opinion was translated directly into public policy. In their use of the term *republic,* the Framers were referring to representative government in which elected officials met in representative institutions to decide policy through extended debate and deliberation.[17]

The Framers' concept of a proper system of representation was similar to an idea put forth by the English theorist Edmund Burke (1729–1797). In his *Letter to the Sheriffs of Bristol,* Burke argued that representatives should act as public **trustees:** they are obliged to promote the interest of those who elected them, but the nature of this interest is for the representatives, not the voters, to decide. Burke was concerned about the ease with which society could degenerate into selfishness, and he thought it imperative for representatives not to surrender their judgment to popular whim.

LIMITED POPULAR RULE

The Constitution provided that all power would be exercised through representative institutions. There was no provision for any form of direct popular participation in the making of policy decisions. In view of the fact that the United States was much too large to be governed directly by the people in popular assemblies, a representative system was necessary. Moreover, the separation of powers meant that the majority's will, again by necessity, would be filtered through an institutional structure. The Framers went beyond what was necessary, however, and placed officials at a considerable distance from the people they represented (see Table 2-2).

TABLE 2-2 Methods of Choosing National Leaders Fearing the concentration of political power, the Framers devised alternative methods of selection and terms of service for national officials.

Office	Method of Selection	Term of Service
President	Electoral College	4 years
U.S. senator	State legislature	6 years (one-third of senators' terms expire every 2 years)
U.S. representative	Popular election	2 years
Federal judge	Nominated by president, approved by Senate	Indefinite (subject to "good behavior")

The House of Representatives was the only institution that would be based on direct popular election—its members would be elected for two-year terms of office through vote of the people. Frequent and direct election of House members was intended to make government sensitive to the concerns of popular majorities.

U.S. senators would be appointed by the legislatures of the states they represented. Because state legislators were popularly elected, the people would be choosing their senators indirectly. Every two years, a third of the senators would be appointed to six-year terms. The Senate was expected to check and balance the House, which, by virtue of the more frequent and direct election of its members, would presumably be more responsive to popular opinion.

Presidential selection was an issue of considerable debate at the Philadelphia convention. Direct election of the president was twice proposed and twice rejected because it linked executive power directly to popular majorities. The Framers finally chose to have the president selected by the votes of electors (the so-called **Electoral College**). Each state would have as many **electoral votes** as it had members in Congress and could select its electors by any method it chose. The president would serve four years and be eligible for reelection.

The Framers decided that federal judges and justices would be appointed rather than elected. They would be nominated by the president and confirmed through approval by the Senate. Once confirmed, they would "hold their offices during good behavior." In effect, they would be allowed to hold office for life unless they committed a crime. The judiciary would be more of a guardian institution than a representative one.[18]

These differing methods of selecting national officeholders would not prevent a determined majority from achieving unbridled power, but control could not be attained easily or quickly. Unlike the House of Representatives, institutions such as the Senate, presidency, and judiciary would not yield to an impassioned majority in a single election. The delay would reduce the probability that government would degenerate into mob rule driven by momentary whims.

Electoral College An unofficial term that refers to the electors who cast the states' electoral votes.

electoral votes The method of voting that is used to choose the U.S. president. Each state has the same number of electoral votes as it has members in Congress (House and Senate combined). By tradition, electoral voting is tied to a state's popular voting. The candidate with the most popular votes in a state (or, in a few states, the most votes in a congressional district) receives its electoral votes.

ALTERING THE CONSTITUTION: MORE POWER TO THE PEOPLE

The Framers' conception of self-government was at odds with what the average American in 1787 believed was appropriate (indeed, most historians conclude

HOW THE NATIONAL POLITICAL SYSTEM WAS MADE MORE RESPONSIVE TO POPULAR MAJORITIES

Earlier Situation	Subsequent Development
Separation of powers, as a means of dividing authority and blunting passionate majorities.	Political parties, as a means of uniting authorities and linking them with popular majorities.
Indirect election of all national officials except House members, as a means of buffering officials from popular influence.	Direct election of U.S. senators and popular voting for president (linked to electoral votes), as a means of increasing popular control of officials.
Nomination of candidates for public office through political party organizations.	Primary elections, as a means of selecting party nominees.

that if George Washington had not presided over the Philadelphia convention and had not been widely expected to become the nation's first president, the Constitution would not have been ratified). It certainly was at odds with the spirit and letter of the state constitutions. Every state but South Carolina held annual legislative elections, and several states also chose their governors through annual election. In this context, the Constitution's provisions for popular rule were rather thin. Richard Henry Lee of Virginia criticized even the House of Representatives, which he said had "very little democracy in it" because each of its members would represent such a large population and area that they would not be in close touch with the people.[19] And it was not long after ratification of the Constitution that Americans sought a stronger voice in their own governing.

Jeffersonian Democracy: A Revolution of the Spirit

Thomas Jefferson, who otherwise admired the Constitution, was among the prominent Americans who questioned its provisions for self-government. And it was Jefferson who may have spared the nation a bloody conflict over the issue of popular sovereignty. Under John Adams, the second president, the national government increasingly favored the nation's wealthy interests. Adams publicly suggested that the Constitution was designed for a governing elite, while Alexander Hamilton urged him to use force if necessary to suppress popular dissent.[20] Jefferson asked whether Adams, with the aid of a strong army, planned soon to deprive ordinary Americans of their freedoms altogether. Jefferson challenged Adams in the next presidential election and, upon defeating him, hailed the victory as the "Revolution of 1800."

Although Jefferson was a champion of the common people, he had no clear vision of how a popular government might work in practice. He believed that congressional majorities were the proper expression of popular majorities and accordingly was reluctant to use his presidency as the instrument of the people.[21] Jefferson also had no illusions about a largely illiterate population's readiness for a significant governing role and feared the ruinous consequences of inciting the masses to contest the moneyed class. Jeffersonian democracy was thus mainly a revolution of the spirit; Jefferson taught Americans to look upon the national government as belonging to all, not just to the privileged few.[22]

Jacksonian Democracy: Linking the People and the Presidency

Not until Andrew Jackson was elected in 1828 did the country have a powerful president who was willing and able to involve the public more fully in government. Jackson carried out the constitutional revolution that Jeffersonian democracy had foreshadowed.

Jackson recognized that the president was the only official who could legitimately claim to represent the people as a whole. Unlike the president, members of Congress were elected from separate states and districts rather than from the entire country. Yet the president's claim to popular leadership was diminished by the existence of the electoral college. Jackson persuaded the states to choose their presidential electors on the basis of popular voting. Jackson's reform, which is still in effect today, basically places the selection of a president in the voters' hands. The winner of the popular vote in each state is awarded its electoral votes; hence, the candidate who wins most of the popular votes in the states is also most likely to receive a majority of the electoral votes. Since Jackson's time, only three candidates—Rutherford B. Hayes in 1876, Benjamin Harrison in 1888, and George W. Bush in 2000—have won the presidency after losing the popular vote. (The electoral college is discussed further in Chapter 14.)

The Progressives: Senate and Primary Elections

The Progressive Era of the early 1900s brought another wave of democratic reforms. The Progressives rejected the Burkean idea (discussed earlier in this chapter) of representatives as trustees; they embraced instead the idea of representatives as **delegates**—officeholders who are obligated to respond directly to the expressed opinions of the people whom they represent.

The Progressives succeeded primarily in changing the way that some state and local governments operate (see "States in the Nation"). Progressive reforms of these governments included nonpartisan local elections; recall elections, which enable citizens through petition to require a particular officeholder to submit to election before the expiration of his or her normal term of office; the initiative, which enables citizens through petition to place legislative measures on the ballot for enactment or rejection through popular voting; and the referendum, which permits legislative bodies to submit measures to the voters for enactment or rejection.

The Progressives also brought about two changes in the role of voters in national politics. One was the direct election of U.S. senators, who before the Seventeenth Amendment was ratified in 1913, had been chosen by state legislatures and were widely perceived as agents of big business (the Senate was nicknamed the "millionaires' club"). Senators who stood to lose their seats in a direct popular vote had blocked earlier attempts to amend the Senate election procedure.

delegates Elected representatives whose obligation is to act in accordance with the expressed wishes of the people whom they represent.

★ STATES IN THE NATION

DIRECT DEMOCRACY: THE INITIATIVE AND REFERENDUM

The Progressive movement's reforms included the initiative (which allows citizens through petition to place legislative measures on the ballot) and the referendum (which permits legislative bodies to submit proposals to the voters for approval or rejection). Not all states adopted these devices or have them today. The initiative and referendum are common in the Midwest and West, where the Progressive movement was strong. They are less prevalent in the Northeast, where the party machines were strong, and in the South, where political elites opposed reforms that would have enabled African Americans and poor whites to exercise more power.

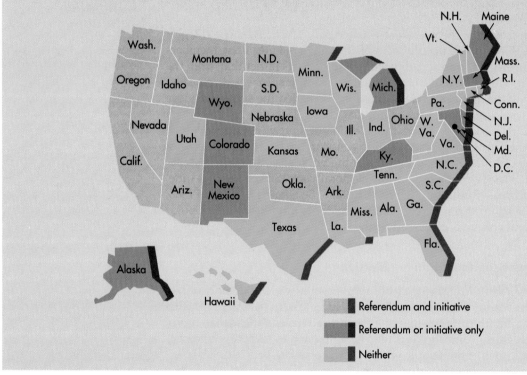

SOURCE: Council of State Governments, *Book of the States*, 1998–1999 (Lexington, Ky.: Council of State Governments, 1999), 210.

Eventually, however, the Senate was persuaded to support an amendment by pressure from the Progressives and by revelations that corporate bribes had influenced the selection of several senators.

A second Progressive reform that affected national politics is the **primary election,** which gives rank-and-file voters the opportunity to select party nominees. Nearly all states in the early 1900s adopted the primary election as a means of choosing nominees for at least some federal and state offices. Before this change, nominees were chosen by party leaders.

The Progressive era spawned attacks on the Framers. A prominent criticism was the historian Charles S. Beard's *Economic Interpretation of the Constitution*.[23]

primary election A form of election in which voters choose a party's nominees for public office. In most states, eligibility to vote in a primary election is limited to voters who are registered members of the party.

CURRENT CONTROVERSIES

SHOULD CONGRESS BE SUBJECT TO TERM LIMITS?

What is the proper relationship between the electorate and its representatives? The question was a major focus of debate at the Philadelphia convention and is still heard today. An example is the term-limit movement, which has sought to restrict the number of years that an officeholder can remain in office. Term limits are intended to protect the public against politicians who would use the power of their office to stay in office indefinitely. Opponents say that term limits are unnecessary because voters have the power at the next election to decide whether an official should be removed from office. Although many states have adopted term limits for their legislatures, the courts have ruled that states do not have the power to restrict the terms of members of Congress. That action would have to originate with Congress. Several term-limit proposals have been introduced in Congress, but none has managed to gain the necessary support.

YES: During the first 150 years of this country's history, term limits were unnecessary. Turnover in the U.S. House of Representatives was routinely over 50 percent. But in recent years, a rapacious desire for power has infiltrated our nation's legislature. Over the last decade we have experienced reelection rates averaging over 90 percent, creating a class of career politicians who have insulated themselves from the public will and grown less and less representative of the people. Like the Founding Fathers, the American people recognize the need for new blood in government. They have decided that it is time for their elected officials to return home at regular intervals. Term limits have seized the hearts and minds of millions of Americans frustrated with an unresponsive and arrogant government.

—U.S. Term Limits organization

NO: The terms of Members of Congress are already limited. We face the voters every other year. We are given only a two-year term in the House. If the voters do not like what we are doing, they can easily kick us out. Elections are the best term limits ever invented. . . . Term limits are [also] unconstitutional. They were specifically considered by our Founding Fathers and specifically rejected, for a whole host of good reasons. . . . They would prohibit voters from voting for a candidate who might otherwise be their first choice. They would prohibit good people from running for office. [Also], very few Members of Congress would be able to develop experience and expertise about important matters on which they were expected to legislate. . . . Term limits solve a problem that does not exist. We should let the voters decide, and not just arbitrarily limit their choices.

—Congressman John J. Duncan Jr. (R-Tenn.)

Arguing that the Constitution grew out of wealthy Americans' fears of the debtor rebellions and noting that many of the Framers were themselves wealthy men, Beard claimed that the Constitution's elaborate systems of power and representation were devices for keeping power in the hands of the rich. Beard's thesis was challenged by other historians, and he later acknowledged that he had not taken the Framers' full array of motives into account. Their conception of separation of powers, for example, was a time-honored governing principle that had previously been incorporated in state constitutions.

Although the Framers did not have great trust in popular rule, it would be a mistake to conclude they were foes of democracy. They were intent on balancing the demands of limited government with those of self-government and, in striking a balance, leaned toward the former, believing that the evil of unrestrained power was the greater danger to a civil society.

Constitutional Democracy Today

constitutional democracy A government that is democratic in its provisions for majority influence through elections, and constitutional in its provisions for minority rights and rule by law.

The type of government created in the United States in 1787 is today called a **constitutional democracy.** It is *democratic* in its provisions for majority influence through elections and *constitutional* in its requirement that power gained through elections be exercised in accordance with law and with due respect for individual rights.

By some standards, the American system of today is a model of *self-government*. The United States schedules the election of its larger legislative chamber (the House of Representatives) and its chief executive more frequently than any other democracy. In addition, it is the only country that relies extensively on primary elections instead of party organizations for the selection of party nominees. The principle of popular election to office, which the writers of the Constitution regarded as a prerequisite of popular sovereignty but to be used sparingly, has been extended further in the United States than anywhere else.

By other standards, however, the U.S. system is less democratic than many others. Popular majorities must work against the barriers to influence—the elaborate system of divided powers, staggered terms of office, and separate constituencies—that were devised by the Framers. In fact, the link between an electoral majority and a governing majority is far less direct in the American system than in nearly all other democratic systems. In the European parliamentary democracies, for example, legislative and executive power are not separated, are not subject to close check by the judiciary, and are acquired through the winning of a legislative majority in national elections. The Framers' vision was a different one, dominated by a concern with *liberty*, and therefore controls on political power, a response to the experiences they brought with them to Philadelphia in the summer of 1787.

www.mhhe.com/patterson5

Self-Quiz

Summary

The Constitution of the United States is a reflection of the colonial and revolutionary experiences of the early Americans. Freedom from abusive government was a reason for the colonies' revolt against British rule, but the English tradition also provided ideas about government, power, and freedom that were expressed in the Constitution and, earlier, in the Declaration of Independence.

The Constitution was designed in part to provide for a limited government in which political power would be confined to proper uses. The Framers wanted to ensure that the government they were creating would not itself be a threat to freedom. To this end, they confined the national government to expressly granted powers and also denied it certain specific powers. Other prohibitions on government were later added to the Constitution in the form of stated guarantees of individual liberties—the Bill of Rights. The most significant constitutional provision for limited government, however, was a separation of powers among the three branches. The powers given to each

branch enable it to act as a check on the exercise of power by the others, an arrangement that, during the nation's history, has in fact served as a barrier to abuses of power.

The Constitution, however, made no mention of how the powers and limits of government were to be judged in practice. In its historic ruling in *Marbury v. Madison*, the Supreme Court assumed the authority to review the constitutionality of legislative and executive actions and to declare them unconstitutional and thus invalid.

The Framers of the Constitution respected the idea of self-government but distrusted popular majorities. They designed a government that they felt would temper popular opinion and slow its momentum, so that the public's "true interest" (which includes a regard for the rights and interests of the minority) would guide public policy. Different methods were established to select members of the House of Representatives, members of the Senate, the president, and federal judges as a means of separating political power from momentary and unreflecting majorities.

Since the adoption of the Constitution, the public has gradually assumed more direct control of its representatives, particularly through measures affecting the way in which officeholders are chosen. Presidential voting (linked to the Electoral College), direct election of senators, and primary elections are among the devices aimed at strengthening the majority's influence. These developments are rooted in the idea, deeply held by ordinary Americans, that the people must have substantial direct control of their government if it is to serve their real interests.

Key Terms

Anti-Federalists
Bill of Rights
checks and balances
constitution
constitutional democracy
delegates
democracy
denials of power
Electoral College
electoral votes
Federalists
grants of power
Great Compromise
inalienable (natural) rights

judicial review
limited government
New Jersey (small-state) Plan
North-South Compromise
primary election
representative democracy
republic
self-government
separated institutions sharing power
separation of powers
trustees
tyranny of the majority
Virginia (large-state) Plan

Suggested Readings

Beard, Charles S. *An Economic Interpretation of the Constitution.* New York: Macmillan, 1941. Argues that the Framers had selfish economic interests uppermost in mind when they wrote the Constitution.

Bianco, William T. *Trust: Representatives and Constituents.* Ann Arbor: University of Michigan Press, 1994. Examines the relationship between representatives and constituents.

Farrand, Max. *The Records of the Federal Convention of 1787.* New Haven, Conn.: Yale University Press, 1966. A four-volume work that includes all the important records of the Philadelphia convention.

Federalist Papers. Many editions, including a one-volume paperback version edited by Isaac Kramnick (New York: Penguin, 1987). A series of essays written by Alexander Hamilton, James Madison, and John Jay under the pseudonym Publius. The essays, published in a New York newspaper in 1787–88, explain the Constitution and support its ratification.

Finegold, Kenneth. *Experts and Politicians: Reform Challenges to Machine Politics in New York, Cleveland, and Chicago.* Princeton, N.J.: Princeton University Press, 1995. A careful study of the successes and failures of party-reform efforts in three major cities during the Progressive era.

Hardin, Russell. *Liberalism, Constitutionalism, and Democracy.* New York: Oxford University Press, 1999. Analysis of the great ideas that underlie the Constitution.

Levin, Daniel. *Representing Popular Sovereignty.* Albany: State University of New York Press, 1999. An analysis of how the Constitution is reflected in popular culture.

Levin, Peter. *The New Progressive Era: Toward a Fair and Deliberative Democracy.* Lanham, Md.: Rowman & Littlefield, 2000. An analysis of current progressive trends and goals.

Sandel, Michael J. *Democracy's Discontent: America in Search of a Public Philosophy.* Cambridge, Mass.: Harvard University Press, 1996. An argument for a community-oriented conception of democracy.

Tocqueville, Alexis de. *Democracy in America*, vols. 1 and 2, ed. J. P. Mayer. New York: Doubleday/Anchor, 1969. A classic analysis (originally published 1835–1840) of American democracy by an insightful French observer.

CHAPTER 3

Federal Government: Forging a Nation

★

The question of the relation of the states to the federal government is the cardinal question of our Constitutional system. It cannot be settled by the opinion of one generation, because it is a question of growth, and each successive stage of our political and economic development gives it a new aspect, makes it a new question.

—Woodrow Wilson[1]

★ ★ ★

*S*enate majority Leader Trent Lott declared it a great day for those who believe that the answers to America's problems are more likely to be found in Albany, Sacramento, and Jackson than in Washington. Senator Daniel Patrick Moynihan, an outspoken critic of the legislation, called it "the most brutal act of social policy since Reconstruction." The Urban Institute estimated that within a decade the legislation would push more than a million children into poverty.[2]

At issue was the nation's program of assistance for poor families and whether the program would be directed by the national government or the states. Since the 1930s, the program had been run out of Washington as an entitlement policy, which meant that every American family who met the eligibility criteria was entitled to assistance. For many liberal Democrats, it was the cornerstone of the idea that no needy American family, wherever it resided, would be denied help. Individual states had some leeway in deciding the amount of support a needy family would receive each month, but all states had to participate in the program and contribute to its funding.

The new legislation ended this federal guarantee of cash assistance and replaced it with a system of cash grants to the states, which would assume responsibility for caring for welfare recipients and getting them into jobs. The legislation fulfilled the long-held desire of conservative Republicans to reduce welfare dependency and move welfare recipients into tax-paying jobs. It also met their goal of reducing the power of the federal government. Under the new program, states would have to support a needy family for five years but could deny benefits if, after two years, an able-bodied adult refused to accept a job or job training. And after five years, a state could unconditionally deny benefits to poor families.

The 1996 Welfare Reform Act is one of thousands of controversies during American history that have hinged on whether national or state authority should prevail. Americans possess what amounts to dual citizenship: they are citizens both of the United States and of the state where they reside. The American political system is a *federal system*, one in which constitutional authority is divided between a national government and state governments: each is assumed to derive its powers directly from the people and therefore to have sovereignty (final authority) over the policy responsibilities assigned to it. The federal system consists of nation *and* states, indivisible and yet separate.[3]

This chapter on American constitutionalism focuses on federalism. The nature of the relationship between the nation and the states was the most pressing issue when the Constitution was written in 1787, and this chapter describes how that issue helped shape the Constitution. The chapter's closing sections discuss

CURRENT CONTROVERSIES

SHOULD CONGRESS HAVE SHIFTED CONTROL OF WELFARE TO THE STATES?

America's federal system divides power between the state and national governments. This arrangement can create conflict over the issue of controlling authority—should a particular policy be entrusted primarily to the states or primarily to the government in Washington? An example is welfare policy. Until passage of the Welfare Reform Act of 1996, the nation's welfare program was run out of Washington and every American who met the eligibility criteria was entitled to assistance. The 1996 legislation shifted authority to the states; they were provided cash grants and charged with moving able-bodied recipients into tax-paying jobs. The shift toward state authority is still controversial, as is evident from an exchange during a televised debate between the leading contenders for the 2000 Democratic presidential nomination, Al Gore and Bill Bradley.

YES: We passed tough welfare reform, which I think has worked . . . People were trapped in the old welfare system. I met earlier with Christine Maguire here, who lives in Portsmouth and has two children. She was trapped in welfare. Now she has a good job. There are millions like her. . . . [It's not a perfect bill but we have] to be willing to really get out there and push the boundaries and try new things.

—Vice President Al Gore

NO: I don't think the answer to the problems of people who are poor in America is to take a pot of money from federal officials and send it to state officials and say "Spend 80 percent of this as best you can." . . . I was out in L.A. not too long ago, in East L.A., . . . and a woman came up to me and said, "What are you going to do about this welfare reform bill?" . . . She said that the people who are going out to work are getting minimum wage jobs. They're not getting any training and, therefore, they're never going to move forward. . . . I don't think that you deal with this problem with this kind of federal shirking of responsibility and states assuming all responsibility.

—Former U.S. Sen. Bill Bradley (D-N.J.)

how federalism has changed during the nation's history and conclude with a brief overview of contemporary federalism. The main points presented in the chapter are the following:

★ *The power of government must be equal to its responsibilities.* The Constitution was needed because the nation's preceding system (under the Articles of Confederation) was too weak to accomplish its expected goals, particularly those of a strong defense and an integrated economy. The Constitution created a stronger national government by granting it significant powers, particularly in the areas of taxation and the regulation of commerce.

★ *Federalism—the Constitution's division of governing authority between two levels, nation and states—was the result of political bargaining.* Federalism was not a theoretical principle, but a compromise made necessary in 1787 by the prior existence of the states.

★ *Federalism is not a fixed principle for allocating power between the national and state governments,* but a principle that has changed over the course of time in response to new political needs. Federalism has passed through several distinct stages during the nation's history.

★ *Contemporary federalism tilts toward national authority, reflecting the increased interdependence of American society.* However, there is a current trend toward reducing the scope of federal authority.

Federalism: National and State Sovereignty

The delegates to the Philadelphia convention in 1787 included many of the nation's most prominent leaders, such as George Washington and Benjamin Franklin. Not all of America's top leaders were at the convention, however, and many of them were steadfastly opposed to a strong national government. When rumors circulated that the convention would propose a new form of government rather than an amended Articles of Confederation, Patrick Henry, an ardent supporter of state-centered government, said that he "smelt a rat." After the convention had adjourned, he realized that his fears were justified. "Who authorized them," he asked, "to speak the language of 'We, the People,' instead of 'We, the States'?"

The question of people versus states was dictated by the previous experience with the Articles of Confederation. The government of the Articles (see Chapter 2) was a union of states rather than also of people. The result was an inherently weak national government because its strength rested entirely on the states' willingness to cooperate. If they refused to contribute to the collective effort, the national government had no sure way to make them comply. Georgia and North Carolina, for example, contributed no money at all to the national treasury between 1781 and 1786, and the national government could do nothing more than to implore them to pay a fair share of the costs of defense, diplomacy, and other national policies. The only realistic solution was a government based on the people. If ordered to pay taxes, individuals would either do so or face

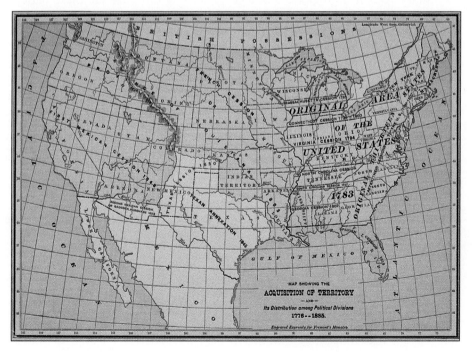

It could take weeks to travel overland or by ship from the most distant points in the American states. The great size of America when compared with European countries was used as an argument by both those who favored a strong union and those who opposed it.

consequences—imprisonment or confiscation of property—that most of them would choose to avoid.

Although the need for a national government based directly on the people was therefore a goal of the writers of the Constitution, they also wanted to preserve the states as governing bodies. When Virginia's George Mason said he would never agree to a union that abolished the states, he was speaking for virtually all the delegates. The Philadelphia convention thereby devised a system of government that came to be known as **federalism.** Federalism is the division of **sovereignty,** or ultimate governing authority, between a national government and regional (that is, state) governments. Each directly governs the people and derives its powers from them.

American federalism is basically a system for dividing authority between sovereign national and state governments (see Figure 3-1). The system gives states the power to address local matters in separate ways, thus providing for a responsiveness to local values and differences. At the same time, federalism gives the national government the power to decide matters of broad national scope on a uniform basis. In practice, there is some overlap between state and national action, but there is also a division of responsibilities. The national government has primary responsibility for national defense and the currency, among other policies, whereas the states have primary responsibilities for such policy areas as public education and police protection. The national and state governments also have some *concurrent powers* (that is, powers exercised over the same areas of policy); for example, each has the power to raise taxes and borrow money.

A federal system is different from a **confederacy,** which is the type of government established by the Articles. A confederacy is a union of states that retain all sovereignty. The authority of the central government is derived from the states, which can, at will, redefine its authority. Federalism is also different from a **unitary system,** in which sovereignty is vested solely in the national government. In a unitary system, all regional and local governing units are subject to national authority. The people are citizens or subjects only of the national government, and the other governments derive their authority from the national government, which can, in theory at least, abolish them or redefine their authority.

Because a federal system invests sovereignty in both the national and state governments, each has powers that are not subject to the other's discretion. For example, each has complete authority over its taxation rates. Moreover, each is protected constitutionally in its existence and from undue interference by the other in the conduct of its lawful affairs.

federalism   A governmental system in which authority is divided between two sovereign levels of government: national and regional.

sovereignty   The ultimate authority to govern within a certain geographical area.

confederacy   A governmental system in which sovereignty is vested entirely in subnational (state) governments.

unitary system   A governmental system in which the national government alone has sovereign (ultimate) authority.

FIGURE 3-1   Federalism as a Governing System: Examples of National, State, and Concurrent Powers
The American federal system divides sovereignty between a national government and the state governments. Each is constitutionally protected in its existence and authority, although their powers overlap somewhat even in areas granted to one level (for example, the federal government has a role in education policy).

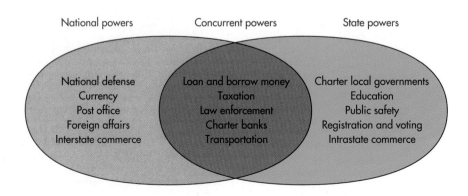

National powers

National defense
Currency
Post office
Foreign affairs
Interstate commerce

Concurrent powers

Loan and borrow money
Taxation
Law enforcement
Charter banks
Transportation

State powers

Charter local governments
Education
Public safety
Registration and voting
Intrastate commerce

🌐 HOW THE UNITED STATES COMPARES

FEDERAL VERSUS UNITARY GOVERNMENTS

Federalism involves the division of sovereignty between a national government and subnational (such as state) governments. It was invented in 1787 in order to maintain the preexisting American states while establishing an effective central government. Since then a number of other countries have established a *federal* government, but most countries have a *unitary* government, in which all sovereignty is vested in a national government. In some cases, countries have developed hybrid versions. Great Britain's government is formally unitary, but Parliament has granted some autonomy to regions. Mexico's system is formally federal, but in actuality nearly all power is concentrated in the national government.

Country	Form of Government
Canada	Federal
France	Unitary
Germany	Federal
Great Britain	Modified unitary
Italy	Modified unitary
Japan	Unitary
Mexico	Modified federal
United States	Federal
Sweden	Unitary

Federalism was invented in America in 1787. It was different not only from a confederate or unitary system but also from any form of government the world had known. The ancient Greek city-states and the medieval Hanseatic League were confederacies. The governments of Europe were unitary in form. The United States of America would be the first nation to be governed through a federal system.

THE ARGUMENT FOR FEDERALISM

Unlike many other decisions made at the Philadelphia convention, federalism had no clear basis in political theory. Federalism was a practical necessity: there was a need for a stronger national government and yet the states existed and were intent on retaining their sovereignty.

Nevertheless, the Framers developed arguments for the superiority of federalism. Federalism, they claimed, would protect liberty, moderate the power of government, and provide the foundation for an effective national government.

Protecting Liberty

Theorists such as Locke and Montesquieu had not proposed a division of power between national and local authorities as a further means of protecting *liberty*. Nevertheless, the Framers came to look upon federalism as part of the Constitution's system of checks and balances (see Chapter 2).

Alexander Hamilton argued in *Federalist* No. 28 that the American people could shift their loyalties back and forth between the national and state governments in order to keep each under control. "If [the people's] rights are invaded by either," Hamilton wrote, "they can make use of the other as the instrument of redress." James Madison wrote in *Federalist* No. 51 that a federal system is a superior form of limited government because power is divided between two

Patrick Henry was a leading figure in the American Revolution ("Give me liberty or give me death!"). He later opposed ratification of the Constitution on grounds that the national government should be a union of states and not also of people.

distinct governments, as well as among the separate branches. "In the compound republic of America, the power surrendered by the people is first divided between two distinct governments, and then the portion allotted to each is subdivided among distinct and separate departments," Madison said. "Hence a double security arises to the rights of the people. The different governments will control each other at the same time that each will be controlled by itself."

Moderating the Power of Government

To the Anti-Federalists (opponents of the Constitution), the sacrifice of states' power to the nation was as unwise as it was unnecessary. They argued that a distant national government could never serve the people's interests as well as the states could. In support of their contention, the Anti-Federalists turned to the French philosopher Montesquieu, who had concluded that a small republic is more likely than a large one to respect and respond to the people it governs. When government encompasses a small area, he argued, its leaders are in closer touch with the people, have a better understanding of their needs, and a greater concern for their interests.

Madison took issue with Montesquieu's small-republic theory. In *Federalist* No. 10 (reprinted in this book's appendix), Madison argued that whether a government serves the common good is a function not of its size but of the range of interests that share political power. The problem with a smaller republic, Madison claimed, is that it is likely to have a dominant faction—whether it be large landholders, financiers, an impoverished majority, or some other group—that is strong enough to take full control of government, using this power to advance its selfish interests. A large republic is less likely to have such an all-powerful faction. If financiers are strong in one area of a large republic, they are likely to be weaker elsewhere, and the same will be true of other interests. By this reasoning, Madison concluded that political control in a large republic could not be won by a single interest but would require a joining of interests, each of which would be forced to limit its demands and to respect the interests of others. "Extend the sphere," said Madison, "and you take in a greater variety of parties and interests; you make it less probable that a majority of the whole will have a common motive to invade the rights of other citizens." (Madison's argument has historical support in the American case. The severest forms of repression, such as enforced racial segregation in the South, have been perpetrated by the state governments.)

Strengthening the Union

The most telling argument in 1787 for a federal system, however, was that it would overcome the deficiencies of the Articles. The Articles had numerous flaws (including the lack of a strong executive and a judiciary independent of the state courts), and two of them were fatal: the government had neither the power to tax nor the power to regulate commerce.

Under the Articles, Congress was given responsibility for national defense but was not granted the power to tax, and so it had to rely on the states for the money to maintain an army and navy. During the first six years under the Articles, Congress asked the states for $12 million but received only $3 million—not even enough to pay the interest on Revolutionary War debts. By 1786 the national government was so desperate for funds that it sold the navy's ships and had fewer than a thousand soldiers in uniform—this at a time when England had an army in Canada and Spain occupied Florida.

Congress was also expected to shape a national economy, yet it was powerless to do so because the Articles forbade interference with the states' commerce policies. States imposed trade barriers among themselves. Connecticut placed a higher tariff on finished goods from Massachusetts than it did on the same goods shipped from England. New Jersey imposed a duty on foreign-made goods shipped from other states. New York responded by taxing goods from New Jersey shipped through New York ports.

The Articles of Confederation showed the fallacy of the adage "That government is best which governs least." The consequences of an overly weak authority were abundantly clear: public disorder, economic chaos, and inadequate defense.

THE POWERS OF THE NATION

The Philadelphia convention met to decide the powers of the national government. The delegates had not been sent to determine how state government should be structured. Accordingly, the U.S. Constitution focuses on the lawful authority of the national government, which is provided through *enumerated* and *implied powers*. Authority that is not in this way granted to the national government is left—or "reserved"—to the states. Thus the states have *reserved powers*.

Enumerated Powers

Article I of the Constitution grants to Congress seventeen **enumerated (expressed) powers.** These powers were intended by the Framers to be the basis

Alexander Hamilton (1757–1804), a strong nationalist, was just thirty-two years old when he served as a delegate to the constitutional convention. Collection of The New York Historical Society, Neg. #6242.

enumerated (expressed) powers
The seventeen powers granted to the national government under Article I, Section 8, of the Constitution. These powers include taxation and the regulation of commerce as well as the authority to provide for the national defense.

for a government strong enough to forge a union that was secure in its defense and stable in its commerce.

Congress's powers to regulate commerce among the states, to create a national currency, and to borrow money, for example, would provide a foundation for a sound national economy. Its power to tax, combined with its authority to declare war and establish an army and navy, would enable it to provide for the common defense. In addition, the Constitution prohibited the states from actions that would interfere with the national government's exercise of its lawful powers. Article I, Section 10, forbids the states to make treaties with other nations, raise armies, wage war, print money, or make commercial agreements with other states without the approval of Congress.

The writers of the Constitution recognized that the lawful exercise of national authority would at times conflict with the actions of the states. In such instances, national law was intended to prevail. Article VI of the Constitution grants this dominance in the so-called **supremacy clause,** which provides that "the laws of the United States . . . shall be the supreme law of the land."

Implied Powers

The Framers of the Constitution also recognized that an overly narrow definition of national authority would result in a government incapable of adapting to change. Under the Articles of Confederation, Congress was strictly limited to those powers expressly granted to it, inhibiting its ability to respond effectively to the country's changing needs after the Revolutionary War. Concerned that the enumerated powers by themselves might be too restrictive of national authority, the Framers added the **"necessary and proper" clause,** or, as it later came to be known, the **elastic clause.** Article I, Section 8, gives Congress the power "to make all laws which shall be necessary and proper for carrying into execution the foregoing [enumerated] powers." This grant gave the national government **implied powers:** the authority to take action that is not expressly authorized by the Constitution but that supports actions that are so authorized.

THE POWERS OF THE STATES

The Framers' preference for a sovereign national government was not shared in 1787 by all Americans. Although Anti-Federalists recognized a need to strengthen defense and interstate commerce, they feared the consequences of a strong central government. The interests of the people of New Hampshire were not identical to those of Georgians or Pennsylvanians, and the Anti-Federalists argued that only state-centered government would protect and preserve this *diversity.*

The Federalists responded by asserting that the national government would have no interest in submerging the states.[4] The national government would take responsibility for establishing a strong defense and for promoting a sound economy, while the states would retain nearly all other governing functions, including oversight of public morals, education, and safety. The national government, James Madison said, would neither want these responsibilities nor have the competence to fulfill them.[5]

This argument did not persuade the Anti-Federalists that their fears of a powerful national government were unfounded. Even some of the Americans

---

supremacy clause Article VI of the Constitution, which makes national law supreme over state law when the national government is acting within its constitutional limits.

"necessary and proper" clause (elastic clause) The authority granted Congress in Article I, Section 8, of the Constitution "to make all laws which shall be necessary and proper" for the implementation of its enumerated powers.

implied powers The federal government's constitutional authority (through the "necessary and proper" clause) to take action that is not expressly authorized by the Constitution but that supports actions that are so authorized.

who were otherwise inclined to support the proposed constitution worried that it would lead to an overly powerful national government. The supremacy and "necessary and proper" clauses were particularly worrisome, because they provided a constitutional basis for future expansions of national authority. Such concerns led to demands for a constitutional amendment that would protect the states against encroachment by the national government. Ratified in 1791 as the Tenth Amendment to the Constitution, it reads: "The powers not delegated to the United States by the Constitution, nor prohibited by it to the States, are reserved to the States." The states' powers under the U.S. Constitution are thus called **reserved powers.***

Federalism in Historical Perspective

Since ratification of the Constitution two centuries ago, no aspect of it has provoked more frequent or bitter conflict than federalism. By establishing two levels of sovereign authority, the Constitution created competing centers of power and ambition, each of which was sure to claim disputed areas as belonging within its realm of authority.

Conflict between national and state authority was also ensured by the brevity of the Constitution. The Framers deliberately avoided detailed provisions, recognizing that brief phrases would give flexibility to the government they were creating. The document does not define what is meant by the "necessary and proper" clause, does not list any of the states' reserved powers, does not indicate whether the supremacy clause allows the states discretionary authority in areas where state and national responsibilities overlap, and does not indicate how *inter*state commerce (which the national government is empowered to regulate) differs from *intra*state commerce (which presumably is reserved for regulation by the states).

Not surprisingly, federalism has been a contentious and dynamic system, its development determined less by constitutional language than by the strength of contending interests and by the country's changing needs. Federalism can be viewed as having progressed through three historical eras, each of which has involved a different relationship between nation and states.

AN INDESTRUCTIBLE UNION (1789–1865)

The issue during the first era, which lasted from the Constitution's beginnings in 1789 through the end of the Civil War in 1865, was the Union's survival.

★ CRITICAL THINKING ★

WHAT'S YOUR OPINION?

National Versus State Powers
The Constitution establishes a system in which authority is divided between the nation and the states. What do you regard as the most important powers assigned to national government? (These powers are listed in Article I, Section 8 of the Constitution, which is reprinted in the back of this book.) Are there any important powers—for example, in the areas of law enforcement and education—that you think should have been assigned to the federal government but were not? What would be different if, say, education policy were established largely by Washington rather than by states and localities?

reserved powers The powers granted to the states under the Tenth Amendment to the Constitution.

---

*A federal system requires relationships not only between the national and state governments but also among the states themselves. The U.S. Constitution defines several state-to-state obligations. One provision is that states are not permitted to enter into commercial arrangements with other states except as approved by Congress. This provision is intended to prevent two or more states from joining together to gain unfair advantage over another state or states. The Constitution also requires each state to grant "full faith and credit" to the legal acts and judgments of other states. This provision means that such legal matters as marriages, wills, court settlements, and contracts rendered in one state are to be upheld by other states. Without the guarantee of full faith and credit, federalism would not work. For example, commerce would grind to a halt if firms incorporated in one state were not allowed to do business in another state or if a party could escape a legal obligation simply by crossing state lines.

A first dispute over federalism was whether the Constitution allowed the creation of a Bank of the United States (shown here in an early nineteenth-century painting). The Constitution had a clause on the printing of currency but not on the establishment of a bank itself.

Given the state-centered history of America before the Constitution, it was inevitable that the states would dispute national policies that threatened their separate interests.

The Nationalist View: *McCulloch v. Maryland*

A first dispute over federalism arose early in George Washington's presidency when his secretary of the treasury, Alexander Hamilton, proposed the creation of a national bank. Thomas Jefferson, Washington's secretary of state, opposed the bank on the grounds that its activities would benefit commercial interests and would harm small farmers, who in Jefferson's view were the backbone of the new nation. Jefferson rejected Hamilton's claim that because the government had constitutional authority to regulate currency, it had the implied power through the "necessary and proper" clause to establish a national bank.

Hamilton's view prevailed when Congress in 1791 established the First Bank of the United States, granting it a twenty-year charter. Congress did not renew the charter when it lapsed in 1811, but, in 1816, established the Second Bank of the United States over the objections of state and local bankers. Responding to their complaints, several states, including Maryland, attempted to drive the Second Bank of the United States out of existence by levying taxes on its operations within their borders. Edwin McCulloch, who was head cashier of the U.S. Bank in Maryland, refused to pay the Maryland tax, and the resulting dispute reached the Supreme Court.

John Marshall, the chief justice of the Supreme Court, was, like Hamilton, a strong nationalist, and in *McCulloch v. Maryland* (1819) the Court ruled decisively in favor of national authority. It was reasonable, Marshall concluded, to infer that a government with powers to tax, borrow money, and regulate commerce could establish a bank in order to exercise those powers properly. Marshall's argument was a clear statement of *implied powers*—the idea that, through the "necessary and proper" clause, the national government's powers extend beyond a narrow reading of its enumerated powers.

Marshall also addressed the meaning of the Constitution's supremacy clause. The state of Maryland argued that it had the sovereign authority to tax the national bank even if the bank was a legal entity. The Supreme Court rejected Maryland's position, concluding that valid national law prevailed over conflicting state law. Because the national government had the power to create the bank, it could also protect the bank from actions by the states, such as taxation, that might destroy it.[6]

The *McCulloch* decision served as precedent for future assertions of national authority, including a second landmark decision by the Marshall Court. In *Gibbons v. Ogden* (1824), the Court ruled on the power of Congress to regulate commerce. The state of New York had granted a monopoly to Aaron Ogden to operate a ferry between New York and New Jersey. When Thomas Gibbons set up a competing ferry under a federal coastal licensing agreement, Ogden tried to prevent Gibbons from operating it. Marshall invalidated the New York monopoly, saying it intruded on Congress's power to regulate commerce among the states. Going further, Marshall ruled that Congress's power extended *into* a state when commerce between two or more states was at issue.[7]

Marshall's opinions asserted that legitimate uses of national power took precedence over state authority and that the "necessary and proper" clause and the commerce clause were broad grants of national power. As a nationalist, Marshall was providing the U.S. government the legal justification for expanding its power in ways that fostered the development of the nation as a nation rather than as a collection of states. This constitutional vision was of utmost significance. As Justice Oliver Wendell Holmes Jr. noted a century later, the Union could not have survived if each state had been allowed to determine for itself the extent to which national authority restricted its actions.[8]

John C. Calhoun (1782–1850) of South Carolina was a champion of states' rights.

The States'-Rights View: The *Dred Scott* Decision

Although John Marshall's rulings helped strengthen national authority, the issue of slavery posed a growing threat to the Union's survival. A resurgence of cotton farming in the early nineteenth century revived the South's flagging dependence on slaves and heightened white southerners' fears that Congress might move to abolish slavery. Southerners consequently did what others have done throughout American history: they devised a constitutional argument to fit their political needs. John C. Calhoun of South Carolina argued that the Constitution had created "a government of states . . . not a government of individuals."[9] This line of reasoning led Calhoun to his famed "doctrine of nullification," which declared that each state had the constitutional right to nullify a national law.

In 1832 South Carolina invoked this doctrine, declaring "null and void" a tariff law that favored northern interests. President Andrew Jackson retorted that South Carolina's action was "incompatible with the existence of the Union," a position that was strengthened when Congress authorized Jackson to use military force against South Carolina. The state backed down when Congress agreed to amend the tariff act slightly.

The clash foreshadowed a confrontation of far greater scope and consequence: the Civil War. The war between the states would not break out for another thirty

www.mhhe.com/patterson5

Graphic

Southern delegates at the constitutional convention sought assurances that Congress would not bar the importation and sale of slaves and that their slave-based agricultural economy would be protected. The photo shows a Civil War–era building in Atlanta that was a site of slave auctions.

Dred Scott (1795?–1858).

years, but in the interim, conflicts over states' rights intensified.[10] Westward expansion and immigration into the northern states were tilting power in Congress toward the free states, which increasingly signaled their determination to outlaw slavery in the United States at some future time. Attempts to find a compromise acceptable to both the North and the South were fruitless. Slavery was too deep and too contentious an issue to be settled by constitutional means.

The Supreme Court's infamous *Dred Scott* decision exemplifies the conflict. Dred Scott, a slave, applied for his freedom when his master died, citing a federal law—the Missouri Compromise of 1820—that made slavery illegal in a free state or territory. Scott had lived in the North four years, but the Supreme Court in a 7–2 decision ruled that slaves were "property" and not "citizens" under the Constitution. The Court also invalidated the Missouri Compromise, declaring that Congress had no authority to outlaw slavery in any part of the United States.[11]

The *Dred Scott* decision outraged many northerners and contributed to a sectional split in the majority Democratic party that enabled the Republican Abraham Lincoln to win the presidency in 1860 with only 40 percent of the popular vote. Lincoln had campaigned for the gradual, compensated abolition of slavery. By the time he assumed office, seven southern states had already seceded from the Union. In justifying his decision to wage civil war on these states, Lincoln said, "The Union is older than the states." In 1865 the superior strength of the Union army settled by force the question of whether national authority would be binding on the states.

The American Civil War was the bloodiest conflict the world had yet known. Ten percent of fighting-age males died in the four-year war, and uncounted others were wounded. The death toll—618,000 (360,000 from the North, 258,000 from the South)—exceeded that of the American war dead in World War I, World War II, the Korean War, and the Vietnam War combined. And this death toll was in a nation with a population that was only one-ninth the size it is today.

DUAL FEDERALISM AND LAISSEZ-FAIRE CAPITALISM (1865–1937)

Although the Civil War preserved the Union, new challenges to federalism were surfacing. Constitutional doctrine held that certain policy areas, such as interstate commerce and defense, were the clear and exclusive province of national authority, while other policy areas, such as public health and intrastate commerce, belonged clearly and exclusively to the states. This doctrine, known as **dual federalism,** was based on the idea that a precise separation of national and state authority was both possible and desirable. "The power which one possesses," said the Supreme Court, "the other does not."[12]

American society, however, was in the midst of changes that raised questions about the suitability of dual federalism as a governing concept. The Industrial Revolution had given rise to large business firms, which were using their economic power to dominate markets and exploit workers. Government was the logical counterforce to this economic power. Which level of government—state or national—would regulate business? There was also the issue of the former slaves. The white South had lost the war but was hardly of a mind to share power and opportunity with newly freed black people. Could the federal government intervene in state affairs to ensure the fair treatment of African Americans?

Dual federalism became a barrier to an effective response to these issues. From the 1860s through the 1930s, the Supreme Court held firm to the idea that there was a sharp line between national and state authority and, in both areas, a high wall of separation between government and the economy. This era of federalism was characterized by state supremacy in racial policy and by business supremacy in commerce policy.

dual federalism A doctrine based on the idea that a precise separation of national power and state power is both possible and desirable.

The Fourteenth Amendment and State Discretion

Ratified after the Civil War, the Fourteenth Amendment was intended to protect citizens (especially black Americans) from discriminatory actions by state governments.[13] A state was prohibited from depriving "any person of life, liberty, or property without due process of law," from denying "any person within its jurisdiction the equal protection of the laws," and from abridging "the privileges or immunities of citizens of the United States."

Supreme Court rulings during subsequent decades, however, helped to undermine the Fourteenth Amendment's promise. The Court held, for example, that the Fourteenth Amendment did not substantially limit the power of the states to regulate rights of person and property,[14] and that the Fourteenth Amendment was not meant to prevent discrimination by private owners of hotels, restaurants, and other accommodations that catered to the general public.[15] Then, in *Plessy v. Ferguson* (1896), the Court issued its infamous "separate but equal" ruling. A black man, Adolph Plessy, had been convicted of violating a

www.mhhe.com/patterson5

Graphic

After the Civil War Reconstruction, the white majority in the South used the power of government to enforce a two-race society in which the public schools and other public facilities for blacks were vastly inferior to those for whites.

Louisiana law that required white and black citizens to ride in separate railroad cars. The Supreme Court upheld his conviction, concluding that state governments could require blacks to use separate railroad cars and other accommodations as long as those facilities were "equal" in quality to those reserved for use by whites. "If one race be inferior to the other socially," the Court concluded, "the Constitution of the United States cannot put them on the same plane." The lone dissenting justice in the case, John Marshall Harlan, had harsh words for his colleagues: "Our Constitution is color-blind and neither knows nor tolerates classes among citizens. . . . The thin disguise of 'equal' accommodations . . . will not mislead anyone nor atone for the wrong this day done."[16]

With its *Plessy* decision, the Court undercut the Fourteenth Amendment and allowed southern states to establish a thoroughly racist system of legalized segregation. Black children were forced into separate schools that seldom had libraries and usually had few teachers, most of whom had no formal training. Hospitals for blacks had few doctors and nurses and almost no medical supplies and equipment. Legal challenges to these discriminatory practices were generally unsuccessful. The *Plessy* ruling had become a justification for the separate and *unequal* treatment of black Americans. For the next seven decades, the states'-rights doctrine was often invoked by white southerners as a guise for the perpetuation of racism.

Judicial Protection of Business

Through its ruling after the Civil War, the Supreme Court also provided a constitutional basis for uncontrolled private power. The Court was dominated by adherents of the doctrine of laissez-faire capitalism (which holds that business should be "allowed to act" without interference), and they interpreted the Constitution in ways that frustrated government's attempts to regulate business activity. In 1886, for example, the Court decided that corporations were "persons" within the meaning of the Fourteenth Amendment, and thus their property rights were protected from substantial regulation by the states.[17] The irony was inescapable. A constitutional amendment that had been enacted to protect the newly freed slaves was ignored for this purpose but was used instead to protect fictitious persons—business corporations.

The Court also weakened the national government's regulatory power by narrowly interpreting its commerce power. The Constitution's **commerce clause** says that Congress shall have the power "to regulate commerce" among the states but does not spell out the economic activities included in the grant of power. When the federal government invoked the Sherman Antitrust Act (1890) in an attempt to break up a monopoly on the manufacture of sugar, the Supreme Court blocked the action, claiming that interstate commerce covered only the "transportation" of goods, not their "manufacture."[18] Manufacturing was deemed part of intrastate commerce and thus, according to the dual federalism doctrine, subject to state regulation only. However, since the Court had previously decided that the states' regulatory powers were restricted by the Fourteenth Amendment, they were relatively powerless to control manufacturing activity.

Although the national government subsequently made some headway in business regulation, the Supreme Court remained an obstacle. An example is the case of *Hammer v. Dagenhart* (1918), which arose from a 1916 federal act that prohibited the interstate shipment of goods produced by child labor. The act was popular because factory owners were exploiting children, working them for long hours at low pay. Citing the Tenth Amendment, the Court invalidated the law, ruling that factory practices could be regulated only by the states.[19] However, in an earlier case, *Lochner v. New York* (1905), the Court had prevented a state from regulating labor practices, concluding that such action was a violation of firms' property rights.[20]

commerce clause The clause of the Constitution (Article I, Section 8) that empowers the federal government to regulate commerce among the states and with other nations.

Between 1865 and 1937, the Supreme Court's rulings severely restricted national power. Narrowly interpreting Congress's constitutional power to regulate commerce, the Court forbade Congress to regulate child labor and other aspects of manufacturing.

Hundreds of men wait in a food line for a sandwich and cup of coffee, the gift of a New York City newspaper. State and local governments could not cope with the enormous problems created by the Great Depression, so the federal government stepped in with its New Deal programs, greatly changing the nature of federal-state relations.

In effect, the Supreme Court had denied both Congress and the states the authority to decide economic issues. Neither was permitted to substantially regulate business. As the constitutional scholars Alfred Kelly, Winifred Harbison, and Herman Belz have concluded, "No more complete perversion of the principles of effective federal government can be imagined."[21]

National Authority Prevails

Judicial supremacy in the economic sphere ended abruptly in 1937. For nearly a decade, the United States had been mired in the Great Depression, which President Franklin D. Roosevelt's New Deal was designed to alleviate. The Supreme Court, however, had ruled much of the New Deal's economic recovery legislation to be unconstitutional. A constitutional crisis of historic proportions seemed inevitable until the Court suddenly reversed its position. In the process, American federalism was fundamentally and forever changed.

The Great Depression revealed clearly that Americans had become a national community with national economic needs. By the 1930s, more than half the population lived in cities (only 20 percent did so in 1860), and more than ten million workers were employed by industry (only one million were so employed in 1860). Urban workers were typically dependent on landlords for their housing, on farmers and grocers for their food, and on corporations for their jobs. Farmers were more independent, but they too were increasingly a part of a larger economic network. Their income depended on market prices and shipping and equipment costs.[22]

This economic interdependence meant that no area of the economy was immune if things went wrong. When the depression hit in 1929, its effects could not be contained. A decline in spending was followed by a drop in production, a loss of jobs, unpaid rents and grocery bills, and a shrinking market for foodstuffs, which led to a further decline in spending, and so on, creating a relentless downward spiral. At the depths of the Great Depression, one-fourth of the nation's work force was unemployed.

The states by tradition had responsibility for welfare, but they were nearly penniless because of declining tax revenues and the growing ranks of poor people. The New Deal programs offered a way out of the crisis; for example, the National Industry Recovery Act of 1933 called for a massive public works program to create jobs and for coordinated action by major industries. However, the New Deal was opposed by economic conservatives (who accused Roosevelt of leading the nation down the road to communism) and by justices of the Supreme Court. In *Schechter v. United States* (1935), the Court invalidated the Recovery Act by a 5–4 vote, ruling that it usurped powers reserved to the states.[23]

Frustrated by the Court, Roosevelt in 1937 proposed his famed "Court-packing" plan. Roosevelt recommended that Congress enact legislation that would permit an additional justice to be appointed to the Court whenever a seated member passed the age of seventy. The number of justices would increase, and Roosevelt's appointees would presumably be more sympathetic to his programs. Roosevelt's scheme was resisted by Congress, but the controversy ended with "the switch in time that saved nine," when, for reasons that have never become fully clear, Justice Owen Roberts abandoned his opposition to Roosevelt's policies and thus gave the president a 5–4 majority on the Court.

Within months, the Court upheld the 1935 National Labor Relations Act, which gave employees the right to organize and bargain collectively.[24] In passing the act, Congress had argued that labor-management disputes were disruptive of the national economy and therefore could be regulated through the commerce clause. In upholding the act, the Supreme Court in effect granted Congress the authority to apply its commerce powers broadly. Several years later, the Court explicitly acknowledged the new constitutional doctrine by saying it has "nothing to do" with regulating commerce and asserted that Congress's commerce power is "as broad as the needs of the nation."[25] Thus the constitutional path was opened to a substantial increase in the national government's authority. During this same period, the Court also relaxed its restrictions on Congress's use of its taxing and spending powers.[26]

In effect, the Supreme Court had finally recognized the obvious: that an industrial economy is not confined by state boundaries and must be subject to some level of national regulation if it is to serve the nation's needs and interests.[27] It was a principle that business itself also increasingly accepted. The nation's banking industry, for example, was saved in the 1930s from almost complete collapse by the creation of a federal regulatory agency, the Federal Deposit Insurance Corporation (FDIC). By insuring depositors' savings against loss, the FDIC gave depositors the confidence to keep their money in banks, enabling many banks to remain solvent despite the depression.

After the depression era and until recently, the Supreme Court gave Congress almost complete discretion in the enactment of policies affecting state governments and business firms. The extent of Congress's power was evident, for example, in the 1964 Civil Rights Act, which forbids racial discrimination by the private operators of hotels and restaurants on the grounds that they provide lodging and food to travelers engaged in interstate commerce.[28]

TOWARD NATIONAL CITIZENSHIP

The fundamental change in the constitutional doctrine of federalism as applied to economic issues that took place in the 1930s is paralleled by similar changes in other areas. One area is civil rights. As will be discussed in Chapter 5, federal authority has compelled states and localities to eliminate government-sponsored discrimination and, in some cases, to create compensatory opportunities for minorities and women. In 1954, for example, the Supreme Court held that racial segregation in public schools was unconstitutional on grounds that it violated the Fourteenth Amendment.[29]

The idea that Americans are equal in their rights regardless of where they reside has also been applied in other areas. As Chapter 4 will discuss, states have been required to broaden individual rights of free expression and fair trial. An example is the Supreme Court's *Miranda* ruling, which requires police officers to inform crime suspects of their rights at the time of arrest.[30]

Of course, important differences remain in the rights and privileges of the residents of the separate states, as could be expected in a federal system. The death penalty, for example, is legal in some states but not others, and states differ greatly in terms of their services, such as the quality of their public schools. Nevertheless, national citizenship—the notion that Americans should be equal in their rights and opportunities regardless of the state in which they live—is a more encompassing idea today than in the past.

Federalism Today

Since the 1930s, the relation of the nation to the states has changed so fundamentally that dual federalism is no longer even a roughly accurate description of the American situation.

An understanding of the nature of federalism today requires a recognition of two countervailing trends. The first is a long-term *expansion* of national authority that began in the 1930s and continued for the next half century. The national government now operates in many policy areas that were once almost exclusively within the control of states and localities. The national government does not dominate these policy areas, but it does have a significant role. Much of this influence stems from social welfare policies that were enacted in the 1960s as part of President Lyndon Johnson's Great Society program, which included initiatives in health care, public housing, nutrition, welfare, urban development, and other areas reserved previously to states and localities.

The second trend is more recent and involves a partial *contraction* of national authority. Known as "devolution," the recent trend involves "the passing down" of authority from the national government to the state and local levels. Devolution has reversed the decades-long increase in federal authority but only in some areas and then only to a modest degree.

★ CRITICAL THINKING ★

WHAT'S YOUR OPINION?

Congress Versus Supreme Court as Protector of the States

In a 1985 decision, the Supreme Court said that the states should look primarily to Congress, and not to the Court, for relief from "undue burdens" placed on them by Washington. This position followed from earlier Supreme Court decisions that said, in effect, that the commerce and taxing powers of the federal government were defined more by national needs than by any constitutional provision.

In your view, is the Supreme Court or Congress better equipped to safeguard America's federal system? Keep in mind that members of the Congress are elected by voters within the states they represent.

Texas Attorney General John Cornya speaks at a gathering of federal, state, and local law enforcement officials. Cooperative federalism brings together officials from all levels of government in joint efforts to solve common problems.

Stated differently, the national government's policy authority has expanded greatly since the 1930s even though that authority has been reduced somewhat in recent years. What follows is an explanation of each of these trends.

INTERDEPENDENCY AND INTERGOVERNMENTAL RELATIONS

Interdependency is a primary reason why national authority increased dramatically in the twentieth century. Modern systems of transportation, commerce, and communication transcend local and state boundaries. These systems are national, even international, in scope, which means that problems affecting Americans in one part of the country are likely also to affect Americans living elsewhere. This situation has required Washington to assume a larger policy role: national problems ordinarily require national solutions.

This situation has also encouraged national, state, and local policy makers to work together to solve policy problems. This collaborative effort has been described as **cooperative federalism**.[31] The difference between this system of federalism and the older dual federalism has been likened to the difference between a marble cake, whose levels flow together, and a layer cake, whose levels are separate.[32]

Cooperative federalism is based on shared policy responsibilities rather than sharply divided ones. An example is Medicaid, which provides health care for the poor. The Medicaid program is jointly funded by the national and state governments, operates within eligibility standards set by the national government, and gives states some latitude in determining the benefits that recipients receive. The Medicaid program is not an isolated example. Literally hundreds of policy programs today are run jointly by the national and state governments. In many cases, local governments are also involved. The characteristics of these programs are the following:

cooperative federalism The situation in which the national, state, and local levels work together to solve problems.

- Jointly funded by the national and state governments (and sometimes by local governments, too)
- Jointly administered, with the states and localities providing most of the direct service to recipients and a national agency providing general administration
- Jointly determined, with both the state and national governments (and sometimes, the local governments) having a say in eligibility and benefit levels, and with federal regulations, such as those prohibiting discrimination, giving an element of uniformity to the various state and local efforts

Cooperative federalism should not be interpreted to indicate that the states are now powerless and dependent. States have retained most of their traditional authority. In fact, the states have a larger influence than Washington does in many policy areas (see Figure 3-2). Nearly 95 percent of the funding for public schools, for example, is provided by states and localities, which also set most of the education standards, from teachers' qualifications to course requirements to the length of the school day. Moreover, the policy areas dominated by the states—such as education, law enforcement, and transportation—tend to be those that have the greatest impact on people's daily lives. Finally, contrary to what many Americans might think, state and local governments have nearly six times as many employees as the federal government. (Chapter 21 describes state and local governments in greater detail.)

Nevertheless, the federal government's involvement in policy areas traditionally reserved for the states has increased its policy influence and has diminished state-to-state policy differences. Before the enactment of the federal Medicaid program in 1965, for example, poor people in many states were not entitled to government-paid health care. Now most poor people are eligible regardless of where in the United States they live.

GOVERNMENT REVENUES AND INTERGOVERNMENTAL RELATIONS

The interdependence of different sectors of modern American society is one of two factors that have propelled a larger federal role in domestic policy. The

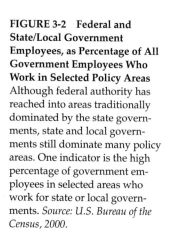

FIGURE 3-2 Federal and State/Local Government Employees, as Percentage of All Government Employees Who Work in Selected Policy Areas
Although federal authority has reached into areas traditionally dominated by the state governments, state and local governments still dominate many policy areas. One indicator is the high percentage of government employees in selected areas who work for state or local governments. *Source: U.S. Bureau of the Census, 2000.*

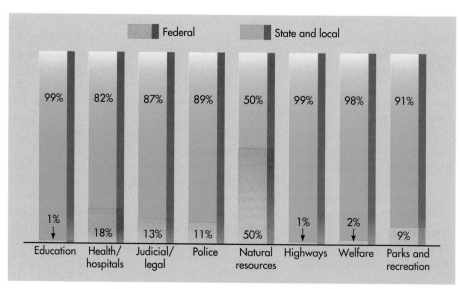

other is the federal government's superior taxing and borrowing capacity. States and localities are in an inherently competitive situation with regard to taxation. People and businesses faced with state or local tax increases can move to another state or locality where taxes are lower. Moreover, the federal government depends almost entirely on forms of taxation, such as personal and corporate income taxes, that automatically increase revenues as the economy expands. State and local governments depend more heavily than does Washington on revenue sources, such as license fees and property taxes, that are relatively inflexible. The overall result is that the federal government raises more tax revenues than do all fifty states and the thousands of local governments combined (see Figure 3-3). Finally, because it controls the American dollar, the federal government has a nearly unlimited ability to borrow money to cover its deficits. States and localities can go bankrupt and therefore cannot as easily find the credit to cover their budget deficits.

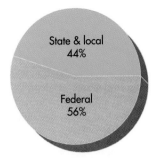

FIGURE 3-3   Federal, State, and Local Shares of Government Tax Revenue
The federal government raises more tax revenues than all state and local governments combined. *Source: U.S. Department of Commerce, 2000.*

Fiscal Federalism

The federal government's revenue-raising advantage has helped make money the basis for many of the relations between the national government and the states and localities. **Fiscal federalism** refers to the expenditure of federal funds on programs run in part through state and local government.[33] The federal government provides some or all the money for a program through **grants-in-aid** (cash payments) to states and localities, which then administer the program.

The pattern of federal assistance to states and localities during the last four decades is shown in Figure 3-4. Federal grants-in-aid increased tenfold during this period. The sharpest rise occurred in the 1960s and early 1970s as a result of President Johnson's Great Society programs. Even at the height of the New Deal, federal aid had accounted for less than 10 percent of state and local spending. With Johnson's Great Society, however, the figure rose above 20 percent and has remained in that range ever since. In other words, roughly one in every five dollars spent by local and state governments in recent decades was raised not by them, but by the government in Washington.

Cash grants to states and localities have extended Washington's influence over policy.[34] Through the funds it provides and the conditions it attaches to the use of those funds, Washington affects the policy choices of state and local governments. State and local governments can reject a grant-in-aid, but if they accept it, they must spend it in the specified ways. And because most grants require states to contribute matching funds, the federal programs in effect determine how states will use some of their own tax dollars. Federal grants have also pressured state and local officials to accept broad national goals, such as the elimination of racial and other forms of discrimination. A building constructed with the help of federal funds, for example, must be accessible to persons with disabilities.

Nevertheless, federal grants-in-aid also serve the policy interests of state and local officials. They have often complained that federal grants contain too many restrictions and infringe too much on their authority, but they have been eager to obtain the money because it permits them to offer services they could not otherwise provide. An example is a 1994 federal grant program that has enabled local governments to put seventy-five thousand additional police officers on the streets.

fiscal federalism   A term that refers to the expenditure of federal funds on programs run in part through states and localities.

grants-in-aid   Federal cash payments to states and localities for programs they administer.

CATEGORICAL AND BLOCK GRANTS

State and local governments receive two major types of assistance, categorical grants and block grants, which are differentiated by the extent to which Washington defines the conditions of their use.

categorical grants   Federal grants-in-aid to states and localities that can be used only for designated projects.

block grants   Federal grants-in-aid that permit state and local officials to decide how the money will be spent within a general area such as education or health.

Categorical grants are the more restrictive; they can be used only for a designated activity. An example is funds directed for use in school-lunch programs. These funds can be used only in support of school lunches; they cannot be diverted for other school purposes, such as the purchase of textbooks or the hiring of teachers. **Block grants** are less restrictive. The federal government specifies the general area in which the funds must be used, but state and local officials select the specific projects. A block grant targeted for the health area, for example, might give state and local officials leeway in deciding whether to use the money on hospital construction, medical equipment, or some other health care activity.

State and local officials have naturally preferred federal money that comes with fewer strings attached, so they have favored block grants. On the other hand, members of Congress have at times preferred categorical grants because this form of assistance gives them more control over how state and local officials will spend federal funds. Recently, however, officials at all levels have looked to block grants as the key to a more workable form of federalism. This tendency is part of a larger trend—that of devolution.

A NEW FEDERALISM: DEVOLUTION

devolution   The passing down of authority from the national government to the state and local governments.

Devolution is the idea that American federalism will be improved by a shift in authority from the federal government to the state and local governments. De-

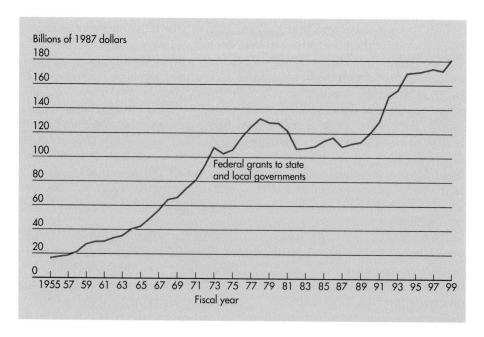

FIGURE 3-4   Federal Grants to State and Local Governments in Constant (1987) Dollars
Federal aid to states and localities has increased dramatically since the 1950s.
Source: Advisory Commission on Intergovernmental Relations.

volution is reshaping American federalism and is attributable to both practical and political developments.

Changing Conditions, Changing Politics

The rapid increase in federal assistance to the states during the 1960s and 1970s did not go unchallenged. Although both major political parties had initiated expansions of federal authority, Republicans had more often questioned both the legitimacy and consequences of federal involvement in policy areas traditionally reserved for the states. Republican presidents Richard Nixon, Ronald Reagan, and George Bush all advocated some version of a "new federalism" in which some areas of public policy for which the federal government had assumed responsibility would be returned to state and local control.[35]

The GOP's philosophical stance as the party of smaller government was behind these proposals, but so too was the fact that Democratic constituencies were the main beneficiaries of many federal grant programs. If the primary effect of fiscal federalism was to strengthen the nation's health, transportation, education, welfare, and public safety systems, a secondary effect was the distribution of a disproportionate share of the benefits to traditionally Democratic constituencies. Many of the grant programs were based on need, which meant that the cities, minorities, and the poor were among the primary beneficiaries.

During the 1980s, the federal government faced huge budget deficits, which buttressed Republican demands for a rollback in federal grants-in-aid. And in fact, federal assistance actually decreased during the 1980s in terms of constant dollars (dollars adjusted to reflect the rate of inflation). By 1990, however, federal grant spending was again on the rise but not as a result of the desire of Washington officials to expand assistance programs. A sharp rise in medical costs was pushing up the cost of the Medicaid grant program, which was by far the most expensive of the federal assistance programs. Because the states paid part of the Medicaid costs, their direct cost was also rising. Yet the economy was weak and budget deficits were still growing, which fueled taxpayer resentment about government spending. Some of the federal grant programs, such as AFDC, food stamps, and housing subsidies, had not been very popular before the fiscal crunch and now came under even heavier criticism.

By the early 1990s, American federalism was positioned for a major change. Two decades earlier, three-fourths of Americans had expressed confidence in Washington's ability to govern effectively. Less than half the public now held this view. A 1993 CBS News/New York Times survey indicated that 69 percent of Americans believed that "the federal government creates more problems than it solves."

The Republican Revolution

The public's declining confidence in the federal government contributed to a sweeping Republican victory in the 1994 congressional elections. The GOP gained control of both the House and the Senate for the first time in four decades. GOP House leader Newt Gingrich declared that "1960s-style federalism is dead," and Republican lawmakers acted quickly to rollback federal authority.

FEDERAL GRANTS-IN-AID AS A PERCENTAGE OF TOTAL STATE REVENUE

Federal assistance accounts for a significant share of state revenue, but the state-to-state variation is considerable. Louisiana is at one extreme: 34.6 percent of its total revenue comes from federal grants. Nevada is at the other extreme: only 14.5 percent of its revenue comes from federal assistance. Ironically, states in the South, where anti-Washington sentiment is relatively high, tend to get a larger percentage of their revenue through federal grants than most other states do. Many of the grant programs are designed to assist people with low incomes, and poverty is more widespread in the South than in other regions. Moreover, southern states have traditionally provided fewer government services, and federal grants therefore constitute a larger proportion of their state budgets.

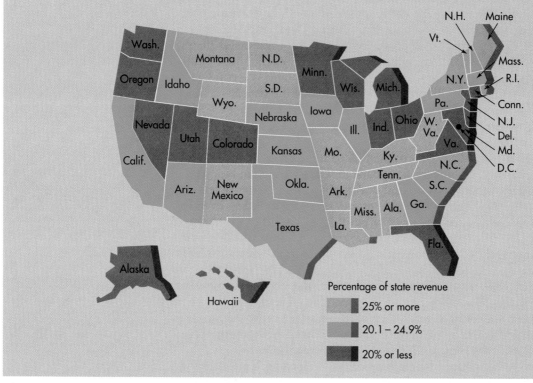

Percentage of state revenue

- 25% or more
- 20.1 – 24.9%
- 20% or less

SOURCE: U.S. Bureau of the Census, 1999.

A first step was a reduction in *unfunded mandates*. These are federal programs that require action by states or localities but provide no or insufficient funds to pay for it. For example, states and localities are required by federal law to make their buildings accessible to the physically handicapped but Washington pays only part of the cost of these accommodations. In the Unfunded Mandates Reform Act of 1995, Congress eliminated some of these mandates, although under threat of a presidential veto it exempted those that deal with civil rights and liberties. The GOP-controlled Congress also took action to lump additional categorical grants into block grants, thus giving states more control over how federal money would be spent.

When the 1994 elections were over, Newt Gingrich declared that "1960s-style federalism is dead." As Speaker of the House of Representatives, Gingrich then helped enact major changes in federal-state relations.

The most significant legislative change came a year later, when the Republican Congress enacted the sweeping 1996 Welfare Reform Act. Its key element is the Temporary Assistance for Needy Families block grant (TANF), which ended the decades-old program that granted cash assistance to every poor family with children. TANF restricts a family's eligibility for federal assistance to five years, and after two years, a family head normally has to go to work or the benefits cease. Moreover, TANF gives states wide latitude in setting benefit levels, eligibility criteria, and other regulations affecting aid for poor families. (TANF and other aspects of the 1996 welfare reform legislation are discussed further in Chapter 19.)

After passage of the 1996 Welfare Reform Act, congressional efforts to rollback federal authority declined sharply. Devolution had hardly rolled back a half century of Washington-centered federalism, nor had it blunted new federal assistance programs. Among the federal initiatives enacted recently are grants for classroom modernization and the hiring of tens of thousands of additional teachers.

Although it is uncertain how far devolution will be extended, American federalism has clearly entered a new stage, where answers to the nation's problems will be sought less in Washington than in the states and localities. Devolution has resulted in a modification of fiscal and cooperative federalism rather than their demise. The federal government will continue to be a part of the answer to problems in policy areas once reserved almost exclusively to the states. Because of the complexity of modern policy issues, and the interdependency of American society, the states will never regain the level of autonomy that they exercised in the early twentieth century. Through devolution, however, they have acquired a greater degree of discretionary authority in some policy areas.

Devolution, Judicial Style

In the five decades after the 1930s, the Supreme Court granted Congress broad discretion in the enactment of policies affecting state and local governments. In *Garcia v. San Antonio Authority* (1985), for example, the Court held that federal minimum wage standards apply even to state and local governments.[36] States and localities are prohibited from paying their employees less than the federally mandated minimum wage.

In recent years, however, the Supreme Court has restricted congressional authority somewhat. Chief Justice William Rehnquist and some of the other Republican appointees on the Supreme Court believe that Congress in some instances has encroached on powers properly reserved to state and local governments. In *United States v. Lopez* (1995), for example, the Court struck down a federal law that prohibited the possession of guns within a thousand feet of a school. Congress had justified the law as an exercise of its commerce power, but the Court stated that the ban had "nothing to do with commerce, or any sort of economic activity."[37] Two years later, in *Printz v. United States* (1997), the Court struck down that part of the federal Handgun Violence Prevention Act (the so-called Brady bill) which required local law-enforcement officers to conduct background checks on prospective handgun buyers. The Court said the provision violated the "principle of separate state sovereignty," arguing that the federal government cannot "command" local officials "to administer or enforce a federal regulatory program."[38] Then, in *Kimel v. Florida Board of Regents* (2000), the Supreme Court held that Congress did not have the authority to require state governments to comply with the federal law that bars discrimination against older workers. Age discrimination is not among the forms of discrimination expressly prohibited by the U.S. Constitution, and the Court declared that states have the power to decide for themselves the age-related policies that will apply to their employees.[39]

Although these Court decisions have restricted federal authority, they have done so only to a limited extent. The Court has not by any means repudiated the principle established in the 1930s that Congress's commerce and spending powers are broad and substantial. In *Reno v. Condon* (2000), for example, the Court ruled that the states have to comply with a federal law barring them from selling to private firms or groups their databases of personal information obtained from automobile license applicants. The majority opinion, which was written by Chief Justice Rehnquist, declared that the information in these databases is "an article of commerce" and thus is subject to regulation through Congress's commerce power. The Court noted that the law also applied to "private resellers" and was aimed at regulating "the owners of databases," which in this case included the states.[40]

The Public's Influence: Setting the Boundaries of Federal-State Power

The ebb and flow in Washington's power in the twentieth century has coincided closely with public opinion. The American people have had a decisive voice in determining the relationship between the federal and state governments.

Through their votes, the American people have had a decisive influence on the balance of power between Washington and the states. Residents of Columbus, Ohio, are shown voting in a midterm election.

During the Great Depression, when it was clear that the states would be unable to help, Americans turned to Washington for relief. For people without jobs and money, the fine points of the Constitution were of little consequence. President Roosevelt's welfare and public jobs programs were a radical departure from the past but quickly gained widespread support. A 1936 Gallup poll indicated, for example, that 61 percent of Americans supported Roosevelt's social security program, whereas only 27 percent opposed it. "The Social Security Act," Andrew Dobelstein noted, "reflected [the new public attitude] that the federal government had responsibility to promote the general welfare through specific public welfare programs funded with federal tax dollars."[41]

The second great wave of federal social programs—President Johnson's Great Society—was also driven by public demands. Income and education levels had risen dramatically after the Second World War, and Americans wanted more and better services from government. When the states were slow to respond, Americans pressured federal officials to act. The Medicaid program is an example of Washington's response.

Public opinion is also behind the more recent rollback in federal authority. The Republican victory in the 1994 midterm elections was in large part a result of Americans' increased dissatisfaction with the federal government. In a 1994 Times Mirror survey, 66 percent of respondents expressed the view that most officials in Washington did not care what people like themselves think.[42]

The public's role in defining the boundaries between federal and state power would come as no surprise to the Framers of the Constitution. For them, federalism was a pragmatic issue, one to be decided by the nation's needs rather than inflexible rules. And indeed, each succeeding generation of Americans has seen fit to devise a balance of federal and state power that would serve its interests. The historian Daniel Boorstin said the true genius of the American people is their pragmatism; their willingness to try new ways when the old ones stop working.[43] In few areas of governing has this ingenuity been more apparent than in Americans' approach to federalism.

www.mhhe.com/patterson5

Self-Quiz

Summary

A foremost characteristic of the American political system is its division of authority between a national government and the states. The first U.S. government, established by the Articles of Confederation, was essentially a union of the states.

In establishing the basis for a stronger national government, the U.S. Constitution also made provision for safeguarding state interests. The result was the creation of a federal system in which sovereignty was vested in both national and state governments. The Constitution enumerates the general powers of the national government and grants it implied powers through the "necessary and proper" clause. Other powers are reserved to the states by the Tenth Amendment.

From 1789 to 1865, the nation's survival was at issue. The states found it convenient at times to argue that their sovereignty took precedence over national authority. In the end, it took the Civil War to cement the idea that the United States was a union of people, not of states. From 1865 to 1937, federalism reflected the doctrine that certain policy areas were the exclusive responsibility of the national government, while other areas belonged exclusively to the states. This constitutional position permitted the laissez-faire doctrine that big business was largely beyond governmental control. It also allowed the states in their public policies to discriminate against African Americans. Federalism in a form recognizable today began to emerge in the late 1930s.

In the areas of commerce, taxation, spending, civil rights, and civil liberties, among others, the federal government now has an important role, one that is the inevitable consequence of the increasing complexity of American society and the interdependence of its people. National, state, and local officials now work closely together to solve the country's problems, a situation that is described as cooperative federalism. Grants-in-aid from Washington to the states and localities have been the chief instrument of national influence. States and localities have received billions in federal assistance; in accepting that money, they have also accepted both federal restrictions on its use and the national policy priorities that underlie the granting of the money.

In recent years, the relationship between the nation and the states has again become a priority issue. Power is shifting downward to the states, and a new balance in the ever-evolving system of U.S. federalism is taking place. This change, as has been true throughout U.S. history, has sprung from the demands of the American people.

Key Terms

block grants
categorical grants
commerce clause
confederacy
cooperative federalism
devolution
dual federalism
enumerated (expressed) powers
federalism

fiscal federalism
grants-in-aid
implied powers
"necessary and proper" clause (elastic clause)
reserved powers
sovereignty
supremacy clause
unitary system

Suggested Readings

Beer, Samuel H. *To Make a Nation: The Rediscovery of American Federalism*. Cambridge, Mass.: The Belknap Press of Harvard University Press, 1993. An innovative interpretive framework for understanding the impact of federalism and nationalism on the nation's development.

Conlan, Timothy. *From New Federalism to Devolution*. Washington, D.C.: Brookings Institution Press, 1998. A careful analysis of the changing nature of modern federalism.

Cornell, Saul. *The Other Founders: Anti-Federalism and the Dissenting Tradition in America*. Chapel Hill: University of North Carolina Press, 1999. An analysis of Antifederalist thought, its origins, and its legacy.

Elkins, Stanley, and Eric McKitrick. *The Age of Federalism: The Early American Republic, 1788–1800*. New York: Oxford University Press, 1993. An award-winning book on the earliest period of American federalism.

Maidment, Richard A. *The Judicial Response to the New Deal: The U.S. Supreme Court and Economic Regulation*. New York: Manchester University Press, 1992. An analysis of a major turning point in the constitutional interpretation of federalism.

O'Toole, Lawrence, ed. *American Intergovernmental Relations*, 3d ed. Washington, D.C.: Congressional Quarterly Press, 2000. A useful set of perspectives on the relationships between federal, state, and local governments.

Peterson, Paul A. *The Price of Federalism*. Washington, D.C.: Brookings Institution, 1995. A careful analysis of how federalism works, including its costs and benefits.

Ross, William G. *A Muted Fury: Populists, Progressives, and Labor Unions Confront the Courts, 1890–1937*. Princeton, N.J.: Princeton University Press, 1993. A valuable study of the political conflict surrounding the judiciary's laissez-faire doctrine in the 1890–1937 period.

Thompson, Tommy. *Power to the People: An American State at Work*. New York: HarperCollins, 1996. An argument for state-centered federalism by one of its leading practitioners, the governor of Wisconsin.

Walker, David B. *The Rebirth of Federalism*, 2d ed. Chatham, N.J.: Chatham House Publishers, 2000. An optimistic assessment of the state of today's federalism.

CHAPTER 4

Civil Liberties: Protecting Individual Rights

★

A bill of rights is what the people are entitled to against every government on earth, general or particular, and what no just government should refuse, or rest on inference.

—Thomas Jefferson[1]

★ ★ ★

*R*obert and Sarisse Creighton and their three children were asleep when FBI agents and local police broke into their home in the middle of the night. Brandishing guns, the officers searched the house for a relative of the Creightons who was suspected of bank robbery. When asked to show a search warrant, they said, "You watch too much TV." The suspect was not there, and the officers left as abruptly as they had entered. The Creightons sued the FBI agent in charge, Russell Anderson, for violating their Fourth Amendment right against unlawful search.

The Creightons won a temporary victory when the Eighth U.S. Circuit Court of Appeals, noting that individuals are constitutionally protected against warrantless searches unless officers have good reason ("probable cause") for a search and unless they have good reason ("exigent circumstances") for conducting that search without a warrant, concluded that Anderson had been derelict in his duty. In the judgment of the appellate court, Anderson should have sought a warrant from a judge, who would have decided whether a search of the Creightons' home was justified.

The Supreme Court of the United States overturned the lower court's ruling. The Court's majority opinion said: "We have recognized that it is inevitable that law enforcement officials will in some cases reasonably but mistakenly conclude that probable cause is present, and we have indicated that in such cases those officials . . . should not be held personally liable." Justice John Paul Stevens and two other justices sharply dissented. He accused the Court's majority of showing "remarkably little fidelity" to the Fourth Amendment.[2] Civil liberties groups claimed that the Court's decision gave police an open invitation to invade people's homes on the slightest pretext. However, the Court's decision was praised by law enforcement officials and conservatives, who contended that a ruling in the Creightons' favor would have made police hesitant to pursue suspects for fear of a lawsuit if a search failed to produce the person sought.

As this case illustrates, issues of individual rights are complex and political. No right is absolute. For example, the Fourth Amendment protects Americans not from *all* searches but from *unreasonable* searches. The public would be unsafe if law officials could never search for evidence of a crime or pursue a suspect into a home. Yet the public would also be unsafe if police could frisk people at will or invade their homes with impunity. Such acts are characteristic of a police state, not of a free society. The challenge to a civil society is to establish a level of police authority that balances the demands of public safety with those of individual freedom. The balance point, however, is always subject to dispute. Did FBI agent Anderson have sufficient cause for a warrantless search of the

civil liberties The fundamental individual rights of a free society, such as freedom of speech and the right to a jury trial, which in the United States are protected by the Bill of Rights.

Bill of Rights The first ten amendments to the Constitution, which set forth basic protections for individual rights to free expression, fair trial, and property.

Creightons' home? Or was his evidence so weak that his forcible entry constituted an unreasonable search? Law enforcement officials and civil liberties groups had widely different opinions on these questions. Nor did the justices of the Supreme Court have a uniform view. Six of the justices sided with Anderson and three backed the Creightons' position.

This chapter examines issues of **civil liberties:** specific individual rights, such as freedom of speech and protection against self-incrimination, that are constitutionally protected against infringement by government. As we saw in Chapter 2, the Constitution's failure to enumerate individual freedoms led to demands for the **Bill of Rights.** Enacted in 1791, these first ten amendments to the Constitution specify certain rights of life, liberty, and property that the national government is obliged to respect. A later amendment, the Fourteenth, became the basis for extending these protections of individual rights to actions by state and local governments.

Rights have full meaning only as protected in law. A constitutional guarantee of free speech, for example, is worth no more than the paper on which it is written if authorities can prevent people from speaking freely. Judicial action is important in defining what people's rights mean in practice and in setting and enforcing limits on official action that may infringe on these rights. In some areas, the judiciary devises a specific test to determine whether government action is lawful. A test applied in the area of free speech, for example, is whether general rules (such as restrictions on the time and place of a public gathering) are applied fairly to all groups. Government officials do not meet this test if they apply one set of rules for groups that they like and a harsher set of rules for those they dislike.

Issues of individual rights have become increasingly complex and important. The writers of the Constitution could not possibly have foreseen the United States of the early twenty-first century, with its huge national government, enormous corporations, pervasive mass media, urban crowding, and nuclear weapons. These developments are potential threats to individual liberty, and the judiciary in recent decades has seen fit to expand the rights to which individuals are entitled. However, these rights are constantly being balanced against competing individual rights and society's collective interests. The Bill of Rights operates in an untidy world where people's highest aspirations collide with their worst passions, and it is at this juncture that issues of civil liberties arise. Should an admitted murderer be entitled to recant a confession? Should the press be allowed to print military secrets whose publication might jeopardize national security? Should prayer be allowed in the public schools? Should extremist groups be allowed to publicize their messages of prejudice and hate? Such questions are among the subjects of this chapter, which focuses on the following major points:

★ *Freedom of expression is the most basic of democratic rights, but like all rights, it is not unlimited.* Free expression recently has been strongly supported by the Supreme Court.

★ *"Due process of law" refers to legal protections (primarily procedural safeguards) that are designed to ensure that individual rights are respected by government.*

★ *During the last half century particularly, the civil liberties of individual Americans have been substantially broadened in law and given greater judicial protection from action by all levels of government.* Of special significance has been the

Exercising their right of free expression, anti-abortion protesters gather outside a government building.

Supreme Court's use of the Fourteenth Amendment to protect these individual rights from action by state and local governments.

★ *Individual rights are constantly being weighed against the demands of majorities and the collective needs of society.* All political institutions are involved in this process, as is public opinion, but the judiciary plays the central role in it and is the institution that is most partial to the protection of civil liberties.

Freedom of Expression

Freedom of political expression is the most basic of democratic rights. Unless citizens can openly express their political opinions, they cannot properly influence their government or act to protect their other rights. They also cannot hear what others have to say and thus cannot judge the merits of alternative views. And without free expression, elections are a sham, a mere showcase for those who control what is on people's lips and in their minds. As the Supreme Court concluded in 1984, "The freedom to speak one's mind is not only an aspect of individual liberty—and thus a good unto itself—but also is essential to the common quest for truth and the vitality of society as whole."[3]

It is for such reasons that the First Amendment provides the foundation for **freedom of expression**—the right of individual Americans to hold and communicate views of their choosing. For many reasons, such as a desire to conform to social pressure or a fear of harassment, Americans do not always choose to express themselves freely. Nevertheless, the First Amendment provides for freedom of expression by prohibiting laws that would abridge the freedoms of conscience, speech, press, assembly, and petition.

freedom of expression
Americans' freedom to communicate their views, the foundation of which is the First Amendment rights of freedom of conscience, speech, press, assembly, and petition.

Supreme Court Justice Oliver Wendell Holmes Jr. (1841–1935).

Freedom of expression, like other rights, is not absolute. It does not entitle individuals to say or do whatever they want, to whomever they want, whenever they want. Free expression can be denied, for example, if it endangers national security, wrongly damages the reputations of others, or deprives others of their basic freedoms. An individual's private thoughts are completely free, but words and actions may not be. The Supreme Court has ruled, for example, that abortion protesters can be arrested if they violate laws or court orders that bar them from protesting within a certain distance of abortion clinics or from physically interfering with a woman's attempt to enter a clinic.[4]

In recent decades, free expression has received broad protection from the courts. Today, under most circumstances, Americans can freely verbalize their political views without fear of governmental interference. In earlier times, however, Americans were less free to express their political views.

THE EARLY PERIOD: THE UNCERTAIN STATUS OF THE RIGHT OF FREE EXPRESSION

The first legislative attempt by the U.S. government to restrict free expression was the Sedition Act of 1798, which made it a crime to print false or malicious newspaper stories about the president or other national officials. Thomas Jefferson called the Sedition Act an "alarming infraction" of the Constitution and, upon replacing John Adams as president in 1801, pardoned those who had been convicted under it. Because the Supreme Court did not review the sedition cases, however, the judiciary's position on free expression remained an open question. The Court also did not rule on free speech during the Civil War era, when the government severely restricted individual rights.

In 1919 the Court finally ruled on a case that challenged the national government's authority to restrict free expression. Two years earlier, Congress had passed the Espionage Act, which prohibited forms of dissent deemed to be harmful to the nation's effort in World War I. Nearly two thousand Americans were convicted for such activities as interfering with draft registration and distributing anti-war leaflets. The Supreme Court upheld one of these convictions in *Schenck v. United States* (1919), ruling unanimously that the Espionage Act of 1917 was constitutional. In the opinion written by Justice Oliver Wendell Holmes, the Court said that Congress could restrict speech that was "of such a nature as to create a clear and present danger" to the nation's security. In a famous passage, Holmes argued that not even the First Amendment would permit a person to falsely yell "fire" in a crowded theater and create a panic that could kill or injure innocent people.[5] Although the **clear-and-present-danger test** has been superseded by a more rigorous standard (the imminent lawless action test, discussed later in this chapter in the context of *Brandenburg v. Ohio*), it served to place a limit on the government's authority over free expression. Political speech that did *not* pose a clear and present danger could *not* be restricted.

THE MODERN PERIOD: PROTECTING FREE EXPRESSION

Until the twentieth century, the tension between national security interests and free expression was not a pressing dilemma for the United States. The country's

clear-and-present-danger test A test devised by the Supreme Court in 1919 in order to define the limits of free speech in the context of national security. According to the test, government cannot abridge political expression unless it presents a clear and present danger to the nation's security.

great size and ocean barriers provided protection from potential enemies, minimizing concerns of internal subversion. World War I, however, intruded upon America's isolation, and World War II brought it to an abrupt end. Since then, Americans' rights of free expression have been defined largely in the context of national security concerns.

Free Speech and Assembly

During the cold war that developed after World War II, many Americans perceived the Soviet Union as bent on destroying the United States through internal subversion and global expansion. In this period, the Supreme Court allowed government to put substantial limits on free expression. In 1951, for example, the Court upheld the convictions of eleven members of the U.S. Communist party who had been prosecuted under a law that made it illegal to advocate the forceful overthrow of the U.S. government.[6]

By the late 1950s, however, fear of internal communist subversion was subsiding, and the Supreme Court expanded the scope of permissible speech.[7] The Court implicitly embraced a legal doctrine first outlined by Justice Harlan Fiske Stone in 1938. Stone argued that First Amendment rights of free expression are the basis of Americans' liberty and ought to have a "preferred position" in the law. If government can control what people know and say, it can manipulate their opinions and thereby deprive them of the right to decide for themselves how they will be governed. Therefore, government should be broadly prohibited from restricting free expression.[8]

This philosophy has led the Supreme Court to rule that government officials must show that national security is directly and substantially imperiled before they can lawfully prohibit citizens from speaking out or assembling. For example, during the Vietnam era, despite the largest sustained protest movement in America's history, not a single individual was convicted solely for voicing objections to the government's war policy. (Some dissenters were found guilty on other grounds, such as inciting riots and assaulting the police.)

The Supreme Court's protection of **symbolic speech** has been less substantial than its protection of verbal speech. For example, the Court in 1968 upheld the conviction of a Vietnam protester who had burned his draft registration card. The Court said that government can prohibit action that threatens a legitimate public interest as long as the main purpose of the policy is not to restrict free expression. The Court concluded that the federal law prohibiting the destruction of draft cards was designed primarily to protect the military's need for soldiers, not to prevent people from criticizing government policy.[9]

symbolic speech Action (for example, the waving or burning of a flag) for the purpose of expressing a political opinion.

The Supreme Court, however, has not granted the government broad power to restrict symbolic speech. In 1989, for example, the Court ruled that the burning of the American flag is a protected form of free expression. The ruling came in the case of Gregory Lee Johnson, a member of the Communist Youth Brigade. Johnson had set fire to a U.S. flag outside the hall in Dallas where the 1984 Republican National Convention was being held. The Supreme Court rejected the state of Texas's argument that flag burning is, in every instance, an imminent danger to public safety. A year later the Court struck down a new federal statute that made it a federal crime to burn or deface the flag.[10] "If there is a bedrock principle underlying the First Amendment," the Court ruled in the *Johnson* case,

Civil rights attorney William Kunstler (*right*), with defendant Gregory Lee Johnson (*second from right*), addresses reporters outside the Supreme Court building. Kunstler defended Johnson in the celebrated case that ultimately established flag burning as a constitutionally protected form of political expression.

"it is that the Government may not prohibit the expression of an idea simply because society finds the idea itself offensive or disagreeable."[11]

Government's authority to regulate activities that are related to free speech is also subject to certain limitations. In its landmark *Buckley v. Valeo* (1976) decision, for example, the Supreme Court held that Congress cannot restrict the amount of their own money that political candidates can spend on their own campaigns. Any such limit, the Court concluded, would infringe on candidates' freedom of speech. Legal limits on individual and group contributions to candidates, however, were upheld on grounds that such limitations were necessary to prevent the appearance and possibly the reality that officeholders would be unduly influenced by large donors.[12] Another example is a 1999 Supreme Court ruling that overturned a Colorado statute that placed restrictions on the process by which petitioners could place initiatives on the state ballot. Colorado had required that all petitioners wear badges bearing their name and be registered Colorado voters. The Supreme Court invalidated these requirements, saying they infringed on the First Amendment's guarantee of "communication with voters."[13]

Press Freedom and Prior Restraint

Freedom of the press has also received strong judicial support in recent decades. In *New York Times Co. v. United States* (1971), the Court ruled that the *Times*'s publication of the "Pentagon papers" (secret government documents revealing official deception about the success of the Vietnam war policy) could not be blocked by the Department of Justice, which claimed that publication would hurt the war effort. The documents had been illegally obtained by anti-war activists, who had turned them over to the *Times* for publication. The Court ruled that "any system of prior restraints" on the press is unconstitutional unless the government can clearly justify the restriction.[14]

prior restraint   Government prohibition of speech or publication before the fact, which is presumed by the courts to be unconstitutional unless the justification for it is overwhelming.

The unacceptability of **prior restraint**—government prohibition of speech or publication before the fact—is basic to the current doctrine of free expression. The Supreme Court has said that any attempt by government to prevent expression carries "a 'heavy presumption' against its constitutionality."[15] News organizations and individuals are legally responsible after the fact for what they report or say (for example, they can be sued by an individual whose reputation is wrongly damaged by their words), but generally government cannot stop them in advance from expressing their views. An exception in rare instances is news coverage of criminal proceedings when intense or inflammatory reporting could make it impossible for the accused to get a fair trial. Another exception is the reporting of military operations. During the Persian Gulf War, U.S. journalists on station in Saudi Arabia had to work within limits placed on them by military authorities. In another exception to the doctrine of prior restraint, the courts have upheld the government's authority to ban uncensored publications by certain past and present government employees, such as CIA agents, who have taken part in classified national security activities.

FREE EXPRESSION AND STATE GOVERNMENTS

In 1790 Congress rejected a proposed amendment to the Constitution that would have applied the Bill of Rights to the states. Thus the freedoms guaranteed in the Bill of Rights were initially protected only from action by the national government, a constitutional arrangement that the Supreme Court upheld in *Barron v. Baltimore* (1833).[16] The effect was that the Bill of Rights had little practical meaning in the lives of ordinary Americans because state and local governments carry out most of the activities, such as law enforcement, where people's rights are at issue.

Not until the twentieth century did the Supreme Court begin to protect individual rights from infringement by state and local governments. The vehicle for this change was the **due process clause of the Fourteenth Amendment** to the Constitution.

due process clause (of the Fourteenth Amendment) The clause of the Constitution that has been used by the judiciary to apply the Bill of Rights to the actions of state governments.

The Fourteenth Amendment and Selective Incorporation

Ratified in 1868, the Fourteenth Amendment includes a clause that forbids a state from depriving any person of life, liberty, or property without due process of law (due process refers to the legal procedures that have been established as a means of protecting individuals' rights). Six decades later, the Supreme Court in *Gitlow v. New York* (1925) decided that the Fourteenth Amendment applied to state action in the area of freedom of expression. The Court upheld Benjamin Gitlow's conviction for violating a New York law that prohibited advocacy of the violent overthrow of the U.S. government, but warned that the states were not completely free to limit expression:

> For present purposes we may and do assume that freedom of speech and of the press—which are protected by the First Amendment from abridgement by Congress—are among the fundamental personal rights and "liberties" protected by the due process clause of the Fourteenth Amendment from impairment by the states.[17]

There is no indication that Congress, when it passed the Fourteenth Amendment after the Civil War, meant it to protect First Amendment rights from state action. The Supreme Court justified its new interpretation in the *Gitlow* case by

selective incorporation The absorption of certain provisions of the Bill of Rights (for example, freedom of speech) into the Fourteenth Amendment so that these rights are protected from infringement by the states.

reference to **selective incorporation**—the absorption of certain provisions of the Bill of Rights, particularly freedom of speech and press, into the Fourteenth Amendment so that these rights would be protected from infringement by the states. The Court reasoned that the Fourteenth Amendment's due-process clause was largely meaningless if states could prohibit their residents from speaking freely.

Having developed in the *Gitlow* case a new interpretation of the Fourteenth Amendment, the Supreme Court proceeded during the next decade to overturn state laws that restricted expression in the areas of speech, press, religion, and assembly and petition (see Table 4-1).[18] The most famous of these judgments is *Near v. Minnesota* (1931). Jay Near was the publisher of a Minneapolis weekly newspaper that regularly made scurrilous attacks on blacks, Jews, Catholics, and labor union leaders. His paper was closed down on authority of a state law that banned "malicious, scandalous, or defamatory" publications. Near appealed the shutdown, and the Supreme Court ruled in his favor, saying that the Minnesota law was "the essence of censorship."[19]

Limiting the Authority of States to Restrict Expression

Since the 1930s, the Supreme Court has broadly protected freedom of expression from action by the states and by local governments, which derive their authority from the states. The Court has held that the states cannot restrict free expression except when such expression is almost certain to result in imminent lawlessness. A leading free speech case was *Brandenburg v. Ohio* (1969). The appellant was a Ku Klux Klan member who, in a speech delivered at a Klan rally, said that "revenge" might have to be taken if the national government "continues to suppress the white Caucasian race." He was convicted of advocating force under an Ohio law prohibiting "criminal syndicalism," but the Supreme Court reversed the conviction, saying the First Amendment prohibits a state from suppressing speech that advocates the unlawful use of force "except where such advocacy is directed to inciting or producing imminent lawless action, and is likely to produce such action."[20] This test—the likelihood of **imminent lawless action**—is a severe restriction on the government's power to restrict expression. It is rare when words alone immediately incite others to act lawlessly.

imminent lawless action test A legal test that says government cannot lawfully suppress advocacy that promotes lawless action unless such advocacy is aimed at producing, and is likely to produce, imminent lawless action.

TABLE 4-1   Selective Incorporation of Rights of Free Expression   In the 1920s and 1930s, the Supreme Court selectively incorporated the free-expression provisions of the First Amendment into the Fourteenth Amendment so that these rights would be protected from infringement by the states.

Supreme Court Case	Year	Constitutional Right at Issue
Gitlow v. New York	1925	First Amendment's applicability to free speech
Fiske v. Kansas	1927	Free speech
Near v. Minnesota	1931	Free press
Hamilton v. Regents, U. of California	1934	Religious freedom
DeJonge v. Oregon	1937	Freedom of assembly and of petition

The Court has broadly held that "hate speech" cannot be silenced. This ruling came in a unanimous 1992 opinion that struck down a St. Paul, Minnesota, ordinance making it a crime to engage in speech likely to arouse "anger or alarm" on the basis of "race, color, creed, religion or gender." The Court said the First Amendment prohibits government from "silencing speech on the basis of its content."[21] This protection of violent *speech* does not, however, extend to violent *crimes*, such as assault, motivated by racial or other forms of prejudice. A Wisconsin law that provided for increased sentences for such crimes was challenged as a violation of the First Amendment. In a unanimous 1993 opinion, the Court said that the law was aimed at "conduct unprotected by the First Amendment" rather than the defendant's speech.[22]

In a key case involving freedom of assembly, the U.S. Supreme Court in 1977 upheld a lower-court ruling against local ordinances of Skokie, Illinois, which had been invoked to prevent a parade there by the American Nazi party.[23] Skokie had a large Jewish population, including many survivors of Nazi Germany's concentration camps. The Supreme Court held that the right of free expression takes precedence over the mere *possibility* that exercising the right may have undesirable consequences. Before government can lawfully prevent a speech or rally, it must offer persuasive evidence that an evil will almost certainly result from the event and must also demonstrate the lack of alternative ways (such as assigning police officers to control the crowd) to prevent the evil from happening.

The Supreme Court has recognized that freedom of speech and assembly may conflict with the routines of daily life. Accordingly, individuals do not have the right to hold a public rally in the middle of a busy intersection during rush hour, nor do they have the right to command immediate access to a public auditorium. The Court has held that public officials can regulate the time, place, and conditions of public assembly, provided that these regulations are reasonable and do not discriminate on the basis of the nature of these gatherings. In a 1992 case, the Court declared unconstitutional a local ordinance that imposed a fee of up to $1,000 to offset the costs of maintaining order at a public assembly; the more trouble expected, the higher the fee a group had to pay for permission to hold the assembly. The Court concluded that the First Amendment denies officials "unbridled discretion" in putting a price on speech "simply because it might offend a hostile mob."[24] Officials have an obligation to accommodate public gatherings and to treat *all* groups—including those that espouse unpopular views—in accordance with reasonable standards.

In general, the Supreme Court's position is that the First Amendment makes any government effort to regulate the *content* of a message highly suspect. In the flag-burning case, Texas was regulating the content of the message—contempt for the flag and the principles it represents. Texas could not have been regulating the act itself, for the government's own method of disposing of worn-out flags is also to burn them. But a content-neutral regulation (no public rally can be held in the middle of a busy intersection at rush hour) is acceptable as long as it is reasonable and does not discriminate against certain groups or ideas.

LIBEL AND SLANDER

The constitutional right of free expression is not a legal license to avoid responsibility for the consequences of what is said or written. If false information that

libel Publication of material
that falsely damages a person's
reputation.

slander Spoken words that
falsely damage a person's
reputation.

greatly harms a person's reputation is published (**libel**) or spoken (**slander**), the injured party can sue for damages.

Libel is the more important issue in the political arena because it affects the news media's ability to openly criticize governing officials. If an official could win a libel judgment any time a news organization made a factually inaccurate statement, the news media would hesitate to say anything critical of officials.

A leading decision in this area is *New York Times Co. v. Sullivan* (1964), in which the Court overruled an Alabama state court that had found the *Times* guilty of libel for printing an advertisement accusing Alabama officials of physically assaulting black civil rights demonstrators. The Court ruled that libel of a public official requires proof of "actual malice," which was defined as a knowing or reckless disregard for the truth.[25] It is *very* difficult to prove that a publication acted with reckless or deliberate disregard for the truth. In fact, no federal official has won a libel judgment against a news organization in the three decades since the *Sullivan* ruling. (The press has less protection against a libel judgment when its target is a "private" person rather than a "public" official. The courts regard the communication of information about private individuals as less basic to the democratic process than information about public officials, and therefore the press must take greater care in ascertaining the validity of claims about an ordinary citizen.)

The *Sullivan* decision notwithstanding, the greatest protection against a libel judgment is truthfulness. The Court has held that expressions of opinion deserve "full constitutional protection" against the charge of libel as long as they do not contain "a provably false factual connotation."[26]

OBSCENITY

In 1990 the director of a Cincinnati museum, Dennis Barrie, was charged with obscenity for holding an exhibit that included homoerotic art by the photographer Robert Mapplethorpe. Barrie was acquitted in a jury trial, but the incident provoked a controversy that extended to Congress. The exhibit was funded in part by a grant from the National Endowment for the Arts (NEA), and Congress enacted a law requiring the NEA to take "decency standards" into account in granting funds. Artists claimed that the law would have a "chilling effect" on artistic expression, but the Supreme Court in 1998 upheld Congress's authority to set limits on the uses of the funds it appropriates.[27]

Obscenity is a form of expression that is not protected by the First Amendment. However, the Supreme Court has found it difficult to define which publicly disseminated sexual materials are obscene and which are not. The Court has struggled to develop a standard that gives predictability to the law without endangering First Amendment rights.

The Court's first test was established in *Roth v. United States* (1957), when the Court defined obscenity as material that "taken as a whole" appealed to "prurient interest" and had no "redeeming social significance." The perspective was to be that of "the average person, applying contemporary community standards."[28] The test proved unworkable. Even the justices, when personally examining allegedly obscene material, would argue over whether it appealed to

This work at the Brooklyn Museum of Art was the center of controversy after it was attacked as obscene by New York mayor Rudy Guliani, who threatened to withdraw city funding for the 1999 exhibit. The work combined a religious icon with elephant dung. A decade earlier an exhibit in Cincinnati spurred national debate over government support for controversial works of art.

prurient interest and was without redeeming social value. In the end, they usually concluded that it had at least some social significance.

In *Miller v. California* (1973), the Court changed the test, saying that instead of having no redeeming social significance, the material had to have "serious literary, artistic, political, or scientific value." The Court also narrowed the "contemporary community standards" to the local level. The court said that what might offend residents of "Mississippi might be found tolerable in Las Vegas."[29] But this test proved too restrictive. The Court subsequently ruled that material cannot be judged obscene simply because the "average" local resident might object to it. "Community standards" were to be judged in the context of a "reasonable person"—someone whose outlook is broad enough to evaluate the material on its overall merit rather than its most objectionable feature. The Court later also modified its content standard, saying that the material must be of a "particularly offensive type."[30] These efforts illustrate the difficulty of defining obscenity and, even more, of developing a legal standard that can be applied evenhandedly by courts when an obscenity case arises.

The Supreme Court has distinguished between obscene materials in public places and in the home. A unanimous ruling in 1969 held that what adults read and watch in the privacy of their homes cannot be made a crime.[31] The Court created an exception to this rule in 1990 by upholding an Ohio law making it a crime to possess pornographic photographs of children.[32] The Court reasoned that purchase and distribution contributed to the spread of the crime of abusing minors through pornography.

The shielding of children from the effects of sexually explicit material has also affected cable television policy. In 1996, the Supreme Court held that although cable operators are not required to scramble the signal of channels that provide "adult" programming, they must do so for individual subscribers who request that the signal be scrambled.[33]

The Internet is also a source of indecent material. To prevent this material from reaching children, Congress in 1996 passed the Communications Decency Act, which made it a federal crime to use the Internet to transmit

The Supreme Court in 1997 invalidated the Communications Decency Act, which had broadly outlawed indecent material on the Internet. The Court held that the law was so broad and so punitive that it would censor "a large amount of speech."

obscene material to someone under eighteen years of age or to post material in a way that made it available to minors. In a key 1997 ruling, *Reno v. ACLU*, the Supreme Court declared the Decency Act to be unconstitutional. "We have repeatedly recognized the governmental interest in protecting children from harmful materials," the Court said. "But that interest does not justify an unnecessarily broad suppression of speech addressed to adults." The Court noted that authorities might apply too restrictive a definition of obscenity and that someone sending a targeted message on the Internet could not be sure that it would reach only its intended recipients. The Court also criticized the harsh penalties for communicating indecent material—up to two years in jail and $200,000 in fines. The Court concluded: "[The Decency Act] effectively suppresses a large amount of speech that adults have a constitutional right to receive and to address to one another."[34] (The Court's decision does not legalize child pornography on the Internet or grant immunity to pedophiles who might prey on children through the Internet; the decision only invalidates the Communications Decency Act as a basis for restricting Internet expression.)

Freedom of Religion

Free religious expression is the precursor of free political expression, at least within the English tradition of limited government. England's Glorious, or Bloodless, Revolution of 1689 centered on the issue of religion and resulted in the Act of Toleration, which gave members of all Protestant sects the right to worship freely and publicly. The English philosopher John Locke (1632–1704) extended this principle, arguing that legitimate government could not inhibit free expression, religious or otherwise. The First Amendment reflects this tradition, providing for freedom of religion along with freedom of speech, press, assembly, and petition.

In regard to religion, the First Amendment reads: "Congress shall make no law respecting an establishment of religion, or prohibiting the free exercise thereof." The prohibition on laws aimed at "establishment of religion" (the establishment clause) and its "free exercise" (the free-exercise clause) applies to states and localities through the Fourteenth Amendment.

CURRENT CONTROVERSIES

SHOULD SEXUALLY EXPLICIT MATERIAL ON THE INTERNET BE TIGHTLY REGULATED?

In 1997, the Supreme Court struck down the Communications Decency Act on grounds that it was overly broad and would have the effect of reducing not only indecent content on the Internet but legitimate expression as well. The Act made it a federal crime to transmit obscene material through the Internet to minors or to post such material in a way that made it accessible to them. The conflict between the congressional majority that enacted the legislation and the Supreme Court majority that invalidated it is part of society's continuing debate over how to regulate obscenity without infringing on First Amendment rights.

YES: Opponents of the new law use harsh language like "censorship" to describe the Communications Decency Act . . . Those who cry censorship hide behind the First Amendment to make defense of those who would give pornography to children and engage children in sexual conversations. What a travesty . . . The Act makes it a crime to send indecent communications to children by means of a computer service or telecommunications device [and] to make indecent communications available to children on an open electronic bulletin board. . . . The heart and soul of the new law is its protections for children. It is not censorship. It is not prudishness. The new law does not prohibit consenting adults from engaging in constitutionally protected speech.

—Former U.S. Senator James Exon (D-Nebr.)

NO: We are persuaded that the [Act] lacks the precision that the First Amendment requires when a statute regulates the content of speech. In order to deny minors access to potentially harmful speech, the [Act] effectively suppresses a large amount of speech that adults have a constitutional right to receive and to address to one another. . . . It is true that we have repeatedly recognized the governmental interest in protecting children from harmful materials. But that interest does not justify an unnecessarily broad suppression of speech addressed to adults. As we have explained, the Government may not "reduc[e] the adult population . . . to . . . only what is fit for children." . . . Knowledge that, for instance, one or more members of a 100-person chat group will be minor—and therefore that it would be a crime to send the group an indecent message—would surely burden communication among adults.

—*Reno v. ACLU* (1997)

THE ESTABLISHMENT CLAUSE

The **establishment clause** has been interpreted by the courts to mean that government may not favor one religion over another or support religion over no religion. (This position contrasts with that of a country such as England, where Anglicanism is the official, or "established," state religion, though no religion is prohibited.) The Supreme Court's interpretation of the establishment clause has been described as maintaining a "wall of separation" between church and state, which includes a prohibition on nondenominational support for religion.[35] The Court has taken a pragmatic approach, however, by permitting some establishment activities but disallowing others. The Court has permitted states to provide secular textbooks for use by church-affiliated schools,[36] for instance, but has forbidden states to pay part of the salaries of teachers in church-affiliated schools.[37] Such distinctions follow no strict logic but are based on judgments of whether government action involves "*excessive* entanglement with religion."[38] In allowing public funds to be used by religious schools for secular textbooks but not for teachers' salaries, the courts have indicated that, whereas

establishment clause The First Amendment provision that government may not favor one religion over another or favor religion over no religion, and that prohibits Congress from passing laws respecting the establishment of religion.

The First Amendment's protection of free expression includes religious freedom, which has led the courts to hold that government should not in most instances promote or interfere with religious practices.

it is relatively easy to ascertain whether the content of a particular textbook promotes religion, it would be much harder to determine whether a particular teacher was promoting religion in the classroom.

In 2000, the Supreme Court expanded the range of permissible support in a ruling that allows federal funds to be used to buy computers and other equipment for parochial school classrooms.[39]

In *Engel v. Vitale* (1962), the Court held that the establishment clause prohibits the reciting of prayers in public schools.[40] A year later the Court struck down Bible readings in public schools.[41] Religion is a strong force in American life, and the Supreme Court's position has evoked strong opposition, particularly from Protestant fundamentalists. An Alabama law attempted to circumvent the prayer ruling by permitting public schools to set aside one minute each day for silent prayer or meditation. In 1985, the Court declared the law unconstitutional, ruling that "government must pursue a course of complete neutrality toward religion."[42] The Court in 2000 reaffirmed the ban by extending it to include organized student-led prayer at public school football games.[43]

THE FREE-EXERCISE CLAUSE

The First and Fourteenth Amendments also prohibit governmental interference with the free exercise of religion. The idea underlying the **free-exercise clause** is clear: Americans are free to hold any religious belief they choose.

free-exercise clause A First Amendment provision that prohibits the government from interfering with the practice of religion or prohibiting the free exercise of religion.

Although people are free to believe what they want, they are not always free to act on their beliefs. The courts have allowed government interference in the exercise of religious beliefs when such interference is the secondary result of an overriding social goal. An example is the legal protection of children with life-threatening illnesses whose parents refuse to permit medical treatment on religious grounds. A court may order that such children be given medical assistance because the social good of saving their lives overrides their parents' free-exercise rights. And in 1986 the Supreme Court concluded that military regulations requiring standard headgear took precedence over an Orthodox Jewish serviceman's practice of wearing a yarmulke.[44] (Congress responded by enacting legislation that permitted yarmulkes.)

In an important 1997 decision, the Court struck down the Religious Freedom Restoration Act, which was passed by a large congressional majority and with the backing of President Clinton. The law said that government at any level could not interfere with religious practices unless a "compelling reason," such as a danger to health or safety, was involved. In striking down the law, which had been challenged in a case where a city wanted to prevent a church from enlarging its building, the Court said that Congress lacked the authority through statute to redefine the meaning of the Constitution. The Court concluded that the law had placed more restrictions on government (for example, denying it the power to regulate construction when a church was at issue) than was required by the First Amendment's guarantee of religious freedom.[45]

In some circumstances, exceptions to certain laws have been permitted on free-exercise grounds. The Supreme Court ruled in 1972 that Wisconsin could not compel Amish parents to send their children to school beyond the eighth grade because this policy violates a centuries-old Amish religious practice of having children leave school and begin work at an early age.[46] In upholding free exercise in such cases, the Court may be said to have violated the establishment clause by granting preferred treatment to people who hold a particular religious belief. The Court has recognized the potential conflict between the free-exercise and establishment clauses and, as in other such situations, has tried to strike a reasonable balance between the competing claims.

When the free-exercise and establishment clauses cannot be balanced, the Supreme Court has been forced to make a choice. In 1987, the Court overturned a Louisiana law requiring that creationism (the Bible's account of how the world was created) be taught along with the theory of evolution in public school science courses. Creationism, the Court concluded, is a religious doctrine, not a scientific theory; thus its inclusion in public school curricula violates the establishment clause by promoting a religious belief.[47] Creationists viewed the Court's decision as a violation of their right to the free exercise of religion; they argued that their children were being forced to study a theory of evolution that contradicts the biblical account of human origins.

The Right of Privacy

Until the 1960s, Americans' constitutional rights were confined largely to those enumerated in the Bill of Rights. This situation prevailed despite the Ninth Amendment, which reads: "The enumeration in the Constitution, of certain rights, shall not be construed to deny or disparage others retained by the people."

In 1965, however, the Supreme Court added to the list of individual rights, declaring that Americans have "a right of privacy." This judgment arose from the case of *Griswold v. Connecticut*, which challenged a state law prohibiting the use of birth control devices, even by married couples. The Supreme Court invalidated the statute, concluding that a state had no business interfering with a married couple's decision regarding contraception. The Court did not base its decision on the Ninth Amendment, but reasoned instead that the freedoms in the Bill of Rights imply an underlying right of privacy. Individuals have, said the Court, a "zone of [personal] privacy" that government cannot lawfully infringe upon."[48]

The right of privacy was the basis for the Supreme Court's ruling in *Roe v. Wade* (1973), which gave women full freedom to choose abortion during the first three months of pregnancy.[49] In overturning a Texas law prohibiting abortion except to save the life of the mother, the Supreme Court said that the right to privacy is "broad enough to encompass a woman's decision whether or not to terminate her pregnancy."

After *Roe,* anti-abortion activists sought to reverse or weaken the Court's ruling. Attempts to pass a constitutional amendment that would ban abortions were unsuccessful, but abortion foes succeeded in a campaign to prohibit the use of government funds to pay for abortions for poor women. Then, in *Webster v. Reproductive Health Services* (1989), the Supreme Court upheld a Missouri law that prohibits abortions in public hospitals and by public employees.[50] The ruling was in part a consequence of the efforts of anti-abortion groups to influence Supreme Court appointments during the Reagan presidency. The Missouri law was upheld by a 5–4 majority and all three Reagan appointees on the Court (Justices O'Connor, Scalia, and Kennedy) voted with the majority.

The *Webster* decision was followed in 1992 by a judgment in the Pennsylvania abortion case *Planned Parenthood v. Casey.* Pennsylvania's law placed a twenty-four-hour waiting period on women who sought an abortion, required doctors to counsel women on abortion and alternatives to abortion, required a minor to have a parent's consent or a judge's approval before having an abortion, and required a married woman to notify her husband before obtaining an abortion. Anti-abortion advocates saw the Pennsylvania law as an opportunity for the Supreme Court to overturn the *Roe* precedent. However, in a decision that surprised many observers, the Court by a 5–4 margin reaffirmed the "essential holding" of *Roe v. Wade:* that a woman, because of the constitutional guarantee of privacy, has a right to abortion during the early months of pregnancy. The Court also ruled, however, that states can regulate abortion as long as they do not impose an "undue burden" on women seeking abortion. The Court concluded that the twenty-four-hour waiting period, physician counseling, and the

Abortion rights activists demonstrate outside the Supreme Court, while the justices inside hear arguments on Pennsylvania's controversial abortion law. By a 5–4 vote, the Court narrowly reaffirmed the principle that a woman has the right to choose an abortion during the early months of pregnancy.

informed-consent requirement for minors were not undue burdens and were therefore permissible. The spousal notification requirement, however, was judged to place a "substantial obstacle" in the path of women seeking abortion and was thereby declared unconstitutional.[51]

In a controversial 2000 ruling, *Stenberg v. Carhart*, the Supreme Court ruled that states may not ban partial-birth abortion (where the fetus's life is terminated during delivery) because it is the most appropriate medical procedure for terminating some pregnancies.

Abortion will certainly be a leading controversy for years to come. The American public is sharply divided on the issue (see Figure 4-1), and there are many deeply committed activists on both sides. As with other rights, the abortion issue is not only, or even primarily, fought out in the courts. Abortion opponents have waged demonstrations outside clinics in an effort to stop the practice. Some of these protests have erupted in violent acts toward women and staff who tried to enter the clinics. In 1994, Congress made it unlawful to block the entrance to abortion clinics or otherwise prevent people from entering.

Although a right of privacy has been established in some areas of personal conduct, the Supreme Court has declined to extend it to other areas. In *Bowers v. Hardwick* (1986), for example, the Court upheld a Georgia law prohibiting sodomy, concluding that the right of privacy did not include homosexual acts among consenting adults.[52] States can choose to permit these acts, but they are not bound to do so by the Constitution of the United States.

The Court has also held that the right of privacy does not extend to the terminally ill who might want medical help in taking their own lives. This ruling came in response to New York and Washington state laws that ban physician-assisted suicide. The Court held that a state has a legitimate interest in protecting vulnerable people. Although the Court did not say so, it hinted in its ruling that a state might choose to permit physician-assisted suicide if there were proper safeguards in its use. But the Court was clear that "liberty" in the Fourteenth Amendment does not include a constitutional *right* to doctor-assisted suicide.[53]

Privacy questions are among the most contentious in American politics because of the moral and ethical issues they raise. Physician-assisted suicide, for example, is seen as a humane act by its proponents. What is the public benefit, they ask, in forcing the dying to accept prolonged and horrible suffering? A majority of Oregon voters in a statewide referendum concluded that there was no public benefit to this suffering and enacted the first state law that permits

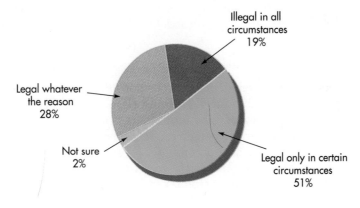

FIGURE 4-1 Opinions on the Abortion Issue
Americans are divided over abortion. Respondents were asked which position best represents their view on abortion. *Source: Gallup, Mar. 30–Apr. 2, 2000.*

Physician-assisted suicide has become a privacy-rights issue as medical advances have made it possible to keep terminally ill patients alive for long periods.

physician-assisted suicide. Opponents argue that society's interest in preserving life outweighs a patient's desire to die. They also worry that laws allowing doctors to assist a suicide would be abused, arguing that doctors and relatives in some instances would persuade terminally ill patients to accept death against their will or that depressed patients who ask to die will be granted their wish rather than be treated for their depression, after which they might choose to live.

Rights of Persons Accused of Crimes

Justice Felix Frankfurter once wrote that "the history of liberty has largely been the history of the observance of procedural guarantees."[54] No system of justice is foolproof; even in the most honest systems, innocent people have been wrongly accused, convicted, and punished with imprisonment or death. But the scrupulous application of procedural safeguards, such as a defendant's right to legal counsel, greatly increases the likelihood that true justice will result.

PROCEDURAL DUE PROCESS

procedural due process   The constitutional requirement that government must follow proper legal procedures before a person can be legitimately punished for an alleged offense.

Due process refers to legal protections that have been established to preserve the rights of individuals. The most significant form of these protections is **procedural due process;** the term refers primarily to procedures that authorities must follow before a person can legitimately be punished for an offense.

The U.S. Constitution provides for several procedures designed to protect a person from wrongful arrest, conviction, and punishment. According to Article I, Section 9, any person taken into police custody is entitled to seek a writ of habeas corpus, which requires law enforcement officials to bring him or her into court and state the legal reason for the detention. The Fifth and Fourteenth Amendments provide generally that no person can be deprived of life, liberty, or property without due process of law. And specific procedural protections for the accused are spelled out in the Fourth, Fifth, Sixth, and Eighth Amendments:

- *The Fourth Amendment* forbids the police to conduct searches and seizures unless they have probable cause to believe that a crime has been committed.
- *The Fifth Amendment* protects against double jeopardy (being prosecuted twice for the same offense); self-incrimination (being compelled to testify against oneself); indictment for a crime except through grand jury proceedings; and loss of life, liberty, and property without due process of law.
- *The Sixth Amendment* provides the right to have legal counsel, to confront witnesses, to receive a speedy trial, and to have a trial by jury in criminal proceedings.
- *The Eighth Amendment* protects against excessive bail or fines and prohibits the infliction of cruel and unusual punishment on those convicted of crimes.

These procedural protections have always been subject to interpretation. The Sixth Amendment, for example, provides the right to have legal counsel. But what if a person cannot afford a lawyer? For most of the nation's history, poor people had almost no choice but to act as their own attorneys. They had a right to counsel but could avail themselves of it only if they had the money to hire a lawyer or could find a public-spirited lawyer who would work for free. Today, if a person is accused of a serious crime and cannot afford a lawyer, the government must provide one. This change came about not through a constitutional amendment but through Supreme Court rulings that gave new meaning in practice to the Sixth Amendment.

www.mhhe.com/patterson5

Graphic

SELECTIVE INCORPORATION OF PROCEDURAL RIGHTS

For most of the nation's history, the procedural protections in the Bill of Rights applied only to the actions of the national government. States in their criminal proceedings were not bound by them. There were limited exceptions, such as a 1932 Supreme Court ruling that a defendant charged in a state court with a crime carrying the death penalty had to be provided with an attorney.[55] The Court's general position, however, was that the states could decide for themselves what procedural rights their residents would have.

A salient case was *Palko v. Connecticut* (1937). A Connecticut court had convicted Frank Palko of killing two policemen, and he was sentenced to life imprisonment. But Connecticut had a statute that permitted law enforcement authorities under certain conditions to appeal a sentence on the grounds that legal errors had been made at the trial. The authorities had wanted Palko to receive the death penalty, so they appealed the decision. Palko was tried again on the same charges and this time was sentenced to death. He appealed to the U.S. Supreme Court, claiming that Connecticut's second trial violated his right not to be tried twice for the same crime. The Fifth Amendment to the U.S. Constitution prohibits double jeopardy, and so do many state constitutions, but at the time Connecticut's did not. The Supreme Court refused to overturn Palko's second conviction, and he was executed.[56]

★ STATES IN THE NATION

THE DEATH PENALTY

Of the rights of the accused, none has proven more difficult to define in practice than the Eighth Amendment's prohibition against "cruel and unusual punishment." A 1972 Supreme Court decision (*Furman v. Georgia*) struck down the death penalty, ruling that its arbitrary application amounted to cruel and unusual punishment. States then revised their death penalty statutes to specify more precisely "the aggravating circumstances" that might justify a sentence of death, and the Supreme Court in *Gregg v. Georgia* (1976) upheld one such law. However, the odds that a convicted murderer will be sentenced to death vary dramatically from state to state and even within states because local prosecutors differ in how aggressively they pursue the death penalty in capital cases. Texas is far and away the leader in executions; roughly a third of all executions in the United States since 1976 have taken place in that state. The uneven application of capital punishment has been a source of recent (but unsuccessful) lawsuits that have charged that the death penalty violates the Eighth Amendment.

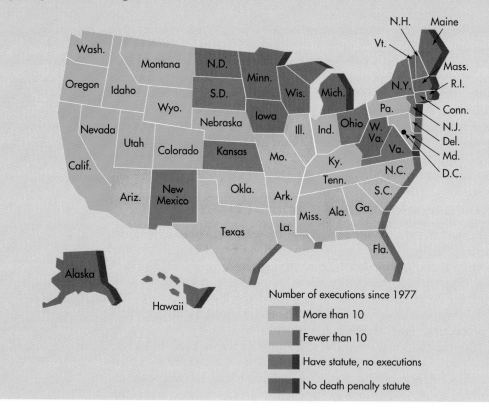

Number of executions since 1977

More than 10

Fewer than 10

Have statute, no executions

No death penalty statute

Justice Benjamin Cardozo wrote the Court's *Palko* opinion, which stated that the Fourteenth Amendment protects rights "fundamental" to liberty but not other rights provided in the Bill of Rights. Free expression is a "fundamental" right, since it is "the indispensable condition of nearly every other form of freedom." Some procedural due-process rights, such as protection against double jeopardy, are not in the same category, Cardozo claimed.

TABLE 4-2 Selective Incorporation of Rights of the Accused In the 1960s, the Supreme Court selectively incorporated the fair-trial provisions of the Fourth through Eighth Amendments into the Fourteenth Amendment so that these rights would be protected from infringement by the states.

Supreme Court Case	Year	Constitutional Right (Amendment) at Issue
Mapp v. Ohio	1961	Unreasonable search and seizure (Fourth)
Robinson v. California	1962	Cruel and unusual punishment (Eighth)
Gideon v. Wainwright	1963	Right to counsel (Sixth)
Malloy v. Hogan	1964	Self-incrimination (Fifth)
Pointer v. Texas	1965	Right to confront witnesses (Sixth)
Miranda v. Arizona	1966	Self-incrimination (Fifth)
Klopfer v. North Carolina	1967	Speedy trial (Sixth)
Duncan v. Louisiana	1968	Jury trial in criminal cases (Sixth)
Benton v. Maryland	1968	Double jeopardy (Fifth)

This view changed abruptly in the 1960s when the Supreme Court broadly required states to safeguard procedural rights. Changes in public education and communication made Americans more aware of their rights, and the civil rights movement dramatized the fact that rights were administered very unequally: the poor and minority group members had many fewer rights in practice than other Americans did. In response, the Supreme Court in the 1960s "incorporated" Bill of Rights protections for the accused in state courts by ruling that these protections are covered by the Fourteenth Amendment's guarantee of due process of law (see Table 4-2).

This selective incorporation process began with *Mapp v. Ohio* (1961). Dollree Mapp's home had been entered by Cleveland police, who, though they failed to find what they were looking for, happened to discover some pornographic material. Mapp's conviction for its possession was overturned by the Supreme Court on the grounds that she had been subjected to unreasonable search and seizure.[57] The Court ruled that illegally obtained evidence could not be used in state courts.

Two years later, the Court's decision in *Gideon v. Wainwright* (1963) required the states to furnish attorneys for poor defendants in all felony cases. Clarence Gideon, an indigent drifter, had been convicted and sentenced to prison in Florida for breaking into a poolroom. He successfully appealed on the grounds that he had been denied due process because he could not afford to pay an attorney.[58]

During the 1960s the Court also ruled that defendants in state criminal proceedings cannot be compelled to testify against themselves,[59] have the rights to remain silent and to have legal counsel when arrested,[60] have the right to confront witnesses who testify against them,[61] must be granted a speedy trial,[62] have the right to a jury trial,[63] and cannot be subjected to double jeopardy.[64] The most famous of these cases is *Miranda v. Arizona* (1966), as a result of which police are required to inform suspects of their rights at the time of arrest. Ernesto Miranda had confessed during police interrogation to kidnapping and raping a young

In recent decades the Supreme Court has restricted the scope of the "exclusionary rule." This rule excludes from use in court proceedings any evidence that is illegally obtained by law enforcement officials.

woman. His confession led to his conviction, which he successfully appealed to the Supreme Court on the grounds that he had not been informed of his rights to remain silent and to have legal counsel present during interrogation. Using other evidence of Miranda's crime, the state of Arizona then retried and convicted him again. He was paroled from prison in 1972 and four years later was stabbed to death in a bar fight. Ironically, Miranda's assailant was read his "Miranda rights" when police arrested him. By now the wording has become familiar: "You have the right to remain silent. . . . Anything you say can and will be used against you in a court of law. . . . You have the right to an attorney."

In a 2000 case, *Dickerson v. United States*, the Supreme Court reaffirmed the *Miranda* decision, saying that because it had established "a constitutional rule," it was not subject to change by legislative action.

RESTRICTING DEFENDANTS' RIGHTS

Although the *Miranda* decision is still intact, the Supreme Court since the 1960s, as a result of political pressures and changes in its membership, has narrowed the protections afforded those accused of crime.

The Exclusionary Rule

exclusionary rule The legal principle that government is prohibited from using in trials evidence that was obtained by unconstitutional means (for example, illegal search and seizure).

The greatest change can be seen in the application of the **exclusionary rule,** which bars the use in trials of evidence obtained in violation of the Fourth Amendment's protection against "unreasonable searches and seizures." The rule was formulated in a 1914 Supreme Court decision,[65] and its application was further expanded in federal cases. The *Mapp* decision extended the exclusionary rule to state trial proceedings as well. Subsequent decisions of the Supreme Court broadened its application to the point where almost any type of illegally obtained evidence was considered inadmissible in a criminal trial.

In the 1980s, the Supreme Court reversed the trend by placing restrictions on the rule's application, concluding that illegally obtained evidence can be admitted in trials if the procedural errors are small, inadvertent, or ultimately inconsequential. In a key 1984 decision, for example, the Court ruled that illegally obtained evidence can be used against a defendant if the prosecution can prove that it would have discovered the evidence anyway.[66]

Recent Supreme Court decisions have further weakened the exclusionary rule. In the 1960s, the Court developed the principle that police had to have a solid basis ("probable cause") for believing that an individual was involved in a specific crime before they could stop a person and engage in search and seizure activity. This principle has been modified. In 1990, for example, the Supreme Court held that roadside checkpoints where police stop drivers to check them for signs of intoxication are legal as long as the action is systematic and not arbitrary (for example, stopping all drivers and not just young drivers).[67]

In a 1999 case, the Court ruled unanimously that police in stopping a speeding motorist do not automatically have the authority to search the vehicle.[68] But in another 1999 case, the Court held that when there is probable cause to search a car, police can search even the personal belongings of a passenger who is not suspected of illegal activity.[69] Two years earlier, the Court ruled that once police have stopped a car for a traffic violation, they can ask the driver's permission to search the car and, if granted, can conduct the search without telling the driver that he or she has the right to refuse the request and then would be free to drive away.[70]

A key ruling that clarified the Supreme Court's determination to give police more discretionary authority was *Whren v. United States* (1996), which unanimously upheld the conviction of an individual who had been found with packets of drugs in the front seat of his car after being stopped for a minor traffic infraction. The police had no evidence (no "probable cause") to believe that drugs were actually in the car but they nonetheless suspected the driver was involved in drug dealing and used the traffic infraction as a pretext to stop and check him. The Supreme Court accepted defense arguments that the police had no clear evidence on which to base their suspicion, that the traffic infraction was not the real reason the individual was stopped, and that police usually do not stop a person for the infraction in question (turning a corner without signaling). But the Court concluded that the officers' motive was irrelevant, as long as an officer in some situations might reasonably stop a car for the infraction that occurred. Thus, the stop and search of the driver was deemed to meet the Fourth Amendment's reasonableness standard.[71]

The Court's objective has been to weaken the exclusionary rule without granting police unbridled discretion. This position was evident in a case that tested the legality of a Chicago anti-loitering ordinance that gave police the authority to arrest a person who refused to obey an order to leave a scene where a suspected gang member was present. In *Chicago v. Morales* (1999), the Court invalidated the ordinance, concluding that it gave the police too much leeway to arrest or harass innocent persons.[72]

The Court has also restricted police entry into people's homes. The Court has declared, for example, that states may not exempt drug-related searches from the general requirement that, when entering a person's home with a search warrant, police must first knock and announce their presence.[73] In 1999, the Court held that police who take news reporters into a home during a lawful search violate "the right of residential privacy at the core of the Fourth Amendment."[74]

When Should Procedural Error Result in a New Trial?
Roger Coleman was convicted of rape and murder in a Virginia court and was sentenced to death. He sought to appeal the conviction on several grounds, including evidence that one of the jurors had told friends he wanted to sit on the jury in order to make sure Coleman was convicted.

Coleman had no money to hire legal counsel, and his appeal was prepared by voluntary attorneys who were not fully familiar with Virginia law. They filed the appeal a day after the deadline set by law. Prosecutors moved to deny the appeal because it was late, and Virginia's highest court upheld the action. Coleman filed a habeas corpus petition to have the appeal heard in federal court. His petition eventually reached the Supreme Court, which turned it down, saying Coleman had forfeited his right to bring the petition because of the procedural error. The Court's ruling overturned a 1963 precedent that had held that state prisoners were entitled to seek federal habeas corpus petitions as long as they had not "deliberately bypassed" state courts. In its decision, the Supreme Court said it was fair to penalize Coleman because, unlike the situation at the trial stage, he had no right to an attorney at the appeal stage.

In your opinion, was Roger Coleman treated justly or unjustly by the courts. Why?

Habeas Corpus Appeals

The Supreme Court has recently restricted habeas corpus appeals to federal courts by individuals who have been convicted of crimes in state courts. (Habeas corpus gives defendants access to federal courts in order to argue that their rights under the Constitution of the United States were violated when they were convicted in a state court.) A 1960s Supreme Court precedent had assured prisoners of the right to have their petitions heard in federal court unless they had "deliberately bypassed" the opportunity to make the appeal in state courts.[75]

This precedent was overturned in 1992, when the Court held that inmates can lose the right to a federal hearing even if a lawyer's mistake is the reason they failed to first present their appeal properly in state courts.[76] Another significant habeas corpus defeat for inmates occurred in 1993 when the Supreme Court held that federal courts cannot overturn a state conviction on the basis of constitutional error unless the prisoner can demonstrate that the error contributed to the conviction.[77] Previously, the burden of proof was on the state: it had to prove that the error did not affect the case's outcome. Then, in *Felker v. Turpin* (1996), the Court upheld a recent federal law that severely restricts federal habeas corpus appeals by state prison inmates who have already filed one.[78]

Through these decisions, the Supreme Court has sought to prevent frivolous and multiple federal court appeals. State prisoners had used habeas corpus appeals to contest even small issues, and some—particularly those on death row—had filed appeal after appeal. An effect was to clog the federal courts and delay other cases. A majority of Supreme Court justices concluded that a more restrictive policy toward these appeals is required. They have held that it is fair to ask inmates to first pursue their options in state courts and then, except in unusual cases,[79] to confine themselves to a single federal appeal. Civil liberties groups have objected to the change, arguing that no procedure that would protect the innocent from wrongful punishment—particularly when the death penalty is at issue—is too big a burden to place on the courts.

However, no one claims that recent decisions mark a return to the lower procedural standards that prevailed before the 1960s. Many of the vital precedents set in that decade remain in effect, including the most important one of all: the principle that procedural protections guaranteed to the accused by the Bill of Rights must be observed by the states as well as by the federal government.

In addition, the Supreme Court in the last decade has extended procedural rights in some areas. Among the key rulings are that African Americans are denied their rights in some instances when prosecuting attorneys use peremptory challenges (that is, rejections without explanation) to exclude black potential jurors so that the trial is conducted with an all-white jury,[80] that police must immediately halt an interrogation if the accused asks for a lawyer,[81] and that patients' discussions with psychotherapists and other mental health professionals do not have to be disclosed in judicial proceedings.[82]

CRIME, PUNISHMENT, AND POLICE PRACTICES

The theory and practice of procedural guarantees are often two quite different things, as Adrienne Cureton discovered on January 2, 1995. She is a plainclothes police officer who, with a uniformed partner, was called to the scene of

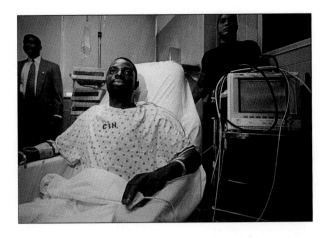

Abner Louima was sodomized with a wooden handle by a New York City police officer after having been taken into custody. Louima's case focused national attention on the issue of police brutality and dramatized the difference that can exist between the theory and reality of constitutional rights.

a domestic dispute. When a struggle ensued, her partner radioed for help. When the officers arrived, Cureton and her partner had already handcuffed the homeowner. The officers barged in and mistook Cureton, an African American, for the other person involved in the dispute. They grabbed her by the collar, dragged her by the hair onto the porch, and clubbed her repeatedly with flashlights, despite her screams that she was a police officer.[83]

There is no reliable estimate of how often Americans' rights are violated in practice, but infringements of one sort or another are commonplace. Minorities and the poor are the more likely victims. Racial profiling (the assumption that certain groups are more likely to commit particular crimes) is a common police practice and results in the unequal treatment of minorities. A 1999 American Civil Liberties Union study found that although minority and white motorists were about equally likely to commit traffic infractions, 80 percent of the motorists stopped and searched by Maryland State Police on Interstate 95 were minorities and only 20 percent were white, despite the fact that white motorists constituted 75 percent of all drivers. A 1999 report by the New Jersey Attorney General's Office revealed a similar pattern in that state.

These tendencies are reflected in a 1999 Gallup poll on racial profiling. Only 6 percent of white respondents, compared with 42 percent of blacks, believed they had been stopped by police just because of their race or ethnic background. On average, blacks who made this claim said they had been stopped by police on at least four occasions for reasons of their race alone. The Gallup poll also demonstrated public awareness of racial profiling: 56 percent of whites and 77 percent of blacks said they believed the practice was "widespread."

Despite the uneven application of justice in America, watchdog groups such as Amnesty International give the United States fairly high marks in its treatment of the criminally accused. Northern European countries are rated higher, partly because they have outlawed capital punishment and have a lower incidence of police misconduct. Yet none of the European democracies has gone as far as the United States in establishing an elaborate set of legal procedures designed to protect the accused.

Another issue of justice in America is whether adherence to proper legal procedures produces reasonable outcomes. The Eighth Amendment prohibits "cruel and unusual punishment" for those convicted of crime, but judgments in

HOW THE UNITED STATES COMPARES

LAW AND ORDER

Individual rights are a cornerstone of the American governing system and receive strong protection from the courts. The government's ability to restrict free expression is severely limited, and the individual's right to a fair trial is protected through elaborate due-process guarantees.

According to Amnesty International, a watchdog group that monitors human rights achievements and violations around the world, the United States has a good record in terms of its constitutional protection of civil liberties. A number of countries in Asia, Africa, eastern Europe, the Middle East, and Latin America are accused by Amnesty International of "appalling human rights catastrophies" that include the execution, torture, and rape of persons accused of crime or regarded as opponents of the government. Amnesty International does not rank the United States as high as the countries of northern Europe in terms of respect for human rights. Among other problems, Amnesty International faults

police in the United States for "excessive force" in their treatment of prisoners and faults U.S. immigration officials for the forcible return of asylum seekers to their country of origin without granting them a hearing.

Although human rights groups admire America's elaborate procedural protections for those accused of crime, they are critical of its sentencing and incarceration policies. The United States is a world leader in the number of people it places behind bars and in the length of sentences for various categories of crime. Defenders of U.S. policy say that although overall crime rates are about the same here as elsewhere, there is more violent crime in America. Critics reply that although the murder rate is high in the United States, it is also true that more than half of the people in prison were convicted of non-violent offenses, such as drug use or a crime against property. Whatever the reasons, the United States is rivaled only by Russia in the proportion of its people who are in prisons.

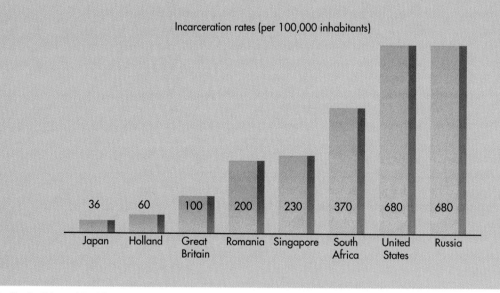

Incarceration rates (per 100,000 inhabitants)

Japan	Holland	Great Britain	Romania	Singapore	South Africa	United States	Russia
36	60	100	200	230	370	680	680

From Elliot Currie, *Crime and Punishment in America*, p. 15. Copyright © 1998. Reprinted by permission.

this area are relatively subjective. Although the Supreme Court has ordered officials to relieve inmate overcrowding and to improve prison facilities in a few instances, it has concluded that inmates cannot sue over prison conditions unless prison officials show "deliberate indifference" to conditions.[84] The severity of a sentence can also be an Eighth Amendment issue. A divided Supreme

Court in 1991 upheld a Michigan law that mandated life imprisonment without parole for a nonviolent first-offense conviction for possession of as little as 1.5 pounds of cocaine.[85] In general, the Court has shied away from decisions about what constitutes cruel and unusual punishment, preferring to leave those decisions to legislative bodies.

In recent years, legislators in the United States have taken a tougher stance on crime. Congress and most states have mandated stiffer sentences, and the number of federal and state prisoners has more than doubled in the past decade. The United States has a larger proportion of its people behind bars than any country besides Russia (see "How the United States Compares"). America's high incarceration rate has resulted in increasingly expensive, overcrowded, and unsafe prisons, which has prompted some officials to call for more lenient sentencing, particularly for nonviolent crimes such as drug use and petty theft.

The Courts and a Free Society

A free and democratic nation has a vital stake in maintaining individual freedoms. The United States was founded on the belief that individuals have an innate right to personal liberty—to speak their minds, to worship as they choose, to be free of police intimidation. The greatest threat to individual rights in a democratic society is a popular majority backed by elected leaders determined to carry out its will. Majorities have frequently preferred policies that would diminish the freedom of those who hold minority views, have unconventional life-styles, or simply "look different" from the majority.

Americans are highly supportive of rights and freedoms expressed in abstract terms but are much less supportive—and in some cases antagonistic—when confronted with these same rights in concrete situations. For example, a Time/CNN survey indicated that nearly as many Americans say that they would allow police to search anyone who merely looked suspicious as say that they would prohibit such a search. This lukewarm respect for individual rights is a reason why there is so little public outrage over official violations of these rights.

Greater support for individual rights exists among the political elite. Those who are most active politically, including officeholders and journalists, are more likely to express strong support for free expression and fair trial rights. They are also better positioned than the ordinary citizen to express their beliefs. However, they are not always willing to act. Often, the exercise of rights involves society's least savory characters—its murderers, rapists, drug dealers, and hate peddlers. Miscreants are hardly the type of person that engenders public support at any level.

The courts are not isolated from the public mood. They inevitably balance society's demand for safety and order against the rights of the individual. Nevertheless, the judicial branch can normally be expected to grant more consideration to the rights of the individual, however unpopular his or her views or actions, than will the general public or elected officials. How far the courts will go in protecting a person's rights depends on the facts of the case, the existing status of the law, prevailing social needs, and the personal views

★ CRITICAL THINKING ★

WHAT'S YOUR OPINION?

The Necessity of the Bill of Rights
The Bill of Rights was added to the Constitution despite the Framers' objection that it was unnecessary. Whose position—the Framers' or those who advocated the Bill of Rights—do you think history supports? Can you think of additional rights that you might have today if the Framers' position had prevailed? Can you think of rights that you might *not* have today if individual rights had not been explicitly written into the Constitution?

of the judges. Nevertheless, the courts regard the protection of individual rights as one of their most significant responsibilities, a perspective that is owed in no small measure to the Bill of Rights. It transformed the inalienable rights of life, liberty, and property into legal rights, thus putting them under judicial protection.[86]

Civil liberties are not blessings that government kindly bestows on the individual. Because of their constitutional nature, these rights are above government. In fact, it can be said that government exists to protect these rights. True, government does not always act lawfully; the temptations of power and the pressures of the majority can at times lead governmental institutions to usurp individual rights. The courts are not immune to these influences and have the added pressure of the obligation to seek an accommodation between the claims of individuals and the collective interests of society (which, of course, include respect for civil liberties). While the courts have not always sided with individuals in their claims to rights, it is at least as noteworthy that they have not always sided with government in its claims against the individual.

Nevertheless, the judiciary alone cannot provide adequate protection for individual rights. A civil society rests also on enlightened representatives and a tolerant citizenry. If, for example, politicians and the public encourage police to infringe the rights of vaguely threatening minorities or nonconformists, the judiciary's protection of persons accused of crimes will not ensure justice. It may be said that the test of a truly civil society is not its treatment of popular ideas and of its best citizens but its willingness to tolerate ideas that the majority detests and to respect equally the rights of its least popular citizens.

www.mhhe.com/patterson5

Self-Quiz

Summary

In their search for personal liberty, Americans added the Bill of Rights to the Constitution shortly after its ratification. These amendments guarantee certain political, procedural, and property rights against infringement by the national government. Freedom of expression is the most basic of democratic rights. People are not free unless they can freely express their views. Nevertheless, free expression may conflict with the nation's security needs during times of war and insurrection. The courts at times have allowed government to limit expression substantially for purposes of national security. In recent decades, however, the courts have protected a very wide range of free expression in the areas of speech, press, and religion.

The guarantees embodied in the Bill of Rights originally applied only to the national government. Under the principle of selective incorporation of these guarantees into the Fourteenth Amendment, the courts extended them to state governments, though the process was slow and uneven. In the 1920s and 1930s, First Amendment guarantees of freedom of expression were given protection from infringement by the states. The states continued to have wide discretion in criminal proceedings until the

early 1960s, when most of the fair-trial rights in the Bill of Rights were given federal protection.

Due process of law refers to legal protections that have been established to preserve individual rights. The most significant form of these protections consists of procedures or methods (for example, the right of an accused person to have an attorney present during police interrogation) designed to ensure that an individual's rights are upheld. A major controversy in this area is the breadth of the exclusionary rule, which bars the use in trials of illegally obtained evidence. The right of privacy, particularly as it applies to the abortion issue, is also a source of controversy.

Civil liberties are not absolute but must be balanced against other considerations (such as national security or public safety) and against one another when different rights come into conflict. The judicial branch of government, particularly the Supreme Court, has taken on much of the responsibility for protecting and interpreting individual rights. The Court's positions have changed with time and conditions, but the Court has generally been more protective of and sensitive to civil liberties than have elected officials or popular majorities.

Key Terms

Bill of Rights
civil liberties
clear-and-present-danger test
due process clause (of the Fourteenth Amendment)
establishment clause
exclusionary rule
free-exercise clause
freedom of expression

imminent lawless action test
libel
prior restraint
procedural due process
selective incorporation
slander
symbolic speech

Suggested Readings

Abraham, Henry J., and Barbara A. Perry. *Freedom and the Court.* New York: Oxford University Press, 1998. A comprehensive analysis of the Supreme Court's work on civil rights and civil liberties.

Bodenhamer, David J. *Fair Trial: Rights of the Accused in American History.* New York: Oxford University Press, 1991. A comprehensive historical survey of the rights of the accused.

Bovard, James. *Freedom in Chains.* New York: St. Martin's Press, 1999. An analysis of the effect of the modern state on citizens' rights.

Epstein, Lee and Thomas G. Walker. *Constitutional Law for a Changing America,* 2d ed. Washington, D.C.: Congressional Quarterly Press, 2000. An accessible introduction to U.S. constitutional law.

Graber, Mark A. *Rethinking Abortion: Equal Choice, the Constitution, and Reproductive Politics.* Princeton, N.J.: Princeton University Press, 1996. Argues that constitutional principles require that all U.S. women be afforded the same abortion rights.

Lewis, Anthony. *Gideon's Trumpet.* New York: Random House, 1964. The riveting story of Clarence Gideon and the effects of his case on the right to legal counsel.

McDonagh, Eileen. *Breaking the Abortion Deadlock.* New York: Oxford University Press, 1996. A forward look at breaking the abortion deadlock.

Murphy, Paul L. *The Shaping of the First Amendment: 1791 to the Present.* New York: Oxford University Press, 1991. A description of the development and application of First Amendment principles in American history.

Nagel, Robert F. *Judicial Power and American Character.* New York: Oxford University Press, 1996. Concludes that the real protection for legal rights resides in political action rather than judicial decisions.

Perry, Michael J. *Religion in Politics: Constitutional and Moral Perspectives.* New York: Oxford University Press, 1997. A constitutional and moral look at the role of religion in politics.

Segers, Mary, and Ted G. Jelen. *A Wall of Separation? Debating the Public Role of Religion.* Lanham, Md.: Rowman & Littlefield, 1997. An assessment of the relationship between church and state as a constitutional issue and in practice.

Uviller, Richard H. *Virtual Justice: The Flawed Prosecution of Crime in America.* New Haven, Conn.: Yale University Press, 1996. A critical analysis of the U.S. criminal justice system.

Wirenius, John F. *First Amendment, First Principles.* New York: Holmes and Meier, 2000. Analysis of verbal acts and freedom of speech.

CHAPTER 5

Equal Rights:
Struggling Toward
Fairness

★

*I have a dream that one day this nation will rise up and live out
the true meaning of its creed: "We hold these truths to be self-
evident: that all men are created equal."*

—Martin Luther King, Jr.[1]

★ ★ ★

*T*he producers of ABC television's *PrimeTime Live* put hidden cameras on two young men, equally well dressed and groomed, and then sent them on different routes to do the same things—search for an apartment, shop for a car, look at albums in a record store. The cameras recorded the reactions the two men received. One was greeted with smiles and was invited to buy, often at good prices. The other man was treated with suspicious looks, was sometimes made to wait, and was often asked to pay more. Why the difference? The explanation was simple: the young man who was routinely well received was white; the young man who was treated badly was an African American.

The Urban Institute had conducted a similar experiment a few months earlier. The experiment used pairs of specially trained white and black male college students who were the same in all respects—education, work experience, speech patterns, physical builds—except for their race. The students responded individually to nearly five hundred classified job advertisements in Chicago and Washington, D.C. The black applicants got fewer interviews, had shorter interviews, and were given fewer job offers than were the white applicants. An Urban Institute spokesperson said, "The level of reverse discrimination [favoring blacks over whites] that we found was limited, was certainly far lower than many might have been led to fear, and was swamped by the extent of discrimination against black job applicants."[2]

These two experiments suggest why some Americans are still struggling for equal rights. In theory, Americans are equal in their rights, but in reality, they are not now equal, nor have they ever been. African Americans, women, Hispanic Americans, the disabled, Jews, American Indians, Catholics, Asian Americans, homosexuals, and members of nearly every other minority group have been victims of discrimination in fact and in law. The nation's creed—"all men are created equal"—has encouraged minorities to believe that they deserve equal justice and has given weight to their claims for fair treatment. But full equality is far from being a universal condition of American life. Inequality is built into almost every aspect of our society. Here is but one example: African Americans with a correctable heart problem are only half as likely to receive the necessary surgery than are whites with the same problem.[3]

This chapter focuses on **equal rights,** or **civil rights**—terms that refer to the right of every person to equal protection under the laws and equal access to society's opportunities and public facilities. Chapter 4 explained that civil liberties refer to specific *individual* rights, such as freedom of speech, that are protected from infringement by government. Equal rights or civil rights have to do with whether individual members of differing *groups*—racial, sexual, and the like—are

civil rights or **equal rights**   The right of every person to equal protection under the laws and equal access to society's opportunities and public facilities.

treated equally by government and, in some areas, by private parties. To oversimplify, civil liberties deal with issues of personal freedom, and civil rights deal with issues of equality.

Although the law refers to the rights of individuals first and to those of groups in a secondary and derivative way, this chapter concentrates on groups because the history of civil rights has been largely one of group claims to equality. The chapter emphasizes the following main points:

★ *Disadvantaged groups have had to struggle for equal rights.* African Americans, women, Native Americans, Hispanic Americans, Asian Americans, and others have all had to fight for their rights in order to come closer to equality with white males.

★ *Americans have attained substantial equality under the law.* They have, in legal terms, equal protection of the laws, equal access to accommodations and housing, and an equal right to vote. Discrimination by law against persons because of race, sex, religion, and ethnicity is now almost nonexistent.

★ *Legal equality for all Americans has not resulted in de facto equality.* African Americans, women, Hispanic Americans, and other traditionally disadvantaged groups have a disproportionately small share of America's opportunities and benefits. Existing inequalities, discriminatory practices, and political pressures are still major barriers to their full equality. Affirmative action and busing are policies designed to help the disadvantaged achieve full equality.

The Struggle for Equality

Equality has always been the least fully developed of America's founding concepts. Not even Thomas Jefferson, who had a deep admiration for the "common man," believed that broad meaning could be given to the claim of the Declaration of Independence that "all men are created equal." To Jefferson, "equality" had a restricted, though significant, meaning: people are of equal moral worth and as such deserve equal treatment under the law.[4] Even then, Jefferson made a distinction between free men, who were entitled to legal equality, and slaves, who were not.

The history of America shows that disadvantaged groups have rarely achieved a greater measure of justice without a struggle.[5] Legal equality has rarely been bestowed by the more powerful upon the less powerful. Their gains have nearly always occurred through intense and sustained political movements, such as the civil rights movement of the 1960s, that have pressured established interests to relinquish or share their privileged status (see Chapter 7).

Disadvantaged groups have a shared history of political exclusion, struggles for empowerment, and policy triumphs, but they also have distinctive histories, as is evident by a brief look at the efforts of African Americans, women, Native Americans, Hispanic Americans, Asian Americans, and other groups to achieve a greater degree of equality.

AFRICAN AMERICANS

Of all America's problems, none has been as persistent as the white race's unwillingness to yield a fair share of society's benefits to members of the black race. The ancestors of most African Americans came to this country as slaves, after having been captured in Africa, shipped in chains across the Atlantic, and sold in open markets in Charleston and other seaports.

It took a civil war to bring slavery to an end, but the battle did not end institutionalized racism. When Reconstruction ended in 1877 with the withdrawal of federal troops from the South, whites in the region regained power and gradually reestablished racial segregation by enacting laws that prohibited black citizens from using the same public facilities as whites.[6] In *Plessy v. Ferguson* (1896), the Supreme Court endorsed these laws, ruling that "separate" facilities for the two races did not violate the Constitution as long as the facilities were "equal." "If one race be inferior to the other socially," the Court argued, "the Constitution of the United States cannot put them on the same plane."[7] The *Plessy* decision became a justification for the separate and *unequal* treatment of African Americans. Black children, for example, were forced into separate schools that rarely had libraries and had few teachers; they were given worn-out books that had been used previously in white schools.

Black leaders challenged these discriminatory state and local policies through legal action, but not until the late 1930s did the Supreme Court begin to respond favorably to their demands. The Court began modestly by ruling that where no public facilities existed for African Americans, they must be allowed to use those reserved for whites.[8]

The *Brown* Decision

Substantial judicial relief for African Americans was finally achieved in 1954 with *Brown v. Board of Education of Topeka*, arguably the most significant ruling in Supreme Court history. The case began when Linda Carol Brown, a black child in Topeka, Kansas, was denied admission to an all-white elementary school that she passed every day on her way to her all-black school, which was twelve blocks farther away. The case was initiated on her behalf by the National Association for the Advancement of Colored People (NAACP) and was argued before the Supreme Court by Thurgood Marshall, who later became the Court's first black justice. In its decision, the Court fully reversed its *Plessy* doctrine by declaring that racial segregation of public schools "generates [among black children] a feeling of inferiority as to their status in the community that may affect their hearts and minds in a way unlikely ever to be undone. . . . Separate educational facilities are inherently unequal."[9]

As a 1954 Gallup poll indicated, a sizable majority of southern whites opposed the *Brown* decision, and billboards were erected along southern roadways that called for the impeachment of Chief Justice Earl Warren. In the so-called Southern Manifesto, southern congressmen urged their state governments to "resist forced integration by any lawful means." In 1957, rioting broke out when Governor Orval Faubus called out the Arkansas National Guard to block the entry of black children to the Little Rock public schools. To restore order and carry out the desegregation of the Little Rock schools, President Dwight D. Eisenhower used his power as the nation's commander in chief to place the

Arkansas National Guard under federal control. For their part, northern whites were neither strongly for nor strongly against school desegregation. A Gallup poll revealed that only a slim majority of whites outside the South agreed with the *Brown* decision.

The Black Civil Rights Movement

After *Brown*, the struggle of African Americans for their rights became a political movement. Perhaps no single event turned national public opinion so dramatically against segregation as a 1963 march led by Dr. Martin Luther King Jr. in Birmingham, Alabama. An advocate of nonviolent protest, King had been leading peaceful demonstrations and marches for nearly eight years before that fateful day in Birmingham.[10] As the nation watched in disbelief on television, police officers led by Birmingham's sheriff, Eugene "Bull" Connor, attacked King and his followers with dogs, cattle prods, and fire hoses.

The modern civil rights movement peaked with the triumphant March on Washington for Jobs and Freedom of August 2, 1963. Organized by Dr. King and other civil rights leaders, it attracted 250,000 marchers, one of the largest gatherings in the history of the nation's capital. "I have a dream," the Reverend King told the gathering, "that my four little children will one day live in a nation where they will not be judged by the color of their skin but by the content of their character."

A year later, after a months-long fight in Congress that was marked by every parliamentary obstacle that racial conservatives could muster, the Civil Rights Act of 1964 was enacted. As discussed later in this chapter, the legislation provided African Americans and other minorities with equal access to public facilities and prohibited job discrimination. Even then, southern states resorted to legal maneuvering and other delaying tactics to blunt the new law's impact.

Two police dogs attack a black civil rights activist (*center left*) during the 1963 Birmingham demonstrations. Such images of hatred and violence shook many white Americans out of their complacency regarding race relations.

The state of Virginia, for example, established a commission to pay the legal expenses of white citizens who were brought to court for violations of the federal act. Nevertheless, momentum was on the side of racial equality. The murder of two civil rights workers during a voter registration drive in Selma, Alabama, helped sustain the momentum.[11] President Lyndon Johnson, who had been a decisive force in the battle to pass the Civil Rights Act, called for new legislation that would end racial barriers to voting.[12] Congress's answer was the 1965 Voting Rights Act.

The Aftermath of the Civil Rights Movement

Although the most significant progress in history toward the legal equality of all Americans occurred during the 1960s, Dr. King's dream of a color-blind society has remained elusive.[13] By some indicators, the status of African Americans has actually deteriorated since Martin Luther King was assassinated in 1968. During this period, for example, the gap in the incomes of black and white Americans has widened, not narrowed. The income of the average African American family today is roughly 60 percent of the average white family's.

Even the legal rights of African Americans do not, in practice, match the promise of the civil rights movement.[14] Studies have found, for example, that African Americans accused of crime are more likely to be convicted and to receive stiffer sentences than are white Americans on trial for comparable offenses. Federal statistics from the National Office of Drug Control Policy and the U.S. Sentencing Commission revealed that in 1997 black Americans accounted for more than 75 percent of crack cocaine convictions but only about 35 percent of crack cocaine users. It is hardly surprising that many African Americans believe that the nation has two standards of justice, an inferior one for blacks and a higher one for whites (see Figure 5-1).

One area where African Americans have made substantial progress since the 1960s is the winning of election to public office (see "States in the Nation"). Although the percentage of black elected officials is still far below the proportion

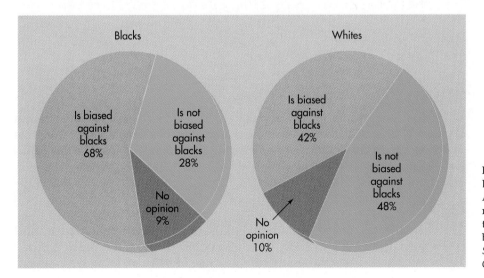

FIGURE 5-1 Opinions on Racial Bias in the Justice System
African Americans are much more likely than white Americans to believe that the courts are biased against black people.
Source: National Center for State Courts, 1999.

★ STATES IN THE NATION

BLACK AND LATINO REPRESENTATION IN STATE LEGISLATURES

For a long period, minorities were barely visible in the state legislatures. The situation began to change after passage of the 1964 Civil Rights Act and the 1965 Voting Rights, but minorities are still underrepresented relative to their numbers in the population. Only 8 percent of state legislators in 2000 were black and a mere 3 percent were Hispanic. Alabama and Mississippi have the highest proportion (25 percent each) of African American state legislators. New Mexico has the highest number (37 percent) of Latino lawmakers. A few states, including Maine and North Dakota, have no legislator from either of these minority groups. Of course, these states have small minority populations while states such as Alabama, Mississippi, and New Mexico have much larger ones.

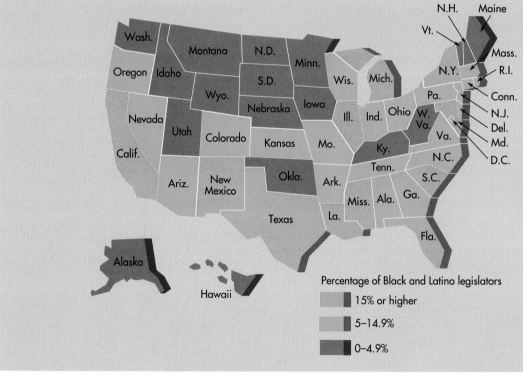

Percentage of Black and Latino legislators

- 15% or higher
- 5–14.9%
- 0–4.9%

SOURCE: National Conference of State Legislatures, 2000.

of African Americans in the population, it has risen sharply over recent decades.[15] As of 2000, there were more than twenty black members of Congress and two hundred black mayors—including the mayors of some of this country's largest cities.

WOMEN

The United States carried over from English common law a political disregard for women, forbidding them to vote, hold public office, and serve on juries.[16] Upon marriage, a woman essentially lost her identity as an individual and

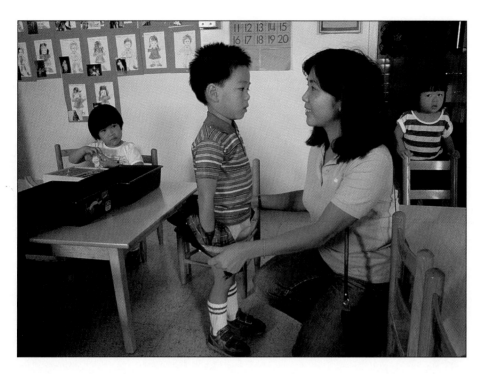

The majority of women with preschool children work outside the home, a situation that has created demands for government support of day care centers, parental leave, and other programs and services.

could not own and dispose of property without her husband's consent. Even the wife's body was not fully hers. A wife's adultery was ruled by the Supreme Court to be a violation of the husband's property rights![17]

The first women's rights convention in America was held in 1848 in Seneca Falls, New York, after Lucretia Mott and Elizabeth Cady Stanton had been barred from the main floor of an anti-slavery convention.[18] Thereafter, however, the struggle for women's rights became closely aligned with the abolitionist movement, but the passage of the post–Civil War constitutional amendments proved to be a setback for the women's movement. The Fifteenth Amendment, for example, said that the right to vote could not be abridged on account of race or color, but said nothing about sex.[19] After decades of struggle, the Nineteenth Amendment was finally adopted in 1920, forbidding denial of the right to vote "by the United States or by any state on account of sex."

Women's Legal and Political Gains

Ratification of the Nineteenth Amendment encouraged leaders of the women's movement to propose in 1923 a constitutional amendment that would guarantee equal rights for women. Congress rejected that proposal and several subsequent ones. In 1973, however, Congress approved the Equal Rights Amendment (ERA) and submitted it to the states for ratification or rejection. The ERA failed by three states to get the three-fourths majority required for ratification.[20]

Although the ERA did not become part of the Constitution, it helped bring women's rights to the forefront at a time when developments in Congress and the courts were contributing significantly to the legal equality of the sexes.[21] Among the congressional initiatives that have helped women are the Equal Pay

HOW THE UNITED STATES COMPARES

WOMEN'S EQUALITY: REPRESENTATION IN NATIONAL LEGISLATURES

Although conflict between groups is universal, the nature of the conflict is often particularized. Racial conflict in the United States cannot readily be compared with, say, religious conflict in Northern Ireland. The one form of inequality common to all nations is that of gender: nowhere are women equal to men in law or in fact. But there are large differences between countries. A study by the Population Crisis Committee ranked the United States third overall in women's equality, behind only Sweden and Finland. The rankings were based on five areas—jobs, education, social relations, marriage and family, and health; U.S. women had an 82.5 percent rating compared with men.

The inequality of women is also underscored by their underrepresentation in public office. There is no country in which women comprise as many as half the members of the national legislature. The Scandinavian countries rank highest in terms of the percentage of female lawmakers. Other northern European countries have lower levels, but the levels are higher than that of the United States. The accompanying figure, estimated from several sources, indicates the approximate percentage of seats held by women in the largest chamber of each country's national legislature:

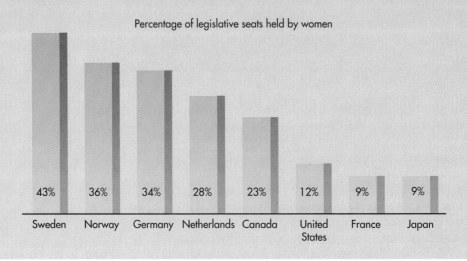

Percentage of legislative seats held by women

Sweden	Norway	Germany	Netherlands	Canada	United States	France	Japan
43%	36%	34%	28%	23%	12%	9%	9%

Act of 1963, which prohibits sex discrimination in salary and wages by some categories of employers; the Civil Rights Act of 1964, which prohibits sex discrimination in programs that receive federal funding; Title IX of the Education Amendment of 1972, which prohibits sex discrimination in education; the Equal Credit Act of 1974, as amended in 1976, which prohibits sex discrimination in the granting of financial credit; and the Civil Rights Act of 1991 and the Family Leave Act of 1993 (discussed later in this chapter).

Women have made clear gains in the area of appointive and elective offices.[22] In 1981, President Reagan appointed the first woman to serve on the Supreme Court, Sandra Day O'Connor. When the Democratic party in 1984 chose Geraldine Ferraro as its vice presidential nominee, it was the first time a woman ran on the national ticket of a major political party. The elections of California's Dianne Feinstein and Barbara Boxer in 1992 marked the first time that women occupied both U.S. Senate seats from a state.

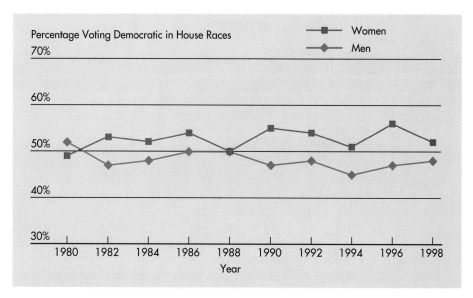

FIGURE 5-2 **The Gender Gap in Congressional Voting** Women and men differ, on average, in their political behavior. For example, women are more likely than men to vote Democratic, as shown by the difference between the women's vote and the men's vote for Democratic candidates in recent U.S. House races. *Source: National Election Studies.*

Despite such signs of progress, women are still a long way from political equality with men.[23] Women occupy only 10 percent of congressional seats and only 20 percent of statewide and city council offices (see "How the United States Compares").

Although women are underrepresented in political office, their vote is becoming increasingly powerful. Until the 1970s, there was almost no difference in the voting patterns of women and men. Today, there is a substantial **gender gap:** Women and men differ substantially in their political attitudes and voting tendencies. Women are more supportive than men of government programs for the poor, minorities, children, and the elderly. They also have a greater tendency to cast their votes for Democratic candidates (see Figure 5-2). In the 1996 presidential race the difference was a record 16 percent. (The gender gap is discussed further in Chapters 6 and 8).

gender gap The tendency of women and men to differ in their political attitudes and voting preferences.

Job-Related Issues: Family Leave, Comparable Worth, and Sexual Harassment

In recent decades, increasing numbers of women have sought employment outside the home. Government statistics indicate that three in five women worked outside the home in 1995 compared with only one in eight in 1950. Women have made gains in many traditionally male-dominated fields. For example, women now make up a third of the new lawyers who enter the job market each year. The change in women's status is also reflected in education statistics. In 1972, more white, black, and Hispanic men than women enrolled in college. By 1991, the reverse was true: more women than men of each race were enrolled.

The increase in the number of women in the workplace has created demands for the expansion of programs such as day care centers and parental leave. In 1993, Congress passed the Family and Medical Leave Act, which provides up to twelve weeks of unpaid leave for employees, male or female, to care for a new baby or a seriously ill family member. Upon return from leave, employees must

Employees in certain job categories dominated by women—day care workers, secretaries, and so on—are paid less than those in male-dominated jobs with similar educational requirements and levels of responsibility. The concept of comparable worth is proposed as a remedy for such inequities.

ordinarily be restored to their original or equivalent positions with equivalent pay, benefits, and other employment terms.

Nevertheless, women are less than equal to men when it comes to job opportunities and benefits. Women increasingly occupy managerial positions, but they are less likely than men to receive top promotions. The term *glass ceiling* refers to the invisible but nonetheless real barrier to advancement that talented women encounter after having reached the middle-management level.

Women also hold a disproportionate number of the low-wage jobs in society. Although the disparity is decreasing, the average pay for full-time women employees is only about three-fourths that of full-time men employees (see Figure 5-3). This situation has led to demands by women for equal pay for work that is of similar difficulty and responsibility and that requires similar levels of education and training—a concept called **comparable worth.** A comparable-worth policy would eliminate salary inequities resulting from the fact that some jobs (for example, secretaries) have traditionally been dominated by women and thus pay less than male-dominated jobs (for example, truck drivers). Advocates of comparable worth gained an early victory when the Supreme Court held in 1981 that female guards at a prison had to be paid the same as male guards even if their work assignments differed.[24] In general, however, proponents of comparable worth have had only limited success in persuading public and private employers to accept their view.[25]

Workplace discrimination against women includes sexual harassment. Lewd comments and unwelcome advances are a part of everyday life for many working women, and the courts have taken an increasingly firm stand against companies that tolerate such behavior. In 1998, the Supreme Court ruled that a firm can be held liable for sexual misconduct by supervisors even if the firm was unaware of the misconduct and even if the employee did not suffer adverse job consequences. The Court also held, however, that a firm's liability is reduced when it has an aggressive program to guard against sexual harassment in the workplace.[26]

Federal law also bars sexual discrimination in schools. In a 1999 ruling, the Supreme Court held that schools that ignore a pattern of persistent and severe sexual harassment are liable for damages. However, in a controversial 2000 decision, the Supreme Court invalidated a provision of the federal Violence

comparable worth The idea that women should get pay equal to men for work that is of similar difficulty and responsibility and that requires similar levels of education and training.

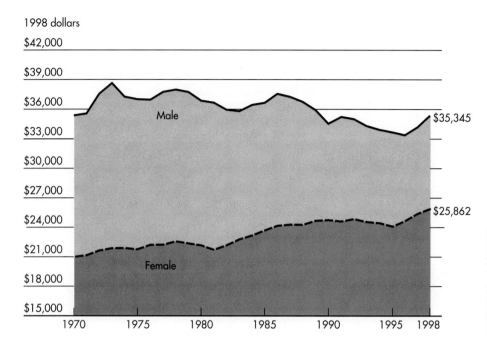

FIGURE 5-3 Median Annual Income of Full-Time Male and Female Workers
Women's income has increased relative to men's income during the past quarter-century but is still substantially lower. *Source: U.S. Bureau of the Census, 2000.*

Against Women Act (VAWA) that permitted victims of domestic violence, rape, and other acts motivated by gender to sue their attackers in federal court. The Court struck down the provision on grounds that it unlawfully infringed on the power of the states. Although the ruling was one in a series of recent decisions that have sought to limit federal power (see Chapter 3), the substance of the case gave it national attention. The implications of the ruling depend on whether a woman lives in a state that itself provides an adequate civil remedy in the case of such attacks. In states that do not provide this legal protection, women will not have an opportunity to seek monetary damages from their attackers.[27]

NATIVE AMERICANS

When white settlers began arriving in America in large numbers during the seventeenth century, nearly ten million Native Americans were living in the territory that would become the United States. By 1900, the Native American population had plummeted to less than one million. Diseases brought by white settlers had taken a toll on the various Indian tribes, but so had wars and massacres. "The only good Indian is a dead Indian" is not simply a hackneyed expression from cowboy movies. It was part of a strategy of westward expansion, as settlers and U.S. troops alike mercilessly drove the eastern Indians from their ancestral lands to the Great Plains and then took those lands as well.

Today Native Americans number more than one million, about half of whom live on or close to reservations set aside for them by the federal government. Reservations are governed by treaties signed when they were established. State governments have no direct authority over reservations and the federal government's authority is limited by the terms of a particular treaty. Although U.S.

Gambling casinos have become a major source of revenue and employment for many Native American reservations. Some Native Americans claim that the casinos are destroying tribal culture and traditions.

policy toward the reservations has changed over time, the current policy is to promote self-government and economic self-sufficiency.[28]

Native Americans are less than half as likely to attend college as other Americans, their life expectancy is more than ten years lower than the national average, and their infant mortality rate is more than three times higher than that of white Americans. In recent years, some Native American tribes have erected gaming casinos on reservation land. The casinos have brought jobs and income to the reservations but have also brought controversy—traditionalists argue that the casinos are destroying their tribal cultures.

The civil rights movement of the 1960s at first did not include Native Americans. Then, in the early 1970s, militant Native Americans occupied the Bureau of Indian Affairs in Washington, D.C., and later seized control of the village of Wounded Knee on a Sioux reservation in southwestern South Dakota, exchanging gunfire with U.S. marshals. These episodes brought attention to the grievances of Native Americans and may have contributed to the passage in 1974 of legislation that granted Native Americans on reservations a greater measure of control over federal programs that affected them. Native Americans had already benefited from the legislative climate created by the civil rights movement of the 1960s. In 1968, Congress had enacted the Indian Bill of Rights, which gives Native Americans on reservations constitutional guarantees that are similar to those held by other Americans.

In recent years Native Americans have filed suit to reclaim lost ancestral lands and have won a few settlements. But they stand no realistic chance of getting back even those lands that had been granted them by federal treaty but were later sold off or simply taken forcibly by federal authorities. Native Americans were not even official citizens of the United States until an act of Congress in 1924. This status came too late to be of much help; their traditional way of life had already been seriously eroded.

HISPANIC AMERICANS

The fastest-growing minority in the United States is that of Hispanic Americans, that is, people of Spanish-speaking background. Hispanics are also one of the country's oldest ethnic groups. Some Hispanics are descendants of people who helped colonize the areas of California, Texas, Florida, New Mexico, and Arizona before they were taken over by the United States. But most Hispanics are recent immigrants or their descendants.

The 2000 census counted over 30 million Hispanics living in the United States, an increase of 35 percent over the 1990 census; and it is projected that Hispanics will soon replace African Americans as the nation's largest racial or ethnic minority group. They have emigrated to the United States primarily from Mexico and the Caribbean islands, mainly Cuba and Puerto Rico. About half of all Hispanics in the United States were born in Mexico or claim a Mexican ancestry. Hispanics are concentrated in their states of entry; thus Florida, New York, and New Jersey have large numbers of Caribbean Hispanics, while California, Texas, Arizona, and New Mexico have many immigrants from Mexico. More than half the population of Los Angeles is of Hispanic—mostly Mexican—descent.

The term *Hispanic* can be misleading if it is construed to mean a group of people who all think alike (see Table 5-1). Hispanics cover a wide political spectrum, from the conservative Republican-leaning Cuban Americans of southern Florida to the liberal Democratic-leaning Puerto Ricans of the Northeast. Hispanic Americans share a common language, Spanish, but they are not monolithic in their politics.[29]

Legal and Political Action

Hispanic Americans have benefited from laws and court rulings aimed primarily at protecting other groups. Thus, although the Civil Rights Act of 1964 was largely a response to the condition of black people, its provisions against discrimination apply broadly to other groups as well.

Nevertheless, Hispanics had their own civil rights movement. Its most publicized actions were the farm workers' strikes of the late 1960s and the 1970s that aimed at achieving basic labor rights for migrant workers. Migrants were working long hours for low pay, were living in shacks without electricity or

TABLE 5-1 Hispanics' Party Identification, by National Origin Hispanics share a common language and ancestry, but differ sharply in their political leanings.

Party Identification	Puerto Rican Americans	Mexican Americans	Cuban Americans
Democratic	64%	60%	19%
Independent	22	24	17
Republican	14	16	64
	100%	100%	100%

From *Latino National Political Survey*, reported in Rudolfo O. de la Garza, Angelo Falcon, F. Chris Garcia, and John A. Garcia, "Hispanic Americans in the Mainstream of U.S. Politics," *The Public Perspective*, July/August 1992, p. 19. © The Roper Center for Public Opinion Research, University of CT. Storrs, CT. Used by permission.

plumbing, and were unwelcome in many local schools and in some local hospitals as well. Farm owners at first refused to bargain with the workers, but a well-organized national boycott of California grapes and lettuce forced that state to pass a law giving migrant workers the right to bargain collectively. The strikes were led in California by Cesar Chavez, who himself grew up in a Mexican-American migrant family. Chavez's tactics were copied in other states, particularly Texas, but the results were less successful.

Hispanics face some distinctive problems. The fact that many do not speak English led to a 1968 amendment to the 1964 Civil Rights Act that funds public school programs offering English instruction in the language of children for whom English is a second language. In addition, many Hispanics are illegal aliens and do not have the full rights of citizens. In *De Canas v. Bica* (1976), for example, the Supreme Court upheld a state law barring illegal aliens from employment.[30]

In 1986, Congress passed the landmark Immigration Reform and Control Act, commonly known as the Simpson–Mizzoli Act, which primarily affected Hispanics. The legislation offered citizenship to illegal aliens who could prove they had lived continuously in the United States for five years. Roughly two million Hispanics received their citizenship in this way. The act also mandated fines on employers who hired aliens without work permits; it was expected that the resulting lack of job opportunities would eliminate a main incentive for aliens to enter the country illegally.

The issue of illegal aliens was also addressed through California's controversial Proposition 187. Placed on the state's ballot in 1994 through a citizen petition, Proposition 187 received the votes of a majority of Californians even though a majority of the state's Mexican Americans voted against it. The initiative aimed to cut off public services to illegal immigrants, the great majority of whom are Mexicans. They would no longer receive state-funded food stamps, welfare, and medical care except in life-threatening circumstances, and they would no longer be eligible for public schooling at any level. Supporters of the initiative claimed it would save the state from bankruptcy (for example, 10 percent of California's primary and secondary school students are illegal aliens, and their education costs the state more than $1 billion annually).[31] To many of the state's Mexican Americans, the initiative was a thinly disguised attempt to keep additional people from Mexico out of the state. The implementation of Proposition 187 was delayed pending a court ruling on its constitutionality, and most of its key provisions were subsequently judged to be unconstitutional.

Growing Political Power

Hispanic Americans are an important political force in several states and communities, and their influence is likely to increase substantially in the future. Hispanics are projected to become the largest single population group in California in the current century. Their political involvement, like that of other immigrant groups, can be expected to increase as they become more deeply rooted in the society and economy. At present, nearly half of all Hispanic adults are not registered to vote, and only about a third actually vote, which limits the group's political power. Nevertheless, the sheer size of the Hispanic population in states such as Texas and California makes the group a potent political force, as was

U.S. Congresswoman Loretta Sanchez (D-CA) represents a part of Orange County, California. Hispanic Americans are growing in political and cultural influence as their numbers increase in California, Arizona, New Mexico, Texas, and other states.

evident in the 2000 presidential campaign when both parties mounted a massive effort to woo Hispanic voters.

More than four thousand Hispanic Americans nationwide hold public office. In 1974, Arizona and New Mexico elected governors of Spanish-speaking background. New Mexico elected its second Hispanic governor in 1982. About twenty Hispanic Americans currently serve in the House of Representatives.

ASIAN AMERICANS

Chinese and Japanese laborers were the first Asians to come to the United States in large numbers. They were brought into western states during the late 1800s to work in mines and to build railroads. When the need for this labor declined, Congress in 1892 ordered a temporary halt to Chinese immigration. Over the next three decades, informal agreements kept all but a few Asians out of the country. In 1921, the United States ended its traditional policy of unlimited immigration and established immigration quotas based on country of origin. Western European countries were given large quotas and Asian countries tiny ones. About 150 Japanese a year were allowed to immigrate until 1930, when Congress excluded them entirely. Japan had protested a California law that prohibited persons of Japanese descent from buying property in the state. Rather than finesse what was called "the California problem," Congress bluntly told Japan that its people were not wanted in the United States.[32]

Discrimination against Asians did not ease substantially until 1965, when Congress enacted legislation that adjusted the immigration quotas to favor those who had previously been disadvantaged. This change in the law was a product of the 1960s civil rights movement, which sensitized national leaders to all forms of discrimination. About half a million people now emigrate to the United States each year, and a majority come from Asian and Latin American countries. Asian Americans numbered about twelve million in the 2000 census,

Asian Americans studying in a high-school classroom. Many Asian American families emphasize academic achievement as a basis of personal advancement.

or between 4 and 5 percent of the total U.S. population. Most Asian Americans live on the West Coast, particularly in California.

The rights of Asian Americans have been expanded primarily by court rulings and legislation, such as the Civil Rights Act of 1964, that were responses to the problems of other minorities. In a few instances, however, the rights of minorities have been defined by actions of Asian Americans. For example, in *Lau v. Nichols* (1974), a case involving Chinese Americans, the Supreme Court ruled that public schools with a large proportion of children for whom English is a second language must offer English instruction in the children's first language.[33]

In 1998, the second-language issue arose in the form of Proposition 227, a California ballot measure that called for a ban on bilingual education in the state's public schools. The measure received the support of a majority of voters despite opposition from teachers' groups and many within California's Hispanic and Asian communities. Children for whom English is a second language would have to take their courses in English after their first year in school. The constitutionality of Proposition 227 was challenged unsuccessfully in the courts, but some teachers have said they would not abide by its provisions.

Asian Americans are an upwardly mobile group. The values of most Asian cultures include a commitment to hard work, which, in the American context, has included an emphasis on academic achievement. For example, Asians make up a disproportionate share of the students at California's leading public universities, which base admission primarily on high school grades and standardized test scores. However, Asian Americans are still underrepresented in certain areas of the workplace. According to U.S. government figures, Asian Americans account for about 5 percent of professionals and technicians, nearly the same as their percentage of the population. Yet they hold less than 2 percent of managerial jobs; past and present discrimination has kept them from obtaining their fair share of top business positions. They are also underrepresented politically. It was not until 1996, for example, that the first Asian American was elected governor of a state other than Hawaii.

OTHER GROUPS AND THEIR RIGHTS

Although civil rights efforts have been directed mainly at women and racial and ethnic minorities, other groups are also involved.

One such group is the roughly 40 million Americans who have a physical or mental disability that prevents them from performing a critical function, such as seeing, hearing, or walking. A goal of the disabled is equal access to society's opportunities, which was facilitated by the 1990 Americans with Disabilities Act. It grants the disabled the same employment and other protections enjoyed by other disadvantaged groups. In addition, the Education for All Handicapped Children Act of 1975 mandates that all children, however severe their disability, receive a free, appropriate education. Before the legislation, 4 million disabled children were getting either no education or an inappropriate one (as in the case of a blind child who is not taught Braille). Government must actively take steps to ensure the education of such children. In a 1999 ruling, for example, the Supreme Court held that students who require special care at school are entitled to that care, provided that a physician is not needed to deliver it.[34] However, government and employers are not required to honor the disability claims of those with correctable impairments, such as nearsightedness or high blood pressure.[35]

The government has also acted to protect the elderly from discrimination. The Age Discrimination Act of 1975 and the Age Discrimination in Employment Act of 1967 prohibit discrimination against older workers in hiring for jobs in which age is not clearly a crucial factor in job performance. More recently, mandatory retirement ages for most jobs have been eliminated by law. Forced retirement for reasons of age is permissible only if justified by the nature of a particular job or the performance of a particular employee.

A group that until very recently had not received substantial legal protection is homosexuals. In *Bowers v. Hardwick* (1986), the Supreme Court upheld a state law banning sexual acts between consenting homosexual adults, ruling that the constitutional right of privacy does not extend to such acts. Gay rights also were dealt a setback when the Supreme Court in 2000 ruled that the Boy Scouts, as a private organization that has a right to freedom of association, can ban gays because homosexuality is prohibited by the Scouts' creed.[36] Gays are also prohibited from serving in the military but can be dismissed only if they engage in overt verbal or behavioral displays of homosexuality (the so-called "don't ask, don't tell" policy).

However, gays gained a significant legal victory when the Supreme Court in *Romer v. Evans* (1996) struck down a Colorado constitutional amendment that nullified all existing and any new legal protections for homosexuals. In a 6–3 ruling, the Court said the Colorado law violated the Constitution's guarantee of equal protection because it subjects individuals to employment and other forms of discrimination simply because of their sexual preference. The Court concluded that the law had no reasonable purpose but was instead motivated by "animus" (hostility) toward homosexuals.[37]

Equality Under the Law

The catchphrase of nearly every group's claim to a more equal standing in American society has been "equality under the law." The importance that people attach to legal equality is understandable. Once secure in their legal rights, people are in a stronger position to seek equality in other arenas, such as the economic sector. Once encoded in law, a claim to equality can also force officials to take positive action on behalf of a disadvantaged group. Americans' claims to legal equality are contained in a great many laws, a few of which are particularly noteworthy.

EQUAL PROTECTION: THE FOURTEENTH AMENDMENT

The Fourteenth Amendment, which was ratified in 1868, declares in part that no state shall "deny to any person within its jurisdiction the equal protection of the laws." Through this **equal protection clause,** the courts have protected such groups as African Americans and women from discrimination by state and local governments.

The Fourteenth Amendment's equal protection clause does not require government to treat all groups or classes of people the same way in all circumstances. In fact, laws routinely treat people unequally. By law, for example, twenty-one-year-olds can drink alcohol but twenty-year-olds cannot. The judiciary allows such inequalities because they are held to be "reasonably" related to a legitimate government interest. In applying this **reasonable-basis test,** the courts give the benefit of doubt to government. It need only show that a particular law has a sound rationale. For example, the courts have held that the goal of reducing fatalities from alcohol-related accidents involving young drivers is a valid reason for imposing a twenty-one-year minimum age requirement for the purchase of alcohol. (The *Romer* decision discussed earlier provides an example of a law that failed the reasonable-basis test. The Supreme Court concluded that Colorado's law affecting gays had "no legitimate government purpose.")

The reasonable-basis test does not apply, however, to racial or ethnic classifications, particularly when these categories serve to discriminate against minority group members (see Table 5-2). Any law that posits a racial or ethnic classification is subject to the **strict-scrutiny test,** under which such a law is unconstitutional in the absence of an overwhelmingly convincing argument that it is necessary. The strict-scrutiny test has virtually eliminated race and ethnicity as permissible classifications when the effect is to put members of a minority group at a disadvantage. The Supreme Court's position is that race and national origin are **suspect classifications**—that such classifications have invidious discrimination as their purpose and therefore any law containing such a classification is in all likelihood unconstitutional.

The strict-scrutiny test emerged after the 1954 *Brown* ruling and became a basis for invalidating laws that discriminated against black people. As other groups, especially women, began to organize and press for their rights in the late 1960s and early 1970s, the Supreme Court gave early signs that it might expand the scope of suspect classifications to include gender. In the end, however, the Court announced in *Craig v. Boren* (1976) that sex classifications were permissible if they served "important governmental objectives" and were "substantially" related to the achievement of those objectives.[38] The Court thus placed sex distinctions in an intermediate (or almost suspect) category, to be scrutinized more closely than some other classifications (for example, income levels) but, unlike racial classifications, justifiable in some instances. In *Rostker v. Goldberg* (1980), for example, the policy of male-only registration for the military draft was upheld on grounds that the exclusion of women from combat duty serves a legitimate and important purpose.[39]

equal protection clause   A clause of the Fourteenth Amendment that forbids any state to deny equal protection of the laws to any individual within its jurisdiction.

reasonable-basis test   A test applied by courts to laws that treat individuals unequally. Such a law may be deemed constitutional if its purpose is held to be "reasonably" related to a legitimate government interest.

strict-scrutiny test   A test applied by courts to laws that attempt a racial or ethnic classification. In effect, the strict-scrutiny test eliminates race or ethnicity as a legal classification when it places minority group members at a disadvantage.

suspect classifications   Legal classifications, such as race and national origin, that have invidious discrimination as their purpose and are therefore unconstitutional.

TABLE 5-2 Levels of Court Review for Laws That Treat Americans Differently

Test	Applies to	Standard Used
Strict-scrutiny	Race, ethnicity	Suspect category—assumed unconstitutional in the absence of an overwhelming justification
Intermediate-scrutiny	Gender	Almost suspect category—assumed unconstitutional unless the law serves a clearly compelling and justified purpose
Reasonable-basis	Other categories (such as age and income)	Not suspect category—assumed constitutional unless no sound rationale for the law can be provided

The imprecise nature of the **intermediate-scrutiny test** has led some scholars to question its validity as a legal principle. Nevertheless, when evaluating claims of sex discrimination, the judiciary applies a stricter level of scrutiny than is required by the reasonable-basis test. Rather than give government broad leeway to treat men and women differently, the Supreme Court has recently invalidated most of the laws it has reviewed that contain sex classifications. A leading case is *United States v. Virginia* (1996), in which the Supreme Court determined that the male-only admissions policy at Virginia Military Institute (VMI), a 157-year-old state-supported college, was unconstitutional. The state had developed an alternative program for women at another college, but the Court concluded it was no substitute for the unique education and other opportunities that attendance at VMI could provide. (The VMI decision also had

intermediate-scrutiny test A test applied by courts to laws that attempt a gender classification. In effect, the test eliminates gender as a legal classification unless it serves an important objective and is substantially related to the objective's achievement.

Although women are excluded by law from having to register for the draft, they serve with distinction in the U.S. military.

the effect of ending the all-male admissions policy of the Citadel, a state-supported military college in South Carolina.)[40]

EQUAL ACCESS: THE CIVIL RIGHTS ACTS OF 1964 AND 1968

The Fourteenth Amendment applies only to action by government. It does not prohibit discrimination by private parties. As a result, for a long period in the nation's history, owners could legally bar black people from restaurants, hotels, and other accommodations, and employers could freely discriminate in their job practices. Since the 1960s private firms have had much less freedom to discriminate for reasons of race, sex, ethnicity, or religion.

Accommodations and Jobs

The Civil Rights Act of 1964 entitles all persons to equal access to restaurants, bars, theaters, hotels, gasoline stations, and similar establishments serving the general public. The legislation also bars discrimination in the hiring, promotion, and wages of employees of medium-sized and large firms. A few forms of job discrimination are still lawful under the Civil Rights Act of 1964. For example, an owner-operator of a small business can discriminate in hiring his or her co-workers, and a religious school can take the religion of a prospective teacher into account.

The Civil Rights Act of 1964 has nearly eliminated the most overt forms of discrimination in the area of public accommodations. Some restaurants and hotels may provide better service to white customers, but outright refusal to serve African Americans or other minority group members is rare. Such a refusal is a violation of the law and could easily be proved in many instances. It is harder to prove discrimination in job decisions; accordingly, the act has been less effective in rooting out employment discrimination—a subject that will be discussed in detail later in this chapter.

Housing

In 1968, Congress passed civil rights legislation designed to prohibit discrimination in housing. A building owner cannot refuse to sell or rent housing because of a person's race, religion, ethnicity, or sex. An exception is allowed for owners of small multifamily dwellings who reside on the premises.

Despite legal prohibitions on discrimination, housing in America remains highly segregated. Less than a third of all African Americans live in a neighborhood that is mostly white. One reason is the fact that the annual income of most black families is substantially below that of most white families. Another reason is the practice of banks. At one time, they contributed to housing segregation by "redlining"—refusing to grant mortgage loans in certain neighborhoods. This practice drove down the selling prices of homes in these neighborhoods, which led to an influx of African Americans and an exodus of whites. Redlining is prohibited by the 1968 Civil Rights Act, but many of the segregated neighborhoods that it helped to create still exist.

Recent studies indicate that minority status is still a factor in the lending practices of some banks.[41] A 1998 report of the U.S. Conference of Mayors indicated that, among applicants with average or slightly higher incomes relative to their

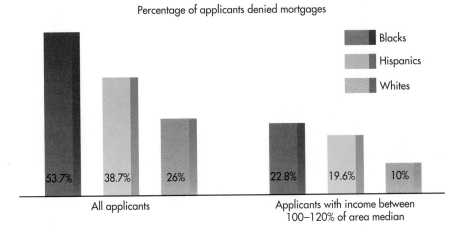

Percentage of applicants denied mortgages

FIGURE 5-4 Mortgage Application Rejections
Blacks and Hispanics are more likely than whites to be rejected for a mortgage, even among applicants with similar incomes. *Source: U.S. Conference of Mayors, 1998.*

community, Hispanics and African Americans were twice as likely as whites to be denied a mortgage (see Figure 5-4).[42]

EQUAL BALLOTS: THE VOTING RIGHTS ACT OF 1965, AS AMENDED

Free elections are perhaps the foremost symbol of American democracy, yet the right to vote has only recently become a reality for many Americans, particularly for African Americans.

The Nineteenth Amendment, which in 1920 gave women the right to vote, effectively ended resistance to women's suffrage; paradoxically, resistance to black suffrage was intensified by the Fifteenth Amendment, which in 1870 gave black persons the right to vote. Southern whites invented a series of devices, including whites-only primaries, poll taxes, and rigged literacy tests to keep African Americans from registering and voting.[43] For example, almost no votes were cast by African Americans between the years 1920 and 1946 in North Carolina.[44]

Barriers to black participation in elections began to crumble in the mid-1940s, when the Supreme Court declared that whites-only primary elections were unconstitutional.[45] Two decades later, through the Twenty-fourth Amendment, poll taxes were outlawed.

The major step toward equal voting rights for African Americans was passage of the Voting Rights Act of 1965, which forbids discrimination in voting and registration.[46] The legislation empowers federal agents to register voters and to oversee participation in elections. The Voting Rights Act, as interpreted by the courts, also eliminates literacy tests: local officials can no longer deny registration and voting for reasons of illiteracy. In fact, in communities where a language other than English is widely spoken, officials are now required by law to provide ballot materials in that language. If most civil rights legislation seldom has a significant and immediate impact on people's behavior, the Voting Rights Act is an exception. In the 1960 presidential election, voter turnout among African Americans was barely more than 20 percent nationwide. In 1968, three years after passage of the legislation, the turnout rate doubled and, in 1972, was within 10 percentage points of the level for white Americans. In 1960, the gap had exceeded 40 percentage points (see Figure 5-5).

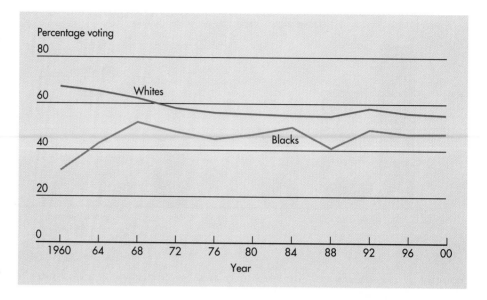

FIGURE 5-5   Voter Turnout in Presidential Campaigns Among Black and White Americans, 1960–2000
Voter turnout among black Americans rose dramatically during the 1960s as legal obstacles to their voting were removed. The 2000 figures are based on preliminary projections. *Source: U.S. Bureau of the Census.*

Congress renewed the Voting Rights Act in 1970, 1975, and 1982. The 1982 extension is noteworthy because it renewed the act for twenty years and requires states and localities to clear with federal officials any electoral change that has the effect, intended or not, of reducing the voting power of a minority group. When congressional district boundaries were redrawn after the 1990 census (see Chapter 13), the 1982 extension became the basis for the creation of districts that included a majority of Hispanic or African American voters. The result was the election of an unprecedented number of minority group members to Congress in 1992; Hispanic and African American representatives increased from 10 and 25 to 17 and 38, respectively.

However, the Supreme Court in 1996 ruled that the redistricting of four congressional districts in Texas and North Carolina was unconstitutional because race had been the "dominant" factor in their creation. The states were directed to redraw the districts. A year earlier, the Court had invalidated a Georgia redistricting plan, holding that the state's Eleventh Congressional District violated the rights of white voters under the Fourteenth Amendment's equal protection clause. The Georgia district stretched from Savannah to Atlanta and had all sorts of twists and turns designed to exclude white residential areas. These rulings have not necessarily settled fully the issue of racial redistricting. The 1996 Texas and North Carolina cases were each decided by a 5–4 majority, and three of the justices in the majority indicated that there *might* be instances in which race, along with other factors, could be taken into account in redistricting decisions. But the Court's majority made it clear that race cannot be the *deciding* factor in redistricting arrangements.[47]

The Court demonstrated its flexibility in a 1999 decision, *Hunt v. Cromartie*, when it unanimously upheld the redistricting of North Carolina's Twelfth Congressional District, even though race had been a consideration in the redistricting. The Court held that the heavily Democratic district was created primarily for partisan political reasons and was therefore acceptable.[48]

Kay Bailey Hutchison was elected to the U.S. Senate from Texas in 1993 to fill the seat vacated by Lloyd Bentsen, who had resigned to become Secretary of the Treasury. Hutchison is among the growing number of women who sit in the U.S. Congress.

Equality of Result

America's disadvantaged groups have made significant progress toward equal rights, particularly during the past few decades. Through acts of Congress and rulings of the Supreme Court, most forms of government-sponsored discrimination—from racially segregated public schools to gender-based pension plans—have been banned.

However, civil rights problems involve deeply rooted conditions, habits, and prejudices and affect whole categories of people. For these reasons, a new civil rights policy rarely produces a sudden and dramatic change in society. Despite their greater equality in law, America's traditionally disadvantaged groups are still substantially unequal in their daily lives. Consider the issue of income disparity (see Figure 5-6). The average Asian American's income is about 90 percent of the average white person's income. But the average falls to 60 percent for African Americans and 55 percent for Hispanic Americans.

Such figures reflect **de facto discrimination,** which is discrimination that is a consequence of social, economic, and cultural biases and conditions. This type of discrimination is different from **de jure discrimination,** which is discrimination based on law, as in the case of segregation in southern public schools during the pre-*Brown* period. De facto discrimination is difficult to root out because it is embedded not in the law but in the very structure of society. **Equality of result** is the aim of policies intended to reduce or eliminate de facto discriminatory effects so that members of disadvantaged groups may obtain the same benefits as members of advantaged groups. Such policies are inherently more controversial because many Americans believe that government's responsibility extends no further than the removal of legal barriers to equality.

de facto discrimination Discrimination on the basis of race, sex, religion, ethnicity, and the like that results from social, economic, and cultural biases and conditions.

de jure discrimination Discrimination on the basis of race, sex, religion, ethnicity, and the like that results from a law.

equality of result The objective of policies intended to reduce or eliminate the effects of discrimination so that members of traditionally disadvantaged groups will have the same benefits of society as do members of advantaged groups.

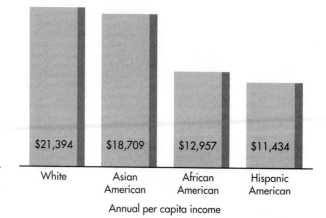

FIGURE 5-6   U.S. per Capita Income, by Race and Ethnicity The average income of white Americans is substantially higher than that of most other Americans. *Source: U.S. Bureau of the Census, 1999.*

This attitude reflects the culture's emphasis on *individualism* and helps explain the lack of any large-scale government effort to reduce the economic and social gaps between Americans of varying racial and ethnic backgrounds. Nevertheless, a few policies—notably affirmative action and busing—have been implemented to achieve equality of result.

AFFIRMATIVE ACTION: WORKPLACE INTEGRATION

The difficulty of converting newly acquired legal rights into everyday realities is evident in the fact that, with passage of the 1964 Civil Rights Act, which prohibited discrimination in employment, women and minorities did not suddenly find it easier to obtain jobs for which they were qualified. Many employers maintained a deliberate though unwritten preference for white male employees, while other employers adhered to established employment procedures that continued to keep women and minorities at a disadvantage; membership in many union locals, for example, was handed down from father to son. Moreover, the Civil Rights Act did not compel employers to show that their hiring practices were not discriminatory. Instead, the burden of proof was on the woman or minority group member who had been denied a particular job. It was costly and often difficult to prove in court that one's sex or race was the reason that one had not been hired. In addition, a victory in court affected only the individual in question; such case-by-case settlements were no remedy for a situation in which established hiring practices kept millions of women and minorities from competing equally for job opportunities.

A broader remedy was obviously required, and the result was the emergence during the late 1960s of affirmative action programs. **Affirmative action** is a deliberate effort to provide full and equal opportunities in employment, education, and other areas for women, minorities, and individuals belonging to other traditionally disadvantaged groups. Affirmative action requires corporations, universities, and other organizations to establish programs designed to ensure that all applicants are treated fairly. Affirmative action also places the burden of proof on the providers of opportunities; to some extent, they must be able to demonstrate that any disproportionate granting of opportunities to white males is not the result of discriminatory practices.

affirmative action A term that refers to programs designed to ensure that women, minorities, and other traditionally disadvantaged groups have full and equal opportunities in employment, education, and other areas of life.

Since its inception in the 1960s, affirmative action policy has been a source of contentious debate but also a source of progress for women and minorities.

Opinions on Affirmative Action

Few issues in recent years have provoked more controversy than has affirmative action.[49] Although most Americans say they believe that minorities and women deserve a truly equal chance at jobs and other opportunities, they also say they worry that aggressive affirmative action programs will discriminate against more qualified males, an outcome that is called *reverse discrimination*.

Although opposition to affirmative action has increased in recent years, it is marked by ambivalence (see Figure 5-7). Americans oppose the making of hiring and admission decisions on the basis of race, yet a majority also indicates that diversity in the workplace and in college is a desirable goal and that special efforts to enable the historically disadvantaged to compete on more equal footing should be made. In a New York Times/CBS News poll, for example, a majority of whites said no to the question, "Do you believe that where there has been job discrimination against blacks in the past, preference in hiring or promotion should be given to blacks today?" But in the same poll, a majority of whites said yes to the question, "Do you believe there should be special educational programs to assist minorities in competing for college admissions?" These opinions are in line with traditional American attitudes (see Chapter 1). Americans generally endorse the idea of equal opportunity and thus tend to support programs that would give people a chance to compete for success. But they oppose policies that would give someone preferential treatment once the competition is underway.

"Which [position on affirmative action programs] comes closer to your own point of view?"

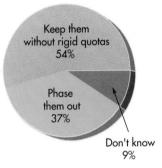

Keep them without rigid quotas 54%

Phase them out 37%

Don't know 9%

FIGURE 5-7 Opinions on Affirmative Action
Americans' support for affirmative action has declined in recent years, but rather than eliminate the policy entirely, Americans prefer to retain it minus the quota or preference aspects. *Source: NBC News, Wall Street Journal Poll, March, 2000.*

Affirmative Action in the Law

Most issues that pit individuals against each other in a struggle over society's benefits eventually end up in the courts, and affirmative action is no exception (see Table 5-3). The policy was first tested before the Supreme Court in *University of California Regents v. Bakke* (1978). Alan Bakke, a white man, had twice been denied admission to a University of California medical school, even though his

TABLE 5-3   Key Decisions in the History of Affirmative Action Policy

Year	Action
1969	Nixon Administration's Department of Labor initiates affirmative action policy
1978	Supreme Court in *Bakke* invalidates rigid quotas for medical school admissions but does not invalidate affirmative action
1980	Supreme Court in *Fullilove* upholds a quota system for minority-owned firms in granting of federal contracts
1980s	Supreme Court in a series of decisions narrows situations in which preferential treatment of minorities will be permitted
1991	In Civil Rights Act of 1991, Congress places burden of proof on business in situations where there is a pattern of white male dominance
1995	Supreme Court in *Adarand* eliminates fixed quotas in the granting of government contracts
1996	California voters enact Proposition 209, which bans public employment, education, and contracting programs based on race, ethnicity, or sex

admission test scores were higher than those of several minority group students who had been accepted. Bakke sued, claiming the school had a "quota" system for minorities that discriminated against white males. The Court ruled in Bakke's favor but did not invalidate affirmative action per se. The Court said only that rigid racial quotas were an impermissible form of affirmative action in determining medical school admissions.[50]

Bakke was followed by two rulings in favor of affirmative action programs, one of which—*Fullilove v. Klutnick* (1980)—upheld a quota system that required 10 percent of federal public works funds to be set aside for minority-owned firms.[51]

In the 1980s, the appointment of more conservative justices to the Supreme Court narrowed the scope of affirmative action policy. The Court held, for example, that preferential treatment of minorities could normally be justified only in cases where discrimination had been severe and that affirmative action could be applied only in a way that did not infringe on the rights of white employees to keep their jobs (thus restricting the use of race as a basis for determining which employees would be terminated in the case of job layoffs).[52]

Proponents of affirmative action succeeded, however, in shifting some of the burden of proof about discrimination from employees to employers. After the Supreme Court in the 1980s allowed business firms more latitude in defending their hiring practices,[53] Congress responded with the Civil Rights Act of 1991, which requires larger firms in some instances to prove why their overwhelmingly male or white work force is the result of business necessity (such as the nature of the work or the locally available labor pool) and not the result of systematic discrimination against women or minorities.

In a key 1995 decision, *Adarand v. Pena*, the Supreme Court sharply curtailed the federal government's affirmative action authority. The case arose when Adarand Constructors filed suit over a federal contract that was awarded to a Hispanic-owned company even though Adarand had submitted a lower bid. The Court in a 5–4 ruling said that the government had to prove that a preference program for minorities was a response to specific past acts of discrimination,

CURRENT CONTROVERSIES

SHOULD AFFIRMATIVE ACTION PREFERENCES END? THE CASE OF ONE FLORIDA

No civil rights policy has provoked more controversy in recent decades than affirmative action has. The application of quotas and preferences has contributed to a perception among some Americans that affirmative action discriminates against people who are white or male. Yet, as supporters of affirmative action have emphasized, the statistics indicate that the more typical victim of discrimination is a minority group member or a woman. In the past few years, opponents of affirmative action have gained ground. Minority preference systems in California and Texas, for example, have been terminated. In early 2000, Governor Jeb Bush proposed that Florida also halt its minority preference systems in college admissions and government contracts. His One Florida plan provoked a protest demonstration that was organized by civil rights leaders, including Jesse Jackson, Martin Luther King III, and the NAACP's Kweisi Mfume.

YES: Today, I am announcing my One Florida initiative. . . . The old solutions have become increasingly controversial and divisive [and they] are no longer producing the kinds of results Floridians deserve. Preferences in higher education are being used to mask the failure of low performing schools in our K–12 system. . . . Likewise, preferences in contracting are failing to increase economic opportunities for minorities in a meaningful way, while discriminating against non-minorities who simply want a level field of competition.
—Governor Jeb Bush (R-Fla.)

NO: [One Florida] is an affront to people of color and women who continue to suffer from discrimination when it comes to education, winning government contracts, and health care. . . . [This protest is about] people's dignity and humanity. We don't want to just expand the economic pie, we want to expand the number of pie eaters. . . . This is not about Florida alone, it's about the nation. The eyes of the nation are upon Florida. . . . The [protest] demonstration you see today did not just happen. You cannot continue to impose policy on [us] without any impact whatsoever.
—Kweisi Mfume, president, NAACP

not just discrimination in a historic sense. This decision essentially reversed earlier precedents that allowed the federal government to give a preference to minority applicants. The Supreme Court held that set-aside contracts for minority applicants are unlawful unless, through costly and conclusive studies, the government can demonstrate past discrimination particular to a situation; and even then, it must devise a program "narrowly tailored" to the problem that is being remedied.[54] In other words, the government cannot issue general requirements (such as a 10 percent set-aside) as a means of remedying past discrimination.

Even supporters of affirmative action concluded that the *Adarand* decision likely marked the end of the era of extensive racial and gender preferences. By holding that affirmative action must be narrowly tailored and based on specific past acts of discrimination, the Court substantially restricted the authority of federal authorities to mandate broad affirmative action remedies. Earlier, the Court had restricted the authority of state and local governments to institute such requirements.

Another blow to affirmative action proponents was the California Civil Rights Initiative, which bans in California any public employment, education, or contracting program that is based on race, ethnicity, or sex. Known as Proposition 209, the initiative was placed on the 1996 ballot by citizen petition and approved 54 to 46 percent by California voters. The vote divided along racial,

Students at a California state university demonstrate against Proposition 209. The initiative proposed to end all racial, ethnic, and gender preferences in the awarding of university admissions, jobs, and government contracts in the state. The initiative passed by a 54 to 46 percent vote margin in 1996.

ethnic, and gender lines, with white males most strongly in favor and blacks and Hispanics most strongly opposed. The constitutionality of Proposition 209 was challenged by opponents, but the Supreme Court upheld it in 1997.

The Board of Regents of the University of California had earlier voted an end to affirmative action in university admissions, a policy that was also instituted at the University of Texas Law School and some other academic institutions. The effect was a dramatic decline in minority enrollment at these institutions. The entering classes at the Berkeley and Los Angeles campuses of the University of California in the fall of 1998, for example, had more than 50 percent fewer African Americans than the previous class. Hispanic enrollment also declined, although less dramatically.

Further restrictions on affirmative action are possible in the future, inasmuch as even some of its supporters believe that it is now heightening white resistance to other civil rights measures and that it is diminishing the accomplishments of women and minorities who would have gotten ahead even without the policy. It is unlikely, however, that affirmative action will be eliminated entirely. Statistical indicators show that women and minorities, as groups, are still at a substantial disadvantage to white males in terms of job hiring, pay, and promotion. In a few occupations, mostly in the professions, well-qualified women and minority group members are in high demand. In most settings, however, these people are at a substantial disadvantage, a situation that creates pressure on policy makers to maintain affirmative action in some form.

In 1998, the state of Texas devised an innovative response to the problem of equal opportunity. Recognizing the disparity in the quality of its public schools and other factors that result in lower average scores on standardized tests for minorities, the state established a policy that guarantees admission at the public university campus of his or her choice to any Texas high school student who graduates in the top 10 percent of the class. The 10 percent rule has met with lit-

www.mhhe.com/patterson5

Simulation

Deacon John Hodge stands at the charred remains of Rising Star Baptist Church in Greensboro, Alabama. His church is one of more than two dozen predominantly black churches that were torched by arsonists in 1996 alone. The burnings are an ugly reminder that racism—"America's curse," in the words of the sociologist Gunner Myrdal—is still the nation's most conspicuous shortcoming.

tle opposition from even the most outspoken critics of affirmative action, and those who favor affirmative action support this program "because it eliminates suspicion that students may have been admitted solely on the basis of race."[55]

SCHOOL INTEGRATION: BUSING

The 1954 *Brown* ruling mandated an end to *forced segregation* of public schools. Government would no longer be permitted to prevent minorities from enrolling in white schools. *Brown* did not, however, mandate school *integration*. Government was not required by *Brown* to take action to require white and minority children to attend school together, and *Brown* did little to change the face of America's schools. Ten years after *Brown*, less than 3 percent of black children were attending schools that were predominantly white. The proportion jumped roughly 20 percent after passage of the 1964 Civil Rights Act, but the fact that black and white children lived in mostly separate neighborhoods meant that they would continue to attend separate schools. This situation set the stage for one of the few public policies that forced whites into close regular contact with blacks: the busing of children to achieve racial balance in schools.

The *Swann* Decision and Its Aftermath

In 1971, the Supreme Court took the controversial step of requiring the busing of children in some circumstances. Affirming a lower-court decision, the Supreme Court held in *Swann v. Charlotte-Mecklenburg County Board of Education* that the busing of children from one neighborhood to another was a permissible way for courts to compel the integration of public schools in which past years of official segregation had created residential patterns that had the effect of keeping the races in separate schools. Busing, the Court said, was allowed as a tool "in the interim period when remedial adjustments are being made to eliminate the dual school system."[56]

Few policies of recent times provoked so much controversy as the introduction of forced busing.[57] Surveys indicated that more than 80 percent of white

Americans and a majority in Congress disapproved of forced busing. Angry demonstrations lasting weeks took place in Charlotte. When busing was ordered in Detroit and Boston, the protests turned violent. Unlike *Brown*, which affected mainly the South, *Swann* also applied to northern communities in which African Americans and whites lived apart as a result of economic and cultural differences as well as discriminatory real estate practices and local housing ordinances. In fact, many of the nation's most segregated communities are in the Northeast and Midwest rather than the South. According to a segregation index created by researchers at the University of Michigan, there is less neighborhood integration in northern cities like Gary, Indiana, and Flint, Michigan, than in southern cities like Fayetteville, North Carolina, and Fort Walton Beach, Florida.

Despite the widespread protests, busing became a part of national policy. Each school day, thousands upon thousands of children were bused out of their neighborhoods to attend school with children of a different color. Busing's application was narrowed, however, by court-imposed restrictions on its use. The Supreme Court in 1974—perhaps in response to the protests over busing—held that it could be applied *across* school districts only in situations where it could be shown that school district boundaries were purposely drawn so as to segregate the races.[58] Because school districts in most states coincide with community boundaries, the effect of this position was to insulate most suburban schools from integration plans.

Does Busing Work?

Studies indicate that busing has contributed to more positive racial attitudes among children. Studies also show that the performance of black children on standardized tests improves when they attend white-majority schools and that the test performance of the white children is not adversely affected.[59]

However, busing has contributed to whites' departure from public schools, which, along with population and residential shifts, has made it increasingly difficult to achieve diversity in city schools. In Boston, for example, less than 20 percent of public school children today are white, compared with more than 50 percent when busing began there in 1974.

Busing also fragmented neighborhoods and forced children into long bus rides to and from school. Many black and white families alike were affected by what came to be called "busing fatigue." Parents asked, in effect, whether busing was worth the costs. That debate led the Prince George's County (Maryland) school board, which had a black majority, to abandon busing in 1998 and replace it with improved funding for neighborhood schools. Alvin Thornton, chair of the Prince George's County school board and a Howard University professor, argued that the change would increase "the sense of community" among the county's African Americans.[60]

Diversity and America's Schools

Prince George's County is among dozens of communities—including Seattle, Jacksonville, Minneapolis, Mobile, and Boston—that have dismantled their school busing programs in recent years. In 1999, the school district where busing policy began—Charlotte-Mecklenburg—joined the list. Federal judge Robert

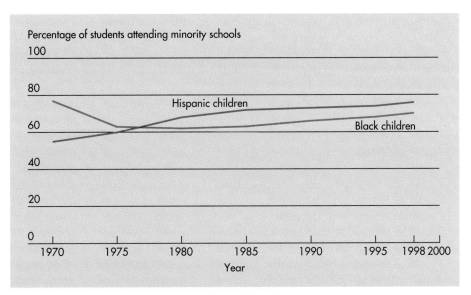

Percentage of students attending minority schools

FIGURE 5-8 Decrease in School Integration
Busing contributed to an increase in the percentage of black children attending predominantly white schools, but the percentage has decreased since the late 1980s, and the percentage of Hispanics in white-majority schools has declined steadily for three decades. *Source: U.S. Department of Education, 1999.*

Potter ruled in an anti-busing lawsuit that the school district could no longer take race into account in "assigning" children to its schools. Potter's decision followed a series of Supreme Court rulings in the 1990s that had held that busing was intended as a temporary, not permanent, solution to the problem of segregated schools;[61] that the performance of black students could not be the criterion for continuation of a busing program;[62] and that communities could devise alternative programs to replace their busing programs.[63]

The cutback in busing contributed to a decrease in school integration. Nationwide, integration peaked in the late 1980s and has declined steadily since then (see Figure 5-8). Only about a third of black children today attend a predominantly white school, which is about the same proportion as in 1970, before busing was initiated. The proportion is even higher for Hispanic children—only about a fourth of them attend a predominantly white school.

Population and residential changes have also contributed to the decrease in school integration. The core cities of most U.S. metropolitan areas are increasingly populated by minorities. The movement of middle-class blacks and Hispanics to suburban communities has resulted in some degree of integration in their school districts, but the trend today is toward a more segregated educational system. The trend is unlikely to be reversed any time soon through public policy because *diversity*, unlike *equality*, has no explicit constitutional status. Government is compelled by the Constitution to treat people equally; it is not required to promote diversity. "Some say that diversity should be a compelling governmental purpose," says George Mason University professor David J. Armor, "but the Supreme Court says no."[64]

As busing recedes, the focus has shifted to parity in school financing. In comparison with predominantly white schools, those schools with mostly minority children have significantly larger classroom sizes, fewer certified teachers, and fewer resources, including library materials, computers, and science laboratories.[65] In Prince George's County and other communities that have dismantled busing programs, local and state governments have promised to increase the funding for predominantly minority schools. The NAACP is among the minority-group organizations that are fearful this promise will not be kept. "We can't go back to where we were before school desegregation," says Maxine Waters, chair of the NAACP's National Education Committee. "Resources have always followed the white child. If we go back to separate facilities, that will happen again.[66]

Persistent Discrimination: Superficial Differences, Deep Divisions

In 1944, the Swedish sociologist Gunnar Myrdal gained fame for his book *An American Dilemma,* whose title referred to deep-rooted racism in a country that proclaimed itself to be the epitome of an equal society.[67] Since then, legal obstacles to the mixing of the races have been nearly eliminated. Public opinion has also changed significantly in the past half century. In the early 1940s, a majority of white Americans believed that black children should not be allowed to go to school with white children; today less than 5 percent of white Americans express this belief. There are also visible signs of black progress. In the past two decades, increasing numbers of African Americans have attended college, received undergraduate degrees, obtained jobs as professional and managers, and moved into suburban neighborhoods.

Nevertheless, true equality for all Americans has remained elusive. The realities of everyday American life are still very different for its white and black citizens. For example, a black child born in the United States has more than twice the chance of dying before reaching his or her first birthday than a white child does. The difference in the infant mortality rates of whites and African Americans reflects differences in their nutrition, medical care, and education—in other words, differences in their access to the most basic resources of a modern society.

Myrdal called discrimination "America's curse." America's professed commitment to equality for all has always had a restricted meaning. No greater challenge faces America in the twenty-first century than the rooting out of disadvantages and prejudice related to race, sex, and ethnicity.

www.mhhe.com/patterson5

Self-Quiz

Summary

During the past few decades, the United States has undergone a revolution in the legal status of its traditionally disadvantaged groups, including African Americans, women, Native Americans, Hispanic Americans, and Asian Americans. Such groups are now provided equal protection under the law in areas such as education, employment, and voting. Discrimination by race, sex, and ethnicity has not been eliminated from American life but is no longer substantially backed by the force of law.

Traditionally disadvantaged Americans have achieved fuller equality primarily as a result of their struggle for greater rights. The Supreme Court has been an important instrument of change for minority groups. Its ruling in *Brown v. Board of Education* (1954), which declared racial

segregation in public schools to be an unconstitutional violation of the Fourteenth Amendment's equal protection clause, was a major breakthrough in equal rights. Through its busing, affirmative action, and other rulings, the Court has also mandated the active promotion of integration and equal opportunities.

However, because civil rights policy involves large issues of social values and the distribution of society's resources, questions of civil rights are politically explosive. For this reason, legislatures and executives as well as the courts have been deeply involved in such issues, siding at times with established groups and sometimes backing the claims of underprivileged groups. Thus, Congress, with the support of President Lyndon Johnson, enacted the landmark Civil Rights Act of 1964; but Congress and recent presidents have been ambivalent about or hostile to busing for the purpose of integrating public schools.

In recent years, affirmative action programs, designed to achieve equality of result for African Americans, women, Hispanic Americans, and other disadvantaged groups, have become a civil rights battleground. Affirmative action has had the strong support of civil rights groups and has won the qualified endorsement of the Supreme Court but has been opposed by those who claim that it unfairly discriminates against white males. Busing is another issue that has provoked deep divisions within American society.

Key Terms

affirmative action
civil rights
comparable worth
de facto discrimination
de jure discrimination
equality of result
equal protection clause

equal rights
gender gap
intermediate-scrutiny test
reasonable-basis test
strict-scrutiny test
suspect classifications

Suggested Readings

Armor, David. *Forced Justice: School Desegregation and the Law.* New York: Oxford University Press, 1995. An evaluation that concludes that the federal courts have overstretched their legal mandate by requiring school integration rather than simply school desegregation.

Bergmann, Barbara A. *In Defense of Affirmative Action.* New York: Basic Books, 1997. An economist's analysis of affirmative action that concludes that policy is necessary for women and broadly beneficial to society.

Cherry, Robert, and William M. Rodgers III. *Prosperity For All?* Analysis of the economic circumstance of America's disadvantaged.

de la Garza, Rudolfo O., Louis DeSipio, F. Chris Garcia, John Garcia, and Angelo Falcon. *Latino Voices: Mexican, Puerto Rican, and Cuban Perspectives on American Politics.* Boulder, Colo.: Westview Press, 1992. A study of the opinions and behaviors of Hispanic Americans.

Fiss, Owen M. *A Community of Equals.* Boston: Beacon Press, 1999. An analysis of the constitutional protections afforded new immigrants.

Hochschild, Jennifer L. *Facing Up to the American Dream: Race, Class, and the Soul of the Nation.* Princeton, N.J.: Princeton University Press, 1995. A careful assessment of what is required of American society if its ideal of equal opportunity is to be realized.

Howard, John R. *The Shifting Wind.* Albany: State University of New York Press, 1999. A review of the Supreme Court and civil rights from Reconstruction to the *Brown* decision.

Kinder, Donald R., and Lynn M. Sanders. *Divided by Color: Racial Politics and Democratic Ideals.* Chicago: University of Chicago Press, 1996. An analysis of the factors that shape people's opinions on race and related issues.

McClain, Charles J. *In Search of Equality: The Chinese Struggle Against Discrimination in Nineteenth-Century America.* Berkeley: University of California Press, 1994. A careful study of how Chinese in nineteenth-century California used the legal system to fight racism and injustice.

Nagel, Joane. *American Indian Ethnic Renewal: Red Power and the Resurgence of Identity and Culture.* New York: Oxford University Press, 1996. Explores the meaning of activism for Native Americans' ethnic identification.

Reeves, Keith. *Voting Hopes or Fears? White Voters, Black Candidates, and Racial Politics in America.* New York: Oxford University Press, 1997. A critical assessment of race and politics in American society.

Skrentny, John David. *The Ironies of Affirmative Action: Politics, Culture, and Justice in America.* Chicago: University of Chicago Press, 1996. An empirical analysis of affirmative action and its impact.

Stavans, Hans. *The Hispanic Condition: Reflections on Culture and Identity in America.* New York: HarperPerennial, 1996. An analysis of the behavioral and cultural differences and similarities among the major Hispanic groups.

Walton, Hanes, Jr. *African American Power and Politics: The Political Context Variable.* New York: Columbia University Press, 1997. An incisive analysis of African-American politics.

Witt, Linda, Karen M. Paget, and Glenna Matthews. *Running as a Woman: Gender and Power in American Politics.* New York: Free Press, 1994. A careful analysis of the way women campaign, and how the process differs from the way men campaign.

PART TWO

Mass Politics

★ ★ ★

We are concerned about public affairs, but immersed in our private ones, Walter Lippmann wrote. Nevertheless, the integrity of the democratic process requires that citizens have significant opportunities to make their voices heard.

Citizens individually participate in public affairs, primarily through voting and by expressing opinions. Their influence is greatest, however, when they join together in common purpose. This joining comes through intermediaries such as political parties, interest groups, and the media.

The chapters in this section explore these avenues of citizen politics. Chapter 6 examines the way Americans think politically and the effect of their opinions on government. Chapter 7 describes the nature and impact of citizen participation. Chapters 8 and 9 look at parties, elections, and campaigns. Interest groups are the subject of Chapter 10, and the news media are addressed in Chapter 11.

All democracies depend on these instruments of popular influence, but the United States does so in relatively unique ways. For example, America's political parties are among the weakest in the world, while its interest groups and media are among the strongest. The consequences are significant. Political action enables Americans to make their voices heard, but the precise nature of this activity determines whose voices will be heard the loudest. ★

CHAPTER 6

Public Opinion and Political Socialization: Shaping the People's Voice

★

To speak with precision of public opinion is a task not unlike coming to grips with the Holy Ghost.

—V. O. Key Jr.[1]

★   ★   ★

When American bombs started falling on Serbia in 1999, most Americans were ill-equipped to pass judgment on what was happening. They had been hearing for months about the war between the Serbs and the ethnic Albanians in Serbia's Kosovo province, but polls indicated they had only a vague notion of what was at issue in the conflict. One poll found that most Americans were unable to say where Kosovo was located.

Surveys taken before the bombing began showed only limited support for U.S. involvement. Asked in a February 1999 Gallup poll whether they thought "the United States needs to be involved in Kosovo in order to protect its own interests," only 37 percent said that it did; 55 percent said it did not. An NBC News poll taken four months earlier showed that only a minority of Americans would support the bombing of Serb targets by the United States and its allies if Serb forces refused to end their aggressive action against the ethnic Albanians.

Once the bombs started falling, President Clinton went on national television to ask Americans to support the attack. He appealed to their conscience, saying that intervention was necessary to stop the "ethnic cleansing" campaign that the Serbs were waging in Kosovo. There was an eerie familiarity to the speech. Three years earlier, Clinton had made a similar speech in reference to air strikes aimed at deterring Serb aggression in Bosnia.

Public opinion quickly shifted. A *Newsweek* poll showed that 53 percent of Americans supported President Clinton's decision to commit U.S. jets and cruise missiles to the NATO operation. Within a few days, polls showed that more than 60 percent of Americans approved of the military intervention and less than 30 percent were opposed. The change occurred despite the public's worries about the outcome. In the *Newsweek* poll, 44 percent said they doubted that the NATO forces could avoid significant casualties, and 59 percent said the attacks were likely to result in a long-term U.S. military commitment in the region. They also believed that the air strikes would not stop Serbian aggression, and only 47 percent said they would support a decision to use U.S. ground troops against the Serbs.

The unfolding of the intervention in Serbia is a revealing example of the influence of public opinion on government. Public opinion rarely compels officials to follow a particular course of action. Clinton was not forced by public opinion to order U.S. planes to bomb Serbia, nor did public opinion erupt into widespread protest when he did. The public, somewhat reluctantly, was willing to follow Clinton's lead, at least until, and if, the conflict turned sour.

Public opinion has an important place in democratic societies because of the idea that democratic government springs from the will of the people.

U.S. soldiers have been deployed to the Balkans twice in recent years in an effort to stop Serb aggression in the region. Their deployment occurred despite the public's ambivalence about the policy.

However, public opinion is a far more elusive phenomenon than conventional wisdom suggests. It is widely assumed that there is a conclusive public opinion on major issues, but in fact, as the Kosovo situation illustrates, public opinion is seldom exact when it comes to questions of how to resolve policy problems. Political leaders typically have leeway in deciding a course of action. They may be held accountable by the public for the results, but the action itself is often theirs to choose.

This chapter discusses public opinion and its influence on the U.S. political system. A major theme is that public opinion is a powerful and yet inexact force in American politics. The policies of the U.S. government cannot be understood apart from public opinion; at the same time, public opinion is not a precise determinant of public policy. This apparent paradox is explained by the fact that *self-government* in a large and complex country requires a division of labor between the public and its representatives. The result is a government that is tied only loosely to its public and a public that ordinarily affects only the general direction of its government. The main points made in this chapter are the following:

★ *Public opinion consists of those views held by ordinary citizens that are openly expressed.* Public officials have many means of gauging public opinion but increasingly have relied on public opinion polls to make this determination.

★ *The process by which individuals acquire their political opinions is called political socialization.* This process begins during childhood, when, through family and school, Americans acquire many of their basic political values and beliefs. Socialization continues into adulthood, during which peers, political institutions and leaders, and the news media are major influences.

Public opinion includes contradictory elements. According to surveys, for example, most Americans say they want lower taxes but also say they want more public services. At a Boston rally, this demonstrator expresses his anger with President Clinton's tax-increase legislation while also demanding that government provide free health care.

★ *Americans' political opinions are shaped by several frames of reference. Four of the most important are ideology, group attachments, partisanship, and political culture.* These frames of reference form the basis for political consensus and conflict among the general public.

★ *Public opinion has an important influence on government but ordinarily does not directly determine what officials will do.* Public opinion works primarily to impose limits and directions on the choices made by officials.

The Nature of Public Opinion

Public opinion is a relatively new concept in the history of political ideas. Not until democracy arose in the eighteenth century did the need arise to take full account of what the people were thinking on political issues. Although the pre-democratic theorist Machiavelli warned that rulers who ignored the people's interests risked assassination and popular unrest, his notion of the public's influence was a far cry from the democratic idea of government as being of and for the people.[2] Public opinion today is central to the practice of democratic government.

WHAT IS PUBLIC OPINION?

Today, *public opinion* is a widely used term. It is typically applied in ways that suggest that the people have a common set of concerns. In fact, it is not very meaningful to lump all citizens together as if they constituted a single coherent public.[3] There is, to be sure, an occasional issue of such power and breadth that it captures the attention of nearly all citizens. The large majority of issues, however, attracts the attention of some citizens but not others.

There are a great many issues in which there is literally no majority opinion. Agricultural conservation programs are a matter of intense concern to farmers but of little interest to city dwellers. In such situations, a form of *pluralist* democracy usually prevails: government responds to the views of the intense minority. In still other cases, *elitist* opinion prevails. On the question of U.S. relations with Madagascar, for example, there is little likelihood of a popular constituency that knows or cares what the federal government does. In such instances, the policy opinions of an elite group of business and policy leaders ordinarily prevail. *Majority* opinion, to the degree it governs policy, is normally confined to those few, broad issues that elicit widespread attention and concern, such as social security and employment. Although this situation may suggest a limited role for popular majorities, such issues, although few in number, typically have the most impact on society as a whole.

Hence, any definition of the term *public opinion* cannot be based on the assumption that all citizens, or even a majority, are actively interested and have a preference about all aspects of political life. **Public opinion** can be defined as those opinions held by ordinary citizens that they are willing to express openly.[4] This expression need not be verbal. It could also take the form, for example, of a protest demonstration or a vote for one candidate rather than another. The crucial point is that a person's private thoughts on an issue become public opinion when expressed openly.

public opinion Those opinions held by ordinary citizens that they express openly.

People's willingness to express their opinions forcefully can affect the outcome of political conflict. Polls taken during the Vietnam War, for example, indicated that, until that last stage of the conflict, a majority of Americans supported the war effort. Yet, of the demonstrators who took to the streets to express their opinions, the vast majority opposed U.S. policy. The Nixon administration used the phrase "silent majority" to refer to those citizens who backed the war but were not publicly heard. In the end, they probably had less influence on Vietnam policy than the vocal demonstrators whom they far outnumbered.

WHAT ROLE SHOULD PUBLIC OPINION PLAY?

A fundamental principle of democracy is that the people's view ought to be the foundation of government. No true democrat, past or present, would reject the idea that a just government rests on the consent of the governed or that the people are in some sense the ultimate source of governing wisdom and strength.[5] Nevertheless, there has always been widespread disagreement about the exact role that public opinion should play in the formulation of public policy.

At one extreme are those analysts who claim that it would be foolish to base policy decisions on whatever the people happen to think at the time. One such analyst, Robert Nisbet, says the idea that "public opinion must somehow govern, must therefore be incessantly studied, courted, flattered and drawn upon . . . is the great heresy . . . of modern democracies." Nisbet claims that government has an obligation to respond only to the enduring and fundamental beliefs that citizens share as members of an ongoing political community. He labels these beliefs "public opinion" and distinguishes them from "popular opinion," which he defines as the transitory thoughts that citizens express on topical issues in the

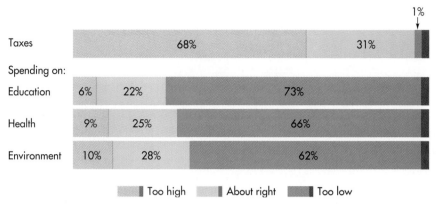

Too high ▮ About right ▮ Too low

FIGURE 6-1 Opinions on Taxing and Spending
People's opinions can be contradictory. Americans say, for example, that taxes are too high and yet also say, when asked about specific policy areas, that government is spending too little. *Used by permission of National Opinion Research Center, University of Chicago.*

polls.[6] Nisbet's view stems from the classical liberal tradition that influenced the *Federalist Papers* (see Chapter 2). James Madison distinguished between the public's momentary passions and its enduring concerns, arguing that government is obliged to represent only the public's "true interest."[7]

In contrast, other analysts contend that almost any opinion held by ordinary citizens—whether stable or fleeting, reasoned or emotional—should be taken into account by government. George Gallup, who founded the public opinion polling industry in the United States, promoted this view. He believed that leaders should be closely in tune with the citizenry. "In a democracy," Gallup said, "the task of the leader is to decide how best to achieve the goals set by the people."[8] Gallup's view belongs to the tradition of the Jacksonian and Progressive movements (see Chapters 2 and 8), which were based on a strong faith in the judgment of ordinary citizens and a deep skepticism toward governing elites.

Most Americans today share Gallup's view: they want government to act in accordance with their views and are disenchanted when they believe government is ignoring public opinion. There are, however, several practical obstacles to government by public opinion in all instances. The most apparent reason is that people have differing opinions; in responding to one side of an issue, government is compelled to reject other preferences. Public opinion is also contradictory in many cases. Polls indicate, for example, that Americans would like better schools, health care, and other public services while they also favor a reduction in taxes (see Figure 6-1). A significant increase in the quantity and quality of social services cannot be accomplished without additional taxes. Which opinion of the people should govern—their desire for more services or their desire for lower taxes?

HOW INFORMED IS PUBLIC OPINION?

Another limitation on the role of public opinion is the public's relatively low level of political information. Some citizens pay close attention to politics, but most do not. As a result, most people are poorly informed about politics.[9]

Most citizens would "flunk" a current affairs test. In 1994, a Times Mirror survey asked a cross-section of Americans five questions on people and events that were currently at the top of the news. Only 6 percent of the respondents answered all five questions correctly, and 9 percent knew four answers; 37 percent

HOW THE UNITED STATES COMPARES

CITIZENS' AWARENESS OF PUBLIC AFFAIRS

Americans' knowledge of public affairs is relatively low. Although most citizens say they follow the news regularly or often, they are not very attentive to what they see and hear. Even the simplest facts sometimes elude the average citizen's grasp. A Gallup poll found, for example, that a third of Americans were unable to name the vice president of the United States.

Low levels of public information are characteristic of most countries, but by some indicators Americans rank lower than do citizens of other western democracies. In a multicountry (including U.S.) survey conducted in 1994 by the Times Mirror Center for the People and the Press, Americans ranked next to last in terms of their ability to respond correctly to five questions about world leaders

and events. Americans did their best on a question that asked them to name the president of Russia: 50 percent said Boris Yeltsin, but this total was far lower than the 94 percent of Germans who named Yeltsin. Americans had difficulty with the question that asked them to name the country that was threatening to withdraw from the nuclear nonproliferation treaty: only 22 percent correctly said Korea or North Korea compared with 45 percent of Germans. In light of America's leading role in the world, its citizens might be expected to be uniquely well informed about international affairs. However, they are less knowledgeable in this area than are Europeans, who live in closer proximity to other countries and who thus may be more attentive to world politics.

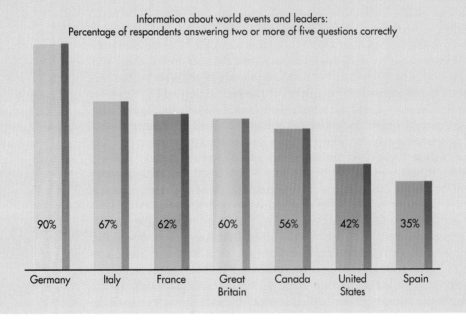

Information about world events and leaders:
Percentage of respondents answering two or more of five questions correctly

Germany	Italy	France	Great Britain	Canada	United States	Spain
90%	67%	62%	60%	56%	42%	35%

could answer none of the questions, and 21 percent answered only one question correctly. In other words, a majority of citizens knew little or nothing when asked relatively simple questions about world developments. (Citizens in several other countries were asked the same five questions; the results are summarized in "How the United States Compares.")

Although people with lower education levels are more likely to be uninformed, many college-educated people also lack basic information. A survey of Ivy League students found that a third could not identify the British prime minister, half could not name both U.S. senators from their state, and three-fourths could not identify Abraham Lincoln as the author of the phrase, "a government of the people, by the people, and for the people."[10]

The public's lack of information is not as significant a factor as might seem the case. Citizens do not necessarily have to be well informed about a situation to have a reasonable opinion about it. Opinions stem more from people's general beliefs, values, and policy orientations than from precise information about policy alternatives. Many people's opinions on the abortion issue, for example, derive from deep-seated religious beliefs. The fact that most individuals have only a foggy notion of Supreme Court rulings on the abortion issue does not make their opinions any less relevant. Similarly, people can have a considered view of how the United States should respond to foreign aggression without a detailed knowledge of the globe or top foreign leaders.

Nevertheless, the public's lack of information restricts the role it can play in policy disputes. Public opinion can direct government toward certain goals, but it rarely provides a detailed guide to the way these goals are to be accomplished. The choice of one course of action over another requires knowledge of the likely consequences of the various alternatives. The average citizen often lacks this knowledge.

The Measurement of Public Opinion

Woodrow Wilson once said he had spent nearly all of his adult life in government and yet had never seen a "government." What Wilson was saying, in effect, was that government is a system of relationships. A government is not a building or a person; it is not tangible in the way that a car or a bottle of soda is. So it is with public opinion. No one has ever seen a "public opinion," and thus it cannot be measured directly. It must be assessed indirectly.

A time-honored method of interpreting public opinion is election returns. The vote is routinely interpreted by the press and politicians as an indicator of the public's mood—whether liberal or conservative, angry or satisfied, quiet or intense. When the Republicans piled up huge gains in the House and Senate in the 1994 congressional elections, pundits labeled it an angry backlash against government and the Democrats, who were in control of Congress and the presidency.

Letters to the editor in newspapers, e-mail messages to elected officials, and the size of crowds at mass demonstrations are other means of judging public opinion. Yet another device is the activity of lobbyists, who bring the concerns of their constituents to government's attention.

All these indicators of public opinion are important and deserve the attention of those in power. These indicators, however, have shortcomings as a guide to what is on the minds of the people. Elections offer the people only a yes-or-no choice between candidates, and different voters will make the same choice for quite different reasons. The winning candidate may claim that the public has based its choice on a particular issue or inclination, but election returns almost always mask a much more complex reality. As for letter writers and demonstrators, they are not at all representative of the general population. Less than 1 percent of Americans participate each year in a mass demonstration, and fewer than 10 percent write to the president or a member of Congress. Studies have found that the views of letter writers and demonstrators are more intense and more extreme than those of other citizens.[11]

★ CRITICAL THINKING ★

WHAT'S YOUR OPINION?

Forming Opinions Without Information
The level of the public's knowledge about some policy issues is shockingly low. How does this situation affect the public discussion of policy problems? What circumstances affect whether a citizen is likely to possess much factual information about a policy issue? Can you think of an issue about which a citizen could have a thoughtful opinion without having much information? How important in general do you think it is for citizens to have substantial information when forming their opinions on policy issues?

PUBLIC OPINION POLLS

In an earlier day, such indicators as elections and letters to the editor were the only means by which public officials could gauge what the public was thinking. Today, they can also rely on polls or surveys, which provide a more systematic method of estimating public sentiment.

public opinion poll   A device for measuring public opinion whereby a relatively small number of individuals (the sample) are interviewed for the purpose of estimating the opinions of a whole community (the population).

In a **public opinion poll,** a relatively few individuals—the **sample**—are interviewed in order to estimate the opinions of a whole **population,** such as the students of a college, the residents of a city, or the citizens of a country. If a sufficient number of individuals are chosen at random, their views will tend to be representative—that is, roughly the same as the views held by the population as a whole.

How is it possible to measure the thinking of a large population on the basis of a relatively small sample? How can interviews with, say, one thousand Americans provide a reliable estimate of what 250 million are thinking? The answer is found in the theory of probability. Opinion sampling is based on the mathematical laws of probability, which can be illustrated by the hypothetical example of a huge jar filled with a million marbles, half of them red and half of them blue. If a blindfolded person reaches into the jar, the likelihood of selecting a marble of a given color is fifty-fifty. And if one thousand marbles are chosen in this random way, it is likely that about half of them will be red and half will be blue.

sample   In a public opinion poll, the relatively small number of individuals who are interviewed for the purpose of estimating the opinions of an entire population.

population   In a public opinion poll, the people (for example, the citizens of a nation) whose opinions are being estimated through interviews with a sample of these people.

sampling error   A measure of the accuracy of a public opinion poll. The sampling error is mainly a function of sample size and is usually expressed in percentage terms.

The accuracy of a poll is usually expressed in terms of **sampling error,** which indicates the likelihood that the responses of the sample accurately represent the view of the population. As would be expected, the larger the size of the sample, the greater the likelihood that the sample's opinions will accurately reflect those of the population. Thus, the larger the sample is, the smaller the sampling error is (see Figure 6-2).

FIGURE 6-2   Relationship Between Sample Size and Sampling Error
The larger a poll's sample is, the smaller is the error in estimating the population from which the sample is taken. These figures are based on a 95 percent confidence level, which means that for a given sample size (e.g., 600), the chances are 19 in 20 (95 percent) that the sample will produce results that are within the sampling error (e.g., ±4 percent) of the results that would have been obtained if the whole population had been interviewed.

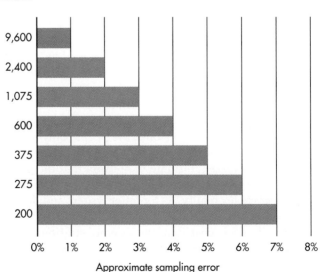

President Harry Truman holds up the early edition *Chicago Tribune* with the headline "Dewey Defeats Truman." The *Tribune* was responding to analysts' predictions that Dewey would win the 1948 election. Dewey's loss aside, the Gallup poll has correctly predicted all presidential election outcomes since 1936.

Many people assume that a poll of the United States, with its 250 million people, must have a much larger sample to achieve the same level of accuracy as, say, a poll of Massachusetts or Arizona. In fact, the mathematics of polling are such that sample size is the critical factor. Thus, a sample of one thousand people will have nearly the same level of accuracy whether the population is that of the nation, a state, or a large city.

A properly drawn sample of one thousand individuals has a sampling error of about plus or minus 3 percent, which is to say that the proportions of the various opinions expressed by the people in the sample are likely to be within 3 percent of those of the whole population. For example, if 55 percent of a sample of one thousand respondents say that they intend to vote for the Republican candidate for president, then the chances are high that 52 to 58 percent (55 percent plus or minus 3 percent) of the whole population plan to vote for the Republican.

The impressive record of the Gallup poll in predicting the outcomes of presidential elections indicates that the theoretical accuracy of polls can be matched in practice. For example, the Gallup poll predicted a 52 to 41 percent victory for Bill Clinton over Bob Dole in 1996. The actual margin was 49 to 41. The Gallup organization has erred badly only once: it stopped polling several weeks before the 1948 election and missed a late trend that carried Harry Truman to victory over Thomas E. Dewey.

PROBLEMS WITH POLLS

Mathematical estimations of poll accuracy require a **probability sample**—a sample in which each individual in the population has a known probability of being selected at random for inclusion. In practice, pollsters can only approximate this ideal. Because pollsters rarely have a list of all individuals in a population from which to draw a random sample, they usually base their sample on telephones or locations. Random-digit telephone sampling is the most commonly used technique. Pollsters use computers to pick random telephone numbers, which

probability sample A sample for a poll in which each individual in the population has a known probability of being selected randomly for inclusion in the sample.

CURRENT CONTROVERSIES

SHOULD THE CENSUS BE CONDUCTED BY STATISTICAL SAMPLING?

Every ten years there is a census of the American population for the purpose of apportioning congressional seats among the states. The census has always been conducted by an actual head count of Americans. This procedure results in an undercounting of hard-to-reach groups, including certain minorities, children, and renters. Because these groups are not evenly distributed across the country and within states, the undercount affects how House district boundaries are drawn and can even affect a state's representation in Congress. Undercounting is severe in New York City and Los Angeles, for example, and might even deprive New York and California of House seats. Accordingly, some people have argued that the census should use polls to obtain population estimates that would be closer to the true population of each state than can be obtained through an actual head count. This procedure has been opposed on political grounds: because the groups that are undercounted tend to vote Democratic, Republican lawmakers have been reluctant to endorse the procedure. When the Clinton administration decided to use statistical sampling for the 2000 census, the Republican majority in the House of Representatives took the issue to court. In *Department of Commerce v. U.S. House of Representatives* (1999), the Supreme Court ruled against statistical sampling. Justice Sandra Day O'Connor, a Republican appointee, wrote the Court's majority decision. Justice Stephen Breyer, a Democratic appointee, wrote a dissenting opinion.

YES: Any special emphasis the Census Bureau might place on including racial and minority neighborhoods among its samples would be justified as an effort to ensure proper counts among groups that history shows have been undercounted. . . . I note that the Census Bureau has never relied exclusively upon headcounts to determine population. [It] has supplemented its headcounts with imputation to some degree for at least the last 50 years. [The Census Act] could not have been intended as a prohibition so absolute as to stop the Census Bureau from imputing the existence of a living family behind the closed doors of an apparently occupied house, should the family refuse to answer the bell. Similarly, I am not convinced that the Act prevents the use of sampling to ascertain the existence of a certain number of the families that fail to mail back their census forms.

—Justice Stephen Breyer

NO: The Constitution's Census Clause authorizes Congress to direct an "actual enumeration" of the American public every 10 years. . . . Pursuant to this authority, Congress has enacted the Census Act [which] provides: "Except for the determination of population for purposes of apportionment . . . , the Secretary [of Commerce] shall, if he considers it feasible, authorize the use of . . . statistical . . . "sampling" in carrying out the [census]. . . . Absent any historical context, the "except/shall" sentence structure . . . might reasonably be read as either permissive or prohibitive. However, the section's interpretation depends primarily on the broader context in which that structure appears. Here, the context is provided by over 200 years during which federal census statutes have uniformly prohibited using statistical sampling for congressional apportionment.

—Justice Sandra Day O'Connor

are then dialed by interviewers to reach respondents. Because the computer is as likely to pick one telephone number as any other and because 95 percent of U.S. homes have a telephone, a sample selected in this way is usually assumed to be representative of the population.

Some polls are not based on probability sampling. For example, news reporters sometimes conduct "people-in-the-street" interviews to obtain individual responses to political questions. Although a reporter may imply that the views of those interviewed are representative of the general public's view, there is a fallacy in this reasoning. The sample will be biased by where and when the reporter chooses to conduct the interviews. For example, interviews conducted on a downtown street at the noon hour will include a disproportionate number of business employees who are taking their lunch breaks. Housewives, teachers, factory workers, and farmers are among the many groups that would be underrepresented in such a sample.

Polls can also be misleading if they include poorly worded questions. A 1992 Roper study received widespread attention when it indicated that more than a fifth of the American public had doubts about whether the Nazi extermination of the Jews actually happened. The *San Francisco Chronicle* described these individuals as "willfully stupid."[12] However, the poll was subsequently criticized for its use of a double-negative question: "Does it seem possible or does it seem impossible to you that the Nazi extermination of the Jews never happened?" Research has shown that double-negative questions confuse respondents. The Gallup organization did a follow-up poll in which half of the respondents were asked the original form of the Roper question and the other half were asked: "Do you doubt that the Holocaust actually happened or not?" In response to the straightforward question, only 9 percent of the respondents (as compared with 33 percent of those asked the double-negative version) expressed doubt about the Holocaust, a clear indication that the form of the Roper question had misled respondents.[13]

Despite these and other sources of error, the poll or survey has become the most relied-upon method of measuring public opinion. More than one hundred organizations are in the business of conducting public opinion polls. Some, like the Gallup organization, conduct polls that are then released to the news media by syndication. Most large news organizations also have their own in-house polls; one of the foremost of these is the CBS News/New York Times poll, which conducts about fifteen surveys annually for use in the *Times* and on CBS's newscasts. Finally, there are polling firms that specialize in conducting surveys for candidates and officeholders.

www.mhhe.com/patterson5

Simulation

CHARACTERISTICS OF PUBLIC OPINION

Polls provide information about public opinion, which must then be summarized if it is to be readily interpreted. It is not enough to interview hundreds or thousands of people; it is necessary also to describe their responses in a systematic way.

The most common way of describing poll results is in terms of *direction,* which is a measure of whether opinion on a particular question is favorable (positive) or unfavorable (negative). A recent Time/CNN poll asked respondents whether they would "favor or oppose building more prisons even if your taxes would be raised significantly." The direction of opinion favored the building of prisons; 60 percent supported this approach to crime and 35 opposed it. Opinions can also be described in terms of *intensity,* which is a measure of the strength of a particular opinion. A person may, for example, favor the building of more prisons but not feel very strongly about it. Another person may hold the same opinion intensely and express anger that more criminals are not behind bars. *Stability* is yet another characteristic of opinions. It refers to whether an opinion is relatively stable or changes over time. Majority opposition in the early 1970s to the death penalty, for example, proved to be unstable. By 1975, a majority was in favor of capital punishment, and support for it has stabilized since then. A recent Harris survey, for instance, indicated that 67 percent of Americans favor "expanding the number of crimes to which the death penalty would apply."

These characteristics affect the degree of attention that particular opinions are likely to receive from government. Opinions of high intensity or one-sided direction tend to get more attention than low-intensity or divided ones. Similarly, officials are generally more responsive to intensely held or stable opinions than to weakly held or fleeting ones.

Political Socialization: How Americans Learn Their Politics

Analysts have long been interested in the process by which public opinion is formed. A century ago James Bryce proposed that opinion formation takes place in stages, beginning with the public's first impression of an issue, continuing through a period of public deliberation on the issue, and concluding with a public action—such as the enactment of legislation—that settles the issue.[14] Analysts now know that the process of opinion formation is far more varied and haphazard than Bryce believed. Citizens arrive at their opinions by any number of routes, most of them quite casual and unreflective and many of them involving elaborate psychological defense mechanisms.

political socialization The learning process by which people acquire their political opinions, beliefs, and values.

The learning process by which people acquire their opinions, beliefs, and values is called **political socialization.** Just as a language, a religion, or an athletic skill is acquired through a learning process, so too are people's political orientations. Political beliefs are not drawn from a hat; they are acquired. Americans are socialized to see the political world in certain ways. For most Americans, the socialization process starts in the family with exposure to the political loyalties and opinions of the parents. The schools later contribute to the process, as do the mass media, friends, and other influences. Political socialization is thus a lifelong process.

THE PROCESS OF POLITICAL SOCIALIZATION

The process of political socialization in the United States has several major characteristics. First, although socialization continues throughout life, most people's political outlook is substantially influenced by their childhood learning. The **primacy tendency** refers to the fact that what is learned first is often lodged most firmly in one's mind.[15] Most people do not reflect deeply on how they acquired their political preferences. Basic ideas about race, gender, and political party, for example, are often formed uncritically in childhood, much in the way that belief in a particular religion, typically the religion of one's parents, is acquired.

primacy tendency The tendency for early learning to become deeply embedded in one's mind.

A second characteristic of political socialization is that it is cumulative. The **structuring tendency** refers to the tendency of earlier learning to structure later learning.[16] This tendency is less a function of age itself than of an accumulated attachment to particular ideas or values. Of course, the fact that the United States is a diverse and mobile society makes a basic change in a person's political views possible, especially when previous and current experiences are at odds with one another. However, individuals have psychological defense mechanisms that protect their ingrained beliefs; when faced with situations that might challenge their original views, they can readily muster reasons for clinging to them.

structuring tendency The tendency of earlier political learning to structure (influence) later learning.

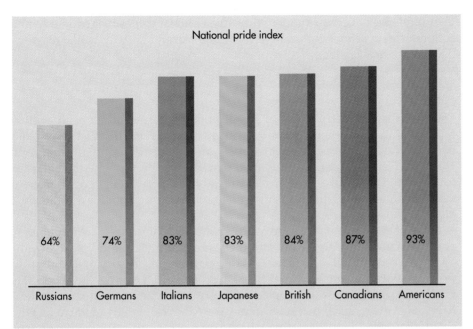

National pride index

Russians	Germans	Italians	Japanese	British	Canadians	Americans
64%	74%	83%	83%	84%	87%	93%

FIGURE 6-3 National Pride Compared with other people, Americans have a very high level of national pride, as indicated by this ten-item index that was based on measures such as people's pride in their nation's political, economic, artistic, sporting, scientific, and other achievements. *Source: Based on International Social Survey Program data in Pippa Norris, "Australian Democracy in Comparative Perspective," in Marion Sawer, ed., The People's Choice (Melbourne, Australia: Allen & Unwin, 2000).*

It is the unusual individual who can step away from the way in which he or she has learned to see the world and see it differently. Dramatic political transformation is uncommon, and when it has occurred on a large scale, it has nearly always been preceded by an extraordinary event that has shaken people out of their complacency. In such instances, it is usually younger adults who are more responsive. Their beliefs are less firmly rooted in past experiences and are therefore more easily changed. The **age-cohort tendency** holds that a significant break in the pattern of political socialization is almost always concentrated among younger citizens. President Franklin Roosevelt's New Deal initiatives, which sought to alleviate the economic hardship of the Great Depression, resulted in a substantial increase in Democratic loyalists among first-time voters, but not among habitual ones.

A noteworthy characteristic of political socialization in the United States is that it is relatively casual. It is not the rigid program of indoctrination that some societies impose on their people. Nevertheless, Americans receive a thorough political education. Their country's values are impressed upon them by every medium of communication: newspapers, daily conversations, television, movies, books.[17] Most Americans believe they have the best governing system in the world; they also believe that their nation's history and achievements are unparalleled. Indeed, Americans have a level of national pride that exceeds that of nearly all other people (see Figure 6-3).

age-cohort tendency The tendency for a significant break in the pattern of political socialization to occur among younger citizens, usually as the result of a major event or development that disrupts preexisting beliefs.

THE AGENTS OF POLITICAL SOCIALIZATION

As has been noted, the socialization process takes place through a variety of influences, including family, schools, peers, mass media, and political leaders and events. It is helpful to consider briefly some ways in which these so-called **agents of socialization** affect the opinions that people have. Although these agents will be discussed separately, it should be kept in mind that, by and large,

agents of socialization Those agents, such as the family and the media, that have a significant impact on citizens' political socialization.

their influences overlap. Many of the same political values that people acquire at home and in school, for example, are emphasized regularly by the mass media and political leaders.

Family

The family is a powerful agent of socialization because children begin with no political attitudes of their own and are likely to accept uncritically those of their parents. The family has a near-monopoly on the attention of the young child, who also places great trust in what a parent says. By the time the child is a teenager and is not likely to listen to any advice a parent might offer, many of the beliefs and values that will stay with the child throughout life are already in place.

Some of these orientations are overtly political. Many adults are Republicans or Democrats today largely because they accepted their parents' party loyalty. They now can give all sorts of reasons for preferring their party to the other. But the reasons come later in life; the loyalty comes first, during childhood. The family also contributes to basic orientations that, while not directly political, have political significance. For example, the American family tends to be more egalitarian than families in other nations, and American children often have a voice in family decisions. Such basic American values as equality, individualism, and personal freedom have their roots in patterns of family interaction.[18]

Opinions on specific issues of public policy are less substantially influenced by childhood experiences.[19] And, of course, a critical event, such as the Great Depression or the Vietnam War, may intervene to disrupt family influences.

School

The school, like the family, has its major impact on children's basic political beliefs and values rather than on specific issues of policy. Teachers at the elementary level describe the exploits of national heroes such as George Washington, Abraham Lincoln, and Martin Luther King Jr. and extol the superiority of the country's economic and political systems.[20] Although students in the middle and high school grades may encounter a more critical perspective in the classroom, they are more likely to receive a fabled version of the country's history and politics (see Chapter 1). U.S. schools are probably more instrumental in building support for the nation than are the schools in other democracies. The Pledge of Allegiance, which is recited daily in many U.S. schools, has no equivalent in European countries. Schools also contribute to Americans' sense of social equality. Most American children, regardless of family income, attend public schools and study a fairly standard curriculum. In many countries, even some in Europe, children are segregated by class in the schools they attend and, once in school, take courses that prepare some of them for manual labor and others for a university education.

America's colleges and universities also have a socializing effect. The sense of a citizen's obligations—to vote, to be active in community affairs, to take an interest in political news—is stronger among college-educated people than among people with less education. Support for individual rights, such as freedom of speech, is also stronger among this group. These tendencies are due in

Students in a North Carolina school reciting the Pledge of Allegiance. Such childhood socialization experiences can have a profound impact on an individual's basic political beliefs.

part to the direct effects of a college education; in the classroom and out, college students learn about and experience civic life. College-educated people are also likely to have more of the skills and contacts that promote political involvement, from which can flow consistent opinions. For example, freedom of expression, like other rights, is prized most highly by those citizens who make active use of it.

Peers

Members of peer groups—friends, neighbors, and co-workers—tend to have similar political views. Belonging to a peer group usually reinforces what a person already believes. One reason is that most people trust the views of their friends and associates. In addition, because members of a peer group share many of the same socializing experiences, they often think along the same lines, with the result that contradictory opinions are not often voiced within the group.

Many individuals are also unwilling to deviate too far from what their peers think. In her book *The Spiral of Silence,* Elisabeth Noelle-Neumann contends that most individuals want to conform and are reluctant to speak out against a dominant opinion, particularly when the issue contains a strong moral component. The effect, she argues, is to make a prevailing opinion appear to be much stronger than it actually is, which can lead public officials to give it more attention than it may deserve.[21]

Mass Media

The mass media are another powerful socializing agent. The media's influence, although diffuse and difficult to measure, is nonetheless substantial. While experts disagree, for example, on the extent to which violence on television

Arizona Senator John McCain, activist Gary Bauer, and Texas governor George W. Bush participate in a televised debate during the 2000 GOP nominating race. The media are an important agent of political socialization.

contributes to the rising level of violence in American society, few hold it entirely blameless.

The media's socializing influence is also felt through its news coverage. Studies indicate that the way in which news stories are "framed" affects people's political perceptions.[22] For example, the public responds more favorably to presidential candidates when they are portrayed as leaders of a political coalition rather than as vote-seeking tacticians. In recent elections, the press has tended to frame candidates in the context of strategic manipulation, with the result that the public thinks less highly of the candidates than it did at an earlier time. (The media's influence is examined more fully in Chapter 11.)

Political Leaders and Political Institutions

People look to political leaders and institutions, particularly the presidency and the political parties, as guides to opinion. The level of public approval of a nuclear arms limitation agreement with the USSR rose in 1987 after President Ronald Reagan endorsed the idea. In broader terms, political leaders play a significant role in shaping political debate and opinion through the symbols and slogans they use.[23]

Their ability to mold opinion, however, has limits. When President Bill Clinton in 1993 proposed to Congress a policy that would have given nearly every American either government- or employer-provided health care, his plan quickly gained the support of 70 percent of the public. Within a year, however, support for the plan had fallen below 40 percent. Opponents had convinced most Americans that the plan was too complicated and too costly and that it would jeopardize both the quality of their medical care and their access to a personal physician. Support for the plan was so weak that it did not even come up for a floor vote in either the House or Senate.

As the Clinton health plan illustrates, people look to leaders for guidance but tend to judge the options in the context of their own lives and values. In the end, Clinton's plan was not supported by most Americans because it conflicted with their view of how medical care should be provided. (Chapters 8, 13, and

15 discuss further the impact of political leaders and institutions on public opinion.)

Churches

From the seventeenth-century Puritans to today's Islamic Nation, churches have been a powerful force in shaping Americans' basic social opinions. Most Americans say they believe in God, most attend church regularly or at least occasionally, and most adhere to a religion that teaches beliefs about the proper nature of society. Moreover, most Americans believe that religion can provide answers to many of today's problems (see Figure 6-4). In all these respects, churches and religion are a more powerful force in the United States than in other Western societies.

Scholars have not studied the impact of church attendance and religious instruction on political socialization as closely as they have studied other influences, such as the schools and the media, but churches are an important source of politically relevant attitudes, including society's obligations to children, the poor, and the unborn. (The impact of religion is discussed further in a later section of this chapter.)

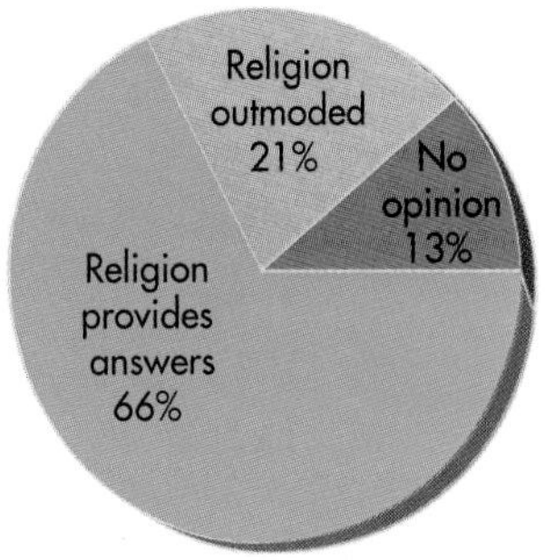

FIGURE 6-4 Opinions on Religion as an Answer to Today's Problems
Most Americans say that religion can answer all or most of today's problems; only a minority believe religion is old-fashioned and out of date. *Source: Gallup poll, March 17–19, 2000. Used with permission.*

Frames of Reference: How Americans Think Politically

What are the frames of reference that guide the political thinking of Americans? The question is important in at least two respects. First, the ways in which citizens think politically provide clues about the way in which public opinion is likely to affect government. The government in a democratic system is expected to act more often in accordance with public opinion than against it.

A second reason it is important to understand how the people think politically is that a shared frame of reference can bring citizens together in the pursuit of a common goal. The opinions of millions of Americans would mean almost nothing if each of these opinions were different from all the others. If enough people think the same way, however, they may be able to exert political power.

The subject of how Americans think politically fills entire books. Outlined here are four of the major frames of reference through which Americans evaluate political alternatives. The first tends to unite Americans; the other three give rise to differences of opinion among them.

CULTURAL THINKING: COMMON IDEAS

As was indicated in Chapter 1, Americans are unusual in their commitment to a common set of ideals that define the nature of the American political experience. Such principles as individualism, equality, and self-government have always meant somewhat different things to different people but nonetheless are a source of opinion consensus. For example, government programs aimed at redistributing wealth from the rich to the poor are common in western Europe but are less appealing for Americans, who have a deeper commitment to individualism.

There are limits, of course, to the degree to which Americans' basic beliefs shape their policy opinions. For nearly two centuries African Americans were inferior by law to white Americans, despite the American creed that "all men are created equal." Such inconsistencies speak to the all-too-human capacity to voice one idea and live another.

Nevertheless, Americans' political ideals are a powerful influence on public opinion. They affect the way in which disputes are argued and affect what people regard as reasonable and desirable. Americans' ideals serve to define the boundaries of acceptable political action and opinion (see Chapter 1).

IDEOLOGICAL THINKING: THE OUTLOOK FOR SOME

Commentators on public opinion in the United States often use such ideological words as *liberal* and *conservative* in describing how ordinary citizens think about political issues. In the early 1980s, for example, analysts spoke of "a conservative tide" that was supposedly sweeping the country and displacing the liberal trend that had dominated American politics for most of the preceding fifty years.

ideology A consistent pattern of opinion on particular issues that stems from a core belief or set of beliefs.

Liberal and *conservative* are ideological terms. So, too, are such terms as *populist, progressive, libertarian, communist,* and *fascist.* An **ideology** is a consistent pattern of opinion on particular issues that stems from a core or basic belief. Communism, for example, is rooted in a belief in material equality, and a communist therefore would be expected to support wage and welfare policies designed to spread wealth more evenly across society.

Although ideological terms are often used to describe mass publics, they do not accurately describe how most people think about politics.[24] Nearly everyone has basic beliefs that affect their opinions, but most people do not apply them consistently across a wide range of issues. They may say, for example, that they favor free trade among nations but then oppose it in particular cases where it works to the disadvantage of U.S. firms or workers. Research indicates that no more than a third of Americans, and perhaps as few as a tenth, have a pattern of opinions on issues that is consistent enough to be described as a manifestation of a true ideology.[25] Further, most Americans are relatively pragmatic in their political judgments. Rather than applying an ideological framework, Americans tend to judge policies by whether they appear to be working or seem likely to work.

Nevertheless, analysts sometimes find it useful to measure the public's ideological tendencies. A standard method is to ask survey respondents whether they think of themselves as liberal, moderate, or conservative. The problem with this approach is that, although people readily label themselves by these terms, many individuals are unable to say what the terms mean or provide inexact or inappropriate definitions. For this reason, pollsters have recently developed an alternative and less-direct method. They ask respondents two questions: Do you support or oppose an activist role for government in determining the distribution of economic benefits in society? and Do you support or oppose activist government as a means of promoting a particular set of social values? This method does not require that respondents know the meaning of ideological terms and yet provides a measure of people's general beliefs about government action in the broad areas of economic and social policy.

Responses to the two questions have been the basis for identifying four ideological types: conservatives, liberals, populists, and libertarians (see Figure 6-5).

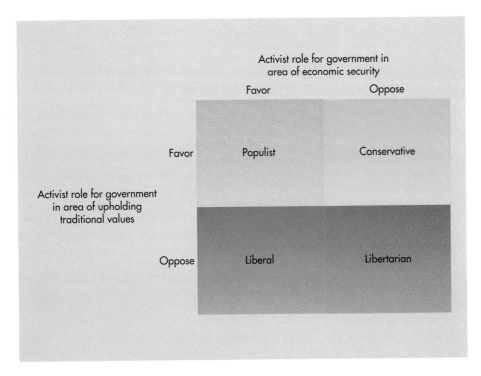

FIGURE 6-5   **Types of Ideologies**
Americans can be classified as liberals, conservatives, populists, or libertarians, depending on their attitudes toward the government's role in the areas of economic security and social values.

Conservatives are defined as individuals who oppose an activist role for government in providing economic benefits but look to government to uphold traditional social values. In contrast, **liberals** favor activist government as an instrument of economic redistribution but reject the notion that government should favor a particular set of social values. True liberals and conservatives could be expected to differ, for instance, on the issues of homosexual rights (a social values question) and government-guaranteed health care (an economic distribution question). Liberals would view homosexuality as a private issue and believe that government should ensure that everyone has access to adequate medical care. Conservatives would oppose government-mandated access to health care and favor government policies that actively discourage homosexual lifestyles. **Populists** are defined as individuals who share with conservatives a concern for traditional values but, like liberals, favor an active role for government in providing economic security. **Libertarians** are opposed to government intervention in both the economic and social spheres.

In sum, libertarians are the most committed to individual freedom, and populists are the most committed to government activism. Conservatives and liberals are committed to individual freedom in one area (the economic sphere for conservatives, the social sphere for liberals) but to government activism in the other (the social sphere for conservatives, the economic sphere for liberals). Of these ideological types, conservatives are the largest group. A Gallup poll, for example, estimated that 31 percent of Americans are conservatives, 24 percent are libertarian, 17 percent are populist, and 13 percent are liberal.[26] (See "Your Turn: What Is Your Ideology?")

conservatives   Those who emphasize the marketplace as the means of distributing economic benefits but look to government to uphold traditional social values.

liberals   Those who favor activist government as an instrument of economic security and redistribution but reject the notion that government should favor a particular set of social values.

populists   Those who favor activist government as a means of promoting both economic security and traditional values.

libertarians   Those who oppose government as an instrument of traditional values and of economic security.

☞ YOUR TURN

WHAT IS YOUR IDEOLOGY?

Most citizens do not have the structured and coherent belief system associated with a true ideology. However, most people do have opinions about traditional values and government activism, which can be used in describing their ideological tendency. To determine your ideology, at least as measured by pollsters, answer the following two survey questions (which are used by the Gallup organization in its surveys):

1. Some people think the government is trying to do too many things that should be left to individuals and businesses. Others think that government should do more to solve our country's problems. Which view is closer to your own?
   a. Government is doing too much
   b. Government should do more
2. Some people think that the government should promote traditional values in our society. Others think the government should not favor any particular set of values. Which view is closer to your own?
   a. Government should promote traditional values
   b. Government should not favor particular values

If you had been a respondent in a poll that asked these questions, you would have been classified as a *conservative* if you agreed with the first statement of each question (1a and 2a); a *liberal* if you agreed with the second statement of each question (1b and 2b); a *libertarian* if

you agreed with the first statement of the first question (1a) and the second statement of the second question (2b); and a *populist* if you agreed with the second statement of the first question (1b) and the first statement of the second question (2a).

You might ask yourself whether you have ever used the applicable label to describe yourself. You might also test whether your label corresponds with your opinions on particular issues (in other words, whether your general attitudes about government correspond with your attitudes in specific situations). For example, if your general and specific attitudes are consistent, you would support policies that protect the rights of homosexuals if you are a liberal or libertarian and oppose such policies if you are a conservative or populist. As another example, if your general and specific attitudes are consistent, you would back a greater role for government in providing health-care services to those who cannot afford such services if you are a liberal or populist and oppose a greater role if you are a conservative or libertarian. Are your general and specific attitudes consistent in these instances? If so, there is a likelihood that you have a true ideology in the sense that your opinions are structured and coherent. If your general and specific attitudes are not consistent, you are probably like most Americans—non-ideological in your beliefs.

GROUP THINKING: THE OUTLOOK OF MANY

An early study of ideology by Philip Converse indicated that groups are a more important reference for Americans than is ideology; subsequent studies have confirmed his finding.[27] Many Americans see politics through the lens of a group to which they belong or with which they identify. These individuals nearly always pay closer attention to issues that affect the group's interests than to more remote issues. Farmers, for example, are more likely to follow agricultural issues than they are labor-management issues. A group outlook is a source of both consensus and conflict. Farmers generally approve of government price supports for commodities; this opinion unites farmers but pits them against other groups, including consumers.

Because of the country's great size, settlement by various immigrant groups, and economic pluralism, Americans are a very diverse people. Later chapters will examine group tendencies more fully, but it is useful here to mention a few of the major group orientations: religion, class, region, race and ethnicity, gender, and age.

Two coal miners, one a man and the other a woman, break for lunch. Economic class affects Americans' opinions. The political views of most union members, for example, are more liberal than those of most Americans.

Religion

Religious differences have always been a source of solidarity within a group and conflict with outsiders. At an earlier time, religion was a bitterly divisive force as newly immigrant Catholics and Jews encountered widespread hostility and discrimination from entrenched Protestant groups. Today, Catholics, Protestants, and Jews share similar opinions on most policy issues.

Nevertheless, some important religious differences remain, although the opposing sides are not always the same. Fundamentalist Protestants and Roman Catholics oppose legalized abortion more strongly than do other Protestants and Jews. In contrast, on some welfare issues, such as food programs for the poor, Catholics and Jews are more supportive than are Protestants, especially those of fundamentalist beliefs. Such differences have at least a partial basis in religious beliefs. A belief in self-reliance, for example, is part of the so-called Protestant ethic. Attitudes on abortion are tied to religious beliefs about whether human life begins at conception or at a later stage in the development of the fetus.

The most powerful religious force in contemporary American politics is the so-called religious right, which consists primarily of individuals who see themselves as born-again Christians and view the Bible as the infallible truth. Their views on such issues as homosexual rights, abortion, and school prayer differ significantly from those of the population as a whole. A Time/CNN survey found, for example, that born-again Christians are 37 percent more likely than other Americans to agree that "the Supreme Court and the Congress have gone too far in keeping religious and moral values like prayer out of our laws, schools, and many areas of our lives."

Class

Economic class has less influence on political opinion in the United States than in Europe, but it is nevertheless related to opinions on certain economic issues. For example, lower-income Americans are more supportive of social welfare programs, business regulation, and progressive taxation than are those in higher-income categories. An obstacle to class-based politics in the United States is that people with similar incomes, but differing occupations, do not share the same opinions. Support for collective bargaining, for example, is substantially higher among factory workers than among small farmers, service workers, and those in the skilled crafts. The interplay of class and opinion will be examined more closely in Chapter 10, which discusses interest groups.

Region

Region has declined as a basis of political opinions. The increased mobility of the U.S. population has resulted in the relocation of millions of Americans from the Northeast and Midwest to the South and West. Their beliefs on issues such as social welfare tend to be more liberal than those of people who are native to these regions. Nevertheless, regional differences are still evident in the areas of social welfare, civil rights, and national defense. Conservative opinions on these issues are more prevalent in the southern and mountain states than elsewhere (see "States in the Nation").

Race and Ethnicity

Race and ethnicity, as Chapter 5 pointed out, have a significant influence on opinions. Whites and African Americans, for example, differ on issues of integration: black people are more in favor of affirmative action, busing, and other measures designed to promote racial equality and integration. Racial and ethnic groups also differ on many pocketbook issues, largely as a result of the differences in their economic situations: African Americans are more supportive of social welfare programs and government-backed job and training programs. The crime issue is another area where opinion differences are pronounced and predictable: minorities are less trusting of police and the judicial system. A 1999 poll conducted for the American Bar Association found, for example, that only 26 percent of non-whites believe that "law enforcement officials and police try to treat whites and minorities alike."

Gender

Although male-female differences of opinion are small on most issues, gender does affect opinion on some questions. Men and women have somewhat different views on issues such as abortion rights and affirmative action. The differences are even larger, however, in two other policy areas: social welfare and the use of force by the state.[28] Women are more supportive of government spending on social welfare (such as for education and poverty programs) and more opposed to state-sponsored force (for example, military power as an instrument of foreign policy). Some analysts have suggested that such differences reflect women's heightened sense of compassion and community responsibility. Men

★ STATES IN THE NATION

CONSERVATIVES AND LIBERALS

Nearly half of Americans describe themselves as moderates. Of the rest, the large majority are conservatives. According to a 1996 poll, liberals outnumber conservatives only in Massachusetts, Vermont, and the District of Columbia. The concentration of conservatives is especially high in the southern, plains, and mountain states where traditionalism and individualism are more widely embraced than in the coastal states of the northeast and west.

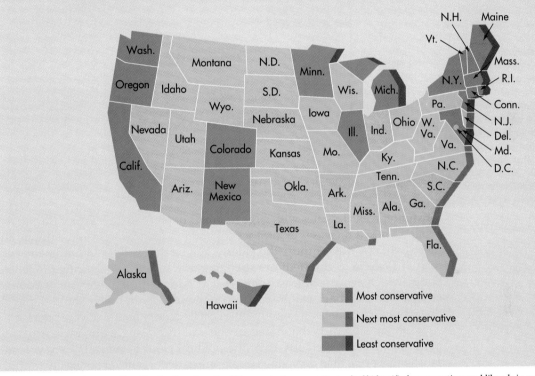

SOURCE: CNN exit polls, 1996. Classification based on the difference in the proportions of self-identified conservatives and liberals in each state.

are said to believe more strongly in self-reliance. In any case, women tend to hold more liberal views than men (see Figure 6-6). This difference is a factor in the *gender gap,* which was discussed in Chapter 5. (The politics of gender is discussed further in Chapters 8 and 14.)

Age

Another division of growing importance is the *age gap.* Young and old have always had somewhat divergent opinions as a consequence of differences in their ages and socialization experiences, but their disagreements are becoming greater. In her book *Young v. Old,* the political scientist Susan MacManus notes that the elderly tend to oppose increases in public school funding while supporting increases in social security and Medicare (government-assisted medical

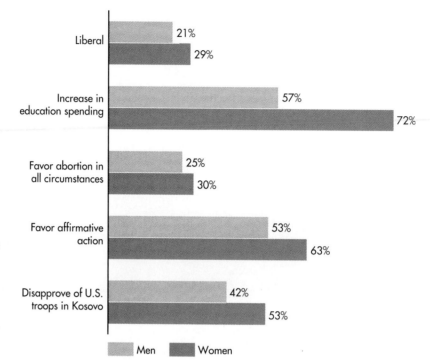

FIGURE 6-6 Gender and Opinion
Compared with men, women are less conservative, more supportive of social welfare services, and more opposed to the use of military force. *Sources (polls, from top to bottom): Gallup, 2000; Washington Post/ABC News, 2000; Gallup, 2000; Gallup, 2000; Washington Post/ABC News, 1999.*

care for retirees). In states with large numbers of retirees, such as Florida and Arizona, proposed increases in local school budgets are regularly voted down, and more than any other group, the elderly helped defeat Republican lawmakers' plan in 1995–96 to cut Medicare spending as a means of balancing the federal budget. Such acts are at least somewhat at odds with the interests of younger adults, who may have children in the public schools and who, through payroll deductions, pay the taxes that fund the social security and Medicare programs.[29]

MacManus predicts that issues of age will increasingly dominate American politics and that the elderly have the political clout to prevail. They vote at a much higher rate than do young people, are better organized politically (through groups such as the powerful American Association of Retired Persons), and are increasing in number as a result of lengthened life spans (the so-called graying of America). (The politics of age is also discussed in Chapters 10 and 18.)

Cross-Cutting Cleavages

Although group loyalties can have a powerful impact on people's opinions, their influence is diminished when identification with one group is offset by identification with other groups. In a pluralistic society such as the United States, groups tend to be "cross-cutting"—that is, each includes individuals from a range of other groups. Cross-cutting cleavages tend to produce moderate opinions. Faced with conflicting feelings arising out of identification with several groups, most people seek a balance between them when forming an opinion. However, in societies such as Northern Ireland where group loyalties are reinforcing rather than cross-cutting (Catholics tend to have much lower incomes, Protestants much higher ones), opinions are intensified by group

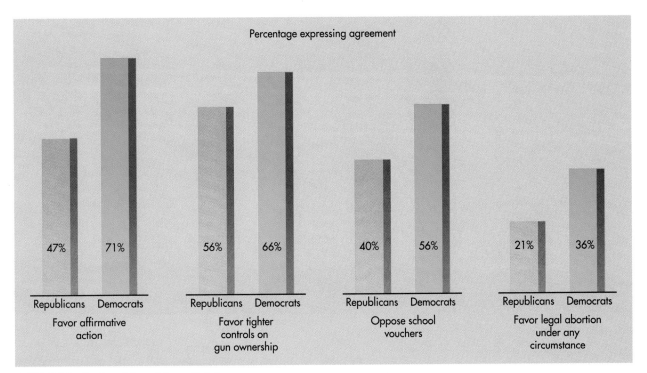

FIGURE 6-7 Partisanship and Issue Opinions
Republicans and Democrats differ significantly in their opinions on many policy issues. *Source: In order of questions: Washington Post/ABC News, 2000; Washington Post/ABC News, 1999; Gallup, 2000; Gallup, 2000.*

identifications and deep hatreds among the opposing camps can result. In America, Catholics and Protestants are not at each other's throats, largely because each group includes people of varying income, education, region, and so on. *Diversity* is a source of differences; it can also be a basis for harmony.

PARTISAN THINKING: THE LINE THAT DIVIDES

In the everyday play of politics, no source of opinion more clearly divides Americans than that of their partisanship. Figure 6-7 provides examples, but they indicate only a few of the differences. On nearly every major issue of economic, social, and foreign policy, Republicans and Democrats have views that are at least somewhat different. In many cases, such as spending programs for the poor, the differences are substantial.

Party identification refers to a person's ingrained sense of loyalty to a political party. Party identification is not formal membership in a party but instead an emotional attachment to a party—the feeling that "I am a Democrat" or "I am a Republican." Scholars and pollsters have typically measured party identification with a question of the following type: "Generally speaking, do you think of yourself as a Republican, a Democrat, an Independent, or what?" About 65 percent of adults call themselves Democrats or Republicans. Of the 35 percent who prefer the label "Independent," most say they lean slightly toward one party or the other.

party identification The personal sense of loyalty that an individual may feel toward a particular political party.

Vice President Al Gore speaks to Democratic activists during his 2000 presidential campaign. Many campaign activists have a strong party identification that was acquired through socialization in a family where one or both parents were strong partisans.

Early studies of party identification concluded that partisan attitudes were highly stable and seldom changed over the course of adult life.[30] Subsequent studies have shown that party loyalties are more fluid than originally believed.[31] Nevertheless, most adults do not switch their party loyalties easily, and a substantial proportion never waver from an initial commitment to a party, which can often be traced to childhood influences.

Once acquired, partisanship affects how people perceive and interpret events. When the independent counsel Kenneth Starr in September 1998 issued his report of impeachment charges in the Clinton-Lewinsky scandal, for example, the responses of Democrats, Independents, and Republicans differed sharply. A Gallup poll indicated that 87 percent of Democrats and 63 percent of Independents wanted Clinton to remain in office, but only 35 percent of Republicans expressed that opinion.

For most people, partisanship is not simply a blind faith in the party of their choice. Some Republicans and Democrats know very little about their party's traditions, policies, or group commitments, and they unthinkingly embrace its candidates. However, party loyalties are not randomly distributed across the population but follow a pattern that would be predicted from the parties' traditions. The Democratic party, for example, has been the driving force behind social welfare and workers' rights polices while the Republican party has been the spearhead for pro-business and tax reform policies. The fact that most union workers are Democrats and most businesspeople are Republicans is not mere coincidence. Their partisanship is rooted in their different life circumstances and the different policy traditions of the two parties.

Partisanship is obviously a strong force in American politics, but its influence is declining. In recent decades, the proportion of voters who identify with the Democratic or Republican party has declined and the proportion of Independents has increased. As a result, elections are more volatile than in the past.

People are less likely to vote on the basis of a long-standing party loyalty and more likely to base their choice on the issues and candidates of the moment. This and other issues of partisanship are examined in depth at various points later in this book, particularly in Chapters 7, 8, 9, 13, and 15.

The Influence of Public Opinion on Policy

Yet unanswered in the discussion is the central question about public opinion: What impact does it have on government?

The fundamental principle of democracy is that the people's view ought to prevail on public issues. This principle is difficult to put into practice. In any society of appreciable size, it is simply not possible for the people to directly formulate public policies and programs. However, democracy can be said to exist once officials take the public's views into account when making policy decisions and once the people have recourse to free and fair elections when they believe their opinions are being ignored.[32]

Some analysts argue that the public's views do not count for enough; the elites, it is claimed, are so entrenched and remote they pay little attention to the preferences of ordinary citizens.[33] The most comprehensive study ever conducted of the relationship between public opinion and policy, however, concluded otherwise. In a study spanning fifty years of trends, Benjamin Page and Robert Shapiro found a substantial relationship between changes in public opinion and subsequent changes in public policy, particularly on highly visible issues. More often than not, policy changed in response to opinion rather than the reverse. In addition, the more important the issue, the more likely that policy adapted to changes in public opinion. Page and Shapiro concluded that U.S. officials are reasonably responsive to public opinion.[34]

Not all scholars have interpreted the evidence on public opinion and policy so favorably,[35] but there is little question that the public's views do have an impact. Public opinion is rarely powerful enough to force officials into a specific course of action, but public opinion does serve as a guiding force in public policy. There are many actions, for example, that officials dare *not* take for fear of public retribution. No politician who wants to stay in office is likely to say, for example, that social security for the elderly should be abolished. And there are many actions that politicians willingly take in order to appeal to the public.[36] In late 1999, for example, the GOP-controlled Congress passed a budget that included funding to hire thousands of new public school teachers. Congressional Republicans had opposed the measure, but education ranked near the top in polls of Americans' policy priorities and the 2000 election was just around the corner. Republicans, reluctant to hand the Democrats a potent campaign issue, enacted the funding measure.

Such examples, however, do not provide an answer to the question of whether government is *sufficiently* responsive to public opinion. This question, as was discussed earlier in the chapter, is a normative one, the answer to which rests on assumptions about the proper relationship between people's everyday opinions and what government does. The question is also complicated by the fact that politics includes a battle over the control of public opinion. People's views are neither fixed nor simply a product of personal circumstances. Public

★ CRITICAL THINKING ★

WHAT'S YOUR OPINION?

Should Leaders Govern According to Opinion Polls? These days, public officials and candidates for public office routinely use public opinion polls to keep track of what the people are thinking. Some observers argue that polls contribute to effective government by keeping political leaders from getting too far out of line with the public's thinking.

Other observers claim that poll results cannot substitute for leadership. Noting that the mass public is usually poorly informed about policy issues, Walter Lippmann concluded that leaders must take the responsibility for devising workable policies that the public, in the long run, will accept.

What is your view on the use of polls in governing? Should leaders rely heavily on public opinion polls in making their governing decisions? Or should leaders mainly apply their own judgments of the public interest?

opinion is dynamic and can be changed, activated, and crystallized through political action.

In fact, one of the best indicators of the power of public opinion is the effort of political leaders to harness it in support of their goals. In American politics, popular demand for a policy is a powerful argument for that policy. For this reason and others, great effort is made to organize and represent public opinion through elections (Chapter 8), political parties (Chapter 9), interest groups (Chapter 10), the news media (Chapter 11), and political institutions (Chapters 12 to 17). Later chapters will also examine the direct impact of public opinion in particular policy areas: the economy (Chapter 18), social welfare (Chapter 19), and foreign affairs (Chapter 20).

www.mhhe.com/patterson5

Self-Quiz

Summary

Public opinion can be defined as those opinions held by ordinary citizens that they openly express. Public officials have many ways of assessing public opinion, such as the outcomes of elections, but have increasingly come to rely on public opinion polls. There are many possible sources of error in polls, and surveys sometimes present a misleading portrayal of the public's views. However, a properly conducted poll can provide an accurate indication of what the public is thinking and can dissuade political leaders from thinking that the views of the most vocal citizens (such as demonstrators and letter writers) are also the views of the broader public.

The process by which individuals acquire their political opinions is called political socialization. During childhood the family and schools are important sources of basic political attitudes, such as beliefs about the parties and the nature of the U.S. political and economic systems. Many of the basic orientations that Americans acquire during childhood remain with them in adulthood, but socialization is a continuing process. Major shifts in opinion during adulthood are usually the consequence of changing political conditions; for example, the Great Depression of the 1930s was the catalyst for wholesale changes in Americans' opinions on the government's economic role. There are also short-term fluctuations in opinion that result from new political issues, problems, and events. Individuals' opinions in these cases are affected by prior beliefs, peers, political leaders, and the news media. Events themselves are also a significant short-term influence on opinions.

The frames of reference that guide Americans' opinions include cultural beliefs, such as individualism, that result in a range of acceptable and unacceptable policy alternatives. Opinions can also stem from ideology, although most citizens do not have a strong and consistent ideological attachment. In addition, individuals develop opinions as a result of group orientations, notably religion, income, occupation, region, race, ethnicity, gender, or age. Partisanship is perhaps the major source of political opinions; Republicans and Democrats differ in their voting behavior and views on many policy issues. However, party loyalty has declined in importance in recent decades as a frame of reference for people's opinions.

Public opinion has a significant influence on government but seldom determines exactly what government will do in a particular instance. Public opinion serves to constrain the policy choices of officials. Some policy actions are beyond the range of possibility because the public will not accept change in existing policy or will not seriously consider policy that seems clearly at odds with basic American values. Evidence indicates that officials are reasonably attentive to public opinion on highly visible and controversial issues of public policy.

Key Terms

age-cohort tendency
agents of socialization
conservatives
ideology
liberals

libertarians
party identification
political socialization
population
populists

primacy tendency
probability sample
public opinion
public opinion poll

sample
sampling error
structuring tendency

Suggested Readings

Delli Carpini, Michael X., and Scott Keeter. *What Americans Know About Politics and Why It Matters.* New Haven, Conn.: Yale University Press, 1996. A synthesis of the American public's knowledge about politics.

Dunn, Charles W., and J. David Woodard. *The Conservative Tradition in America.* Lanham, Md.: Rowman & Littlefield, 1996. A study of the philosophical and political roots of conservatism from its origins to the present.

Jacobs, Lawrence, and Robert Shapiro. *Politicians Don't Pander.* Chicago: University of Chicago Press, 2000. An analysis that concludes politicians are not driven by polls.

Just, Marion R., Ann N. Crigler, Dean E. Alger, Timothy E. Cook, Montague Kern, and Darrell M. West. *Crosstalk: Citizens, Candidates, and the Media in a Presidential Campaign.* Chicago: University of Chicago Press, 1996. An exhaustive study of the factors that shape campaign information and how citizens use this information.

Lupia, Arthur, and Mathew D. McCubbins. *The Democratic Dilemma: Can Citizens Learn What They Need to Know?* New York: Cambridge University Press, 1998. An insightful analysis of the conditions under which citizens need information to make decisions.

MacManus, Susan A. *Young v. Old: Generational Combat in the Twenty-First Century.* Boulder, Colo.: Westview Press, 1996. A study of the emerging conflict in the political self-interest of younger and older Americans.

Noelle-Neumann, Elisabeth. *The Spiral of Silence.* 2d ed. Chicago: University of Chicago Press, 1993. An intriguing theory of how public opinion is formed and muted.

Stimson, James A. *Public Opinion in America,* 2d ed. Boulder, Colo.: Westview Press, 1999. A valuable overview of American public opinion.

Traugott, Michael W., and Paul J. Lavrakas. *The Voter's Guide to Election Polls,* 2d ed. Chatham, N.J.: Chatham House, 1999. A clear guide to survey methods and analysis with an emphasis on election polling.

Zaller, John R. *The Nature and Origins of Mass Opinion.* New York: Cambridge University Press, 1992. A superb analysis of the nature of public opinion.

CHAPTER 7

Political Participation and Voting: Expressing the Popular Will

★

We are concerned in public affairs, but immersed in our private ones.

—Walter Lippmann[1]

★ ★ ★

*A*t stake in the 2000 elections was control of the White House and Congress. Which party would have the leading voice on issues of education, health, welfare, and the environment? Which party would have the greater say in how America responded to the challenges and opportunities of the domestic and global economies? Which party would be entrusted with national security? With so much at stake, it might be thought that Americans would have been eager to cast their ballots for the party of their choice. But, in fact, roughly half of American adults did not vote in the 2000 elections. Despite a concerted get-out-the-vote campaign by the news media and public service groups, the number of people who did not vote was far greater than the number of votes the winning party received in either the presidential or congressional races.

Voting is a form of **political participation**—a sharing in activities designed to influence public policy and leadership. Political participation involves other activities in addition to voting, such as joining political parties and interest groups, writing to elected officials, demonstrating for political causes, and giving money to political candidates.

Democratic societies are distinguished by their emphasis on citizen participation. The concept of self-government rests on the idea that ordinary people have a right, even an obligation, to involve themselves in the affairs of state. A political system that claims to represent the public's interest is not necessarily a truly democratic system; citizens must also be given meaningful opportunities to participate in the process. From this perspective, the extent of political participation—how much and by whom—is a measure of how fully democratic a society is.[2]

The question of participation also extends to the reasons people are politically involved or not involved. It is one thing if political participation is like attendance at a rock concert, which is mostly a matter of individual taste and proximity, and quite another if participation is like attendance at an elite prep school, which is mostly a matter of social privilege. A democratic political system implies that society will not place substantial barriers in the way of those who want to participate. As we will see in this chapter, differences in the extent of political participation among Americans are explained by both individual and systemic factors, although the latter are more influential in the United States than in most other Western democracies. One result is that the participation rate in U.S. elections is less than that of other countries, particularly among citizens of lower income and less education. The major points made in this chapter are the following:

political participation   A sharing in activities designed to influence public policy and leadership, such as voting, joining political parties and interest groups, writing to elected officials, demonstrating for political causes, and giving money to political candidates.

★ *Voter turnout in U.S. elections is low in comparison with that of other democratic nations.* The reasons for this difference include the nature of U.S. election laws, particularly those pertaining to registration requirements and the scheduling of elections.

★ *Most citizens do not participate actively in politics in ways other than voting.* Only a small proportion of Americans can be classified as political activists.

★ *Most Americans make a sharp distinction between their personal lives and national life.* This attitude reduces their incentive to participate and contributes to a pattern of participation dominated by citizens with higher levels of income and education.

Voter Participation

suffrage   The right to vote.

At the nation's founding, **suffrage**—the right to vote—was restricted to property-owning males. Tom Paine ridiculed this policy in *Common Sense.* Observing that a man whose only item of property was a jackass would lose his right to vote if the jackass died, Paine asked, "Now tell me, which was the voter, the man or the jackass?" It was not until 1840 that all states extended suffrage to propertyless white males, a change made possible by their continued demand for the vote and by the realization on the part of the wealthy that the nation's abundance and openness were natural protections against an assault on property rights by the voting poor.

Women did not secure the vote until 1920, with the ratification of the Nineteenth Amendment. In the 1870s, Susan B. Anthony tried to vote in her hometown of Rochester, New York, asserting that she had a right to do so as a U.S. citizen. The men who placed her under arrest charged her with "illegal voting" and insisted that her proper place was in the home. By 1920, men had run out of pretexts for keeping the vote from women. The best argument that the antisuffragists could muster was that women should not vote because they had no

After a hard-fought, decades-long campaign, American women finally won the right to vote in 1920.

voting experience. Senator Wendell Phillips expressed the pro-suffrage view: "One of two things is true: either woman is like man—and if she is, then a ballot based on brains belongs to her as well as to him. Or she is different, and then man does not know how to vote for her as she herself does."[3]

African Americans had to wait nearly fifty years longer than women to be granted full suffrage. Blacks seemed to have won the right to vote with passage of the Fifteenth Amendment after the Civil War, but as we saw in Chapter 5, they were effectively disenfranchised in the South by a number of electoral tricks, including poll taxes, literacy tests, and whites-only primary elections. The poll tax was a fee of several dollars that had to be paid before one could register to vote. Since most blacks in the South were too poor to pay it, the poll tax barred them from voting. Not until the ratification of the Twenty-fourth Amendment in 1964 was the poll tax outlawed in federal elections. Supreme Court decisions and the Voting Rights Act of 1965 swept away other legal barriers to fuller participation of African Americans.

In 1971, the Twenty-sixth Amendment extended voting rights to include those eighteen years of age or older. Previously, nearly all states had restricted voting to those twenty-one years of age or older.

Today virtually any American—rich or poor, man or woman, black or white—who is determined to vote can legally and actually do so. Americans attach great importance to the power of their votes. They claim that voting is their greatest source of influence over political leadership and their strongest protection against an uncaring or corrupt government.[4] They also claim that voting is a basic act of citizenship (see Table 7-1). In view of this attitude and the historical struggle of various groups to gain voting rights, the surprising fact is that Americans are not active voters. Millions of them choose not to vote regularly, a tendency that sets them apart from citizens of most other Western democracies.

TABLE 7-1 Opinions on Obligations of Citizens   Americans rank voting as one of the essential obligations of citizenship.

	Essential Obligation	Very Important Obligation	Somewhat Important	Personal Preference
Treating all people equally regardless of race or ethnic background	57%	33%	6%	4%
Voting in elections	53	29	9	9
Working to reduce inequality and injustice	41	42	12	6
Being civil to others with whom we may disagree	35	45	14	6
Keeping fully informed about the news and other public issues	30	42	19	10
Donating blood or organs to help with medical needs	20	37	18	26
Volunteering time to community service	16	42	26	16

SOURCE: Used by permission of the Survey of American Political Culture, James Davison Hunter and Carol Bowman, Directors, University of Virginia.

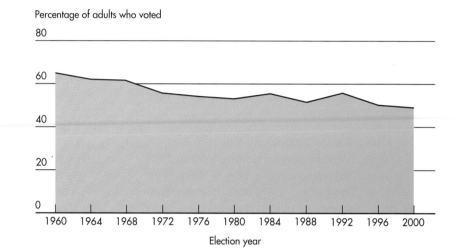

Percentage of adults who voted

FIGURE 7-1   Voter Turnout in
Presidential Elections, 1960–2000
Voter turnout has declined substantially since the 1960s.
*Source: U.S. Bureau of the Census,
1960–1968; Federal Election Commission, 1972–1996; 2000 figure
based on preliminary estimates.*

Election year

FACTORS IN VOTER TURNOUT:
THE UNITED STATES IN COMPARATIVE PERSPECTIVE

voter turnout   The proportion of
persons of voting age who
actually vote in a given election.

Voter turnout is the proportion of persons of voting age who actually vote in a
given election. Since the 1960s the turnout level in presidential elections has not
reached 60 percent (see Figure 7-1). In the 1996 and 2000 elections, only about
half of adults cast a vote for president.

Turnout is even lower in the midterm congressional elections that take place
between presidential elections. Midterm election turnout has not reached 50
percent since 1920, nor made it past the 40 percent mark since 1970. After one
midterm election, the cartoonist Rigby showed an election clerk eagerly asking
a stray cat that had wandered into a polling place, "Are you registered?"[5]

Nonvoting is far more prevalent in the United States than in nearly all other
democracies (see "How the United States Compares"). In recent decades,
turnout in major national elections has averaged less than 60 percent in the
United States, compared with more than 90 percent in Belgium, more than 80
percent in France and Denmark, and more than 70 percent in Great Britain and
Germany.[6] The disparity in turnout between the United States and other nations
is not as great as these official voting rates indicate. Some nations calculate
turnout solely on the basis of eligible adults, whereas the United States bases its
figures on all adults, including noncitizens and other ineligible groups. Nevertheless, even when such statistical disparities are corrected, turnout in U.S. elections remains low in comparison with that of nearly every other Western
democracy.

Voting does not require vast amounts of time. It takes most people longer to
go to a video store and select a movie than it takes to go to the neighborhood
polling place and cast a ballot. Thus, the explanation for the relatively low
turnout rate of Americans must entail considerations other than the time it takes
to vote. The major factors that depress turnout in U.S. elections in comparison
with other democracies include registration requirements, the frequency of elections, and the lack of clear-cut differences between the political parties.

HOW THE UNITED STATES COMPARES

VOTER TURNOUT

The United States ranks near the bottom among the world's democracies in the percentage of eligible citizens who participate in national elections. One reason for the low voter turnout is that individual Americans are responsible for registering to vote, whereas in most other democracies, voters are automatically registered by government officials. In addition, unlike some other democracies, the United States does not encourage voting by holding elections on the weekend or by imposing penalties, such as fines, on those who do not participate.

Another factor affecting the turnout rate in the United States is the absence of a major labor or socialist party, which would serve to bring lower-income citizens to the polls. In democracies where such parties exist, the turnout difference between upper- and lower-income groups is relatively small. In the United States, however, lower-income persons are much less likely to vote than higher-income persons are.

Country	Approximate Voter Turnout	Automatic Registration?	Social Democrat, Socialist, or Labor Party?	Election Day a Holiday or Weekend Day?
Belgium	90%	Yes	Yes	Yes
Italy	90%	Yes	Yes	Yes
Denmark	85%	Yes	Yes	No
Austria	80%	Yes	Yes	Yes
France	80%	No	Yes	Yes
Germany	80%	Yes	Yes	Yes
Great Britain	70%	Yes	Yes	No
Canada	65%	Yes	No	No
Japan	60%	Yes	Yes	Yes
United States	50%	No	No	No

SOURCE: Foreign embassies, except data on United States, which is based on Federal Elections Commission information.

Registration Requirements

Before Americans are allowed to vote, they must be registered—that is, their names must appear on an official list of eligible voters. **Registration** began around 1900 as a way of preventing voters from casting more than one ballot during an election. Fraudulent voting had become a favorite tactic of political party machines in communities where the population was too large for residents to be personally known to poll watchers. However, the extra effort involved in registering placed an added burden on honest citizens. Because citizens could now vote only if they had registered beforehand, those people who forgot or otherwise failed to do so found themselves unable to participate on election day. Turnout in U.S. elections declined steadily after registration was instituted.[7]

Although other democracies also require registration, they place this responsibility on government. In most European nations, public officials have the duty to enroll citizens on registration lists. The United States—in keeping with its *individualistic* culture—is the one of the few democracies in which registration is the individual's responsibility.[8] In addition, registration laws have traditionally been established by the state governments, and some states make it relatively difficult for citizens to qualify. Registration periods and locations are usually not highly publicized, and many citizens simply do not know when or where to register.[9] Eligibility can also be a problem. In most states, a citizen must establish

registration The practice of placing citizens' names on an official list of voters before they are eligible to exercise their right to vote.

CURRENT CONTROVERSIES

SHOULD VOTING THROUGH THE INTERNET BE ALLOWED?

As nonvoting has increased and Internet use has spread, it was only a matter of time before voting through the Internet would be considered. In 2000, Arizona voters had the opportunity to vote online in the state's Democratic presidential primary. Several states are moving toward online voting for all elections, and the U.S. military has established a pilot online voting option for troops overseas. Advocates see online voting as the answer to the downward trend in voter turnout. Not everyone agrees that Internet voting is the solution. Opponents say that Internet voting would lead to a sharp increase in election fraud. They also note that Internet voting would disadvantage groups, primarily the poor and minorities, that have limited access to the Internet.

YES: Voting is an important example of an information activity that could be improved with the help of the Internet. Where I live, we vote for judges, but I often don't know who deserves my ballot, since little information about their judicial records is available. I look forward to an Internet-based alternative. Instead of voting in person or mailing in an absentee ballot, I expect to be able to vote from my PC. While pondering the choices at my leisure, I'll be able to see what the candidates say about themselves, listen to speeches they've given, check their judicial records, read or watch news reports, survey their endorsements or the recommendations of nonpartisan groups, or even ask individuals I trust who they intend to vote for—all electronically. The result will be a better-informed vote, and probably greater participation.

—Bill Gates, Chairman, Microsoft Corporation

NO: Statistics on Internet use raise concerns that Internet voting will only increase access for a limited population group. Although Internet use is rapidly expanding, the typical user is still an under-35 affluent male college graduate, and there is growing concern about the disparity of access for certain population groups. . . . For Internet voting to become a reality, it must be able to meet the same requirements that current public elections are required (though increasingly fail) to meet—guarantee of ballot secrecy, guarantee of ballot sanctity, and universal availability. . . . Only when the critical issues of security, access, and public confidence have been fully addressed should any U.S. jurisdiction open the Pandora's box that Internet voting could represent.

—The Voting Integrity Project

legal residency by living in the same place for a minimum period, usually thirty days but sometimes as long as fifty days, before becoming eligible to register.

States with a tradition of lenient registration laws generally have a higher turnout than other states do. Idaho, Maine, and Minnesota, which are among the states that allow people to register at their polling place on election day, have high turnout rates. Those states that have erected the most barriers are in the South, where restrictive registration was originally intended to prevent black people from voting. These historical differences continue to be reflected in state voter turnout levels (see "States in the Nation").

One reason all states have not simplified their registration procedures is that many state and local officials, regardless of what they may say publicly, are not deeply interested in adding lots of new voters to the registration lists. Registration is not merely an administrative issue but also a political one. An increase or decrease in voter turnout can alter the outcome of elections. Poor and less educated voters are particularly discouraged by registration requirements. They are less likely to know when and where to register and, when they do, to have the time and transportation to get there. "The rich have the capacity to participate with or without assistance," Benjamin Ginsberg writes. "When assistance is given, it is primarily the poor who benefit."[10]

★ STATES IN THE NATION

STATE-BY-STATE VOTER TURNOUT IN PRESIDENTIAL ELECTIONS

Southern states have a tradition of more restrictive registration laws, and even today they tend to have lower rates of voter turnout. States with large recent immigrant populations, such as California and New York, also have lower turnout. Categories are based on turnout average in recent presidential elections.

Relatively high turnout
Moderate turnout
Relatively low turnout

In 1993, in an effort to increase registration levels nationwide, Congress enacted a voting registration law known as "motor voter." Its supporters predicted that the legislation, so named because it requires states to permit people to register to vote when applying for a driver's license (it also requires states to provide registration through mail and at certain state welfare offices), would add as many as 50 million new voters to registration rolls by the end of the century. The prediction seemed optimistic, because state agencies cannot compel applicants to register. Congressional Republicans made their support of the legislation contingent on this nonmandatory provision. They had blocked the bill for several years, fearing that it would help the Democrats by adding mainly lower-income Americans to the registration rolls. For the same reason, Republican governors in several states, including California and South Carolina, delayed putting the law into effect. Partisan concerns have always played a role in shaping registration laws, but in this case they appear miscalculated. Registrations under the motor-voter law have been about evenly divided between the Republican and Democratic parties.

Judge Robert Rosenberg of Broward County (Florida) Canvassing Board inspects an uncounted presidential ballot. Tens of thousands of such ballots went uncounted in Florida's decisive presidential vote contest.

By the time of the 2000 presidential election, more than 20 million people had been registered as part of the motor-voter law. Yet the increase did not result in a higher turnout rate; it actually declined between 1992 and 2000. Clearly, registration is only one of the factors underlying America's low turnout rate.

Ballots Cast but Not Counted

In the 2000 election, more than 100 million votes were officially recorded as having been cast for president. However, more than a million other votes were cast but not counted. Some could not be read by a voting machine because the voter had not marked the ballot clearly or had placed a mark outside the designated space. Some were punch-card ballots that could not be read because the hole in the card was not punched through completely.

It has been estimated that 1 to 2 percent of all ballots cast in U.S. elections are spoiled for one reason or another. These votes rarely get attention because they do not affect an election's outcome. In the 2000 presidential election, however, they may have been decisive. George W. Bush won the presidency on the basis of a 930-vote victory in Florida, where tens of thousand of ballots went uncounted. His opponent, Al Gore, mounted a legal challenge to get the ballots counted, but it failed when the U.S. Supreme Court intervened to stop a hand recount on the grounds that the standards for determining a legal ballot were vague (see Chapter 17). The Florida vote highlighted a glaring weakness in the conduct of U.S. elections. Many communities are unable or unwilling to invest public funds in balloting systems that have a low error rate. Most of the inadequate machinery is found in minority areas. In Chicago, for example, the error rate is three times lower in white neighborhoods than in African-American neighborhoods, where older and less reliable balloting methods are used. By comparison, many Western European countries have uniform national standards for balloting and, apparently, a smaller percentage of uncounted ballots than does the United States.

Frequency of Elections

The United States holds more elections than any other nation. No other democracy has elections for the lower chamber of its national legislature (the equivalent of the U.S. House of Representatives) as often as every two years, and none schedules elections for chief executive as often as every four years.[11] In addition, elections of state and local officials in the United States are often scheduled separately from national races. Two-thirds of the states elect their governors in nonpresidential election years,[12] and 60 percent of U.S. cities hold elections of municipal officials in odd-numbered years.[13]

This staggered scheduling reflects in some cases a deliberate effort by state and local officials to insulate their election races from the possible effects of other campaigns. During Franklin D. Roosevelt's four terms as president, for example, Republicans in several states, including New York and Connecticut, backed constitutional amendments that required gubernatorial races to be held in nonpresidential years. The purpose was to prevent other Democratic candidates from riding into office on Roosevelt's coattails. Several Democratic-

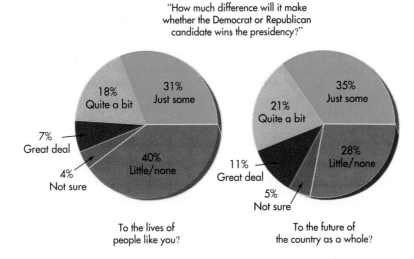

FIGURE 7-2 The Perceived Effect of Electing a Republican or Democratic President Most Americans believe that their lives and the country as a whole will not be greatly affected by whether the Republican or Democratic candidate wins the presidency. *Source: Used by permission of the Shorenstein Center Poll for the Vanishing Voter Project.*

controlled legislatures took similar action in the 1950s, when the popular Republican Dwight D. Eisenhower was president.

The frequency of U.S. elections reduces turnout by increasing the effort required to participate in all of them.[14] Most European nations have less frequent elections, and the responsibility of voting is thus less burdensome. Many European nations also schedule their elections on Sundays or declare election day to be a national holiday, thus making it more convenient for working people to vote. In the United States, elections are traditionally held on Tuesdays, and most people must vote before or after work.

The contrast with European practice is especially marked in the case of primary elections. The United States is the only democratic nation in which party nominees are commonly chosen by voters through primary elections rather than by party leaders.[15] Consequently, Americans are asked to vote twice to fill a single office. Many voters skip the primaries, preferring to vote just once, in the general election.

Party Differences

A final explanation for low voter turnout in the United States has to do with voters' perception that there is not much difference between the major political parties (see Figure 7-2). More than half of Americans claim that it does not make a big difference whether the Republicans or the Democrats gain control of government.[16] This belief is not entirely unfounded. The two major American political parties do not normally differ greatly in their policies. Each party depends on citizens of all economic interests and social backgrounds for support; consequently, neither party can afford to take an extreme position that would alienate any sizable segment of the electorate. For example, both parties share a commitment to the private enterprise system and to social security for the elderly (see Chapter 9).

Parties in Europe tend to divide more sharply over economic policies. There the choice between a conservative party and a socialist party may mean a choice between private and government ownership of major industries. Studies indicate that turnout is higher in nations whose political parties represent clear-cut alternatives, particularly when religious or class divisions are involved. Conversely, turnout is lower when, as in the United States, a nation's parties compete for the loyalty of voters of all religions and classes.[17] European parties, particularly those on the left, are also more closely tied to other organizations, such as labor unions, which assist in the mobilization of the electorate.[18]

WHY SOME AMERICANS VOTE AND OTHERS DO NOT

Even though turnout is lower in the United States than in other democracies, some Americans do vote in all or nearly all elections. But other Americans seldom or never vote. What accounts for such *individual* differences?

The factors that account for differences in public opinion (see Chapter 6) are not in all cases related to turnout differences. The turnout rates of men and women, for example, are similar.[19] Race was once a very significant predictor of turnout but has become less important. African Americans still have a lower turnout rate than do whites, but the difference, which is less than 10 percent in presidential elections, is much lower than the 40 percent difference that existed in 1960 (see Chapter 5).

Large differences in voter turnout are associated with citizens' sense of civic involvement, age, education, and economic class.

Feelings of Civic Duty, Apathy, and Alienation

civic duty The belief of an individual that civic and political participation is a responsibility of citizenship.

Regular voters are characterized by a strong sense of **civic duty**—that is, they regard participation in elections as one of the main responsibilities of citizenship. By election day in 1996, it was clear from the polls that Bill Clinton would handily defeat Bob Dole, yet regular voters were undeterred. Although they knew their votes would not sway the election, they voted anyway in order to fulfill their duty as citizens. This sense of duty is an attitude that is usually acquired as part of adolescent and childhood political socialization. When parents vote regularly and take an interest in politics, their children are likely to grow up viewing the vote as an important expression of their citizenship. Schools reinforce this belief by stressing the importance of the right to vote.

apathy A feeling of personal noninterest or unconcern with politics.

Many citizens do not have a strong sense of civic duty, and some of them display almost no interest in politics. **Apathy** is the term that describes a general lack of interest in or concern with politics. Just as some people would not attend the Super Bowl even if it were free and being played across the street, some people would not bother to vote even if a ballot were delivered to their door. As with civic duty, a sense of apathy is often the consequence of adolescent and childhood socialization. When parents disparage voting and other forms of political participation, their children are likely to hold a similar view when they reach voting age.

However, voter turnout is also affected by the degree to which people believe that their participation will make a difference. The level of turnout tends to increase when citizens have a high degree of trust in government and to fall when they are politically disillusioned.[20] Turnout in U.S. presidential elections dropped by 10 percentage points between 1958 and 1980, a period in which Americans' trust in Washington declined sharply under the onslaught of the Vietnam War, the Watergate scandal, economic stagnation, and other national problems (see

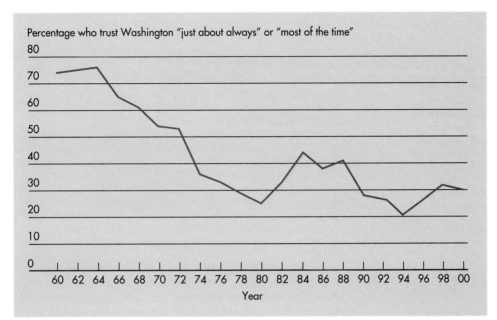

Percentage who trust Washington "just about always" or "most of the time"

FIGURE 7-3 Confidence in the National Government
Americans' trust in Washington has declined sharply in recent decades. This growing sense of alienation has been paralleled by a decline in voter turnout. *Source: National Election Studies, 1960–1992; various sources, 1993–2000.*

Figure 7-3). After 1980, the public's confidence in the national government rose somewhat but at no time came close to reaching its earlier level. Trust in government began to fall again in 1988 and reached a record low of less than 20 percent in 1994. A recent rise in the level of trust is largely attributable to increased economic growth. When the economy is relatively strong, citizens have a rosier view of government than when the economy is in a tailspin.

Alienation is the term that describes a sense of personal powerlessness that includes the notion that government does not care about the opinions of people like oneself.[21] Alienation diminishes people's interest in political participation.[22] It might be thought foolish for people to withdraw from politics when they believe government is inept and uncaring. Yet, for some individuals, the vote is as much an affirmation of citizenship as it is an opportunity to influence the direction of government. Most people know that their single vote is unlikely to affect the outcome of an election. When disgusted with government, they may choose simply to retreat from politics. In a recent CBS News/New York Times poll, more than half the respondents said there was not a single politician they truly admired. When people are so thoroughly disillusioned, it becomes understandable why some of them reject everything about politics, including the exercise of their right to vote.

alienation A feeling of personal powerlessness that includes the notion that government does not care about the opinions of people like oneself.

Age

When viewers tuned in MTV at various times in the 2000 presidential campaign, they might have thought at first that they had selected the wrong channel. Rather than a video of their favorite rock star, they saw the presidential candidates urging young people to vote.

Young adults have the lowest voter turnout rate of any major demographic group. Efforts to increase their participation include MTV's "Rock the Vote" campaign, which often features celebrity participants. Pictured here are (from left to right) humorist Bill Maher and singers Macy Gray and Moby.

The candidates had targeted the right audience for their get-out-the-vote message. Young adults are much less likely to vote than middle-aged citizens are. Even senior citizens, despite the infirmities of old age, have a far higher turnout rate than do voters under the age of thirty. Young people are less likely to have the political concern that can accompany such life-style characteristics as homeownership, a permanent career, and a family.[23] In fact, citizens under the age of thirty have a lower turnout rate than do all other demographic groups of comparable size.

Young voters have also contributed disproportionately to the decline in voter turnout in recent decades. Of the eligible eighteen- to twenty-four-year-olds, about half voted in 1972 compared with less than a third in 2000. On the other hand, turnout among those forty-five years of age and older declined only a few percentage points during this period.

Education

What does your college education mean? One thing it means is that you have a higher likelihood of becoming an active citizen. The difference is striking. Persons with a college education are about 40 percent more likely to vote than are persons with a grade school education. Researchers have concluded that education generates a greater interest in politics, a higher level of political information, a greater confidence that one can make a difference politically, and peer pressure to participate—all of which are related to the tendency to vote.[24]

Education, in fact, is the single best predictor of voter turnout. This fact led some analysts in the 1950s to conclude that increasing the overall level of education was the way to increase levels of turnout. Paradoxically, the overall education level of the American people has increased since then, but turnout has dropped. Political scientists have concluded that the positive effect of increased education levels has been more than offset by people's declining political interest and party loyalties.

Economic Class

Turnout is also strongly related to economic status, as measured by income level (see Figure 7-4). Americans at the bottom of the economic ladder are about

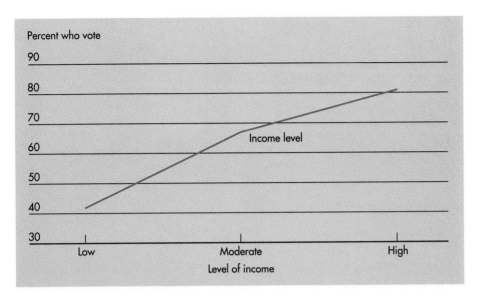

Percent who vote

Income level

Level of income

FIGURE 7-4 **Voter Turnout and Level of Income**
Americans of lower income are much less likely to vote. *Source: U.S. Bureau of the Census.*

one-third less likely to vote in presidential elections than are those at the top.[25] The difference is even larger in primaries and nonpresidential elections.[26]

In European democracies, economic status does not affect turnout to such a high degree. Europeans of lower income levels are encouraged to participate by class-based organizations and traditions—strong socialist parties, politically oriented trade unions, and class-based political ideologies.[27] In Britain, for example, the Labour party emerged with the growth of trade unionism and enrolled many manual laborers. Since 1918 the Labour party's membership card has carried a broad pledge "to secure for the workers by hand or by brain the full fruits of their industry." When the Labour party came to power in 1945, it made good on this promise to the working class by placing key industries under government ownership and adopting new social welfare programs. A major policy was government-paid medical care for all Britons, which was of particular benefit to lower-income people.

Although social class has declined in importance, European political traditions and institutions continue to encourage lower-class voter participation in ways that the U.S. political system does not.[28] The United States does not have, and never has had, a major socialist or labor party.[29] The Democratic party by and large represents poorer Americans, but their interests tend to be subordinated to the party's concern for the American middle class, which, because of its size and voting regularity, is the key to victory in U.S. elections.

Some analysts point out that once education level is controlled, income is a small factor in Americans' participation level. However, this observation does not adequately account for the absence of a lower-class political party in the U.S. system. The real test of the impact of income is whether poor people would turn out at a higher level if the party alternatives were different. Voting patterns during the Great Depression of the 1930s suggest that they would. In response to social security, public works projects, and other unprecedented class-based New Deal programs, turnout rose sharply among lower-income citizens.[30] Their

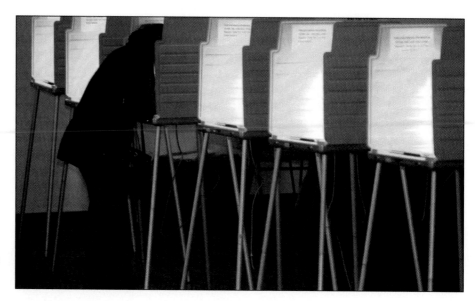

Voters turned out in relatively low numbers in the 2000 presidential election, continuing a pattern that has characterized recent U.S. elections.

voting rate stayed high through the 1950s because the New Deal agenda remained the focus of the domestic policy debate. As class-based appeals declined after 1960, turnout among those at the bottom of the economic ladder dropped by 25 percent from its 1960 level. Turnout at the top declined by only 4 percent. Today less than 40 percent of unemployed and working-class Americans vote even in a presidential election.[31]

THE IMPACT OF THE VOTE

Through their votes, the people choose the representatives who will govern in their name. But what is the relationship between the vote and the actions of government? What influence does the vote have on public policy? Fuller answers to these questions will be provided later (see Chapters 8, 13, and 15), but it is useful to consider at least a partial response at this point.

Elections do *not* ordinarily produce a popular mandate for the policies advocated by the winning candidate. A mandate requires voters to consciously choose between candidates on the basis of the promises they make during the campaign. A difficulty with this interpretation of election results is that voters are not usually well informed about candidates' policy positions. In U.S. House campaigns, less than half the voters can recall on their own the names of the two major-party nominees in their district and even fewer can identify these candidates' positions on major issues.[32] In presidential races, the voters are better informed, but most of them cannot readily recall more than a few of the differences in the candidates' platforms.

Several influences combine to limit the voters' awareness of issues. The candidates do not always make their positions altogether clear, either because they fear that taking a firm stand will lose them votes or because they do not have specific policies in mind. Many candidates have dodged the abortion issue in recent years by expressing personal opposition to it while at the same time promising to uphold a woman's right to choose as long as the courts permit it.

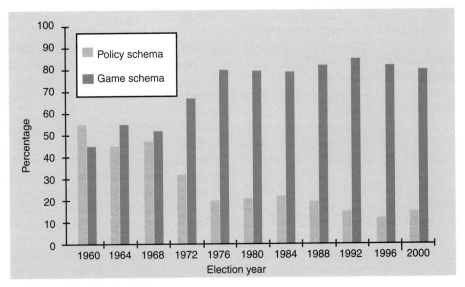

FIGURE 7-5   The Game-Centered Nature of Election News
In their reporting of elections, the media tend to place candidates and issues in the context of the game—who's winning and why—rather than in the context of policy proposals and problems. *Source: From* OUT OF ORDER *by Thomas F. Patterson. Copyright © 1993 by Thomas E. Patterson. Reprinted by permission of Alfred A. Knopf, a Division of Random House Inc.*

Additionally, the news media have increasingly focused their election coverage not on issues but on the strategic aspects of the candidates' pursuit of office (see Figure 7-5). By covering campaigns as if they were a strategic game, the media deemphasize substantive issues of policy, thereby making it more difficult for the voters to discover where the candidates stand.

Finally, voters can hardly be aware of issues if they are personally inattentive to politics. Most citizens do not follow campaigns closely and do not necessarily gain knowledge of even highly publicized issues.[33] In the 1994 congressional elections, voters cited excessive federal spending as a reason why they favored GOP candidates over their Democratic opponents. Polls indicated that nearly 60 percent of Americans believed that the budget deficit had increased during the first two years of the Clinton presidency. In fact, because of budget-deficit legislation developed by Clinton and enacted by Congress, the deficit had fallen two straight years for the first time since the mid-1980s.

There are, to be sure, some voters who are highly informed on the issues and cast their ballots on this basis. **Prospective voting** is a term used to describe this forward-looking type of voting. Prospective voting occurs when voters know the issue positions of the candidates and choose the candidate whose promises best match their own issue preferences.

A more prevalent form of voting is **retrospective voting,** which is the situation in which voters support the incumbent party or candidate when they are pleased with the performance, and reverse their position when they are displeased. Bill Clinton's victories in 1992 and 1996 illustrate the importance that voters attach to past governmental performance. The U.S. economy in 1992 was in its longest recession since World War II, and the situation soured voters on the incumbent president George Bush. Three-fourths of the American public expressed dissatisfaction with his handling of the economy, and their dissatisfaction translated into Bush's defeat. He lost by a substantial margin to Clinton, who, despite widespread reservations about his personal character, represented the prospect of change. According to the National Election Studies survey, about

prospective voting   A form of electoral judgment in which voters choose the candidate whose policy promises most closely match their own preferences.

retrospective voting   A form of electoral judgment in which voters support the incumbent candidate or party when their policies are judged to have succeeded and oppose the candidate or party when their policies are judged to have failed.

★ CRITICAL THINKING ★

WHAT'S YOUR OPINION?

Is It Better to Vote Retrospectively Than Prospectively?
The civics-book model of voting suggests that voters should choose among the candidates on the basis of the positions they take on the issues of the campaign. V. O. Key Jr. argued that this model has two basic drawbacks: it places extraordinary information demands on voters and requires them to accept at face value the promises that candidates make.

In Key's view, voters would be better advised to select their candidates retrospectively. They should consider the incumbent's past performance and, depending on whether they judge the performance to be effective, vote for or against the incumbent's party. The retrospective model places fewer information demands on voters and is based on the actual performance of government rather than on promises of future action.

Do you agree with Key's assessment? Are there particular times when prospective voting or retrospective voting is the more advisable basis of decision? Do you tend to judge parties and candidates on their performance or on future promises?

80 percent of the voters who supported Bush in 1988 but who deserted him in 1992 believed that the economy was the nation's most important problem.

By 1996, the nation's economy had recovered. Economic growth was strong, jobs were plentiful, and consumer confidence was high. Clinton's opponent, Bob Dole, tried to persuade voters that Clinton's personal character was reason enough to deny him a second term. But voters were satisfied with Clinton's handling of the economy and returned him to office.

As in these cases, economic conditions are usually the key factor in the electorate's retrospective judgments. When voters' confidence in the in-party's handling of the economy has been high, its nominee has usually won the presidential election. Conversely, its nominee has usually lost when the voters are dissatisfied with the economy.[34] Congressional elections are affected to a lesser extent by national conditions because these races often hinge on local issues and incumbents' superior funding and name recognition (see Chapter 12). Nevertheless, House and Senate elections can be affected by the public's view of the federal government's performance. Voters' disenchantment with Washington politics was the catalyst for the Republicans' sweeping victory in the 1994 midterm congressional races.

Retrospective voting is a somewhat weaker form of public control than prospective voting, because it occurs after the fact: government has already acted, and nothing can change what has taken place. Nevertheless, retrospective voting can be an effective form of popular control over policy because it forces public officials to anticipate the voters' likely response in the next election. The fear that they might be voted out of office by an electorate upset with their policies is a powerful constraint on elected representatives.[35]

Conventional Forms of Participation Other Than Voting

In one sense, voting is an unrivaled form of citizen participation. Free and open elections are the defining characteristic of democratic government, so voting is regarded as the most basic duty of citizens.[36] Voting is also the only form of citizen participation engaged in by a majority of adults in every democratic country.[37]

In another sense, however, voting is a restricted form of participation. Citizens have the opportunity to vote only at a particular time and place, and only on those predetermined items listed on a ballot. Voting takes up less than an hour a year for most citizens, and there is no guarantee that candidates will be able to keep the promises they made to the voters during the campaign. Other forms of participation offer a greater opportunity for personal influence or involvement. These may be divided into campaign activities, community activities, lobbying group activities, attentiveness to the news, and "virtual" participation.

CAMPAIGN ACTIVITIES

A citizen may engage in such campaign-related activities as working for a candidate or a party, attending election rallies or meetings, contributing money, and wearing a candidate's campaign button. The more demanding of these activities, such as doing volunteer work for a candidate or a party, require a lot more time and effort than voting does. These activities are also less imbued with notions of civic duty than is voting.[38] Not surprisingly, the proportion of citizens who engage in these activities is relatively small. For example, less than one in twenty adult Americans say they worked for a party or a candidate within the past year. Most of these citizens are strong partisans with a keen interest in politics.

Nevertheless, campaign participation is higher in the United States than in Europe. A five-country comparative study found that Americans ranked ahead of citizens of Germany, Austria, the Netherlands, and Great Britain in such activities as volunteering to work for a party or a candidate during an election campaign.[39] One reason Americans, even though they vote at a lower rate than Europeans do, are more likely than Europeans to work in a campaign is that they have more opportunities to do so.[40] Elections take place more often in the United States, and citizens can become involved in an election campaign by volunteering to work for either a party or a candidate (see Chapter 9). In Europe, campaigns are organized through the parties, and participation opportunities for those who are not party members are restricted. Moreover, the United States is a federal system, which results in campaigns for national, state, and local offices. A citizen who wishes to participate is almost certain to find an opportunity at one level of office or another. Most of the governments of Europe are unitary in form (see Chapter 2), which means that there are fewer elective offices and thus fewer campaigns in which to participate.

COMMUNITY ACTIVITIES

Many Americans participate in public affairs, not through campaigns and political parties, but through local organizations such as parent-teacher associations, neighborhood groups, Rotary clubs, church-affiliated groups, and hospital auxiliaries. Apart from their other purposes, these organizations also serve as a means to influence the public life of the community. Through such organizations, citizens can work to accomplish community goals and inform officials of their opinions on issues affecting the community.

Youthful volunteers work to fix up a children's playground. Americans are more likely than citizens of other democracies to take part in voluntary community activities.

The actual number of citizens who participate actively in a community group is difficult to estimate, but the number is surely in the tens of millions. The United States has a tradition of community participation that goes back to colonial days. Moreover, compared with local communities in Europe, those in the United States have more authority over policy issues, which is an added incentive to participation. Because of increased mobility and other factors, Americans may be less tied to their local communities than in the past and therefore less involved in community action. Nevertheless, half of Americans claim that they volunteer time to groups and community causes, compared with 20 percent or less in most European countries. When it comes to donating money to a group, Americans also have an edge on Europeans (see Figure 7-6).

In a widely publicized book entitled *Bowling Alone*, Harvard's Robert Putnam claims that America is undergoing a decline in its **social capital** (the sum of the face-to-face civic interactions among citizens in a society).[41] Putnam argues that there has been a continuing erosion of civic engagement. The relationships fostered by this participation are the foundation of democratic life. They bring citizens together, broaden and deepen people's understanding of other points of view, and provide the skills that foster continued participation in public affairs. Putnam attributes the decline to television and other factors that are drawing people inward and away from participation in civic and political groups. Not all scholars accept Putnam's interpretation of trends in civic participation (some indicators point toward a rise in certain types of participation),[42] but no one challenges his assumption about the importance of high levels of civic participation. And no democratic theorist has suggested that there can be "too much" community involvement. Indeed, in an earlier study, *Making Democracy Work*, Putnam found that the more abundant a society's voluntary associations are, the more likely it is that its public institutions will act in the public interest. Putnam uses the term *civic community* to describe a society where voluntary associations flourish.[43]

social capital   The sum of face-to-face interactions among citizens in a society.

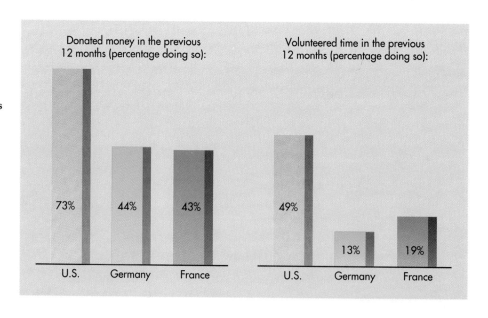

FIGURE 7-6   Conventional Participation in Three Countries Americans are more actively involved in volunteering time and donating money to groups and community causes than are the French or Germans. *Source: From Helmut I. Anheier, Lester M. Salamon, and Edith Archambault, "Participating Citizens; U.S.–Europe Comparisons in Volunteer Action,"* The Public Perspective, *March/April 1994. © The Roper Center for Public Opinion Research, University of CT, Storrs, CT. Used by permission.*

Donated money in the previous 12 months (percentage doing so):

U.S. 73%   Germany 44%   France 43%

Volunteered time in the previous 12 months (percentage doing so):

U.S. 49%   Germany 13%   France 19%

LOBBYING GROUP ACTIVITIES

Increasingly, Americans are also involved in public affairs through membership in lobbying groups. This form of participation seldom consists of more than the contribution of annual dues that enable a national organization to pressure government officials or otherwise attempt to influence public policy. Examples of these groups are the National Organization for Women, Common Cause, the Christian Moral Government Fund, the American Civil Liberties Union, and the National Conservative Political Action Committee. Chapter 10 discusses lobbying groups more fully.

FOLLOWING POLITICS IN THE NEWS

Campaign work and community participation are active forms of political involvement. There is also a passive form of participation: following politics by reading newspapers and newsmagazines and by listening to news reports on television or radio. It can safely be said that no act of political participation takes up more of people's time than does news consumption. The news is important to citizen participation: if people are to participate effectively and intelligently in politics, they must be aware of what is taking place in their communities, in their nation, and in the world.

News about politics is within easy reach of nearly all Americans. More than 95 percent of U.S. homes have a television set, and about 50 percent of Americans receive a daily newspaper. However, the regular audience for news is much smaller than these figures suggest. The mere fact of having a television or getting a daily paper does not mean that a person pays close attention to the news these media provide. If the regular audience for politics is defined as those who read a newspaper's political sections or watch television newscasts on a regular basis, then about a third of Americans can be classified as closely attentive to the news. Another third follows the news intermittently, catching an occasional newscast or scanning a paper's news sections somewhat often. The final third pays no appreciable attention to the news either on television or in a newspaper.

Television is the medium through which most Americans get most of their news (see Figure 7-7). In recent decades, citizens who say television is their main source of news have substantially outnumbered those who rely mainly on a newspaper. Radio and magazines account for even smaller proportions. The

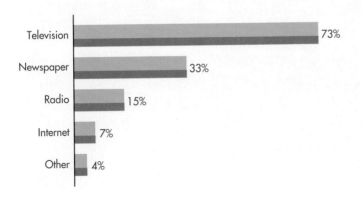

FIGURE 7-7 Americans' Major News Sources
When Americans are asked where they get most of their news, they mention television most often. *Source: Pew Research Center for the People and the Press, February 2000. Asked in context of presidential campaign. Adds to more than 100% due to multiple responses.*

figures are somewhat misleading in that people are asked where they get "most" of their news, not how much news they actually get. Some of the people who say they get "most" of their news from television do not watch the news a lot. They do not read a newspaper at all, so that even a little exposure to television news makes it their leading news source.

The news audience has shrunk considerably in size in recent years. Newspapers have lost audience to television newscasts, which in turn have lost audience to television entertainment programs. Before cable television was widely available, many television viewers had no alternative to a newscast during the dinner hour. With cable, viewers always have a wide variety of choices, and many viewers, as many as 40 percent by some estimates, choose to ignore the news unless a sensational event occurs, such as the Oklahoma City bombing in 1995 that killed more than a hundred people. To be sure, cable has also fostered a core of news junkies who immerse themselves in the Cable News Network (CNN), C-SPAN, and other news and public affairs programming. The more significant effect of cable, however, has been to contribute to a substantial decrease in the size of the news audience.

Young Americans in particular are ignoring the news. Americans under thirty years of age know less and care less about politics and pay less attention to newspapers than did each previous generation of the last half-century. Young people today are inclined toward television use generally but do not pay much attention to television news. Many of them apparently cannot be bothered with news in any form.[44]

VIRTUAL PARTICIPATION

The prospect of an entire generation of politically inattentive citizens is a disturbing one to many observers. Yet there is a glimmer of hope—the Internet. It is used more heavily by younger people and is packed with political information and participation possibilities.

A UCLA student works on the computer in her room. The Internet has vast but as yet unrealized potential as an instrument of mass political participation.

Nevertheless, it is unclear whether the Internet will actually serve as an entry into the world of politics for large numbers of citizens. Most people use it primarily for entertainment, school assignments, shopping, and personal and business communication. On the other hand, there are thousands of chat rooms where politics and public affairs are discussed. In addition, nearly every major interest group has its own website, and many groups have developed a capacity to inform and activate their membership through e-mail. Finally, candidates for public office have developed websites to promote their campaigns; in the 2000 presidential election, the candidates used their sites to raise funds and enlist campaign volunteers.

Reliable data are not available on the extent of political participation through the Internet, but according to a recent survey, 7 percent of Americans claimed they get most of their news of public affairs from the Internet. The full impact of this new medium on citizen participation, however, is not likely to be known until its technological capacity is fully developed and today's computer-literate generation reaches adulthood.

THE MIDDLE-CLASS BIAS OF CONVENTIONAL PARTICIPATION

Citizens who work in campaigns, who take an active part in the community, or who pay close attention to the news have the same general characteristics as those who vote regularly. Compared with the population as a whole, they are older, have higher incomes, are more highly educated, are more likely to have a strong sense of civic duty, and are less likely to feel politically alienated or apathetic.

The class bias of conventional participation is particularly noteworthy. Citizens of higher economic status are by far the most politically active individuals. They are most likely to possess the financial resources and communication skills that encourage participation and make it personally rewarding. Among citizens who are most active in politics, three times as many have incomes in the top third as in the bottom third.[45] This tendency is predictable. Less-advantaged Americans find it harder to contribute to organized activity even when they desire to do so. They often lack the money, information, contacts, and communication skills required to participate effectively. On the other hand, educated and affluent Americans possess the personal resources that enhance participation in public affairs.

It is a mistake, however, to assume that middle-class Americans are politically involved. The proportion of the citizenry who participate beyond the act of voting or occasional attendance at a community forum is relatively small. Involvement in partisan politics is particularly uncommon. The political scientist W. Russell Neuman concludes: "Roughly speaking, only one in twenty Americans can confidently be described as actively involved. . . . Such activities as attending campaign meetings [and] contributing to political organizations . . . are, all things considered, rare phenomena."[46]

Unconventional Activism: Social Movements and Protest Politics

Before mass elections became prevalent, the public often resorted to revolts and disorders as a way of expressing dissatisfaction with government. Tax and food

★ CRITICAL THINKING ★

WHAT'S YOUR OPINION?

What Kind of Citizens Will Young Adults Become? Recent surveys indicate that young Americans differ significantly from older citizens in ways that suggest a decline in democracy. Today's Americans under thirty years of age pay less attention to politics than did each generation of young people since polling began in the 1930s. Surveys by Peter D. Hart Research Associates found that fewer than 15 percent of those between the ages of fifteen and twenty-five believed that voting was an essential part of good citizenship. About half of them defined good citizenship in terms of caring personal relationships.

What do you make of these findings? Why are today's young people less committed to public life than their parents and grandparents were? What might be the long-term consequences for American democracy? What steps might be taken to instill in young people a greater sense of civic duty?

riots were common forms of popular protest. The advent of elections allowed the masses to communicate their views in an institutionalized and less disruptive way. Elections are double-edged, however. Although they are commonly viewed as a means by which the people control the government, *elections are also a means by which the government controls the people.*[47] Because they have been freely chosen by the people to rule, representatives can claim that their policies reflect the popular will. It is difficult for people to claim they are justified in rioting against government policy that has been enacted by representatives they themselves placed in office.

Voting in elections is also limited to the options listed on the ballot. America's voters effectively have only two choices: they can back the Democratic or Republican party. No other party has much chance of victory, and any citizen who is dissatisfied with the major parties realistically has no way to express a policy preference through the ballot.

social (political) movements
Active and sustained efforts to achieve social and political change by groups of people who feel that government has not been properly responsive to their concerns.

Social movements are an alternative form of influence. **Social movements,** or **political movements,** as they are sometimes called, refer to broad efforts to achieve change by citizens who feel that government is not properly responsive to their interests.[48] Their efforts are sometimes channeled through traditional forms of participation, such as political lobbying, but citizens can also take to the streets in protest against government. Perhaps the most dramatic recent example occurred in late 1999 when a host of activists—trade unionists, environmentalists, and others—engaged police in what became known as the "Battle in Seattle." The World Trade Organization (WTO) was meeting in Seattle to discuss global economic issues, and the activists were protesting the weak environmental and labor provisions that had marked earlier trade agreements. Their actions disrupted the WTO's meeting and earned a promise that, somehow, their views would be incorporated in future WTO deliberations.[49]

Social movements do not always succeed, but they sometimes assist otherwise politically weak persons to force government to respond to their desires. For example, the timing and scope of the landmark 1964 Civil Rights Act and 1965 Voting Rights Act can be explained only as a response by Congress to the pressure created by the civil rights movement. The movement was in great part nonviolent, but it existed outside established channels—civil disobedience was one of its techniques—and it challenged existing power structures. Another effective social movement in the 1960s was the farm workers' movement, whose protests led to landmark legislation and court decisions that improved the working and living conditions of migrant workers.

The son of Mexican immigrants, Cesar Chavez organized a social movement in the early 1960s to fight for better pay and working conditions for migrant farm workers and to protest discrimination against Hispanics. Chavez (left) is shown here with Walter Reuther (right), president of the United Auto Workers, during a march protesting the low wages of grape pickers.

Protest can pose a serious threat to established authority, and government at times has responded violently to dissent. In May 1970, during demonstrations against the Vietnam War, several unarmed students at Kent State University and Jackson State College were shot to death and others were wounded by national guardsmen who had been sent onto the campuses to restore order. In such situations, the majority of the general public usually sides with authorities. In a *Newsweek* poll, 58 percent of respondents blamed the Kent State killings on the student demonstrators, while only 11 percent blamed the guardsmen.

Most citizens apparently believe that the proper way to express disagreement over public policy is through voting and not through protesting, despite the First Amendment's guarantee of the right "peaceably to assemble." In a 1972 University of Michigan survey, only 15 percent of those interviewed ex-

TABLE 7-2   Opinions About Peace Demonstrations During the Gulf War, 1991
Most Americans believed that protests against the war were a "bad thing."

	ARE CURRENT DEMONSTRATIONS . . . ?		
	A Bad Thing	*Not a Bad Thing*	*No Opinion*
All respondents	63%	34%	3%
Male	58	40	2
Female	67	28	5
18–29 years	57	40	3
30–49 years	58	39	3
50 years and over	72	23	5
College grads	47	47	6
Some college	59	37	4
High school grads	68	30	2
Not high school grads	76	20	4
Republicans	71	26	3
Democrats	61	35	4
Independents	57	40	3

SOURCE: Used by permission of The Gallup Organization.

pressed approval of the Vietnam protests. Only 1 to 2 percent of the American public took to the streets in protest at any time during the 1960s and 1970s. Public opinion about demonstrations against the Gulf War was also negative, although less so than for protests against the Vietnam War, perhaps because U.S. involvement in the Gulf was shorter and more successful. A Gallup poll in early 1991 indicated that by a 2-to-1 margin Americans believed it was "a bad thing for Americans to be demonstrating against the war when U.S. troops are fighting overseas." This view was particularly pronounced among women, older persons, Republicans, and persons with lower education levels (see Table 7-2).

Recent American history would be very different if the civil rights, women's rights, Vietnam protest, and other major social movements had not pressed their claims on government. Social movements have been an effective way for groups outside the political mainstream to make significant claims on society.

Protest politics in America goes back to the Boston Tea Party and earlier, but it has taken on new forms in recent years. Protest was traditionally a desperate act that began, often spontaneously, when a group had lost hope that it could succeed through more conventional methods. Today, however, protest is usually a calculated act—a means of bringing added attention and impetus to a cause.[50] These tactical protests often involve a great deal of planning, including, in some instances, the busing of thousands of people to Washington for a rally staged for television. Civil rights, environmental, agricultural, and pro- and antiabortion groups are among those that have staged tactical protests in Washington within the past few years.

Citizens who participate in social movements tend to be younger than non-participants, which is a reversal of the situation with voting. In fact, age is the best predictor of protest activity.[51] Participants in social movements also tend to emphasize nonmaterial values more than do nonparticipants. Social movements often develop in response to real or perceived injustices and thus attract idealists.[52]

Participation and the Potential for Influence

Although Americans claim that political participation is important, most of them do not practice what they preach. As we have seen, most citizens take little interest in participation except to vote, and a significant minority cannot even be persuaded that voting is worth their while. However, Americans are not completely apathetic: many millions of them give their time, effort, and money to political causes, and roughly a hundred million go to the polls in presidential elections.

Yet sustained political activism does not engage a large proportion of the public. Moreover, many of those who do participate are drawn to politics by a habitual sense of civic duty rather than by an intense concern with current issues. The emphasis that American culture places on *individualism* tends to discourage a sense of urgency about political participation. "In the United States, the country of individualism *par excellence*," William Watts and Lloyd Free write, "there is a sharp distinction in people's minds between their own personal lives and national life."[53] Although wars and severe recessions can lead the American public to turn to government, most people under most conditions expect to solve their own problems. This is not to say that Americans have a disdain for collective action. In their communities particularly, citizens frequently take part in collective efforts to support a local hospital, improve the neighborhood, and the like. But most Americans tend not to see their material well-being as greatly dependent on involvement in politics of the traditional kind.[54]

This tendency contributes to a class bias in American politics. For one thing, it helps maintain a relatively sharp distinction between that which is properly public (political) and that which is properly private (economic). The private component, which includes most economic relationships, is largely beyond the realm of political debate and action. Americans, said political scientist Robert Lane, have a preference for market justice rather than political justice.[55] They prefer to see benefits distributed primarily through the economic marketplace rather than through the policies of government. The nation's health care system is an example. Unlike the systems of Europe, which provide government-paid coverage for everyone, access to medical care in the United States is to some degree based on a person's ability to pay for it. There are about thirty-eight million Americans who do not have access to adequate health care because they cannot afford health insurance.

America's individualistic culture also contributes to a class bias by its effect on the participation level of lower-income groups. As we have seen, citizens of lower economic status are substantially less involved politically than are those of higher status. The difference is much greater in the United States than elsewhere. In other Western democracies, the government assists poorer citizens in participating by assuming the burden of registering voters and by fostering class-based political organizations. By comparison, the poor in the United States

Police and protestors face off in 1999 at the World Trade Organization (WTO) meeting in Seattle. Although protest movements are an American tradition, they rarely receive strong public support.

must arrange their own registration and must choose between two political parties that are attuned primarily to middle-class interests.

During the 1950s and 1960s, many political scientists argued that the low turnout rate of lower-income Americans was largely immaterial because their preferences in regard to policies and candidates were not greatly different from those of other citizens. This viewpoint continues to have its advocates but is less persuasive today. As the income gap between lower- and upper-income Americans has widened in recent decades, so has the gap in their political opinions. As Walter Dean Burnham notes, "It is no longer possible to assume a quiet consensus, a happy apathy."[56]

The relatively low participation rate of the poor tends to reduce the influence of their opinions on public policy. Studies indicate that representatives are more responsive to the demands of participants than to those of nonparticipants,[57] although it must be kept in mind that participants do not always promote only their own interests. It would be a mistake, however, to conclude that large numbers of people regularly support policies that would mainly benefit others. A turning point in the defeat of President Bill Clinton's health care reform proposal came when middle-class Americans decided that it might increase the cost and reduce the quality of their own medical care. According to Time/CNN polls, support for the Clinton plan dropped from 57 to 31 percent in favor to 49 to 37 percent opposed between September 1993 and July 1994. Although this decline reflected a loss of support among all groups, the drop was particularly acute among higher-income groups. By mid-1994, those Americans with incomes over $20,000 were opposed to the Clinton plan by a 3-to-2 ratio. In contrast, a majority of those individuals with incomes under $20,000 still favored the plan. They would have been the principal beneficiaries of the Clinton plan, which called for universal health care insurance. On the other hand, most middle-class voters already had health insurance, either through an individual policy or an employment-related group policy.

www.mhhe.com/patterson5

Self-Quiz

In sum, the pattern of individual political participation in the United States parallels the distribution of influence that prevails in the private sector. Those who have the most power through participation in the marketplace also have the most power through participation in the political arena. However, the issue of individual participation is only one piece of the larger puzzle of who rules America and for what purposes. Subsequent chapters will provide additional pieces.

Summary

Political participation is involvement in activities designed to influence public policy and leadership. A main issue of democratic government is the question of who participates in politics and how fully they participate.

Voting is the most widespread form of active political participation among Americans. Yet voter turnout is significantly lower in the United States than in other democratic nations. The requirement that Americans must personally register in order to establish their eligibility to vote is one reason for lower turnout among Americans; other democracies place the burden of registration on government officials rather than on the individual citizen. The fact that the United States holds frequent elections also discourages some citizens from voting regularly. Finally, the major American political parties, unlike many of those in Europe, do not clearly represent the interests of opposing economic classes; thus the policy stakes in American elections are correspondingly lower. Some Americans do not vote because they think that policy will not change greatly regardless of which party gains power.

Prospective voting is one way the people can exert influence on policy through their participation. It is the most demanding approach to voting: voters must develop their own policy preferences and then educate themselves about the candidates' positions. Most voters are not well-enough informed about the issues to respond in this way. Retrospective voting demands less from voters: they need only decide whether the government has been performing well in terms of the goals and values they hold. The evidence suggests that the electorate is, in fact, reasonably sensitive to past governmental performance, particularly in relation to economic prosperity.

Only a minority of citizens engage in the more demanding forms of political activity, such as work on community affairs or on behalf of a candidate during a political campaign. The proportion of Americans who engage in these more demanding forms of activity exceeds the proportion of Europeans who do so. Nevertheless, only about one in every four Americans will take an active part in a political organization at some point in their lives. Most political activists are individuals of higher income and education; they have the skills and material resources to participate effectively and tend to take greater interest in politics. More than in any other Western democracy, political participation in the United States is related to economic status.

Social movements are broad efforts to achieve change by citizens who feel that government is not properly responsive to their interests. These efforts sometimes take place outside established channels; demonstrations, picket lines, and marches are common means of protest. Protesters are younger and more idealistic on average than are other citizens, but they are a very small proportion of the population. In addition, protest activities do not have much public support, despite the country's tradition of free expression.

Overall, Americans are only moderately involved in politics. They are concerned with political affairs but mostly immersed in their private pursuits, a reflection in part of our culture's emphasis on individualism. The lower level of participation among low-income citizens has particular significance in that it works to reduce their influence on public policy and leadership.

Key Terms

alienation
apathy
civic duty
political participation
prospective voting
registration

retrospective voting
social capital
social (political) movements
suffrage
voter turnout

Suggested Readings

Conway, M. Margaret, Gertrude A. Steuernagel, and David Ahern. *Women and Political Participation: Cultural Change in the Political Arena.* Washington, D.C.: Congressional Quarterly Press, 1997. An analysis of women and political participation.

Entman, Robert. *Democracy Without Citizens: Media and the Decay of American Politics.* New York: Oxford University Press, 1989. A critical evaluation of citizen involvement in the context of news about politics and public affairs.

Kryzanek, Michael J. *Angry, Bored, Confused.* Boulder, Colo.: Westview Press, 1999. An assessment and handbook of contemporary citizen politics.

Neuman, W. Russell, Marion R. Just, and Ann N. Crigler. *Common Knowledge: News and the Construction of Meaning.* Chicago: University of Chicago Press, 1992. An assessment of how citizens interpret and use the news they receive.

Nie, Norman H., Jane Junn, and Kenneth Stehlik-Barry. *Education and Democratic Citizenship in America.* Chicago: University of Chicago Press, 1996. A study of the relationship between education and political participation.

Putnam, Robert. *Bowling Alone.* New York: Simon and Schuster, 2000. A provocative analysis of the trend in civic participation.

Rimmerman, Craig A. *The New Citizenship: Unconventional Politics, Activism, and Service.* Boulder, Colo.: Westview Press, 1997. An assessment of citizenship in the modern age.

Schudson, Michael. *The Good Citizen: A History of American Civic Life.* New York: Free Press, 1998. A thoughtful history of civic participation in America.

Tate, Katherine. *From Protest to Politics: The New Black Voters in American Elections.* Enlarged ed. Cambridge, Mass.: Harvard University Press, 1994. A study of the transformation of a social movement into a conventional form of political participation.

Verba, Sidney, Kay Schlozman, and Henry Brady. *Voice and Equality.* Cambridge, Mass.: Harvard University Press, 1995. A careful study of political attitudes and participation.

Woliver, Laura R. *From Outrage to Action: The Politics of Grass Roots Dissent.* Urbana: University of Illinois Press, 1993. A valuable case study of the impact of grassroots protest.

CHAPTER 8

Elections and the Two-Party System: Defining the Voters' Choice

★

*Political parties created democracy and . . . modern democracy is
unthinkable save in terms of the parties.*

—E. E. Schattschneider[1]

★   ★   ★

*O*n opposite coasts and two weeks apart, they faced off, each offering their own plan for a better America.

The Republicans met first, in Philadelphia. Their 2000 platform included a steep cut in personal income taxes, a limit on abortions, parental choice of schools, business deregulation, a partial privatization of the social security system, and a delegation of authority to state and local governments. The Republicans chose Texas governor George W. Bush, the son of former President George Bush, as their presidential nominee.

The Democrats met in Los Angeles, the same city where thirty-two years earlier Robert F. Kennedy had been assassinated at the end of a bitter Democratic nominating campaign that had nearly torn the party apart over the issue of the Vietnam War. This time, however, the Democrats were a united party. The Democrats chose Vice President Al Gore as their presidential nominee. The Democrats' lengthy platform included tax benefits for low- and middle-income families, restrictions on handguns, protection of social security, reproductive freedom for women, and pledges to strengthen the nation's environmental, educational, and health systems.

The political parties, as their nominees and platforms illustrate, are in the business of offering the voting public a choice. Each party seeks to define itself in a way that will attract majority support.

Competition between political parties is the foundation of the public's influence through elections. The party is the one institution that develops broad policy and leadership choices and then presents them to the public to accept or reject. This process is what gives the citizens an opportunity, through elections, to influence how they will be governed. Although many Americans distrust political parties and question their value, the fact is that democracy would be nearly impossible in practice without them.

Parties are not the only means by which the public can exert influence. Interest groups such as the AFL-CIO and the American Medical Association provide individuals with the opportunity to act collectively. However, most such groups articulate the narrow and specific demands of a *minority* interest in society. In the United States, with its individualistic culture and tradition of freedom of association, group activity is more fragmented than in many other nations. Major political parties function in a different way. The party's goal is to create a *majority* by bringing together individuals with diverse interests. A **political party** is an ongoing coalition of interests joined together to try to get their candidates for public office elected under a common label.[2] Parties pull diverse interests together and in the process offer the public competitive policy and leadership alternatives.

political party   An ongoing coalition of interests joined together to try to get their candidates for public office elected under a common label.

two-party system   A system in which only two political parties have a real chance of acquiring control of the government.

multiparty system   A system in which three or more political parties have the capacity to gain control of government separately or in coalition.

In the American case, this competition takes place between two major parties, the Republicans and the Democrats. Because these parties have long dominated U.S. elections and are the only parties with any realistic chance of acquiring political control, Americans nearly take their **two-party system** for granted. However, most democracies have a **multiparty system,** in which three or more parties have the capacity to gain control of government separately or in coalition. Even democracies that have what is essentially a two-party system typically have important smaller parties as well. For example, Great Britain's Labour and Conservative parties have dominated that nation's politics since early in this century, but they have had competition from the Liberal party and, more recently, the Liberal Democrats.

America's two-party system has important consequences for the nation's politics. Neither major party can win an election by drawing its votes from only a small sector of the population; as a result, the two parties tend to appeal to many of the same interests. The policy traditions and tendencies of the Republican and Democratic parties do not regularly differ sharply. For example, each party is committed to social security for the elderly and to substantial expenditures for national defense. Parties in European multiparty systems tend to be more programmatic. Each party has its distinctive platform and voting bloc. Of course, once in power, European parties are forced to adjust their programs to the prevailing realities. Germany's Social Democratic party, for example, won power in 1998 by attacking the center-right parties for failing to protect the

Democratic nominee Al Gore is surrounded by party faithful during the 2000 presidential campaign. Political parties have responsibility for selecting nominees and submitting them to the voters for acceptance or rejection. Competition between the parties gives the voters an opportunity to influence the direction of government.

living standards of working-class and middle-class citizens, but the nation's economic problems forced the Social Democrats to retain many of the free-market policies of the previous government. Nevertheless, European multiparty systems usually offer voters a more clear-cut set of choices than does the American two-party system.

To critics, the American parties' failure to take sharply different policy positions means that they offer the public "no genuine alternatives." To their admirers, however, America's major parties provide political stability and yet are different enough to give voters "a real choice." This chapter investigates America's two-party system and the type of choice it actually provides the public. It argues that the Republican and Democratic parties do offer a real and significant choice, but only at particular times and on particular issues. The main points discussed in this chapter are the following:

★ *Party competition is the mechanism that enables voting majorities to have a substantial influence on the direction of government.* This competition peaks during periods of realignment but at all times is a vital aspect of democratic government.

★ *Throughout most of the nation's history, political competition has centered on two parties.* This two-party tendency is explained primarily by the nature of America's electoral system. Minor parties exist in the United States but have been unable to compete successfully for governing power.

★ *The Republican and Democratic coalitions are very broad.* Each includes a substantial proportion of nearly every economic, ethnic, religious, and regional grouping in the country.

★ *To win an electoral majority, each of the two major parties must appeal to a diverse set of interests; this necessity normally leads them to advocate moderate and somewhat overlapping policies and to avoid taking detailed positions on controversial issues.* Only during periods of stress are America's parties likely to present the electorate with starkly different policy alternatives.

Party Competition and Majority Rule

Political parties give direction and strength to the people's votes. Through their numbers, citizens have the potential for great influence, but that potential cannot be realized unless they have the capacity to act together. Parties give them that capacity. When Americans go to the polls, they have a choice between the Republican and Democratic parties. This **party competition** narrows their options to two and in the process enables people with different opinions to render a common judgment. In electing a party, the voters choose its candidates, its philosophy, and its policies over those of the opposing party.

It is not always a choice that Americans find satisfying. In a national poll conducted during the 2000 campaign, the Shorenstein Center at Harvard found that more than 80 percent of respondents agreed with the statement "most presidential candidates will say whatever it takes to get elected."[3] Such views are not groundless, but party competition is basic to democratic government. Parties

party competition   A process in which conflict over society's goals is transformed by political parties into electoral competition in which the winner gains the power to govern.

give weight to the preferences of ordinary people. Because they have the strength of numbers, citizens have the potential for great influence in a democracy, but that potential cannot be realized unless they have a way to express a collective judgment. Parties are *the* way. When Americans go to the polls to elect a president or member of Congress, they can choose the Republican or Democratic alternative. This choice channels a great many different opinions into just two and in the process enables people to act together.

The history of democratic government is virtually synonymous with the history of parties. When the countries of eastern Europe gained their freedom a few years ago, one of their first steps toward democracy was the legalization of parties. When the United States was founded two centuries ago, the formation of parties was also a first step toward the erection of its democracy. In case after case, democracies have found that they cannot do without parties and for the simplest of reasons: it is the competition between parties that gives popular majorities a chance to determine how they will be governed.

ORIGINS OF THE AMERICAN PARTY SYSTEM

Parties had not yet been invented when George Washington took office in 1789. Factions were known, however, and they were widely despised. Washington warned the nation of the "baneful effects" of factions. The term *faction* connoted a self-interested group bent on getting its own way at the expense of all others. Although America's first leaders were wary of any organized form of advocacy, they soon recognized the need to organize those who held similar political views.[4] Out of this recognition came the world's first parties. James Madison at first had likened parties to factions, but his misgivings gradually gave way to a grudging admiration. He saw that parties were the only effective way for likeminded people to jointly promote their vision of how the new nation should be governed.

The First Parties

America's parties originated in the rivalry within George Washington's administration between Thomas Jefferson and Alexander Hamilton (see Figure 8-1). Jefferson defended states' rights and small landholders, while Hamilton promoted a strong national government and wealthy interests. When Hamilton's ideas prevailed in Congress, Jefferson and his followers formed a political party, the Republicans. By adopting this label, which was associated with popular government, the Jeffersonians sought to portray themselves as the rightful heirs to the American Revolution's legacy of self-government and political equality.

Hamilton responded by organizing his supporters into a formal party—the Federalists—and in the process created America's first competitive party system. The Federalists took their name from the faction that had supported ratification of the Constitution, thereby implying that they were the Constitution's true defenders. However, the Federalists' preoccupation with commercial and wealthy interests fueled Jefferson's claim that the Federalists were bent on establishing a government for the rich and wellborn. After Adams's defeat by Jefferson in the election of 1800, the Federalists and their philosophy never again held sway.

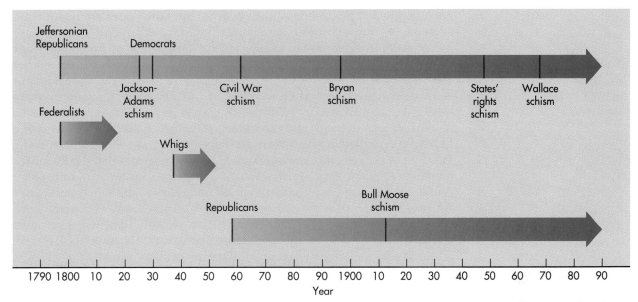

FIGURE 8-1 A Graphic History of America's Major Parties

During the so-called Era of Good Feeling, when James Monroe ran unopposed in 1820 for a second presidential term, it appeared as if the nation might exist without parties. Yet by the end of Monroe's second term, policy differences had split the Republicans. The dominant faction, led by Andrew Jackson, retained Jefferson's commitment to the interests of small farmers, tradespeople, and shopkeepers. To better reflect its base among ordinary citizens, this faction called itself Democratic Republicans, later shortened to Democrats. Thus, the Republican party of Jefferson is the forerunner of today's Democratic party rather than today's Republican party.

Andrew Jackson and Grassroots Parties

For all its shortcomings, competition between parties is the only system that can regularly mobilize collective influence on behalf of the many who are individually powerless against those few who have extraordinary wealth and prestige.[5] This realization led Jackson during the 1820s to develop a **grassroots party.** Whereas Jefferson's party had been well organized only at the leadership level, Jackson sought a party that was built from the bottom up. Jackson's Democratic party consisted of committees and clubs at the national, state, and local levels, with membership open to all eligible voters. These organizational activities, along with more liberal suffrage laws, contributed to a nearly fourfold rise in voter turnout during the 1830s.[6] At the peak of Jacksonian democracy, Alexis de Tocqueville wrote, "The People reign in the American political world as the Deity does in the universe."[7] Although Tocqueville exaggerated the people's true power, he caught the spirit of popular government that was behind the development of grassroots parties under Andrew Jackson.

In this period, a new opposition party, the Whigs, emerged to challenge the Democrats. The Whigs formed a residual party of sorts. Its followers were united

grassroots party A political party organized at the level of the voters and dependent on their support for its strength.

Abraham Lincoln said that this portrait of him by Mathew Brady, which he used in his campaign literature, contributed to his election to the presidency as a Republican in 1860.

not by a coherent philosophy of their own but by their opposition for one reason or another to the philosophy and policies of the Jacksonian Democrats.

Competition between the Whigs and the Democrats was relatively short-lived. During the 1850s, the slavery issue began to tear both parties apart. In 1860, the Democratic party's northern faction nominated for president Stephen A. Douglas, who held that the question of whether a new territory permitted slavery was for a majority of its voters to decide, while the southern faction nominated John C. Breckinridge, who called for the legalization of slavery in all territories. The Democratic vote in the fall election was split sharply along regional lines between these two candidates—with the result that the Republican nominee, Abraham Lincoln, was able to win the presidency with only 40 percent of the popular vote. The Republicans had eclipsed the Whigs and become America's other major party. However, the U.S. party system essentially collapsed in 1860, for the only time in the nation's history.[8] The issues of slavery and union were too powerful to be settled peaceably through political compromise and competition between political parties.

REPUBLICANS VERSUS DEMOCRATS: REALIGNMENTS AND THE ENDURING PARTY SYSTEM

After the Civil War, the nation settled into the pattern of competition between the Republican and Democratic parties that has prevailed ever since. The durability of these two parties is due not to their ideological consistency but to their remarkable capacity to adapt during periods of crisis. By abandoning at these crucial times their old ways of doing things, the Republican and Democratic parties have essentially remade themselves—with new bases of support, new policies, and new public philosophies.

These periods of great political change are known as "realignments." A **party realignment** involves four basic elements:

party realignment An election or set of elections in which the electorate responds strongly to an extraordinarily powerful issue that has disrupted the established political order. A realignment has a lasting impact on public policy, popular support for the parties, and the composition of the party coalitions.

1. The disruption of the existing political order because of the emergence of one or more unusually powerful and divisive issues
2. An election contest in which the voters shift their support strongly in favor of one party
3. A major change in policy through the action of the stronger party
4. An enduring change in the party coalitions, which works to the lasting advantage of the dominant party

Realignments are relatively rare. A simple change of power from one party to the other does not constitute a realignment, which is defined instead by the fullness and longevity of its effects. A realignment affects not just one election, but later elections as well. By this standard, there have been three realignments since the 1850s, and some observers believe the United States is now in the midst of a fourth.

The Civil War Realignment

The Civil War resulted in a realignment along sectional lines. The Republicans were the dominant party in the larger and more populous North and were therefore also the nation's majority party. The Democratic party was left with a stronghold in what became known as "the Solid South." During the next three decades the Republicans controlled the presidency except for Grover Cleveland's two terms, and they held a majority in one or both houses of Congress for all but four of those years. Cleveland's initial victory in 1884 was made possible only by a split in Republican ranks. The GOP denied nomination to its own incumbent, Chester A. Arthur, and turned instead to James G. Blaine ("the Man from Maine"), who, it appears, had the support neither of progressive Republicans nor of his own running mate, John A. Logan.

The 1890s Realignment

The election of 1896 resulted in a further realignment of the Republican-Democratic party system. Three years earlier, an economic panic following a bank collapse had resulted in a severe depression. The Democrat Cleveland was president when the panic occurred, and that circumstance worked to the advantage of the Republicans. They gained strength in the East particularly because of fear of cheap credit, a policy advocated by the Democrats' 1896 presidential nominee, William Jennings Bryan. During the four decades between the 1890s realignment and the next one in the 1930s, the Republicans held the presidency except for Woodrow Wilson's two terms and had a majority in Congress for all but six years. As was the case with Cleveland, Wilson could not have won except for dissension within Republican ranks. In the election of 1912, the Republican vote for incumbent William Howard Taft was split by the Bull Moose party candidacy of Theodore Roosevelt, which enabled Wilson to win with less than 45 percent of the total vote.

The new order begins: Franklin D. Roosevelt rides to his inauguration with outgoing president Herbert Hoover after the realigning election of 1932.

The Great Depression and the 1930s Realignment

The Great Depression of the 1930s triggered a thoroughgoing realignment of the American party system. The Republican Herbert Hoover was president when the stock market crashed in 1929, and many Americans blamed Hoover, his party, and its business allies for the economic catastrophe that followed. The Democrats became the country's majority party, and their political and policy agenda favored a significant social and economic role for the national government. Franklin D. Roosevelt's presidency was characterized by unprecedented policy initiatives in the areas of business regulation and social welfare (see Chapters 3, 15, and 16). His election in 1932 began a thirty-six-year period of Democratic presidencies that was interrupted only by Dwight D. Eisenhower's two terms in the 1950s. During this period, the Democrats also dominated Congress, losing control only in 1947–1948 and 1953–1954.

The reason realignments have such a substantial effect on future elections is that they affect voters' *party identification* (see Chapter 6). Young voters in particular are likely to identify with the newly ascendant party, and they tend to maintain that identity, giving the party a solid base of support for years to come. In the 1930s, for example, the Democratic party's image as the party of the common people, jobs, and social security was vastly more appealing to young voters than the Republican party's image as the party of business and wealthy interests. First-time voters in the 1930s came to identify by a 2-to-1 margin with the Democratic party, which established it as the nation's majority party and enabled it to dominate national politics for the next three decades.[9] Even in recent elections, Americans who reached voting age during the depression era were more supportive of the Democratic party than were people who reached voting age earlier or later (see Figure 8-2).

A NEW REALIGNMENT OR A DEALIGNMENT?

A party realignment inevitably loses strength over time, because the issues that gave rise to it cannot remain dominant indefinitely. By the late 1960s, when the

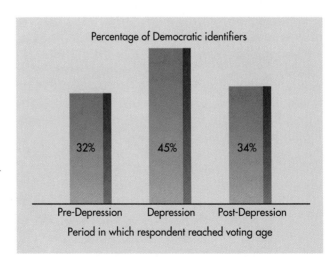

FIGURE 8-2 The Enduring Effects of Partisan Realignment Even today, Americans who reached voting age during the depression era are more likely to support the Democratic party than are those who reached voting age either earlier or later. *Source: Estimated by author from various polls.*

Percentage of Democratic identifiers

32%   45%   34%

Pre-Depression   Depression   Post-Depression

Period in which respondent reached voting age

Republican presidential nominee George W. Bush reaches out to shake a voter's hand during the early months of the 2000 campaign. Bush sought to reverse Republican losses in recent elections by positioning the GOP closer to the political center.

Democratic party was divided over the Vietnam War and civil rights, it was apparent that the era of New Deal politics was over.[10]

Yet Republican inroads were otherwise less dramatic or temporary. After 1968, the Republicans held the presidency for more years than the Democrats did and in 1994 won a landslide midterm election victory that gave the GOP control of both Houses of Congress for the first time in four elections. But at no time has the GOP been able to dominate presidential and congressional elections the way that Democrats did during the height of the New Deal era. Nor has the GOP succeeded in gaining a decisive edge in terms of party identification. The proportion of Americans who call themselves Democrats has typically equaled or exceeded those who say they are Republicans. A lasting realignment favorable to the Republican party could be taking place, but if so, it is unlike past ones—slower, more fitful, and less encompassing. And if such a realignment is taking place, it will be evident only after Republicans enjoy a period of sustained dominance.

An alternative explanation for what has been happening in American elections is put forth by advocates of the dealignment thesis. They suggest that the U.S. electoral system, rather than undergoing a realignment strongly favorable to one party, has been in the process of **dealignment,** a partial but enduring movement of voters away from partisan loyalties.[11] The process is characterized by an electorate that wavers in its support of the parties, sometimes favoring one party and sometimes the other.

Parties, in fact, have a weaker hold on the voters than in the past. As was noted in Chapter 6, the number of voters who describe themselves as independents has increased significantly in recent decades (see Figure 8-3). Moreover, people who today identify with a party are more likely to say it is only a weak attachment. These changes are reflected in increased **split-ticket voting** (see Figure 8-4), where the voter selects candidates of both parties for different offices when casting a ballot. A few decades ago, the large majority of voters engaged in **straight-ticket voting,** supporting candidates of one party only.

dealignment   A situation in which voters' partisan loyalties have been substantially and permanently weakened.

split-ticket voting   The pattern of voting in which the individual voter in a given election casts a ballot for one or more candidates of each major party.

straight-ticket voting   The pattern of voting in which the individual voter in a given election supports only candidates of one party.

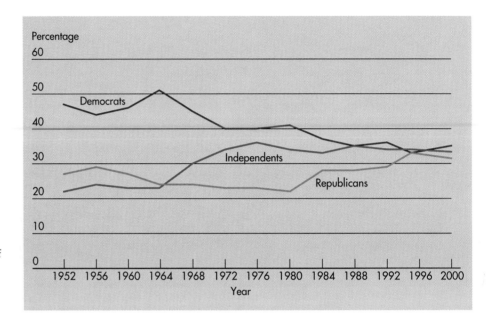

FIGURE 8-3   Partisan Identification
Party loyalties weakened in the late 1960s, and the proportion of independents increased. *Source: National Election Studies, 1952–1992; various surveys, 1993–2000.*

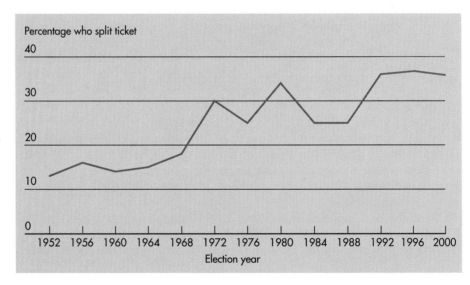

FIGURE 8-4   Split-Ticket Voting in Presidential and House Races
The proportion of voters who split their ballot in presidential and House races has increased substantially in recent decades as a result of the decline in the strength of partisan loyalties. *Source: National Election Studies, 1952–1996; 2000 election data based on preliminary estimates.*

The decline of partisanship began during the 1960s and 1970s when divisive issues arose and disrupted existing loyalties. The civil rights issue, for example, was unsettling not only to many southern Democrats but also to some white northern Democrats, particularly blue-collar workers from newer immigrant groups who felt that African Americans were making progress at their expense.[12] Vietnam, abortion, social welfare, and a host of other issues also divided followers of each party. Americans' trust in their elected representatives declined, as did their faith in parties.

Party loyalties have been weak ever since, and some analysts see little likelihood of a dramatic reversal. For one thing, voters of today are better educated and more likely to believe they can judge the candidates for themselves, on the basis of what they hear through the media rather than on the basis of party labels. Moreover, people today are protected by programs like social security and Medicare from the economic hardships that in the past fueled party realignments. Finally, Americans today want higher incomes and lower taxes, but they also want a cleaner environment, services for the elderly, and better schools. As a result, they are less likely to be drawn fully to either the Republican argument for a less active government or the Democratic argument for a more active one.[13]

If advocates of the dealignment thesis are correct, neither party in the foreseeable future will enjoy the prolonged success of the type the Democratic party had from the 1930s on. The predicted scenario is one of shifting support, with the Republicans prevailing at some times and the Democrats at other times.

Electoral and Party Systems

The United States traditionally has had a *two-party system:* Federalists versus Republicans, Whigs versus Democrats, and Republicans versus Democrats. Every now and then, as in the case of Ross Perot's 1992 and 1996 candidacies, a third choice joins the fray, but two-party competition has been the rule. Why two parties? Most democracies have a *multiparty* system in which three or more parties compete regularly for power (see "How the United States Compares"). Why does the United States have only two major parties? Another question: What role do minor parties or independent candidates such as Perot play in the American system? This section addresses these questions.

THE SINGLE-MEMBER-DISTRICT SYSTEM OF ELECTION

A major reason for the persistence of America's two-party system is the fact that the nation chooses its officials through plurality voting in **single-member districts.**[14] Each constituency elects a single candidate to a particular office, such as U.S. senator or representative. Only the party that gets the most votes (a plurality) in a district wins the office. This system discourages minor parties. Assume, for example, that a minor party received exactly 20 percent of the vote in each of the nation's 435 congressional races. Even though one in five voters nationwide backed the minor party, it would not win any seats in Congress because none of its candidates placed first in any of the 435 single-member-district races. The winning candidate in each case would be the major-party candidate who received the larger proportion of the remaining 80 percent of the vote.

By comparison, most European democracies use some form of **proportional representation,** in which seats in the legislature are allocated according to a party's share of the popular vote. This type of electoral system provides smaller parties an incentive to organize and compete for power. In the 1998 German elections, the Green party won slightly more than 5 percent of the national vote and received a proportionate number of the seats in the Bundestag, the German parliament. If the Greens had been competing under American electoral rules, they would not have won any seats and would have had no chance of exercising a

single-member districts The form of representation in which only the candidate who gets the most votes in a district wins office.

proportional representation A form of representation in which seats in the legislature are allocated proportionally according to each political party's share of the popular vote. This system enables smaller parties to compete successfully for seats.

HOW THE UNITED STATES COMPARES

PARTY SYSTEMS

For nearly 160 years, electoral competition in the United States has centered on the Republican and Democratic parties. By comparison, most democracies have a multiparty system, in which three or more parties receive substantial support from voters. The difference is significant. In a two-party system, the parties tend to have overlapping coalitions and programs, because each party must appeal to the middle-of-the-road voters who provide the margin of victory. In multiparty systems, particularly those with four or more strong parties, the parties tend to separate themselves, as each tries to secure the enduring loyalty of voters who have a particular viewpoint.

Whether a country has a two-party or a multiparty system depends on several factors, but particularly the nature of its electoral system. The United States has a single-member plurality district system in which only the top vote getter in a district gets elected. This system is biased against smaller parties; even if they have some support in a great many races, they win nothing unless one of their candidates places first in an electoral district.

By comparison, proportional representation systems enable smaller parties to compete; each party acquires legislative seats in proportion to its share of the total vote. All the countries in the chart that have four or more parties also have a proportional representation system of election.

NUMBER OF COMPETITIVE PARTIES

Two	Three	Four or More
United States	Canada (at times)	Belgium
	Great Britain	Denmark
		France
		Germany
		Italy
		Netherlands
		Sweden

share of legislative power. In this case, the Greens even gained a share of executive power. The Social Democratic party won the most legislative seats in the 1998 German election but failed to gain an outright majority. The Social Democrats formed a coalition with the Green party, which received cabinet posts in return for its backing of a Social Democrat-led government.

The adverse effect of electoral laws on U.S. minor parties is evident also in the election of the president. A presidential race is a winner-take-all contest, and only a strong party has any chance of gaining the office. The presidency can be won with less than a majority of the popular vote, as was the case in 1992 when Democrat Bill Clinton was elected with only a 43 percent plurality. In that election, Ross Perot won 19 percent of the national vote, but his relatively strong showing gave him no share of executive power. By comparison, in France there must be a runoff election between the two candidates who receive the most votes if neither receives a majority—50 percent or more—of the vote. Minor parties that fare poorly in the first election can bargain with the final contenders, trading support in the runoff election for policy concessions or cabinet positions in the new government. In this way, the French system—unlike the American one—provides an incentive for smaller parties to compete.

The Republican and Democratic parties have institutionalized their hold on the U.S. party system with policies that are designed to promote their candidates. In the 1970s, for example, Congress established a system of public funding for presidential elections. Each major-party candidate receives a substantial sum of money (roughly $70 million in 2000) with which to conduct a general election campaign. Minor-party or independent candidates get funding only if they receive at least 5 percent of the vote, which means that, unless they obtained that level of support in the previous election, they do not receive funds, if at all, until after the election. Moreover, they receive funds only in an amount equal to the ratio of their total vote to the average total vote of the two major-party candidates. Thus, in 1980, independent candidate John Anderson received $4.2 million after he won 7 percent of the presidential vote, compared to the nearly $30 million awarded the Republican nominee Ronald Reagan and the Democratic nominee Jimmy Carter. Anderson ran his campaign on borrowed money and would have received no public funding if his vote total had dropped below the 5 percent level. In 1992, the billionaire Ross Perot campaigned on his own money, which made him ineligible for public funding (a candidate loses eligibility if he or she spends more than $50,000 in personal funds on the general election campaign). However, because he received 19 percent of the vote in 1992, Perot was eligible for and accepted public funding in 1996. He received $29 million. This amount was slightly less than half as much as Clinton or Dole received and reflected the fact that in 1992 Perot got slightly less than half of the average vote of the Republican and Democratic candidates.

Germany's electoral system allocates legislative seats on the basis both of single-district voting and of the overall proportion of votes a party receives. This system requires that the German voter cast two ballots in legislative races: one to choose among the candidates in the particular district and one to choose among the parties. Shown here is a ballot from a German election. The left column lists the candidates for the legislative seat in a district, and the right column lists the parties. (Note the relatively large number of parties on the ballot.)

MINOR PARTIES

Although the U.S. electoral system discourages the formation of third parties, the nation has always had minor parties—more than a thousand during the nation's history.[15] Most of them have been short-lived, and only a few have had a lasting impact. Only one minor party, the Republican party, has ever achieved majority status.

Minor parties in the United States have formed largely to advocate positions that their followers believe are not being adequately represented by either of the two major parties. This approach is both the strength and weakness of minor parties. Their followers are motivated by issue positions that are vital to them but less attractive to other voters. To increase its following, a minor party must broaden its platform; in so doing, however, it risks alienating its original supporters. Yet if it remains small, it cannot win elections and may eventually wither away.

In addition to providing a haven for those with atypical political views, minor parties increase the Republican and Democratic parties' responsiveness. A major party is always somewhat captive to its past, which is the source of many of its ideas and most of its followers. When conditions change, major parties are often slow to respond, which can enable a minor party to capitalize on the emerging issues. If the minor party should gain a relatively large following, which has happened a few times in history, the major parties are forced to pay attention to the problems that are driving people to look elsewhere for leadership. The best example recently is Ross Perot's 1992 candidacy, which was fueled by the widespread perception that Washington had lost touch with the interests of the middle class. Both major parties saw the advantage they would gain if they could draw Perot's backers to their side in future elections. In 1994, the Republicans succeeded in doing so, at least temporarily. Exit polls indicated

CURRENT CONTROVERSIES

SHOULD THE BROADCAST NETWORKS BE REQUIRED TO TELEVISE THE POLITICAL PARTY CONVENTIONS?

Until the 1970s the most prominent symbol of America's major political parties was the televised presidential nominating convention. Scheduled during the summer of a presidential election year, the convention was a major national event and drew a huge audience. Nearly 80 percent of American families reported watching the televised convention, and the average adult logged nearly ten hours of convention viewing. Since then, the convention audience has declined sharply. The conventions are less appealing because they have become ratifying conventions for decisions made in the state presidential primaries and caucuses that precede them. Moreover, television viewers now have numerous options, and many people choose not to watch the conventions. As a result, the broadcast networks have dramatically reduced the number of hours that they televise the conventions, and some network executives believe they should terminate their coverage completely except for the nominees' acceptance speeches. Critics say that the networks have a public-service obligation to televise the conventions. And if the conventions are televised only on cable, 25 percent of Americans—those without cable—will have no opportunity to watch.

YES: For more than twenty years, the televised convention was a public event. People didn't just watch; they talked about what went on. . . . Our democracy may not depend on it, but with the erosion of public engagement in politics already far advanced, the disappearance of the televised convention is something we simply can't afford.

—Zachary Karabell, author

NO: We're not going to cover the convention the way we have in the past. You have to be living on Mars to not know we're living in a new era of fiscal reality. . . . From our point of view it matters much more the quality of what's being done than the number of hours on the air . . . We're going straight to cable in the next election. . . . There's not enough news at the convention to justify the effort.

—Network executives (composite statement)

that more than 60 percent of the Perot supporters voted Republican in the midterm elections.

Viewed historically, minor parties have formed in response to the emergence of a single controversial issue, out of a commitment to a certain ideology, or as a result of a rift within one of the major parties.

Single-Issue Parties

Some minor parties form around a single issue of overriding concern to their supporters, such as the present-day Right-to-Life party, which was formed to oppose the legalization of abortion. Some single-issue parties have seen their policy goals enacted into law. The Prohibition party contributed to the ratification in 1919 of the Eighteenth Amendment, which prohibited the manufacture, sale, and transportation of alcoholic beverages (but was repealed in 1933). Single-issue parties usually disband when their issue is favorably resolved or fades in importance.[16]

Ideological Parties

Other minor parties are characterized by their ideological commitment, or belief in a broad and radical philosophical position, such as redistribution of economic resources. Modern-day ideological parties include the Reform Party, the Green Party, and the Libertarian party, each of which has its loyal followers.

One of the strongest ideological parties in the nation's history was the Populist party. Its candidate in the 1892 presidential election, James B. Weaver, gained 8.5 percent of the national vote and won twenty-two electoral votes in six western states. The party, which is classified as a "protest party" by some scholars, began as an agrarian protest movement in response to an economic depression and the anger of small farmers over low commodity prices, tight credit, and the high rates charged by railroad monopolies to transport farm goods.[17] The Populists' ideological platform called for government ownership of the railroads, a graduated income tax, low tariffs on imports, and elimination of the gold standard. The Populist party in 1896 endorsed the Democratic presidential nominee, William Jennings Bryan, and its support probably hurt the Democrats nationally. Large numbers of "Gold Democrats" abandoned their party in fear of the inflationary consequences of Bryan's advocacy of the free coinage of silver.[18]

Factional Parties

The Republican and Democratic parties are relatively adept at managing internal conflict. Although each party's support is diverse, the differences among its varying interests can normally be reconciled. However, there have been times when factional conflict within the major parties has led to the formation of minor parties.

The most successful of these factional parties at the polls was Theodore Roosevelt's Bull Moose party. In 1908, Roosevelt, after having served eight years as president, declined to seek a third term and handpicked William Howard Taft for the Republican nomination. When Taft as president showed neither Roosevelt's enthusiasm for a strong presidency nor his commitment to the goals of the Progressive movement, Roosevelt decided to challenge Taft for the 1912

What If the United States Had Proportional Representation? Politics is a game played under certain rules. These rules are often regarded as neutral in their effect: they define how the game is played and won but do not themselves influence the outcome. However, this view is naive. The rules can and do affect who wins and who loses.

A clear example is electoral systems. The United States has a single-member-district system in which the election winners are those candidates who get the most votes in a district. Most European countries, by comparison, have proportional representation systems, in which seats in the national legislature are distributed according to each party's share of the popular vote. The European system makes it possible for smaller parties to win legislative seats. In contrast, the American system discourages smaller parties. A party that receives 15 percent of the national vote might win no seats in Congress.

Which system—the proportional or the single-member district—do you prefer? Why? Is one system inherently better suited to the United States than the other? Why?

In 1896, the Populist party—a strong ideological party—nominated William Jennings Bryan as its presidential candidate. Bryan was also the Democratic nominee in that election. This Puck cartoon shows the Democratic party being swallowed by a Bryan-headed Populist snake.

Republican nomination. Progressive Republicans backed Roosevelt, but Taft won the nomination with the support of conservative Republicans and the Republican National Committee. Roosevelt led a Progressive walkout to form the Bull Moose party (a reference to Roosevelt's claim that he was "as strong as a bull moose"). Roosevelt won 27 percent of the presidential vote to Taft's 25 percent, but the split within Republican ranks enabled the Democratic nominee, Woodrow Wilson, to win the presidency.

The States' Rights party in 1948 and the American Independent party in 1968 are other examples of strong factional parties. Each of these parties was formed by southern Democrats who were angered by northern Democrats' support of racial desegregation.

Deep divisions within a party give rise to factionalism and can lead eventually to a change in its coalition. The conflict over civil rights that began within the Democratic party during the Truman years continued for the next quarter-century, which initially led many southern whites to support Republican presidential candidates and later to shift their party loyalty to the Republican party.

Independent Candidates

Campaigns have increasingly been shaped by money and media, a development that has enabled candidates to seek high-level office without a party's backing. The most successful independent candidacy was Texas billionaire Ross Perot's 1992 presidential bid, which gained 19 percent of the vote (second only to Roosevelt's 1912 percentage among candidates who were not major-party nominees). Perot's campaign was based on middle-class discontent with the major parties and was conducted almost entirely on television. Perot ran again in 1996 but as the nominee of the Reform party, which he founded. He ran a media-based campaign that attracted 8 percent of the vote.

Perot chose not to run again in 2000, which enabled Pat Buchanan, a former Republican officeseeker and television commentator, to gain the party's presidential nomination. His nomination alienated many Reform party regulars, and

Jesse Ventura, who was chosen Minnesota's governor in 1998, is one of the few independent or third-party candidates to win a major elective office in the United States. Such candidates normally cannot surmount the built-in advantages possessed by major party nominees.

he drew less than 1 percent of the presidential vote, enabling the Green party and its nominee, Ralph Nader, who received 3 percent of the vote, to claim the position of America's strongest third party.

Policies and Coalitions in the Two-Party System

The overriding goal of a major American party is to gain power by getting its candidates elected to office. Because there are only two major parties, however, the Republicans or Democrats can win consistently only by attracting majority support. In Europe's multiparty systems, a party can hope for a share of power if it has the firm backing of a minority faction. This is not so in the United States. If either party confines its support to a narrow segment of society, it forfeits its chance of gaining control of government.

SEEKING THE CENTER, USUALLY

This situation encourages both parties to stay near the center of the political spectrum and to avoid the minority position on deeply divisive issues. The two parties typically try to develop stands that will have broad appeal or at least will not alienate significant blocs of voters. Any time a party makes a pronounced shift toward either extreme, the middle is left open for the opposing party. For this reason, congressional Republicans in 1998 advocated a moderate cut in taxes. They wanted to center the 1998 elections on the tax issue but feared that Democrats, who wanted to use most of the federal budget surplus to shore up the social security system, would exploit a GOP tax-cut proposal to gain the support of elderly voters.

Nevertheless, there are factors that can push the parties toward the extremes. Democratic activists are more liberal than other Democrats, and Republican activists are more conservative than other Republicans—and either group can lead its party away from the center. The conservative views of Republican activists in 1992 contributed to an uncompromising anti-abortion plank in the GOP platform, which contributed to George Bush's weak showing among women voters in the November election. Nevertheless, many activists and most candidates are more pragmatic than ideological. They normally try to avoid positions that will alienate moderate voters. They seek victory and do not knowingly embrace positions that will ruin all chances of achieving it.

It is impossible to understand the dynamics of the U.S. party system without a recognition that the true balance of power in American elections rests with America's pragmatic and moderate voters rather than those who hold more extreme views. When congressional Republicans mistook their 1994 election victory as a mandate to trim assistance programs for the elderly, poor, and children, they alienated many of the moderate voters who had contributed to their 1994 victory. These voters wanted "less" government but not a government that neglected society's most vulnerable citizens. After weak showings in the 1996 and 1998 elections, congressional Republicans shifted course. They unseated Speaker Newt Gingrich, replacing him with a more pragmatic conservative, Dennis Hastert. "We still need to prove that we can be conservative without being mean," was how one Republican member of Congress described the change in strategy.[19] The change in Republican outlook was also evident in GOP presidential candidate George W. Bush's campaign slogan of "compassionate conservatism." These adjustments reflect a basic truth about U.S. politics: party ideology is acceptable as long as it is tinged with moderation.

Nonetheless, the Republican and Democratic parties do offer somewhat different alternatives and, at times, a clear choice. When Roosevelt was elected president in 1932, Johnson in 1964, and Reagan in 1980, the parties were relatively far apart in their priorities and programs. Roosevelt's New Deal, for example, was an extreme alternative within the American political tradition and caused a decisive split along party lines. A lesson of these periods is that the center of the American political spectrum can be moved. Candidates risk a crushing defeat by straying too far from established ideas during normal times, but they may do so with some chance of victory during turbulent times.

Another lesson of such periods is that public opinion is the critical element in partisan change. Critics who say that the Democratic and Republican parties fail to offer the voters a real choice ignore the parties' tendency to tailor their appeals to majority opinion.[20] When the public's mood shifts, the parties usually also shift. The Republicans' Contract with America in 1994, for example, was a response to public discontent with the federal government's taxing and spending policies. When the Republicans won in 1994, many Democratic officeholders also embraced cutbacks in federal power, thus shifting the entire party system toward the right. President Clinton, a Democrat, summed up the change in his 1996 State of the Union address when he said: "The era of big government is over."

PARTY COALITIONS

party coalition The groups and interests that support a political party.

The groups and interests that support a party are collectively referred to as the **party coalition.** In multiparty systems, each party is supported by a relatively narrow range of interests. European parties tend to divide along class lines, with the center and right parties drawing most of their votes from the middle and upper classes and the left parties drawing theirs from the working class. By comparison, America's two-party system requires each party to accommodate a wide range of interests in order to gain the voting plurality necessary to win elections. The Republican and Democratic coalitions are therefore very broad. Each includes a substantial proportion of voters of nearly every ethnic, religious, regional, and economic grouping. There are only a few sizable groups that are tightly aligned with a party. African Americans are the clearest example; they vote about 90 percent Democratic in national elections.

Although the Republican and Democratic coalitions overlap, they are hardly identical (see Figure 8-5). Each party likes to appear to be all things to all Americans, but in fact each builds its coalition through a process of both unification and division. If a party did not stand for something—if it never took sides—it would lose all support.

Since the 1930s, the major policy differences between the Republicans and the Democrats have involved the national government's role in solving social and economic problems. Each party has supported government action to promote economic security and social equality, but the Democrats have consistently favored a greater degree of governmental involvement. Virtually every

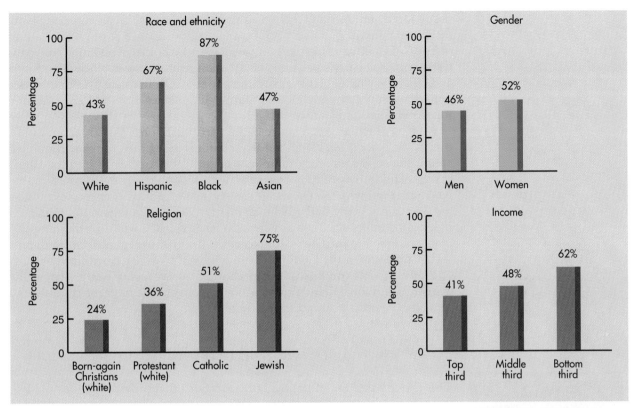

FIGURE 8-5 The Vote of Selected Demographic Groups in Recent Presidential Elections Although the Democratic and Republican coalitions overlap substantially, there are important differences, as illustrated by the Democratic party's percentage of the two-party vote among some major demographic groups in recent elections. *Source: Compiled by author from NES and other surveys.*

major assistance program for the poor, elderly, and low-wage workers has been initiated by the Democrats. To some extent, the Democratic coalition draws support disproportionately from society's "underdogs"—blacks, union members, the poor, city dwellers, Hispanics, Jews, and other "minorities."[21] For a long period, the Democratic party was also the clear choice of the nation's elderly as a result of its support for old-age assistance programs and because the basic political loyalties of the elderly were acquired during the New Deal era, a period favorable to the Democrats. Recently, however, elderly voters have split their vote nearly evenly between the parties.

The Democratic party's biggest gains recently have been with women, who traditionally had a voting pattern very similar to men. In recent elections, however, there has been a gender gap (see Chapter 6). Women have voted disproportionately for the Democratic party, apparently as a result of its positions on issues such as abortion rights, education spending, employment policies, and gun control.

The Republican coalition consists mainly of white middle-class Protestants. The GOP has historically been the party of tax cuts and business incentives. The GOP has also been more supportive of traditional values, as reflected, for example, in its support of school prayer and its opposition to abortion. Not surprisingly, the GOP has generally been the stronger party in the suburbs and other areas, such as the West and Midwest, where traditional values and a desire for lower taxes and less government regulation of economic activity are more pronounced.

The GOP has made big gains in recent decades among white fundamentalist Christians. The party's positions on abortion, school prayer, affirmative action, and other social issues have drawn them to the GOP. In recent presidential elections, the Republican nominee has garnered the votes of roughly 70 percent of fundamentalist Christians.

There is a self-limiting feature to the party coalitions. The larger a party becomes, the greater the likelihood that conflict among the groups within it will occur. The New Deal, for example, brought black Americans into the Democratic coalition, where they coexisted with the white southern conservatives who had sided with the Democratic party since the Civil War. However, when the Democratic party in the 1950s and early 1960s began to respond to the civil rights issues of its black constituents, it alienated many white southerners, who then gravitated to the GOP. More recently, the growing number of fundamentalist Christians in the GOP has been a source of division within that party. Their strong views on issues such as abortion and school prayer are not shared by many traditional Republicans, which has enabled Democratic candidates in some races to attract support from these voters.

Popular Influence and America's Two-Party System

The religious right is a major force within the Republican party. The Rev. Pat Robertson (left) introduces former interior secretary Don Hodel (center left) as the new president of the Christian Coalition. It was also announced that former GOP congressman Randy Tate (center right) would replace Ralph Reed (right) as the coalition's executive secretary.

"It is the competition of political organizations that provides the people with the opportunity to make a choice," E. E. Schattschneider once wrote. "Without this opportunity popular sovereignty amounts to nothing."[22] Thus the competitive nature of America's two major parties is a central issue in any evaluation of the nation's politics. Do the parties in fact give the public a meaningful choice?

Critics who contend that public policy in America is controlled by a wealthy elite argue that the two parties do not offer a real alternative.[23] These critics emphasize the tendency of Republican and Democratic policies to converge.[24] For nearly a century, for example, Europe has had major socialist parties, whereas the U.S. party system has never offered socialism as a serious alternative. Each U.S. major party has embraced private enterprise to a degree not found elsewhere. Of course, the American public has shared this attachment to private initiative, although from time to time polls have indicated public support for social welfare alternatives. In the two decades following World War II, for example, the American public, by a bare majority and apparently without much intensity, indicated a preference for a comprehensive system of government-paid health care. President Truman did propose legislation for such a health care system in the late 1940s, but the plan never came close to receiving the necessary congressional approval.

Noting such examples, leftist critics argue that America's major parties are tools of upper-class interests. Ironically, the Republican and Democratic parties have not been spared by critics on the right, either. After all, it was George Wallace, a conservative, who made the slogan "Not a dime's worth of difference between them" the basis for a third-party campaign. Wallace contended that the Republican and Democratic parties were both overly solicitous of the opinions

★ STATES IN THE NATION

PARTY CONTROL OF STATE GOVERNMENT

The strength of the major parties varies substantially among states. An indicator of party dominance is whether one party controls all elected institutions: the governor's seat and the two legislative chambers (except in Nebraska, which has a unicameral, nonpartisan legislature). As of 2000, the Republican party had an edge on the Democrats.

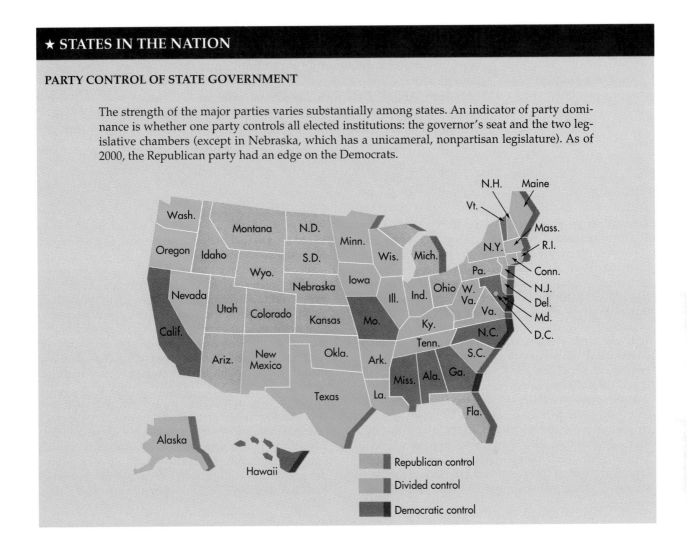

Republican control

Divided control

Democratic control

of minorities and liberals. Indeed, until Ronald Reagan's election in 1980, most of the attacks on the parties from political circles (as opposed to academic circles) came from the right, not the left.

Nonetheless, as I have explained in this chapter, the Republican and Democratic parties do offer somewhat different alternatives and, at times, a clear choice. When the parties have later converged again, that trend was always in large part a reflection of a change in the public's attitudes.

The continuous adjustment of America's two parties to the mood of the electorate reflects their competition for power.[25] Each party has a realistic chance of winning a national election and thus has an incentive to respond to changes in public opinion. Viewed differently, a competitive opposition party is the public's best protection against an unresponsive government; the out-party provides the electorate with an alternative. Even in its weakened position after the Roosevelt years, the Republican party was strong enough to provide an alternative when the public's dissatisfaction with the Democrats rose, as in 1952,

www.mhhe.com/patterson5

Self-Quiz

1968, and 1980 at the presidential level and in 1946, 1952, and 1980 at the congressional level. And the GOP made a strong breakthrough at the congressional level in 1994 as a direct result of the public's anger with the performance of government.

In sum, America's parties do offer the public a real choice, even if the alternatives are not so sharply defined as those in some other democratic nations. Without political parties, the American public would be in a weak position to influence the broad direction of public policy through elections.

Summary

Political parties give elections their force and direction. Through competition for the people's votes, parties give voters an opportunity to influence the policies of government. The people's voice is particularly decisive during realigning periods when the parties search for responses that will satisfy the public's desire for change. The policies that emerge typically define the nation's politics for years to come.

In the United States, party competition takes place within the confines of a two-party system; only the Democratic and Republican parties have any chance of winning control of government. Most other democracies have a multiparty system. The fact that the United States has only two major parties is explained by several factors: an electoral system—characterized by single-member districts—that makes it difficult for third parties to compete for power; each party's willingness to accept political leaders of differing views; and a political culture that stresses compromise and negotiation rather than ideological rigidity. America's two major parties are also maintained by laws and customs that support their domination of elections.

Because the United States has only two major parties, each of which seeks to gain majority support, they normally tend to avoid controversial or extreme political positions. The parties typically pursue moderate and somewhat overlapping policies. Their appeals are designed to win the support of a diverse electorate with moderate opinions. This form of party competition is reflected in the Republican and Democratic coalitions. Although the two parties' coalitions are not identical, they do overlap significantly: each party includes large numbers of individuals who represent nearly every significant interest in the society. Nonetheless, the Democratic and Republican parties sometimes do offer sharply contrasting policy alternatives, particularly in times of political unrest. It is at such times that the public has its best opportunity to make a decisive difference through its vote.

Key Terms

dealignment
grassroots party
multiparty system
party coalition
party competition
party realignment

political party
proportional representation
single-member districts
split-ticket voting
straight-ticket voting
two-party system

Suggested Readings

Aldrich, John H. *Why Parties? The Origin and Transformation of Political Parties in America*. Chicago: University of Chicago Press, 1995. An insightful analysis of what parties are and how they emerge and develop.

Flanigan, William H., and Nancy H. Zingale. *Political Behavior of the American Electorate*. 9th ed. Washington, D.C.: Congressional Quarterly Press, 1998. An analysis of political behavior of the American electorate.

Keith, Bruce E., David B. Magleby, Candice J. Nelson, Elizabeth Orr, Mark C. Westlye, and Raymond E. Wolfinger. *The Myth of the Independent Voter*. Berkeley: University of California Press, 1992. An analysis that asserts that independent voters are actually not very "independent" in their voting patterns.

Lijphardt, Arend. *Electoral Systems and Party Systems: A Study of Twenty-Seven Democracies, 1945–1990.* New York: Oxford University Press, 1994. A comprehensive study of the relationship between electoral systems and party systems.

Manza, Jeffins, and Clem Brooks. *Social Cleavages and Political Change: Voter Alignment and U.S. Party Coalitions.* New York: Oxford University Press, 1999. A systematic look at groups in the context of the party coalitions.

Milkis, Sidney M. *The President and the Parties: The Transformation of the American Party System Since the New Deal.* New York: Oxford University Press, 1993. A careful assessment of how presidential politics has affected the party system.

Patterson, Kelly D. *Political Parties and the Maintenance of Liberal Democracy.* New York: Columbia University Press, 1996. A systematic look at the effects of political parties on American government and politics.

Pomper, Gerald M. *Passions and Interests: Political Party Concepts of American Democracy.* Lawrence: University Press of Kansas, 1992. A broad theoretical analysis of American political parties.

Rosenstone, Steven J., Roy L. Behr, and Edward H. Lazarus. *Third Parties in America.* 2d ed. Princeton, N.J.: Princeton University Press, 1996. An analysis of America's third parties and their impact on the two-party system.

Stonecash, Jeffrey. *Class and Party in American Politics.* Boulder, Colorado: Westview Press, 2000. A provocative analysis that shows the relationship of class and party has been getting stronger.

CHAPTER 9

Political Parties, Candidates, and Campaigns: Contesting Elections

★

By the standards of political parties of most Western democracies, the American party organizations are comparatively weak and insubstantial.

—Frank J. Sorauf[1]

★ ★ ★

*W*here's the party? The question could have been asked as the candidates prepared to battle in the 2000 election for a U.S. Senate seat from New York. One contender was the first lady of the United States. Hillary Clinton brought to the campaign a national reputation and a loyal personal following, but she had never sought public office and had not even resided in the state until a year before the election. But she had enough popular support and money-raising capacity to dissuade other Democrats from challenging her for the Senate nomination. Her opponent initially was Mayor Rudy Giuliani, who had defied the odds of getting elected and reelected as a Republican in heavily Democratic New York City. Giuliani was a party maverick who had angered party leaders when during his first term he endorsed the Democrat candidate for governor. Yet he had a strong electoral base and plenty of campaign money and no Republican stepped forward to challenge him for the Republican nomination. Six months before the election, however, Giuliani was diagnosed with prostate cancer and was under heavy criticism for an extramarital affair. He withdrew from the race, prompting U.S. Representative Rick Lazio to immediately declare his candidacy. Lazio was a relatively junior member of the House, but he had raised a substantial amount of money for a campaign and had the backing of New York Governor George Pataki. Two other Republican House members had also expressed interest in the Senate race, but Lazio's entry dissuaded them from making a run for the nomination.

The New York Senate race in 2000 is an example of the tendency in American politics toward **candidate-centered politics.** Even though candidates compete under the banner of the Democratic or Republican party, they raise most of their own funds, form their own campaign organizations, and decide for themselves when they will run for office and on what issues. This situation is different from the one that exists in Europe. There, a form of **party-centered politics** exists. The party itself decides what the campaign issues will be and how campaign funds will be allocated. The party also chooses the candidates who will seek office under its label. European countries do not have primary elections. The United States has had them since the early 1900s and, as a result, U.S. **party organizations** are among the weakest in the world and U.S. candidates are among the most independent.

This chapter will examine the role of parties and candidates in U.S. politics and describe how modern election campaigns are conducted. The following points are emphasized in the chapter:

Hillary Clinton is the only first lady to seek elective office. She moved to New York to compete in the state's U.S. Senate race in 2000. Clinton is shown here campaigning on the streets of New York City.

candidate-centered politics Election campaigns and other political processes in which candidates, not political parties, have most of the initiative and influence.

party-centered politics Election campaigns and other political processes in which political parties, not individual candidates, hold most of the initiative and influence.

party organizations The party organizational units at national, state, and local levels; their influence has decreased over time because of many factors.

★ *The ability of America's party organizations to control nominations, campaigns, and platforms has declined substantially.* Although the parties continue to play an important role, elections are now controlled largely by the candidates, each of whom is relatively free to go his or her own way.

★ *U.S. party organizations are decentralized and fragmented. The national organization is a loose collection of state organizations, which in turn are loose associations of autonomous local organizations.* This feature of U.S. parties can be traced to federalism and the nation's diversity, which have made it difficult for the parties to act as instruments of national power.

★ *Party organizations, particularly at the state and national levels, have recently made a comeback of sorts by adapting to the money and media demands of modern campaigns.* However, their new relationship with candidates is more of a service relationship than a power relationship.

★ *Candidate-centered campaigns are based on the media and the skills of professional consultants.* Money, strategy, and televised advertising are key components of the modern campaign.

★ *Candidates' relative freedom to run campaigns of their own making lends flexibility to U.S. politics but diminishes the electorate's capacity to influence national policy in a predictable direction.* The choice of a candidate made by voters in any one constituency has no strong relationship to the choices of voters in other constituencies.

The Weakening of Party Control

Party organizations engage in a variety of activities, including public education. But the raison d'être of the party organization is the contesting of elections. Parties recruit candidates, conduct campaigns, and formulate platforms. Other organizations, including interest groups, also do some or all these things (see

Chapter 10). But parties alone owe their existence to the pursuit of electoral success.

Ironically, U.S. party organizations do not dominate any aspect of campaigns, not even the selection of the candidates who run under their banners. Candidates who are not recruited by the party often run and sometimes win. They become the party's choice, whether the organization likes it or not. Even candidates who have the party's enthusiastic backing are often more concerned with marketing themselves than with promoting the party.[2]

In the nineteenth and early twentieth centuries, the situation was different. The party organizations were in control of nominations, elections, and platforms. The story of how and why they lost their commanding position is basic to an understanding of the parties' present role and influence.

CONTROL OF NOMINATIONS

Nomination refers to the selection of the individual who will run as the party's candidate in the general election. The legendary William Marcy ("Boss") Tweed of New York City's Tammany Hall machine once remarked, "I don't care who does the electing just so I can do the nominating."[3] Tweed was stating the obvious. His Democratic machine so thoroughly dominated New York City elections in the late nineteenth century that his hand-picked nominees were virtually guaranteed election. Even in constituencies where the parties are competitive, the nominating decision is a critical choice because it narrows a large field of potential candidates down to the final two, one Republican and one Democrat.

Until the early twentieth century, nominations were the responsibility of party organizations. In smaller communities where voters had personal knowledge of potential candidates, the parties often had no practical alternative but to nominate popular individuals who wanted to run. In the cities, however, the party organizations were in a commanding position. Party label was the prime influence on urban voters, so it was essential for candidates to have party backing. To receive nomination, an individual had to be loyal to the party organization, a requirement that included a willingness to share with it the spoils of office—government jobs and contracts. The situation allowed party organizations to acquire campaign workers and funds but also enabled unscrupulous party leaders to extort money from those seeking political favors. Reform-minded Progressives argued for *party democracy*, claiming that party organizations should operate according to the same principle that governs elections: power should rest with ordinary voters rather than the party bosses (see Chapter 2).

The most serious assault of the Progressives on the party organizations was the introduction of the **primary election** (or **direct primary**) as a method of choosing nominees. In place of party-designated nominees, the primary system placed nomination in the hands of voters. *Primaries are the severest impediment imaginable to the strength of the party organizations.* If primaries did not exist, candidates would have to work through party organizations in order to gain nomination, and they could be denied renomination if disloyal to the party's goals. Because of primaries, however, candidates have the option of seeking

nomination The designation of a particular individual to run as a political party's candidate (its "nominee") in the general election.

primary election (direct primary) A form of election in which voters choose a party's nominees for public office. In most primaries, eligibility to vote is limited to voters who are registered members of the party.

Senator Robert M. La Follette, Sr., of Wisconsin pushed for Progressive reforms, including the use of primary elections to select party nominees. La Follette is shown here near the end of his lengthy political career, speaking on radio as the Progressive party's 1924 presidential nominee.

office on their own, and once elected (with or without the party's help), they can build an independent electoral base that effectively places them beyond the party's direct control.

Today all states have primary elections for contested nominations for U.S. Senate and House seats (in Alabama, Georgia, South Carolina, and Virginia, the parties can nominate through the convention method if they choose to do so). Nearly forty states use primaries to select their delegates to the presidential nominating conventions. The other states use the caucus method, in which voters assemble at local sites to discuss the candidates before expressing their preference for one of them. (The presidential selection process is discussed further in Chapter 14.)

Primary elections take a number of different forms. Most states conduct closed primaries, in which participation is limited to voters registered or declared at the polls as members of the party whose primary is being held. Other states use open primaries, a form that allows independents and voters of either party to vote in a party's primary, although voters are prohibited by law from participating in both parties' primaries simultaneously. A few states have a third form of primary, known as the blanket primary. These states provide a single primary ballot listing both the Republican and Democratic candidates by office. Each voter can cast only one vote per office, but can select a candidate of either party. Louisiana has a variation on this form in which all candidates are listed on the ballot but are not identified by party.

In most states, the winner of a primary election is the candidate who receives the largest number of votes, even if not a majority. In some border and southern states, however, there is a provision for a runoff primary if no candidate receives a majority of the vote (or, in North Carolina, 40 percent of the vote) in the regular primary. Slightly more than half the states have a sore-loser law that prevents a candidate who loses a primary from running as an independent or third-party candidate in the general election.

Primaries have not completely eclipsed the party organizations. Many politicians begin their careers as party volunteers. In this capacity they gain the attention of party leaders, who help them win their first elective office. Having established their political career, they then move up the ladder on their own initiative. Additionally, many party organizations actively try to influence the outcome of primary elections by putting forward their preferred candidate. Nevertheless, primaries are an obstacle to party-centered elections. Without the ability to control who runs under its label, the party is in a weak position to demand that a candidate uphold its governing philosophy.

In the process of taking control of nominations, candidates also have acquired control of most campaign money. At the turn of the century, when party machines were at their peak, most campaign funds passed through the hands of party leaders. Today, more than 80 percent of the money spent on congressional and presidential campaigns goes to the candidates without first passing through the parties.

The absence of primaries in Europe is one of the main reasons the parties there have remained strong (see "How the United States Compares"). They control nominations, and European candidates must operate within the party organizations. A popular leader will be given fairly wide latitude by the party, but it is the parties, not the candidates, that dominate elections. The European

HOW THE UNITED STATES COMPARES

PRIMARY ELECTIONS AND STRONG PARTIES

Primary elections are a defining characteristic of U.S. political campaigns. Primaries were invented in the United States and are used in elections to a wide variety of offices, from president of the United States to city council members. A small number of other countries, including Venezuela, hold primaries for a few offices, but most democracies select their nominees through party organizations.

Nominations are a key element in establishing a party's strength. When a party controls its nominations, it is in a strong position relative to its candidates. Ambitious politicians must work through the party in order to gain office. This situation enables the party to demand loyalty to its platform and also enables it to control other electoral resources, including money and workers. In contrast, primary elections weaken the party. Aspiring politicians can seek nomination directly through a primary, thereby circumventing the party organization. And once elected, incumbents are usually beyond the party's control. Their direct ties to the voters make it difficult for the party to unseat them. From their strong position, candidates are also able to control campaign resources; about 80 percent of campaign funds in U.S. elections are raised directly by the candidates. Not surprisingly, U.S. candidates run on platforms of their own choosing. Although most of them are loyal to the party's traditions, they have wide latitude in deciding where they stand on any particular issue.

Country	Method of Choosing Nominees	Strength of Party Organizations
Canada	Party organizations	Moderate
France	Party organizations	Strong
Germany	Party organizations	Strong
Great Britain	Party organizations	Strong
Italy	Party organizations	Strong
Japan	Party organizations	Strong
Mexico	Party organizations	Strong
United States	Primary elections	Weak

philosophy of party democracy is different from that of the United States. Rather than impose external restrictions on party decisions, European democracies allow the parties to regulate their own affairs, counting on the threat of electoral defeat to keep them in line. By most accounts, European party organizations are no less honest than their U.S. counterparts and are considerably stronger.[4]

CONTROL OF ELECTION WORKERS

Workers have always been a key resource in campaigns, but their relative importance has changed over time, as has their control by parties and candidates.

From their grassroots inception in the Jacksonian era, U.S. parties have depended on a relatively small number of active members. The parties have never had the large dues-paying memberships that characterize some European socialist and labor parties. Even the party machines in their heyday did not attempt to enroll the party electorate as active members. The machine's lowest organizational echelon was the precinct-level unit. Each precinct had several hundred voters but only two party workers, a precinct captain and an assistant.

Patronage was the traditional source of party workers. To get or keep government employment, individuals had to work for the party during election campaigns. Instituted during Andrew Jackson's presidency, this spoils system was a perennial target of reformers, and when antiparty sentiment intensified around 1900, the Progressives demanded that merit-based hiring be expanded. As government jobs shifted from the patronage to the merit system, the party organizations lost some of their vigor. Today, because government has expanded in size, thousands of patronage jobs still exist. Their occupants help staff the parties, but many of them are more loyal to the politician for whom they work than to a party organization. The people who work for members of Congress, for example, are all patronage employees, but they owe their jobs and their loyalty to their senator or representative, not their party.

The parties also get help from volunteers. Volunteers are an important resource, but they are less reliable than patronage employees as campaign workers. Volunteers are more often interested in debating issues than in distributing leaflets, and they cannot be compelled to perform tedious campaign tasks or to work a set number of hours during a campaign. Moreover, volunteers are often more concerned about a particular candidate or issue than about the party's cohesiveness.[5] In 1994, religious-rights activists took over the Minnesota Republican convention and endorsed for governor one of their own people, Allen Quist, even though the party already controlled the governorship. The GOP incumbent, Arne Carlson, subsequently beat Quist in a primary and then won reelection, but the insurgency caused a rift within the Minnesota Republican party.

CONTROL OF PARTY PLATFORMS

Beginning in the 1830s and for more than a century thereafter, U.S. parties had control of the national platforms adopted at the presidential nominating conventions held every four years. Each state party sent a delegation to the national

A campaign volunteer works the phone on behalf of George W. Bush's 2000 presidential campaign. Campaign volunteers are often more interested in a particular issue or candidate than a party.

A century ago, party bosses so dominated the electoral process in some cities that they were regularly accused of stuffing the ballot boxes and pillaging the public treasury. This 1875 cartoon shows New York City's Boss Tweed being released from jail after a new jury found him not guilty of embezzlement. Tweed's organization was widely believed to have rigged the trial.

convention, and most of the delegates were high-ranking organizational and elected party officials. The first real business at each convention was the formulation of the policy proposals that made up the platform, and the delegates took the platform seriously as a statement of their common interests and commitments. (Ticket balancing—the practice of choosing a vice presidential nominee from a different region and wing of the party than the presidential choice—served the same purpose.)

Today the national convention is controlled by the candidate who has accumulated a majority of delegates in the state primaries and caucuses preceding it. Accordingly, the platform is tailored to the policy positions of the nominee-to-be. In an attempt to foster party unity, recent nominees have worked out platform compromises with their opponents and have even made concessions to their own delegates. Nominees, however, insist that major planks in the platform conform to their views and that controversial minor planks be omitted.

National platforms have never been officially binding on presidential candidates, much less on candidates for the House and Senate, who have traditionally embraced, ignored, or rejected platform planks as it suited their purposes. However, the transition from party-centered to nominee-centered conventions has reduced the applicability of the national platform to congressional campaigns. When the parties' organizational and elected leaders, including members of Congress, had control of the platform, they aimed to persuade the delegates to approve planks on which they could campaign. Today, candidates for Congress pretty much ignore the national platform, running instead on platforms of their own devising.

In European democracies, a party's candidates are expected to campaign on the national platform and, if elected as a governing majority, to support its planks, which are formulated in conjunction with organizational leaders. A candidate who repudiates the party's platform is likely to be denied renomination in the next election.

The Structure and Role of Party Organizations

Although the influence of party organizations has declined, parties are not about to die out. Political leaders and activists need a stable organization through which they can work together, and the parties serve that purpose. Moreover, certain activities, such as voter registration drives and get-out-the-vote efforts on election day, benefit all of a party's candidates and are therefore more efficiently conducted through the party organization. Indeed, parties have staged a comeback of sorts.[6] National and state party organizations in particular have developed the capacity to assist candidates with fundraising, polling, research, and media production, which are costly but essential ingredients of a successful modern campaign.

Structurally, U.S. parties are loose associations of national, state, and local organizations (see Figure 9-1). The national parties cannot dictate the decisions of the state organizations, which in turn do not control the activities of local organizations. However, there is communication between the levels, which have a common interest in strengthening the party's position. By comparison, European parties tend to be hierarchical: national parties in Great Britain, for example, have the power to select parliamentary nominees, although they usually follow the recommendations of the local organizations. The major reason that U.S. parties are not hierarchical is the nation's federal system and tradition of local autonomy. Because each governing level in the United States is a competing center of power and ambition, the parties at the national, state, and local levels are able to reject the authority of other levels.

LOCAL PARTY ORGANIZATIONS

In a sense, U.S. parties are organized from the bottom up, not from the top down. There are about 500,000 elective offices in the United States, of which fewer than 500 are contested statewide and only two—the presidency and vice presidency—are contested nationally. All the rest are local offices, so not surprisingly, at least 95 percent of party activists work within local organizations. In addition, as former Speaker of the House Thomas P. "Tip" O'Neill often said, "All politics is local." Distant events may interest voters, but local conditions are more likely to affect how they vote.

It is difficult to generalize about local parties because they vary greatly in their structure and activities. But local parties tend to be strongest in urban areas and in the Northeast and Midwest, where parties traditionally have been more highly organized. In any case, local parties tend to specialize in elections that coincide with local electoral boundaries. Campaigns for mayor, city council, state legislature, county offices, and the like activate local parties to a greater degree than do congressional, statewide, and national contests.

For many Americans, local party organizations are synonymous with the party machines that once flourished in the nation's cities. Well-staffed and

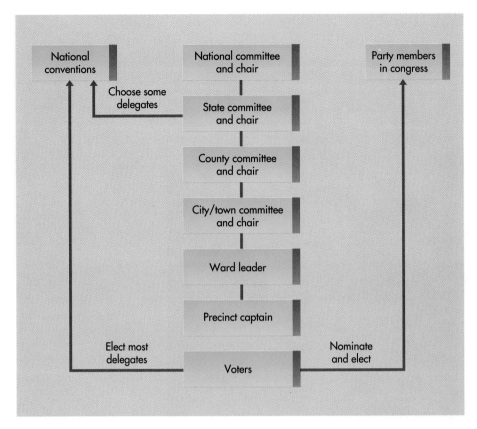

FIGURE 9-1 Formal Organization of the Political Party
U.S. parties are loosely structured alliances of national, state, and local organizations; most local parties are not as well organized as the formal chart implies.

tightly disciplined, the machines were welfare agencies for the poor, vehicles of upward mobility for newly arrived immigrant groups, and brokers of public jobs, contracts, and policies for those willing to meet the price. But above all, the machines could win elections. They were well organized, kept close tabs on voters, and got them to the polls on election day.

The party machines were powerful, but they should not be viewed as representative of party politics in America. Their reign was relatively short: machines flourished during the latter half of the nineteenth century and within a few decades were in retreat in the face of economic and political changes. Moreover, the party machines were located primarily in the big cities of the Northeast and Midwest. Many southern and western cities did not have machinelike parties, and smaller communities rarely had highly organized parties.

Only a few local parties today, including the Democratic organizations in Albany, Philadelphia, and Chicago, bear even a remote resemblance to the old-time machines. In most urban areas the party organizations do not have enough workers to staff even a majority of local precincts (voting districts) on an ongoing basis. However, they do become active during campaigns, when they open campaign headquarters, conduct voter registration drives, send mailings or deliver leaflets to voters, and help get out the vote. These activities are not trivial. Most local campaigns are not well funded, and the party's backing of a candidate can make a critical difference.

Chicago mayor Richard Daley speaks at a campaign event. He is the son of the legendary Chicago mayor of the same name, who headed the last of the big-city party machines. The earlier Mayor Daley "ruled" Chicago during a twenty-year, six-term reign that ended in the 1970s.

In most suburbs and towns, the party's role is less substantial. The parties exist organizationally but typically have little money and few workers; hence they cannot operate effectively as electoral organizations. The individual candidates must carry nearly the entire burden.

STATE PARTY ORGANIZATIONS

At the state level, each party is headed by a central committee made up of members of local party organizations and local and state officeholders. These state central committees do not meet regularly, and they provide only general policy guidance for the state organizations. Day-to-day operations are directed by a chairperson, who is a full-time, paid employee of the state party. The central committee appoints the chairperson, but it often accepts the individual recommended by the party's leading politician, usually the governor or a U.S. senator.

In recent decades the state parties have expanded their budgets and staffs considerably and, therefore, have been able to play a more active electoral role. In contrast, thirty years ago about half of the state party organizations had no permanent staff at all. The increase in state party staff is largely due to improvements in communication technology, such as computer-assisted direct mail, which have made it easier for political organizations of all kinds, parties included, to raise funds. Having acquired the ability to pay for permanent

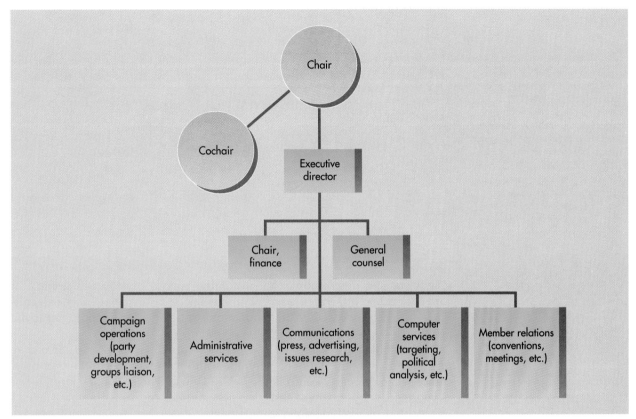

FIGURE 9-2 Organization Chart of the Republican National Committee.
Source: Used by permission of Republican National Committee, 2000.

staffs, state parties have used them to expand their activities, which range from polling to issues research to campaign management. (These activities are discussed in greater detail later in this chapter.)

State party organizations concentrate on statewide races, including those for governor and U.S. senator,[7] and also focus on races for the state legislature. They play a smaller role in campaigns for national or local offices, and in most states they do not endorse candidates in statewide primary contests.

NATIONAL PARTY ORGANIZATIONS

The national party organizations are structured much like those at the state level: they have a national committee, a national party chairperson, and a support staff (see Figure 9-2). The national headquarters for the Republican and Democratic parties are located in Washington, D.C. Although in theory the national parties are run by their committees, neither the Democratic National Committee (DNC) nor the Republican National Committee (RNC) has great power. The RNC (with more than 150 members) and the DNC (with more than 300 members) are too cumbersome to act as deliberative bodies. They meet only periodically, and their power is largely confined to setting organizational

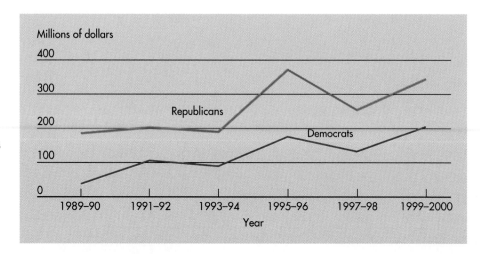

FIGURE 9-3   National Party Expenditures, 1989–2000
Over the years, the Republican party has significantly outspent the Democratic party. The figures include spending by the DNC, RNC, DCCC, NRCC, DSCC, and NRSC. Soft-money (nonfederal) spending is not included.
Source: Federal Elections Commission. The 2000 figures are based on preliminary estimates.

policy, such as determining the site of the party's presidential nominating convention and the rules governing the selection of convention delegates. They have no power to decide nominations or to determine candidates' policy positions.

The national party's day-to-day operations are directed by a national chairperson chosen by the national committee, although it defers to the president's choice when the party controls the White House. The national chairperson is supported by a permanent staff that concentrates on providing assistance in presidential and congressional campaigns.

This focus began in the 1970s when Republican leaders decided that a revamped national party organization could play a contributing role in today's campaigns. The RNC developed campaign-management "colleges" and "seminars" for candidates and their staffs, compiled massive amounts of computer-based electoral data, sent field representatives to assist state and local party leaders in modernizing their operations, and established a media production division. The range of services the RNC provides is substantial. For example, the RNC tapes and catalogues C-SPAN's televised coverage of congressional debate and can instantly retrieve the statement of any speaker on any issue. Republican challengers use this material to create attack ads directed at Democratic incumbents, while Republican incumbents use it to show themselves acting forcefully on issues of concern to their constituents.

The DNC in the early 1980s followed the Republicans' model, but its less affluent political base have kept the Democrats behind (see Figure 9-3). Modern campaigns operate on money, and Democrats have access to less of it. The Republican model has also filtered down to the state Republican and Democratic party committees, which, in varying degrees, provide the types of media, data-research, and educational services that the national committees offer.

The Parties and Money

The national parties' major role in campaigns is the raising and spending of money. The RNC and DNC are major sources of campaign funds, as are

Al Gore walks with Buddhist Master Hsing Yum (left) and Maria Hsia at the Hsi Lai Temple outside Los Angeles during the 1996 campaign. Fundraising activities at this event were probed during a Senate investigation. The charge that Gore had violated campaign finance laws was used against him by opponents during the 2000 campaign.

the party campaign committees in the House and Senate: the Democratic Congressional Campaign Committee (DCCC), National Republican Congressional Committee (NRCC), Democratic Senatorial Campaign Committee (DSCC), and National Republican Senatorial Committee (NRSC).

These party units had a relatively small fundraising role until a loophole developed in the 1970s campaign finance laws. A court ruling gave the parties a nearly unlimited opportunity to raise and spend campaign funds, provided the funds are not channeled directly to a party's candidates.

A party can legally give $10,000 directly to a House candidate and $17,500 to a Senate candidate. This funding, along with the money a candidate receives from individual contributors ($1,000 is the maximum per contributor) and interest groups ($5,000 is the maximum per group), is termed **hard money** since it goes directly to the candidate and can be spent as he or she chooses.

hard money Campaign funds given directly to candidates to spend as they choose.

Party organizations also provide what is known as soft money, which is where the loophole in campaign finance regulation enters the picture. Although federal law limits how much an individual can give directly to a candidate, the loophole permits a contributor to give an unlimited amount to a party. Thus, whereas a wealthy contributor could legally give a candidate only $1,000, that same contributor could give $1 million or more to the candidate's party. By law, this **soft money** is to be spent only on party activities, such as the funding of registration drives and party advertising campaigns. But, of course, this money in the end actually helps particular candidates because it funds campaign activities of benefit to them.

soft money Campaign contributions that are not subject to legal limits and are given to parties rather than directly to candidates.

The existence of soft money is also a temptation to skirt the law and connect party spending to a particular candidacy. During the 1996 presidential election, the Democratic party spent nearly $100 million on "issue" advertising that paralleled the "candidate" advertising of the Clinton campaign. The party ads did not directly urge voters to support Clinton, but his picture appeared in the ads, which featured his accomplishments as president. After the election, the Justice Department launched an investigation into whether the Democratic party ads

CURRENT CONTROVERSIES

SHOULD SOFT MONEY BE OUTLAWED?

Federal law limits the amount that an individual can contribute directly to a presidential or congressional candidate but, as of the 2000 elections, did not restrict the amount that an individual could give a political party. This loophole in the campaign finance laws is the route through which large donors have funneled millions of dollars in soft money into recent campaigns, which has led some politicians to propose the outlawing of these contributions. Others resist a ban, saying it would restrict free expression or hurt the Republican party because it receives a disproportionate share of the soft money. In their battle for the 2000 Republican presidential nomination, George W. Bush and John McCain expressed opposing positions on the issue, as in these excerpts from a candidate debate in Iowa.

YES: The American people need [their government back]. And they're not going to get it back until we get it out of the hands of the special interests, these huge six- and seven-figure donations, the $100,000 checks, the $200,000 checks that have basically taken the government away from the people and put it into the hands of the special interests. . . . [George W. Bush] and I can stop that tonight. We can commit, as nominees of the party, that we will have nothing to do with soft money, with these huge $100,000 checks. We can stop it now. We commit to that and we can get the special-interest money out of American politics. We can give the government back to the people.

—U.S. Senator John McCain (R-Ariz.)

NO: Here's my worry with [McCain's] plan. It's going to hurt the Republican Party. . . . The Democrat Party is really the Democrat Party and the labor unions in America. . . . We do nothing about saying to labor, "You can't take a laboring man's money and spend it the way you see fit." And yet, under this vision [McCain's] got, . . . it's okay that they just take their money and spend it the way they want to spend it. I don't think it's fair. And I think that's unilateral disarmament. . . . There'd better be paycheck protection. Otherwise our Republican Party and our conservative values don't have a shot.

—Governor George W. Bush (R-Texas)

were, in effect, Clinton ads and therefore in violation of the law. The question raised by the Democratic ads is one of several troubling issues surrounding the role of soft money. Many reform advocates believe that soft money threatens the integrity of the entire system of campaign finance regulation and gives wealthy contributors far too much influence over the electoral process.

A ban on soft money was the major issue of Senator John McCain's surprisingly strong bid for the 2000 Republican presidential nomination. Although most citizens favor a ban, efforts to close the soft-money loophole have been unsuccessful, as have efforts generally to restrict the role of money in U.S. campaigns. An obstacle to reform is that the individuals who have the power to change the laws—incumbent officeholders—are the same individuals who benefit the most from the existing system of campaign finance. They raise far more money than their challengers do (see Chapters 10 and 12).

In any event, money is now the greatest source of power for the national parties. The sums involved are enormous. During the last week alone of the 1998 congressional elections, for example, the GOP spent more than $20 million on issue ads for its candidates; most of the money was spent on races where Republican candidates were locked in close fights with their Democratic opponents.

A Service Relationship

Although campaign fundraising and spending is a source of power for the party, its alliance with the candidates is more of a **service relationship** than a power relationship.[8] The party offers help to virtually any of its candidates who has a chance of victory. Without the ability to control the nominating process, the party has little choice but to embrace nearly all candidates who run under its banner. At a minimum, this approach increases the likelihood that the party will gain a congressional majority and thus acquire control of the committees and top leadership positions in the House and Senate (see Chapter 12). The party may also acquire some additional loyalty from officeholders as a result of the contributions it makes to their campaigns. But, because the party is more or less willing to support any candidate, whatever his or her policy positions, its money does not automatically give it much control over how party members conduct themselves after they take office.

service relationship
The situation where party organizations assist candidates for office but have no power to require them to accept or campaign on the party's main policy positions.

The Candidate-Centered Campaign

Although competition between the Republican and Democratic parties provides the backdrop to today's campaigns, the campaigns themselves are largely controlled by the candidates, particularly in congressional, statewide, and presidential races. Each candidate has a personal organization, created especially for the campaign and disbanded once it is over.

RUNNING FOR OFFICE

Today's candidates tend to be self-starters. Some candidates still rise through the ranks of the party or are drafted because no other qualified person is willing to run. But most candidates seek high office because they aspire to a career in politics. They are entrepreneurs who play what the political consultant Joe Napolitan called "the election game."[9] The game begins with money, lots of it.

Seeking Funds: "The Money Chase"

Campaigns for high office are expensive, and the costs keep rising. In 1980, about $250 million was spent on all Senate and House campaigns combined. The figure had jumped to $425 million by 1990 and topped $800 million in 1998.

Because of the high cost of campaigns, candidates are forced to spend much of their time raising funds, which come primarily from individual contributors, interest groups (through PACs, discussed in Chapter 10), and political parties. The **money chase** is relentless.[10] A U.S. senator must raise $20,000 a week on average throughout the entire six-year term in order to raise the $6 million or so that it takes to run a competitive Senate campaign in most states. A Senate campaign in a large state can cost several times that amount. Incumbent senator Al D'Amato and his challenger, Charles Schumer, combined to spend $36 million on the New York Senate race in 1998. In the same state two years later, Hillary Rodham Clinton and Rick Lazio combined to spend nearly double that amount on their Senate race. House campaigns are less costly, but expenditures of $1 million or more are commonplace.[11] As for presidential elections, even the

money chase A term used to describe the fact that U.S. campaigns are very expensive and that candidates must spend a great amount of time raising funds in order to compete successfully.

nominating race is expensive. It has generally been thought that a candidate needs at least $20 million to have a realistic chance of gaining nomination, but even that figure may need revising. In 2000, Texas governor George W. Bush raised $75 million for his nominating campaign. (In presidential races, but not congressional ones, candidates in the general election are eligible to receive federal funds, a topic discussed in Chapter 14. Also see "States in the Nation.")

As might be expected, incumbents have a distinct advantage in fundraising. They have contributor lists from past campaigns and have acquired the public visibility and political clout that donors like. In recent House and Senate races, incumbents have outspent their challengers by more than 2 to 1.[12]

Creating Organization: "Hired Guns"

The "old politics" emphasized party rallies and door-to-door canvassing, which required organizations built around campaign volunteers. The "new politics" is based on the mass media and requires a much different kind of organizational structure. The key operatives are campaign consultants, pollsters, media producers, and fundraising specialists. They are **hired guns** who charge hefty fees for their services.

hired guns A term that refers to the professional consultants who run campaigns for high office.

Some of them are specialists in campaign management. Inexperienced candidates often think that campaigns are simple to run and entrust the job to an amateur, who is often a relative or friend. They soon discover that their campaign is headed nowhere. At this point, if they have the money, they hire a seasoned professional. Over the years, some of these operatives, like James Carville, Joe Napolitan, Ed Rollins, Dick Morris, and Roger Ailes, have developed almost legendary reputations.

Fundraising specialists are also part of the new politics. Direct mail operators have developed contributor lists for every state and nearly every type of candidacy, and they flood the mail with computer-generated letters. There are

In organizing their campaigns, candidates for major office depend more heavily on professional consultants than on party leaders. One of these consultants is James Carville, who ran the Clinton campaign's "war room" in 1992. Carville used the slogan "It's the economy, stupid" as a means of keeping the campaign effort focused on the nation's economic problems.

★ STATES IN THE NATION

PUBLIC FUNDING OF STATE ELECTIONS

Public funding of federal elections is limited to the presidential campaign. The funds are given directly to presidential candidates who meet the qualifying criteria. About half the states also have public funding of election campaigns. Some of these states give the money to the political parties, which then allocate it to candidates or spend it on party activities, such as get-out-the-vote efforts. Other states give funds directly to candidates, although funding is often provided only to candidates for designated offices, such as governor. Many states use the same method of raising these funds that the federal government does; in filing their tax returns, residents can check a box indicating they are willing to have a few of their tax dollars spent on campaigns.

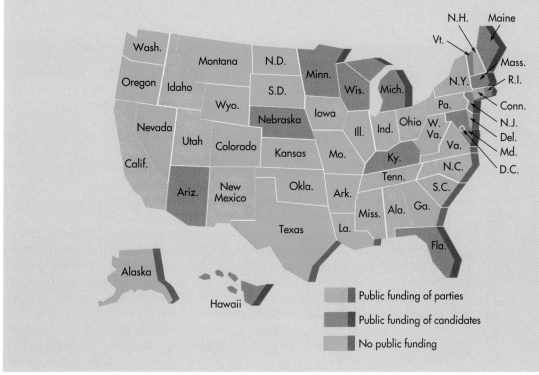

- Public funding of parties
- Public funding of candidates
- No public funding

SOURCE: Common Cause, 2000.

also numerous specialty mailing lists, such as EMILY's List (*early money is like yeast*, "it makes the dough rise"). EMILY's List was started in the 1980s to provide seed money for liberal women candidates. Effective fundraisers also know how to tap into the networks of large contributors and interest groups who give to election campaigns (see Chapter 10).

Polling is another essential component of the modern campaign. Although candidates make use of the public polls conducted by Gallup, the news media, and other organizations, they also hire their own pollsters.[13] They also rely on focus groups, which are small groups of voters assembled to talk at length about the issues and candidates and, in some instances, to evaluate proposed themes and materials, such as televised political ads. Polls and focus groups enable candidates to identify messages that are likely to resonate with the voters. At one point in the 2000 presidential race, for example, George W. Bush shifted from the issue of taxes to issues of education and health care after polls indicated these issues were of greater concern to undecided voters.

Media consultants are another feature of the modern campaign. These experts are adept at producing televised political advertising and creating the "photo-ops" and other staged events that attract news coverage. They also teach the candidates how to use the media properly. Inexperienced candidates soon discover that they cannot "just be themselves" when talking with journalists or participating in a televised debate. They have to conform to the demands of the media, such as the preference of television journalists for sound bites—short, pithy statements that add zest and zing to a news story.[14]

Devising Strategy: "Packaging the Candidate"

In the old days, candidates were nearly prepackaged. They were labeled as Democrats or Republicans, which was about all the guidance most voters wanted or needed. Party labels are still meaningful, but today's campaigns are also based on media images.

Often depicted as hollow deceptions, images are more typically rooted in factual claims.[15] They are constructed by placing aspects of the candidate's partisanship, policy positions, record, and personality in the context of the voters' "ideal" candidate, a process known as the **packaging** of a candidate. The voters want a representative who is honest, able, straightforward, resolute, and responsive to their interests, but there are limits on the claims a candidate can reasonably make. It would be difficult, for example, for Democratic incumbents who have been long-time advocates of welfare spending to convincingly portray themselves as fiscal conservatives. Instead, they would base their images as responsive legislators on other issues such as social security and education. In any case, officeseekers try to create a favorable portrayal of their candidacy that is also plausible. In a way, this type of packaging is as old as politics itself. Andrew Jackson's self-portrayal as "the champion of the people" is an image that any modern candidate could appreciate. What is new is the need to fit the image to the requirements of a media campaign. It must conform to a world of sound bites, thirty-second ads, and televised debates.

Most candidates also try to pin an image on their opponent. It is, predictably, a negative image. Studies indicate that attack messages are based heavily on factual statements about an opponent's personal and political record.[16] There is also evidence to suggest that, message for message, negative appeals may have more impact than positive ones. Unfortunately, one effect of negative campaigning may be to depress voter turnout. By driving up an opponent's negatives, a candidate can allegedly drive down the proportion of the opponent's potential supporters who actually vote on election day.[17]

Going Public: "Air Wars" and "Spin"

The battleground of the modern campaign is the mass media. Televised advertising in particular enables candidates to communicate directly, and on their

packaging   A term of modern campaigning that refers to the process of recasting a candidate's record into an appealing image.

www.mhhe.com/patterson5

Simulation

own terms, with the voters. Candidates spend heavily on the production and airing of televised ads, which account for more than half the expenditures in every presidential campaign and most congressional races. Indeed, televised ads are usually cited as the main reason for the high cost of U.S. campaigns. In most democracies, televised campaigning on behalf of candidates takes place through the parties, which receive *free* air time to make their appeals to voters. Many democracies even prohibit the purchase of televised advertising time by individual candidates (see Table 9-1).

Air wars is the term that the political scientist Darrell West applies to candidates' use of televised ads. Candidates increasingly play off each other's ads, seeking to gain the strategic advantage.[18] Modern production techniques enable well-funded candidates to get new ads on the air within a few hours' time, which allows them to rebut attacks and exploit fast-breaking developments. *Rapid-response* was the term used by the Clinton campaign in 1992 and 1996 for its capacity to counter Republican charges. For example, when Bush ads in the 1992 campaign accused Clinton of having raised taxes when governor of Arkansas, Clinton aired an immediate rebuttal based on his interpretation of his tax record.[19] Rapid-response has become a standard tactic in high-profile contests; both the Gore and Bush campaigns employed the tactic in 2000.

air wars A term that refers to the fact that modern campaigns are often a battle of opposing televised advertising campaigns.

The media campaign also takes place through news vehicles, but coverage varies depending on the race and location. Many House candidates are nearly ignored by their local news media. The New York City media market, for example, includes more than a score of House districts in New York, New Jersey, Pennsylvania, and Connecticut, and candidates in these districts get little or no coverage from the New York media. The presidential campaign, in contrast, gets daily coverage from both national and local media. Between these extremes are Senate races and House races in less populated areas; they always get some news coverage and, if hotly contested, may get heavy coverage.

Candidates try to put a positive spin on their news coverage. They also try to campaign in ways that will lessen the negative spin they have come to expect from journalists. The news is mostly critical in tone, and a candidate's blunder or misstatement can result in a torrent of bad news.[20] As a result, candidates

TABLE 9-1 Television Campaign Practices in Selected Democracies In many democracies, free television time is provided to political parties, and candidates are not allowed to buy advertising time. The United States provides no free time to parties and allows candidates to purchase air time. Television debates are also a feature of many U.S. campaigns.

Country	Paid TV Ads Allowed?	Unrestricted Free TV Time Provided?	Are TV Debates Held?
Canada	Yes	Yes	Yes
France	No	Yes	Yes
Germany	Yes	Yes	Yes
Great Britain	No	Yes	No
Italy	No	Yes	Yes
Netherlands	No	No	Yes
United States	Yes	No	Yes

increasingly rely on scripted statements rather than spontaneous remarks when dealing with the press.

The media campaign also includes debates and talk-show appearances. Debates are particularly important because they often attract a large and attentive audience. But they are also risky encounters because they provide a chance to directly compare the candidates. A weak or bumbled performance can seriously damage a candidate's chances in a close race. To reduce the risks, candidates often spend the day or two before a debate rehearsing their presentation.

Internet Politics: "In the Web"

New communication technology usually makes its way into campaign politics, and the Internet is no exception. Every presidential candidate in 2000 had a website. Each site was packed with information, but its main purposes were to generate public support, raise money, and attract and organize volunteers. Republican candidate John McCain raised more than $1 million for his campaign through Internet contributions.

Although television is still the principal mechanism of election politics, some observers believe that the Internet may eventually replace it, particularly in congressional races. E-mail is much cheaper than television advertising (or, for that matter, traditional mail) and can be more easily directed at supporters and swing voters. Because it is a targeted medium, the Internet may become the channel through which candidates attack each other with charges they feel are not adequately voiced through other channels. This tactic was used, for example, by Republican hopeful Steve Forbes in his unsuccessful effort to derail George W. Bush's nominating campaign. In one instance, the Forbes campaign e-mailed subscribers a copy of a newspaper column that mocked a Bush speech to teenagers that described "a drunken college escapade when he [Bush] stole a

The home pages of the websites of the Democratic National Committee (DNC) and the Republican National Committee (RNC).

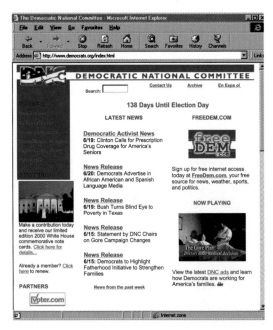

Christmas wreath." The message claimed that the "real lesson" in Bush's remarks was that "the criminal justice system works for rich, white men."[21]

Parties, Candidates, and the Public's Influence

Strong political parties give the public its greatest potential for influence. When a party is cohesive and disciplined enough to adopt a common national platform that is accepted by all its candidates, the electorate has a straightforward opportunity to influence the policies by which the nation will be governed. Voters in all constituencies have a common choice and thus can act collectively with relative ease.

Because European parties are strong national organizations, they periodically offer this type of choice to their electorates. U.S. parties do not provide it. U.S. candidates of the same party in different constituencies run on issues of their own choosing. Of course, U.S. elections produce governing majorities, and it is safe to assume that most elected officials of a particular party share certain ideas. There are common bonds among elected representatives of the same party even when they run and win on their own.[22] But these common bonds are a far cry from a system in which voters everywhere are offered the same choice.

Candidate-centered campaigns have some advantages. First, they provide flexibility and new blood to electoral politics. When political conditions and issues change, self-directed candidates quickly adjust, bringing new ideas into the political arena. Strong party organizations are rigid by comparison. Until recently, for example, the British Labour party was controlled by old-line activists who refused to concede that changes in the British economy called for changes in the party's trade unionist and economic policies. The result was a series of humiliating defeats to the Conservative party that ended only after Tony Blair and other proponents of "New Labour" successfully updated the party's image.

Second, candidate-centered campaigns encourage national officeholders to be responsive to local interests. In building personal followings among their state and district constituents, members of Congress respond to local needs. Nearly every significant domestic program enacted by Congress is adjusted to accommodate the interests of states and localities that would otherwise be hurt by the policy. Members of Congress are not obliged to support the legislative position of their party's majority, and they often extract favors for their constituents as the price of their support. Where strong national parties exist, overarching national interests take precedence over local concerns. In both France and Britain, for example, the pleas of representatives of underdeveloped regions have often gone unheeded by their party's majority.

In other respects, however, candidate-centered campaigns have some real disadvantages. They are fertile ground for powerful special interests, which contribute much of the money that underwrites them.[23] In a party-based system, power can rest on sheer numbers, and so heavy emphasis is placed on appeals to the mass electorate. In a candidate-based system, by contrast, superior campaign funding is prized. In U.S. elections, money increasingly has come from special interests; their financial contributions in congressional campaigns are now three times that of the parties. Many of these special interests give money to incumbents of both parties, which helps to insulate them from an

U.S. Senator Barbara Boxer gestures as she speaks at the 1998 California Democratic State Convention. Boxer was running for reelection in a campaign in which millions of dollars were spent by each side.

election's outcome. Whether the Republicans win or the Democrats win, these groups are assured of having friends in high places. (Chapter 10 discusses the role of interest groups more fully.)

Finally, candidate-centered campaigns can easily degenerate into personality contests. When the emphasis is on the individual candidate rather than broad party differences, there is a tendency to focus on individual traits. Candidates try to portray themselves as virtuous and their opponents as deeply flawed characters. In 1990s elections in New York, Virginia, Massachusetts, Maryland, and other states, the sex life of candidates dominated campaigns. U.S. Senator Charles Robb's reelection campaign in 1994 was greatly weakened by accusations of marital infidelity; Robb won only because his opponent, Oliver North, carried an even more negative image because of his role in the Iran-Contra scandal. Some observers characterize the modern campaign as the era of "attack politics," where negative appeals based on personality and narrow issues are the main thrust.

Candidate-centered campaigns also blur the connection between electing and governing.[24] If national policy goes awry, the individual member of Congress can always blame the problem on others in Congress or on the president. By comparison, lawmakers in a party-centered system cannot easily evade responsibility for what the government has done. In such systems, public dissatisfaction with the performance of government often leads to the majority party's defeat in the next election.

The problem of accountability in the U.S. system is illustrated by surveys that have asked Americans about their confidence in Congress. Although few citizens hold Congress as a whole in high esteem, most citizens say they have confidence in their own representatives. This paradoxical attitude prevails in so many districts that the net result in most elections is a Congress whose membership is not greatly changed from the previous one (see Chapter 12).

In sum, candidate-centered campaigns strengthen the relationship between the voters and their individual representative while at the same time weakening the relationship between the full electorate and their representative institutions. Whether this arrangement serves the public's interest is debatable. Most citizens are not even sure. A Gallup poll found that 81 percent of Americans agreed with the statement that today's politics "seem more like theater or entertainment than like something to be taken seriously." Nevertheless, it is clear that Americans do not want truly strong parties. Parties survived the shift to candidate-centered campaigns and will persist, but their heyday has passed. (Congressional and presidential campaigns are discussed further in Chapters 12 and 14, respectively.)

www.mhhe.com/patterson5

Self-Quiz

Summary

America's political parties are relatively weak organizations. They lack control over nominations, elections, and platforms. Candidates can bypass the party organization and win nomination through primary elections. Individual candidates also control most of the organization and money necessary to win elections and run largely on personal platforms.

Primary elections are a major reason for the organizational weakness of America's parties. Once the parties lost their hold on the nominating process, they became subordinate to candidates. More generally, the political parties have been undermined by election reforms, some of which were intended to weaken the party and others of which have unintentionally done so. Recently the state and national party organizations have expanded their capacity to provide candidates with modern campaign services and are again playing a prominent role in election campaigns. Nevertheless, party organizations at all levels have few ways of controlling the candidates who run under their banners. They assist candidates with campaign technology, workers, and funds but cannot compel candidates' loyalty to organizational goals.

America's parties are decentralized, fragmented organizations. The relationship among local, state, and national party organizations is marked by paths of common interest rather than lines of authority. The national party organization does not control the policies and activities of the state organizations, and they in turn do not control the local organizations. The fragmentation of parties prevents them from acting as cohesive national organizations. Traditionally the local organizations have controlled most of the party's work force because most elections are contested at the local level. Local parties, however, vary markedly in their vitality.

American political campaigns, particularly those for higher-level office, are candidate centered. Most candidates are self-starters who become adept at "the election game." They spend much of their time raising campaign funds, and they build their personal organizations around hired guns: pollsters, media producers, and election consultants. Strategy and image-making are key components of the modern campaign, as is televised political advertising, which accounts for roughly half of all spending in presidential and congressional races.

Because America's parties cannot control their candidates or coordinate their policies at all levels, they are unable to consistently present the voters with a coherent, detailed platform for governing. The national electorate as a whole is thus denied a clear choice among policy alternatives and has difficulty exerting a decisive and predictable influence through elections.

Key Terms

air wars
candidate-centered politics
hard money
hired guns
money chase
nomination

packaging
party-centered politics
party organizations
primary election (direct primary)
service relationship
soft money

Suggested Readings

Allswang, John. *Bosses, Machines, and Urban Voters*. Baltimore: Johns Hopkins University Press, 1986. A penetrating study of the party machines that once flourished in America's cities.

Corrado, Anthony, Thomas E. Mann, Dan Ortiz, Trevor Potter, and Frank Sorauf, eds. *Campaign Finance Reform: A Sourcebook*. Washington, D.C.: Brookings Institution Press, 1997. An informative reference guide about campaign finance reform.

Ehrenhalt, Alan. *The United States of Ambition*. New York: Times Books, 1991. A provocative book that claims that self-starting politicians are the reason the U.S. government has a scarcity of sound leadership.

King, Anthony. *Running Scared: The Victory of Campaigning over Governing in America*. New York: Free Press, 1997. An analysis of why America's leaders have succumbed to the pressure of the permanent campaign.

Menefee-Libey, David. *The Triumph of Campaign-Centered Politics*. New York: Chatham House, 2000. A study that examines the dominance of candidate-centered politics.

Sabato, Larry, and Glenn Simpson. *Dirty Little Secrets: The Persistence of Corruption in American Politics*. New York: Times Books, 1996. Argues that money is the main problem in elections and that strict reforms are needed.

Schlesinger, Joseph. *Political Parties and the Winning of Office*. Ann Arbor: University of Michigan Press, 1991. An evaluation of the parties' role in elections.

Wattenberg, Martin P. *The Decline of American Political Parties, 1952–1996*. New York: Free Press, 1998. A study that documents the declining strength of the parties.

West, Darrell M. *Air Wars: Television Advertising in Election Campaigns, 1952–1996*. 2d ed. Washington, D.C.: Congressional Quarterly Press, 1997. An innovative and updated study of the role advertising plays in political campaigns.

Interest Groups: Organizing for Influence

★

The flaw in the pluralist heaven is that the heavenly chorus sings with a strong upper-class bias.

—E. E. Schattschneider[1]

★ ★ ★

*T*hey launched their attack within hours of the announcement that congressional Republicans had included Medicare in their balanced-budget proposal. The GOP lawmakers planned a $1.1 trillion reduction in federal spending over seven years, including a $270 billion cut in health care for the elderly. Senior-citizen groups assailed the plan and quickly organized a mass demonstration outside the Capitol. The next step was an orchestrated campaign of thousands of angry calls, letters, telegrams, and faxes from retirees to their congressional representatives.

President Clinton sided with the seniors' lobby, promising to veto the Republican bill, which led to a showdown between Congress and the White House that forced a temporary shutdown of the federal government. In January 1996, after a six-week battle and with their poll ratings dropping almost daily, Republican lawmakers shelved their balanced-budget proposal.

The campaign against the Republicans' Medicare initiative suggests why interest groups are both admired and feared. On the one hand, groups have a legitimate right to express their views on public policy issues. It is entirely appropriate for senior citizens or any other group—whether farmers, consumers, business firms, or college students—to actively promote their interests through collective action.

In fact, the *pluralist* theory of American politics (see Chapter 1) holds that society's interests are most effectively represented through the efforts of groups. An extreme statement of this view is Arthur F. Bentley's claim in 1908 that society is "nothing other than the complex of groups that compose it."[2] Although modern pluralists make far less sweeping claims, they do contend that the group process, on balance, is open to a great range of interests, nearly all of which benefit from organized activity in one significant way or another.

Yet groups can wield too much power. If a group gets its way at an unreasonable cost to the rest of society, the public interest is harmed. When the Republican budget package was prepared in Congress, polls indicated that most Americans wanted a balanced federal budget and were willing to bear a fair share of the costs. Did the senior-citizen lobby, in pursuit of its own narrow interest, derail a sound budgetary proposal? Or did the Republican package, which also included tax cuts for upper-income Americans, place on the elderly too much of the burden of a balanced budget?

Opinions on these questions differ widely, but there is no doubt that the special interest in some cases wrongly prevails over the general interest. Indeed, most observers are of the opinion that groups have achieved too much influence over public policy in recent decades. Some analysts describe the situation as the triumph of **single-issue politics:** separate groups organized around nearly

single-issue politics The situation in which separate groups are organized around nearly every conceivable policy issue and press their demands and influence to the utmost.

interest group A set of individuals who are organized to promote a shared political interest.

every conceivable policy issue, with each group pressing its demands and influence to the utmost, at whatever cost to the broader society. The structure of the American political system provides fertile ground for group influence, particularly when a group seeks to protect government benefits it already receives. The system's elaborate checks and balances make it relatively easy for a group, if it has support even within a single institution, to block efforts to cut its benefits. (This "Madisonian dilemma" will be explored more fully in the chapter's concluding section.)

An **interest group** can be defined as a set of individuals who organize to promote a shared political interest. Also called a "faction" or "pressure group" or "special interest," an interest group is characterized by its formalized organization and by its pursuit of policy goals that stem from its members' shared interest. Thus, a bridge club or an amateur softball team is not an interest group because it does not seek to influence the political process. Organizations such as the Association of Wheat Growers, Common Cause, the National Organization for Women, the World Wildlife Fund, the National Rifle Association, and the Anti-Defamation League of B'nai B'rith are interest groups because, despite their differences, they all meet the definition's two criteria: each is an organized entity and each seeks to further its members' interests through political action.

Interest groups promote public policies, encourage the political participation of their members, support candidates for public office, and work to influence policy makers. Interest groups are thus similar to political parties in certain respects, but the two types of organizations differ in important ways. Major political parties address a broad range of issues so as to appeal to diverse blocs of voters. Parties exist to contest elections. They change their policy positions as the voters' preferences change; for the party, winning is almost everything. In comparison, interest groups focus on specific issues of immediate concern to their members; farm groups, for example, concentrate on agricultural policy. A group may involve itself in elections, but its purpose is to influence public policy.

This chapter examines the degree to which various interests in American society are represented by organized groups, the process by which interest groups exert influence, and the costs and benefits of group politics in regard to the public good. The main points made in the chapter are the following:

★ *Although nearly all interests in American society are organized to some degree, those associated with economic activity, particularly business enterprises, are by far the most thoroughly organized.* Their advantage rests on their superior financial resources and on the fact that they offer potential members private goods (such as wages and jobs).

★ *Groups that do not have economic activity as their primary function often have organizational problems.* They pursue public or collective goods (such as a safer environment) that are available even to individuals who are not group members, and so individuals may choose not to pay the costs of membership.

★ *Lobbying and electioneering are the traditional means by which groups communicate with and influence political leaders.* Recent developments,

The American Association of Retired Persons (AARP) has roughly thirty million members and is the largest citizens' group. The AARP's membership benefits include a magazine, *Modern Maturity*.

HOW THE UNITED STATES COMPARES

GROUPS: "A NATION OF JOINERS"

"A nation of joiners" is how the Frenchman Alexis de Tocqueville described the United States during his visit to this country in the 1830s.

Even today, Americans are more actively involved in groups and community causes than are Europeans. The American tradition of group activity is only one reason. Another is the structure of the U.S. political system. Because of federalism and the separation of powers, the American system offers numerous points at which groups can try to influence public policy. If unsuccessful with legislators, groups can turn to executives or the courts. If thwarted at the national level, groups can turn to state and local governments. By comparison, the governments of most other democratic nations are not organized in ways that facilitate group access and influence. France's unitary government, for example, concentrates power at the national level.

Such differences are reflected in citizens' participation rates. Americans are more likely to belong to groups than, for example, the French, Italians, British, or Germans, as the accompanying figures from the World Values Survey indicate.

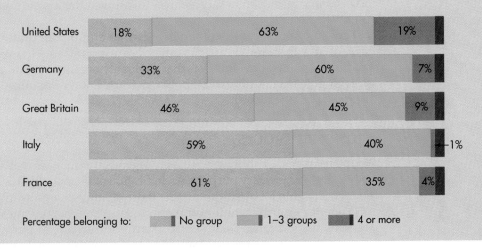

	No group	1–3 groups	4 or more
United States	18%	63%	19%
Germany	33%	60%	7%
Great Britain	46%	45%	9%
Italy	59%	40%	1%
France	61%	35%	4%

Percentage belonging to: ■ No group ■ 1–3 groups ■ 4 or more

including grassroots lobbying and PACs, have given added visibility to groups' activities.

★ *The interest-group system overrepresents business interests and higher-income groups and fosters policies that serve a group's interest more than the public interest.* Thus, although groups are an essential part of the democratic process, they also distort that process.

The Interest-Group System

In the 1830s, the Frenchman Alexis de Tocqueville wrote that the "principle of association" was nowhere more evident than in America.[3] The country's tradition of free association has always made it easy for Americans to join together for political purposes, and their diverse interests have given them reason to seek influence through specialized groups. Few nations have as many separate economic, ethnic, religious, social, and geographic interests as the United States (see "How the United States Compares"). Moreover, because of federalism and separation of powers, numerous political institutions at all levels of government are available for groups to lobby. Not surprisingly, manufacturing, labor, agriculture, and other leading interests have not only national organizations but also separate state and local lobbies. In recent years, for example, tobacco firms have spent millions of dollars to lobby state governments in an effort to defeat or dilute legislation aimed at restricting the sale of cigarettes.

The extraordinary number of groups in the United States does not indicate, however, that the nation's various interests are equally well organized. Organizations develop when people with shared interests have the opportunity and the incentive to join together. Some individuals have the skills, money, contacts, or time to participate effectively in group politics, but others do not. Some groups are inherently more attractive to potential members than others are and thus find it easier to build large or devoted followings. Organizations also differ in their access to financial resources and thus differ also in their capacity for political action.

Therefore, a first consideration in regard to group politics in America is the issue of how thoroughly various interests are organized. Group politics is the politics of organization. Interests that are highly organized stand a good chance of having their views heard by policy makers. Poorly organized interests run the risk of being ignored.

ECONOMIC GROUPS

No interests are more fully or effectively organized than those that have economic activity as their primary purpose. An indication of their advantage is the fact that their Washington lobbyists outnumber those of other groups by more than 2 to 1.

Economic groups include corporations, labor unions, farm groups, and professional associations. They exist primarily for economic purposes: to make profits, provide jobs, improve pay, or protect an occupation. For the sake of discussion, such organizations will be called **economic groups,** although it is important to recognize that their political goals can include policies that transcend the narrow economic interests of their members. Thus, the AFL-CIO concentrates on labor objectives, but it also takes positions on broader issues of foreign and domestic policy.

economic groups Interest groups that are organized primarily for economic reasons, but that engage in political activity in order to seek favorable policies from government.

An Organizational Edge

One reason for the abundance of economic groups is their access to financial resources. Political activity does not come cheap. If a group is to make its views known, it normally must have a headquarters, an expert staff, and communication facilities. Economic groups can obtain the requisite money and expertise from their economic activities. Corporations have the greatest natural advantage. They do not have to charge membership dues or conduct fundraisers to get money to support their lobbying. Their political money comes from the goods and services they produce and sell.

Some economic groups do depend on dues for their support, but they can offer prospective members a powerful incentive to join: **private (individual) goods,** which are the benefits that a group can grant directly to the individual

private (individual) goods Benefits that a group (most often an economic group) can grant directly and exclusively to individual members of the group.

member. For example, workers in the state of Michigan cannot hold automobile assembly jobs unless they belong to the United Auto Workers (UAW). The UAW has a **material incentive**—the economic lure of high wages—to attract potential members. Economic groups are highly organized in part because they serve the individual economic needs of potential members. The predominance of economic interests was predicted in *Federalist* No. 10, in which James Madison declared that property is "the most common and durable source of factions." Stated differently, nothing seems to matter quite so much to people as their pocketbooks and livelihoods.

material incentive An economic or other tangible benefit that is used to attract group members.

Types of Economic Groups

Most economic groups are of four general types: business groups, labor groups, agricultural groups, and professional groups.

Business Groups.   Writing in 1929, E. Pendleton Herring noted, "Of the many organized groups maintaining offices in [Washington], there are no interests more fully, more comprehensively, and more efficiently represented than those of American industry."[4] Although corporations do not dominate the group system to the same degree that they did in the past, Herring's general conclusion still holds: more than half of all groups formally registered to lobby Congress are business organizations. Nearly all large corporations and many smaller ones are politically active. They concentrate their activities on policies that touch directly on business interests, such as tax, tariff, and regulatory decisions.

Business firms are also represented through associations. Some of these associations, such as the U.S. Chamber of Commerce, which represents nearly 3 million businesses of all sizes, seek to advance the general interests of business and to articulate a business perspective on broad policy issues. Other business associations, such as the American Petroleum Institute, are confined to a single trade or industry. Because each trade association represents a single industry, it can promote the interests of member corporations even when these interests conflict with those of business generally. Thus, while the Chamber of Commerce promotes a global free trade policy, some trade associations seek protective tariffs because their member firms want barriers against foreign competition.

Business interests have the advantage of what the economist Mancur Olson calls "the size factor."[5] Although large groups can claim that government should pay more attention to them because they represent more people, small groups are usually more cohesive. Everyone is a consumer, but most consumers do not see any benefit in belonging to a consumer advocacy group. On the other hand, because business firms in a particular industry are few in number, they are likely to recognize the significance of their individual contribution to a collective effort. When the "Big Three" U.S. automakers—General Motors, Ford, and Chrysler—fought federally mandated safety and mileage-efficiency standards, the defection of any one of them would likely have meant defeat. But they stayed together and won concessions from the government. In the process, each automaker saved hundreds of millions of dollars in design and production costs on new autos. In one instance, the automakers gained a multiyear delay in the installation of air bags in all new cars. Their gain came at an unknown cost to consumers, whose newly purchased automobiles were less safe than they could have been.

Labor Groups.   Since the 1930s, organized labor has been politically active on a large scale. Its goal has been to promote policies that benefit workers in general and union members in particular. Although some independent unions, such as the United Mine Workers, lobby actively, the dominant labor group is the AFL-CIO, which maintains its national headquarters in Washington, D.C. The AFL-CIO has more than thirteen million members in its ninety-seven affiliated unions, which include the International Brotherhood of Electrical Workers, the Sheet Metal Workers, the Communication Workers of America, and, as of 1987, the giant International Brotherhood of Teamsters.

At one time, about a third of the U.S. work force was unionized, but today only about one-seventh of all workers belong to unions. Skilled and unskilled laborers have been the core of organized labor, and their numbers are decreasing while professionals, technicians, and service workers are increasing in number. Professionals have shown little interest in union organization, perhaps because they identify with management or see themselves as economically secure. Service workers and technicians are also more difficult for unions to organize than traditional laborers are because they work closely with managers and, often, in small offices.

Nevertheless, unions have made some inroads in recent decades in their efforts to organize service and public employees. Teachers, postal workers, police, firefighters, and social workers are among the public employee groups that have become increasingly unionized. Today, the nation's largest unions are those that represent service and public employees rather than skilled and unskilled laborers (see Table 10-1).

Agricultural Groups.   Farm organizations represent another large economic lobby. The American Farm Bureau Federation is the largest of the farm groups, with more than four million members. The National Farmers Union, the National Grange, and the National Farmers Organization are smaller farm lobbies. Agricultural groups do not always agree on policy issues. For instance, the Farm Bureau sides with agribusiness and owners of large farms, while the Farmers Union promotes the interests of smaller "family" farms.

TABLE 10-1   The Largest Labor Unions, 1950 and 2000   The largest labor unions today represent service and public employees; in the past the largest unions represented skilled and unskilled workers.

1950	2000
1. United Auto Workers	1. National Education Association
2. United Steel Workers	2. International Brotherhood of Teamsters
3. International Brotherhood of Teamsters	3. United Food and Commercial Workers International
4. United Brotherhood of Carpenters & Joiners	4. American Federation of State, County, & Municipal Employees
5. International Association of Machinists	5. Service Employees International

SOURCE: U.S. Department of Labor.

This 1873 lithograph illustrates the benefits of membership in the National Grange, an agricultural interest group.

There are also numerous specialty farm associations, including the Association of Wheat Growers, the American Soybean Association, and Associated Milk Producers. Each association acts as a separate lobby to try to obtain policies beneficial to its members' narrow agricultural interests.

Professional Groups.   Most professions have lobbying associations. Perhaps the most powerful of these groups is the American Medical Association (AMA), which, with nearly 300,000 members, represents about half the nation's physicians. The AMA has consistently opposed any government policy that would limit physicians' autonomy. Other professional groups are the American Bar Association and the American Association of University Professors, each of which maintains a lobbying office in Washington.

CITIZENS' GROUPS

Although economic interests are the best organized groups, they do not have a monopoly on group activity. There are a great number and variety of other organized interests, which are referred to collectively as **citizens' groups** (or **noneconomic groups**). The members of groups in this category are drawn together not by the promise of direct economic gain but by **purposive incentives**—opportunities to promote a cause in which they believe.[6] Whether a group's goal is to protect the environment, reduce the threat of nuclear war, return prayer to the public schools, feed the poor at home or abroad, or

citizens' (noneconomic) groups Organized interests formed by individuals drawn together by opportunities to promote a cause in which they believe but that does not provide them significant individual economic benefits.

purposive incentive An incentive to group participation based on the cause (purpose) that the group seeks to promote.

Environmental activists protest against automobile and truck emissions, which are a leading cause of air pollution. Although environmental groups have been quite successful in attracting public support, they still confront the so-called free-rider problem—the fact that people will gain the benefit of a group's effort even if they do not contribute to it.

whatever, there are citizens who are willing to participate simply because they believe the policy goal is a worthy cause.[7]

In comparison with economic groups, citizens' groups have a harder time acquiring the resources necessary for organization. These groups do not generate profits or fees as a result of economic activity. Moreover, the incentives they offer prospective members are not exclusive. Unlike the private or individual goods provided by many economic groups, most noneconomic groups offer **collective goods** (or **public goods**) as an incentive for membership. Collective goods are, by definition, benefits that must be shared; they cannot be allotted on an individual basis. The air we breathe and the national forests we visit are examples of collective goods. They are available to one and all, those who pay dues to a clean-air group or a wilderness group and those who do not.

collective (public) goods
Benefits that are offered by groups (usually citizens' groups) as an incentive for membership, but that are nondivisible (e.g., a clean environment) and therefore are available to nonmembers as well as members of the particular group.

free-rider problem   The situation in which the benefits offered by a group to its members are also available to nonmembers. The incentive to join the group and to promote its cause is reduced because nonmembers (free riders) receive the benefits (e.g., a cleaner environment) without having to pay any of the group's costs.

The Free-Rider Problem

This characteristic of collective goods creates what is called the **free-rider problem:** individuals can receive the good even when they do not contribute to the group's effort. Take the case of an environmental group that successfully lobbies Congress for tougher air pollution laws. The collective good produced by the legislation—cleaner air—is available to group members and nonmembers alike. Public broadcasting is another example. Although its programs are funded in part through viewers' donations, those who do not contribute can also watch the programs. The noncontributors are free riders: they receive the benefit without paying any of the costs of providing it. About 90 percent of those who regularly view or listen to public broadcasting do not contribute to their local station.

As the economist Mancur Olson notes, it is not rational, in a purely economic sense, for individuals to contribute to a citizens' group, because they can obtain the benefit without paying for it.[8] Moreover, the dues paid by any single member are too small to affect the group's success one way or another. Why pay dues to a clean-air group when any improvement in air quality from its lobbying efforts is available to everyone and when one's contribution is too small to make a real difference? Although many people do join such groups anyway, there is no doubt that the free-rider problem is a reason why citizens' groups are less highly organized than economic ones.

TABLE 10-2 Advantages and Disadvantages Held by Economic and Citizens' Groups Compared with economic groups, citizens' groups have fewer advantages and more disadvantages.

Economic Groups	Citizens' Groups
Advantages	*Advantages*
Economic activity provides the organization resources necessary for political action.	Members are likely to support leaders' political efforts because they joined the group in order to influence policy.
Individuals are encouraged to join the group because of economic benefits they individually receive (e.g., wages).	*Disadvantages*
	The group has to raise funds especially for its political activities.
Disadvantages	Potential members may choose not to join the group because they get collective benefits even if they do not join (the free-rider problem).
Persons within the group may not support leaders' political efforts because they did not join the group for political reasons.	

Citizens' groups try to surmount the free-rider problem by creating individual benefits, akin to those offered by economic groups, to make membership more attractive. Organizational newsletters and social activities are among the individual benefits that citizens' groups offer as a lure to membership. Computer-assisted direct mail has also helped citizens' groups attract members. Group organizers buy mailing lists and flood the mails with computer-typed "personal" letters asking recipients to pay a small annual membership fee. For some individuals, a fee of $25 to $50 annually represents no great sacrifice and offers the personal satisfaction of supporting a cause in which they believe. Until the computer era, citizens' groups had great difficulty in identifying and contacting potential members, which is a reason why the number of such groups was so much smaller in the past than is true today. On the whole, however, the organizational advantages rest with economic groups. In nearly all respects, they have the upper hand on citizens' groups (see Table 10-2).

One area where citizens' groups have gained an edge is the Internet, which has made it easier for these groups to contact their members. Nearly every citizen group of any size has its own website, and many have developed the capacity to reach individual members with urgent and periodic messages. One of the most successful citizen campaigns in history was conducted largely through the Internet. It was a global campaign aimed at the elimination of land mines, and its chief organizer, Jody Williams, received the Nobel Peace Prize in 1997 for her work. Through the Web, she linked together activists and groups throughout the world and, in the end, succeeded in getting one hundred countries to agree to an international treaty that bans the use of land mines and the destruction of those already in the ground.

www.mhhe.com/patterson5

Simulation

Types of Citizens' Groups

Most citizens' groups are of three general types: public interest groups, single-issue groups, and ideological groups.

Public Interest Groups.   Public interest groups are those that claim to represent the broad interests of society as a whole. Despite their label, public interest groups are not led by people elected by the public at large, and the issues they target are ones of their own choosing, not the public's. Just what constitutes the "public interest" is often a subject on which people disagree. And if there is disagreement, can either side truly claim to represent the "public interest"? Moreover, even narrowly self-interested groups often claim that their goals are somehow in the "public interest," as, for example, when a manufacturing firm argues that a tax break it seeks will save workers' jobs. Nevertheless, there is a basis for distinguishing the so-called public interest groups from economic groups: the latter seek direct material benefits for their members, while the former seek benefits that are less tangible and more broadly shared. For example, the National Association of Manufacturers, an economic group, seeks policies favorable to large corporations, while the League of Women Voters, a public interest group, seeks policies—such as simplified voter registration—that can benefit the public in general.

The League of Women Voters has existed for decades, but more than half of the currently active public interest groups were established after 1960. One of these newer organizations is Common Cause, which has more than 200,000 members. Their annual dues help support a seventy-person national staff of lobbyists, attorneys, and public relations experts. Founded by John Gardner, a former cabinet secretary, Common Cause, which describes itself as "a national

Jody Williams won the Nobel Peace Prize in 1997 for organizing a worldwide lobby of citizens' groups in a successful campaign to ban the use of land mines. The Internet was her primary means of organization.

citizens' lobby," concentrates on political reform in such areas as campaign finance. It has been a principal advocate of public funding of congressional campaigns. Its ongoing "People vs. PACs" campaign is aimed at reducing the influence of interest groups on elections.

Single-Issue Groups. A single-issue group is organized to influence policy in just one area. Notable current examples are the National Rifle Association and various right-to-life and pro-choice groups that have formed around the issue of abortion. The number of single-issue groups has risen sharply in the past two decades, and they now lobby on almost every conceivable issue, from nuclear arms to day care centers to drug abuse. Single-issue groups with a national membership are the most prominent, but many single-issue groups are organized and operate autonomously on the local level.

Environmental groups are sometimes classified as public interest groups, but they may also be considered single-issue organizations in that most of them seek to influence public policy in a specific area, such as pollution reduction, wilderness preservation, or wildlife protection. The Sierra Club is one of the oldest of such groups. It was formed in the 1890s to promote the preservation of scenic areas. Also prominent are the National Audubon Society, the Wilderness Society, the Environmental Defense Fund, Greenpeace U.S.A., and the Izaak Walton League. Between 1960 and 1970, membership in environmental groups tripled in response to increased public concern about the quality of the environment.[9] Since then, membership in environmental groups has continued to grow.

Ideological Groups. Single-issue groups have a narrowly focused policy agenda. Other groups take a broader view, usually from the perspective of a general philosophical or moral stance. These groups have been labeled ideological groups. An example is the Christian Moral Government Fund, which was organized to restore "Christian values" to American life and politics. Americans

Gary Bauer is a leading conservative activist who helped mold elements of the Christian right into a powerful interest group. He sought the GOP presidential nomination in 2000 on an anti-abortion platform.

for Democratic Action (ADA) is another example of an ideological group. The ADA supports liberal positions on a wide range of social, economic, and foreign policy issues. Ideological groups on both the left and right have increased substantially in number since the 1960s.

Groups such as the National Organization for Women and the National Association for the Advancement of Colored People (NAACP) can also be generally classified as ideological groups. Their aim is to promote the broad interests of a particular demographic segment of society. The NAACP was formed in 1909 to promote the political interests of racial minorities, primarily through initiating lawsuits on their behalf.

A SPECIAL CATEGORY OF INTEREST GROUP: GOVERNMENTS

While the vast majority of organized interests in the United States represent private concerns, a growing number of interest groups represent governments, both foreign and subnational.

The U.S. federal government makes policies that directly affect the economic development, political stability, and security of nations throughout the world. Arms sales, foreign aid, immigration, and import restrictions and other trade practices have a great impact on foreign nations. For this reason, most foreign nations supplement the political efforts made through their embassies with the services of paid lobbying agents in Washington. Although lobbying by foreign governments is subject to some restrictions, most governments have managed to circumvent these vague regulations. In addition to sending their own agents to Washington, many countries hire American lobbyists to assist their efforts. Roughly one thousand registered agents represent foreign nations' interests in Washington.[10]

States, cities, and other governmental units within the United States also lobby heavily. Although most major cities across the United States and two-thirds of the states have at least one Washington lobbyist, cooperative lobbying is perhaps more important. The intergovernmental lobby includes such groups as the Council of State Governments, the National Governors Conference, the National Association of Counties, the National League of Cities, and the U.S. Conference of Mayors. These organizations are, in essence, the trade associations of subnational governments. They represent the broad interests of cities and states while still allowing individual member cities and states to lobby for their particular interests. A second component of the intergovernmental lobby consists of organizations representing the concerns of bureaucratic specialists at the subnational level—for example, highway engineers, county welfare directors, and housing and redevelopment officials.

The interests of subnational governments vary greatly. The problems of frostbelt states differ from those of sunbelt states; cities in the industrial Northeast face problems that are almost unknown in cities of the Southwest. These differences impose limits on the effectiveness of the intergovernmental lobby. Nonetheless, its presence in Washington has demonstrably influenced many major policy decisions that affect state and local governments.[11] An example is the welfare reform legislation that Congress enacted in 1996. The state governors lobbied hard for a bill that would not unduly shift the costs of the new program to the states. The legislation was also shaped by lessons learned from experimental state programs, such as Wisconsin's welfare-to-work program.

Inside Lobbying: Seeking Influence Through Official Contacts

Modern government provides a supportive environment for interest groups. First, modern government is involved in so many issues—business regulation, income maintenance, urban renewal, cancer research, and energy development, to name only a few—that hardly any interest in society could fail to benefit significantly from having influence over federal policies or programs. Moreover, most of what government does is decided without much publicity and with the participation of a relatively small group of officials. These conditions, as E. E. Schattschneider noted, are conducive to group influence.[12]

Second, modern government is oriented toward action. Officials are inclined to look for policy solutions to problems rather than to let problems linger. For example, when brush fires raged out of control in New Mexico in 2000 and destroyed property worth millions, Washington immediately granted assistance and funds to residents who had incurred losses and cleanup costs.

A group's ability to gain the government's support depends on any number of factors, including its size, its financial strength, and the nature of its policy demands.[13] Groups seek support through **lobbying,** a term that refers broadly to efforts of groups to influence public policy through contact with public officials. According to Norman Ornstein and Shirley Elder, the two main lobbying strategies may be labeled as "inside lobbying" and "outside lobbying."[14] Each strategy involves communication between public officials and group lobbyists, but the strategies differ as to what is communicated, who does the communicating, and who receives the communication. Let's begin by discussing **inside lobbying,** which is based on group efforts to develop and maintain close ("inside") contacts with policy makers. (Outside lobbying will be described in the next section.)

> **lobbying** The process by which interest-group members or lobbyists attempt to influence public policy through contacts with public officials.

> **inside lobbying** Direct communication between organized interests and policy makers, which is based on the assumed value of close ("inside") contacts with policy makers.

ACQUIRING ACCESS TO OFFICIALS

Inside lobbying is designed to give a group direct access to officials in order to influence their decisions. Access is not the same as influence, which is the capacity to affect policy decisions. But access is a critical first step in the influence process.[15]

Lobbying once depended significantly on tangible inducements, sometimes including indirect or even outright bribes. This old form of lobbying survives today. Through personal and family contributions, Charles H. Keating Jr., owner of Lincoln Savings and Loan, contributed hundreds of thousands of dollars to the campaigns of five U.S. senators, each of whom interceded on his behalf with the Federal Home Loan Bank Board, which was investigating Lincoln's finances. When asked whether his contributions helped him, Keating said, "I certainly hope so." The investigation of Lincoln Savings lagged for two years, costing taxpayers an estimated $1.3 billion. But modern lobbying generally involves more subtle and sophisticated methods than providing money or personal favors to officials.

A group's chances of success improve if it has effective lobbyists working on its behalf. Some of the best lobbyists are longtime Washington lawyers from prestigious firms who have built effective working relationships with top

Lobbyists meet with a U.S. senator in his office on Capitol Hill. Access to public officials is crucial to effective inside lobbying.

officials. Former members of Congress are also in great demand as lobbyists. They have the unique right to go directly onto the floor of the House or Senate to speak with current members. Former members usually represent groups with which they had close ties while they were in office. Representative Bob Livingston (R-La.), chair of the House Appropriations Committee, resigned from Congress in 1999 and soon thereafter started the Livingston Group, which lobbies Congress on behalf of business firms.

For the most part, inside lobbying is directed at policy makers who are inclined to support the group rather than those who have opposed it in the past. This tendency reflects both the difficulty of persuading opponents to change long-held views and the advantage of having trusted allies who will actively support the group's position in policy deliberations. Thus, union lobbyists work mainly with pro-labor officials, just as corporate lobbyists work mainly with policy makers who support business interests.

Money is the essential ingredient of inside lobbying efforts. The American Petroleum Institute, for example, with its abundant financial resources, can afford a downtown Washington office staffed by lobbyists, petroleum experts, and public relations specialists who help the oil companies maintain access to and influence with legislative and executive leaders.[16] Many groups spend $1 million or more annually on lobbying. Other groups survive with much less, but it is hard to run an effective lobbying effort on less than $100,000 a year. Given the costs of maintaining a Washington lobby, the domination by corporations and trade associations is understandable. They have the money to retain high-priced lobbyists, while many other interests do not.

The targets of inside lobbying are officials of all branches—legislative, executive, and judicial.

Lobbying Congress

The benefits of a close relationship with members of Congress are substantial. With support in Congress, a group can obtain the legislative help it needs to achieve its policy goals. By the same token, members of Congress also gain from working closely with lobbyists. The volume of legislation facing Congress is enormous, and members rely on trusted lobbyists to identify bills that deserve their attention and support. When Republican lawmakers took control of Congress in 1995, they invited corporate lobbyists to participate directly in drafting legislation affecting business. Congressional Democrats complained loudly, but Republicans said they were merely getting help from those who best understood business's needs and accused Democrats of having engaged in the same practice with organized labor when they were in power.

Lobbyists' effectiveness with members of Congress depends in part on their reputation for fair play. Congressional action normally requires compromise among competing interests. If a group is adamant about getting everything it wants—"my way or no way"—it is likely to end up with nothing. Lobbyists are also expected to play it straight. Said one congressman: "If any [lobbyist] gives me false or misleading information, that's it—I'll never see him again."[17] Arm-twisting is another unacceptable practice. During the debate over the North American Free Trade Agreement in 1993, the AFL-CIO threatened retaliation against congressional Democrats who supported the legislation. The backlash from these Democrats was so intense that the union backed down on its threat. The safe lobbying strategy is the aboveboard approach: provide information, rely on longtime allies among members of Congress, and push steadily but not too aggressively for legislative goals.

Lobbying Executive Agencies

As the scope of the federal government has expanded, lobbying of the executive branch has increased in importance. Bureaucrats make key administrative decisions and develop policy initiatives that the legislative branch later makes into law. By working closely with government agencies, groups can influence policy decisions at the implementation and initiation stages. In return, groups assist government agencies by providing information and lending support when their programs are reviewed by Congress and the president.

Nowhere is the link between groups and the bureaucracy more evident than in the regulatory agencies that oversee the nation's business sectors. For example, the Federal Communications Commission (FCC), which regulates the nation's broadcasters, uses information provided by broadcast organizations to decide many of the policies governing their activities. The FCC is sometimes cited as an example of agency capture. The capture theory suggests that regulatory agencies pass through a series of phases that constitute a life cycle. Early in an agency's existence, it regulates an industry on the public's behalf, but as the agency matures, its vigor declines until at best it protects the status quo and at worst it falls captive to the very industry it is supposed to regulate.[18] In the 1950s, the commercial networks successfully lobbied the FCC in a campaign against the establishment of a strong public sector television system. For example, public stations were assigned UHF frequencies while commercial stations

The broadcast industry is regulated by the Federal Communications Commission (FCC), which at times has been a captive agency. Over the years, broadcasters have obtained a great many favorable decisions from the FCC.

held the more powerful VHF frequencies, which were also the only ones that most television sets of the 1950s were programmed to receive. Without access to a large audience, public television was in a weak position to request additional funding from Congress. Without more funds, it had to struggle to develop the type of programming that would attract a larger audience. The consequences of this vicious circle linger today. Compared with Europe, where public broadcasting was established early and on a solid footing, the U.S. system is very weak.

Research has shown that the capture theory describes only some agencies—and then only some of the time.[19] Agencies selectively cooperate with or oppose interest groups, depending on which strategy better suits agency purposes.[20] Agency officials are aware that they can lose support in Congress, which controls agency funding and program authorization, if they show too much favoritism toward an interest group.

Although instances of favoritism occur, the U.S. bureaucracy ranks high in comparison with other national bureaucracies in terms of its efficiency and honesty.[21] Its dealings with lobbying groups are important to effective administration, which includes an understanding of the impact of programs on affected interests. From the viewpoint of the interest group, the bureaucracy's need for information is a lobbying opportunity.

Lobbying the Courts

Court rulings in areas such as education and civil rights have made interest groups recognize that the judiciary, too, can help them reach their goals.[22] Interest groups have several judicial lobbying options, including efforts to influence the selection of federal judges. Right-to-life groups pressured the Reagan and Bush administrations to make opposition to abortion a prerequisite for nomination to the federal bench. The Clinton administration faced the opposite type of pressure from pro-choice groups on its judicial nominations.

Amicus curiae ("friend of the court") briefs are another method of judicial lobbying. An amicus brief is a written document in which a group brings its position on a particular case to a court's attention. For example, in the landmark affirmative action case *Regents of the University of California v. Bakke* (1978), fifty-eight amicus briefs representing the positions of more than one hundred organizations were filed with the Supreme Court at its invitation.

Groups typically try to influence public policy through the courts by filing lawsuits. For some organizations, such as the National Association for the Advancement of Colored People (NAACP) and the American Civil Liberties Union, legal action is the primary means of lobbying government. The NAACP, for example, has emphasized legal action since its founding in 1909 because it recognizes that minorities often lack influence with elected officials. The NAACP financed the 1954 *Brown* case, in which the Supreme Court declared that racial segregation of public schools is unconstitutional. Had the NAACP tried to achieve the same result by lobbying state legislators in the South, it almost certainly would have failed.

As interest groups increasingly resort to legal action, they often find themselves facing one another in court. Such environmental litigation groups as the Sierra Club Legal Defense Club, the Environmental Defense Fund, and the Natural Resources Defense Council have frequently sued oil, timber, and mining corporations.

WEBS OF INFLUENCE: GROUPS IN THE POLICY PROCESS

Lobbying efforts provide an incomplete picture of how groups obtain influence. To get a fuller picture, it is necessary to also consider two policy processes—iron triangles and issue networks—in which many groups are enmeshed.

Iron Triangles

An **iron triangle** consists of a small and informal but relatively stable set of bureaucrats, legislators, and lobbyists who seek to develop policies beneficial to a particular interest.[23] The three "corners" of one such triangle are the Department of Veterans Affairs (bureaucrats), the veterans' affairs committees of Congress (legislators), and veterans' groups such as the American Legion and the Veterans of Foreign Wars (lobbyists), which together determine many of the policies affecting veterans. Of course, the support of others, including the president and a majority in Congress, is needed to enact new programs to benefit veterans. However, they often defer to the policy views voiced by the veterans' triangle, whose members have the most knowledge of the programs, problems, and policy needs of veterans.

A group in an iron triangle has an inside track to those legislators and bureaucrats who are in the strongest position to promote its cause. And because it can offer something of value to each of them in return, the relationship tends to be ironclad. The group provides lobbying support for the agency's funding and programs, and gives campaign contributions to its congressional allies. Agricultural groups, for example, contributed millions of dollars to congressional

iron triangle A small and informal but relatively stable group of well-positioned legislators, executives, and lobbyists who seek to promote policies beneficial to a particular interest.

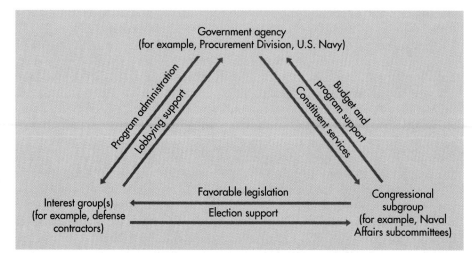

FIGURE 10-1   How an Iron Triangle Benefits Its Participants An iron triangle works to the advantage of each of its participants—an interest group, a congressional subgroup, and a government agency.

candidates in the 2000 campaign. Most of the money was given to incumbents, and of these contributions, most went to the campaigns of members of the House and Senate agriculture committees. Figure 10-1 summarizes the benefits that flow to each member of an iron triangle.

Issue Networks

issue network An informal and relatively open network of public officials and lobbyists who have a common interest in a given area and who are brought together by a proposed policy in that area. Unlike an iron triangle, an issue network disbands after the issue is resolved.

Iron triangles represent the pattern of influence only in certain policy areas and are less dominant than in the past. A more common pattern of influence today is the **issue network,** which is an informal grouping of officials, lobbyists, and policy specialists (the "network") who are brought together temporarily by their shared interest in a particular policy problem (the "issue").

Issue networks are a result of the increasing complexity and interconnectedness of policy problems. The complexity of modern issues often makes it essential that a participant have specialized knowledge of the issue at hand in order to join in the debate. Thus, unlike iron triangles, where one's position is everything, an issue network is built around specialized interests and information. On any given issue, the participants might come from a variety of executive agencies, congressional committees, interest groups, and institutions such as universities or think tanks. And, unlike iron triangles, issue networks are less stable and less clearly defined. As the issue develops, new participants may join the debate and old ones drop out. Once the issue is resolved, the network disbands.[24]

An example of an issue network is the set of participants who would come together over the issue of whether a large tract of old forest should be opened to logging. A few decades ago, that issue would have been settled in an iron triangle consisting of the timber companies, the U.S. Forest Service, and some members of the House and Senate agriculture committees. But as forestlands have diminished and environmental concerns have grown, such issues can no longer be contained within the cozy confines of an iron triangle. Today, an issue network would form that included logging interests, the U.S. Forest Service, House and Senate agriculture committee members, research scientists, and

The policy issues surrounding the technological revolution are extraordinarily complex, and issue networks tend to form when policy issues of this type arise.

representatives of environmental groups, the housing industry, and animal-rights groups. Unlike the old iron triangle, which was confined to like-minded interests, this issue network would include opposing interests (for example, the loggers and the environmentalists). And unlike an iron triangle, the issue network would dissolve once the issue was resolved; after it was settled, the separate parties would go their separate ways.

Issue networks, then, differ substantially from iron triangles. In an iron triangle, it is a shared interest that brings the participants together in a stable, long-lasting, and mutually beneficial relationship. In an issue network, it is an immediate issue that brings the participants together in a temporary network that is based on their ability to address the issue in a sophisticated way and where they play out their separate interests before disbanding once the issue is settled. Iron triangles and issue networks, however, do have one thing in common. They are arenas in which organized interests operate. The interests of the general public may be taken into account in these webs of influence, but its direct role is ordinarily a small one.

Outside Lobbying: Seeking Influence Through Public Pressure

Although an interest group may rely solely on Washington lobbying, this approach is not likely to be successful unless it can demonstrate convincingly that its concerns reflect those of a vital constituency. Accordingly, groups make use of constituency connections when it is advantageous to do so. They engage in **outside lobbying,** which involves bringing public ("outside") pressure to bear on policy makers.[25] The outside approach typically takes the form of either *constituency advocacy* or *electoral action* (see Table 10-3).

outside lobbying A form of lobbying in which an interest group seeks to use public pressure as a means of influencing officials.

TABLE 10-3   Tactics Used in Inside and Outside Lobbying Strategies   Inside and outside lobbying are based on different tactics.

Inside Lobbying	Outside Lobbying
Developing contacts with legislators and executives	Encouraging group members to write or phone their representatives in Congress
Providing information and policy proposals to key officials	Seeking favorable coverage by news media
Forming coalitions with other groups	Encouraging members to support particular candidates in elections
	Targeting group resources on key election races
	Making PAC contributions to candidates

CONSTITUENCY ADVOCACY: GRASSROOTS LOBBYING

grassroots lobbying   A form of lobbying designed to persuade officials that a group's policy position has strong constituent support.

Some groups depend heavily on **grassroots lobbying**—that is, pressure designed to convince government officials that a group's policy position has strong public support. To mobilize constituents, groups can mount advertising and public relations campaigns through the media. They can also encourage their members to write or call their elected representatives, or even see their representatives personally.

No group illustrates grassroots lobbying better than the American Association of Retired Persons (AARP). With more than thirty million members and a staff of 1,600 employees, AARP has been a powerful lobby on issues affecting the elderly. Pressure from the AARP is a major reason that social security and Medicare are politically explosive issues whenever proposals to reduce the federal budget are discussed. AARP members are so responsive to policies affecting them that they generate more mail to Congress than any other group.[26]

As with other forms of lobbying, the precise impact of grassroots campaigns is usually difficult to assess. Some members of Congress downplay its influence, but all congressional offices monitor letters and phone calls from constituents as a way of tracking their views. Most members receive hundreds of

Grassroots lobbying is based on pressure from constituents. These farmers traveled to Washington to protest the low prices they were getting for agricultural goods.

Former White House press secretary James Brady, who was shot and partially paralyzed during the 1981 assassination attempt on President Reagan, celebrates a hard-fought victory over the National Rifle Association (NRA), a powerful gun lobby. Despite the NRA's opposition, the Senate had just passed a bill requiring a five-day waiting period for handgun purchases.

letters and phone calls each week from constituents, not counting fax messages, computer-generated mail, and organized grassroots postcard campaigns.

ELECTORAL ACTION: VOTES AND PAC MONEY

"Reward your friends and punish your enemies" is a political adage that loosely describes how interest groups view election campaigns. As part of an "outside" strategy, organized groups work to elect their supporters and defeat their opponents. The possibility of electoral opposition from a powerful group can keep an officeholder from openly obstructing its goals. For example, opposition from the three-million-member National Rifle Association is a major reason the United States has lagged behind other Western societies in its handgun control laws, although polls show that most Americans favor such laws.

The principal way in which interest groups try to gain influence through elections is by contributing money to candidates' campaigns. As one lobbyist said, "Talking to politicians is fine, but with a little money they hear you better."[27] Money does not literally "buy" votes in Congress, but it does buy access. Members of Congress listen to the groups that fund their campaigns.

The vehicle for group contributions is the **political action committee (PAC).** A group cannot give organizational funds (such as corporate profits or union dues) to candidates; but through its PAC, a group can raise money for election campaigns by soliciting voluntary contributions from members or employees. A PAC is legally limited in the amount it can contribute to the campaign of a candidate for federal office. As of 2000, the ceiling was $10,000 per candidate— $5,000 in the primary campaign and $5,000 in the general election campaign; there was no legal limit on the number of candidates a PAC could support. These financial limits do not apply to candidates for state and local office. Their

political action committee (PAC) The organization through which an interest group raises and distributes funds for election purposes. By law, the funds must be raised through voluntary contributions.

★ STATES IN THE NATION

LIMITS ON PAC CONTRIBUTIONS IN STATE ELECTIONS

Elections for state office are regulated by the states, which in some cases limit how much a PAC can give to a candidate. Of the states that limit contributions, only New York and Nevada allow contributions in excess of $10,000.

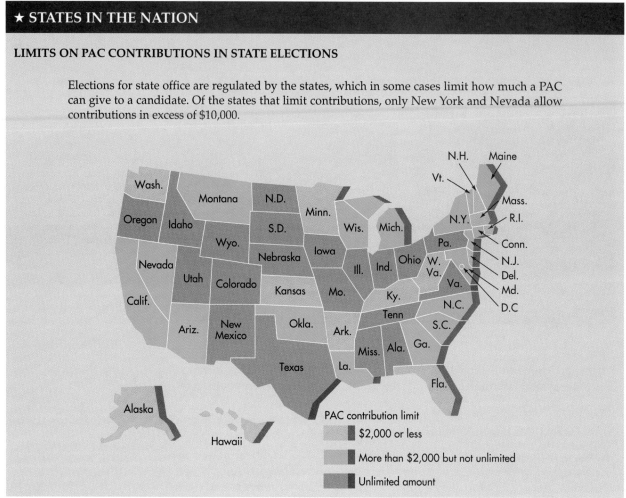

PAC contribution limit
- $2,000 or less
- More than $2,000 but not unlimited
- Unlimited amount

SOURCE: Federal Elections Commission.

campaigns are regulated by state laws, and many states allow PACs to make unlimited campaign contributions (see "States in the Nation").

PACs mushroomed in the 1970s as a result of favorable changes in campaign finance laws (see Figure 10-2). There are now more than four thousand PACs, and PAC contributions account for roughly a third of total contributions to congressional campaigns. Because PAC money can be raised earlier and more quickly than money from individual contributors, PACs have become a critical factor in getting congressional campaigns off the ground. Their role is less significant in presidential campaigns, which are larger in scale and publicly funded in part and therefore less dependent on PAC contributions.

PACs target most of their support to congressional incumbents (see Figure 10-3). PACs typically contribute more than five times as much money to incumbents as to their challengers. PACs are well aware of the fact that incumbents are likely to win and thus to remain in a position to make policy. One PAC

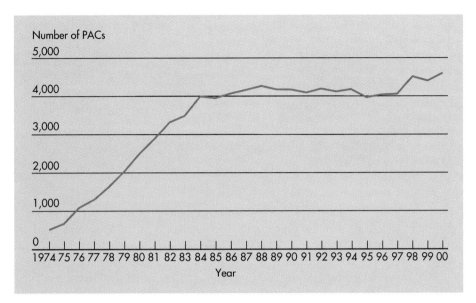

FIGURE 10-2   Growth in the Number of PACs, 1974–2000
The number of PACs began to increase sharply after campaign finance reforms were enacted in the early 1970s. *Source: Federal Elections Commission.*

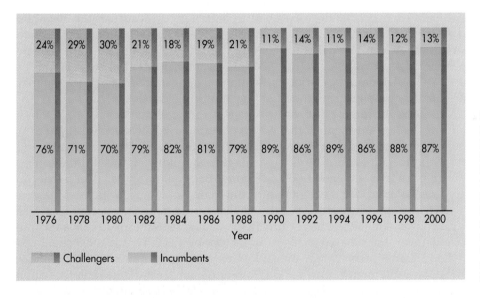

FIGURE 10-3   Allocation of PAC Contributions Between Incumbents and Challengers in Congressional Races That Included an Incumbent, 1974–2000
In allocating campaign contributions, PACs favor incumbent members of Congress over their challengers by a wide margin. *Source: Federal Elections Commission; 2000 figures based on preliminary estimates.*

director, expressing a common view, said, "We always stick with the incumbent when we agree with them both."[28]

The tendency of PACs to back incumbents has to some extent blurred longstanding partisan divisions in campaign funding. Business interests are the most pragmatic. Although they generally favor Republican candidates and strongly supported them in 1994 when it became clear the GOP would sweep the congressional elections, business groups are reluctant to anger Democratic incumbents. The result is that Democratic incumbents, particularly in House races, have received substantial support over the years from business-related

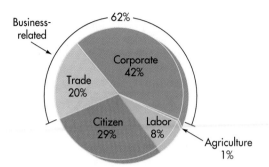

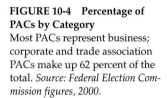

FIGURE 10-4   Percentage of PACs by Category
Most PACs represent business; corporate and trade association PACs make up 62 percent of the total. *Source: Federal Election Commission figures, 2000.*

PACs.[29] Other PACs, especially those organized to promote a particular public policy or ideology, are less pragmatic. The Christian Moral Government Fund, for example, backs only candidates who take conservative stands on issues such as school prayer and abortion.

More than 40 percent of all PACs are associated with corporations (see Figure 10-4). Examples include the Ford Motor Company Civic Action Fund, the Sun Oil Company Political Action Committee (Sunpac), and the Coca-Cola PAC. The next largest group of PACs consists of those linked to citizens' groups (that is, public interest, single-issue, and ideological groups), such as the liberal People for the American Way and the conservative NCPAC (National Conservative Political Action Committee). Ranking third are PACs tied to trade and professional associations, such as AMPAC (American Medical Association) and R-PAC (National Association of Realtors). Labor unions were once the major source of group contributions, but they now rank fourth.

Among the largest PAC contributors in recent elections have been tobacco firms. As lawsuits against the industry mounted, tobacco firms sought a congressional settlement that would grant them immunity from class-action suits and protection against punitive damages. The industry was willing to pay a high price for a settlement—$300 billion to $500 billion spread over twenty-five years—in return for legal immunity. But many in Congress opposed the grant, at least without legislative provisions that would have the effect of sharply reducing smoking, particularly among the young. In its efforts to gain a favorable settlement, the tobacco industry in the period from 1995 to 1998 spent more than $50 million on congressional lobbying and gave more than $12 million in PAC and soft money contributions to congressional candidates and the national political parties. Its lobbying team included Haley Barbour, former chair of the Republican National Committee, and Howard Baker, a retired lawmaker who was Senate majority leader in the 1980s.[30]

Advocates of PACs claim that groups have a right to be heard, which includes the right to express themselves with money. Advocates also say that a campaign finance system based on pooled contributions by individuals is superior to one in which candidates rely on a few wealthy donors.[31]

Critics argue, however, that PACs give interest groups altogether too much influence over public officials.[32] The opposition to PACs has increased in the last few years, as citizens have come to associate the influence of interest groups with what they see as costly federal programs. Although members of Congress deny that they are unduly influenced by PAC contributions, there has been a growing sentiment within Congress to place some restrictions on PACs.

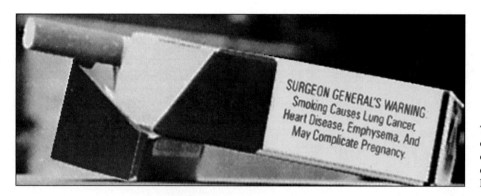

Tobacco firms have been leading contributors to recent congressional campaigns in an effort to gain protection from lawsuits.

As this 1889 cartoon by Joseph Koppler shows, at the end of the last century big business attempted to run the show in Congress through its enormous (and unregulated) campaign contributions. *Source: Collection of The New-York Historical Society, Neg. #44166*

Agreement on the changes, however, has been difficult to achieve because of differences between Democrats and Republicans in the way they would reform the process and also because some incumbents are unwilling to support any change that would significantly alter the advantage they have under the present system.

The Group System: Indispensable but Biased

As was noted in the introduction to this chapter, pluralist theory holds that organized groups provide for the representation of society's many and diverse interests. On one level, this claim is beyond dispute. Without groups to carry the message, most of society's interests would find it difficult to gain government's attention and support. Yet the issue of representation is also a question of whether all interests in society have a fair chance to succeed, and here the pluralist argument is less compelling.

CURRENT CONTROVERSIES

HAVE INTEREST GROUPS HIJACKED THE INITIATIVE PROCESS?

The initiative was pioneered by the Progressives of the early twentieth century, who saw it as a way to wrest power from the political bosses and corporate robber barons and place it in the hands of ordinary citizens. Twenty-four states allow the initiative, which requires the gathering of a sufficient number of citizens' signatures to place a legislative proposal (initiative) on the ballot. If a majority of voters approve it, the initiative becomes law, just as if it had been enacted by the legislature itself. In recent years, however, the initiative process has been used by interest groups to advance their policy agendas. They have the money to pay for the signature-gathering phase and to conduct a campaign for enactment of the initiative. To some observers, this tendency has corrupted the initiative process. Other observers claim that the initiative remains a bulwark of citizen-based politics.

YES: [The initiative process is] now being driven very much by money. With their own political agendas, interest groups of all kinds have latched onto the device as a way of writing the law the way they would like it written without having to go through all the hoops of the normal governmental process. . . . I think it's particularly ironic that a device that was introduced into this country as a way of fighting special interest influence and the power of money now has been largely taken over by those same interest groups and by very wealthy millionaires who have the resources that it takes now to get an initiative on the ballot and to fight these campaigns to get them passed or defeated in the states.

—David S. Broder, author and journalist

NO: The initiative and referendum process has been a critical tool to check the power of unresponsive and unaccountable government at the state and local level for 100 years. Through its use, women gained the right to vote, we can directly elect our U.S. Senators, we have direct primaries, term limits on 18 state legislatures, tax and spending limits, the eight-hour work day, environmental reforms and much, much more. In 1998 alone, the 100th anniversary of initiative and referendum, voters were heard on such issues as affirmative action, animal rights, term limits, tax limits, and medical marijuana, to name a few.

—The Initiative and Referendum Institute

THE CONTRIBUTION OF GROUPS TO SELF-GOVERNMENT: PLURALISM

Group activity is an essential part of self-government. A major obstacle to popular sovereignty is the many difficulties that public officials encounter in trying to discover what the people want from government. To determine their wishes, lawmakers consult public opinion polls, meet with constituents, and assess the meaning of recent elections. Organized groups are an additional means of determining popular sentiment because they provide policy makers with a better picture of the policy concerns of various interests in society.[33] On any given issue, the policy positions that are likely to be expressed most clearly and intensely are those held by organized interests.

Moreover, government does not exist simply to serve majority interests. The fact that most people are not retirees or labor union members or farmers or college students or Hispanics does not mean that the special needs and concerns of such "minorities" are undeserving of attention. And what better instrument exists for promoting the interests of such "minorities" than organizations formed around them? Groups are not antithetical to the democratic process: they are basic to it.

Some pluralists even question whether such terms as "the common good" and "the collective interest" are very useful. If people disagree on society's goals and priorities, as they always do, how can it be said that people have a "common" or "collective" concern? As an alternative, pluralist theory would substitute the sum of people's varied (that is, plural) interests as a rough approximation of society's collective interest. The logic of this proposition is that, because society has so many interests, the common good is ultimately served by a process that enables a great many interests to gain favorable policies. Thus, if manufacturing interests prevail on one issue, environmentalists on another, farmers on a third, minorities on a fourth, and so on until a wide range of particular interests is served, the collective interest of society will have been promoted.[34]

Finally, interest groups often take up issues that are neglected by the party system. Party leaders typically shy from issues, such as affirmative action and abortion, on which the party's voters disagree. Such issues would get less notice if not for the groups that promote them. And when groups succeed in drawing attention to these issues, the parties are nearly compelled also to address them. In this sense, as the political scientist Jack Walker noted, the party and group systems "are complementary and together constitute a much more responsive and adaptive system than either would be if they somehow operated on their own."[35]

FLAWS IN PLURALISM: INTEREST-GROUP LIBERALISM AND ECONOMIC BIAS

Although pluralist theory offers some compelling arguments, it also has questionable aspects. In a direct attack on pluralism, Theodore Lowi argues that there is no concept of society's collective interest in a system that allows special interests to determine for themselves which policy benefits they receive, regardless of how many interests are served.[36] When each group makes its own choice, the basis of decision in each case is not majority (collective) rule but minority (special-interest) rule.

It is seldom safe to assume that what a popular majority favors is what a special-interest group wants. Consider the case of the federal law that required auto dealers to list the known defects of used cars on window stickers. The law was repealed after an extensive lobbying campaign financed by contributions of more than $1 million by the National Association of Automobile Dealers to the reelection campaigns of members of Congress. Although an overwhelming majority of the general public would surely have favored retention of the law, the car dealers' view prevailed.

Lowi uses the term **interest-group liberalism** to describe the tendency of officials to support the policy demands of the interest group or groups that have a special stake in a policy. Interest-group liberalism constitutes a partial abdication by government of its authority over policy. In practical terms, it is the group as much as the government that decides policy. The adverse effects include a weakening of majoritarian institutions and an inefficient use of society's resources: groups get what they want, whether or not their priorities match those of society as a whole.

Another flaw in the pluralist argument resides in its claim that the group system is representative. Pluralists recognize that better-organized interests have more influence but argue that the group process is relatively open and that few

interest-group liberalism The tendency of public officials to support the policy demands of self-interested groups (as opposed to judging policy demands according to whether or not they serve a larger conception of "the public interest").

Sometimes the interests of a group clearly diverge from majority opinion, as when the National Association of Auto Dealers lobbied successfully against legislation that would have required automobile dealers to inform customers about any defects in used cars.

interests are at a serious disadvantage. These claims contain an element of truth but are far from the complete truth.

As this chapter has pointed out, organization is a political resource that is distributed unequally across society. Economic interests, particularly corporations, are the most highly organized, and some analysts argue that group politics works almost entirely to the advantage of business.[37] This generalization is less valid today. In fact, many of the public interest groups formed in the past three decades were deliberately created to check and balance the influence of existing groups, particularly corporate lobbies.[38]

Big government has also brought the group political system into closer balance. Groups form not only to influence policy but also in response to policy. When new programs were created in the 1960s for the benefit of less advantaged interests in society, these interests mobilized to protect their newly acquired benefits. The National Welfare Rights Organization was formed during the 1960s after new welfare programs were established.[39] Many of the newer interest groups have had a significant impact in areas such as civil rights, the environment, social welfare programs for the elderly and the poor, public morality, national security, and business regulation. Moreover, policy today is less often decided by the actions of one or a few groups. The group system is thus not closed and rigid; it is open to new interests and new patterns of influence.

Nevertheless, interests differ significantly in their level of organization. Well over half of all lobbying groups in Washington are still business-related. The interest-group system is biased toward America's economically oriented groups, particularly its corporations.

The group system is also slanted toward upper-middle-class interests. Studies indicate that individuals of higher socioeconomic status are disproportionately represented among group members and even more so among group leaders. These tendencies are predictable. Educated and affluent Americans have the skills and money that give organizational form to special-interest politics. Less advantaged Americans lack the money, information, contacts, and communication skills to participate even when they desire to do so. The poor, minorities, women, and the young are greatly underrepresented in the group politics system. A lack of organization does not ensure an interest's failure, just as the existence of organization does not guarantee success. However, organized interests are obviously in a better position to make their views known.

The business and class bias of the group system is especially significant because the most highly organized interests are, in a sense, those least in need of political clout. Corporations and affluent citizens already benefit from the distribution of society's material resources.

A MADISONIAN DILEMMA

James Madison recognized the dilemma inherent in group activity. Although he worried that government would fall under the control of a dominant interest, whether of the majority or of the minority, he realized that a free society is obliged to permit the advocacy of self-interest. Unless people can promote the separate opinions that stem from differences in their talents, needs, values, and possessions, they do not have liberty.

Ironically, Madison's constitutional solution to the problem of factions has become part of the problem. The American system of checks and balances, with a separation of powers at its core, was designed primarily to prevent a majority faction from trampling on the interests of others. Indeed, throughout the nation's history, majorities have been frustrated in their efforts to gain full power by America's elaborate system of divided government.

This same system, however, makes it relatively easy for minority factions—or, as they are called today, special-interest groups—to protect the government benefits they receive. Benefits are hard to eliminate because concerted action by the executive and both houses of Congress is usually required. If a group has strong support in even a single institution, it can usually fend off attempts to terminate its benefits. This support is ordinarily easy to acquire, because the group can provide resources—money or votes—in return. Jonathan Rauch uses the term *demosclerosis* to describe the debilitating effect on government: its resources are increasingly absorbed by entrenched interests and it consequently undergoes a progressive loss in its ability to respond to new needs. Like the arteriosclerosis that slowly deprives the human body of the oxygen-laden blood it needs to survive, demosclerosis slowly robs government of its capacity to respond.[40] Chapters 12 and 13 will discuss further the issue of interest-group power.

Many citizens' groups lack the financial resources to publicize their needs, so they must rely on dramatic protest to attract media attention to their cause. These disabled Americans are demonstrating in front of the White House to urge passage of the Americans with Disabilities Act.

www.mhhe.com/patterson5

Self-Quiz

Summary

A political interest group is composed of a set of individuals organized to promote a shared political concern. Most interest groups owe their existence to factors other than politics. They form for economic reasons, such as

the pursuit of profit, and maintain themselves by making profits (in the case of corporations) or by providing their members with private goods, such as jobs and wages. Such interest groups include corporations, trade associations, labor unions, farm organizations, and professional associations. Collectively, economic groups are by far the largest set of organized interests. The group system tends to favor interests that are already economically and socially advantaged.

Citizens' groups do not have the same organizational advantages as economic groups. They depend on voluntary contributions from potential members who may lack interest and resources or who recognize that they will get the collective good from a group's activity even if they do not participate (the free-rider problem). These citizens' groups include public interest, single-issue, and ideological groups. Their numbers have increased dramatically since the 1960s despite their organizational problems.

Organized interests seek influence largely by lobbying public officials and contributing to election campaigns. Using an inside strategy, lobbyists develop direct contacts with legislators, government bureaucrats, and members of the judiciary in order to persuade them to accept their group's perspective on policy. Groups also use an outside strategy, seeking to mobilize public support for their goals. This strategy relies in part on grassroots lobbying—encouraging group members and the public to communicate their policy views to officials. Outside lobbying also includes efforts to elect officeholders who will support group aims. Through political action committees (PACs), organized groups now provide nearly a third of all contributions received by congressional candidates.

The policies that emerge from the group system bring benefits to many of society's interests, and in some instances these benefits also serve the general interest. But when groups can essentially dictate policies, the common good is not served. The majority's interest is subordinated to group (minority) interests. In most instances, the minority consists of individuals who already have a substantial share of society's benefits. As E. E. Schattschneider noted, the group system has "a strong upper-class bias."

Key Terms

citizens' (noneconomic) groups
collective (public) goods
economic groups
free-rider problem
grassroots lobbying
inside lobbying
interest group
interest-group liberalism
iron triangle

issue network
lobbying
material incentive
outside lobbying
political action committee (PAC)
private (individual) goods
purposive incentive
single-issue politics

Suggested Readings

Berry, Jeffrey M. *The New Liberalism: The Rising Power of Citizen Groups*. Washington, D.C.: Brookings Institution Press, 1999. An exploration of the influence that citizen groups exercise.

Browne, William P. *Cultivating Congress: Constituents, Issues, and Interests in Agriculture Policymaking*. Lawrence: University Press of Kansas, 1995. An analysis of the limits of "iron triangles" as a description of congressional policy making.

Cigler, Allan J., and Burdett A. Loomis. *Interest Group Politics*, 5th ed. Washington, D.C.: Congressional Quarterly Press, 1998. A comprehensive analysis of interest group politics.

Gais, Thomas L. *Improper Influence: Campaign Finance Law, Political Interest Groups, and the Problem of Equality*. Ann Arbor: University of Michigan Press, 1996. An analysis of how PACs have changed the process of representation through groups.

Gerber, Elisabeth R. *The Populist Paradox: Interest Group Influence and the Promise of Direct Legislation*. Princeton, N.J.: Princeton University Press, 1999. An analysis that challenges the notion that groups have captured the initiative process.

Herrnson, Paul S., Ronald G. Shaiko, and Clyde Wilcox, eds. *The Interest Group Connection: Electioneering, Lobbying and Policymaking in Washington*. Chatham, N.J.: Chatham House Publishers, 1998. Essays and commentaries on groups and officials and the linkages between them.

Kollman, Ken. *Outside Lobbying*. Princeton, N.J.: Princeton University Press, 1998. An analysis of why and when groups seek to mobilize the public.

Olson, Mancur, Jr. *The Logic of Collective Action*, rev. ed. Cambridge, Mass.: Harvard University Press, 1971. A pioneering analysis of why some interests are more fully and easily organized than others.

Rauch, Jonathan. *Demosclerosis: The Silent Killer of American Government*. New York: Times Books, 1994. An attack on groups as the main cause of government's ineffectiveness in responding to society's emerging needs.

Rothenberg, Lawrence S. *Linking Citizens to Government: Interest Group Politics at Common Cause*. New York: Cambridge University Press, 1992. A careful case study of a leading lobbying group.

Rozell, Mark J., and Clyde Wilcox. *Interest Groups in American Campaigns*. Washington, D.C.: Congressional Quarterly Press, 1999. A look at the powerful role that groups play in elections.

Walker, Jack L., Jr. *Mobilizing Interest Groups in America: Patrons, Professions, and Social Movements*. Ann Arbor: University of Michigan Press, 1991. An insightful analysis of how interest groups form and how they flourish or fail.

CHAPTER 11

The News Media: Communicating Political Images

★

The press in America . . . determines what people will think and talk about—an authority that in other nations is reserved for tyrants, priests, parties, and mandarins.

—Theodore H. White[1]

★ ★ ★

*E*arly on the morning of April 22, 2000, CNN interrupted its coverage to report a breaking story from Miami. Federal agents had just broken into the home where six-year-old Elian Gonzalez was staying and had taken him to a waiting plane that would fly him to Washington to be reunited with his father. Video pictures of the armed seizure followed almost immediately, and the story was soon playing on nearly every television news program in the country. As the day unfolded, viewers were to see Elian arriving in Washington while crowds of Cuban Americans gathered in Miami to protest the Justice Department's actions. For the next week, Elian's seizure and reactions to it filled the airwaves and front pages.

The seizure was the latest episode in a running news story that had begun months earlier when Elian was rescued at sea after his mother had drowned while trying to escape Cuba by boat. The young boy became the object of a political tug-of-war between Florida's Cuban American community and Cuba's Fidel Castro. Every move and countermove provoked a torrent of news coverage.

Not all developments receive such intensive news coverage. More new immigrants have arrived in the United States in the past two decades than during any comparable period in the nation's history. Their sheer number has strained the capacity of schools and other public organizations. In some communities, trailer houses have been converted into makeshift schoolrooms simply to get a roof over all students' heads. The impact of this great wave of immigration has been enormous and will affect the United States for years to come. Yet this development has only occasionally been mentioned in the news, let alone emblazoned in the headlines month after month.

Although the news has been compared to a mirror held up to society, it is actually a highly selective portrayal of reality. The **news** is mainly an account of overt, obtruding events, particularly those that are *timely* (new or unfolding developments rather than old or static ones), *dramatic* (striking developments rather than commonplace ones), and *compelling* (developments that arouse people's concerns and emotions as opposed to remote ones).[2] These characteristics of the news have a number of origins, not the least of which is that the news is a business. News organizations seek to make a profit, which leads them to prefer news stories that will attract and hold an audience. Thus, Elian Gonzalez became headline news the instant he was plucked from the sea, and he remained newsworthy while the political and legal process surrounding his status unfolded. The larger issue of the influx of immigrants into the United States during the past two decades is not considered particularly newsworthy, because it is a slow and steady process, dramatic only in its long-term implications. The columnist George Will notes that a

news The news media's version of reality, usually with an emphasis on timely, dramatic, and compelling events and developments.

press (news media) Those print and broadcast organizations that are in the news-reporting business.

development requires a defining event before it can become big news.[3] Without such an event, reporters have no peg on which to hang their stories.

News organizations and journalists, of either the print media (newspapers and magazines) or the broadcast media (radio and television), are referred to collectively as the **press** or the **news media.** The press is an increasingly important political actor. Its heightened influence is attributable in part to changes within the media. New technology, from television to cable to satellites, has dramatically increased the reach and speed of communication. In addition, the press has filled some of the void created by the decline in political parties and other political institutions.

Like political parties and interest groups, the press is a key link between the public and its leaders. In some ways, the press is better positioned than parties or groups to influence the public. On a daily basis, Americans connect to politics more through the news that is produced by the media than through the activities of parties or groups.

This chapter argues, however, that the news media are a very different kind of intermediary than either parties or interest groups and that problems arise when the press is asked to perform the same functions as these organizations. The chapter begins with a review of the media's historical development and the current trends in news reporting. It concludes with an analysis of the roles the press can and cannot perform adequately in the American political system. The main ideas represented in this chapter are the following:

★ *The American press was initially tied to the nation's political party system (the partisan press) but gradually developed an independent position (the objective press).* In the process, the news shifted from a political orientation, which emphasizes political values and ideas, to a journalistic orientation, which stresses newsworthy information and evaluations.

★ *Although the United States has thousands of separate news organizations, they present a common version of the news that reflects journalists' shared view of what*

Allegations in 1998 of a sexual relationship between Monica Lewinsky and President Bill Clinton unleashed a media feeding frenzy that disrupted the White House's policy agenda.

the news is. Freedom of the press in the United States does not result in a robust marketplace of ideas.

★ *In fulfilling its responsibility to provide public information, the news media effectively perform three significant roles—those of signaler (the press brings relevant events and problems into public view), common carrier (the press serves as a channel through which political leaders can address the public), and watchdog (the press scrutinizes official behavior for evidence of deceitful, careless, or corrupt acts).* These roles are within the news media's capacity because they fit with the values, incentives, and accountability of the press.

★ *The press cannot do the job of political institutions, even though it increasingly tries to do so.* The nature of journalism as it has evolved is incompatible with the characteristics required for the role of public representative.

The Development of the News Media: From Partisanship to Objective Journalism

Democracy requires a free flow of information. Communication enables a free people to keep in touch with one another, with their leaders, and with important events. Recognizing the vital role of the press in the building of a democratic society, Thomas Jefferson wrote in 1787, "Were it left to me to decide whether we should have a government without newspapers, or newspapers without a government, I should not hesitate a moment to prefer the latter."[4]

America's early leaders were quick to see the advantages of promoting the establishment of newspapers. At Alexander Hamilton's urging, the *Gazette of the United States* was founded by John Fenno to promote the policies of George Washington's administration. Hamilton was secretary of the treasury and supported Fenno's paper by granting it the Treasury Department's printing contracts. Jefferson, who was secretary of state and Hamilton's adversary, complained that the newspaper's content was "pure Toryism." Jefferson persuaded Philip Freneau to start the *National Gazette* as the opposition Republican party's publication and supported it by granting Freneau authority to print State Department documents. When Jefferson resigned his post as secretary of state in 1793, Freneau lost his financial base and was forced to close down his newspaper.

Early newspapers were printed on hand presses, a process that limited production and kept the cost of each copy beyond the reach of ordinary citizens—most of which were illiterate anyway. Leading papers such as the *Gazette of the United States* had fewer than 1,500 subscribers and could not have survived without party support. Not surprisingly, the "news" they printed was a form of party propaganda.[5] In this era of the **partisan press,** publishers openly took sides on partisan issues. Their employees were expected to follow the party line. President James K. Polk once persuaded a leading publisher to fire an editor who was critical of Polk's policies.[6]

partisan press Newspapers and other communication media that openly support a political party and whose news in significant part follows the party line.

FROM A PARTISAN PRESS TO AN "OBJECTIVE" ONE

Technological changes helped bring about the gradual decline of America's partisan press. After the invention of the telegraph in 1837, editors could receive timely information on developments in Washington and the state capital, and

★ STATES IN THE NATION

IN THE NEWS, OR OUT?

A few major media outlets dominate news production in the United States. The stories they carry tend to set the news agenda for other media. *The New York Times* is generally regarded as the most powerful of these agenda setters. Not surprisingly, since it is based in New York City, the *Times* includes a disproportionate amount of coverage of New York and surrounding states, such as New Jersey and Connecticut. But what about other states? How much attention do they receive in the *Times*? The fact is, coverage varies with events of the moment. The news highlights events that are colorful, sensational, or significant. A natural disaster can bring a state into the national media spotlight, but it may fade from view as soon as the crisis has passed. The map indicates the relative frequency with which the states were mentioned in the *Times* during the first month of 2000. It was the period of the first presidential primaries and caucuses, and thus New Hampshire and Iowa were among the most newsworthy states, even though they ordinarily do not get close attention from the national media.

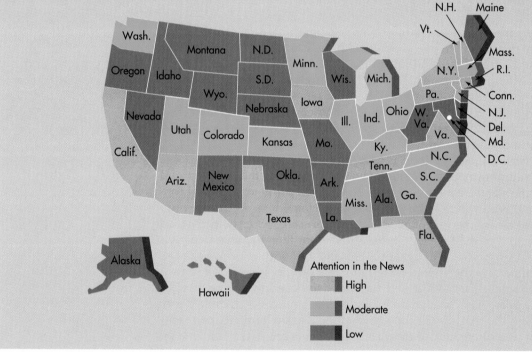

SOURCE: Data compiled by author from Nexis.

they had less reason to fill their pages with partisan harangues.[7] Another major innovation was the rotary press (invented in 1815), a breakthrough that enabled commercially minded publishers to print their newspapers rapidly and cheaply and thus to increase their profit potential.[8] The *New York Sun* was the first paper to pass on the benefit of high-speed printing to subscribers by reducing the price of a daily copy from six cents to a penny. The *Sun*'s circulation rose to five thousand in four months and to ten thousand in less than a year.[9] Increased

Yellow journalism was characterized by its sensationalism. William Randolph Hearst's *New York Journal* whipped up public support for a war in Cuba with Spain through inflammatory reporting on the sinking of the battleship *Maine* in Havana Harbor in 1898.

circulation and revenues gave newspapers independence from government and parties, a change that some political leaders welcomed. "The freedom and independence of the press," a congressional committee concluded in 1873, "is best maintained by the people, and their subscriptions are a more legitimate means of support than the patronage of the federal government."[10]

By the late nineteenth century, several American newspapers were printing 100,000 or more copies a day, and their large circulation enabled them to charge high prices for advertising. The period marked the height of newspapers' power and the nadir in their sense of public responsibility.[11] A new style of reporting—"yellow journalism"—had emerged as a way of boosting circulation.[12] The "yellow" press—so called because some of these newspapers were printed on cheap yellow paper—emphasized "a shrieking, gaudy, sensation-loving, devil-may-care kind of journalism which lured the reader by any possible means."[13] A circulation battle between William Randolph Hearst's *New York Journal* and Joseph Pulitzer's *New York World* is believed to have contributed to the outbreak of the Spanish-American War through sensational (and largely inaccurate) reports on the cruelty of Spanish rule in Cuba. A young Frederic Remington (who later became a noted painter and sculptor), working as a news artist for Hearst, planned to return home because Cuba appeared calm and safe, but Hearst cabled back, "Please remain. You furnish the pictures and I'll furnish the war."[14]

The excesses of yellow journalism led some publishers to consider ways of reporting the news more responsibly. One step was to separate the newspaper's advertising department from its news department, thus reducing the influence

objective journalism A model of news reporting that is based on the communication of "facts" rather than opinions and that is "fair" in that it presents all sides of partisan debate.

of advertisers on news content. A second development was a new model of reporting called **objective journalism,** which was based on the reporting of "facts" rather than opinions and was "fair" in that it presented both sides of partisan debate.[15]

A chief advocate of this new form of journalism was Adolph Ochs of *The New York Times.* Ochs bought the *Times* in 1896, when its circulation was 9,000; four years later, its readership had grown to 82,000. Ochs told his reporters that he "wanted as little partisanship as possible . . . as few judgments as possible."[16] The *Times*'s approach to reporting appealed particularly to educated readers, and by the early twentieth century it had acquired a reputation as the country's best newspaper. Objective reporting was also promoted through newly formed journalism schools. Among the first of these professional schools were those at Columbia University and the University of Missouri. The Columbia School of Journalism opened in 1912 with a $2 million grant from Pulitzer.

interpretive reporting The style of reporting that aims to explain *why* something is taking place or has occurred.

Objective journalism is still a component of news coverage. Although most newspapers have a partisan bias on their editorial pages, they tend to treat the Republican and Democratic parties equally on their news pages. Nevertheless, the influence of objective journalism is waning. Newspapers increasingly rely on an **interpretive style of reporting,** in which the journalist's job is to analyze, evaluate, and explain developments rather than merely report them. The older form of objective journalism (called **descriptive reporting,** because of its straightforward description of events) required that reporters stick to the "facts." The newer interpretive style allows them to speculate on what the facts mean. As we will see later in the chapter, interpretive reporting has greatly increased journalists' ability to shape the news to fit their own views, including their skeptical opinion of politicians' motives and accomplishments.

descriptive reporting The style of reporting that aims to describe *what* is taking place or has occurred.

THE DEVELOPMENT OF THE BROADCAST MEDIA

Radio and Television: The Truly National Media

Until the early twentieth century, the print media were the only form of mass communication. Within a few decades, however, there were hundreds of radio stations throughout the nation, many of which were linked in national networks, such as the Red and Blue networks of the National Broadcasting Corporation (NBC). Franklin D. Roosevelt used radio for his famous fireside chats with the American people. When business-minded newspaper editors were critical of his New Deal programs, Roosevelt used radio as a way of getting his messages directly to the people without having to filter them through editors and reporters. Broadcasting was also revolutionary in a second way: it was the first truly national mass medium. Newspapers had local circulation bases, whereas radio could reach millions of Americans across the country simultaneously.

Television followed radio, and by the late 1950s more than 90 percent of American homes had a television set. The political potential of television was evident as early as 1952, when seventeen million homes tuned in to the national Republican and Democratic party conventions.[17] However, television newscasts of the 1950s were brief, lasting no more than fifteen minutes, and relied on news gathered by other organizations, particularly the Associated Press and other wire services. In the early 1960s, the three commercial networks—CBS, NBC, and ABC—expanded their evening newscasts to thirty minutes, and

Franklin D. Roosevelt was the first president to make effective use of the radio to communicate directly with the American people. He broadcast a series of fireside chats that reached millions of listeners across the country.

their audience ratings increased.[18] Simultaneously, they increased the size and funding of their news divisions, and television soon became the principal news medium of national politics.

Today, television provides a twenty-four-hour forum of political news and information. The advent of the Cable News Network (CNN) and C-SPAN in the late 1970s brought Americans round-the-clock communication. Television talk shows, such as *Larry King Live*, have broadened the range of choices available to politically interested viewers. A parallel development is the emergence of radio talk shows. Nearly a sixth of the American public claims to listen regularly to a politically oriented radio talk show, most of which have a conservative slant. The best known radio talk show host is Rush Limbaugh, who is known for his scathing attacks on Democratic politicians.

Even more so than their newspaper counterparts, television journalists rely on an interpretive style of reporting. The reason is that television journalists use a narrative or storytelling mode in order to appeal to an audience accustomed to entertainment programming. "Facts" alone do not tell a story; they have to be interpreted in a way that makes them into a story. Reuven Frank, a network executive and pioneer in television journalism, once told his correspondents: "Every news story should, without any sacrifice of probity or responsibility, display the attributes of fiction, of drama. It should have structure and conflict, problem and denouement, rising action and falling action, a beginning, a middle and an end."[19]

Government Licensing and Regulation of Broadcasters

At first the government did not carefully regulate broadcasting. The result was chaos. Nearby stations often used the same or adjacent radio frequencies, interfering with each other's transmissions. Finally, in 1934, Congress passed the Communications Act, which requires that broadcasters be licensed and meet certain performance standards. Congress established the Federal Communications Commission (FCC) to administer the act through regulations pertaining to such matters as signal strength, advertising rates and access, and political coverage.

The principle of scarcity justifies the licensing and regulation of broadcast media. Because the number of available broadcasting frequencies is limited, those few individuals who are granted a broadcasting license are expected to serve the public interest in addition to their own. In principle, licensing is a means of controlling broadcasting. If a station fails to comply with federal broadcast regulations, the FCC can withdraw its license. However, the FCC seldom even threatens to revoke a license, for fear of being accused of restricting freedom of the press. A broadcast station can apply for renewal of its license by postcard and is virtually guaranteed FCC approval, which covers seven years for radio and five for television.

Because broadcast frequencies are a scarce resource, licensees are required by law to be somewhat evenhanded during election campaigns. Section 315 of the Communications Act imposes on broadcasters an "equal-time" restriction, which means that they cannot sell or give air time to a political candidate without granting equal opportunities to the other candidates running for the same office. (Election debates are an exception; broadcasters can sponsor them and limit participation to nominees of the Republican and Democratic parties only.)

At an earlier time, broadcasters were also bound by the "fairness doctrine," an FCC regulation that compelled broadcasters to air opposing opinions on major public issues. In 1987, broadcasters, on the grounds that the fairness doctrine infringed on press freedom, persuaded the FCC to rescind it.

The Emergence of the Internet

Although the First Amendment protects each individual's right to press freedom, the right in practice has been reserved for a tiny few. The journalist A. J. Liebling wrote that freedom of the press belongs to those with the money to own one.[20] Even a modest-sized broadcast station or daily newspaper costs millions to buy; the largest media conglomerates are multibillion-dollar enterprises.

Access to the Internet is no substitute for ownership of a major news outlet, but it provides ordinary citizens at least the opportunity to exercise their free-press rights. By creating a website, the ordinary citizen can post information about public affairs, harangue officials, argue for public policies, and attempt to mobilize the support of others. There is no assurance of a wide audience, and in fact, most citizens have neither a personal website nor, if they do, a large following. But the Internet has reduced the barriers to citizen communication to a level not seen since the colonial days, when citizen-produced pamphlets were the major form of political expression.

The Internet has also provided political leaders and organizations a direct channel to the public. At all political levels, officeholders, parties, and interest groups now have websites that are used to inform and mobilize their followers. The Internet has reduced somewhat the traditional media's capacity to control

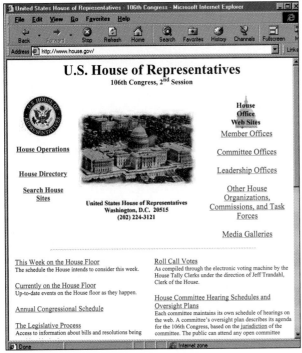

The Internet has weakened the traditional news media's control of the political information that Americans receive. Through the Internet, citizens and political leaders alike can communicate widely without having their messages filtered by the news media. Pictured here are the home pages of the U.S. House and Senate.

the news agenda. Editors and reporters are "gatekeepers" who decide what will make the news and what will not. Although they still play this role, Internet communication has in some instances virtually forced "stories" upon them. The best known web outlet is likely the "Drudge Report," which was created by Matt Drudge and became a prime source of information for enterprising reporters. The Clinton-Lewinsky scandal, for example, surfaced in the "Drudge Report" four days before it appeared in the mainstream press.

Freedom and Conformity in the U.S. News Media

Some democracies impose significant legal restraints on the press. The news media in Britain are barred from reporting on anything that the government has labeled an "official secret," and the nation's tough libel laws inhibit the press from publishing unsubstantiated personal attacks.

In the United States, as we saw in Chapter 4, the First Amendment gives the press substantial protection. The courts have consistently upheld the right of U.S. newspapers to report on politics as they choose. Broadcasters, as the equal-time restriction indicates, have less freedom under the law, but they are subject to much less government control than are broadcasters in Europe. In the case of both U.S. newspapers and broadcasters, the government cannot block publication of a news story unless it can convincingly demonstrate in court that the information would jeopardize national security. U.S. libel laws also strongly favor

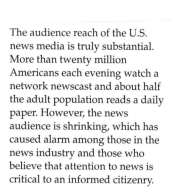

The audience reach of the U.S. news media is truly substantial. More than twenty million Americans each evening watch a network newscast and about half the adult population reads a daily paper. However, the news audience is shrinking, which has caused alarm among those in the news industry and those who believe that attention to news is critical to an informed citizenry.

the press. A public figure who is attacked in a news story cannot collect libel damages unless he or she can demonstrate convincingly that the news organization was false in its accusations and knowingly or recklessly careless in its search for the truth.

Moreover, the U.S. government provides the news media with indirect economic support. Newspapers and magazines have a special postal rate that helps them keep their circulation costs low, and broadcasters pay only a few dollars annually in license fees. Such policies have contributed to the development of a truly enormous news industry in the United States: 1,600 daily newspapers, 8,500 weeklies, 9,500 radio stations, 6 national television news networks, 850 local television stations, and 10,500 cable television systems.[21]

The audience reach of leading news organizations is substantial. Each weekday evening, more than twenty million Americans tune into a network newscast. *Time* and *Newsweek* magazines reach over three million readers each week. *U.S. News & World Report*'s weekly circulation exceeds two million copies. *The New York Times, The Wall Street Journal, USA Today*, and the *Los Angeles Times* have daily circulations exceeding one million readers. Another three dozen newspapers have circulations in excess of 250,000 readers. The average daily circulation of America's newspapers is roughly forty million; on Sunday, newspaper circulation jumps to sixty million.[22]

In view of the great number and the freedom of news organizations in the United States, it might be expected that Americans would have a lot of choice in the news they receive. However, the opposite is true. Each day, newspapers and broadcast stations from coast to coast tend to highlight the same national news stories and to interpret them in similar ways. Any number of terms—pack journalism, groupthink, media concentration—have been used to describe the fact that news reporting is fairly homogeneous.

The basic reason the news is pretty much the same everywhere is that America's reporters, unlike their counterparts in some European democracies, do not take sides in partisan disputes. They do sometimes differ on which facts, events, and issues are more important than others, but these polite disagreements are a far cry from the disputes and diversity that characterized the nineteenth-century partisan press.

Of course, today's news organizations differ in the way they tell a given story. Broadcast news tends to be, in effect, headline news with pictures. A thirty-minute network news broadcast typically presents a dozen or so stories in the twenty-two minutes allotted to news content (the other eight minutes being devoted to commercials). Newspapers have the space to present news developments in greater depth; some, like *The New York Times* (which labels itself "the newspaper of record"), provide substantial detail. The reporting styles of news organizations also vary. Although most of them present the news in an understated way, others tend toward sensationalism. For example, when Jeffrey Dahmer, a convicted murderer who had cannibalized his victims, was himself murdered in a Wisconsin prison in 1994, the *New York Post* gave its whole front page to the headline: "Death of a Monster." *The New York Times,* in contrast, gave the story a standard-size front-page headline, "Jeffrey Dahmer, Multiple Killer, Is Bludgeoned to Death in Prison." Such differences in approach, however, do not disguise the fact that most news organizations tell their audiences the same stories each day.

DOMINATION OF NEWS PRODUCTION

Another reason for the lack of diversity in national news reporting is that a few news organizations generate most of it. The quintessential case of concentrated news production is radio, with its "canned" network-provided news; almost no local radio station in the country produces its own national news reports.

The Associated Press (AP) is the major producer of news stories. It has three hundred full-time reporters stationed throughout the country and the world to gather news stories, which are relayed by satellite to subscribing newspapers and broadcast stations. More than 95 percent of the nation's dailies are serviced by AP, and some also subscribe to other wire services, such as Reuters and the New York Times.[23] Smaller dailies lack the resources to gather news outside their own localities and thus depend almost completely on wire service reports for their national and international coverage.[24] They may give these reports a local or partisan slant, but most of what they say is a rehash of wire service dispatches.

Television news production is similarly dominated by just a few organizations. The six major networks—ABC, CBS, NBC, PBS, Fox, and CNN—generate most of the news coverage of national and international politics. For news of the nation and the world, local stations depend on video transmissions fed to them by the networks.

NEWS VALUES AND IMPERATIVES

Competitive pressures also lead the producers of news to report the same stories. No major news organization wants to miss an important story that others are reporting.[25] The pressure *not* to be different is substantial. "Even at the best newspapers," Timothy Crouse notes, "the editor always gauges his own reporters' stories against the expectations that the stories [of other news organizations] have aroused."[26]

CNN is one of six major networks that dominate news coverage of national and international events. CNN correspondent Mike Hannan and film crew are shown on location in Zaire, Africa.

The networks, wire services, and a few elite dailies, including *The New York Times*, the *Washington Post*, *The Wall Street Journal*, *Los Angeles Times*, and *Chicago Tribune*, establish a national standard of story selection. Whenever one of them highlights an important story, the others jump on the bandwagon. The chief trendsetter among news-gathering organizations is *The New York Times*, which has been described as "the bulletin board" for other major newspapers, news-magazines, and television networks.[27] Herbert Gans notes, "When editors and producers are uncertain about a selection decision, they will check whether, where, and how the *Times* has covered the story; and story selectors see to it that many of the *Times*'s front-page stories find their way into television programs and magazines."[28]

The imperatives of the fast pace of daily journalism also tend to make the news homogeneous.[29] Journalists have the task each day of filling a newspaper or broadcast with stories. Thus editors assign reporters to such beats as the White House and Congress, which can be relied on for a steady supply of news. On these beats the reporters of various news organizations see and hear the same things, exchange views on what is important, and not surprisingly, produce similar news stories.

Finally, shared professional values guide journalists in their search for news.[30] Reporters are on the lookout for aspects of situations that lend themselves to interesting news stories—novel, colorful, and compelling developments.[31] Long practice at storytelling leads journalists to develop a common understanding of what the news is.[32] After the White House press corps has listened to a presidential speech, for example, nearly all the journalists in attendance are in agreement on what was most newsworthy about the speech, often only a single statement within it.

DO MEDIA MERGERS SERVE THE PUBLIC INTEREST? THE CASE OF AOL AND TIME WARNER

Giant corporations now control most of the nation's communication capacity. Most large newspapers and all three broadcast networks are embedded in media conglomerates. For example, the American Broadcasting Company (ABC) is owned by the entertainment giant Disney. The largest merger of all was announced in 2000 when AOL and Time Warner (owner of CNN, *Time* magazine, and dozens of other news outlets) agreed to merge. Are such concentrations of media power in the public interest? Advocates of these mergers claim that they foster the production and distribution of information on an unprecedented scale and with unparalleled benefit to society. Critics say that media concentration sacrifices diversity and the free flow of information to corporate profits. These differences are reflected in claims that were made when the AOL and Time Warner merger was announced.

YES: This strategic combination with AOL accelerates the digital transformation of Time Warner by giving our creative and content businesses the widest possible canvas. The digital revolution has already begun to create unprecedented and instantaneous access to every form of media and to unleash immense possibilities for economic growth, human understanding, and creative expression. AOL Time Warner will lead this transformation. . . . The opportunities are limitless for everyone connected to AOL Time Warner—shareholders, consumers, advertisers, the creative and talented people who drive our success, and the global audiences we serve.

—Jerry Levin, CEO, Time Warner

NO: Consumers do not want to be beholden to a giant media-Internet dictatorship, even if it promises to be a benevolent one. This is the sad result of [a] weak competition policy that has allowed enormous consolidations, which are likely to leave consumers with fewer choices, limited competition, and higher prices. . . . We want the FCC [Federal Communication Commission] to require open access, regardless of the promises made by the players. Long-term diversity of views, choices, service, and competitive prices require public responsibilities, not just wheeling and dealing among the parties.

—joint statement by Consumers Union, Consumer Federation of America, Media Access Project, and Center for Media Education

"MEGAMEDIA": MERGERS, PROFITS, AND THE NEWS

Over the past two decades and at an accelerating pace, media ownership has become increasingly concentrated. The trend reflects the high profitability of the media business and the economies of scale—the larger the media organization, the more it can leverage advertisers and achieve efficiencies in the production of news and entertainment. The net result has been the emergence of huge media conglomerates. Although *The New York Times* remains a family-controlled paper, nearly all other major news organizations have been absorbed into larger corporate entities. The ABC network and its news division, for example, is part of the Disney corporation, while CNN is part of Time Warner. The list could be extended but the point would be the same: U.S. news is largely in the hands of what the political scientist Dean Alger calls the "megamedia."[33]

One issue that surrounds this development is whether it is healthy to a democracy to have concentrated ownership of the means of public communication (see "Current Controversies"). Should so few entities control so much of what Americans see and hear through the mass media? Some observers say that the change is not all that significant because there is still competition between news organizations and because there is a degree of independence for news organizations within their corporate structures. Alger is not convinced: "It is . . . vital for democracy to have a truly diverse set of media sources present in the public arena, a variety of alternative information and perspectives representing a real competition of approaches to news definitions and thoughts on the direction in which society should head. The continued advance of megamedia and their increasing domination of the prime mass media spell a profound constriction of that diversity and a severe diminution of the marketplace of ideas, and thus a danger to democracy."[34]

Another issue is the impact of media conglomerates on the quality of news content. As news organizations have become a part of larger corporations, they have increasingly had to adapt to the demands of the economic market. The news organization or division is only one part, and usually a relatively small part, of a very large corporation. A result has been a cutback in news-gathering capacity. ABC, CBS, and NBC News, for example, have closed many of their overseas news bureaus; the assumption is that international news is not of great interest to Americans and, therefore, that its production is not a high priority. News divisions have also been directed to compete more aggressively for audiences, because audience size determines advertising revenues. As a consequence, the news has become increasingly entertainment oriented. Critics say it is "infotainment" rather than real news. A study of network evening newscasts found that, over the past decade, the amount of news time devoted to government, politics, and public affairs has declined significantly while the amount given to life-style issues, celebrities, and human-interest subjects has risen sharply.[35] There has also been a substantial increase in "soft" public affairs programming, such as NBC's *Dateline* and ABC's *20/20*. These programs use news journalists to gather and present their stories, but they are aimed at the prime-time viewing audience. They contain some news, but their standard fare is exposé and human-interest stories.

Although this programming is popular with television audiences, it has contributed to a growing disenchantment with the news media. The public believes that journalists are now less professional and less moral, that the news is now more biased and less accurate, and that the news media's contribution to a healthy democracy has declined (see Figure 11-1).

The News Media as Link: Roles the Press Can and Cannot Perform

When the objective model of reporting came to dominate American news coverage, the relationship between the press and the public was fundamentally altered. The nineteenth-century partisan press gave its readers overt cues as to how to evaluate political issues and leaders. In the presidential election campaign of 1896, the *San Francisco Call* devoted 1,075 column-inches of photographs to the Republican ticket of McKinley-Hobart and only 11 inches to the Democrats, Bryan and Sewell.[36] Many European newspapers still function in this way, guiding their readers by applying partisan or ideological values to

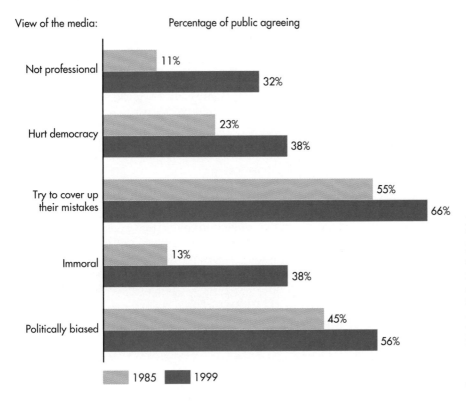

FIGURE 11-1 **The Public's View of the "New" News** In recent years as news organizations have competed more aggressively to attract an audience, the news has become more sensational, more personal, and more negative. In the process, the public's view of the news has become less favorable. *Source: Pew Research Center for the People and the Press, February 25, 1999.*

current events. The *Daily Telegraph,* for example, is an unofficial but fiercely loyal mouthpiece of Britain's Conservative party (see "How the United States Compares").

In contrast, U.S. news organizations do not routinely and consistently take sides in partisan conflict. Their main task is to report and analyze events. The media are thus very different from political parties and interest groups, the other major links between the public and its leaders. The media are driven by the search for interesting and revealing stories; parties and interest groups exist to articulate particular political opinions and values.

This distinction provides a basis for determining what roles the media can and cannot be expected to perform. The press is capable of fulfilling only those public responsibilities that are compatible with journalistic values: the signaler role, the common-carrier role, and the watchdog role. The media are less successful in their attempts to perform a fourth, politically oriented role: that of public representative.

THE SIGNALER ROLE

As journalists see it, one of their responsibilities is to play the **signaler role,** alerting the public to important developments as soon as possible after they happen: a state visit to Washington by a foreign leader, a bill that has just been passed by Congress, a change in the nation's unemployment level, a demand by dairy farmers for higher milk prices, a terrorist bombing in a foreign capital.

signaler role The accepted responsibility of the media to alert the public to important developments as soon as possible after they happen or are discovered.

HOW THE UNITED STATES COMPARES

PARTISAN NEUTRALITY AS A NEWS VALUE

In the nineteenth century, the United States had a partisan press. Journalists were partisan actors, and news was a blend of reporting and advocacy. Facts and opinions were freely intermixed in news stories. This type of reporting gradually gave way to a model of journalism that emphasizes the "facts" and covers the two parties more or less equally. American journalists, through both print and television, seek impartiality in their daily news reporting. For example, a political scandal, whether it involves a Democrat or Republican, is a big story for any major U.S. news organization.

European news organizations are less committed to partisan neutrality. Many European newspapers are aligned with a party, and although they focus on events, their coverage has a partisan component. In Great

Britain, for example, the *Daily Telegraph* often serves as a voice of the Conservative party, while the *Guardian* favors the liberal side. Broadcasters in most European countries are politically neutral by law and practice, but there are exceptions, as in the case of the French and Italian broadcasters.

The difference between the U.S. and European media is evident in a five-country survey that asked journalists whether they agreed with the following directive: "Journalists should make sure they are not perceived as trying to influence the outcome of the conflict between political parties over the issues." Compared with their counterparts in Great Britain, Germany, Sweden, and Italy, U.S. journalists were more likely to express agreement with the statement.

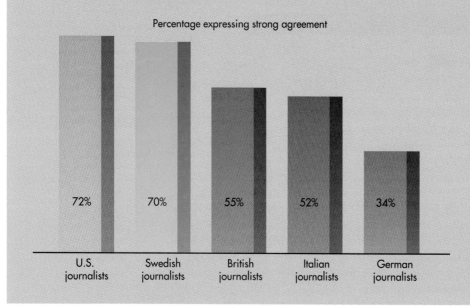

SOURCE: Thomas E. Patterson, Media and Democracy Project, in progress.

The signaler role is one that the American media perform relatively well. The press is poised to converge on any fast-breaking major news event anywhere in the nation and nearly anywhere in the world. For instance, as the United States prepared to intervene forcefully in Haiti in 1994, dozens of U.S. journalists went to that trouble-ridden Caribbean nation to report from the scene. The NBC and CBS networks even sent their news anchors, Tom Brokaw and Dan Rather, despite a possible risk to their personal safety.

Through their similar role, the news media alert the public to developments in the nation and the world. Shown here U.S. journalists taking pictures of a refugee in war-torn Kosovo.

The media are particularly well suited to signal developments from Washington. More than half of all reported national news emanates from the nation's capital, most of it from the White House and Congress. Altogether, more than ten thousand people in Washington work in the news business. The key players are the leading correspondents of the television networks and major newspapers, the heads of the Washington news bureaus, and a few top editors.[37]

The press, in its capacity as signaler, has the power to focus the public's attention. The term **agenda setting** has been used to describe the media's ability to influence what is on people's minds.[38] By covering the same events, problems, issues, and leaders—simply by giving them space or time in the news—the media place them on the public agenda.[39] The press, as Bernard Cohen notes, "may not be successful much of the time in telling people what to think, but it is stunningly successful in telling them what to think about."[40] This influence is most obvious in such situations as the Persian Gulf War, an event that quickly aroused widespread attention. When the allies started their air raid on Baghdad, the broadcast networks began an unprecedented forty-two hours of continuous coverage. News of the war was almost inescapable.

The press's agenda-setting influence is also evident in less dramatic circumstances. In 1993, crime news doubled from its level in the previous year. On network television, crime accounted for 12 percent of 1993 news coverage, overshadowing all other issues, including the economy, health care, and the Bosnian crisis.[41] This emphasis was triggered by several high-profile cases, including the arrest of serial killer Joel Rifkin in New York, the parent-killing trial of the Menendez brothers, the kidnap-murder of twelve-year-old Polly Klaas in California, and a crazed gunman's shooting spree on a Long Island commuter train that killed six people and wounded nineteen. The media's focus on crime continued into 1994, fed by new cases such as the Simpson murder. The media's crime coverage had a dramatic impact on the public's agenda. At no time in the previous decade had more than 10 percent of Americans named crime as the nation's most important problem. Opinion polls in 1994, however, indicated that crime had become the public's leading concern (see Figure 11-2). The only

agenda setting The power of the media through news coverage to focus the public's attention and concern on particular events, problems, issues, personalities, and so on.

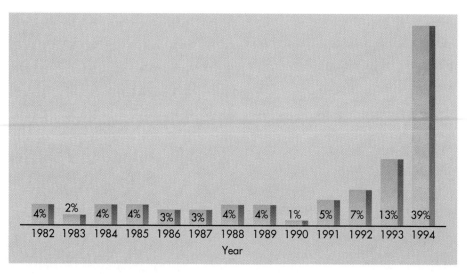

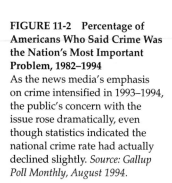

FIGURE 11-2   Percentage of Americans Who Said Crime Was the Nation's Most Important Problem, 1982–1994
As the news media's emphasis on crime intensified in 1993–1994, the public's concern with the issue rose dramatically, even though statistics indicated the national crime rate had actually declined slightly. *Source: Gallup Poll Monthly, August 1994.*

feasible explanation for this heightened concern is the media's saturation coverage of the crime issue: Justice Department statistics indicate that the actual level of crime in America decreased by 2 percent in the 1993–1994 period.

THE COMMON-CARRIER ROLE

common-carrier role   The media's function as an open channel through which political leaders can communicate with the public.

Journalists base many of their news stories on the words of public officials. The press thus plays what is labeled a **common-carrier role,** providing a channel through which political leaders can reach the public. The importance of this role to officials and citizens alike is obvious. Citizens cannot very well support or oppose a leader's plans and actions if they do not know about them. And leaders need news coverage if they are to get the public's attention.

Not surprisingly, political leaders make a great effort to get coverage. They hold news conferences, issue press releases, and stage events in an effort to garner the media's attention.[42] Indeed, national news is mainly about the actions of political leaders and institutions, as is reflected in the hundreds of reporters who station themselves regularly at the Capitol and White House.

Officials try to get the most favorable news coverage they can. For example, the White House Press Office and the White House Office of Communication try to shape information in a way favorable to the president. Sometimes they succeed in placing their "spin" (that is, the president's interpretation) on the media's coverage of events.

However, the press today is less deferential to political leaders than in the past. Even though the president and Congress can expect coverage, the press increasingly places its own "spin" on these stories. Journalists, because of their increased celebrity status, their heightened skepticism of politicians since Vietnam and Watergate, and the greater latitude afforded them by the interpretive style of reporting, have become accustomed not only to covering what newsmakers say but also to having their own say. In 1998, as the Clinton White House was trying to focus coverage on the president's policy accomplishments and plans, the press was devoting most of its coverage to the Monica Lewinsky

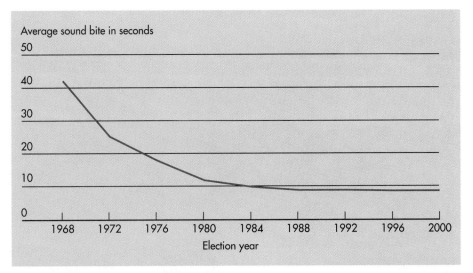

Average sound bite in seconds

FIGURE 11-3 The Shrinking Sound Bite of Television Election Coverage
The average length of time that presidential candidates are shown speaking without interruption on television newscasts has declined sharply in recent elections. *Source: Adapted from Daniel C. Hallin, "Sound Bite News: Television Coverage of Elections 1968–1988," Journal of Communication 42 (Spring 1992): 6. The 1992–2000 data were provided by the Center for Media and Public Affairs.*

scandal. President Clinton, to no avail, pleaded with the press to pay more attention to the nation's policy problems.

In fact, the news today is as much journalist centered as it is newsmaker centered. For every minute that the presidential candidates spoke on the network newscasts during coverage of the 2000 campaign, for example, the journalists who were covering them talked for five minutes. It was once the case that a candidate's "sound bite" (the length of time within a television story that the candidate speaks without interruption) was about forty-five seconds in length on average.[43] In recent campaigns, the average sound bite has been less than ten seconds, which is barely enough time for the candidate to utter a full sentence (see Figure 11-3).

THE WATCHDOG ROLE

Traditionally, the American press has accepted responsibility for protecting the public from deceitful, careless, incompetent, and corrupt officials.[44] In this **watchdog role,** the press stands ready to expose any official who violates accepted legal, ethical, and performance standards. The role is a vital one. Officials cannot always be trusted to act properly, and the press is a check on impropriety. The First Amendment grants the press the freedom and independence to scrutinize government action and to tell the American people when their representatives have strayed from acceptable practices.

watchdog role The accepted responsibility of the media to protect the public from deceitful, careless, incompetent, and corrupt officials by standing ready to expose any official who violates accepted legal, ethical, or performance standards.

The most notable exercise of the watchdog role in recent decades took place during the Watergate scandal. Bob Woodward and Carl Bernstein of the *Washington Post* spent months uncovering evidence that high-ranking officials in the Nixon White House were lying about their role in the burglary of the Democratic National Committee's headquarters and in the subsequent cover-up. Virtually all the nation's media picked up on the *Post*'s revelations. Nixon was forced to resign, as was his attorney general, John Mitchell. The Watergate episode is a dramatic reminder that a vigilant press is one of society's best safeguards against abuses of political power.

Presidential politics is a favorite topic of the press. Here, Republican presidential nominee George W. Bush is surrounded by reporters during a 2000 campaign stop.

www.mhhe.com/patterson5

Simulation

There is an inherent tension between the watchdog role and the common-carrier role. The watchdog role demands that the journalist maintain a skeptical view of political leaders and keep them at a distance. The common-carrier role requires the journalist to maintain close ties with political leaders. In the period before Watergate, the common-carrier role was clearly the dominant orientation. It perhaps still is, but journalists have become increasingly critical of political leaders and institutions.

Some of this criticism revolves around scandals such as the Iran-Contra affair (President Reagan) and the Whitewater, Paula Jones, and Monica Lewinsky allegations (President Clinton). Most of the criticism, however, is leveled at the day-to-day conduct of politics. Journalists are intent on publicizing the missteps of political leaders. Given the enormous size of the U.S. government, there is plenty to criticize if journalists want to focus on it. The media's preference for "bad news" can be seen, for example, in the fact that negative coverage of presidential candidates has risen steadily in recent decades and now exceeds their positive coverage (see Figure 11-4).

"Bad news" characterizes the coverage of Democrats and Republicans alike. Although surveys indicate that most journalists lean toward the Democratic party in their personal beliefs, studies have found partisan bias to be a relatively small factor in political coverage.[45] Other influences, including the norm of objectivity, counterbalance the effect of partisanship on journalists' news decisions. On the other hand, journalists' skeptical view of politicians is not offset by other factors. There is no rule that limits negativity.[46] Coverage of the Democrat-controlled Congress of 1993–1994 by the national media was nearly 70 percent negative; when the Congress shifted to Republican hands in 1995–1996, its coverage too was nearly 70 percent negative in tone.[47] The fact is, the real bias of the

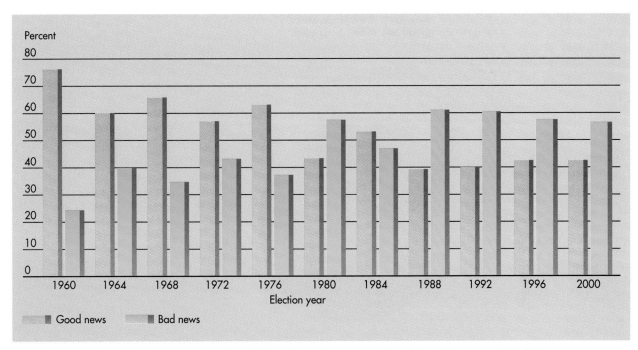

FIGURE 11-4 **"Bad News" Coverage of Presidential Candidates Compared to "Good News" Coverage, 1960–2000**
In the 1960s, candidates received largely favorable news coverage. Today, their coverage is mostly negative. *Source: Thomas E. Patterson, Out of Order (New York: Vintage, 1994), 20, for 1960–1992 coverage; Center for Medic Public Affairs, 1996; author's estimate based on preliminary data, 2000.*

press is not liberal as opposed to conservative, but a pronounced tendency to report what is wrong with politics and politicians rather than what is right. "Bad news is good news" is an old adage of the press, and in recent years, it has become its guiding principle.

Critics argue that the press has gone too far in its search for bad news, claiming that it now faults nearly everything that politicians say and do, thereby undermining the public trust on which effective leadership is built. Critics also complain that the press no longer has any respect for public officials' private lives—that everything from their bedroom behavior to decades-old "skeletons in the closet" are grist for news stories. Journalists claim that they are merely doing their job—that the public is better served by a highly skeptical and intrusive press than a compliant one. CNN correspondent Bob Franken said, "We historically are not supposed to be popular, and it's almost our role to be bearer of bad news."[48]

The public is ambivalent about the news media's skepticism. A 1997 Pew Research Center poll found that most Americans believe that press skepticism is a factor in keeping politicians from abusing public office. Yet the same poll also indicated that most Americans believe that the press gets in the way of efforts to solve society's problems. The press skepticism is thus seen as both an obstacle to effective governance and a form of protection against wayward politicians. Yet the press may actually be undermining its watchdog role by its zealous pursuit of scandal. When the public is deluged day after day with

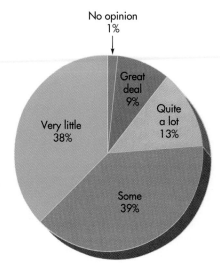

"How much trust and confidence
do you have in the news media?"

FIGURE 11-5 Public Confidence in the News Media From a high in the early 1970s when the Watergate scandal was in the news, the public's trust in the press has declined. Today, the media are among the lowest ranked institutions in the public's view. *Source: Survey sponsored by National Public Radio, Henry V. Kaiser Family Foundation, and Harvard University's Kennedy School of Government, June 2000.*

stories of wrongdoing in high places, its expectations of public officials decline and its confidence in the media's judgment diminishes (see Figure 11-5). An effect is that the public may reject the media's outcries. Such was the public reaction to the news media's initial reporting of the Clinton-Lewinsky scandal. Even though the press intimated that the president would have to resign, the public reacted differently. The news coverage was so sensational, so lurid, and so rooted in hearsay that a majority of Americans concluded that it was unfair to Clinton and said that he should remain in office.

THE PUBLIC REPRESENTATIVE ROLE

public representative role
A role whereby the media attempt to act as the public's representatives.

Traditionally, the **public representative role**—that of spokesperson for and advocate of the public—has belonged to political leaders, political institutions, and political organizations. Today, however, many reporters believe they also have a mandate to represent the public. "[Our] chief duty," newscaster Roger Mudd claims, "is to put before the nation its unfinished business."[49]

Although the press has to some degree always acted as a stand-in for the people, the desire of journalists to play the role of public advocate has increased significantly since the 1960s.[50] As journalists' status rose, they became more assertive, a tendency sharpened by the trend toward interpretive reporting. Vietnam and Watergate also contributed to the change; these events convinced many journalists that their judgments were superior to those of political leaders. James Reston of *The New York Times* said of Vietnam, "Maybe the historians will agree that the reporters and cameras were decisive in the end. They brought the issue of the war to the people, before the Congress and the courts, and forced the withdrawal of American power from Vietnam."[51]

Nevertheless, there are at least two basic reasons for concluding that journalists are not nearly as well suited as political leaders to the role of public

NBC anchorman Tom Brokaw walks with President Bill Clinton, followed by Secret Service agents. Network anchors such as Brokaw, Dan Rather, and Peter Jennings are more familiar to Americans than is nearly any politician except the president.

representative. First, the news media are not subject to the level of public accountability required of a public representative. Political institutions are made responsible to the public by a formal mechanism of accountability—elections. The vote gives officeholders a reason to act in the majority's interest, and it offers citizens an opportunity to boot from office anyone they feel has failed them. Thousands of elected officials have lost their jobs this way. The public has no comparable hold over the press. Journalists are neither chosen by the people nor removable by them. Irate citizens can stop watching a news program or buying a newspaper that angers them, but no major daily newspaper or television station has gone out of business as a result.

A second obstacle to journalists' attempts to play the role of public representative is that representation requires a point of view. Politics is essentially the mobilization of bias—that is, it involves the representation of particular values and interests. Political parties and interest groups, as we saw in Chapters 8 and 9, exist to represent particular interests in society. But what political interests do the media represent? CBS News executive Richard Salant once said that his reporters covered stories "from nobody's point of view."[52] What he was saying, in effect, was that journalists do not consistently represent the political concerns of any segment of society. They respond to news opportunities, not to political interests. Above all, they prize good stories.

The O. J. Simpson murder-trial story is a prime example. The former football star's trial received more news coverage in 1994–95 than any public policy issue, foreign or domestic. Judged by the media's priorities, Simpson's fate was more important than health care, unemployment, Haiti, drug abuse, education, and every other national problem. The Clinton-Lewinsky-Starr saga is another example. In the first month, January 1998, the scandal filled a third of the news time on the network evening newscasts. It had to compete for time with the Winter Olympics, a papal visit to Cuba, the possibility of renewed war with Iraq, and the ravaging effects of the El Niño weather system.[53] Yet it received more coverage than all these developments combined. And it remained the top news story every month thereafter, even in periods when there were no new revelations or when more pressing issues arose, such as a financial crisis in Asia that threatened to weaken the U.S. economy.

Underlying the press's search for the dramatic story is the media's quest for profits. The bottom line, rather than the public interest, increasingly drives news coverage. Audience competition has intensified with the spread of cable television, and the news has become increasingly sensational. "All Monica All the Time" was how some critics described the press's coverage of the Lewinsky scandal. One network, MSNBC, even chose to make the scandal nearly the sole focus of its programming, hoping that higher audience ratings and correspondingly higher advertising revenues would be the result.

The relentless search for attention-getting stories weakens the press's ability to provide citizens a clear understanding of what is broadly at issue in politics. It is a difficult job to formulate society's problems in a way that allows citizens to understand and act on them. The news media cannot do the job consistently well. The journalist Walter Lippmann put it plainly when he said:

> The press is no substitute for [political] institutions. It is like the beam of a searchlight that moves restlessly about, bringing one episode and then another out of darkness into vision. Men cannot do the work of the world by this light alone. They cannot govern society by episodes, incidents, and interruptions.[54]

Organizing the Public in the Media Age

Lippmann's point was not that news organizations are somehow inferior to political organizations but that each has a different role and responsibility in society. Democracy cannot operate effectively without a free press that acts

Independent counsel Kenneth Starr is shown here during the peak of the media feeding frenzy that surrounded allegations of a sexual affair between President Clinton and the White House intern Monica Lewinsky. Starr's tactics and motives were widely criticized in the press.

effectively in its signaler, common-carrier, and watchdog roles. To keep in touch with one another and with the government, citizens must have access to timely and uncensored news about public affairs. In other words, the media must do their job well if democratic government is to succeed. However, the media cannot also be asked to do the job of political institutions. For reasons already noted, the task is beyond the media's capacity.

As previous chapters have emphasized, the problem of citizen influence is the problem of organizing the public so that people can act together effectively. The news media merely appear to solve this problem. The fact that millions of people each day receive the same news about their government does not mold them into an organized community. The news creates a pseudo-community: citizens feel they are part of a functioning whole until they try to act on their news awareness. The futility of media-centered democracy was dramatized in the movie *Network* when its central character, a television anchorman, became enraged at the nation's political leadership and urged his viewers to go to their windows and yell, "I'm mad as hell and I'm not going to take it anymore!" Citizens heeded his instructions, but the main effect was to raise the network's ratings. It was not clear what officials in Washington were expected to do about several million people leaning out their windows and shouting a vague slogan at the top of their lungs. The film vividly illustrated the fact that the news can raise public consciousness as a prelude to action, but the news itself cannot organize the public in any meaningful way. When public opinion on an issue is already formed, the media can serve as a channel for the expression of that opinion. But when society's choices are in their formative stage, the media are not ordinarily an adequate guide to the action that should be taken or the priority they should be given.[55]

www.mhhe.com/patterson5

Self-Quiz

Summary

In the nation's first century, the press was allied closely with the political parties and helped the parties mobilize public opinion. Gradually the press freed itself from this relationship and developed a form of reporting, known as objective journalism, that emphasizes the fair and accurate reporting of newsworthy developments. The foundation of modern American news rests on the presentation and evaluation of significant events, not on the advocacy of partisan ideas. The nation's news organizations do not differ greatly in their reporting; broadcast stations and newspapers throughout the country emphasize many of the same events, issues, and personalities, following the lead of the major broadcast networks, a few elite newspapers, and the wire services.

The press performs four basic roles in a free society. In their signaler role, journalists communicate information to the public about events and problems that they consider important, relevant, and therefore newsworthy. The press also serves as a common carrier in that it provides political leaders with a channel for addressing the public.

Third, the press acts as a public protector, or watchdog, by exposing deceitful, careless, or corrupt officials. The American media can and, to a significant degree, do perform these roles adequately.

The press is less well suited, however, to the other role it plays, that of public representative. This role requires a consistent political viewpoint and public accountability, neither of which the press possesses. The media cannot be substitutes for effective political institutions. The press's strength lies ultimately in its capacity to inform the public, not in its attempts to serve as their representative.

Key Terms

agenda setting
common-carrier role
descriptive reporting
interpretive reporting
news
objective journalism

partisan press
press (news media)
public representative role
signaler role
watchdog role

Suggested Readings

Alger, Dean. *Megamedia: How Giant Corporations Dominate Mass Media, Distort Competition, and Endanger Democracy.* Lanham, Md.: Rowman & Littlefield, 1998. A look at the effect of media concentration on the quality of news.

Cook, Timothy E. *Governing with the News: The News Media as a Political Institution.* Chicago: University of Chicago Press, 1997. An analysis of the news media as a political institution.

Fallows, James. *Breaking the News: How the Media Undermine American Democracy.* New York: Pantheon, 1996. A leading journalist's critique of his profession.

Kovach, Bill, and Tom Rosenstiel. *Warp Speed: America in the Age of Mixed Media.* New York: The Century Foundation Press, 1999. A careful account of how the "new" news was revealed in reporting of the Lewinsky scandal.

Kurtz, Howard. *Spin Cycle: Inside the Clinton Propaganda Machine.* New York: Free Press, 1998. A look at the Clinton White House's attempts to manage its news coverage.

Maltese, John Anthony. *Spin Control: The White House Office of Communications and the Management of Presidential News.* Chapel Hill: University of North Carolina Press, 1994. An assessment of how presidents attempt to manage news coverage.

McChesney, Robert W. *Rich Media, Poor Democracy.* Urbana: University of Illinois Press, 1999. An award-winning analysis of the media's political impact.

Patterson, Thomas E. *Out of Order.* New York: Vintage Books, 1994. An analysis of how election news coverage has changed in recent decades.

Sabato, Larry J., Mark Stencel, and S. Robert Lichter. *Peep Show: Media and Politics in the Age of Scandal.* Lanham, Md.: Rowman & Littlefield, 2000. A penetrating critique of today's news.

Sparrow, Bartholomew H. *Uncertain Guardians.* Baltimore, Md.: Johns Hopkins University Press, 1999. A systematic assessment of the news media's political role and tendencies.

Walsh, Kenneth T. *Feeding the Beast: The White House Versus the Press.* New York: Random House, 1996. A journalist's view of the relationship between the president and the press.

PART THREE

Governing Institutions

★ ★ ★

merican democracy is often described as government by the
people. But direct democracy is a practical impossibility in a nation the size of the United States. Americans are governed largely
through institutions.

A debate has long raged over the proper relationship between a people and
their representatives. One view holds that representatives should follow the
expressed opinions of the governed, for if they do not, they will promote their
own narrow interests. Another view, first elaborated by the English theorist
Edmund Burke, holds that representatives should exercise their best judgment in deciding policy; if they listen too closely to those who elected them,
they will serve parochial interests rather than the general interests of society.

The governing system of the United States embodies both conceptions of
representation. The presidency is a truly national office that, as Chapters 14
and 15 will describe, encourages its incumbent to take a national view of issues. On the other hand, Congress, as Chapters 12 and 13 will show, is both a
national institution and a body that is subject to powerful local influences.

Americans are also governed through unelected bureaucrats and appointed judges. Their decisions, as Chapters 16 and 17 will describe, can in
some instances be as far reaching as those made by the people's elected
representatives. ★

CHAPTER 12

Congressional Election and Organization: Sharing the Power

★

Whether . . . safe or marginal, cautious or audacious, congressmen must constantly engage in activities relating to reelection.

—David Mayhew[1]

★ ★ ★

*A*s Speaker of the House of Representatives, Newt Gingrich was the chamber's most powerful member. In fact, he was often called the most powerful congressional leader of modern times. He had led the Republican party to a dramatic victory in the 1994 midterm elections and had molded the GOP majority in the House into a powerful political bloc. But Gingrich's "revolution" faltered after its early success. He pressed a budget showdown with the Clinton White House that backfired, resulting in a temporary shutdown of the federal government that was widely unpopular and may have cost the GOP its chance to win the presidency in 1996. His public popularity plummeted, fueled by people's dislike of his confrontational style and blunt words. When the GOP then lost House seats in the 1998 midterm election amid expectations that it would gain seats, Gingrich's Republican colleagues rebelled against him, forcing him out of the Speaker's post. He also resigned his seat in the House.

The Gingrich story illustrates the influence that elections have on the outlook of members of Congress. They seek a career in Congress, not just a temporary stay. Anything or anybody that might jeopardize their career is a cause for alarm. Elections also determine whether they will be part of the majority or minority party in Congress, and there is a large difference between the two. The majority party selects the chairs of the committees and subcommittees, which are positions of great power and prestige. Gingrich was dumped because he had become a liability; his leadership was jeopardizing the reelection chances of Republican House members and was threatening the GOP's position as the House majority.

This chapter explains the roles of elections and organization in the makeup and operations of the Congress of the United States. The next chapter will focus on congressional policymaking. The following points are emphasized in this first of two chapters on Congress:

★ *Congressional elections tend to have a strong local orientation and to favor incumbents.* Congressional office provides incumbents with substantial resources (free publicity, staff, and legislative influence) that give them (particularly House members) a major advantage in election campaigns. However, incumbency also has some liabilities that contribute to turnover in congressional membership.

★ *Congress is organized in part along political party lines; its collective leadership is provided by party leaders of the House of Representatives and the Senate.* These leaders do not have great formal powers. Their authority rests mainly on shared partisan values and on the fact that they have been entrusted with leadership responsibility by other senators or representatives of their party.

★ *The work of Congress is done mainly through its committees and subcommittees, each of which has its leader (a chairperson) and its policy jurisdiction.* The committee system of Congress allows a broad sharing of power and leadership, which serves the power and reelection needs of Congress's members but fragments the institution.

Congress as a Career: Election to Congress

In the nation's first century, service in the Congress was not a career for most of its members. Before 1900 at least a third and sometimes as many as half of the seats in Congress changed hands at each election. Most members left voluntarily. Because travel was slow and arduous, serving in the nation's capital required them to spend months away from their families. And because the national government was not the center of power and politics that it is today, many politicians preferred to serve in state capitals.

The modern Congress is very different. Most of its members are professional politicians, and a seat in the U.S. Senate or House is as far as most of them can expect to go in politics. The pay (about $135,000 a year) is reasonably good, and the prestige of their office is substantial, particularly if they serve in the Senate. An extended stay in Congress is what most of its members aspire to attain.

Incumbents have a good chance of being reelected (see Figure 12-1). They are not a sure bet to win again, but the odds are on their side. In the last decade, the reelection rate of House incumbents seeking another term has exceeded 90 percent, as has the reelection rate of Senate incumbents.

These figures overestimate somewhat an incumbent's chances of reelection. Some incumbents retire from Congress when faced with a campaign they fear

Like all other members of Congress, Senator Dianne Feinstein of California tries to win reelection by serving the interests of her constituents. Here, Feinstein talks to the press about proposed military base closings in California. She pledged support for the California communities and workers adversely affected by cutbacks in defense spending.

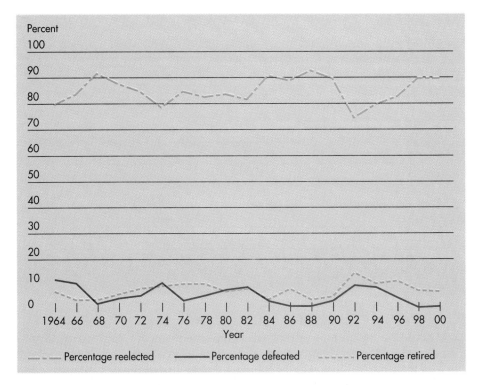

FIGURE 12-1 Reelection Rates of House Incumbents
U.S. House incumbents have a very high rate of reelection, although the percentage declined somewhat in the early 1990s.
Source: Congressional Quarterly Weekly Report, *various dates.*

they will lose. Moreover, incumbents must stand for reelection again and again if they intend to make Congress a career. A single loss will halt or interrupt this goal. Over the period of a few elections, a substantial number of congressional seats can change hands. The 1992 and 1994 congressional elections are an extreme example: the turnover in House membership in these two elections was a combined 188 seats, the highest total of any two consecutive elections since World War II.

On balance, however, incumbents have a clear edge over their opponents, as their margin of victory indicates. In recent elections, most House incumbents (see Figure 12-2) and nearly half of Senate incumbents seeking reelection have received 60 percent or more of the vote. Even when voters are convinced that Congress as an institution is performing badly, they reelect a large majority of its members. One reason is that many congressional districts and a few states are so lopsidedly Democratic or Republican that the candidate of the weaker party has no realistic chance of victory. In the 2000 elections, dozens of House members ran unopposed for reelection. All incumbents, however, gain important reelection advantages from the office they hold, a subject to which we now turn.

USING INCUMBENCY TO STAY IN CONGRESS

Getting reelected is a high priority for members of Congress.[2] They may be more interested in issues of public policy than in reelection activities, but they must stay in Congress if they are to realize their policy goals. In Lawrence Dodd's phrase, members of Congress strive for **electoral mastery**—a strong base of popular support that will free them from constant worry over reelection

electoral mastery A strong base of popular support that frees a congressional incumbent from constant worry over reelection.

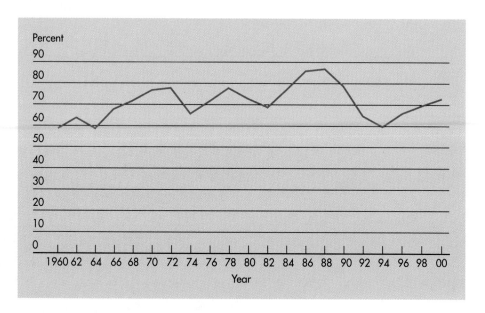

FIGURE 12-2 Percentage of House Incumbents Who Were Reelected by 60 Percent or More of the Vote, 1960–2000 The majority of House incumbents are reelected by a wide margin of votes. *Source:* Congressional Quarterly Weekly Report, *various dates.*

and allow them to pursue other goals.[3] Some members of Congress acquire electoral mastery the easy way—through election in a constituency that lopsidedly favors their party. Most members have to make use of the advantages of their office in order to attain electoral mastery.

Pork, Favors, and Publicity

constituency The individuals who live within the geographical area represented by an elected official. More narrowly, the body of citizens eligible to vote for a particular representative.

Members of Congress promote their reelection prospects by serving their **constituency**—the body of citizens eligible to vote in their state or district. Members of Congress pay close attention to constituency opinions when casting their votes on legislation, and they work hard to get their share of **pork barrel projects,** a term that refers to legislation that funds a special project for a particular locale, such as a new roadway or hospital. (*Pork* was the term for political graft or corruption in the late nineteenth century. When legislators adopted the practice of placing numerous items of pork into a single bill, people began to say, "Now the pork is all in one barrel.") Although pork barrel politics is often ridiculed by the public, the voters themselves are a main reason it continues. Constituents may disagree on issues of national policy, but they ordinarily do not object when federal money is spent on a project in their area.

pork barrel projects Laws whose tangible benefits are targeted at a particular legislator's constituency.

service strategy Use of personal staff by members of Congress to perform services for constituents in order to gain their support in future elections.

Members of Congress also boost their reelection chances by catering to their constituents' individual needs, a practice known as the **service strategy.**[4] When constituents seek information about a government program, express an opinion about pending legislation, or want help in obtaining a federal benefit, their representative usually responds. A representative or senator can often prod the bureaucracy to respond more quickly to a citizen who is encountering a delay or other obstacle in applying for social security or other federal benefits.[5] Congressional observers disagree on exactly how many votes can be won through these small favors,[6] but there is no doubt that constituency service helps—particularly in House races, where the incumbent's attentiveness to local people and problems is often a major campaign issue.

The U.S. Capitol in Washington, D.C., with the House wing in the foreground. The Senate meets in the wing at the right of the central rotunda (under the dome). The offices of the House and Senate party leaders—Speaker, vice president, majority and minority leaders and whips—are located in the Capitol. Other members of Congress have their offices in nearby buildings.

The service strategy is made possible by the staff resources provided to members of Congress. Each House member receives an office suite and an office allowance of more than $750,000 a year, which supports a personal staff of about twenty full-time employees. Senators have larger budgets whose size depends on the population of the state they represent. Senators' personal staffs average about forty employees. Members of Congress are also provided office space in their state or district and, in the case of senators, a mobile office as well. The personal staffs of members of Congress spend the bulk of their time not on legislative matters but on constituency relations.

Congressional staffs also churn out newsletters and press releases designed to publicize the member for whom they work. Television and radio materials are part of the publicity effort; members have free use of broadcast facilities located in the Capitol. Members also promote their image through personal appearances in their home states and districts. At public expense, each House member is allowed about thirty visits to his or her district each year and each senator can take about forty trips home.

Finally, each member of Congress is permitted several free mailings annually to constituent households, a privilege known as the *frank*. The average House member sends out more than a million pieces of frank mail in an election year (although members are barred from sending franked mail within sixty days of the election).[7] Some congressional offices are quite shameless in their use of the frank. Certain House members, for example, routinely send congratulatory letters to all graduating high school seniors in their districts, an effort that is designed to impress these newly eligible voters and their parents. The letters are individually signed—by a machine that duplicates the member's signature.

Campaign Spending

Incumbents also have a decided advantage when it comes to raising campaign funds. The cost of running for Congress has risen sharply in recent decades as

FIGURE 12-3   Congressional Campaign Expenditures
The cost of running for congressional office has risen sharply as campaign techniques—television advertising, opinion polling, and so on—have become more elaborate and sophisticated. The increase in spending can be seen from a comparison of the approximate average spending by both candidates per House or Senate seat at ten-year intervals, beginning in 1980. *Source: Federal Election Commission; 2000 figures based on preliminary projections.*

1980 House $300,000
Senate $3,000,000

1990 House $630,000
Senate $5,300,000

2000 House $1,250,000
Senate $10,600,000

campaign techniques, such as televised advertising and polling, have become increasingly sophisticated and costly (see Figure 12-3). Today, a successful House campaign will often cost the winner $500,000 or more. The price of victory in competitive Senate races is much higher, ranging from several million dollars in smaller states to $15 million or more in the largest states.

Incumbents are usually better funded than their challengers. The political scientist Paul Herrnson concludes that the most successful candidates essentially run two campaigns: one in Washington where they appeal for campaign funds and one in the state or district where they appeal for votes.[8] Incumbents have a decided advantage in the first of these campaigns, which usually begins far in advance of the second. Incumbents' fundraising advantage starts with their past campaigns and constituent service, which enables them to create mailing lists of potential contributors. Individual contributions, most of which are $100 or less, account for about 50 percent of all campaign funds and are obtained mainly through direct mail solicitation. Incumbents also have an edge, when they need it, with the party campaign committees (see Chapter 9). These committees, though not the main contributors to congressional campaigns, do make sizable and timely contributions that can make a difference in close races.

Incumbents fare even better with political action committees (PACs, discussed in detail in Chapter 10), which contribute about 30 percent of campaign funds. Incumbents are well positioned to help PACs achieve their legislative goals. Not surprisingly, PACs are a prime source of incumbents' campaign funds. More than half the U.S. senators seeking reelection in 2000 received $1 million or more from PACs, and more than a dozen House members received half a million dollars or more. Many PACs are hesitant to oppose an incumbent unless it is clear that the candidate is vulnerable. More than 85 percent of PAC contributions in recent elections have been given to incumbents; their challengers got less than 15 percent.[9] "Anytime you go against an incumbent, you take a minute and think long and hard about what your rationale is," said Desiree Anderson, director of the Realtors PAC.[10]

Though money has been called "the mother's milk of politics," money does not always decide an election; in most elections it is not even the main factor. The political scientist Gary Jacobson has demonstrated that money is no higher than third in importance, ranking behind partisanship and incumbency.[11]

CURRENT CONTROVERSIES

SHOULD CONGRESSIONAL CAMPAIGNS BE PUBLICLY FUNDED?

U.S. congressional campaigns are funded entirely through private sources—individual contributors, political parties, interest groups, and candidates' own money. These campaigns are also extremely expensive. As a result, House and Senate candidates spend an inordinate amount of time on fundraising. The financing system also raises the question of whether large contributors acquire too much influence over the policy decisions of those who win election to Congress. Some candidates and observers believe that public funding of congressional campaigns is the answer. Others oppose the idea of public funding, either in principle or on pragmatic grounds.

YES: [America needs] to completely break the dependence of politicians on special interests' campaign cash by creating an alternative source of disinterested "clean" funding for their campaigns. Here in Washington, such a step might induce heart attacks . . . but out across the country, the states are leading the way. [Voters in Maine approved] a sweeping proposal that created a system of "clean election" financing for qualified candidates who agree not to take any private money and abide by spending limits. . . . The concept is pretty simple. In baseball we don't allow the players, the managers, or individual owners to pay the umpires, for obvious reasons. For the same reasons special interests should not be financing politicians' campaigns.

—Ellen Miller, Executive Director, Public Campaign

NO: To achieve a reduction of special interest influence— if you want to do that, I think that is not a good idea at all, it is blatantly unconstitutional, and the wrong thing to do. . . . For reality ever to square with reformer rhetoric, the Constitution would have to be amended . . . to give the Government the power to restrict all spending, and in support of or in opposition to candidates. . . . [What this] comes down to is an effort to have the Government control all spending.

—Senator Mitch McConnell (R-Ky.)

Nevertheless, the flow of money in congressional campaigns is significant both in itself and as an indicator of the other crucial factors, particularly the advantages of incumbency. The Federal Election Commission reported that more than half of House incumbents in recent elections outspent their challengers by a ratio of at least 5 to 1.

Many challengers are able to raise only enough money for a token campaign. "Spending is particularly important for non-incumbents," political scientist Barbara Hinckley notes. "It significantly increases recognition and affects the vote."[12] Challengers who spend heavily have at least a chance of victory; those who spend little are almost certain to lose. In contrast, incumbents normally spend heavily only when they face a serious challenger.

Senate races tend to attract well-funded challengers, but incumbents still derive a financial advantage from a variety of funding sources, including individual contributors, PACs, and political party sources. In recent years, Senate incumbents have filled large campaign "war chests" well in advance of their reelection campaigns, partly in order to discourage potentially strong challengers from running against them. A year before his 2000 Senate race, Edward M. Kennedy (D-Mass.) had already raised four million dollars; faced with the prospect of a tough campaign against a strong incumbent, the Republicans nominated a relatively weak candidate and Kennedy won easily.

New York Mayor Rudolph Guliani speaking at an event before his withdrawal from the 2000 senate race against Hillary Clinton. With or without Guliani, the New York race shaped up as one of the most expensive campaigns in congressional history.

open-seat election An election in which there is no incumbent in the race.

A race without an incumbent—called an **open-seat election**—usually brings out a strong candidate from each party and involves heavy spending, especially when party competition in the state or district is strong. In 1998, for example, the major-party candidates spent on average more than a million dollars between them in open-seat House races.

Open-seat contests can be critically important to shifts in power in Congress. The Republican party's stunning victory in the 1994 midterm elections, for example, was achieved primarily through its success in open-seat races. There were fifty-two open House seats and nine open Senate seats in 1994, and the GOP won 80 percent of these races. Without these victories, the Republicans would not have gained control of either the House or Senate.

THE PITFALLS OF INCUMBENCY

Incumbency is not without its liabilities. The potential pitfalls include troublesome issues, personal misconduct, variation in turnout, strong challengers, and for some House members, redistricting.

Troublesome Issues

Disruptive issues are a potential threat to incumbents. Although most elections are not waged against the backdrop of strong issues, those that are tend to produce the largest turnover in Congress. In the 1992–1994 period, when the public was angry over economic and social conditions and believed Congress was performing poorly, the number of incumbents who were defeated exceeded 10 percent. After that, the economy improved and the number dropped to roughly 5 percent.

Personal Misconduct

Members of Congress can also fall prey to scandal. Life in Washington can be fast paced, glamorous, and expensive, and some members of Congress get

CONSTITUTIONAL QUALIFICATIONS FOR SERVING IN CONGRESS

Representatives: "No personal shall be a Representative who shall not have attained to the age of twenty-five years, and been seven years a citizen of the United States, and who shall not, when elected, be an inhabitant of that State in which he shall be chosen" (Article I, section 2).

Senators: "No personal shall be a Senator who shall not have attained to the age of thirty years, and been nine years a citizen of the United States, and who shall not, when elected, be an inhabitant of the State for which he shall be chosen" (Article I, section 3).

caught up in influence peddling, sex scandals, and other forms of misconduct. These acts if discovered receive close attention from the news media and are a major threat to the reelection of incumbents. Roughly a fourth of House incumbents who lost their bid for reelection in the past decade were shadowed by ethical questions. "The first thing to being reelected is to stay away from scandal, even minor scandal," says the political scientist John Hibbing.[13]

Midterm Elections: A Special Problem for Incumbents of the President's Party

Historically, the party holding the presidency has usually lost seats in the midterm elections, particularly in the House of Representatives. The 1998 midterm elections, which were waged against the backdrop of the House impeachment inquiry into President Clinton's affair with Monica Lewinsky, were a surprising exception. His Democratic party gained a small number of House seats, which some analysts attributed to a robust economy and to a voting public that wanted Congress to scale down the impeachment inquiry and focus instead on issues such as education, social security, and taxes. As Figure 12-4 shows, however, the president's party nearly always suffers a net loss of House seats. This tendency is not a function of the president's personal popularity. Although the losses tend to be greater when the president's public approval rating is low, the pattern holds even when confidence in the president is high.

The pattern is attributable to a dropoff in turnout for midterm elections.[14] The voters who go the polls only during presidential election years tend to have weaker party loyalties and are therefore more responsive to the issues of the moment. In any given election, these issues tend to favor one party, which contributes to the success of its congressional candidates as well as its presidential nominee. Most of the party's congressional candidates who win narrowly owe their margin of victory to these voters. However, these voters stay home during midterm elections. Thus, unless these incumbents can make inroads among midterm voters who backed their opponent two years earlier, they stand a good chance of losing. Since many of these voters are strong partisans, they are not easily swayed, and the typical result is the midterm defeat of a significant number of these incumbents.

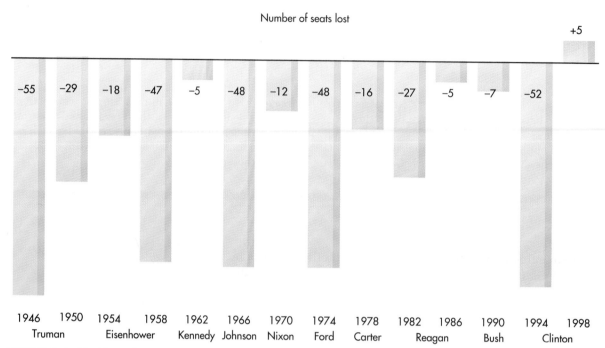

FIGURE 12-4 **Net House Seats Lost by Presidential Party in Midterm Elections, 1946–1998**
Historically, the party holding the White House has lost seats in the midterm elections.

Strong Challengers: A Special Problem for Senators

Incumbents are also vulnerable to strong challengers. Senators are particularly likely to face formidable opponents: after the presidency, the Senate is the top rung of the political ladder. Governors and House members are frequent challengers for Senate seats, and they have the electoral base, reputation, and experience to compete effectively. Moreover, the U.S. Senate lures wealthy challengers. Michael Huffington spent nearly $25 million of his own money in California's 1994 Senate race and came within one percentage point of defeating incumbent Dianne Feinstein. The willingness of strong challengers to take on Senate incumbents is a major reason that Senate campaigns have remained somewhat competitive in recent decades.

House incumbents have less reason to fear strong challengers. A House seat is often not attractive enough to induce prominent local politicians, such as mayors or state legislators, to risk their political careers in a challenge to an incumbent. Political scientists Linda Fowler and Robert McClure speak of "the unseen candidates"—potentially strong House challengers who end up deciding that the costs of a campaign outweigh the benefits.[15] This situation leaves the field open to weak opponents with little or no governmental or political experience. Both parties in the 2000 elections had difficulty finding strong challengers who were willing to take on a House incumbent. Potential candidates for Congress, however, are not unmindful of political developments, and when favorable conditions exist, they are more inclined to run. The GOP anticipated that it would gain seats in 1994, which brought a stronger-than-normal group of

U.S. Representative William (Bill) Clay represents a heavily Democratic district in St. Louis. The biggest reelection obstacles for House members from one-sided districts are redistricting, scandal, and a well-funded primary election opponent.

Republican challengers into the campaign and further increased the party's chances of success.

Redistricting: A Problem for House Members

Every ten years, after each population census, the 435 seats in the House are re-allocated among the states in proportion to their population. States that have gained population since the last census may acquire additional House seats, while those that have lost population may lose seats. New York and Illinois are among the states that will lose seats in the 2002 elections as a result of the 2000

When Massachusetts was redistricted in 1812, Governor Elbridge Gerry had the lines of one district redrawn in order to ensure that a candidate of his party would be elected. The cartoonist Elkanah Tinsdale, noting that the strangely shaped district resembled a salamander, called it a "Gerry-mander."

reapportionment The reallocation of House seats among states after each census as a result of population changes.

redistricting The process of altering election districts in order to make them as nearly equal in population as possible. Redistricting takes place every ten years, after each population census.

gerrymandering The process by which the party in power draws election district boundaries in a way that advantages its candidates.

census; Arizona and Washington are among the states that will gain. This reallocation process is called **reapportionment.** (The Senate is not affected by population change, since each state has two senators regardless of its size.)

The responsibility for redrawing House election districts after a reapportionment—a process called **redistricting**—rests with the state governments. States are required by law to make their districts nearly equal in population. There are many ways, however, to divide a state into districts of equal size, and the party in power in the state legislature will do so in a way that favors its candidates (a process called **gerrymandering**). A common method is to create a few districts that contain overwhelming numbers of voters of the opposing party, which results in "wasted" votes in these districts and thereby makes the opposing party less competitive in other districts. The courts have placed some limits on gerrymandering (for example, very oddly shaped districts may be ruled unacceptable), but it is a common practice.

Reapportionment, redistricting, and gerrymandering are a potential threat to House incumbents. Turnover in House elections is typically higher after a new census than in previous elections. The newly redrawn districts include voters who are unfamiliar with the incumbent, thereby diminishing an advantage that incumbents typically have over their challengers. Moreover, when a state loses congressional seats, there are fewer districts than there are incumbents, who may end up running against each other.

SAFE INCUMBENCY AND REPRESENTATION

Although the obstacles to an incumbent's reelection can be substantial, the advantage in most congressional races clearly rests with the incumbent. As a result, Congress is somewhat insulated from political change. Democracy depends on periodic shifts in power between the parties to bring public policy closer into line with shifts in public opinion. Research indicates that changes in congressional voting patterns occur primarily around the replacement of defeated or retiring lawmakers with new members.[16] Incumbents tend to hold relatively stable policy positions during their time in office. Because the advantages of incumbency are so substantial, Congress does not change nearly so rapidly as public moods. It is worth noting that national legislators in other democracies do not have the large personal staffs and the substantial travel and publicity budgets that members of Congress have. Elsewhere, incumbents tend to win or lose on the popularity of their political party, not on their capacity to generate voter support through constituent service. The large turnover in legislative membership that sometimes occurs in elections in other democracies and that once also characterized U.S. congressional elections is now very rare in the United States.

WHO ARE THE WINNERS IN CONGRESSIONAL ELECTIONS?

Although members of the House and Senate are elected to represent their constituents, the average representative is very different from the average American in virtually every respect.[17] Although only one in every 350 Americans is a lawyer, about one in three members of Congress has studied law. Attorneys are attracted to politics in part by Congress's role in lawmaking and by the public visibility that a campaign for office helps build, which can make a private law practice more successful. Along with lawyers, professionals such as business executives, educators, bankers, and journalists account for more than 90 percent of congressional membership.[18] Blue-collar workers, clerical employees, and home-makers are seldom elected to Congress. Farmers and ranchers are not as rare; a fair number of House members from rural districts have agricultural backgrounds.

Finally, members of Congress are disproportionately white and male. Minority group members and women each account for less than 15 percent of the Congress (see Chapter 5). This proportion, however, is twice that of a decade ago. The 1992 elections were particularly important to the change. Reapportionment and the retirement of an unusually high number of incumbents contributed to the election to Congress of more than thirty additional women and minority group members. Safe incumbency is a major obstacle to the election to Congress of more women and minorities. They have been no more successful than other challengers in dislodging congressional incumbents. In elections to state and local office, where incumbency is less important, women and minority candidates have made greater inroads (see "States in the Nation").[19]

Congressional Leadership

The way in which Congress works is related to the way in which its members win election. Because of their independent power base in their state or district, members of Congress have substantial independence within the institution they serve. The Speaker of the House and the other top leaders in Congress are crucial to its operation, but unlike their counterparts in European legislatures, they cannot demand the loyalty of the members they lead. Speaker Newt Gingrich's extraordinary success in pushing the Contract with America through the House in 1995 was based less on the formal powers of his office than on the galvanizing force of the ideas the contract contained. There is an inherent tension in Congress between the institution's need for strong leadership at the top and the individual members' need to exercise power on behalf of constituents. The result is an institution where power is dispersed although not evenly: the top party and committee leaders exercise more power than do the other members.

PARTY LEADERSHIP IN CONGRESS

The House and Senate are organized along party lines. When members of Congress are sworn in at the start of a new two-year session, they automatically are members of either the Republican or Democratic **party caucus** in their chamber. The caucuses are critical bodies within the Congress. Through them, the Democrats and Republicans in each chamber meet periodically to plan strategy and air their differences in the process of settling on the party's legislative program. The caucuses also select the **party leaders**, who represent the party's interests in the chamber and give direction to the party's goals.

party caucus A group that consists of a party's members in the House or Senate and that serves to elect the party's leadership, set policy goals, and determine party strategy.

party leaders Members of the House and Senate who are chosen by the Democratic or Republican caucus in each chamber to represent the party's interests in that chamber and who give some central direction to the chamber's deliberations.

The House Leadership

The main party leaders in the House are the Speaker, majority leader, majority whip, minority leader, and minority whip. The Constitution provides only for the post of Speaker, who is to be chosen by a vote of the entire House. In practice, this provision means that the Speaker is selected by the majority party's

★ STATES IN THE NATION

WOMEN IN THE STATE LEGISLATURE

Men have traditionally dominated elective office, but women are slowly gaining ground, particularly in local and state government. In 1969, fewer than 5 percent of state legislators were women. By 1999, there were 1,652 women state legislators—22.3 percent of the total. Washington state has the highest proportion of women legislators—40.8 percent. Alabama with 7.9 percent has the lowest, although the number of women in its legislature nearly doubled in the 1998 elections. The northeastern, plains, and western states tend to have a higher proportion of women in their legislatures than do states in other regions.

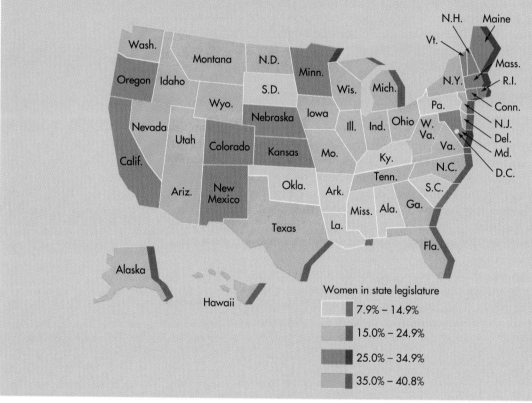

Women in state legislature

▮	7.9% – 14.9%
▮	15.0% – 24.9%
▮	25.0% – 34.9%
▮	35.0% – 40.8%

SOURCE: Center for the American Woman and Politics (CAWP), National Information Bank on Women in Public Office, Eagleton Institute of Politics, Rutgers University, 1999.

members, because only they have enough votes to choose one of their own. (Table 12-1 shows the party composition of Congress during the past two decades.)

The Speaker is often said to be the second most powerful official in Washington, after the president.[20] The Speaker has the right to speak first on legislation during House debate and has the power to recognize members—that is, give them permission to speak from the floor. Because the House places a time limit on floor debate, not everyone has a chance to speak on a bill, and the

TABLE 12-1 Number of Democrats and Republicans in House of Representatives and Senate, 1981–2002

	81–82	83–84	85–86	87–88	89–90	91–92	93–94	95–96	97–98	99–00	01–02
House											
Democrats	243*	269*	253*	258*	262*	268*	259	205*	207*	212*	213
Republicans	192	166	182	177	173	167	176	230	228	223	222
Senate											
Democrats	47	45	47	54*	55*	56*	56	46*	45*	45*	50
Republicans	53	55	53	46	45	44	44	54	55	55	50

*Chamber not controlled by the president's party. House Independents are included in the total for the party with which they caucused.

Speaker can sometimes influence legislation simply by exercising the power to decide who will speak and when. The Speaker also chooses the chairperson and majority-party members of the powerful House Rules Committee, which controls the scheduling of bills for debate. Legislation that the Speaker wants passed is likely to reach the floor under conditions favorable to its enactment; for example, the Speaker may ask the Rules Committee to delay sending a bill to the floor until there is enough support for its passage. The Speaker has other ways of directing the work of the House. The Speaker assigns bills to committees, places time limits on the reporting of bills out of committees, and assigns members to conference committees. (The importance of these powers over committee action will become apparent later in this chapter and in the next.)

The Speaker is active in developing the party's position on issues and in persuading party members in the House to follow his or her lead.[21] The Speaker chairs the Steering Committee, which has ongoing responsibility for developing and promoting the majority party's legislative program. Although the Speaker cannot compel party members to support this program, they look to the Speaker for leadership. The Speaker can draw on shared partisan views and has a few rewards on hand for cooperative party members; the Speaker can, for instance, help them obtain public spending projects for their districts and favorable committee assignments for themselves.

The Speaker is assisted by the House majority leader and the House majority whip, who are elected by the majority party's members. The majority leader acts as the party's floor leader, organizing the debate on bills and working to line up legislative support. Typically, the majority leader is an experienced and skilled legislator.[22]

The majority-party whip has the important job of soliciting votes from party members and of informing them when critical votes are scheduled. Whips have been known to track down members who are out of town and persuade them to rush back to Washington for an important vote. As voting is getting under way on the House floor, the whip will sometimes stand at a location that is easily seen by party members and let them know where the leadership stands on the bill by giving them a thumbs-up or thumbs-down signal.

The minority party has its own leaders in the House. The House minority leader heads the party's caucus and policy committee and plays the leading role in developing the party's legislative positions. If the president is also of the

House Speaker Dennis Hastert bangs his gavel during the opening session of the 106th Congress. Because of the House's large size and restrictive rules, the Speaker's position is a relatively powerful position. Ultimately, however, the power of the Speaker and other party leaders in the House and Senate rests on the trust placed in them by members of their party.

minority party, the minority leader will work closely with the president on legislative issues. The minority leader is assisted by a minority whip, who is responsible for lining up party members' support on legislation and informing them when votes are scheduled.

The Senate Leadership

In the Senate, the most important party leadership position is that of the majority leader, who heads the majority-party caucus. The majority leader's role is much like that of the Speaker of the House, in that the majority leader formulates the majority's legislative policies and strategies and seeks to develop influential relationships with colleagues. Like the Speaker, the Senate majority leader chairs the party's policy committee and acts as the party's voice in the chamber.[23] The majority leader works closely with the president in developing legislative programs if they are of the same party. When Howard Baker was the Senate majority leader, he said that part of his job was to act as President Reagan's "point man" in the Senate.[24] For example, when the Reagan administration in 1981 sought congressional approval for the sale of AWACS surveillance planes to Saudi Arabia, Baker advised the White House not to press for a vote in order to give undecided senators enough time to study the effect of the sale on the security of Israel. Reagan agreed to hold off, and the sale was eventually approved.[25]

Unlike the Speaker of the House, the Senate majority leader is not the chamber's presiding officer. The Constitution assigns this responsibility to the vice president of the United States. However, because the vice president is allowed to vote in the Senate only to break a tie, the vice president seldom presides over Senate debates. The Senate has a president *pro tempore,* who, in the absence of the vice president, has the right to preside over the Senate. President *pro tempore* is largely an honorary position that by tradition is usually held by the majority party's senior member. The presiding official has limited power, since each senator has the right to speak at any length on bills under consideration.

The vice president's tie-breaking vote in the Senate had added significance after the 2000 election because the Senate was evenly divided between the parties: there were 50 Republican and 50 Democratic senators. Senate Democrats asked for a full power-sharing arrangement that would acknowledge the equal division. They sought equal representation on committees, equal claim to staff resources, and co-leadership positions. Republicans initially rejected the Democrats' proposal, saying that Vice President Dick Cheney's vote gave them a majority and therefore the power to determine how the Senate would be organized. Republicans argued that one party ought to take responsibility for the Senate's leadership and its legislative successes and failures. However, Republicans altered their position when the new Congress convened. Recognizing that Americans were expecting bipartisanship in Washington after the divisive 2000 presidential election, GOP senators decided that compromise would serve their interests and those of the nation. They accepted equal representation on committees and a more equal sharing of staff resources but retained the top party and committee leadership positions. Although Senate Democrats did not get the full equality they sought, they took consolation in the fact that Senate rules make it very difficult for a narrow majority to impose its will on the minority. Democrats knew, for example, that they could use the power of unlimited debate to bring Senate business to a halt if their views on legislation were repeatedly ignored.

The Senate's tradition of unlimited debate stems mainly from its relatively small size (only 100 members, compared with the House's 435 members). Moreover, senators like to view themselves as the equals of all others in their chamber and are thus reluctant to take orders from their leadership. For such reasons, the Senate majority leader's position is weaker than that of the Speaker of the House. One former Senate majority leader, Robert Byrd, jokingly called himself a "slave," saying that he served his fellow Democrats' needs without commanding their votes.[26] The Senate majority leader's actual power depends significantly on bargaining and leadership skills.[27]

Like the House, the Senate has a majority whip; however, this position is less important in the Senate because that body's members are less subject to persuasive tactics. Nevertheless, the Senate majority whip sees to it that members know when important votes are scheduled and ensures that the party's strongest advocates on a legislative measure are present for the debate.

Finally, the Senate has a minority leader and minority whip, whose roles are comparable to those performed by their counterparts in the House. As befits "a chamber of equals," the majority leadership in the Senate usually consults the minority leadership on the scheduling of legislation.

Party Leaders and Followers

The power of all party leaders, in the Senate and House alike, rests largely on the trust placed in them by the members of their party. They do not have the strong formal powers of parliamentary leaders, but they are expected to lead. If they are adept at promoting ideas and building coalitions, they can exercise considerable power within their chamber.

They also are positioned to influence national debate. They are recognized by the news media as their party's chief spokespersons within the House and Senate, a role that is magnified when their party does not control the White House. In that circumstance, they are the closest thing to an opposition leader (a mainstay of European parliamentary politics) that the U.S. system has. They are pressed by journalists to respond to White House initiatives and to lay out the plans of their own party. When they are of the same party as the president, however, they are of less interest to the press. It sees the president, not the party's leaders in Congress, as the party's national voice.

Party leaders are in a stronger position today than a few decades ago as a result of changes in the composition of the congressional parties. The GOP once had a substantial progressive faction within it, but this faction has been eclipsed by its conservative wing. At the same time, the Democratic party's conservative wing, represented by its southern lawmakers, has withered away almost entirely. As congressional Republicans have become more alike in their thinking and different from congressional Democrats, each group has found it easier to band together and to stand against the opposing party. Accordingly, the party leaders through the party caucus have found it easier to bring their party's lawmakers together on legislative issues.

At the same time, House and Senate members are less deferential to their leaders than in the past. Until a few decades ago, congressional folkways dictated that newer members, particularly on the House side, would mostly listen and learn, awaiting the day when through seniority they were positioned to

www.mhhe.com/patterson5

Simulation

assume a larger role in the institution. There were always a few mavericks who were unwilling to respect this unwritten norm, but most new members willingly took a back seat. Of course, a back seat in the Senate was not the same as one in the House. Because the Senate is a small body and operates on rules that are more egalitarian, a junior senator could rise to prominence more quickly than a junior House member. Nevertheless, the Senate, too, had a tight inner circle dominated by its more senior members.[28]

Today, junior House and Senate members pursue their own agendas more aggressively. They were elected in a system that rewards self-starters and encourages them to pursue a constant reelection campaign. They seek the visibility that attends a more active legislative role. They also are increasingly likely to have forged close ties with the special interests that support their campaigns, and they are expected by these groups to vigorously pursue legislative goals.[29] Moreover, because the two parties have become more polarized at the activist level, the newer members of Congress have been more ideological and less pragmatic in their beliefs and thus more eager to express their views.[30] Finally, television has provided a path to prominence for junior members who are articulate and engaging. The visibility they obtain outside Congress through the media magnifies their voice within the institution. The old axiom that junior members, particularly in the House, "should be seen and not heard" is hardly an accurate description of today's Congress.

COMMITTEE CHAIRPERSONS: THE SENIORITY PRINCIPLE

Party leaders are not the only important leaders in Congress. Most of the work of Congress takes place in the meetings of its thirty-five standing (permanent) committees and their numerous subcommittees, each of which is headed by a chairperson. A committee chair schedules committee meetings, determines the order in which committee bills are considered, presides over committee discussions, directs the committee's majority staff, and can choose to lead the debate when a committee bill reaches the floor of the chamber for a vote by the full membership. (The process by which a bill becomes a law is discussed in Chapter 13.)

seniority A member of Congress's consecutive years of service on a particular committee.

Committee chairs are always members of the majority party, and they usually have the most **seniority**—the most consecutive years of service on a particular committee. Seniority is based strictly on time served on a committee, not on time spent in Congress. If a member switches committees, the years spent on the first committee do not count toward seniority on the second one.

The seniority principle was instituted in the Senate in the mid-nineteenth century but was not formally applied in the House until the early twentieth century. The seniority principle remained virtually absolute until the House Democratic majority decided in the early 1970s that committee chairs would henceforth be chosen by secret ballot. Abuses by some committee chairs led to the change. Virginia's Howard Smith, who chaired the House Rules Committee in the 1950s and 1960s and was opposed to racial change, would sometimes leave Washington for his Virginia farm when civil rights legislation reached his committee. Because the Rules Committee could not meet unless he called it into session, Smith's absence was sometimes enough to persuade the full committee to "table" a bill, or set it aside. A committee chair now has less power; for example, a majority of the committee members can vote to convene meetings in the chair's absence.

Although the seniority principle is no longer absolute, the congressional majorities usually abide by it.[31] Exceptions took place in 1995 when, at Speaker Gingrich's request, House Republicans bypassed some veteran members, most notably Representative Carlos Moorhead of California, who was the most senior Republican on both the Judiciary and Commerce committees. Gingrich wanted a more forceful individual than Moorhead as chair of these major committees.

The seniority system persists because it has several important advantages: it reduces the number of bitter power struggles that would occur if the chair were decided by open competition, it provides experienced and knowledgeable committee leadership, and it enables members to look forward to the reward of a position as chair after years of service on the same committee. A drawback of the seniority system is that it places the committee chairs largely outside the reach of House or Senate's elected leaders.

Congressional organization and leadership extend into subcommittees, which are smaller units within each committee formed to conduct specific aspects of the committee's business. Altogether there are about two hundred subcommittees in the House and Senate, each with a chairperson who decides its order of business, presides over its meetings, and coordinates its staff. In both chambers, a subcommittee chair is often the most senior member on the panel, but seniority is not as important in these appointments as it is in the designation of committee chairs.

OLIGARCHY OR DEMOCRACY: WHICH PRINCIPLE SHOULD GOVERN?

In 1995, House Republicans gave committee chairs the power to select the chairs of their subcommittees and to appoint all majority-party staff members, including those who work for the subcommittees. The changes were designed to give committee chairs more control over legislation. "If you're going to ask someone to lead, you've got to give him some leverage," said Republican Whip Tom DeLay. "This notion that we've got to have 100 and some odd [subcommittee] fiefdoms is over."[32]

The changes reversed House reforms of the 1970s that were designed to weaken the hold that chairs had on their committees. At that time, selection of subcommittee chairs was removed from the committee chair and placed in the hands of the majority-party members of each committee.[33] Other actions were also taken to give House subcommittees a substantial degree of independence from their committee and its chair. (The Senate in the 1970s also granted more autonomy to its subcommittees, but the changes were less consequential because the Senate relies less heavily on subcommittees in its work.)

The reforms of the 1970s were premised on the idea that Congress should be more democratic in its organization. By granting greater authority to each subcommittee and by freeing its chairperson from control by the committee chair, power and leadership in Congress were more widely distributed. The reforms also happened to serve the personal reelection and power needs of individual members. They would no longer have to wait many years to acquire the seniority that would place them in a position of institutional authority.

★ CRITICAL THINKING ★

WHAT'S YOUR OPINION?

National Office, Local Orientation: Good or Bad?
Whereas legislators in most other democracies are preoccupied with national affairs, members of the U.S. Congress divide their attention between national and local concerns. Membership in Congress provides U.S. senators and representatives with the large personal budgets and staffs they need to retain the support of constituents in the home state or district—support that they must have if they are to be reelected. Incumbency also makes it relatively easy for members of Congress to raise money for their reelection campaigns.

In contrast, members of the Canadian House of Commons concentrate on national issues because their chances of reelection depend heavily on their party's nationwide popularity. Members of the House of Commons have almost no staff help and spend only small amounts of money on their campaigns.

What are the relative merits of the American system? In serving their constituencies, do members of Congress also serve the interests of the country as a whole better than they would if they were preoccupied with national-level problems? Does the existence of a president in the U.S. system (Canada has no separate executive branch) lessen your concern about the local orientation of most members of Congress?

HOW THE UNITED STATES COMPARES

LEGISLATIVE LEADERSHIP AND AUTHORITY

The U.S. House and Senate are separate and coequal chambers, each with its own leadership and rules. This type of legislative structure is not found in most democracies. Although many other democracies have a bicameral legislature like the U.S. Congress, nearly all power is vested in just one of the two chambers. In the British Parliament, for example, the House of Commons is far more powerful than the House of Lords; the latter can delay legislation but cannot kill it. In such a situation, legislative power is more concentrated and easier to exercise. Thus, in Great Britain, the party that controls the House of Commons decides legislative policy. In the United States, a party must control both the House of Representatives and the Senate if it is to exercise such power.

The U.S. Congress is fragmented in other ways as well: it has elected leaders with limited formal powers, a network of relatively independent and powerful committees, and members who are free to follow or ignore other members of their party. Most Democrats and Republicans vote with a majority of their party on major bills, but it is not uncommon for a fourth or more of a party's legislators to vote against their party's position on important legislative issues. In contrast, European

legislatures have a centralized power structure: top leaders have substantial authority, the committees are weak, and the parties are unified. European legislators are expected to support their party unless granted permission to vote otherwise on a particular bill. Legislative leadership is much easier to exercise in Europe's hierarchical parliaments than in America's "stratarchical" Congress.

Country	Form of Legislature
Canada	One house dominant
France	One house dominant
Germany	One house dominant (except on regional issues)
Great Britain	One house dominant
Israel	One house only
Italy	Two equal houses
Japan	One house dominant
Mexico	Two equal houses
United States	Two equal houses

Although "more democratic" internally, the postreform Congress may have been less democratic externally. In order to get Congress to respond to majority sentiment on broad national issues, top leaders had to work against the separate agendas of committee and subcommittee leaders. Delay was common, and concessions were often necessary to get their support.

The Republican reforms of 1995 were designed to strengthen the House's capacity to act as a *majoritarian* institution. Committee and subcommittee leaders would still wield considerable power, but they would also be tied more closely to leaders at the next level. Party leaders would derive their power from the party's members and, as Gingrich's downfall illustrates, would have to retain their loyalty. But once entrusted with leadership, they were expected to exercise it aggressively on the majority's behalf.

The opposing conceptions of Congress embedded in the 1970s and 1995 reforms have played themselves out many times in the history of Congress. The institution is at once a place for conducting the nation's business and for promoting constituency interests. At times, the position of top leaders has been strengthened. At other times, the position of rank-and-file members has been enhanced. At all times, there has been an attempt to create a workable balance of the two. The result is an institution very different from European parliaments, where power is thoroughly concentrated at the top (an arrangement reflected even in the name for rank-and-file members—"backbenchers"). The distinguishing feature of congressional leadership is its dispersion across the membership, with provision for added power at the top (see "How the United States Compares").

The Committee System

When Congress first met in 1789, it had no committees. However, committees formed within a few years in the House, and the first Senate committees were established in 1816. At present there are nineteen standing committees in the House and sixteen in the Senate (see Table 12-2). A **standing committee** is a permanent committee with responsibility for a particular area of public policy. Both the House and the Senate, for example, have a standing committee that specializes in handling foreign policy issues. Other important standing committees are those that deal with agriculture, commerce, the national budget, the interior (natural resources and public lands), defense, government spending, labor, the judiciary, and taxation. House committees, which average about thirty-five to forty members each, are about twice the size of the Senate committees. Each standing committee has legislative authority in that it can draft and rewrite

standing committee A permanent congressional committee with responsibility for a particular area of public policy. An example is the Senate Foreign Relations Committee.

TABLE 12-2 The Standing Committees of Congress

House of Representatives	Senate
Agriculture	Agriculture, Nutrition, and Forestry
Appropriations	Appropriations
Armed Services	Armed Services
Banking and Financial Services	Banking, Housing, and Urban Affairs
Budget	Budget
Commerce	Commerce, Science, and Transportation
Education and the Workforce	Energy and Natural Resources
Government Reform	Environment and Public Works
House Administration	Finance
International Relations	Foreign Relations
Judiciary	Governmental Affairs
Resources	Health, Education, Labor, and Pensions
Rules	Judiciary
Science	Rules and Administration
Small Business	Small Business
Standards of Official Conduct	Veterans' Affairs
Transportation and Infrastructure	
Veterans' Affairs	
Ways and Means	

proposed legislation and can recommend to the full chamber the passage or defeat of the legislation it considers.

Each standing committee in Congress has its own staff, which altogether totals about 1,000 employees in the Senate and 1,300 in the House. Unlike the members' personal staffs, which concentrate on constituency relations, the committee staffs perform an almost entirely legislative function. They help draft legislation, prepare reports, organize hearings, and participate in altering bills within committee.

In addition to its standing committees, Congress also has a number of *select committees*, which are created to perform specific tasks and are disbanded after they have done so; *joint committees*, composed of members of both houses, which perform advisory or coordinating functions for the House and the Senate; and *conference committees*, which are joint committees formed temporarily to work out differences in House and Senate versions of a particular bill. The role of conference committees is discussed more fully in the next chapter.

Congress could not possibly handle its workload without the help of its committee system. About ten thousand bills are introduced during each two-year session of Congress. The sheer volume of this legislation would paralyze the institution if it did not have a division of labor. Yet the very existence of committees and subcommittees helps fragment Congress: each of these units is relatively secure in its power, jurisdiction, and membership.

COMMITTEE POWER

At times, particularly when bills dealing with major issues are introduced, the full membership of Congress takes decisive action. On most bills, however, the full chamber merely votes to confirm or modify decisions made previously by committees and subcommittees. When a committee recommends passage of a bill, the measure has about a 90 percent chance of being approved by the full House or Senate, although about a third of these bills are amended on the floor.[34] Moreover, committees are the burial ground of most legislation introduced in Congress. Only about 10 percent of the bills that committees consider reach the floor for a vote; the others are "killed" when committees decide that they do not warrant further consideration and table them. The full House or Senate can overrule these committee rejections but seldom does so. Most bills die in committee because they are of little interest to anyone other than a few members of Congress or are so poorly conceived that they lack merit. Some bills are not even supported by the members who introduce them. A member may submit a bill to appease a powerful constituent group and then quietly inform the committee to ignore it.

In the House particularly, most of the detailed legislative work—hearings, debates, and basic reworking of bills—is done by the subcommittees rather than by the full committees. Unless a subcommittee's members are seriously divided or have highly unrepresentative views, their general response to a bill usually prevails when it is considered by the full committee. Senate subcommittees, in contrast, serve more as advisory bodies to the full committees than as separate working bodies within the committees.[35]

Although the power of committees and subcommittees should not be underestimated, statistics on their influence can be misleading. The fact that committee

With their staff members looking on, Senators Edward Kennedy (D-Mass.) and Nancy Kassenbaum (R-Kans.) of the Labor and Human Resources Committee talk during a break in hearings. The Labor and Human Resources Committee has jurisdiction over health issues in the Senate.

recommendations are followed about 90 percent of the time does not mean that committees hold 90 percent of the power in Congress. In making their decisions, committees are mindful that their positions can be reversed by the full chamber, just as subcommittees recognize that the full committee can overrule their actions. Consequently, committee and subcommittee decisions are made in anticipation of the probable responses of other members of Congress. Committee and subcommittee members must always ask whether their colleagues are likely to accept their recommendations. Moreover, a committee rarely decides fully the fate of legislation that is important to the majority party or its leadership. As will be discussed in the next chapter, the top leadership is deeply involved in key legislative issues.

COMMITTEE JURISDICTION

The 1946 Legislative Reorganization Act requires each bill introduced in Congress to be referred to the proper committee. An agricultural bill introduced in the Senate must be assigned to the Senate Agriculture Committee, a bill dealing with foreign affairs must be sent to the Senate Foreign Relations Committee, and so on. This requirement is a major source of each committee's power. Even if its members are known to oppose certain types of legislation, bills clearly within its **jurisdiction**—the policy area in which it is authorized to act—must be sent to it for deliberation.

However, policy problems are increasingly complex, and jurisdiction has accordingly become an increasingly contentious issue, particularly on major bills. Which House committee, for example, should handle a major bill addressing the role of financial institutions in global trade? Is it the Banking Committee? Or the Commerce Committee? Or the International Relations Committee? Since all committees seek legislative influence and since each is jealous of its jurisdiction,

jurisdiction (of a congressional committee) The policy area in which a particular congressional committee is authorized to act.

bills that overlap committee boundaries provoke conflict. The political scientist David King describes these conflicts as "turf wars." They also involve the party leaders, who are in charge of assigning bills to committee. The party leaders can take advantage of these situations by shuttling a bill to the committee that is most likely to handle it in the way they would like. But party leaders depend on the committee chairs for support, so they cannot regularly ignore a committee that has a strong claim to a bill. At times, party leaders have responded by dividing up a bill, handing over some of its provisions to one committee and other provisions to a second committee.

House subcommittees have secure jurisdictions like those of the committees: bills must be referred to the appropriate subcommittees within two weeks of their arrival in committee. The Senate has a similar policy. Thus responsibility in Congress is thoroughly divided, with each subcommittee having formal authority over a small area of public policy. The House International Relations Committee, for instance, has five subcommittees: International Economic Policy and Trade, International Operations and Human Rights, Asia and the Pacific, Western Hemisphere, and Africa. Each subcommittee has about a dozen members, and these few individuals do most of the work and have the major voice in the disposition of most bills in their policy domain.

COMMITTEE MEMBERSHIP

Each committee includes Republicans and Democrats, but the majority party holds the majority of seats on each committee and subcommittee. The ratio of Democrats to Republicans on each committee is approximately the same as the ratio in the full House or Senate, but there is no fixed rule on this matter, and the majority party sets the proportions as it chooses (mindful that at the next election it could become the chamber's minority). Members of the House typically serve on only two committees. Senators often serve on four, although they can sit on only two major committees, such as Foreign Relations and Finance. There are also limits on subcommittee assignments; no House member, for example, can serve on more than five subcommittees.

Each standing committee has a fixed number of members, and a committee must have a vacancy before a new member can be appointed. These vacancies usually occur at the start of a new congressional session, when the committee positions of members who have retired or been defeated for reelection are reallocated. On nearly all committees, members retain their seats unless they decide to relinquish them or are forced to do so by changes in party ratios or committee size. The biggest change in committee memberships comes when a party loses control of the House or Senate; many Democrats had to relinquish committee assignments when the Republicans took control of Congress in 1995.

Each party has a special committee in the House and Senate that has responsibility for deciding who will fill vacancies on standing committees. Several factors influence these decisions, including the preferences of the legislators themselves. Most newly elected members of Congress receive a committee assignment that they have requested. New members usually ask for assignment to a committee on which they can serve their constituents' interests and at the same time increase their reelection prospects.[36] For example, when Phil Gramm was first elected to the Senate from Texas, a state that depends heavily on the defense industry, he requested and received a position on the Armed Services Committee.

Members of Congress also prefer membership on one of the most important committees, such as Foreign Relations or Finance in the Senate and Ways and Means or Appropriations in the House. Such factors as members' intelligence, experience, party loyalty, ideology, region, length of congressional service, and work habits weigh heavily in the determination of appointments to these prestigious committees. In both the House and the Senate, however, the choice rests with the special party committees established for the purpose of deciding standing-committee assignments.[37] House Republicans broke with tradition in 1995 by assigning an unusually high number of freshmen legislators to the top committees. Many of the coveted spots went to members who had defeated Democratic incumbents and were expected to face tough reelection races in 1996. The assignments also momentarily strengthened Speaker Gingrich's position, since many of the new members felt they owed their election and therefore also their allegiance to Gingrich.

Subcommittee assignments are handled differently. The members of each party on a committee decide who among them will serve on each of its subcommittees. The members' preferences, seniority, and personal backgrounds and the interests of their constituencies are key influences on subcommittee assignments.

Institutional Support for the Work of Congress

The range and complexity of the policy issues that Congress must confront have greatly increased in this century. As an initial response to policy complexity, Congress gave the president additional staff and authority (see Chapter 14). This approach gradually placed Congress at a substantial disadvantage to the president. The withholding of crucial information about the progress of the Vietnam War by presidents Johnson and Nixon persuaded many members of Congress that they could not maintain their institution as a coequal branch unless it had a larger and more expert staff. Accordingly, Congress increased its committee staffs and expanded its legislative bureaucracy, which consists of three agencies: the General Accounting Office, the Congressional Research Service, and the Congressional Budget Office.

The General Accounting Office (GAO), with about 3,500 employees, is the largest congressional agency. Formed in 1921, it has the primary responsibility of overseeing executive agencies' spending of money that has been appropriated by Congress. The GAO has made news by bringing abuses by defense contractors to Congress's attention. (In one notorious instance, the GAO reported that the government was paying more than $1,000 apiece for wrenches available in hardware stores for less than $10.) Congress has recently broadened the GAO's responsibilities to include program evaluations, such as a major study on the need to reform government-paid health programs.

Created in 1914, the Congressional Research Service (CRS) is the oldest congressional agency and is part of the Library of Congress. The CRS is a nonpartisan reference agency. If a member of Congress wants historical or statistical information for a speech or bill, the CRS will provide it. It also prepares reports

on pending legislative issues, although it makes no recommendations as to what action Congress should take. Finally, the 1,000-member staff of the CRS provides members with status reports and summaries of all bills currently under consideration in Congress.

The Congressional Budget Office (CBO) is the newest agency, created by the Congressional Budget and Impoundment Control Act of 1974. The main role of the CBO's two hundred employees is to provide Congress with projections of the nation's economic situation and of government expenditures and revenues. The Office of Management and Budget (OMB) furnishes similar projections to the president, who incorporates them into the annual budget submitted to Congress. The CBO's figures enable Congress to scrutinize the president's budget proposals more thoroughly.

www.mhhe.com/patterson5

Self-Quiz

Congressional agencies have strengthened Congress's ability to act as a policymaking body. Before the CBO was established, for example, Congress was dependent on the executive branch's Office of Management and Budget (OMB) for economic and budgetary estimates. The CBO now also provides these estimates, which can be compared with those produced by OMB. The change has helped Congress to more accurately assess the budgetary claims made by the White House. The next chapter will explore more fully this and other issues of Congress's role in the making of national policy.

Summary

Members of Congress, once elected, are likely to be reelected. Members of Congress have large staffs and can pursue a service strategy of responding to the needs of individual constituents. They also can secure pork barrel projects for their state or district and thus demonstrate their concern for constituents. House members gain a greater advantage from these activities than do senators, whose larger constituencies make it harder for them to build close personal relations with voters and whose office is more likely to attract a strong challenger. Incumbency does have some disadvantages. Members of Congress must take positions on controversial issues, may blunder into a political scandal or indiscretion, or face strong challengers; any of these conditions can reduce their reelection chances. By and large, however, the advantages of incumbency far outweigh the disadvantages, particularly for House members. Incumbents' advantages extend into their reelection campaigns. Their influential positions in Congress make it easier for them to raise campaign funds.

Congress is a fragmented institution. It has no single leader; the House and Senate have separate leaders, neither of whom can presume to speak for the other chamber. The principal party leaders of Congress are the Speaker of the House and the Senate majority leader. These party leaders derive their influence less from their formal authority than from their having been entrusted by other members of their party with the tasks of formulating policy positions and coordinating party strategy. Individual party members can choose to follow or ignore their leaders' requests.

The committee system is a network of about thirty-five committees and two hundred subcommittees, each with its separate chairperson. Although the seniority principle is not absolute, the chair of a committee is usually the member from the majority party who has the longest continuous service on the committee.

It is in the committees that most of the work of Congress is conducted. Each standing committee of the House and Senate has jurisdiction over congressional policy in a particular area (such as agriculture or foreign relations), as does each of its subcommittees. In most cases, the full House and Senate accept committee recommendations about passage of bills, although amendments to bills are quite common and committees are careful to take other members of Congress into account when making legislative decisions. Moreover, party leaders and caucuses rather than committees are the real locus of power on most major legislative initiatives.

Congress is supported by three agencies of its own: the General Accounting Office, which oversees executive spending and performance; the Congressional Research Service, which serves as a reference agency for congressional members; and the Congressional Budget Office, which provides budget and economic estimates.

Key Terms

constituency
electoral mastery
jurisdiction
open-seat election
party caucus
party leaders

pork barrel projects
reapportionment
redistricting
seniority
service strategy
standing committee

Suggested Readings

Campbell, James E. *The Presidential Pulse of Congressional Elections,* 2d ed. Lexington: University of Kentucky Press, 1997. Analysis of presidency's impact on congressional elections.

Fowler, Linda L. *Candidates, Congress, and the American Democracy.* Ann Arbor: University of Michigan Press, 1994. An insightful analysis of congressional recruitment and its impact on representation.

Herrnson, Paul S. *Congressional Elections: Campaigning at Home and in Washington,* 3rd ed. Washington, D.C.: Congressional Quarterly Press, 2000. A thorough study of the changing nature of congressional campaigns.

Jacobson, Gary C. *The Politics of Congressional Elections,* 4th ed. New York: Longman, 1997. A thorough assessment of the congressional election process.

King, David C. *Turf Wars: How Congressional Committees Claim Jurisdiction.* Chicago: University of Chicago Press, 1997. An innovative study on how congressional committees claim jurisdiction.

Krasno, Jonathan S. *Challenges, Competition, and Reelection: Comparing Senate and House Elections.* New Haven,

Conn.: Yale University Press, 1995. A comparison of the competitiveness of House and Senate races that uses National Election Study (NES) data as evidence.

Sinclair, Barbara. *Legislators, Leaders, and Lawmaking: The U.S. House of Representatives in the Postreform Era.* Baltimore, Md.: Johns Hopkins University Press, 1995. A richly documented study of party leadership in Congress.

Smith, Steven S., and Christopher J. Deering. *Committees in Congress,* 3d ed. Washington, D.C.: Congressional Quarterly Press, 1997. A comprehensive look at the House and Senate committee systems.

Swain, Carol M. *Black Faces, Black Interests: The Representation of African Americans in Congress.* Cambridge, Mass.: Harvard University Press, 1993. A critical assessment of the role of race in elections and representation.

Witt, Linda, Karen M. Paget, and Glenna Matthews. *Running as a Woman: Gender and Power in American Politics.* New York: Free Press, 1993. A comprehensive study of the problems faced by women candidates.

CHAPTER 13

Congressional Policymaking: Balancing National Goals and Local Interests

★

There are really two Congresses, not just one. Often these two Congresses are widely separated; the tightly knit, complex world of Capitol Hill is a long way from the world of [the member's district or state]—not only in miles, but in perspective and outlook as well.

—Roger Davidson and Walter Oleszek[1]

★ ★ ★

*T*he congressional action on the $200 billion transportation bill revealed a lot about the institution. For the first time in a generation, the federal government had the luxury of a budget surplus. How would it be used? To cut taxes? To safeguard the future of the social security system? To provide a cushion against some future day when the economy turned sour and federal expenditures exceeded revenues?

As it happened, a first use of the surplus was to help fund the most expensive transportation bill in the nation's history. It was hard to argue that it was a bad use of the money. The nation's transportation infrastructure had been neglected for years, and there were plenty of bridges, roads, and mass transit systems in need of repair and expansion. Yet the $200 billion transportation bill was attractive to Congress in part because it provided public works projects and jobs for virtually every state and every congressional district in the nation. It was a good policy, but it was also very good politics in an election year.

The story of the 1998 transportation bill illustrates the dual nature of Congress: it is both a lawmaking institution for the country and a representative assembly for states and districts.[2] Members of Congress have both an individual duty to serve the interests of their separate constituencies and a collective duty to protect the interests of the country as a whole. Attention to constituency interests is the common denominator of a national institution in which each member must please the voters back home in order to win reelection. Congressional elections have been described as "local events with national consequences."[3]

The role of Congress in national policymaking is examined in this chapter. Because Congress is a large, complex organization whose members vary widely in their concerns and positions, the observations made in this chapter are necessarily broad. Nevertheless, there are discernible patterns to the policy actions of Congress and its members. One of the most significant is the pattern that emerged in deliberations over the transportation bill—the adjustment of broad national goals to more specific local concerns.

This chapter describes the patterns of congressional policymaking in the context of Congress's three major functions: lawmaking, representation, and oversight. The main points made in the chapter are the following:

★ *Congress is limited by the lack of direction and organization usually necessary for the development of comprehensive national policies.* Congress looks to the president to initiate most broad policy programs but exerts a substantial influence on the timing and content of those programs.

★ *Congress is well organized to handle policies of relatively narrow scope.* Such policies are usually worked out by small sets of legislators, bureaucrats, and interest groups.

★ *Individual members of Congress are extraordinarily responsive to local interests and concerns, although they also respond to national interests.* These responses often take place within the context of party tendencies.

★ *Congress oversees the bureaucracy's administration of its laws, but this oversight function is of less concern to members of Congress than is lawmaking or representation.*

★ *Congress is admired by those who favor negotiation, deliberation, and the rewarding of many interests, particularly those with a local constituency base. Critics of Congress say that it hinders majority rule, fosters policy delay, and caters to special interests.*

The Lawmaking Function of Congress

lawmaking function   The authority (of a legislature) to make the laws necessary to carry out the government's powers.

The Framers of the Constitution expected Congress to be the leading branch of the national government. It was to the legislature—the embodiment of representative government—that the people were expected to look for policy leadership. Moreover, Congress was granted the **lawmaking function**—the authority to make the laws necessary to carry out the powers granted to the national government. During most of the nineteenth century, Congress, not the president, was clearly the dominant national institution.[4] Aside from a few strong leaders such as Jackson and Lincoln, presidents did not play a major legislative role. In fact, Congress frequently made it clear that presidential advice was not wanted. Then, as national and international forces combined to place greater leadership and policy demands on the federal government, the president became a vital part of the national legislative process.

Today, Congress and the president substantially share the lawmaking function. However, their roles differ greatly. The president's major contribution is made on the small number of broad legislative measures that arise each year in response to overarching national problems, although Congress also plays a large part in the disposition of such bills. In addition, Congress has the lead—and in many cases nearly the full say—on the narrower legislation that constitutes the great majority of the roughly ten thousand bills introduced during a two-year congressional session.

An understanding of Congress's lawmaking role begins with an awareness of how laws are made. Lawmaking is an elaborate process that reflects the organizational complexity of Congress and the diffusion of power within it.

HOW A BILL BECOMES LAW

bill   A proposed law (legislative act) within Congress or another legislature.

The formal process by which bills become law is summarized in Figure 13-1. The first step in the legislative process is the creation of a bill. A **bill** is a proposed legislative act. Many bills are prepared by executive agencies, interest

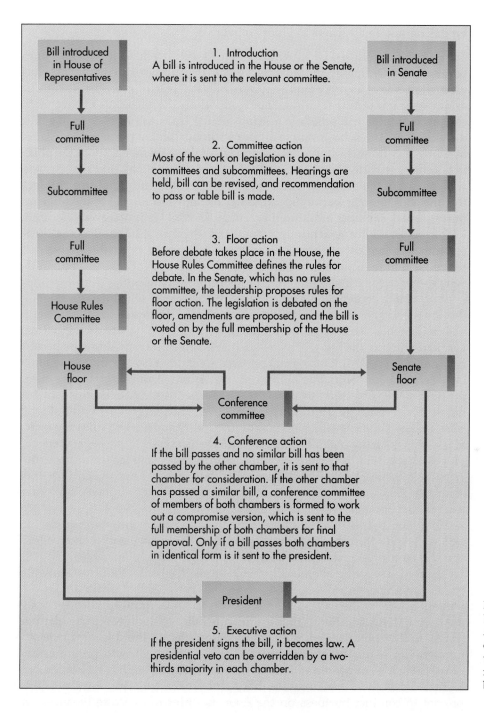

FIGURE 13-1 How a Bill Becomes a Law
Although the legislative process can be short-circuited in many ways, this diagram describes the most typical way in which a bill becomes law.

groups, or other outside parties, but members of Congress also draft bills and only they can formally submit a bill for consideration by their chamber. If a bill is passed by both the House and Senate and signed by the president, it becomes a **law** and thereby takes effect.

law (as enacted by Congress) A legislative proposal, or bill, that is passed by both the House and Senate and is either signed or not vetoed by the president.

From Committee Hearings to Floor Debate

Once a bill is introduced by a member of the House or Senate, it is given a number and a title. Ordinarily, the bill is then sent to the appropriate committee, which assigns it to one of its subcommittees. Most bills that reach a subcommittee are set aside on the grounds that they are not worthwhile. If a bill seems to have merit, the subcommittee will schedule hearings on it. This is a critical stage in a bill's development. The subcommittee invites testimony on the proposed legislation by lobbyists, administrators, and experts who inform members about the policy in question, provide an indication of the support the bill has, and may disclose weaknesses in the proposal. After the hearings, if the subcommittee still feels that the legislation is warranted, members recommend the bill to the full committee, which can hold additional hearings. The full committee may decide to kill the bill by taking no action on it but usually agrees with the subcommittee's recommendation, although it often alters specific provisions. In the House, both the full committee and a subcommittee can "mark up," or revise, a bill; in the Senate, markup is usually reserved for the full committee.

Once a bill is reported out of committee, it needs to be scheduled for floor debate by the full chamber. In the House, the Rules Committee has the power to determine when the bill will be voted on, how long the debate on the bill will last, and whether the bill will receive a "closed rule" (no amendments permitted), an "open rule" (members can propose amendments relevant to any of the bill's sections), or something in between (for example, only certain sections of the bill will be subject to amendment). The Rules Committee has this scheduling power because the House is too large to operate effectively without strict rules for the handling of legislation by the full chamber. The rules are also a means by which the majority party controls legislation. House Democrats employed closed rules to prevent Republicans from proposing amendments to major bills, a tactic House Republicans said they would forgo when they took control in 1995. Once in control, however, the Republicans applied closed rules to a number of major bills. The tactic was too effective to ignore.

Most House bills of importance are scheduled for floor action under the Union Calendar, which sets the order of debate for finance and economic bills, and the House Calendar, which covers nonfinancial and noneconomic bills. There are also separate calendars for noncontroversial bills and private bills. On certain days, noncontroversial and private bills can be called up for a floor vote without action by the Rules Committee. (Private bills grant privileges or payments to individuals. For example, a private bill might allow a particular person to settle in the United States even though he or she does not meet the immigration requirements. In contrast, public bills deal with programs and broad categories of people and are what is normally meant by "legislation.")

The House and Senate require that a quorum (a majority of members) be present to conduct business on the floor. In order to expedite business, the House often adjourns to the Committee of the Whole. This committee consists of all House members and meets on the floor of the House but requires a quorum of only one hundred members and has relatively informal procedures. Once agreement is reached in the Committee of the Whole, the House will reconvene and proceed to vote on the legislation at hand.

The Senate has no Rules Committee, relying instead on the majority leader to schedule its bills. All Senate bills are subject to unlimited debate unless a three-

Members of the Senate Budget Committee discuss the nation's budget. Most of the legislative work in Congress takes place in committees, which also decide the fate of most bills.

fifths majority of the full Senate votes for **cloture,** which limits debate to thirty hours. Cloture is a way of thwarting a Senate **filibuster,** a procedural tactic whereby a minority of senators prevent a bill from coming to a vote by holding the floor and talking until other senators give in and the bill is withdrawn from consideration. Filibustering is a Senate tradition that dates to the mid-1800s, and cloture was rarely invoked until recently. Cloture has become more common because filibustering itself has become more common. Two-thirds of the filibusters in the nation's history have taken place since the 1960s, and Senate majorities have invoked cloture dozens of times in this period in order to force legislation to a vote. A number of senators attempted unsuccessfully in 1995 to get the Senate to adopt a rule that would have banned filibustering entirely.

The Senate also differs from the House in that its members can propose *any* amendment to *any* bill. Unlike House amendments, those in the Senate do not have to be germane to a bill's content. For example, a senator may propose an anti-abortion amendment to a bill dealing with defense expenditures. Such amendments are called **riders,** and they are frequently introduced.

Leadership and Floor Action

Committee action is decisive on bills that address small issues. If a majority of committee members favor such a bill, it normally is passed by the full chamber, often without amendment. In a sense, the full chamber merely votes to confirm or modify decisions made previously by committees and subcommittees. Of course, committees do not operate in a vacuum. In making their decisions, they

cloture A parliamentary maneuver which, if a three-fifths majority votes for it, limits Senate debate to thirty hours and has the effect of defeating a filibuster.

filibuster A procedural tactic in the U.S. Senate whereby a minority of legislators prevent a bill from coming to a vote by holding the floor and talking until the majority gives in and the bill is withdrawn from consideration.

rider An amendment to a bill that deals with an issue unrelated to the content of the bill. Riders are permitted in the Senate but not the House.

take into account the fact that their positions can be reversed by the full chamber, just as subcommittees recognize that the full committee can overrule their decisions.

On major bills, the party leaders are the critical actors. They will have worked closely with the committee during its deliberations and may assume leadership of the bill when it clears the committee. (In the case of "minor" bills, leadership during floor debate is normally provided by committee members.)

In her book *Unorthodox Lawmaking: New Legislative Processes in the U.S. Congress*, Barbara Sinclair notes that the majority party's leaders (particularly in the House) have increasingly set the legislative agenda and defined the debate on major bills.[5] They shape the bills' broad outlines and set the boundaries of the floor debate. In these efforts, they depend on the support of party members. To obtain it, they consult their members informally and through the party caucus. **Party discipline**—the willingness of a party's House or Senate members to act together as a cohesive group—is increasingly important in congressional action and is the key to party leaders' ability to shape major legislation. (The role of parties in Congress is discussed further in a later section of the chapter.)

Conference Committees and the President

For a bill to pass, it must receive the support of a simple majority (50 percent plus one) of the House or Senate members voting on it. To become a law, however, a bill must be passed in identical form by both the House and the Senate. About 10 percent of all proposals that are approved by both chambers—the proportion is larger for major bills—differ in important respects in their House and Senate versions and are referred to a **conference committee** to resolve their differences. Each conference committee is formed temporarily to handle a particular bill; its

party discipline The willingness of a party's House or Senate members to act together as a cohesive group and thus exert collective control over legislative action.

conference committee A temporary committee that is formed to bargain over the differences in the House and Senate versions of a bill. The committee's members are usually appointed from the House and Senate standing committees that originally worked on the bill.

U.S. Senator Orrin Hatch (R-Utah) presides over a Judiciary Committee hearing. Most of the legislative work of Congress is done in committees and their subcommittees.

members are usually appointed from the House and Senate standing committees that worked on the bill originally. The conference committee's job is to bargain over the differences in the House and Senate versions and to develop a compromise version. It then goes to the House and Senate floors, where it can be passed, defeated, or returned to conference, but not amended.

Legislation that is passed by the House and the Senate is not assured of becoming a law. The president also has a role. If the president exercises the **veto,** a refusal to sign a bill, it is sent back to its originating chamber with the president's reasons for the veto. Congress can override a veto by a two-thirds vote of each chamber; the bill then becomes law. If the president fails to sign a bill within ten days and Congress has adjourned for the term, the bill does not become law. This last situation is called a *pocket veto* and forces Congress in its next session to start from the beginning: the bill must again pass both chambers and is again subject to presidential veto.

veto A veto occurs when the president refuses to sign a bill, thereby keeping it from becoming law unless Congress overrides the veto.

www.mhhe.com/patterson5

Simulation

CONGRESS'S POLICY ROLE

The formal process by which a bill becomes law provides a clue about Congress's policy role. A lot of separate and successful actions in different legislative arenas—subcommittees, committees, and the House and Senate floors—are required to move a bill through the Congress. It might be thought, as a result, that it is difficult to enact major legislation on which there are strong differences of opinion. The presumption is correct. Major legislation nearly always takes a great deal of time to make its way through Congress. More often than not, the legislation fails to make it. The total overhaul of the social welfare system that Congress enacted in 1996 was in committee for more than a year before it became law. Even more revealing is the fact that major efforts to reform the nation's welfare system began in Congress during the 1970s. With the exception of a 1987 law, none of them survived the congressional hurdles until the Welfare Reform Act of 1996.

Broad Issues: The Limits of Fragmentation on Congress's Role

Congress is structured in a way that makes agreement on large issues difficult to obtain. Congress is not one house, but two, each with its own authority and constituency base. Neither the House nor the Senate can enact legislation without the other's approval, and they are hardly two versions of the same thing. California and North Dakota have exactly the same representation in the Senate, but in the House, which is apportioned by population, California has fifty-two seats compared to North Dakota's one (see "States in the Nation").

Congress also includes a lot of people: 100 members of the Senate and 435 members of the House. They come from different constituencies and represent different and sometimes opposing interests. Since each member has a separate power base, and depends on it for reelection, the members can be expected to take different positions on legislative issues, even when they agree on the general goal. Nearly every member of Congress, for example, supports the principle of global free trade. When it comes to specific trade provisions, however, they often disagree. Foreign competition has a different meaning for manufacturers that produce automobiles, computer chips, and underwear; it has a

★ STATES IN THE NATION

ONE PERSON, ONE VOTE? NOT IN THE ELECTION OF SENATORS

The U.S. Congress is a true bicameral legislature. Yet the House and Senate are hardly twin institutions; they differ not only in size and procedures but also, most importantly, in their method of apportionment. The Senate is apportioned by geography: each state, regardless of population, has two U.S. senators. The House is apportioned by population. Thus, California, the largest state, has a much larger number of representatives in the House than, say, Vermont, which has only one. In fact, California has more House members (fifty-two) than all twenty-one of the least populated states combined (see map for the identity of these states, which together have a total of forty-nine House members). Yet, these same twenty-one states have a total of forty-two U.S. senators compared to just two for California. The "one-person, one-vote" concept that otherwise characterizes U.S. elections clearly does not apply to Senate elections. Vermont's six hundred thousand people have the same power in voting for senators as do California's thirty-three million voters. In other words, one Vermont voter is equal to fifty-five California voters when it comes to choosing a U.S. senator.

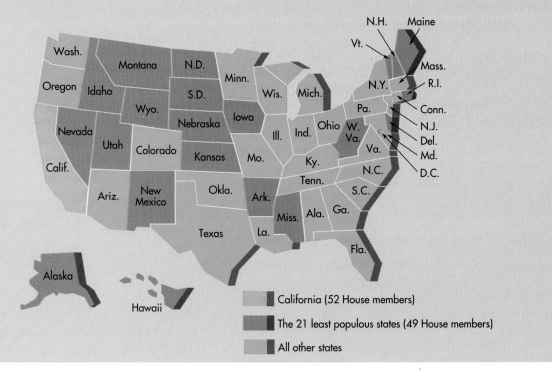

California (52 House members)

The 21 least populous states (49 House members)

All other states

different meaning for farmers who produce corn, sugar, and grapes; and it has a different meaning for firms that deal in international finance, home insurance, and student loans. And because it has different meanings for different people in different parts of the country, members of Congress who represent these areas have conflicting views on what the nation's trade policy should be.

For such reasons, Congress has difficulty taking the lead on broad issues of national policy. A legislative institution can easily lead on such issues only if it assigns this authority to its top leadership. Although the rise in party discipline in Congress has strengthened leaders' role, the fact remains that House and Senate members are relatively free to go their separate ways if they so choose. For this reason Congress ordinarily struggles when faced with the task of developing comprehensive policies that address broad national problems.

To imagine the problem, assume that your college established a committee of 535 students (the same number as sit in the House and Senate) to redesign the core course requirements for all freshmen and sophomores. The members of the committee include students of all majors, from political science to physics to literature. Imagine further that each student on the committee represented a group of other students who, if unhappy with the outcome, have the authority to kick their representative out of the university (similar to voters' ability to vote their representative out of office). What would the outcome of such a process be? Would the new curriculum favor the hard sciences, the social sciences, or the humanities? And how long would the process take? Consider the difficulty of getting 535 students to work together on the task. It is a large group, several times larger than even the largest lecture class at most colleges. If you were on the committee, had a proposal, and wanted to talk about it for just fifteen minutes with each of the other 534 committee members, you would need three weeks to complete your discussions. And that would be merely a starting point in the deliberations. Many of the other 534 members would have their own plan and, in most cases, prefer it to yours.

In short, Congress, like the hypothetical college committee, is not well designed to handle broad issues of policy. To be sure, Congress sometimes takes the lead on large issues. The Contract with America, which House Republicans ran on in 1994 and then sought to govern on in 1995–1996, included several broad measures, including the historic welfare-reform bill that was enacted in 1996. Moreover, except during Roosevelt's New Deal, Congress has been a chief source of major labor legislation, including the Taft-Hartley Act of 1947 (which legalized state right-to-work laws), the Landrum-Griffin Act of 1959 (which holds union officials to sound administrative and democratic practices), and plant-closing legislation in 1988 (which requires companies to notify workers sixty days before a plant closing or mass layoff). Congress also developed the Clean Air Act of 1963, the Water Quality Act of 1965, and other environmental legislation. Federal aid to education and urban development are other areas in which Congress has at times played a leading role.[6]

By and large, however, Congress with its separate chambers and many voices is not an easy place in which to develop comprehensive programs and carry them through to passage. "Congress," Arthur Maass notes, "is limited by the lack of resources and organization typically needed for these tasks."[7]

In general, Congress depends on the president to initiate broad policy proposals, and for good reason: the presidency has characteristics that are very different from those of Congress and better suited to the task.

First, whereas Congress's authority is fragmented, the president is a singular authority.[8] The president seeks the advice of others within the executive branch, but has sole authority to make the final decision. The decision may not be easy: some national problems are difficult to understand fully, let alone to manage effectively.[9] Runaway inflation admittedly bewildered President Jimmy Carter, who proposed program after program—five in all—in a frantic effort to control it. Nevertheless, the president does not have to have a majority consensus within

Newt Gingrich and three hundred Republican congressional candidates stand in front of the Capitol to dramatize their Contract with America. After their stunning victory in the 1994 elections, they launched an aggressive attempt to reduce the scope of the federal government, illustrating that, in some instances, Congress can take the lead on broad national issues.

the executive branch in order to act. As sole chief executive, the president can unilaterally choose a course of action and direct assistants to prepare a proposal for implementing it. Accordingly, the presidency is capable of a degree of policy planning and coordination that is far beyond the normal capacity of Congress. "It is the difference," one member of Congress said, "between an organization headed by one powerful [individual] and a many-headed organization."[10]

Another advantage that presidents enjoy is a national political base, which focuses public attention on their actions and lends a national perspective to their choices. The president must take regional and state concerns into account, but these concerns do not affect the president's decisions as much as they influence those of members of Congress. In a way, the president's situation is the reverse of that of a member of Congress: the president cannot ignore specific state and local interests but must concentrate on broad national ones in order to retain power.

These differences are also reflected in news coverage of the two institutions. As a nationally elected official and sole head of the executive branch, the president ordinarily gets considerably more attention from the press than any member of Congress. In fact, during most periods, the president gets more news coverage than all Senate and House members combined,[11] a situation that contributed to Congress's decision to establish its own cable network, C-SPAN (Cable Satellite Public Affairs Network). Congressional debates and hearings are carried live on C-SPAN, and journalists are authorized to use the televised material for reporting purposes.

Presidential leadership means that Congress will pay attention to White House proposals, not that it will adopt them. Congress typically accepts a presidential initiative only as a starting point in its deliberations. It may reject the proposal outright—particularly when the president is from the opposite

President Bill Clinton speaks about the Mexican financial crisis during an address at the Treasury Department, as Treasury Secretary Robert Rubin (center) and U.S. Trade Representative Mickey Kantor listen. Despite the backing of Republican congressional leaders Newt Gingrich and Robert Dole, Clinton's proposed bailout plan for Mexico failed to gain quick approval in Congress, which forced Clinton to pursue another approach. In Congress, it is ordinarily easier for opponents to block legislation than it is for proponents to obtain quick passage of a bill.

party—but any such proposal provides Congress a tangible bill on which to focus. If the proposal is at all close to what a congressional majority would regard as acceptable, Congress will modify it in large or small ways to fit the demands of its membership.

The president's leverage is greatest when prompt legislative action is imperative. When Congress must act or face the public's wrath, the presidential veto comes into play. Congress is nearly forced into taking the president's position into account in shaping the legislation since it is exceedingly difficult to muster the two-thirds majority in each chamber that is required to override a presidential veto. Of course, Congress can dare the president to veto the bill, hoping that public anger will be directed at the White House. But any such showdown is risky, and Congress and the White House normally bargain their way to a bill that accommodates their separate interests. (The legislative roles of Congress and the president are discussed further in Chapter 15.)

Organizational changes have improved Congress's ability to evaluate and modify presidential proposals. Of particular importance is the Congressional Budget Office (CBO), which was created as part of the Budget Impoundment and Control Act of 1974. Before this time, the president, through the Office of Management and Budget (OMB), had a significant advantage in budgetary matters. Congress had no independent way to systematically assess the president's budgetary proposals or their projected impact. The CBO gives Congress this capacity. Its two hundred employees provide Congress with general economic projections, overall estimates of government expenditures and revenues, and specific estimates of the costs of proposed programs. Since the CBO's inception, its calculations have often been at odds with those of the OMB. For example, the OMB's estimates of the cost of presidential initiatives are usually optimistic, and the CBO's figures have been a basis by which Congress has trimmed or rejected these proposals. (The budgetary process, and the CBO's role in it, are described more fully in Chapter 18. The OMB is discussed further in Chapters 15 and 16.)

CONGRESS IN THE LEAD: NARROW POLICY ISSUES

Only a small proportion of the bills addressed by Congress deal with broad national issues of widespread interest. The rest cover smaller problems of less general interest. The leading role in the disposition of these bills falls not on the president but on Congress and, in most cases, on a relatively small number of its members.

Congress's standing committees and their subcommittees decide most legislative issues.[12] Interest groups and bureaucratic agencies with a stake in a particular policy issue tend to concentrate their persuasive efforts on the committee that is responsible for formulating legislation in that policy area. Hearings on proposed legislation are held by a committee or subcommittee, not by the full membership of Congress. The testimony introduced at the hearings is published, but transcripts of congressional hearings run to over a million pages annually, far more than any member of Congress could read. Members of Congress consequently have little choice but to trust the judgment of committees and subcommittees.

Of course, committees and subcommittees do not operate in a vacuum.[13] Other members of Congress look for signs of trouble, as when a committee's vote divides sharply along party or ideological lines. In such a case the committee's recommendation on a bill is more likely to be debated, amended, or defeated on the floor. Committees also develop reputations for fair play. A committee that regularly seeks excessive benefits for a special interest can expect all its bills to start receiving close scrutiny on the floor. Some committees, such as the House Ways and Means Committee, pride themselves on drafting

There are dozens of informal caucuses in Congress that aim to represent the concerns of particular constituencies. Pictured here is U.S. Representative Loretta Sanchez (D-CA), a member of the Hispanic caucus.

legislation that the full chamber will find acceptable. A question in each case is whether the committee has done its job in weighing the needs of a special interest against the general interest. For example, most members of Congress are not opposed in principle to special tax incentives for individuals and firms engaged in risky ventures, but they do not always feel that these entrepreneurs should be given tax breaks at the expense of other taxpayers.

Big government and social complexity have increased the pressure on committees to weigh the effects of their decisions on other policy areas and to respond to the views of people outside the committee. As we saw in Chapter 10, *iron triangles* (small, stable sets of bureaucrats, lobbyists, and legislators with a shared policy commitment) have given way in large part to *issue networks* (relatively open and fluid networks of bureaucrats, lobbyists, legislators, and policy specialists who are linked by a shared policy expertise, not by a common policy goal). Unlike iron triangles, issue networks cut across committee boundaries, with the result that members of a committee now operate less independently than they once did. Major environmental issues, for example, will draw the close attention of representatives and senators from most states and several committees.

Another congressional subgroup of importance is the unofficial *caucus*, which is an informal group of legislators with a shared interest who meet periodically to exchange information and coordinate a legislative strategy designed to foster that interest. (These caucuses should not be confused with the *party caucuses*, which were discussed in Chapter 12 and are composed of the party members in each chamber.) Some of these caucuses are regional. For example, there is a Northeast-Midwest Caucus as well as a Sunbelt Caucus. The black, Hispanic, and women's caucuses consist of members of Congress who belong to these demographic groups. Many caucuses have formed around constituency interests of members of Congress; the textile, steel, automotive, and agricultural caucuses are examples. (These caucuses are not official bodies of the Congress and are restricted in the use of congressional resources to support their activities.)

★ CRITICAL THINKING ★

WHAT'S YOUR OPINION?

Representation of National and Local Interests
Members of Congress are representatives both of the nation and of particular states and districts. These representative roles often complement each other but sometimes conflict. When should a representative place the needs of the nation ahead of the needs of his or her particular state or district? When should local needs dominate? Try to place your answers in the context of a specific issue, such as energy, global trade, or defense-spending policy.

Members of Congress are keenly sensitive to local opinion on issues of personal interest to their constituents. The representatives from urban areas are more supportive of gun control than those from rural areas, where sport hunting is widespread.

Whether the major influence on a particular bill comes from a subcommittee, committee, iron triangle, issue network, or caucus, the crucial point in each case is that a subset of Congress's members is essentially making national policy on behalf of the whole institution. Woodrow Wilson described Congress as a system of "little legislatures," referring to its dependence on subsets of members to do its work. Many of the bills that these "little legislatures" formulate will pass the full House or Senate with little or no alteration by other members. Because the legislative issues with which subsets of legislators deal are often narrow and technical, other members of Congress may neither know enough nor care enough to examine bills closely as long as they believe that the specialists are doing an acceptable job.

Congress's ability to lead on narrow issues is a substantial strength. In other democracies, the complexity of modern policymaking has led to a clear-cut subordination of the legislature to the executive. The legislature serves as an arena of debate and acts as a check on executive power but is in reality not a fully independent body. By comparison, the U.S. Congress has retained a significant lawmaking role, in part because of its constitutional separation from the executive, but also in part because its committee system gives it an independent source of policy leadership and expertise. The fragmented structure of Congress has, paradoxically, protected it from capture by the executive while at the same time granting the executive the lead on most issues of overarching national concern.

The point can be overstated, however. When the White House and Congress are controlled by opposite parties, the legislature's willingness to accept presidential leadership is greatly reduced. It is also the case that the recent changes in congressional organization and leadership (see Chapter 12) have made it easier for the majority party in Congress to give direction to national policy. By and large, however, Congress's strength is its extraordinary capacity to tackle many narrow issues simultaneously, a capacity made possible by its fragmented lawmaking structure.

The Representation Function of Congress

In the process of making laws, the members of Congress represent various interests within American society, giving them voice and attention in the national legislature. Congress, with its individually elected, constituent-based membership and its decentralized system of power and work, has been characterized as a representative body par excellence. It expresses the concerns of countless interests, from those that would protect a local landmark from the wrecking ball to those that would devise a new banking system in the wake of the savings and loan scandal. The various members of Congress spread their time and energy across a wide range of interests. Congress is superb as a forum of expression for diverse interests.

representation function The responsibility of a legislature to represent various interests in society.

The proper approach to the **representation function** has been debated since the nation's founding. The writers of the Constitution tied members of Congress to their home states and districts so that the interests of these entities would be represented in national politics. The diversity of America was to be reflected in its Congress, which would also respond to broad national concerns. A recurrent issue has been whether the primary focus of a representative should be the interests of the nation as a whole or those of his or her constituency. These interests always overlap to some degree but rarely coincide exactly. Policies that are of maximum benefit to the full society are not always equally advantageous to particular localities and can even cause harm to some constituencies. To the writers of the Constitution, the higher duty was to the nation. James Madison said in *Federalist* No. 10 that members of Congress should be those persons "least likely to sacrifice" the national interest to "local prejudice."

The local-national distinction was discussed in Chapter 3 in terms of the trustee and delegate models of representation. The trustee model holds that elected representatives are obligated to act in accordance with their own judgment as to what policies are in the best interests of society. The delegate model claims that elected representatives are obligated to carry out the expressed wishes of those who elected them to office. The choice is not a simple one, even for a legislator who is inclined toward either the delegate or trustee orientation. To be fully effective, a member of Congress must be reelected time and again, a necessity that compels him or her to pay attention to local demands. Yet, as part of the nation's legislative body, no member can easily put aside his or her judgment as to the nation's needs. In making the choice, most members of Congress, it appears, tend toward a local orientation, albeit one that is modified by both overarching and partisan concerns, as the following discussion explains.

REPRESENTATION OF STATES AND DISTRICTS: CONSTITUENCY POLITICS

Many members of Congress say that they are in Washington primarily to serve the interests of the state or district that elected them.[15] As natural as this claim may appear, it is noteworthy that members of the British House of Commons or the French National Assembly would not be likely to say the same thing: they consider their chief responsibility to be service to the nation, not to their localities. The unitary governments and strong parties of Britain and France give their politics a national orientation. The federal system and weak parties of the United States force members of Congress to take responsibility for their own reelection campaigns and to be wary of antagonizing local interests. They are particularly reluctant to oppose local sentiment on issues of intense concern.[16] Support for gun control legislation, for example, has always been much lower among members of Congress from rural areas where sporting guns are part of the fabric of everyday life.

The committee system of Congress also promotes representation of local rather than national interests.[17] Although recent studies of committees indicate that the views of committee members are not radically different from the views of the full House or Senate membership,[18] committee membership is hardly random. Many senators and representatives sit on committees and subcommittees with policy jurisdictions that coincide with state or district interests. For example, farm-state legislators dominate the membership of the House and Senate Agriculture committees, and westerners dominate the Interior committees (which deal with federal lands and natural resources, most of which are concentrated in the West).

CURRENT CONTROVERSIES

IS MINORITY REDISTRICTING UNCONSTITUTIONAL?

Through their representatives, Americans' views are taken into account in the making of public policy. Nevertheless, congressional representatives are not equally responsive to all constituency opinions. They tend naturally to favor the views of the voting majority that elected them. This tendency can result in the underrepresentation of minority group members because only rarely will those members constitute an electoral majority in a congressional district. In 1982, Congress said that race could be taken into account in congressional redistricting, and after the 1990 census, the boundaries of some House districts were drawn so that black Americans were a voting majority. This "minority redistricting" was controversial, and the issue eventually reached the Supreme Court. It held that race cannot be the determining factor in redistricting decisions, although there might be circumstances in which it could be considered along with other factors. The following are selections from the Supreme Court opinions in one of the redistricting cases, *Shaw v. Hunt* (1996).

YES: [The District Court] held that the North Carolina redistricting plan did classify voters by race, but that the classification survived strict scrutiny and therefore did not offend the Constitution. We [the Supreme Court majority] now hold that the North Carolina plan does violate the Equal Protection Clause because the State's reapportionment scheme is not narrowly tailored to serve a compelling state interest. . . . Racial classifications are antithetical to the Fourteenth Amendment, whose "central purpose" was "to eliminate racial discrimination emanating from official sources in the States." . . . For the foregoing reasons, the judgment of the District Court is reversed.
—Chief Justice William Rehnquist

NO: A majority's attempt to enable the minority to participate more effectively in the process of democratic government should not be viewed with the same hostility that is appropriate for oppressive and exclusionary abuses of political power. . . . We have a duty to respect Congress' considered judgment that such a policy may serve to effectuate the ends of the constitutional Amendment that it is charged with enforcing. We should also respect North Carolina's conscientious effort to conform to that congressional determination. . . . I find no basis for this Court's intervention into a process by which federal and state actors, both black and white, are jointly attempting to resolve difficult questions of politics and race that have long plagued North Carolina.
—Justice John Paul Stevens

logrolling The trading of votes between legislators so that each gets what he or she most wants.

Constituency interests are also advanced by **logrolling,** the practice of trading one's vote with another member so that each gets what he or she most wants. The term dates to the early nineteenth century, when a settler would ask neighbors for help in rolling logs off land being cleared for farming, with the understanding that the settler would reciprocate when the neighbors were cutting trees. In Congress, logrolling occurs most often in committees where constituency interests vary. It has not been uncommon, for example, for agriculture committee members from livestock-producing states of the North to trade votes with committee members from the South where crops such as cotton, tobacco, and peanuts are grown.

Nevertheless, representation of constituency interests has its limits. A representative's constituents have little interest in most issues that come before Congress and even less information about them. Whether the government should appropriate a few million dollars in foreign aid for Bolivia or should alter patent requirements for copying machines is not the sort of issue that local people are likely to know or care about. Moreover, members of Congress often have no choice but to go against the wishes of a significant portion of their constituency. The interests of small and large farmers in an agricultural state, for example, can differ considerably.

REPRESENTATION OF INTERESTS: GROUP POLITICS

Congress is almost ideally designed to represent interest groups. Its committees and subcommittees have legislative responsibility for policies that touch directly on particular groups, and members of Congress are receptive to lobbying efforts.

At one time, the representation of groups was nearly synonymous with the representation of constituents. The relationship of a farm-state senator to agricultural interests is an example. Such relationships are still important, but as society has become increasingly complex and interdependent, interests have cut across constituency boundaries. The representation of groups has accordingly taken on new dimensions. One indicator is the emergence in recent decades of "outside lobbying"—pressure from the grass roots (see Chapter 10). Some of this pressure comes from the member's constituents, but much of it comes from networks of like-minded people who have a shared goal, not by virtue of living in the same state or district but by virtue of shared values. Environmental issues, for example, typically transcend election districts.

Studies indicate that lobbying and PAC money result in "representation" for groups.[19] Indeed, research by Richard Hall and Frank Wayman suggests that, in some policy areas, committee members are more responsive to organized interests than to the views of unorganized voters within their districts.[20]

REPRESENTATION OF THE NATION: PARTY POLITICS

When a clear-cut and vital national interest is at stake, members of Congress can be expected to respond to that interest. The difficulty of using the common good as a routine basis for thinking about representation, however, is that Americans often disagree on what constitutes the common good and what government should do to further it.

Most Americans believe, for example, that the nation's education system requires strengthening. The test scores of American schoolchildren on standardized reading, math, and science examinations are significantly below those of children in many industrial democracies. This situation creates pressure for political action. But what action is necessary and desirable? Does more money have to be funneled into public schools, and which level of government—the federal, state, or local—would provide it? Or does the problem rest with teachers? Should they be subject to higher certification and performance standards? Or is the problem a lack of competition for excellence? Should schools be required to compete for students and the tax dollars they represent? Should private schools be part of any such competition, or would their participation wreck the public school system? There is no general agreement on such issues. The quality of America's schools is of vital national interest, and quality schools would serve the common good. But the means to that end are subjects of endless dispute.

In Congress, debates over national goals occur primarily along party lines. Republicans and Democrats have different perspectives on national issues

★ CRITICAL THINKING ★

WHAT'S YOUR OPINION?

Party Unity and Fragmentation in Congress
The best predictor of the way individual members of Congress will respond to legislation is their party affiliation, Republican or Democratic. In view of this fact, do you think it makes sense for voters in congressional elections to "vote for the person, not the party"? Why, or why not? Then consider this question: Can anything but party unity overcome the fragmentation that besets Congress?

because their parties differ philosophically and politically. In the end-of-the-year budget negotiations in 1998 and 1999, for example, Republicans and Democrats were deadlocked on the issue of new funding to hire thousands of public schoolteachers. The initiative had come from President Clinton and was supported by congressional Democrats but opposed by congressional Republicans who objected to spending federal (as opposed to state and local) funds for that purpose and who also objected to the proposed placement of the new teachers (they would be placed in overcrowded schools, most of which are in Democratic constituencies). Democrats and Republicans alike agreed that more teachers were needed, but they disagreed on how that goal should be reached. In the end, through concessions in other areas, Clinton and the congressional Democrats obtained federal funding for new teachers, but it was obtained through an intensely partisan process.

Partisanship is the main source of division within Congress. There are real and substantial differences between members of the two parties, such that they often vote on the opposite sides of legislative issues (see Figure 13-2). Party-line voting has increased in recent decades, reflecting the rise of party discipline in Congress and the widening gap between the Democrats and Republicans who serve there. There are now in Congress fewer liberal Republicans and fewer conservative Democrats, as well as fewer moderates of both parties. As a result, congressional debate is more rancorous and legislative deadlock is more common.

Partisanship also affects the president's relationship with Congress. Presidents serve as legislative leaders not so much for the whole Congress as for members of their own party. More than half the time, opposition and support for presidential initiatives divide along party lines. Accordingly, the president's legislative success can depend on which party controls the Congress. After Republicans took control of Congress from the Democrats in 1995, for example, President Clinton's legislative victories declined sharply (see Chapter 15).

In short, any accounting of representation in Congress that minimizes the influence of party is faulty. If constituency interests drive the thinking of many members of Congress, so do partisan values. In fact, constituent and partisan

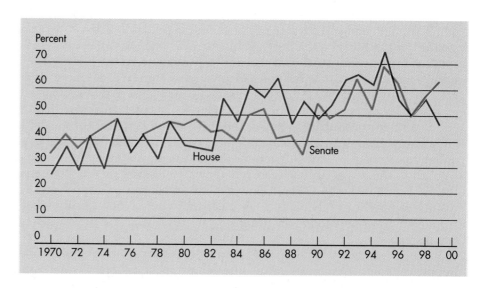

FIGURE 13-2 Percentage of Roll-Call Votes in House and Senate in Which a Majority of Democrats Voted Against a Majority of Republicans Democrats and Republicans in Congress are often on opposite sides of issues; party-line voting has increased in recent years. *Source:* Congressional Quarterly Weekly, *various dates.*

influences are often difficult to separate in practice. In the case of conflicting interests within their constituency, members of Congress naturally side with those that align with their party. When local business and labor groups take opposing sides on issues before Congress, for example, Republican members tend to back business's position while Democratic members tend to line up with labor.

The Oversight Function of Congress

Although Congress enacts the laws governing the nation and appropriates the money to implement them, the administration of these laws is entrusted to the executive branch. Congress has the responsibility to see that the executive carries out the laws faithfully and spends the money properly, a supervisory activity that is referred to as the **oversight function** of Congress.

> **oversight function** A supervisory activity of Congress that centers on its constitutional responsibility to see that the executive carries out the laws faithfully and spends appropriations properly.

THE PROCESS OF LEGISLATIVE OVERSIGHT

Oversight is carried out largely through the committee system of Congress and is facilitated by the parallel structure of the committees and the executive bureaucracy: the House International Relations and Senate Foreign Relations committees oversee the work of the State Department, the House and Senate Agriculture committees look after the Department of Agriculture, and so on. The Legislative Reorganization Act of 1970 spells out each committee's responsibility for overseeing its parallel agency:

> Each standing committee shall review and study, on a continuing basis, the application, administration, and execution of those laws, or parts of laws, the subject matter of which is within the jurisdiction of that committee.

However, oversight is easier to mandate than to carry out. If congressional committees were to try to monitor all the federal bureaucracy's activities, they would have no time or energy to do anything else. Most members of Congress are more interested in working out new laws and looking after constituents than in laboriously keeping track of the bureaucracy. Although Congress is required by law to maintain "continuous watchfulness" over programs, committees have little incentive to take a hard look at programs that they have enacted or on which their constituent groups depend. Oversight normally is not pursued aggressively unless members of Congress are annoyed with an agency, have discovered that a legislative authorization is being grossly abused, or are reviewing a program for possible major changes.[21]

If a committee believes that an agency has mishandled a program, it can investigate the matter. Congress's investigative power is not listed in the Constitution, but the judiciary has not challenged the power, and Congress has used it extensively. The Watergate, Iran-Contra, and Whitewater affairs prompted congressional investigations, which have also been used to focus attention on national problems such as crime, poverty, and health care.

When serious abuses by an agency are suspected, a committee is likely to hold hearings. Except in cases involving "executive privilege" (the right to withhold confidential information affecting national security), executive branch

HOW THE UNITED STATES COMPARES

NATIONAL LEGISLATURES: GOOD INFLUENCE OR BAD?

The past quarter century has been a difficult period for Western democracies. Although they have seen the triumph of democratic capitalism over communist socialism abroad, they have faced disruptive social and economic forces at home. Perhaps at no time in history has social and economic change occurred at such a rapid pace, straining the capacity of governments to respond. Traditional institutions, from political parties to families, have weakened dramatically, and the global marketplace, postindustrial dislocation, and the surge of women into the work force have radically altered economic relationships. The comfortable policies of the past have been inadequate to the new challenges.

In any period of disruptive change, the public tends to express its anxieties through dissatisfaction with governing institutions. The public response is exaggerated in modern times by the expectation that government should be able to resolve society's problems. Although history suggests that adaptation to major social and economic change is slow and costly, there is a tendency today to believe that it can occur quickly and painlessly if government will only do its job properly. When the adaptation is neither quick nor painless, the predictable response is to blame government. Congress has also been a target of the public's anxieties; confidence in the institution has declined substantially from the level of three or four decades ago. Citizens elsewhere are also not very happy with their national legislatures, as indicated by a Times Mirror Center survey that asked respondents in several Western democracies whether their national legislature has been mainly a good influence or bad influence on the way things are going in the country:

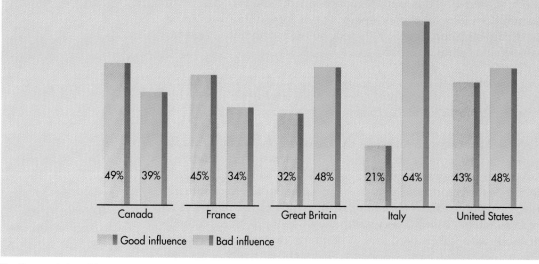

Canada	France	Great Britain	Italy	United States
49% 39%	45% 34%	32% 48%	21% 64%	43% 48%

■ Good influence   ■ Bad influence

Used by permission of the Pew Research Center for the People and the Press.

officials are compelled to testify at these hearings. If they refuse, they can be cited for contempt of Congress, which is a criminal offense. In 1990, in response to allegations that former Secretary of Housing and Urban Development (HUD) Samuel R. Pierce Jr. and other HUD officials had granted illegal loans and otherwise conspired to defraud the government, a House subcommittee concluded that Pierce had channeled government funds to friends and lied to Congress about his actions. The subcommittee recommended that the special prosecutor investigating the HUD scandal explore the charge of perjury and bring Pierce to account if the allegation was substantiated. The investigative work of Congress and the special prosecutor helped bring about administrative and personnel changes within HUD.

Most federal programs must have their funding renewed every year, a requirement that gives Congress crucial leverage in its ongoing oversight function. If an agency has acted improperly, Congress may reduce the agency's appropriation or tighten the restrictions on the way its funds can be spent. A major difficulty is that the House and Senate Appropriations committees must review nearly the entire federal budget, a task that limits the amount of attention they can give any particular program. Some programs are also reviewed for renewal each year by the House and Senate committees that authorized them. These committees, however, are busy with new legislation and are not greatly interested in conducting annual reviews of existing programs. They prefer to wait until administrative problems surface and then respond with investigations.

LEGISLATIVE DEVICES FOR RESTRAINING THE BUREAUCRACY

Oversight conducted after the bureaucracy has acted has an obvious drawback: if a program has been administered improperly, some damage has already been done. For this reason, Congress in recent years has developed ways of limiting the bureaucracy's discretion in advance. One method is to include detailed instructions in appropriations bills. Department of Defense appropriations, for example, now often specify cost-accounting procedures that bureaucrats must use. Such instructions limit bureaucrats' flexibility when they spend funds on programs and provide a firmer basis for holding them accountable if they disregard the intent of Congress.

Another oversight device is the "sunset law," which fixes a date on which a program will end (or "fade into the sunset") unless it is renewed by Congress. Such laws are a response to the fact that any program, once established, tends to be perpetuated by the bureaucrats who run it and by the interests that gain from it. Sunset provisions help prevent a program from outliving its usefulness because, once its expiration date is reached, Congress can reestablish it only by passing a new law.

The "legislative veto" is a more intrusive and controversial oversight tool. It requires that an executive agency have the approval of Congress before it can take a specified action. The Department of Defense, for example, cannot close a military facility unless Congress permits it to do so. Legislative vetoes are under challenge as an unconstitutional infringement on executive authority, and their future is unclear. (Congress's oversight tools are discussed more fully in Chapter 16.)

As indicated in Chapter 12, Congress has come to rely heavily on the General Accounting Office (GAO) to oversee executive agencies' spending and, more recently, their program performance. Some of the more blatant misuses of federal funds, particularly in the Department of Defense, have been uncovered by the GAO and then referred to the appropriate committees of Congress.

OBSTACLES TO OVERSIGHT

Members of Congress acknowledge the importance of their oversight function but find the task a somewhat unrewarding and troublesome one. Because they depend on the bureaucracy to do their own work effectively, members of Congress prefer harmonious relations with administrators. Oversight works against such relationships; it involves surveillance and the prospect of conflict between bureaucrats and members of Congress.

The biggest obstacle to effective oversight is the sheer magnitude of the task. With its hundreds of agencies and thousands of programs, the bureaucracy is beyond comprehensive scrutiny. Even some of Congress's most publicized oversight activities are relatively trivial when viewed against the sheer scope of the bureaucracy. For example, congressional investigations into the Defense Department's purchase of small hardware items, such as wrenches and hammers, at many times their market value do not begin to address the issue of whether the country is overspending on the military. Overpriced hand tools represent pocket change in a defense budget of billions of dollars. The real oversight question is whether the defense budget as a whole provides cost-effective national security. It is a question that Congress has neither the capacity nor the determination to investigate fully.

Congress's zeal for oversight changes dramatically when allegations of scandal or wrongdoing engulf the presidency. Then, members of the opposing party in Congress can be expected to use the oversight process to embarrass, pressure, or rebuke the president to the fullest possible extent. When independent counsel Kenneth Starr's report was submitted to Congress in late 1998, Republican lawmakers quickly approved a formal impeachment inquiry. House Republicans refused to strike a compromise with congressional Democrats and voted unanimously for an inquiry that would be unlimited by time or subject. This procedure would give Congress as a whole the chance to weigh any and all charges against Clinton but also was designed to give congressional Republicans leeway in their efforts to criticize the President. Although formal presidential impeachment inquiries are rare (there have been only three), the opposing party in Congress has rarely overlooked an opportunity to use the oversight

Senate Majority Leader Trent Lott of Mississippi (left) addresses the Senate impeachment trial on the day that the Senate voted to acquit President Clinton on two articles of impeachment.

process to seek political advantage over the incumbent administration. (Chapter 15 describes the impeachment process in detail.)

Congress: Too Much Pluralism?

Congress is an institution divided between service to the nation and to the separate constituencies within it. Its members have responsibility for the nation's laws. Yet they depend for reelection on the voters of their states and districts and are highly responsive to constituency interests. This focus is facilitated by the committee system, which is organized around particular interests. Agriculture, labor, education, banking, and commerce are among the interests represented through this system. It is hard to conceive of a national legislature structured to respond to special interests more closely than does the Congress of the United States. It is even harder to conceive of a national legislature that gives as much real power to these interests through committees as does Congress.

Pluralists admire this feature of Congress. They argue that the United States has a majoritarian institution in the presidency and that Congress is a place where a *diversity* of interests are represented. Critics of this view say that Congress is sometimes so responsive to particular interests that the overall national interest is neglected. This criticism is blunted from time to time by a strong majoritarian impulse in Congress. The current period is one of these moments. The high level of party discipline in recent years, coupled with a widening ideological gap between the parties, has placed Congress at the center of many national policy debates, including the issue of the balance of power between Washington and the states.

The fact is, Congress cannot at once be an institution that is highly responsive both to diverse interests and to the national interest. These interests often conflict, as the rise and fall of Speaker Gingrich illustrates. He sought to make the Republican congressional majority into the driving force in American national politics but lost his position when the conflicts generated by this goal began to threaten the GOP's support in the states and districts. This inherent tension between Congress's national role and local base has replayed itself many times in U.S. history. In a real sense, the strengths of Congress are also its weaknesses. The features of congressional election and organization that make Congress responsive to separate constituencies are often the very same ones that make it difficult for Congress to act as a strong instrument of a national majority. The perennial challenge for members of Congress is to find a workable balance between what Roger Davidson and Walter Oleszek call the "two Congresses"—the one embodied by the Capitol in Washington and other embodied by the members' separate districts and states.[22]

www.mhhe.com/patterson5

Self-Quiz

Summary

The major function of Congress is to enact legislation. Congress is not well suited to the development of broad and carefully coordinated policy programs. Its divided chambers, fragmented leadership, and committee structure, as well as the concern of its members with state and district interests, make it difficult for Congress to routinely initiate solutions to broad national problems. Congress often looks to the president for such proposals but has strong influence on the timing and content of major national programs.

Congress is better designed to handle legislation dealing with problems of narrow interest. Legislation of this sort is decided mainly in congressional committees, where interested legislators, bureaucrats, and groups concentrate their efforts on issues of mutual concern. Narrowly focused bills emerging from committees usually win the support of the full House or Senate. Committee recommendations are always subject to checks on the floor, and larger policy groups—issue networks and caucuses—have increasingly intruded on the committee process. Nevertheless, most narrow policy issues are settled primarily by subgroups of legislators rather than by the full Congress, although the success of these subgroups in the long run can depend on their responsiveness to broader interests.

A second function of Congress is the representation of various interests. Members of Congress are highly sensitive to the state or district on which they depend for reelection. As a result, interest groups that are important to a member's state or district are strongly represented in Congress. Members of Congress do respond to overriding national interests, but for many of them, local concerns generally come first. National representation tends to work through party representation, particularly on issues that have traditionally divided the Democratic and Republican parties and their constituencies.

Congress's third function is oversight, the supervision and investigation of the way the bureaucracy is implementing legislatively mandated programs. Oversight is usually less rewarding than lawmaking or representation and receives correspondingly less attention from members of Congress.

Congress is a slow and deliberative institution. It is also a powerful one. The process by which a bill becomes law is such that legislative proposals can be defeated or stymied rather easily. Congress is admired by those who believe that broad national legislation should reflect a wide range of interests, including local ones; that policies developed through a lengthy process of compromise and negotiation are likely to be sound; and that minorities should be able to obtain selective benefits and should have ways of blunting the impulses of the majority. Critics of the congressional process argue that, too often, it serves special interests, blunts majority opinion, and impedes a timely response to pressing national needs.

Key Terms

bill
cloture
conference committee
filibuster
law
lawmaking function

logrolling
oversight function
party discipline
representation function
rider
veto

Suggested Readings

Crabb, Cecil Van Meter. *Congress and the Foreign Policy Process: Modes of Legislative Behavior.* Baton Rouge: Louisiana State University Press, 2000. An analysis of Congress's role in foreign policy.

Davidson, Roger H., and Walter J. Oleszek. *Congress and Its Members,* 7th ed. Washington, D.C.: Congressional Quarterly Press, 2000. A comprehensive text on Congress and its members.

Hammond, Susan Webb. *Congressional Caucuses in National Policymaking.* Baltimore, Md.: Johns Hopkins University Press, 1998. A critical assessment of the role congressional caucuses play in national policymaking.

Hibbing, John R., and Elizabeth Theiss-Morse. *Congress as Public Enemy: Public Attitudes Toward American Political Institutions.* New York: Cambridge University Press, 1995. An analysis through survey and focus group data of Americans' attitudes toward Congress.

Johnson, Loch K. *A Season of Inquiry.* Chicago: Dorsey Press, 1988. An insightful study of congressional oversight of intelligence activities.

Mayer, R. Kenneth, and David T. Canon. *The Dysfunctional Congress? The Individual Roots of an Institutional Dilemma.* Boulder, Colo.: Westview Press, 1999. An exploration of the tension between Congress's institutional and individual imperatives.

Palazzolo, Daniel J. *The Speaker and the Budget: Leadership in the Post-Reform House of Representatives.* Pittsburgh, Pa.: University of Pittsburgh Press, 1992. An extensive analysis of the role of the Speaker in the budgetary process.

Shull, Steven A., and Thomas C. Shaw. *Explaining Congressional-Presidential Relations: A Multiple Perspectives Approach.* Albany: State University of New York Press, 1999. A careful look at executive-legislative relations.

Sinclair, Barbara. *Unorthodox Lawmaking: New Legislative Processes in the U.S. Congress,* 2nd ed. Washington, D.C.: Congressional Quarterly Press, 2000. A detailed analysis of the American legislative process.

Thomas, Sue. *How Women Legislate.* New York: Oxford University Press, 1994. A well-researched study that indicates women legislators pursue different policy agendas than do men legislators.

CHAPTER 14

Presidential Office and Election: Leading the Nation

★

[The president's] is the only voice in national affairs. Let him once win the admiration and confidence of the people, and no other single voice will easily overpower him.

—Woodrow Wilson[1]

★ ★ ★

*W*hen November 7 finally arrived, Al Gore and George W. Bush could look back on their election campaigns and only shake their heads. For a year and a half, they had traveled the length and breadth of America, often campaigning on a few hours of sleep and rarely getting a day off. They had met thousands of people, delivered hundreds of speeches, and endured countless fundraising events. If the prize had been anything less than the presidency, it is nearly inconceivable that Bush, Gore, or any other politician would have undertaken the grinding effort that the journalist Jules Witcover has called a "marathon."[2]

Yet the process of presidential selection is a critical component of the presidency's power. The Constitution vests executive authority in a single chief executive.[3] The Framers debated briefly the possibility of a three-person executive (one president each from the northern, middle, and southern states) but rejected the idea on the grounds that a joint office would be sapped of its energy by constant infighting. The Framers worried that a single executive might become too powerful but believed that adequate protection against such a threat was provided by the separation of powers and the president's selection by electors. The president would represent the people but would not be chosen directly by them. This arrangement would deny the president the reserve of power that popular election could confer.

The Framers did not anticipate that popular voting would someday take a place alongside the electoral vote in the selection of the president. The Framers also did not foresee all the leadership implications of the president's national office. Senators and representatives are chosen by voters within a single state or district, a limitation that diminishes the claim of any one of them to national leadership. Moreover, since the House and the Senate are separate bodies, no member of Congress can speak for the whole institution. The president, in contrast, is a nationally elected official and the sole chief executive.

These two features of the presidency—*national election* and *singular authority*—have enabled presidents to make use of changing demands on government to claim the position of *national leader.* It is a claim that no other official can routinely make, and it is a key to understanding the role and power of the presidency.

This chapter explains why the presidency has become a stronger office than the Framers envisioned. The chapter also examines the presidential selection process and the staffing of the modern presidency, both of which contribute to the president's prominence in the American political system. The main ideas of the chapter are these:

Cruise missile is launched toward Serbia from a U.S. bomber. American intervention against Serb forces in the Kosovo conflict was based on a presidential directive.

★ *Public expectations, national crises, and changing national and world conditions have required the presidency to become a strong office.* Underlying this development is the public support that the president acquires from being the only nationally elected official.

★ *The modern presidential election campaign is a marathon affair in which self-selected candidates must plan for a strong start in the nominating contests and center their general election strategies on media, issues, and a baseline of support.* The lengthy campaign process heightens the public's sense that the presidency is at the center of the U.S. political system.

★ *The modern presidency could not operate without a large staff of assistants, experts, and high-level managers, but the sheer size of this staff makes it impossible for the president to exercise complete control over it.*

Foundations of the Modern Presidency

Over the course of American history, each of the president's constitutional powers has been extended in practice beyond the Framers' intention. For example, the Constitution grants the president command of the nation's military, but only Congress can declare war. In *Federalist* No. 69, Alexander Hamilton wrote that a surprise attack on the United States was the only justification for war by presidential action. President Thomas Jefferson disputed even this exception, claiming that he could respond to invasion with only defensive action unless Congress declared war. Since Jefferson, however, the nation's presidents have sent troops into military action abroad more than two hundred times. Of the twelve wars included in that figure, only five were declared by Congress.[4] Each of America's most recent wars—the Korean, Vietnam, Persian Gulf, and Kosovo conflicts—was undeclared.

The Constitution also empowers the president to act as diplomatic leader with the authority to receive ambassadors and the power to initiate diplomatic relations with other nations. The president is further empowered to appoint U.S. ambassadors and to negotiate treaties with other countries, subject to approval by the Senate. The Framers anticipated that Congress would have responsibility for developing foreign policy, while the president's job would be to oversee its implementation.[5] However, the president has become the principal

THE PRESIDENT'S CONSTITUTIONAL AUTHORITY

Commander in chief. Article II, section 2: "The President shall be commander in chief of the Army and Navy of the United States, and of the militia of the several states."

Chief executive. Article II, section 2: "He may require the opinion, in writing, of the principal officer in each of the executive departments, upon any subject relating to the duties of their respective offices, and he shall have power to grant reprieves and pardons for offences against the United States, except in cases of impeachment."

Article II, section 2: "He shall have power, by and with the advice and consent of the Senate, to make treaties, provided two thirds of the senators present concur; and he shall nominate, and by and with the advice and consent of the Senate, shall appoint ambassadors, other public ministers and consuls, judges of the Supreme Court, and all other officers of the United States, whose appointments are not herein otherwise provided for, and which shall be established by law."

Article II, section 2: "The President shall have power to fill up all vacancies that may happen during the recess of the Senate, by granting commissions which shall expire at the end of their next session."

Article II, section 3: "He shall take care that the laws be faithfully executed, and shall commission all the officers of the United States."

Chief diplomat. Article II, section 2: "He shall have power, and with the advice and consent of the Senate, to make treaties, provided two thirds of the senators present concur."

Article II, section 3: "He shall receive ambassadors and other public ministers."

Legislative promoter. Article II, section 3: "He shall from time to time give to the Congress information of the state of the Union, and recommend to their consideration such measures as he shall judge necessary and expedient; he may, on extraordinary occasions, convene both houses, or either of them, and in case of disagreement between them, with respect to the time of adjournment, he may adjourn them to such time as he shall think proper."

---

architect of U.S. foreign policy and has even acquired the power to make treaty-like arrangements with other nations, in the form of executive agreements. In 1937, the Supreme Court ruled that such agreements, signed and approved only by the president, have the same legal status as treaties, which require approval by a two-thirds vote of the Senate.[6] Since World War II, presidents have negotiated more than ten thousand executive agreements, as compared with fewer than one thousand treaties ratified by the Senate.[7]

The Constitution also vests "executive power" in the president. This includes the responsibility to execute the laws faithfully and to appoint major administrators, such as heads of the various departments of the executive branch. In *Federalist* No. 76, Hamilton indicated that the president's real authority as chief executive was to be found in this appointive capacity. Presidents have indeed exercised substantial power through their appointments, but they have found their administrative authority—the power to execute the laws—to be of even greater value, because it enables them to determine how laws will be interpreted and applied. President Ronald Reagan used his executive power to *prohibit* the use of federal funds by family-planning clinics that offered abortion counseling. President Bill Clinton exerted the *same* power to *permit* the use of federal funds for this purpose. The *same* act of Congress was the basis for each of these actions. The act authorizes the use of federal funds for family-planning services but neither requires nor prohibits their use for abortion counseling, which enables the president to decide this issue.

Finally, the Constitution provides the president with legislative authority, including use of the veto and the opportunity to recommend proposals to Congress. The Framers expected this authority to be used in a limited and largely negative way. George Washington acted as the Framers anticipated: he proposed only three legislative measures and vetoed only two acts of Congress. Modern presidents have a different, more activist view of their legislative role. They routinely submit legislative proposals to Congress and often veto legislation they find disagreeable. The champion of the veto was Franklin D. Roosevelt, who during his twelve years in office rejected 635 acts of Congress.

The presidency is a more powerful office than the Framers envisioned for many reasons, but two features of the office in particular—national election and singular authority—have enabled presidents to make use of changing demands on government to claim the position of national leader.

AN EMERGING TRADITION OF STRONG PRESIDENTS

The first president to assert forcefully a claim to popular leadership was Andrew Jackson, who had been swept into office in 1828 on a tide of public support that broke the hold that the upper classes had had on the presidency until then. Jackson used his popular backing to challenge Congress's claim to national policy leadership, contending that he was "the people's tribune."

Whig theory A theory that prevailed in the nineteenth century and held that the presidency was a limited or restrained office whose occupant was confined to expressly granted constitutional authority.

Jackson's view of the presidency, however, was not shared by most of his successors during the nineteenth century, because national conditions did not routinely call for strong presidential leadership. The prevailing conception of the presidency was the **Whig theory.** In this view, the presidency was a limited or constrained office whose occupant was confined to the exercise of expressly granted constitutional authority. The president had no implicit powers for dealing with national problems but was primarily an administrator, charged with carrying out the expressed will of Congress. "My duty," said President James Buchanan, a Whig adherent, "is to execute the laws . . . and not my individual opinions."[8]

Theodore Roosevelt rejected the Whig tradition when he took office in 1901. He attacked the business trusts, pursued an aggressive foreign policy, and pressured Congress to adopt progressive domestic policies. Roosevelt embraced the **stewardship theory,** which calls for a strong, assertive presidential role that is confined only at points specifically prohibited by law, not by undefined inherent restrictions.[9] As "steward of the people," Roosevelt said, he was permitted "to do anything that the needs of the Nation demanded unless such action was forbidden by the Constitution or by the laws."[10]

stewardship theory A theory that argues for a strong, assertive presidential role, with presidential authority limited only at points specifically prohibited by law.

Roosevelt's image of a strong presidency was shared by Woodrow Wilson, but his other immediate successors reverted to the Whig notion of the limited presidency.[11] Herbert Hoover's restrained conception of the presidency prevented him from taking decisive action even during the economic devastation that followed the Wall Street crash of 1929. Hoover argued that he lacked the constitutional authority to establish public relief programs for jobless and penniless Americans.

Hoover's successor, Franklin D. Roosevelt, shared the stewardship theory of his distant cousin Theodore Roosevelt, and FDR's New Deal signaled the end of the limited presidency. Today the presidency is an inherently strong office.[12] The

The Mochida family awaits forced evacuation. The children are wearing identification tags that were required by authorities. The Mochidas and thousands of other Japanese Americans were shipped from the West Coast to inland detention camps during World War II. The forced evacuation was ordered by President Roosevelt and upheld as constitutional by the Supreme Court.

modern presidency becomes a more substantial office in the hands of a persuasive leader such as Lyndon Johnson or Ronald Reagan, but even a less forceful person such as Jimmy Carter or Gerald Ford is now expected to act assertively. This expectation is not only the legacy of former strong presidents but also the result of the need for presidential leadership in periods of national crisis and of changes that have occurred in the federal government's national and international policy responsibilities.

THE NEED FOR PRESIDENTIAL LEADERSHIP IN NATIONAL CRISES

National crises have enabled presidents to assume powers beyond those provided in the Constitution. Emergencies usually demand speed of action and singleness of purpose. The president, as sole head of the executive branch, has this capacity. Abraham Lincoln's response to the outbreak of the Civil War is a notable example. Acting on his own authority, Lincoln called up the militia, blockaded southern ports, increased the size of the Army and Navy, ordered conscription, suspended the writ of habeas corpus, and placed part of the nation under martial law. Some of these actions (for example, suspension of the writ of habeas corpus) are not clearly assigned to the president by the Constitution. Nevertheless, when Congress convened in 1861, after Lincoln's war orders had already taken effect, it acknowledged the validity of his actions by passing a law stating that his directives had the same authority "as if they had been issued and done under the previous express authority and direction of the Congress of the United States."[13]

Similarly, Congress formally endorsed Franklin Roosevelt's directive, issued in the wake of the Japanese attack on Pearl Harbor in 1941, that ordered the evacuation of 135,000 Japanese Americans living on the West Coast. Fearing subversive activities among these Japanese Americans, Roosevelt instructed federal authorities to seize their property and relocate them in detention camps farther inland until the war's end. Japanese Americans challenged the legality

★ CRITICAL THINKING ★

WHAT'S YOUR OPINION?

The Increase in Presidential Power
It has been said that constitutionality bends to necessity. How does the axiom help explain the increased power and responsibility that the president has acquired during the twentieth century? Is the axiom strictly accurate, given that the provisions for presidential authority in Article II of the Constitution are relatively vague in any case?

of Roosevelt's order, but the Supreme Court upheld their forced evacuation from coastal areas (although it voided their involuntary detention).[14]

In such instances, the other branches of government have had little choice but to accept presidential claims to extraordinary powers. Constitutionality has given way to perceived necessity in times of crisis. Lincoln's critics called him a dictator, but a congressional majority affirmed that his extraconstitutional actions were necessary if the Union was to be saved.

National crises have had a lasting impact on the conduct of the executive office. Modern presidents are expected to be powerful in part because some of their predecessors assumed extraordinary powers in critical times. Lincoln, Roosevelt, and other strong presidents left a legacy for later presidents. Every strong president has seen the power of the office as flowing from a special relationship with the American people. As Harry S Truman noted in his memoirs, "I believe that the power of the President should be used in the interest of the people and in order to do that the President must use whatever power the Constitution does not expressly deny him."[15]

THE NEED FOR PRESIDENTIAL LEADERSHIP OF AN ACTIVIST GOVERNMENT

During most of the nineteenth century, the United States did not need a strong president. The federal government's policymaking role was small, as was its bureaucracy. Moreover, the nation's major issues were of a sectional nature (especially the North-South split over slavery) and thus suited to action by Congress, which represented state and local interests. The U.S. government's role in world affairs was also small.

Today the situation has greatly changed. The federal government has such broad national and international responsibilities that strong leadership from presidents is essential.

Foreign Policy Leadership

The president has always been the foreign policy leader of the United States, but during the nation's first century that role was a rather undemanding one. The United States avoided getting entangled in the turbulent politics of Europe, and though it was involved in foreign trade, its major preoccupation was its internal development. By the end of the nineteenth century, however, the nation was seeking to expand the world market for its goods, and the size and growing industrial power of the United States was attracting more attention from other nations. President Theodore Roosevelt advocated an American economic empire, looking south toward Latin America and west toward Hawaii, the Philippines, and China (the "Open Door" policy) for new markets. However, the United States' tradition of isolationism remained a powerful influence on national policy. The United States fought in World War I but immediately thereafter demobilized its armed forces. Over President Woodrow Wilson's objections, Congress then voted against the entry of the United States into the League of Nations.

World War II fundamentally changed the nation's international role and the president's role in foreign policy. In 1945 the United States emerged as a global

Harry S Truman's presidency was characterized by bold foreign policy initiatives. He authorized the use of nuclear weapons against Japan in 1945, created the Marshall Plan as the basis for the economic reconstruction of postwar Europe, and sent U.S. troops to fight in Korea in 1950. Truman is shown here greeting British Prime Minister Winston Churchill at a Washington airport in early 1952.

superpower, a giant in world trade, and the recognized leader of the noncommunist world. The United States today has a military presence in nearly every part of the globe and an unprecedented interest in trade balances, energy supplies, and other international issues affecting the nation.

The effects of these developments on America's political institutions have been largely one-sided. Because of the president's constitutional authority as chief diplomat and military commander and the special demands of foreign policy leadership, the president, not Congress, has taken the lead in addressing the United States' increased responsibilities in the world. Foreign policy requires singleness of purpose and, at times, fast action. Congress—a large, divided, and often unwieldy institution—is poorly suited to such a response. In contrast, the president, as sole head of the executive branch, can act quickly and speak authoritatively for the nation as a whole in its relations with other nations.

This capacity was evident during the cold war when the threat of Soviet communism bolstered presidential leadership of U.S. foreign policy. Since then, global economic issues have become increasingly important, and Congress has been less deferential to the president. In 1998, for example, Congress refused to extend the president's authority to negotiate comprehensive trade agreements with other countries; members of Congress wanted a stronger say over these agreements since they have implications for U.S. firms and workers. It is also the case that America's traditional allies have been less willing to let the president define their foreign policy agendas. During the cold war, they regularly deferred to the United States because its military might was the foundation of their national security. But as global economic issues have risen to the fore, their interests compete with those of the United States. Nevertheless, the president

HOW THE UNITED STATES COMPARES

HEADS OF STATE AND HEADS OF GOVERNMENT

Most democracies divide the executive office between a head of state, who is the ceremonial leader, and a head of government, who is the policy leader. In Great Britain, these positions are filled by the queen and the prime minister, respectively. In democracies without a hereditary monarchy, the position of head of state is usually held by an individual chosen by the legislature. Germany's head of state, for example, is a president, who is elected by the Federal Assembly; the head of government is a chancellor, who is chosen by the majority party in the lower house (Bundestag) of the Federal Assembly. The United States is one of a few countries in which the roles of head of state and head of government are combined in a single office, the presidency. The major disadvantage of this arrangement is that the president must devote considerable time to ceremonial functions, such as hosting dinners for visiting heads of state. The major advantage is that the president alone is the center of national attention.

Country	Head of State	Head of Government
Canada	Governor general (representative of the British monarch)	Prime minister
France	President	Premier
Germany	President	Chancellor
Great Britain	Queen	Prime minister
Italy	President	Prime minister
Japan	Emperor	Prime minister
Mexico	President	President
Sweden	King	Prime minister
United States	President	President

remains the dominant force in U.S. foreign policy and the leader to whom many countries turn when global problems surface.

Domestic Policy Leadership

The change in the president's domestic leadership has also been substantial. Throughout most of the nineteenth century, Congress jealously guarded its constitutional powers, making it clear that domestic policy was its business. James Bryce wrote in the 1880s that Congress paid no more attention to the president's views on legislation than it did to the editorial positions of prominent newspaper publishers.[16]

By the early twentieth century, however, the national government was taking on regulatory and policy responsibilities imposed by the nation's transition from an agrarian to an industrial society, and stronger presidential leadership was becoming necessary. In 1921, Congress conceded that it lacked the centralized authority to coordinate the growing national budget and enacted the Budget and Accounting Act, which provided for an executive budget. Federal departments and agencies would no longer submit their annual budget requests directly to Congress. The president would oversee the initiation of the budget, developing the various agencies' requests into a comprehensive budgetary proposal that would then be submitted to Congress as a baseline for its deliberations.

During the Great Depression of the 1930s, Franklin D. Roosevelt's New Deal responded to the public's demand for economic relief with a broad program that involved a level of policy planning and coordination that was beyond the capacity of Congress. In addition to initiating public works projects and social welfare programs aimed at providing immediate relief, the New Deal made the government a partner in nearly every aspect of the nation's economy. If economic regulation was to work, unified and continuous policy leadership was needed, and only the president could provide it. Later, Congress institutionalized the president's economic role with the Employment Act of 1946, which assigns to the federal government an ongoing responsibility "to use all practicable means . . . to promote maximum employment, production, and purchasing power."

Roosevelt's power, like that of the strong presidents before him, rested on the support of the American people.[17] In the early 1930s, the nation was in such desperate condition that Americans would have supported almost anything Roosevelt did. "If he burned down the Capitol," said the humorist Will Rogers, "we would cheer and say 'Well, we at least got a fire started.' "[18]

Presidential authority has continued to grow since Roosevelt's time. In response to pressures from the public, the national government's role in such areas as education, health, welfare, safety, and protection of the environment has expanded greatly, which in turn has created additional demands for presidential leadership.[19] Big government, with its emphasis on comprehensive planning and program coordination, favors executive authority at the expense of legislative authority. All democracies have seen a shift in power from their legislature to their executive. In Britain, for example, the prime minister has taken on responsibilities that once belonged to the cabinet or the parliament.

The president's preeminence as domestic policy leader does not mean that Congress no longer plays a significant role. As we saw in Chapter 13, major policy initiatives do emanate from Congress, which also modifies or rejects many presidential proposals. Moreover, Congress tends to seek the president's leadership only on particular types of legislative measures—principally those that address truly national issues from a national perspective. (The president's domestic and foreign policy roles are discussed further in Chapter 15.)

Choosing the President

As the president's policy and leadership responsibilities changed during the nation's history, so did the process of electing presidents. The changes do not parallel each other exactly, but they are related politically and philosophically. As the presidency drew ever closer to the people, their role in selecting the president grew ever more important.

THE DEVELOPMENT OF THE PRESIDENTIAL SELECTION SYSTEM

The process by which the United States selects its chief executive has evolved through four cumulative systems (summarized in Table 14-1 and described here), each of which resulted from popular reforms that were aimed chiefly at granting the American people a larger say in choosing the president. The justification for each of the reforms was **legitimacy,** the idea that the selection of the president should be based on the will of the people as expressed through their votes.[20]

legitimacy (of election) The idea that the selection of officeholders should be based on the will of the people as expressed through their votes.

TABLE 14-1   The Four Systems of Presidential Selection

Selection System	Period	Features
1. Original	1788–1828	Party nominees are chosen in congressional caucuses.
		Electoral College members act somewhat independently in their presidential voting.
2. Party convention	1832–1900	Party nominees are chosen in national party conventions by delegates selected by state and local party organizations.
		Electoral College members cast their ballots for the popular-vote winner in their respective states.
3. Party convention, primary	1904–1968	As in system 2, except that a *minority* of national convention delegates are chosen through primary elections (the majority still being chosen by party organizations).
4. Party primary, open caucus	1972–present	As in system 2, except that a *majority* of national convention delegates are chosen through primary elections.

The First and Second Systems: Electors and Party Conventions

The delegates to the constitutional convention of 1787 were steadfastly opposed to popular election of the president. They feared that popular election would make the office too centralized and too powerful, which would undermine the principles of federalism and separation of powers. The Framers devised a novel system, which came to be called the Electoral College. Under the Constitution, the president is chosen by a vote of electors who are appointed by the states. Each state is entitled to as many electors as it has members of Congress. The candidate who receives the majority of electoral votes is elected president.

In the first two presidential elections, the electors unanimously selected George Washington, the only presidential candidate in history to receive the votes of all electors. Nevertheless, the Framers anticipated that in some elections no candidate would gain the electoral majority required by the Constitution, in which case the House of Representatives (with each state having one vote) would select the president from among the top five vote getters (later changed to the top three by the Twelfth Amendment). The House soon did decide an election, choosing Thomas Jefferson in 1800.

Jefferson's election by the House resulted from a development that the Framers had not foreseen. In its original form, the Constitution provided that each elector would cast two ballots. The candidate who placed first, provided that the candidate received the votes of a majority of electors, became president, and the second-place candidate became vice president. The Framers had not anticipated the emergence of political parties and the formation of party tickets. In 1800, Jefferson teamed with vice presidential candidate Aaron Burr on the

Republican party's ticket, and each elector who voted for Jefferson also voted for Burr. This strategy led to a tie and nearly a constitutional crisis when Burr tried to persuade the Federalists in Congress to elect him as president. Jefferson finally prevailed on the thirty-sixth House ballot. After he took office, the Twelfth Amendment was enacted to prevent ties in the Electoral College. The amendment provides that each elector shall cast one ballot for a presidential candidate and one ballot for a vice presidential candidate.

In the 1790s, party members in Congress assumed the power to name a presidential nominee. Their choice was not binding on the electors, who could vote as they pleased; but the need for party unity and the prestige of the Congress led some electors to follow the recommendation of their party's congressional caucus, earning it the title of "King Caucus."[21]

In choosing the nation's first presidents, electors often acted somewhat independently, exercising their own judgment in casting their votes. This pattern changed after the election in 1828 of Andrew Jackson, who believed the people's will had been denied four years earlier when he placed first in the popular voting but failed to gain an electoral majority. Jackson could not persuade Congress to support a constitutional amendment that would have eliminated the Electoral College but did obtain the next-best alternative: he persuaded the states to tie their electoral vote to the popular vote. U.S. elections are regulated primarily by state law, and state legislatures are empowered by the Constitution to determine the method of selection of their state's electors. Under Jackson's reform, which is still in effect today, each party in a state has a separate slate of electors who gain the right to cast a state's electoral votes if their party's candidate places first in the state's popular voting. Thus the popular vote for the candidates directly affects their electoral vote. Although the same candidate is likely to win both forms of the presidential vote, there have been several elections, including the one in 2000, where the popular-vote winner has either lost or nearly lost the electoral vote.

Jackson also eliminated King Caucus. In 1832, he convened a national party convention to nominate the Democratic presidential candidate. The parties had their strength at the grass roots, among the people, whereas Congress was dominated by the wealthy interests against which Jackson was fighting. Since Jackson's time, presidential nominees have been formally chosen at national party conventions.

The Third and Fourth Systems: Primaries and Open Races

The system of presidential selection that Jackson had created remained intact until the early twentieth century, when the Progressives initiated primary elections as a way of wresting control over presidential nominations from party bosses (see Chapter 3). However, most states either stayed with the older system of party selection or adopted nonbinding primaries. As a result, party leaders continued to control a majority of the convention delegates who selected the presidential nominees.

Through 1968, a strong showing in the primaries enabled a candidate to demonstrate popular support but did not guarantee nomination. In 1952, for example, Senator Estes Kefauver beat President Harry Truman in New Hampshire's opening primary and went on to win twelve of the thirteen primaries he

John F. Kennedy was the first president whose nomination clearly derived from victories in the primaries. As a Catholic and a junior senator, Kennedy had no chance of winning the Democratic presidential nomination in 1960 unless his primary campaign was successful. Kennedy is shown campaigning in West Virginia, a heavily Protestant state whose primary he won.

open party caucuses   Meetings at which a party's candidates for nomination are voted on and that are open to all the party's rank-and-file voters who want to attend.

entered. However, Kefauver was denied nomination by party leaders, who believed that his views were inconsistent with the party's traditions.

In 1968, the Democratic nomination went to Vice President Hubert Humphrey, who had not entered a single primary and was closely identified with the Johnson administration's Vietnam war policy. After Humphrey narrowly lost the 1968 general election to Richard Nixon, reform-minded Democrats forced changes in the nominating process. The new rules gave rank-and-file party voters more control by requiring that states choose their delegates through either primary elections or **open party caucuses** (meetings open to any registered party voter who wants to attend). Although the Democrats initiated the change, the Republicans were also affected by it. Most states that adopted a presidential primary in order to comply with the Democrats' new rules also required Republicans to select their convention delegates through a primary.

Today it is the voters in state primaries and open caucuses who play the decisive role in the selection of the Democratic and Republican presidential nominees.[22] A state's delegates are awarded the candidates in accordance with how well they do in the state's primary or caucus. Thus, to win the majority of national convention delegates necessary for nomination, a candidate must place first in a lot of states and do at least reasonably well in most of the rest. (In recent presidential elections, about three-fourths of the states have chosen their delegates through a primary election while one-fourth have used a caucus system.)

In sum, the presidential election system has changed from an elite-dominated process to one that is based on popular support. The voters, in effect, choose both the president and the presidential nominees. This arrangement has

CURRENT CONTROVERSIES

SHOULD THE ELECTORAL COLLEGE BE ABOLISHED?

As the votes in the 2000 election were counted, the country was thrown into turmoil by the exisxtence of the electoral vote system. The president is chosen by an indirect system of election. Voters cast ballots for candidates but their votes choose only each state's electors, whose subsequent ballots then result in the actual selection of the president. Electoral votes are apportioned by states based on their representation in Congress (see pages 392-393), which creates the possibility that the canadiate who gets the most popular votes will not get the most electoral votes and thus not be elected president. The 2000 election renewed calls for the abolition of the electoral vote system.

YES: Only the President and Vice President of the United States are currently elected indirectly by the Electoral College—and not by the voting citizens of this country. All other elected officials, from the local officeholder up to United States senator, are elected directly by the people. Our bill will replace the complicated electoral college system with the simple method of using the popular vote to decide the winner of a presidential election. By switching to a direct voting system, we can avoid the result of electing a President who failed to win the popular vote.

—U.S. Representative Ray LaHood (R-Illinois)

NO: [The electoral college has outgrown its usefulness] only if we think the states as semi-sovereign entities have outgrown their usefulness, which many people believe but many do not. Wyoming with its 479,000 people gets the same two senators as California with its 33 million. The electoral college is designed to reflect the same idea. And it is an idea that is also reflected in the way in which each country gets one vote in the General Assembly of the United Nations and [in] the system of representation of the European Union. The electoral college recognizes the equal status of the states, regardless of their population.

—Frederick Schauer, Harvard University professor

strengthened the president by providing the office with the reserve of power that popular election confers on democratic leadership.

THE CAMPAIGN FOR NOMINATION

The modern presidential selection process is a long and grinding process that bears almost no resemblance to the way in which other democratic countries select their chief executives. When Tony Blair gained the office of British prime minister in 1997, the formal campaign lasted just a few weeks. By comparison, a U.S. presidential campaign officially spans nine months and actually starts much earlier. The main reason the U.S. campaign lasts so long is that the voters choose the nominees as well as the final winner. No European democracy uses primary elections as a means of choosing its nominees for public office.

The fact that the voters pick the nominees has made the nominating races more competitive than ever before. The system is basically open to any politician with the energy and resources to run a major national campaign. Nominating campaigns, except those in which an incumbent president is seeking reelection, often attract a half-dozen or more candidates. The 2000 Republican race, for

Presidential nominating campaigns often attract a large number of contenders. Early in the 2000 presidential race, there were nearly a dozen GOP candidates. By the time of the first contests in Iowa and New Hampshire, six candidates still remained. Pictured here in one of their televised debates are (left to right) activist Gary Bauer, Senator John McCain, Governor George W. Bush, publisher Steve Forbes, former ambassador Alan Keyes, and Senator Orrin Hatch.

example, at one time included nearly a dozen contenders, including a governor (Bush), a former governor (Alexander), a former vice president (Quayle), two U.S. senators (McCain and Hatch), a former cabinet member (Dole), a former ambassador (Keyes), a political advocate (Bauer), and a millionaire publisher (Forbes).

Media and Momentum

momentum   A strong showing by a candidate in early presidential nominating contests, which leads to a buildup of public support for the candidate.

A key to success in the nominating campaign is **momentum**—a strong showing in the early contests that leads to a buildup of public support in subsequent ones. If candidates start off poorly, reporters will lose interest in covering them, contributors will deny them funding, political leaders will not endorse them, and voters will not give further thought to supporting them. For these reasons, presidential contenders now give extraordinary attention to the early contests, particularly the first caucuses in Iowa and the first primary in New Hampshire.

Voting in primaries is not affected by partisan loyalties, since all candidates are of the same party. Without partisanship as an anchor, vote swings in response to momentum can be substantial. After Michael Dukakis won the New Hampshire primary in 1988, his nationwide support among Democratic voters in polls doubled. Most New Hampshire winners have, like Dukakis, gained significant public support after the primary.

Money is a critical factor in the nominating races. Money has long been a key to success in presidential politics, and its importance has grown in the last decade as states have moved their primaries and caucuses to the early weeks of the nominating period in order to increase their influence on the outcome. For example, in the first two months of the year 2000 presidential campaign, thirty-five state contests were scheduled. To compete effectively in so many contests in such a short period, candidates need money—lots of it. A candidate can be in only one place at a time, which requires that the campaign be carried to other voters through televised political advertising. Ads are expensive to produce and air, and analysts claim that it takes at least $20 million to run a competitive nominating campaign. George W. Bush raised more than $70 million in 2000 for his successful nominating campaign, far more than any of his Republican rivals.

Although money and momentum help explain nominating outcomes, they do not account for initial success or enduring appeal. Why does one candidate start strongly or maintain strength while another does not? There is no single answer, but a candidate must have strength of one kind or another to prevail. Issues can be important: the main reason George McGovern won the Democratic nomination in 1972 was that his anti-Vietnam stance attracted a stable and committed voting bloc.

Name recognition is another factor. Robert Dole owed much of his success in 1996 to the fact that he was better known than his challengers when the campaign began. Al Gore's label as "the early front-runner" for the 2000 Democratic nomination was a result of the name recognition he had acquired as vice president. Since 1968, the preprimary poll leader in contested nominations has won most of the time.

Candidates in primary elections are assisted by the Federal Election Campaign Act of 1974 (as amended in 1979). This act gives federal "matching funds" to any candidate who raises at least $5,000 in individual contributions of up to $250 in each of twenty states. Candidates who accept matching funds must agree to limit their expenditures to a set amount, which is adjusted each election year to account for inflation. The spending limit for each candidate in the nominating stage of the 2000 presidential campaign was roughly $40 million. (Because Bush went over the spending limit, he was ineligible for matching funds.)

www.mhhe.com/patterson5

Simulation

The National Party Conventions

After the state primaries and caucuses have been held, the national party conventions occur. These were once tumultuous affairs during which lengthy, heated bargaining took place before a presidential nominee was chosen. An extreme case was the Democratic convention of 1924, at which delegates took 103 ballots and ended up nominating an unknown "dark horse," John W. Davis. Today's conventions are relatively tame; not since 1952 has a nomination gone past the first ballot. The leading candidate has usually acquired enough delegates in the primaries and caucuses to lock up the nomination before the convention even begins. Nevertheless, the party convention is a major event. It brings together the delegates elected in state caucuses and primaries, who then vote to approve a party platform and to nominate the party's presidential and vice presidential candidates. National conventions are occasions for cementing party unity and building bridges to party voters. As many as 50 million Americans watch part of the proceedings on national television, and for many of them it is a time of decision. About a fifth of voters solidify their presidential choice during the conventions, and most of them decide to back the nominee of their preferred party.[23]

All recent nominees have received a "bounce" in the polls from their party's convention. In 1992, Bill Clinton was deadlocked in the polls going into the convention but came out with a big lead. Ross Perot's abrupt (though temporary) withdrawal from the race and a show of party unity at the convention combined to give Clinton a twenty-seven-point lead over George Bush. The 1992 Republican National Convention was a more heated gathering that focused on

George W. Bush waves to convention delegates after his speech accepting the 2000 Republican nomination. Laura Bush, the candidate's wife, is on the left; on the right is Dick Cheney, the Republican vice-presidental nominee.

social issues such as abortion and illegitimacy, and it had a polarizing effect on the electorate. Bush gained eight points during the convention week but lost most of this gain after only a few days. Clinton's bounce in 1992 was the highest ever recorded by polls, while Bush's net gain was among the lowest. In 2000, both Al Gore and George W. Bush received a sizeable convention bounce, but Gore's was the larger one and thrust him into a lead in the race which he held until the October presidential debates.

The party conventions choose the vice presidential nominees as well as those for president. By tradition, the vice presidential selection rests with the presidential nominee. Critics have argued that the vice presidential nomination should be decided in open competition, because the vice president stands a good chance of becoming president someday. The chief argument for keeping the existing system is that the president needs a trusted and like-minded vice president.

THE CAMPAIGN FOR ELECTION

The winner in the November general election is almost certain to be either the Republican or the Democratic nominee. A minor-party or independent candidate can draw votes away from the major-party nominees but stands almost no chance of defeating them. A major-party nominee has the critical advantage of support from the party faithful. Although party loyalty has declined in recent decades (see Chapters 6 and 8), two-thirds of the nation's voters still identify themselves as Democrats or Republicans, and a substantial majority of them support their party's presidential candidate.[24] Even Democrat George McGovern, who had the lowest level of party support among recent nominees, was backed in 1972 by 60 percent of his party's voters.

Perot's presidential bids illustrate the problem of the independent candidate (see Figure 14-1). In 1992, he was able to woo only 15 percent of Democratic and Republican identifiers to his column. The percentage was even lower in 1996.

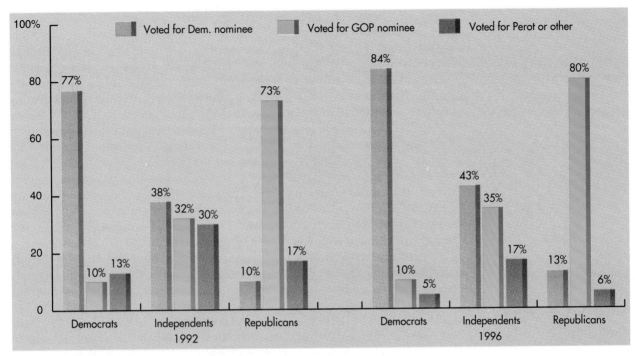

FIGURE 14-1 Partisanship and the Presidential Vote, 1992–1996
The major-party nominees have a built-in advantage over independent and third-party candidates: two-thirds of voters identify with a major party and most of them vote for their party's nominee.
Source: National Election Studies.

Perot ran strongly among independent voters in 1992, but because they constitute only a third of the electorate, he effectively had no chance of beating either Clinton or Bush.

Election Strategy

Presidential candidates act strategically. In deciding on a course of action, they try to estimate its likely impact on the voters. For incumbents and challengers alike, some of these issues will be questions of past performance. During the 1992 campaign, a sign on the wall of Clinton's headquarters read, "The Economy, Stupid." The slogan was the idea of James Carville, Clinton's chief strategist, and was meant as a reminder to keep the campaign focused on the nation's sluggish economy, which ultimately was the issue that got Clinton elected. In 2000, past performance was an issue for both sides—Al Gore played up the booming economy while George W. Bush played up White House morals.

Other issues will be questions of future performance. In 1996, Dole based his campaign on a proposed 15 percent cut in personal income taxes. The proposal did not boost Dole's candidacy as much as he had hoped, perhaps because it appeared to contradict his earlier pledge to give priority to balancing the federal budget but most likely because he was running against an incumbent when the economy was strong. This situation is the most difficult of all for a challenger: it nearly always ends in defeat.

Candidates try to project a strong leadership image. Whether voters accept this image, however, depends more on external factors than on a candidate's personal characteristics. In 1991, after the Persian Gulf War, Bush's approval rating reached

91 percent, the highest level recorded since polling began in the 1930s. A year later, with the Gulf War a receding memory and the nation's economy in trouble, Bush's approval rating dropped below 40 percent. Bush tried to stir images of his strong leadership of the war, but voters remained preoccupied with the economy.

The candidates' strategies are shaped by many considerations, including the constitutional provision that each state shall have electoral votes equal in number to its representation in Congress. Each state thus gets two electoral votes for its Senate representation and a varying number of electoral votes depending on its House representation (see "States in the Nation"). Altogether, there are 538 electoral votes (including three for the District of Columbia, even though it has no voting representatives in Congress). To win the presidency, a candidate must receive at least 270 votes, an electoral majority. (If no candidate receives a majority, the election is decided in the House of Representatives. No president since 1824 has been elected in this way. The procedure is defined by the Constitution's Twelfth Amendment, which is reprinted in this book's appendix.)

unit rule   The rule that grants all of a state's electoral votes to the candidate who receives most of the popular votes in the state.

The importance of the electoral votes is magnified by the existence of the **unit rule;** all the states except Maine and Nebraska grant all their electoral votes as a unit to the candidate who wins the state's popular vote. For this reason, candidates are particularly concerned with winning the most populous states, such as California (with 54 electoral votes), New York (33), Texas (32), Florida (25), Pennsylvania (23), Illinois (22), and Ohio (21). Victory in the eleven largest states alone would provide an electoral majority, and presidential candidates therefore spend most of their time campaigning in those states.[25]

The electoral vote system creates the possibility that the winner of the popular vote may lose the election. This is a significant, though infrequent, limit to the popular election of a president. In the 2000 campaign, the presidential election hung in the balance because of the electoral vote. Al Gore narrowly was the popular vote nationwide but the election came down to Florida with its 25 electoral votes. Neither Gore nor his Republican opponent, George W. Bush, had a clear-cut claim to victory in Florida, which cast both the question of the next president and the legitimacy of that presidency into doubt. The Bush–Gore election stirred calls for an end to the electoral vote system. Most Americans say they would favor a change but the difficult process of constitutional amendment leaves open the question of whether the electoral college will still be in effect in 2004.

Media and Money

The modern presidential campaign is a media campaign. At one time, candidates relied heavily on party organization and rallies to carry their messages to the voters, but now they rely on the media, particularly television. Candidates strive to produce the pithy ten-second sound bites that the television networks prefer to highlight on the evening newscasts. In recent elections, they have also discovered the power of the "new media," appearing on such television programs as *Larry King Live* and establishing their own Internet sites.

Television is the forum for the major confrontation of the fall campaign—the presidential debates. The first televised debate took place in 1960 between Kennedy and Nixon, and an estimated one hundred million people saw at least one of their four debates.[26] Televised debates resumed in 1976 and have become an apparently permanent fixture of presidential campaigns. Studies indicate that presidential debates influence the votes of only a small percentage of the

★ CRITICAL THINKING ★

WHAT'S YOUR OPINION?

The New Elite in the Nomination Process
The process of choosing presidential nominees has greatly changed in the past few decades. Among other things, the old elite of party leaders—governors, mayors, members of Congress, and party chairs—has given way to a new elite of journalists and the candidates' hired consultants—pollsters, media specialists, and the like. What are the implications of this shift? In regard to this change alone, is the new system an improvement over the old?

★ STATES IN THE NATION

ELECTORAL VOTES AND THE 2000 ELECTION

There are a total of 538 electoral votes, and a candidate must receive a majority to win the presidency. In 2000, George W. Bush was elected with 271 electoral votes—one more than required. Bush finished second in the popular voting, receiving 50.5 million popular votes to Al Gore's 51.0 million. Electoral votes are linked to popular votes—the winner of the popular vote in a state gets its electoral votes. (Exceptions are Maine and Nebraska where the statewide winner gets two votes and congressional district winners get one vote for each district they win.) Because electoral votes are allocated on a state-by-state basis, the loser of the national popular vote can gain an electoral-vote majority. Bush is the first president since Benjamin Harrison in 1888 to win the presidency in this way. The 2000 election was decided by the Florida vote. Bush received Florida's 25 electoral votes by virtue of a 930-vote popular margin that excluded ballots that could not be read by voting machines. The U.S. Supreme Court blocked a count of these ballots (see Chapter 17).

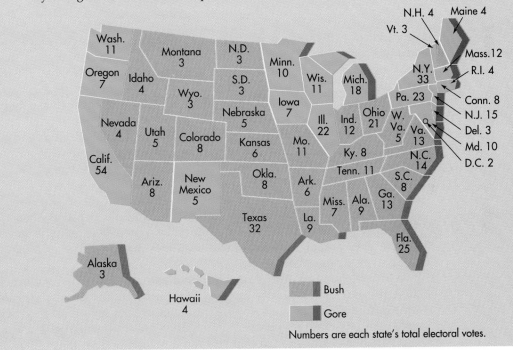

Numbers are each state's total electoral votes.

electorate. However, presidential elections are sometimes decided by a small margin, and the debates can then make a difference. In 2000, Gore had an edge in the polls before the first debate. He was also the more experienced debater and had a firmer grasp of policy issues. But Gore drew a negative response from viewers when he huffed and grimaced while Bush was talking. Meanwhile, Bush gave a stronger performance than pundits had expected, which led them to conclude he had helped his candidacy. Gore was unable in the second and third debates to overcome fully the image created by his performance in the first debate, which some analysts believe was a key turning point in the 2000 campaign.

The television campaign includes political advertising. Televised commercials are by far the most expensive part of presidential campaign politics. Since 1976, political commercials on television have accounted for about half the

Television is the principal medium of presidential politics, although some analysts predict that the Internet may someday have that position. Pictured here is a televised political ad for the 2000 Democratic presidential hopeful Bill Bradley. Senator Daniel Patrick Moynihan (D-NY) is shown speaking on Bradley's behalf.

candidates' expenditures in the general election campaign. Kathleen Hall Jamieson describes the role of advertising in the modern campaign as "packaging the presidency."[27] In 2000, Bush and Gore each spent more than $30 million on advertising in the general election.

The importance that candidates attach to televised ads rests partly on the unreliability of news coverage. Journalists tend to emphasize the strategic game played by the candidates—who's ahead and who's behind, and why—rather than the candidates' policy positions or leadership capabilities. Election news also has a negative slant: "bad news" takes precedence over "good news."[28] Rumors and allegations of marital infidelity made their way into the news of the Clinton campaigns in 1992 and 1996, and the Bush campaign in 2000 had to deal with allegations of cocaine and alcohol abuse. Candidate blunders also prompt a media feeding frenzy. When Dole fell off a stage during the 1996 campaign, he got bigger headlines than he did when announcing most of his major policy stands.

Televised political advertising is also a source of negative messages. Although candidates typically emphasize their own candidacies, they do not shrink from attacking their foes. Media consultants have perfected what is called the "attack ad"—a blistering assault on the opponent. A classic example is a 1988 Bush campaign ad that showed a revolving door that was meant to represent the Massachusetts prison furlough program. The ad implied that Dukakis, Bush's opponent and the governor of Massachusetts, was personally responsible for the actions of furloughed prisoners. One such prisoner was the notorious Willie Horton, who raped a Maryland woman and brutalized her husband after escaping during a prison furlough. The "revolving door" ad has been credited with helping Bush defeat Dukakis, who at one point in the race led by as many as fifteen percentage points. Such advertising may do more than turn voters away from a candidate. Research suggests that it may discourage some people from voting on election day.[29]

The Republican and Democratic nominees are each eligible for federal funding of their general election campaigns. The grant was set at $20 million in 1975 and has been adjusted for inflation in succeeding elections. The major-party

---

FORMAL AND INFORMAL REQUIREMENTS FOR BECOMING PRESIDENT

Formal Requirements. Article II of the U.S. Constitution requires a president to be:
• At least thirty-five years old
• A natural-born U.S. citizen
• A resident in the United States for at least fourteen years

Informal Requirements. In the nation's history, presidents have been:
• Male, without exception
• White, without exception

• Protestant, with the exception of John F. Kennedy
• Married, with the exceptions of James Buchanan and Grover Cleveland (who married in the White House)
• Career public servants—four were army generals, thirteen were vice presidents (seven succeeded upon a president's death, one upon a president's resignation), eight were federal administrators, and the remainder were U.S. senators, U.S. representatives (only one), or state governors.

---

nominees in the 2000 presidential election each received more than $65 million. The only string attached to this money is that candidates who accept it can spend no additional funds on their campaigns (although the party can spend additional money on their behalf; see Chapter 9).

Candidates can choose not to accept public funding, in which case the amount they spend is limited only by their ability to raise money privately. However, all major-party nominees since 1976 have accepted public funding. Other candidates for the presidency qualify for federal funding if they receive at least 5 percent of the vote and do not spend more than $50,000 of their own money on the campaign. In 1992, Perot spent over $60 million of his own money and thus was ineligible for federal funding. He accepted federal funding in 1996, receiving about half as much as the major-party nominees, since in 1992 his vote total was roughly half that averaged by the two major-party candidates. In 2000, Perot's party, the Reform party, received more than $10 million in federal funding by virtue of Perot's 8 percent of the vote in 1996.

The Winners

The Constitution specifies only that the president must be at least thirty-five years old, a natural-born U.S. citizen, and a U.S. resident for at least fourteen years. Yet the winners of all recent presidential elections, as it has been throughout the nation's history, have been white males. The great majority of presidents have also been well-to-do Anglo-Saxon Protestants. Only one Catholic (Kennedy) has been elected. Except for four army generals, no person has won the presidency who has not first held high public office (see Table 14-2). Nearly a third of the nation's presidents had previously been vice presidents, and most of the rest were former U.S. senators, state governors, or top federal executives. The vice presidency in particular has been the inside track to the presidency. About a third of the nation's presidents had first served as vice president.

www.mhhe.com/patterson5

Graphic

TABLE 14-2 The Path to the White House

President	Years in Office	Highest Previous Office	Second-Highest Office
Theodore Roosevelt	1901–1908	Vice president*	Governor
William Howard Taft	1909–1912	Secretary of war	Federal judge
Woodrow Wilson	1913–1920	Governor	None
Warren G. Harding	1921–1924	U.S. senator	Lieutenant governor
Calvin Coolidge	1925–1928	Vice president*	Governor
Herbert Hoover	1929–1932	Secretary of commerce	War relief administrator
Franklin D. Roosevelt	1933–1945	Governor	Assistant secretary of Navy
Harry S Truman	1945–1952	Vice president*	U.S. senator
Dwight D. Eisenhower	1953–1960	None (Army general)	None
John F. Kennedy	1961–1963	U.S. senator	U.S. representative
Lyndon Johnson	1963–1968	Vice president*	U.S. senator
Richard Nixon	1969–1974	Vice president	U.S. senator
Gerald Ford	1974–1976	Vice president*	U.S. representative
Jimmy Carter	1977–1980	Governor	State senator
Ronald Reagan	1981–1988	Governor	None
George Bush	1989–1992	Vice president	Director, CIA
Bill Clinton	1993–2000	Governor	State attorney general
George W. Bush	2001–	Governor	None

*Became president on death or resignation of incumbent.

Staffing the Presidency

On election day, Americans are actually choosing more than a president. They are also picking a secretary of state, an FBI director, and a host of other executives, all of whom are presidential appointees. Newly elected presidents gain important advantages through their appointment power. First, their appointees are a source of ideas and information that can help guide policy decisions. Second, these appointees extend the president's reach into the huge federal bureaucracy, exerting influence on the day-to-day workings of the agencies they head.

Not surprisingly, presidents have tended to appoint individuals who can further their goals. In his initial appointments, President George W. Bush sought to create a team of experienced officials who could help to offset his lack of Washington experience. His appointees included General Colin Powell and Donald Rumsfeld, both of who had held top positions in earlier Republican administrations. For his initial appointments, President Clinton chose many individuals who had played leading roles in his election campaign. Clinton, like Bush, also used diversity as a criterion, seeking to appoint

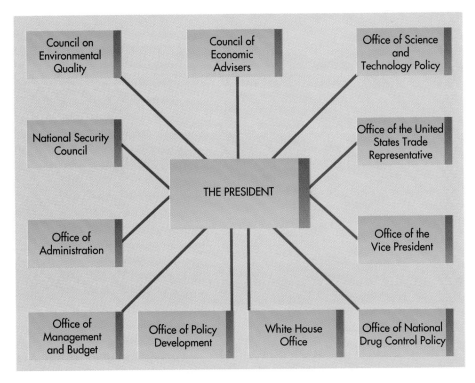

FIGURE 14-2 Executive Office of the President (EOP)
The EOP helps the president manage the rest of the executive branch and promotes the president's policy and political goals.
Source: U.S. Government Manual.

a significant number of women and minorities to executive positions. Among recent presidents, Ronald Reagan was the most adamant about ideological agreement as a criterion for appointment. He perceived career bureaucrats as being hostile to his ideas and believed that he needed Republicans who shared his philosophy in top positions.[30] Of Reagan's first-term appointees, only 18 percent were independents or from the opposing party. By comparison, 42 percent of President Jimmy Carter's appointees were in this category.[31] Reagan also rejected many Republicans who had worked in the Nixon and Ford administrations because he thought they were not conservative enough.

The Executive Office of the President

The key staff organization is the Executive Office of the President (EOP), which Congress created in 1939 to provide the president with the staff necessary to coordinate the activities of the executive branch.[32] The EOP has since become the command center of the presidency.[33] It consists of the Office of the Vice President and ten other organizational units (see Figure 14-2). They include the White House Office (WHO), which consists of the president's closest personal advisers; the Office of Management and Budget (OMB), which consists of experts who formulate and then administer the federal budget; the National Security Council (NSC), which assists the president on foreign and military affairs; and the Council of Economic Advisers (CEA), which advises the president on the national economy.

The Constitution assigns no policy authority to the vice president, whose role is determined by the president. Recent vice presidents, including Dick Cheney, pictured here with President Bush, have been assigned major policy responsibilities. Earlier vice presidents played smaller roles.

The vice president works in the White House, but no executive constitutional authority comes along with this office. Accordingly, the president decides the role the vice president will play. Earlier presidents often refused to assign any significant duties to their vice presidents, which diminished the office's appeal. Nomination to the vice presidency was refused by many leading politicians, including Daniel Webster and Henry Clay. Said Webster, "I do not propose to be buried until I am really dead."[34] Recent presidents, however, have assigned important duties to the vice president. George W. Bush, for example, chose Dick Cheney as his running mate in part because Cheney had ably served as White House chief of staff during the presidency of Bush's father. Cheney was expected to provide Bush with policy advice and to help him in the day-to-day operations of his presidency.

Of the EOP's ten other organizations, the White House Office serves the president most directly and personally. The WHO consists of the president's personal assistants, including close personal advisers, press agents, legislative and group liaison aides, and special assistants for domestic and international policy. They work in the White House, and the president can hire and fire them at will. The personal assistants do much of the legwork for the president and serve as a main source of advice. Because of their closeness and loyalty to the president, they are among the most powerful individuals in Washington. They are usually savvy political operatives. The formal powers of the presidency are somewhat limited, which means that presidents must find ways to get others to follow their lead (see Chapter 15). Presidential assistants help in this process. They are skilled at developing political strategy, recognizing political opportunities, and communicating with the public, Congress, key groups, and the news media.

The president is also served by the policy experts in the EOP's other organizations, who include economists, legal analysts, national security specialists, and others. The president is advised on economic issues, for example, by the

Council of Economic Advisers, headed by three economists who are appointed by the president and assisted by an expert staff. The CEA gathers information to develop indicators of the economy's strength and applies economic theories to various policy alternatives. Modern policymaking cannot be conducted in the absence of such expert advice and knowledge.

CABINET AND AGENCY APPOINTEES

The heads of the executive departments, such as the Department of Defense and the Department of Agriculture, constitute the president's **cabinet.** They are appointed by the president, subject to confirmation by Congress.

cabinet A group consisting of the heads of the (cabinet) executive departments, who are appointed by the president, subject to confirmation by the Senate. The cabinet was once the main advisory body to the president but no longer plays this role.

The cabinet is a tradition but has no formal authority, because the Constitution says nothing about it. When Abraham Lincoln was once unanimously opposed by his cabinet, he said, "Seven nays and one aye—the ayes have it." Although the cabinet once served as the president's main advisory group, it has not played this role since Herbert Hoover's administration. Dwight D. Eisenhower tried in the 1950s to restore the cabinet to its former prominence, but he eventually gave up. As national issues have become increasingly complex, the cabinet has become outmoded as a policymaking forum: department heads are likely to understand issues only in their respective policy areas.[35] Cabinet meetings have been largely reduced to gatherings at which only the most general matters are discussed.

Although the cabinet as a collective decision-making body is a thing of the past, the cabinet members, as individuals who head major departments, are important figures in any administration. They understand that their first responsibility is to carry out the president's instructions. Nevertheless, the president chooses most of them for their prominence in politics, business, government, or the professions. They may also bring to their office a high level of policy expertise

Through their appointments, presidents are able to choose executive leaders who can assist them in developing and administering policy. Pictured here is General Colin Powell. He was President George W. Bush's first cabinet selection; Bush nominated Powell for secretary of state.

and a group commitment.[36] Their stature and ideas can sometimes lead them to pursue their own agendas. President Carter believed that he had no choice in 1978 but to fire Joseph Califano, his secretary of health, education, and welfare, for disloyalty after Califano had repeatedly expressed disagreement with Carter's policies in statements to reporters and members of Congress.

In addition to cabinet secretaries, the president appoints the directors and top deputies of federal agencies, members of federal commissions, and heads of regulatory agencies (see Chapter 16). Altogether, the president appoints more than five thousand executive officials. However, most of these appointees are selected at the agency level or are part-time workers. This still leaves nearly seven hundred appointees who serve the president more or less directly, which is a much larger number than any other democracy's chief executive appoints.[37]

The Problem of Control

Although the president's appointees are a valuable asset, they also pose a problem: because they are so numerous, the president has difficulty controlling them. Most appointees are not under the president's direct supervision and have considerable freedom to act on their own initiative—not necessarily in accord with the president's wishes. President Truman had a wall chart in the Oval Office listing more than one hundred officials who reported directly to him and often told visitors, "I cannot even see all of these men, let alone actually study what they are doing."[38] Since Truman's time, the number of bureaucratic agencies has more than doubled, compounding the problem of presidential control over subordinates.[39]

The nature of the control problem varies with the type of appointee. The advantages of having the advice of policy experts, for example, is offset somewhat by the fact that they often have little political experience and tend to exaggerate the importance of their particular policy interests. As a result, their proposals are sometimes impractical or politically unacceptable. On the other hand, top political appointees, while adept at politics, have a tendency to act too independently. WHO assistants tend naturally to skew information in a direction that supports the course of action they favor. At times they even presume to undertake important actions without first obtaining clearance from the president or a chief assistant, leading others to question the president's authority or performance.[40] In 1996, for example, President Clinton found himself embroiled in controversy when it became known that a low-ranking White House assistant, Craig Livingstone, had unlawfully requested hundreds of personnel files from the FBI, many of them on high-ranking Republicans from the Reagan and Bush administrations. "Filegate," as the incident came to be called, resulted in congressional hearings and news stories that were highly critical of Clinton's administrative oversight.

The problem of presidential control is even more severe in the case of appointees who work outside the White House, in the departments and agencies. The loyalty of agency heads and cabinet secretaries is often split between a desire to help achieve the president's goals and an interest in boosting themselves or the agency they lead. Lower-level appointees within the departments and agencies pose a different type of problem. The president rarely, if ever, sees them, and they are typically political novices (most have fewer than two years of government experience) and not very knowledgeable about policy. These appointees are often "captured" by the agency in which they work because they depend for advice on the agency's career bureaucrats. (Chapter 16 examines further the relationship between presidential appointees and career bureaucrats.)

ORGANIZING THE EXTENDED PRESIDENCY

Effective use of appointees by the president requires two-way communication. The president cannot possibly meet regularly with all appointees or personally oversee their activities. Yet to be in control, the president must receive essential advice from these subordinates and must have means of communicating with them.

The Pyramid Approach

Presidents have relied on a variety of techniques to regulate the flow of information to and from the Oval Office. One arrangement, used by most of the post–World War II Republican presidents, resembles the way the military and most corporations are organized. It places the president at the top of an organizational pyramid and the personal assistants, each of whom is assigned specific responsibilities, at the next levels (see Figure 14-3). All information and recommendations from lower levels must be submitted to these top aides, who decide whether the reports should be forwarded to the president. This hierarchical arrangement, with its multiple levels of supervision, permits more effective control of subordinates. The pyramid form of organization also has the advantage of freeing the president from the need to deal with the many minor issues that reach the White House.

A major disadvantage of the pyramid form is the danger that presidential advisers will make decisions themselves that should be passed along for the president to make. Another disadvantage is that the pyramid form can result in misdirected or blocked information. The president may be denied access to opinions that close advisers decide are wrong or unimportant. The risk is that the president will not be able to take important views and facts into account in making policy decisions.[41]

The Hub-of-the-Wheel Approach

A second approach to staff organization was developed by Franklin D. Roosevelt and adapted by most of his Democratic successors. Each placed himself at the center of the organization, accessible to a fairly large number of advisers (see Figure 14-4). This "hub-of-the-wheel" (or circular) form allows more information to reach the president, providing a greater range of options and opinions. Roosevelt and Kennedy were particularly adept at operating within this organizational framework; each surrounded himself with talented advisers and knew how to make them work together as a team even while they generated competing ideas.

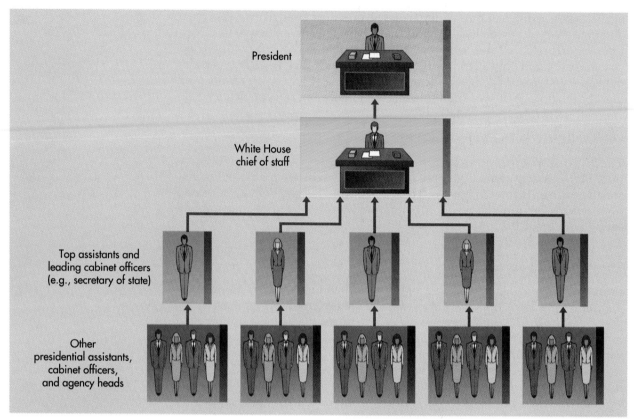

President

White House
chief of staff

Top assistants and
leading cabinet officers
(e.g., secretary of state)

Other
presidential assistants,
cabinet officers,
and agency heads

FIGURE 14-3   Managing the Presidency: The Pyramid (Hierarchical) Form of Organization

In the pyramid form that some presidents have used to organize their staffs, information and recommendations that lower-level advisers wish to communicate to the president must be transmitted through—and thus "filtered" by—first top-level aides and then the White House chief of staff.

Unfortunately, this system encourages personal rivalries. As assistants vie for the president's attention and for control of policy areas, their competition can undermine the team effort the president is looking for. Moreover, the president may become so overloaded with staff opinions that larger issues do not get the proper attention. This criticism was often leveled at President Carter. It was said that Carter knew the details of every policy issue but had difficulty establishing priorities and placing policies in the broad context that leads to effective action. Carter himself came to recognize that his hub-of-the-wheel organization was overloading him with detail, and he changed to a more hierarchically organized staff. The results, however, were not notably different. Ford and Clinton also replaced their collegial staff systems with a more hierarchical one. They faced criticisms that their presidencies lacked direction, and each turned to a strong chief of staff for help.

THE INSOLUBLE PROBLEM

Ultimately the problem of presidential control is beyond an organizational solution.[42] The responsibilities of the Oval Office are so broad that presidents cannot do the job without hundreds of assistants who cannot possibly be supervised directly no matter how they are organized. The modern presidency is thus a

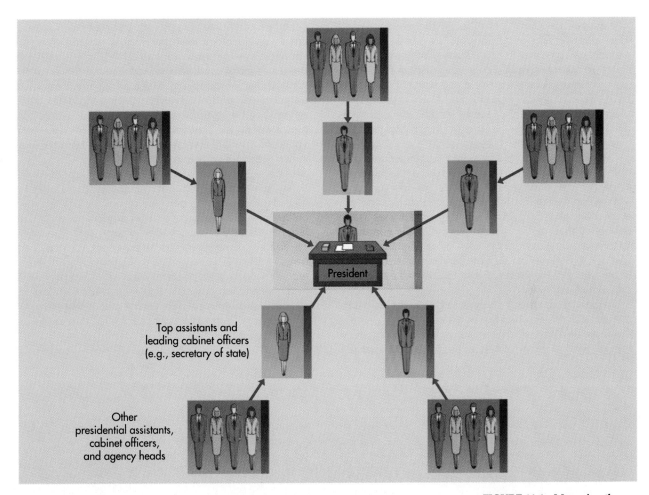

FIGURE 14-4 Managing the Presidency: The Hub-of-the-Wheel (Circular) Form of Organization
In the hub-of-the-wheel form of organization, the president is at the center of a circle composed of a fairly large number of top-level aides, each of whom has direct access to the president. Lower-level advisers have correspondingly closer access to the president than they do in the pyramidal form.

Labels within figure:
Top assistants and leading cabinet officers (e.g., secretary of state)
Other presidential assistants, cabinet officers, and agency heads
President

double-edged sword. Presidents today have greater responsibilities than their predecessors, and the increase in responsibilities expands their opportunities to exert power. At the same time, the range of these responsibilities is so broad that they must rely on staffers who may or may not act in the best interests of the president. The modern president's recurring problem is to find some way of making sure that aides serve the interests of the presidency above all others. The subject of presidential control of the executive branch will be discussed further in Chapter 16.

Summary

The presidency has become a much stronger office than the Framers envisioned. The Constitution grants the president substantial military, diplomatic, legislative, and executive powers, and in each case the president's authority has increased measurably. Underlying this change is the president's position as the one leader chosen by the whole nation. The public's support and expectations underlie presidential claims of broad authority.

National crises have contributed to the growth of presidential power. The public looks to the president during national emergencies, in part because Congress is poorly suited to the decisive and continuous action that emergencies require. Changing world and national conditions have also enhanced the presidency. These changes have placed new and greater demands on the federal government, demands that the president is in some ways better able than Congress to meet.

The nation has had four systems of presidential selection. The first centered on Congress and the Electoral College, the second on party conventions, the third on a convention system with some state primaries, and the current one on state primaries and open caucuses as the dominant method of choosing presidential nominees. Each succeeding system has been more "democratic" in that it was designed to give the public greater influence in the choice of the president and thus to make the selection more legitimate.

To gain nomination, a strong showing in the early primaries is necessary because news coverage and other resources flow toward winning candidates. This momentum is a critical factor in nominating races but normally benefits a candidate who by virtue of past record, stands on issues, ideology, or other factors already is in the strongest position to win nomination. Once nominated, the major-party candidates receive federal funds for the general election campaign. Much of this money is spent on televised political advertising. The candidates themselves spend their time traveling around the nation, concentrating on the states with large numbers of electoral votes and trying to get favorable coverage from the journalists who follow their every move.

Although the campaign tends to personalize the presidency, the responsibilities of the modern presidency far exceed any president's personal capacities. To meet their obligations, presidents have surrounded themselves with large staffs of advisers, policy experts, and managers. These staff members enable the president to extend control over the executive branch while providing the information necessary for policymaking. All recent presidents have discovered, however, that their control of staff resources is incomplete and that some actions that others do on their behalf actually work against what they are trying to accomplish.

Key Terms

cabinet
legitimacy (of election)
momentum
open party caucuses

stewardship theory
unit rule
Whig theory

Suggested Readings

Haskell, John. *Fundamentally Flawed: Understanding and Reforming Presidential Primaries.* Lanham, Md.: Rowman & Littlefield, 1996. An analysis that argues the presidential nominating process is flawed and requires major reform.

Kendall, Kathleen E. *Communication in the Presidential Primaries.* Westport, Conn.: Praeger, 2000. A look at communication in the 1912–2000 nominating campaigns.

Kraus, Sidney. *Televised Presidential Debates and Public Policy*, 2d ed. Mahwah, N.J.: Lawrence Erlbaum Publishers, 2000. An analysis by one of the leading presidential debates experts.

Patterson, Thomas E. *Out of Order.* New York: Vintage, 1994. A study of the news media's coverage of presidential campaigns.

Pfiffner, James P. *The Strategic Presidency: Hitting the Ground Running*, 2d ed. Lawrence: University Press of Kansas, 1996. An analysis of the way a newly elected president can convert electoral support into power in office.

Ponder, Daniel E. *Good Advice.* College Station: Texas A&M University Press, 2000. An examination of the role of information in White House policy making.

Walch, Timothy, ed. *At the President's Side: The Vice Presidency in the Twentieth Century.* Columbia: University of Missouri Press, 1997. An assessment of the vice presidency and its twentieth-century occupants.

Walcott, Charles E., and Karen M. Hult. *Governing the White House: From Hoover Through LBJ.* Lawrence: University Press of Kansas, 1995. An innovative study of how the organization of the White House affects presidential performance.

Warshaw, Shirley Anne. *The Domestic Presidency.* Boston: Allyn and Bacon, 1997. Analysis of domestic policy-making in the White House.

Weko, Thomas J. *The Politicizing Presidency: The White House Personnel Office, 1948–1994.* Lawrence: University Press of Kansas, 1995. A careful study of the presidential appointment process and the institutionalization of the presidency.

CHAPTER 15

Presidential Policymaking: Eliciting Support

★

The president's job in the constitutional system is not to lead a followership; it is to elicit leadership from the other institutions of self-government and help make that leadership effective.

—Hugh Heclo[1]

★ ★ ★

*B*ill Clinton was riding high when 1998 began. He was the first president of his party to have won reelection since Franklin Roosevelt in the 1930s. His reelection had enabled him to work his way back to the center of the political stage, a position he had relinquished when the Republicans swept the congressional election of 1994 and pushed a bold new policy agenda. The first year of his second term had been a quiet one. Pundits suggested he was suffering from the second-term malaise that had characterized so many presidents before him. But Clinton had merely been taking the time to build a set of new and bold initiatives of his own. In the first weeks of January, he unleashed them one by one: Medicare would be extended to early retirees, day care would be expanded through a $20 billion federal program, classroom size in the public schools would be reduced through a $30 billion grant program. The State of the Union Address in late January would include additional proposals that would promote Clinton's goals and solidify his place in history.

On Wednesday morning, January 21, the Clinton presidency abruptly changed. The *Washington Post* had an explosive story: the president was alleged to have had a sexual relationship with a White House intern, Monica Lewinsky. The "scandal of the '90s," as some observers described it, cast a pall over the White House. Clinton gave a stirring State of the Union speech that rallied public support behind him, but the damage was done, and there was more to come. In the months ahead, there would be additional revelations, and the White House would mount a counterattack. Clinton's ambitious policy agenda, however, was shuttled to the side. The president's energies would be spent defending himself from the charges, and the Republican Congress was content to ignore his domestic policy ideas.

The Clinton story is but one in the saga of the ups and downs of the modern presidency. Lyndon Johnson's and Richard Nixon's dogged pursuit of the Vietnam War led to talk of "the imperial presidency," an office so powerful that constitutional checks and balances were no longer an effective constraint on it.[2] Within a few years, because of the undermining effects of Watergate and of changing international conditions during the Ford and Carter presidencies, the watchword was "the imperiled presidency," an office too weak to meet the nation's demands for executive leadership.[3] Reagan's policy successes before 1986 renewed talk heard in the Roosevelt and Kennedy years of "a heroic presidency," an office that is an inspirational center of American politics.[4] After the Iran-Contra scandal in 1986, Reagan was more often called a lame duck. George Bush's handling of the Gulf crisis—leading the nation into a major war and emerging from it with the highest public approval rating ever recorded for a president—bolstered the heroic conception of the office. A year later, Bush was on his way to being removed from office by the voters.

No other political institution has been subject to such varying characterizations as the modern presidency. One reason is that the formal powers of the office are somewhat limited, and thus presidential power changes with national conditions, political circumstances, and the office's occupant.[5] The American presidency is always a central office in that the president is constantly a focus of national attention. Yet the presidency is not an inherently powerful office in the sense that presidents always get what they want. Presidential power is conditional. It depends on the president's personal capacity but even more on the circumstances—on whether the situation demands strong leadership and whether the political support for that leadership exists. When conditions are favorable, the president will appear to be almost invincible. When conditions are adverse, the president will seem vulnerable. This chapter examines the correlates of presidential success and failure in policymaking, focusing on the following main points:

★ *Presidential influence on national policy is highly variable.* Whether presidents succeed or fail in getting their policies enacted depends heavily on the force of circumstance, the stage of their presidency, partisan support in Congress, and the foreign or domestic nature of the policy issue.

★ *The president's election by national vote and position as sole chief executive ensure that others will listen to the president's ideas; but to lead effectively, the president must have the help of other officials and, to get their help, must respond to their interests as they respond to the president's.*

★ *Presidents have often found it difficult to maintain the high level of public support that gives force to their leadership.* The American people have unreasonably high policy expectations of their presidents and tend to blame them for national problems.

Factors in Presidential Leadership

The president operates within a system of separate institutions that share power. Significant presidential action normally depends on the approval of Congress, the cooperation of the bureaucracy, and sometimes the acceptance of the judiciary. Since other officials also have priorities, presidents do not always get their way. The responsibility to initiate and coordinate policy places the president at the center of attention, but other institutions have the authority that can make presidential leadership effective. Congress in particular—more than the courts or the bureaucracy—holds the key to presidential success. Without congressional authorization and funding, most presidential proposals are nothing but ideas, empty of substance.

Given that presidents must elicit support from others if they are to succeed, what is the record of presidential success? One way to judge is to measure the extent to which Congress backs legislative initiatives developed by the White House. No president has come close to getting enactment of all the programs that he placed before Congress. The average success rate is just below 50 per-

HOW THE UNITED STATES COMPARES

SYSTEMS OF EXECUTIVE POLICY LEADERSHIP

The United States instituted a presidential system in 1789 as part of its constitutional checks and balances. This form of executive leadership was copied in Latin America but not in Europe. European democracies adopted parliamentary systems, in which executive leadership is provided by a prime minister, who is a member of the legislature. In recent years, some European prime ministers have campaigned and governed as if they were a singular authority rather than the head of a collective institution. France in the 1960s created a separate chief executive office but retained its parliamentary form of legislature.

The policy leadership of a president can differ substantially from that of a prime minister. As a singular head of an independent branch of government, a president does not have to share executive authority but nevertheless depends on the legislative branch for support. By comparison, a prime minister shares executive leadership with a cabinet, but once agreement within the cabinet is reached, he or she is almost assured of the legislative support necessary to carry out policy initiatives.

Presidential System	Presidential/Parliamentary System	Parliamentary System
Mexico	Finland	Australia
United States	France	Belgium
Venezuela		Canada
		Germany
		Great Britain
		Israel
		Italy
		Japan
		Netherlands
		Sweden

cent, but there has been wide variation. Johnson saw 69 percent of his 1965 initiatives enacted, whereas Nixon attained only 20 percent in 1973. Moreover, presidents have had markedly less success on their more ambitious proposals than on lesser ones.[6]

Whether a president's initiatives are likely to succeed or fail depends on several factors, including the force of circumstance, the stage of the president's term, the type of policy issue, the president's support in Congress, and the level of public support for the president's leadership. Let us examine each of these factors.

THE FORCE OF CIRCUMSTANCE

During his first months in office and in the midst of the Great Depression, Franklin D. Roosevelt accomplished the most sweeping changes in domestic policy in the nation's history. Congress moved quickly to pass nearly every New Deal initiative he proposed. In 1964 and 1965, Lyndon Johnson pushed landmark civil rights and social welfare legislation through Congress on the strength of the civil rights movement, the legacy of the assassinated President Kennedy, and large Democratic majorities in the House and Senate. When Reagan assumed the presidency in 1981, high unemployment and inflation had greatly weakened the national economy and created a mood for significant change, which enabled Reagan to persuade Congress to enact some of the most substantial taxing and spending changes in history.

President Lyndon Johnson addresses a joint session of Congress in 1965. Johnson had an extraordinary record of success with Congress, which adopted the great majority of his legislative proposals.

From presidencies such as these has come the popular impression that presidents single-handedly decide national policy. However, each of these periods of presidential dominance was marked by a special set of circumstances: a decisive election victory that gave added force to the president's leadership, a compelling national problem that convinced Congress and the public that bold presidential action was needed, and a president who was mindful of what was expected and who vigorously advocated policies consistent with those expectations.

When conditions are favorable, the power of the presidency appears awesome. The problem for most presidents is that conditions are not normally conducive to strong leadership. The political scientist Erwin Hargrove suggests that presidential influence depends largely on circumstance.[7] Some presidents serve in periods when important problems are surfacing in American society but have not yet become critical. Such a situation, Hargrove contends, works against a president's efforts to accomplish significant policy change. Kennedy was one such president; he recognized that federal intervention would be necessary to bring social justice to black Americans, but because conditions were unfavorable, he could not get Congress to act. The legislation was passed after his death, when Lyndon Johnson was president.

Of course, presidents have some control over their fate. Through effective leadership they can sometimes rally the public and Congress behind goals that they believe are important. In general, however, presidential achievement is heavily dependent on circumstance. Had Franklin Roosevelt been elected in 1960 rather than 1932, his place in American history would be very different and probably much less conspicuous. Roosevelt's genius lay in the devising of extraordinary policies, not in the creation of conditions that led to their acceptance. In 1994, reflecting on the constraints of budget deficits and other factors beyond his control, Clinton said he had no choice but "to play the hand that history had dealt him."

THE STAGE OF THE PRESIDENT'S TERM

If conditions conducive to great accomplishments occur infrequently, it is nonetheless the case that nearly every president has favorable moments. Such moments tend to come during the first months in office. Most newly elected presidents enjoy a **honeymoon period** during which Congress, the press, and the public anticipate initiatives from the Oval Office and are more predisposed than usual to support these initiatives. The honeymoon is never an entirely smooth one. While Congress expects a flurry of legislative programs from new presidents, it does not always treat these proposals kindly. And the media can be downright tough on a new president.[8] The press kept a close eye on George W. Bush's initial decisions because of the controversy surrounding his election. Nevertheless, presidents can normally expect a more unqualified form of support during their inaugural period rather than at later times.

> **honeymoon period** The president's first months in office, a time when Congress, the press, and the public are more inclined than usual to support presidential initiatives.

Not surprisingly, presidents have put forth more new programs in their first year in office than in any subsequent year. James Pfiffner uses the term "strategic presidency" to refer to a president's need to move quickly on priority items to take advantage of the policy momentum that is gained from the election. Later in their terms, presidents tend to do less well in presenting initiatives and getting them enacted.[9] They may run out of good ideas or, more likely, deplete their political resources—the momentum of their election is gone and sources of opposition have emerged. Furthermore, if they blunder or if conditions turn sour—and it is hard for any president to serve for any length of time without a serious setback of one kind or another—they will lose some of their credibility and public support. Even highly successful presidents like Johnson and Reagan tend to have weak records in their final years. Franklin Roosevelt began his presidency with a remarkable period of achievement—the celebrated "Hundred Days"—but during his last six years in office, few of his major domestic proposals were enacted.

An irony of the presidency, then, is that presidents are most powerful when they are least knowledgeable—during their first months in office. These months can, as a result, be times of risk as well as times of opportunity. An example is the Bay of Pigs fiasco during the first year of John Kennedy's presidency, in which a U.S.-backed invasion force of anti-communist Cubans was easily defeated by Fidel Castro's army.

THE FOREIGN OR DOMESTIC NATURE OF THE POLICY PROPOSAL

In the 1960s, the political scientist Aaron Wildavsky wrote that although the nation has only one president, it has two presidencies: one domestic and one foreign.[10] Wildavsky was referring to Congress's differential responses to presidential initiatives in the areas of foreign and domestic policy. He found that since World War II, only 40 percent of presidential proposals in the domestic policy area had been enacted by Congress, compared with 70 percent of foreign policy initiatives. It must be noted that Wildavsky was looking back on a period when there was general agreement on U.S. foreign policy objectives. After World War II, Republican and Democratic leaders alike were largely united on the desirability of containing Soviet communism and establishing U.S. diplomatic, military, and economic influence around the world (see Chapter 20). Accordingly, presidents had strong backing for their foreign policy leadership. In 1964, for example, Lyndon Johnson urged Congress to ratify the Gulf of Tonkin resolution, which he then used as a mandate to escalate the Vietnam War. The resolution was passed unanimously in the House and with only two dissenting votes in the Senate.

By the late 1960s, however, the Vietnam War had gone sour, and the bipartisan consensus on foreign policy was disrupted. Those deep divisions have endured. The January 1991 authorization of the use of military force in the Gulf War was the first time Congress had voted directly for offensive military action since the Gulf of Tonkin resolution. Bush had asked for the vote (even though he said he would pursue the war regardless of what Congress decided) in order to strengthen his threat to use military force if Iraq did not withdraw from Kuwait. This time Congress was divided in its response to the president's request. The approval of military action in the Gulf was passed by margins of 52 to 47 in the Senate and 250 to 183 in the House.

Wildavsky's two-presidencies thesis is now regarded as a time-bound conception of presidential influence. Today, many of the same factors, such as the party composition of Congress, that affect a president's success on foreign policy also affect success on domestic policy. Nevertheless, presidents are somewhat more likely to get what they want when the issue is foreign policy because they get more support from the opposite party in Congress.[11] The clash between powerful interest groups that occurs on many domestic issues is less prevalent in the foreign policy area. Moreover, foreign policy often springs from negotiations between nations. The president is recognized by other nations as America's voice in world affairs, and even when members of Congress disagree with the president's position, they sometimes accept it out of a concern for America's credibility abroad. In some cases, Congress effectively has no choice but to accept presidential action. When President Bush secretly ordered a military invasion of Panama in 1989, even those members of Congress who might have opposed the invasion had little choice but to express their support for U.S. troops and, by implication, for Bush's policy.

During the cold war, the threat of Soviet military power strengthened the president's hand in foreign affairs. Congress was reluctant to contest presidential initiatives for fear that it would be seen as a sign of national weakness. And for most of the cold war period, public opinion would predictably rally around presidential action whenever there was an appearance that the national interest was threatened by the Soviet Union or another communist state. Since the end of the cold war, however, Congress has been less deferential to presidential leadership and at times has even tried to assume leadership on foreign policy in areas such as military spending, human rights, and international trade.

The president still retains an advantage, however, in the foreign policy area. Some of that advantage can be traced to the increased importance of the global economy. As the chief executive of the nation's most powerful economic nation, the president is expected by the American people and other nations to provide leadership on international economic issues. When Asian economies went into

---

★ CRITICAL THINKING ★

WHAT'S YOUR OPINION?

Foreign Policy: The President Versus Congress
In 1998, President Clinton urged Congress "not to tie his hands" by imposing mandatory sanctions on countries that had engaged in practices disagreeable to members of Congress. Clinton argued that mandatory sanctions deprive the United States of the negotiating flexibility it needs when working out trade and security agreements with other countries and even when trying to get them to mend their ways. Presidents Bush, Reagan, Carter, and Ford had similar complaints, holding that the president should have broad discretion in carrying out foreign policy. Should Congress take an active role in setting precise limits on foreign policy, or should the president have this responsibility? What are the advantages and disadvantages of each arrangement?

CURRENT CONTROVERSIES

SHOULD THE PRESIDENT HAVE FAST-TRACK AUTHORITY ON TRADE?

The president has always been the nation's foreign policy leader. Negotiations with other countries require that the nation speak as with one voice so that these countries know where the United States stands on the issue under discussion. Nevertheless, Congress has been unwilling to grant presidents a free hand in the area of foreign policy negotiations. It is not surprising that Congress has taken a keen interest in issues of international trade, because such trade has direct implications for U.S. firms and workers. An example is the recent congressional resistance to granting the president fast-track authority on global trade. With this authority, the President can negotiate a trade agreement, which Congress then must accept or reject in its entirety. Without it, Congress retains the power to reject specific provisions of an agreement, which weakens this nation's hand in international negotiations because the president cannot guarantee that an agreement negotiated with the United States will be accepted in its entirety.

YES: Fast-track trading authority . . . grants the administration authority to negotiate and implement trade agreements with other nations, which Congress would either support or vote down unamended. . . . Fast track is a necessary step to strengthen the U.S. economy at home—helping producers, workers, and consumers. The agreements made as a result of fast track will expand our markets far beyond our shorelines . . . In the past, fast track has been derailed by special interests, who lack the foresight to see that the general interest of our Nation will benefit from free and open trade—a status that can be greatly assisted by extending traditional trading authority to this administration.

—U.S. Representative Philip M. Crane (R-Ill.)

NO: We have negotiated several trade agreements under fast track. All of them have been abysmal failures, terrible failures. . . . Now we have an enormous trade deficit with Mexico. What has happened to American jobs? They go to Mexico. . . . Fast track—the traditional approach to trade negotiating authority—has been decisively rejected by Congress and the American people. Trade negotiations are increasingly complex, and Congress must have a stronger consultative role. Congressional certification that objectives have been met at each stage must be required before the negotiations can proceed.

—U.S. Senator Byron Dorgan (D-N.D.)

a tailspin in 1998 and threatened to drag down the world economy, President Clinton led the U.S. response, which included a proposed $18 billion grant to the International Monetary Fund. Although the grant was delayed for months by congressional opponents, Congress eventually relented in the face of mounting pressures from the White House, the international financial community, and foreign governments. But the global economy does not give a president the leverage that the cold war provided. Economic issues often engage opposing domestic interests. Business and labor, for example, have been sharply at odds over trade policy (see Chapter 20). Moreover, whenever domestic interests are divided, Congress is usually also divided, which compounds the problems of presidential leadership.

Presidents gain some leverage in foreign and defense policy because of their commanding position with the defense, diplomatic, and intelligence agencies. These are sometimes labeled "presidential agencies." As chief executive, the president is in charge of all federal agencies, but in practice the president's influence is strongest in those agencies that connect with his constitutional authority as chief diplomat and commander in chief, such as the Departments of

Presidents rely heavily on their top-ranking cabinet officers and personal assistants in making major policy decisions. During the Cuban missile crisis in 1962, this group of advisers to President John F. Kennedy met regularly to help him decide on a naval blockade as a means of forcing the Soviet Union to withdraw its missiles from Cuba.

State and Defense and the CIA. These agencies have a tradition of deference to presidential authority that is not found in agencies that deal primarily with domestic policy. The Department of Agriculture, for example, responds to presidential direction but is also responsive (perhaps even more responsive) to farm-state senators and representatives. As Chapter 16 describes, bureaucratic support is important to a president's success with Congress, and that support is more likely to be forthcoming when the agency in question is part of the defense, diplomatic, or intelligence bureaucracy.

Relations with Congress

Although the presidency is not nearly as powerful as most Americans assume, the capacity of presidents to influence the agenda of national debate is unrivaled, reflecting their unique claim to represent the whole country. Whenever the president directs attention to a particular issue or program, the attention of others usually follows. But will those others follow the president's lead? As we have noted, a president's support varies with conditions, some of which clearly cannot be controlled. Yet presidents are not entirely at the mercy of circumstance. As sole chief executive, a president can increase the chance of success by striving to build support in Congress and with the American people.

CONGRESSIONAL SUPPORT

As the center of national attention, presidents can easily start to believe that their ideas should prevail over those of Congress. This line of reasoning invariably gets any president into trouble. Jimmy Carter had not held national office before he was elected in 1976, so he had no clear understanding of how Washington operates.[12] Soon after taking office, Carter deleted from his budget nine-

The White House contains, on the first floor, the president's Oval Office, other offices, and ceremonial rooms. The first family's living quarters are on the second floor.

teen public works projects that he believed were a waste of taxpayers' money, ignoring the importance that members of Congress attach to obtaining federally funded projects for their constituents. Carter's action set the tone for a conflict-ridden relationship with Congress.

In order to get the help of members of Congress, the president must respond to their interests as they respond to the president's. The political scientist Fred Greenstein concludes that "whatever else his qualities, the president needs to be a working politician who can work with or otherwise win over the Washington community."[13]

The use of the presidential veto illustrates the point. Presidents can sometimes force Congress to accommodate their views through the use or threatened use of the veto. Congress can seldom muster the two-thirds majority in each chamber required to override a presidential veto (see Table 15-1), and so the threat of a veto can make Congress more responsive to the president's demands. When a major civil rights bill was being debated in Congress in 1991, for example, George Bush said flatly that he would veto any bill that imposed "hiring quotas" on employers; his ultimatum forced Congress to alter provisions of the bill. Yet the veto is more effective as a presidential restraint on Congress than as a device by which Congress can be forced to take positive action on the president's proposals. The presidential scholar Richard Neustadt argues that the veto is more a sign of presidential weakness than strength, because it usually comes into play when Congress has refused to go along with the president's ideas.[14]

In 1996, Congress enacted legislation that gave the president a line-item veto of spending bills. The president could void (subject to override by a two-thirds vote of the House and Senate) specific spending items without vetoing the entire bill. In 1998, however, the Supreme Court in a 6–3 decision struck down the

TABLE 15-1   Number and Override of Presidential Vetoes

President	Years in Office	Number of Vetoes	Number of Vetoes Overridden by Congress
Franklin Roosevelt	1933–1945	635	9
Harry Truman	1945–1952	250	12
Dwight Eisenhower	1953–1960	181	2
John Kennedy	1961–1963	21	0
Lyndon Johnson	1963–1968	30	0
Richard Nixon	1969–1974	43	7
Gerald Ford	1974–1976	66	12
Jimmy Carter	1977–1980	31	2
Ronald Reagan	1981–1988	78	9
George Bush	1989–1992	46	1
Bill Clinton	1993–2000	31	2

SOURCE: *Congressional Quarterly Weekly Report,* January 7, 1989. Bush figures were provided by the White House Office of Legislative Affairs; Clinton figures were provided by White House Office and cover through May 2000.

www.mhhe.com/patterson5

Graphic

line-item veto, concluding that it violates that part of the Constitution that requires Congress to submit every bill to the president for approval or full veto. Writing for the Court in *Clinton v. City of New York,* Justice John Paul Stevens said that "the procedures authorized by the line-item veto are not authorized by the Constitution." Stevens went on to say that such a veto could only be established through a constitutional amendment. "If there is to be a new procedure in which the president will play a different role in determining the text of what may become a law, such change must come not by legislation but through the amendment procedures set forth in Article V of the Constitution."[15]

The Power to Persuade

According to Neustadt, the most basic fact about presidential leadership is that it takes place in the context of a system of divided powers. Although the president gets most of the attention, Congress has most of the constitutional authority in the American system. The powers of the presidential office are insufficient by themselves to keep the president in a strong position. Congress is a constituency that all presidents must serve if they expect to get its support.[16]

Neustadt's classic illustration of what presidents can do to help themselves with Congress is the Marshall Plan, a program to aid European countries devastated by World War II. The plan was enacted by Congress in 1948 at the request of Harry S Truman. Truman had become president upon the death of Franklin Roosevelt and was widely regarded in Washington as just a caretaker president who would be replaced by a Republican. (The Republicans had made substantial gains in the 1946 congressional elections.) Truman knew he could not simply demand that Congress make a commitment to the postwar rebuilding of Europe, in view of the cost of such a program (roughly $100 billion in today's dollars) and of its novelty (historically, the United States had stayed free of permanent European entanglements). Truman succeeded in getting congressional approval by subordinating his position to that of others.

First, rather than announce the program himself, Truman gave the task to General George C. Marshall, who had been chief of staff of the armed forces during World War II and was one of America's most widely admired leaders. Second, Truman made a special effort to gain the support of Arthur Vandenberg, a leading Republican senator and chairman of the Senate Foreign Relations Committee. Truman accepted Vandenberg's request that "politics" not be allowed to bog down the plan. He followed Vandenberg's advice on changes in financial and administrative aspects of the plan; and he allowed Vandenberg to choose a Republican, Paul Hoffman, to head the U.S. agency responsible for administering the plan. Through Vandenberg's backing, Truman gained the Republican congressional support that made the Marshall Plan possible.

From cases such as the Marshall Plan, Neustadt concluded that presidential power, at base, is "the power to persuade."[17] Like any singular notion of presidential power, Neustadt's has limitations. Presidents at times have the power to command and to threaten. But Congress can never be taken for granted. Theodore Roosevelt expressed the wish that he could "be the president and Congress, too," if only for a day, so that he would have the power to enact as well as propose laws.

Partisan Support in Congress

For most presidents, the next-best-thing to being "Congress, too" is to have a Congress filled with members of their own party. The sources of division within Congress are many. Legislators from urban and rural areas, wealthier and poorer constituencies, and different regions of the country often have very different views of the national interest. To obtain majority support in Congress, the president must find ways to overcome these differences.

No source of unity is more important to presidential success than partisanship is. Presidents are more likely to succeed when their own party controls Congress (see Figure 15-1). Between 1954 and 1992, each Republican president—Eisenhower, Nixon, Ford, Reagan, and Bush—had to contend with a Democratic majority in one or both houses of Congress. Congress passed a smaller percentage of the initiatives supported by each of these presidents than by any Democratic president of the period—Kennedy, Johnson, or Carter.[18]

Democratic presidents have not always had an easy time with Congress, either. A chief obstacle has been southern Democrats, who tend to be more conservative than congressional Democrats from other regions and thus more likely to break party ranks and vote with their Republican colleagues. On such issues as social welfare and individual rights, southern Democrats have sometimes combined with Republicans (in the "conservative coalition") to block the legislative initiatives of Democratic presidents. Nevertheless, Democratic majorities in Congress provided Democratic presidents an advantage. In his first year in office, Bill Clinton was able to persuade Congress to pass a deficit reduction bill, a feat that George Bush was unable to accomplish in his four years as president. As a Democrat, Clinton had more support in Congress with

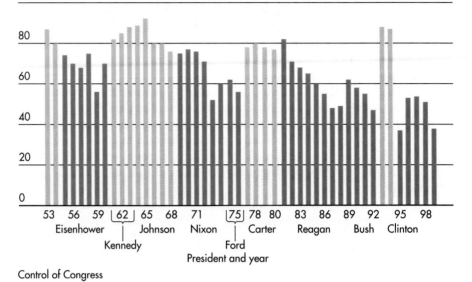

Percentage of bills on which Congress
supported president's position

FIGURE 15-1   Percentage of Bills Passed by Congress on Which the President Announced a Position, 1953–1999
In most years, presidents have been supported by Congress on a majority of policy issues on which they have taken a stand. Presidents fare better when their party controls Congress. *Source: Congressional Quarterly Weekly Report*, December 11, 1999. Used by permission.

which to work. His deficit reduction bill was supported by 85 percent of congressional Democrats, which was all the help he needed. No Republican voted for the bill.

After Republicans took control of Congress in 1995, Clinton's legislative success rate sank to the lowest of any recent Democratic president, a dramatic illustration of how presidential power is affected by whether the president's party controls Congress.

Colliding with Congress

On rare occasions, presidents have pursued their goals so zealously that Congress has felt that it had no choice but to take steps to curb their use of power. The ultimate sanction of Congress is its constitutional power to impeach and remove the president from office. The House of Representatives decides whether the president should be impeached (placed on trial), and the Senate conducts the trial and then votes on the president's guilt, with a two-thirds vote required for removal from office. In 1868, Andrew Johnson was impeached and came within one Senate vote of being removed from office for his opposition to Congress's harsh Reconstruction policies in the wake of the Civil War. In 1974, Richard Nixon's resignation halted congressional proceedings on the Watergate affair that would almost certainly have ended in his impeachment and removal from office.

The prospect of impeachment was raised again in 1998 when the House of Representatives by a vote of 258 to 176 authorized an investigation of President

★ STATES IN THE NATION

DIVIDED POWER IN THE EXECUTIVE

The president operates in a system of divided power where joint action by Congress is often required for the president's programs to be adopted. The chief executives in the American states are the governors, and nearly all of them must contend with a further division—a separation of power within the executive itself. Maine and New Jersey are the only states where executive power is vested solely in a governor. Five other states have separately elected and (unlike the vice president) constitutionally empowered lieutenant governors. In most of the other states, other major executive officials, such as the attorney general and secretary of state, are also elected. Finally, there are twelve states in which even minor executive officials, such as the commissioner of education, are chosen by the voters. In the case of the federal government, these other major and minor officials are appointed by the president.

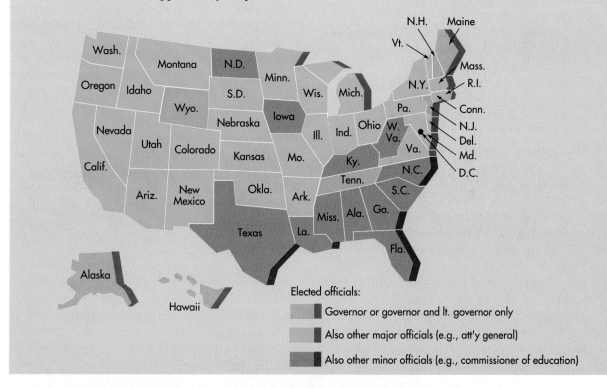

Elected officials:

■ Governor or governor and lt. governor only

■ Also other major officials (e.g., att'y general)

■ Also other minor officials (e.g., commissioner of education)

Clinton's conduct. He was accused of lying under oath about his relationship with Monica Lewinsky and of obstructing justice by trying to conceal the affair. The gravity of the allegations was leavened by the circumstances. The charges had grown out of an extramarital affair rather than a gross abuse of executive power and were tied to a controversial five-year, $50-million investigation by independent counsel Kenneth Starr. For their part, the American people were ambivalent about the whole issue. Most people approved of Clinton's handling of the presidency and did not believe that his actions warranted removal from

IMPEACHING, CONVICTING, AND REMOVING THE PRESIDENT

In October 1998, for only the third time in American history, Congress authorized an official impeachment investigation of the president of the United States. Bill Clinton joined Andrew Johnson and Richard Nixon as presidents whose legacy will be forever linked with the word *impeachment.*

Although *impeachment* technically applies only to the indictment stage of congressional action, it is commonly used to refer also to the conviction stage. But these are separate stages, and the Constitution divides the responsibility for them. The House is granted under Article I, Section 2 of the Constitution the power to impeach (indict) the president. The Senate under Article I, Section 3 has the power to try, convict, and remove the president.

The Constitution is not overly specific on the presidential acts that would justify the removal from office. Article II, Section 4 states that impeachable acts are "Treason, Bribery, or Other High Crimes and Misdemeanors" but does not spell out what these other high crimes and misdemeanors shall include. Any such definition in the context of the presidential office would necessarily be somewhat subjective. As a result, the impeachment process is inevitably a political as well as a constitutional one. Nevertheless, it can be assumed that the contemporary use of the term *misdemeanors* includes lesser crimes (such as a speeding ticket) than the writers of the Constitution would have had in mind. It is also clear from the historical record that the Framers deliberately created a process that would make it difficult to remove the president from office in order to discourage Congress from seeking to get rid of a president for purely political reasons.

The steps that Congress would take in removing the president from office are the following:

1. The House of Representatives by simple majority vote would authorize an investigation of the president.
2. The House Judiciary Committee would conduct the inquiry and submit its findings to the full House.
3. The House through simple majority vote would indict the president on one or more charges (thus "impeaching" the president).
4. The Senate would hold a trial on the charges. The chief justice of the Supreme Court would preside over the trial, and the senators would be under oath to express themselves truthfully.
5. The Senate through a two-thirds majority would convict, causing the president's removal from office. The Senate would be prohibited from imposing any additional penalty (although subsequent action against the president in a court of law would not be precluded).

The Clinton impeachment process ended with step four; the Senate did not vote to convict. The course of Andrew Johnson's impeachment was the same, although the Senate, in his case, came within one vote of conviction. Nixon resigned shortly before the House vote (step three) on impeachment.

office, but they were also sharply critical of his relationship with Lewinsky. Not surprisingly, congressional Republicans and Democrats differed sharply on the impeachment issue. At all formal stages of the process—the House vote to authorize an inquiry, the House vote on the articles of impeachment, and the Senate vote on whether to convict the president—the vote divided largely along party lines. In the end, Clinton was acquitted by the Senate, but his legacy will forever be tarnished by his impeachment in the House.

The gravity of impeachment action makes it an unsuitable basis for curbing presidential power except in rare instances. More often, Congress has responded legislatively to executive abuses. Congress's most significant effort in history to curb presidential power is the War Powers Act. During the Vietnam War, Presidents Johnson and Nixon repeatedly misled Congress, supplying it with intelligence estimates that painted a falsely optimistic picture of the military situation. This information contributed to the willingness of Congress to appropriate the funds necessary for continuation of the war. However, congressional support changed abruptly in 1971 with *The New York Times*'s publication of classified government documents (the so-called Pentagon Papers) that revealed that Johnson and Nixon had systematically lied to Congress in order to pursue the war as they saw fit.

To prevent future presidential wars, Congress in 1973 passed the War Powers Act. Nixon vetoed the measure, but Congress overrode his veto. The act requires the president to notify Congress of the reason for committing combat troops within forty-eight hours of their deployment; requires that hostilities must end within sixty days unless Congress extends the period; gives the president an additional thirty days to withdraw the troops from hostile territory, although Congress can shorten the period; and requires the president to consult with Congress whenever feasible before dispatching troops into a hostile situation.

Every president since Nixon has claimed that the act unlawfully infringes on his constitutional power as commander in chief, and each has refused to accept it fully. They have complied with the forty-eight hour notification provision, but in several instances, including Bush's intervention in Panama in 1989 and Reagan's invasion of Grenada in 1983, Congress was not formally notified in advance. Recent presidents have also rejected the idea that Congress has constitutional authority to determine the initiation, scope, or timetable of military intervention.

Nevertheless, the lessons of Vietnam have been a significant curb on presidential war making. Congress has shown no willingness to give the president anything approaching a free hand in the use of military force. This posture was plainly evident when it became known in late 1986 that officials in the Reagan administration had attempted illegally and covertly to trade weapons for hostages held by the fundamentalist regime in Iran and had then used profits from the weapons sales to sneak arms to the Contra rebels fighting against the Sandanista government in Nicaragua. These policies violated a legislative prohibition on any form of military aid to the Contras, and Congress launched an immediate investigation that brought the unlawful practices to an abrupt halt, produced administrative changes designed to prevent such abuses of executive authority, and subjected President Reagan to sharp criticism and a loss of public support.

Thus, the effect of executive efforts to circumvent congressional authority is heightened congressional opposition. Even if presidents gain in the short run by acting on their own, they undermine their capacity to lead in the long run by failing to keep in mind that Congress is a coequal branch of the American governing system.

www.mhhe.com/patterson5

Simulation

Nurturing Public Support

Harry Truman kept a sign on his desk that read, "The buck stops here"—a reference not only to the president's ultimate responsibility for the decisions of his administration but also to the public's tendency to hold the president responsible for national success or failure. Therein lies an axiom of presidential power. As much as from any constitutional grant, executive authority derives from the president's position as the sole official who can claim to represent the whole American public. With public backing, the president's leadership cannot easily be dismissed by other Washington officials. If public support sinks, they are inclined to accept presidential leadership.[19]

presidential approval rating A measure of the degree to which the public approves or disapproves of the president's performance in office.

Every recent president has had the public's confidence at the very start of the term of office. When asked in polls whether they "approve or disapprove of how the president is doing his job," a majority have expressed approval during the first months of the term. Sooner or later, however, all **presidential approval ratings** have slipped below this high point, and fewer than half of recent presidents have left office with a final-year average higher than 50 percent.

CHARACTER OR CONDITIONS?

The president's personal character plays some part in the public's response. Charges of adultery and financial misconduct dogged Clinton throughout his presidency. Polls showed that Americans had misgivings about his ethical and moral standards and that a majority thought he lacked the level of personal character that is desirable in a president. This perception weakened Clinton's claim to leadership on moral issues and led some Americans to disapprove of his presidency.

The question is the degree to which character issues affect a president's approval ratings. Clinton's approval ratings averaged only 50 percent the first year. Other presidents have averaged about 60 percent or higher during this period (see Table 15-2). Yet Clinton's rating rocketed to the 70 percent level during the early weeks of the Lewinsky matter after dipping initially. Analysts attributed the public's response in part to a backlash against what was widely perceived as excesses in both the news media's coverage of the story and the actions of Kenneth Starr, the independent counsel who was leading the investigation. Even more critical was the fact that the economy was booming and most people were satisfied with the president's policies. In general, a president's personal traits have a smaller influence on presidential approval ratings than do national conditions. The same George Bush who had an approval rating of 91 percent at one point in his presidency had a 41 percent rating the next year. Bush's support peaked with the successful Gulf War in 1991 but declined as the nation's economy swooned.

Economic downswings tend to sharply reduce the public's confidence in the president. Ford, Carter, and Bush experienced precipitous declines in popularity in conjunction with deepening economic problems. A poor economy probably cost Ford a second term and was clearly the key factor in the failed bids for reelection of both Presidents Carter and Bush. In contrast, Clinton's popularity rose in 1995 and 1996 as the economy strengthened, contributing to his reelec-

TABLE 15-2 Percentage of Public Expressing Approval of President's Performance
Presidential approval ratings are generally higher at the beginning of the term than at the end.

President	Years in Office	Average During Presidency	First-Year Average	Final-Year Average
Harry Truman	1945–1952	41%	63%	35%
Dwight Eisenhower	1953–1960	64	74	62
John Kennedy	1961–1963	70	76	62
Lyndon Johnson	1963–1968	55	78	40
Richard Nixon	1969–1974	49	63	24
Gerald Ford	1974–1976	46	75	48
Jimmy Carter	1977–1980	47	68	46
Ronald Reagan	1981–1989	53	58	57
George Bush	1989–1992	61	65	40
Bill Clinton	1993–2000	57	50	60

SOURCE: Averages compiled from Gallup polls.

tion in 1996, just as an improving economy had carried Reagan to reelection in 1984. Apparently the best thing that a president can do to ensure political success is to preside over a healthy economy. It was no surprise that George W. Bush declared early in 2001 that policies designed to keep the economy from faltering would be his administration's highest priority.

The irony, of course, is that presidents do not actually have all that much control over the economy. If they did, it would always be strong. Nevertheless, their popularity moves up and down with the economy and so does the strength of their claim to national leadership.

THE PUBLIC'S RESPONSE TO CRISES

International crises nearly always have the effect of increasing the president's public standing, at least in the short run.[20] Threats from abroad tend to produce a patriotic "rally 'round the flag" reaction that initially creates widespread support for the president. Nearly every foreign policy crisis in the past four decades has conformed to this pattern. Even foreign policy disasters increase public support for the president. Reagan's popularity rose by several percentage points in 1983 after a terrorist bomb killed 241 U.S. Marines whom he had ordered into Lebanon in the midst of its civil war.

Yet ongoing crises can eventually erode a president's support. Within a month after Iranian extremists invaded the U.S. embassy in Teheran in November 1979 and took fifty-nine Americans hostage, Carter's public approval rating jumped from 32 to 51 percent.[21] The change revived Carter's prospects for reelection. Before the crisis began, he had fared badly in polls that asked Americans whether they would like to see him reelected. As months passed without a resolution of the hostage crisis, however, Carter's popularity began to sink and the collapse of hostage negotiations on the eve of the November balloting contributed to his defeat in the 1980 election.

Blindfolded American hostage Jerry Niele is paraded through the streets of Teheran by Iran's revolutionary guards. Although foreign policy crises ordinarily rally public support behind the president, the Iranian hostage crisis lasted a year and contributed to President Carter's defeat in the 1980 election.

Carter's problem stemmed from the public's high expectations of the president—the widespread belief that the president is the one who gets things done. As Godfrey Hodgson puts it, the president is expected to "conduct the diplomacy of a superpower . . . manage the economy, command the armed forces, serve as a spiritual example . . . [and] respond to every emergency."[22]

The Televised Presidency and the Illusion of Presidential Government

A major advantage that presidents enjoy in their efforts to nurture public support is their guaranteed access to the media, particularly television.[23] The television medium exalts personality, and the president is ordinarily the most compelling and familiar figure in the American political system. Only the president can expect the television networks to provide free air time for a major address. Moreover, the presidency receives roughly half again as much coverage as Congress does.[24]

The political scientist Samuel Kernell calls it "going public" when the president bypasses inside bargaining with Congress and promotes "himself and his policies by appealing to the American public for support."[25] Such appeals are at least as old as Theodore Roosevelt's use of the presidency as a bully pulpit but have increased substantially in recent years.[26] As the president has moved from an administrative leader to a policy advocate and agenda setter, public support has become increasingly important to presidential success.[27] Television has made it easier for presidents to go public with their programs. Ronald Reagan was called the "Great Communicator" in part because of his ability to use television to generate public support for his initiatives. Reagan's strength was the delivery of prepared speeches. Because he lacked a command of policy details, he did not perform well in informal settings, particularly when he had to respond to questioning. In one form or another, however, the president must find ways to communicate effectively with the public.[28]

The "going public" strategy is sometimes very effective. In 1998, President Clinton traveled to China amid criticisms that he was too soft on the issue of

China's human rights record. His primary goal was to strengthen economic ties between the two countries as part of the administration's global trade strategy. While there, however, he publicly argued that China would progress more rapidly economically if it allowed free expression and free elections. The trip did not silence all his critics but was widely seen as successful for its economic benefits and its staunch defense of American values.[29]

Critics have charged that presidents are sometimes more concerned with speaking out about problems than with working to solve them. During the second half of his presidency, for example, Reagan sent budgets to Congress that he knew had no chance of approval and then "went public" to make his point that the national government had become too large and expensive. Reagan's budgets were a statement about big government rather than a blueprint for spending in the next fiscal year.

The fact that presidents are the center of media attention does not mean it will always work to their advantage. The news media are highly critical of politicians and of the political process. During Clinton's first year, for example, the press roundly criticized him for reneging on his campaign promises. However, a Knight-Ridder summary showed he had kept or was actively pursuing in Congress 75 percent of the promises he had made during his election campaign. His accomplishments included a tax increase on upper incomes, gun control, an end to the ban on abortion counseling in federally funded clinics, and budget-deficit reduction. The press's version of reality was based on broken promises on a couple of problems that would not go away. Clinton had backed away from a pledge to open the nation's shores to the Haitian boat people, and each tide of immigrants produced additional stories on his broken promise. In contrast, the promises he kept were in the news only a day or two and then not mentioned again. Kept promises are not nearly as newsworthy as broken ones.

Clinton press secretary Mike McCurry held his daily briefings for reporters in the cramped space of the White House Briefing Room. Effective communication is an indispensable part of the modern presidency.

★ CRITICAL THINKING ★

WHAT'S YOUR OPINION?

Presidential "Character"
In his classic book *The Presidential Character*, political scientist James David Barber suggests that a president's orientation toward power ("active" or "passive," in Barber's terms) and politics ("positive" or "negative") affects the capacity to lead.

In Barber's view, "active" presidents are more effective than "passive" presidents are. Active presidents have a drive to lead and succeed. Passive presidents do not make full use of the office's resources. Barber also regards "positive" presidents as more effective. Positive presidents thrive on the give-and-take of politics. Negative presidents are driven by a compulsive sense of duty.

In fact, the presidents that Barber classifies as active-positive have tended to be relatively successful. Franklin D. Roosevelt and Harry Truman are examples. Barber regards active-negative presidents as potentially the most dangerous. Although driven to succeed, their negative traits of compulsiveness and distaste for the routines of politics can result in confrontation, stalemate, or deviousness. Woodrow Wilson and Richard Nixon are presidents in this category.

Do you accept Barber's conclusions? Why, or why not?

Ronald Reagan became known as the "Great Communicator" because of his skillful televised appeals to the public for support of his policies.

www.mhhe.com/patterson5

Self-Quiz

Presidents have no choice but to respond to critical coverage with their own version of events. If they do not, they would be entirely on the defensive, responding to others' interpretations. No recent administration has been more adept at putting its "spin" on events than Clinton's has. By 1995, the White House had become, as some in the press described it, "masters of the message."[30] Each day, Mike McCurry, the president's press secretary, would determine what the media's major political story would be, how the White House wanted it told, and what had to be done to put this "spin" on the story. By McCurry's own estimate, the White House succeeded about half the time—a remarkable record in view of the fact that other political actors and journalists themselves were also trying to control the story.[31]

A public relations effort can carry a president only so far, however. National conditions ultimately determine the level of public confidence in the president. Indeed, presidents run a risk by trying to build up their images through public relations. Through their frequent news appearances and claims of success, presidents contribute to the public's belief that the president is in charge of the national government, a perception that the political scientist Hugh Heclo calls "the illusion of presidential government."[32]

Because the public expects so much from its presidents, they get too much credit when things go well and too much blame when things go badly. Therein lies an irony of the presidential office. More than from any constitutional grant, more than from any statute, and more than from any crisis, presidential power derives from the president's position as the only official who can routinely claim to represent the whole nation. Yet because presidential power rests on a popular base, it erodes when public support declines. The irony is that the presidential office typically grows weaker as problems mount: just when the country could most use effective leadership, that leadership is often hardest to achieve.[33]

Summary

Presidents' records of success in getting their initiatives through Congress have varied considerably. The factors in a president's success include the presence or absence of national conditions that require strong leadership from the White House, the stage of the president's term (success usually comes early), the strength of the president's party in Congress, and the focus on the policy issue (presidents do somewhat better in the area of foreign policy than in domestic policy).

As sole chief executive and the nation's top elected official, the president is in a position to exert leadership. However, other institutions, particularly Congress, have the authority to make this leadership effective. A president who is to succeed over the long run must have a proper conception of the presidency. Even more important, the president must have the help of other officials and, to get their cooperation, he must respond to their concerns. Presidents operate within a system of divided powers and are almost sure to fail if they try to go it alone.

To retain an effective leadership position, the president also depends on the strong backing of the American people. Recent presidents have made extensive use of the media to build public support for their programs. Yet they have had difficulty maintaining that support throughout their terms of office. A major reason is that the public expects far more from its presidents than they can deliver.

Key Terms

honeymoon period   presidential approval rating

Suggested Readings

Burns, James MacGregor, Georgia J. Sorenson, Robin Gerber, and Scott W. Webster. *Dead Center: Clinton-Gore Leadership and the Perils of Moderation.* New York: Scribner, 1999. A critical analysis of presidential leadership in the context of the Clinton presidency.

Cohen, Jeffrey E. *Presidential Responsiveness and Public Policy-making: The Public and the Policies that Presidents Choose.* Ann Arbor: University of Michigan Press, 1997. An accounting of presidential responsiveness and public policymaking.

Gelderman, Carol W. *All the President's Words.* New York: Walker, 1997. A look at the presidency as a bully pulpit.

George, Alexander L., and Juliette L. George. *Presidential Personality and Performance.* Boulder, Colo.: Westview Press, 1998. A psychological study of the relationship of presidential personality and performance.

Jones, Charles. *Separate But Equal Branches.* New York: Chatham House, 1999. An insightful analysis of presidential power in a system of divided powers.

Kernell, Samuel. *Going Public: New Strategies of Presidential Leadership,* 3d ed. Washington, D.C.: Congressional Quarterly Press, 1997. An examination of presidential use of going public to gain support.

Light, Paul C. *The President's Agenda: Domestic Policy Choice from Kennedy to Clinton,* 3d ed. Baltimore, Md.: Johns Hopkins University Press, 1999. An assessment of the process of presidential agenda-setting, based on interviews with presidential staff members from Kennedy to Clinton.

Neustadt, Richard E. *Presidential Power and the Modern Presidents: The Politics of Leadership from Roosevelt to Reagan.* New York: Free Press, 1990. The classic analysis of the nature of presidential power.

Rose, Richard. *The Postmodern President,* 2d ed. Chatham, N.J.: Chatham House, 1991. An incisive analysis of the challenges that changing international conditions pose to the president.

Stuckey, Mary E. *The President as Interpreter-in-Chief.* Chatham, N.J.: Chatham House, 1991. A careful look at the president's power of communication.

Tulis, Jeffrey K. *The Rhetorical Presidency.* Princeton, N.J.: Princeton University Press, 1987. Argues that the modern presidency is split between its institutional and rhetorical aspects and that this division limits the president's effectiveness.

CHAPTER 16

The Federal Bureaucracy: Administering the Government

★

[No] industrial society could manage the daily operations of its public affairs without bureaucratic organizations in which officials play a major policymaking role.

—Norman Thomas[1]

★ ★ ★

*E*arly on the morning of September 7, 1993, a truck pulled up to the south lawn of the White House and unloaded pallets stacked with federal rules and regulations. The display was the backdrop for a presidential speech announcing the completion of the National Performance Review or, as it is commonly called, NPR. The federal regulations piled atop the pallets symbolized bureaucratic red tape, and NPR was a statement of the Clinton administration's effort to make government more responsive. "Our goal," said Clinton, "is to make the entire federal government both less expensive and more efficient, and to change the culture of our national bureaucracy away from complacency and entitlement toward initiative and empowerment. We intend to redesign, to reinvent, to reinvigorate the entire national government."[2]

The origins of the National Performance Review were plain enough. For years, the federal bureaucracy had been derided as too big, too expensive, and too intrusive. These charges gained weight as federal budget deficits increased and the public became increasingly dissatisfied with the performance of the government in Washington. Reform attempts in the 1970s and 1980s had some success but did not stem the tide of federal deficits or markedly improve the bureaucracy's performance. Clinton campaigned on the issue of "reinventing government" and acted swiftly on the promise. During the transition phase, Vice President–elect Al Gore was placed in charge of the National Performance Review. Once in office, Gore assembled more than two hundred career bureaucrats who knew firsthand how the bureaucracy operated and organized them into "reinventing teams" that would recommend ways of improving government administration. The NPR's report included 384 specific recommendations, which were grouped into four broad imperatives: reducing red tape, putting customers first, empowering administrators, and cutting government back to basic services.[3]

NPR is the latest in a lengthy list of major twentieth-century efforts to remake the federal bureaucracy. NPR was different in its particulars, but its claim to improve administration while saving money was consistent with the claims of earlier reform panels, including the Brownlow, Hoover, and Volcker commissions.[4] Like those efforts, NPR addressed an enduring issue of American politics: the bureaucracy's efficiency, responsiveness, and accountability.

Modern government would be impossible without a bureaucracy. It is the government's enormous administrative capacity that makes it possible for the United States to have such ambitious programs as space exploration, social security, environmental protection, interstate highways, and universal postal service. Yet the bureaucracy is also a problem. Even those who work in federal agencies agree that current bureaucratic systems are not working all that well.

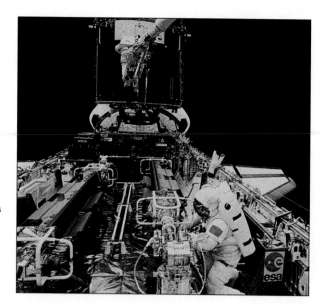

The bureaucracy's responsibilities include the space exploration program. The National Aeronautics and Space Administration (NASA) is the federal agency in charge of the program.

Both these elements, the need for bureaucracy and the problems associated with it, must be taken into account in any effort to understand the bureaucracy's place in modern American politics.

This chapter describes the nature of the federal bureaucracy and the politics that surrounds it. The discussion initially aims to clarify the bureaucracy's responsibilities, organizational structure, and management practices. But the chapter also shows that the bureaucracy is very much a part of the play of politics. Bureaucrats necessarily and naturally take an "agency point of view," seeking to promote their agency's objectives. The three constitutional branches of government impose a degree of accountability on the bureaucracy, but the sheer size and fragmented nature of the U.S. government confound the problem of control and make efforts to reform the bureaucracy a high priority. The main points discussed in this chapter are the following:

★ *Bureaucracy is an inevitable consequence of complexity and scale.* Modern government could not function without a large bureaucracy. Through authority, specialization, and rules, bureaucracy provides a means of managing thousands of tasks and employees.

★ *The bureaucracy is expected simultaneously to respond to the direction of partisan officials and to administer programs fairly and competently.* These conflicting demands are addressed through a combination of personnel management systems—the patronage, merit, and executive leadership systems.

★ *Bureaucrats naturally take an "agency point of view," which they promote through their expert knowledge, support from clientele groups, and backing by Congress or the president.*

★ *Although agencies are subject to scrutiny by the president, Congress, and the judiciary, bureaucrats are able to achieve power in their own right.* The issue of bureaucratic power and responsiveness is a basis of current efforts at "reinventing" government.

Federal Administration: Form, Personnel, and Activities

For many Americans, the word *bureaucracy* brings to mind waste, mindless rules, and rigidity. This image is not unfounded, but it is one-sided. Bureaucracy is also an efficient and effective method of organization. Although Americans tend to equate bureaucracy with the federal government, bureaucracy is found wherever there is a need to manage large numbers of people and tasks. Bureaucracy alone facilitates the coordination of a large work force. All large-scale, task-oriented organizations—public and private—are bureaucratic in form.[5] General Motors is a bureaucracy, and so is the Catholic church and every large medical complex and educational institution. The state governments are every bit as "bureaucratic" as the federal government (see "States in the Nation").

In formal terms, **bureaucracy** is a system of organization and control that is based on three principles: hierarchical authority, job specialization, and formalized rules. **Hierarchical authority** refers to a chain of command whereby the officials and units at the top of a bureaucracy have authority over those in the middle, who in turn control those at the bottom. In a system of **job specialization,** the responsibilities of each job position are explicitly defined, and there is a precise division of labor within the organization. **Formalized rules** are the standardized procedures and established regulations by which a bureaucracy conducts its operations.

These features are the reason that bureaucracy, as a form of organization, is the most efficient means of getting people to work together on tasks of great magnitude and complexity. Hierarchy speeds action by reducing conflict over the power to make decisions: the higher an individual's position in the organization, the more decision-making power he or she has. Specialization yields efficiency because each individual is required to concentrate on a particular job: workers acquire specialized skills and knowledge. Formalized rules enable workers to make quick and consistent judgments because decisions are made on the basis of preestablished guidelines rather than by deliberation and personal inclination.

These organizational characteristics are also the cause of bureaucracy's pathologies. Administrators perform not as whole persons but as parts of an organizational entity. Their behavior is governed by position, specialty, and rule. At its worst, bureaucracy grinds on, heedless of the feelings and needs of its members or their clients. Fixed rules come to dominate everything.[6]

If bureaucracy is an indispensable condition of large-scale organization, gross bureaucratic inefficiency and unresponsiveness are not, or at least that is the assumption underlying current efforts to reform the administration of government, a topic that will be examined later in this chapter.

bureaucracy A system of organization and control based on the principles of hierarchical authority, job specialization, and formalized rules.

hierarchical authority A basic principle of bureaucracy that refers to the chain of command within an organization whereby officials and units have control over those below them.

job specialization A basic principle of bureaucracy that holds that the responsibilities of each job position should be explicitly defined and that a precise division of labor within the organization should be maintained.

formalized rules A basic principle of bureaucracy that refers to the standardized procedures and established regulations by which a bureaucracy conducts its operations.

THE FEDERAL BUREAUCRACY IN AMERICANS' DAILY LIVES

The U.S. federal bureaucracy has more than 2.5 million employees, who have responsibility for administering thousands of programs. The president and Congress may get far more attention in the news, but it is the bureaucracy that has the more immediate impact on the daily lives of Americans. The federal bureaucracy performs a wide range of functions: for example, it delivers the daily mail, maintains the national forests and parks, administers social security,

★ STATES IN THE NATION

THE SIZE OF STATE BUREAUCRACIES

Although the federal bureaucracy is often criticized as being "too big," it is actually smaller on a per capita basis than even the smallest of the state bureaucracies. There are 1.0 federal employees for every 100 Americans. California, with 1.2 state employees for every 100 residents, has the smallest state bureaucracy on a per capita basis. Hawaii, with 5.0 state employees per 100 residents, has the largest. In general, the least populous states, and especially those that are larger geographically, have the largest bureaucracies on a per capita basis. This pattern reflects the fact that a state, whatever its population, has basic functions (such as highway maintenance and policing) that it must perform.

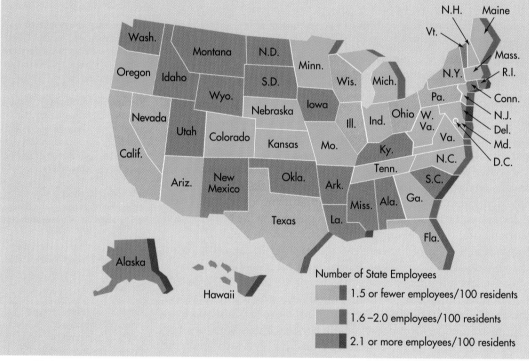

Number of State Employees

- 1.5 or fewer employees/100 residents
- 1.6–2.0 employees/100 residents
- 2.1 or more employees/100 residents

SOURCE: U.S. Bureau of the Census, 1999.

builds dams and generates hydroelectric power, enforces environmental protection laws, develops the country's defense systems, provides foodstuffs for school lunch programs, and regulates the stock markets.

TYPES OF ADMINISTRATIVE ORGANIZATIONS

The chief organizational feature of the U.S. federal bureaucracy is its division into areas of specialization. One agency handles veterans' affairs, another specializes in education, a third is responsible for agriculture, and so on. No two units are exactly alike. Nevertheless, most of them take one of five general forms: cabinet department, independent agency, regulatory agency, government corporation, or presidential commission.

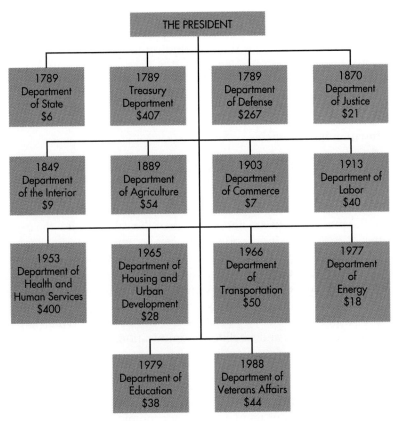

FIGURE 16-1 Cabinet (Executive) Departments
Each executive department is responsible for a general policy area and is headed by a secretary or, in the case of Justice, the attorney general, who serves as a member of the president's cabinet. Shown are each department's year of origin (above the title) and annual budget in billions of dollars (below the title). *Source: U.S. Office of Management and Budget, FY2000.*

Cabinet Departments

The major administrative units are the fourteen **cabinet** (or **executive**) **departments** (see Figure 16-1). Except for the Department of Justice, which is headed by the attorney general, the top official in each department is its secretary (for example, the secretary of defense), who serves as a member of the president's cabinet and is responsible for establishing the department's general policy and overseeing its operations.

Cabinet departments vary greatly in their visibility, size, and importance. The Department of State is one of the oldest and most prestigious departments, but it is also one of the smallest, with approximately twenty-five thousand employees. The Department of Defense has the largest work force, with more than seven hundred thousand civilian employees (apart from the more than 1.3 million uniformed members of the armed services). The Treasury Department has the largest budget, primarily because it pays the interest on the national debt. The Department of Health and Human Services has the next largest budget; its activities account for more than a fourth of all federal spending, much of it for social security benefits. The Department of Veterans Affairs is the newest department, dating from 1988.

Each cabinet department has responsibility for a general policy area. But executive departments are not monoliths: each department has a number of

cabinet (executive) departments The major administrative organizations within the federal executive bureaucracy, each of which is headed by a secretary or, in the case of Justice, the attorney general. Each department has responsibility for a major function of the federal government, such as defense, agriculture, or justice.

www.mhhe.com/patterson5

Graphic

semiautonomous operating units that typically carry the label of "bureau," "agency," "division," or "service." The Department of Justice, for example, has thirteen such operating units, including the Federal Bureau of Investigation (FBI), Immigration and Naturalization Service (INS), and Drug Enforcement Administration (DEA). In short, the Department of Justice is itself a large, complex bureaucracy.

Independent Agencies

independent agencies
Bureaucratic agencies that are similar to cabinet departments but usually have a narrower area of responsibility. Each such agency is headed by a presidential appointee who is not a cabinet member. An example is the National Aeronautics and Space Administration.

Independent agencies resemble the cabinet departments, but most of them have a narrower area of responsibility. They include such organizations as the Central Intelligence Agency (CIA) and the National Aeronautics and Space Administration (NASA). The heads of these agencies are appointed by and report to the president but are not members of the cabinet. Like the executive departments, each of the independent agencies is divided into smaller operating units. In general, the independent agencies exist apart from cabinet departments because their placement within a department would pose symbolic or practical policy problems. NASA, for example, could conceivably be located in the Department of Defense, but this positioning would suggest that the space program is intended for military purposes and not also for civilian purposes such as space exploration and satellite communication.

Regulatory Agencies

regulatory agencies
Administrative units, such as the Federal Communications Commission and the Environmental Protection Agency, that have responsibility for the monitoring and regulation of ongoing economic activities.

Regulatory agencies are created when Congress recognizes the importance of close and continuous regulation of an economic activity. Because such regulation requires more time and expertise than Congress can provide, the responsibility is delegated to a regulatory agency. The Securities and Exchange Commission (SEC), which oversees the stock and bond markets, is a regulatory agency. So is the Environmental Protection Agency (EPA), which monitors and prevents industrial pollution. Table 16-1 lists some of the regulatory agencies and other noncabinet units of the federal bureaucracy.

Beyond their executive functions, regulatory agencies have certain legislative and judicial functions. They issue regulations, implement them, and then judge whether individuals or organizations have followed them. Some regulatory agencies, particularly the older ones, are "independent" by virtue of their relative freedom from ongoing political control. They are headed by a commission of several members who are appointed by the president and confirmed by Congress but who are not subject to removal by the president. Commissioners serve a fixed term, a legal stipulation intended to free their agencies from political interference. The newer regulatory agencies lack such autonomy. Most are headed by a presidential appointee who can be removed at the president's discretion. (Regulatory agencies are discussed more fully in Chapter 18.)

Government Corporations

government corporations
Bodies, such as the U.S. Postal Service and Amtrak, that are similar to private corporations in that they charge for their services, but different in that they receive federal funding to help defray expenses. Their directors are appointed by the president with Senate approval.

Government corporations are similar to private corporations in that they charge clients for their services and are governed by a board of directors. However, government corporations receive federal funding to help defray operating expenses,

TABLE 16-1 Selected U.S. Regulatory Agencies, Independent Agencies, Government Corporations, and Presidential Commissions

Central Intelligence Agency	National Labor Relations Board
Commission on Civil Rights	National Railroad Passenger Corporation (Amtrak)
Consumer Product Safety Commission	
Environmental Protection Agency	National Science Foundation
Equal Employment Opportunity Commission	National Transportation Safety Board
Export-Import Bank of the United States	Nuclear Regulatory Commission
Farm Credit Administration	Occupational Safety and Health Review Commission
Federal Communications Commission	
Federal Deposit Insurance Corporation	Office of Personnel Management
Federal Election Commission	Peace Corps
Federal Emergency Management Agency	Securities and Exchange Commission
Federal Maritime Commission	Selective Service System
Federal Reserve System, Board of Governors	Small Business Administration
Federal Trade Commission	U.S. Arms Control and Disarmament Agency
General Services Administration	
National Aeronautics and Space Administration	U.S. Information Agency
	U.S. International Development Cooperation Agency
National Archives and Records Administration	U.S. International Trade Commission
National Foundation on the Arts and the Humanities	U.S. Postal Service

SOURCE: *The U.S. Government Manual.*

and their directors are appointed by the president with Senate approval. The largest government corporation is the U.S. Postal Service, with roughly 800,000 employees. Other government corporations include the Federal Deposit Insurance Corporation (FDIC), which insures savings accounts against bank failures, and the National Railroad Passenger Corporation (Amtrak), which provides passenger rail service.

Presidential Commissions

Some **presidential commissions** are permanent commissions that provide ongoing recommendations to the president in particular areas of responsibility. Two such commissions are the Commission on Civil Rights and the Commission on Fine Arts. Other presidential commissions are temporary and disband after making recommendations on specific issues. An example is the commission on racial reconciliation that was appointed by President Clinton in 1997; it concluded its work in 1998.

presidential commissions
Organizations within the bureaucracy that are headed by commissioners appointed by the president. An example of such a commission is the Commission on Civil Rights.

FEDERAL EMPLOYMENT

The roughly 2.5 million civilian employees of the federal government include professionals who bring their expertise to the problems of governing a large

Shown here is the main building of the Department of Housing and Urban Affairs (HUD). HUD, a cabinet-level federal agency, is headquartered at L'Enfant Plaza in the District of Columbia.

and complex society, service workers who perform such tasks as the typing of correspondence and the delivery of mail, and middle and top managers who supervise the work of the various federal agencies.

More than 90 percent of federal employees are hired by merit criteria, which include educational attainment, employment experience, and performance on competitive tests (such as the civil service and foreign service examinations). The merit system is intended to protect the public from the inept or discriminatory administrative practices that can result if partisanship is the employment criterion. A 1990 Supreme Court ruling prohibits patronage in all personnel operations (hiring, firing, transfers, promotions, training, and so on) unless the government can convincingly show that party affiliation is *positively* related to effective performance in a particular position.[7] This beneficial relationship can be demonstrated in some cases, but not in the large majority of personnel operations, which are thereby off limits to partisan politics.

Although federal employees were once greatly underpaid in comparison with their counterparts in the private sector, they now receive somewhat more competitive salaries, except at the top levels. The large majority of federal employees have a GS (Graded Service) job ranking. The rankings range from GS-1 (the lowest rank) to GS-18 (the highest). College graduates who enter the federal service usually start at the GS-5 level, which provides a salary of about $22,000 for a beginning employee. With a master's degree, the level is GS-9 at a $33,000 salary. Federal employees' salaries increase with rank and length of service. Public employees receive substantial fringe benefits, including full health insurance, liberal retirement plans, and generous vacation time and sick leave.

Public service has its drawbacks. Federal employees have few rights of collective action. They can join labor unions, but their unions by law have limited authority: the government maintains full control of job assignments, compensation, and promotion. Moreover, the Taft-Hartley Act of 1947 prohibits strikes by federal employees and permits the firing of workers who do go on strike. There are also some limits on the partisan activities of civil servants. The Hatch Act of 1939 prohibited them from holding key positions in election campaigns. In 1993,

Unlike union members in the private sector, federal employees are prohibited by law from going on strike and can be fired if they do so. President Reagan summarily fired members of the air traffic controllers union (PATCO) who went on strike in 1981. President Clinton offered reinstatement in 1993, but by then most of them had retired or started other careers. The union was back in the news again in 1998 when it opposed congressional action that changed the name of Washington National Airport to the Reagan National Airport.

Congress relaxed this prohibition but retained it for certain high-ranking career bureaucrats (including those in the Senior Executive Service, which is discussed later in the chapter).

THE FEDERAL BUREAUCRACY'S POLICY RESPONSIBILITIES

The Constitution mentions executive departments but does not grant them any powers. Their authority derives from grants of power to the three constitutional branches: Congress, the president, and the courts. Nevertheless, the bureaucracy is far more than an administrative extension of the three branches. It never merely follows orders. The primary function of administrative agencies is **policy implementation,** which is to say that they carry out the authoritative decisions of Congress, the president, and the courts.

Although implementation is sometimes described as "mere administration," it is a highly significant and creative function. Many ideas for legislative programs are initiated by the bureaucracy. In the course of their work, administrators come up with policy ideas that are then brought to the attention of the president or members of Congress. Administrative agencies also develop public policy in the process of implementing it. The decisions of Congress, the president, and the courts typically need to be fleshed out by the bureaucracy.[8] Most legislative acts identify general goals, which bureaucrats must then translate into specific programs. The Telecommunications Act of 1996, for example, had the stated goal "to promote competition and reduce regulation in order to secure lower prices and higher quality services for American telecommunication consumers and encourage the rapid deployment of new telecommunications technologies." Although the act included specific provisions, its implementation was left in large part for the Federal Communications Commission (FCC)

policy implementation
The primary function of the bureaucracy—it refers to the process of carrying out the authoritative decisions of Congress, the president, and the courts.

As one of thousands of services provided by the federal bureaucracy, the National Hurricane Service monitors hurricane activity and provides early warning to affected coastal areas.

to decide. The FCC decided, for example, that regional telephone companies (the Bell companies) had to open their networks to AT&T and other competitors at wholesale rates that were far below what they were charging their retail customers. The purpose was to enable AT&T and other carriers to compete with the Bell companies for local phone customers; in other words, the FCC was responding to its legislative mandate to promote "competition." But it was the FCC, not Congress, that determined the wholesale rates and many of the interconnection rules. This development of policy—often through *rule making*—is perhaps the chief way that administrative agencies exercise real power. To an important degree, they decide how the law will operate in practice.

Agencies are also charged with the delivery of services—carrying the mail, processing welfare applications, approving government loans, and the like. Such activities are governed by rules, and in most instances the rules decide what gets done. But some services allow agency employees enough discretion that laws end up being applied arbitrarily, a situation that Michael Lipsky describes as "street-level bureaucracy."[9] For example, FBI agents are more diligent in their pursuit of organized crime than of white-collar crime, even though the law does not designate white-collar criminals as somehow more deserving of more lenient treatment.

In sum, administrators necessarily exercise discretion in carrying out their policy responsibilities. They initiate policy, develop it, evaluate it, apply it, and determine whether others are complying with it. The bureaucracy does not simply administer policy, it also *makes policy*.

Development of the Federal Bureaucracy: Politics and Administration

The organization and staffing of the bureaucracy have been administrative and political issues throughout the country's history. Agencies are responsible for carrying out programs that serve the society, and yet each agency was created and is maintained in response to partisan interests. Each agency thus confronts

CURRENT CONTROVERSIES

DO BUREAUCRATS HAVE TOO MUCH DISCRETION? THE CASE OF THE FDA AND TOBACCO

The bureaucracy is more than an administrative body. It is also a policymaking body. In implementing and interpreting the policy decisions of Congress, the president, and the courts, bureaucrats necessarily make choices that affect the everyday lives of Americans. Even if this responsibility is an inevitable consequence of bureaucracy, there are differences of opinion on just how much latitude bureaucrats should have. These disputes are never simply the clash of opposing philosophies of government. More often, they are the result of a particular bureaucratic decision and whether it works to one side's political advantage. One such conflict took place regarding whether the Food and Drug Administration (FDA) had authority to regulate tobacco products. The Supreme Court ruled in *FDA v. Brown & Williamson Tobacco Co.* (2000) that the FDA did not have the authority. The majority and dissenting opinions in the case illustrate the conflict.

YES: Regardless of how serious the problem an administrative agency seeks to address, . . . it may not exercise it's authority "in a manner that is inconsistent with the administrative structure that Congress enacted into law." And although agencies are generally entitled to deference in the interpretation of statutes that they administer, a reviewing "court, as well as the agency, must give effect to the unambiguously expressed intent of Congress." In this case, we believe that Congress has clearly precluded the FDA from asserting jurisdiction to regulate tobacco products. Such authority is inconsistent with the intent that Congress has expressed in the . . . overall regulatory scheme and in the tobacco-specific legislation that it has enacted. . . In light of this clear intent, the FDA's assertion of jurisdiction is impermissible.

—Justice Sandra Day O'Connor, for the majority

NO: The Food and Drug Administration (FDA) has the authority to regulate "articles (other than food) intended to affect the structure or any function of the body . . ." Unlike the majority, I believe that tobacco products fit within this statutory language. . . . [T]he statute's basic purpose—the protection of public health—supports the inclusion of cigarettes within its scope. . . . I believe that the most important indicia of statutory meaning—language and purpose—along with the . . . legislative history are sufficient to establish that the FDA has authority to regulate tobacco. . . . [T]he Court today holds that a regulatory statute aimed at unsafe drugs and devices does not authorize regulation of a drug (nicotine) and a device (a cigarette) that the Court itself finds unsafe . . . [T]his particular drug and device risks the life-threatening harms that administrative regulation seeks to rectify.

—Justice Stephen G. Breyer, in dissent

two simultaneous but incompatible demands: that it administer programs fairly and competently and that it respond to partisan claims.

Historically, this conflict has worked itself out in ways that have made the organization of the modern bureaucracy a blend of the political and the administrative. This dual line of development is clearly reflected in the mix of management systems that characterizes the bureaucracy today—the *patronage, merit,* and *executive leadership* systems.

SMALL GOVERNMENT AND THE PATRONAGE SYSTEM

The federal bureaucracy was originally small (three thousand employees in 1800, for instance). Under the U.S. Constitution, the states retained responsibility for nearly all domestic policy areas. The federal government's role was confined mainly to defense and foreign affairs, currency and interstate commerce, and the delivery of the mail. The nation's first six presidents, from George Washington through John Quincy Adams, believed that only distinguished men should be entrusted with the management of the national government. Nearly all top presidential appointees were men of education and political experience, and many of them were members of socially prominent families. They often remained in their jobs year after year.

The nation's seventh president, Andrew Jackson, did not share his predecessors' admiration for the wellborn. In Jackson's view, government would be more responsive to the people if it were administered by common men of good sense.[10] Jackson also believed that top administrators should remain in office for short periods, so that there would be a steady influx of fresh ideas.

Jackson's version of the **patronage system** was popular with the public, but critics labeled it a **spoils system**—a device for placing political cronies in government office as a reward for partisan service. Although Jackson was motivated as much by a concern for democratic government as by his desire to reward partisan supporters, later presidents were often more interested in distributing the spoils of victory. Jackson's successors extended patronage to all levels of administration.[11]

patronage system   An approach to managing the bureaucracy whereby people are appointed to important government positions as a reward for political services they have rendered and because of their partisan loyalty.

spoils system   The practice of granting public office to individuals in return for political favors they have rendered.

GROWTH IN GOVERNMENT AND THE MERIT SYSTEM

Because the government of the early nineteenth century was relatively small and limited in scope, it could be managed by employees who had little or no administrative training or experience. As the century advanced, however, the nature of the bureaucracy changed rapidly, as did the bureaucracy's personnel needs.

An impetus for change was the Industrial Revolution, which was creating a truly national economy and was prompting economic groups to pressure Congress to protect and promote their interests. Farmers were one of the groups that looked to the federal government for market and price assistance. In response, Congress created the Department of Agriculture in 1889. Business and labor interests also pressed their claims, and in 1903 Congress established the Department of Commerce and Labor to "promote the mutual interest" of the nation's firms and workers. (The separate interests of business and labor proved stronger than their shared concerns, and so in 1913 Labor became a separate department.)[12]

Because of the increased need for continuous administration of government, an ever-larger bureaucracy was required (see Figure 16-2). By 1930, federal employment had reached six hundred thousand, a sixfold increase over the level of the 1880s.[13] During the 1930s, as a result of President Franklin Roosevelt's New Deal, the federal work force increased enormously, to 1.2 million. Roosevelt's programs were generated in response to public demands for relief from the economic hardship and uncertainty of the Great Depression. Administration of these programs necessitated the formation of economic and social welfare agencies such as the Securities and Exchange Commission and the Social Security Board. The effect was to give the federal government an ongoing role in promoting Americans' economic well-being.

merit (civil service) system   An approach to managing the bureaucracy whereby people are appointed to government positions on the basis of either competitive examinations or special qualifications, such as professional training.

A large and active government requires skilled and experienced personnel. In 1883, Congress passed the Pendleton Act, which established a **merit system** (or **civil service system**) whereby certain federal employees were hired through

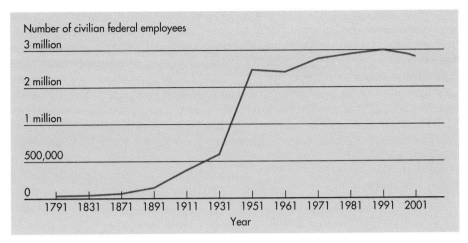

FIGURE 16-2   Number of Persons Employed by the Federal Government
The federal bureaucracy grew slowly until the 1930s, when an explosive growth began in the number of programs that required ongoing administration by the federal government. *Source: Historical Statistics of the United States and Statistical Abstract of the United States, 1986, 322; recent figures from U.S. Office of Personnel Management.*

competitive examinations or by virtue of having special qualifications, such as an advanced degree in a particular field. The transition to a career civil service was gradual. Only 10 percent of federal positions in 1885 were filled on the basis of merit. But the pace accelerated when the Progressives (see Chapter 2) promoted the merit system as a way of eliminating partisan graft and corruption in the administration of government. By 1920, as the Progressive era was concluding, more than 70 percent of federal employees were merit appointees. Since 1950, the proportion of merit employees has not dipped below 80 percent.[14]

The Pendleton Act created the Civil Service Commission to establish job classifications, administer competitive examinations, and oversee merit employees. The commission was replaced by two independent agencies in 1978. The Merit Service Protection Board handles appeals of personnel actions, and the Office of

The assassination of President James A. Garfield in 1881 by Charles Guiteau, a disappointed office seeker, did much to end the spoils system of distributing government jobs.

Personnel Management (OPM) supervises the hiring and classification of federal employees. The National Performance Review dramatically altered OPM's role. At the insistence of Vice President Gore, OPM deleted about two-thirds of the *Federal Personnel Manual,* which governs employee management practices. The effect was to move power out of the OPM to the agency level. Agencies and departments are freer to adapt personnel procedures to their particular needs. For its part, OPM is now less in the business of trying to manage a highly centralized personnel system and more in the business of advising agencies on their personnel policies, such as training programs for entry-level and mid-career employees.[15]

neutral competence The administrative objective of merit-based bureaucracy. Such a bureaucracy should be "competent" in the sense that its employees are hired and retained on the basis of their expertise and "neutral" in the sense that it operates by objective standards rather than partisan ones.

The administrative objective of the merit system is **neutral competence.**[16] A merit-based bureaucracy is "competent" in the sense that employees are hired and retained on the basis of their skills, and it is "neutral" in the sense that employees are not partisan appointees and thus are expected to do their work on behalf of everyone, not just those who support the incumbent administration.

Although the merit system contributes to the impartial and proficient administration of government programs, it has its own sources of bias and inefficiency. Career bureaucrats tend to place their agency's interests ahead of those of other agencies and typically oppose substantial efforts to trim their agency's activities. They are not partisans in the sense of Democratic or Republican politics, but they are partisans when it comes to protecting their own positions and agencies, as will be explained more fully later in the chapter.

BIG GOVERNMENT AND THE EXECUTIVE LEADERSHIP SYSTEM

executive leadership system An approach to managing the bureaucracy that is based on presidential leadership and presidential management tools, such as the president's annual budget proposal.

As problems with the merit system surfaced after the early years of the twentieth century, reformers looked to a strengthened presidency—an **executive leadership system**—as a means of coordinating the bureaucracy's activities to increase its efficiency and responsiveness.[17] The president was to provide the general leadership that would overcome agency fragmentation and provide a common direction. As we saw in Chapter 12, Congress in 1939 provided the president with some of the tools needed for improved coordination of the bureaucracy. The Office of Management and Budget (OMB) was created to give the president the authority to coordinate the annual budgetary process. Agencies would be required to prepare their budget proposals under the direction of the president, who would then submit the overall budget to Congress for its approval and modification. The president was also empowered to reorganize the bureaucracy, subject to congressional approval, in order to reduce duplication of activities and strengthen the chain of command from the president to the agencies. Finally, the president was authorized to develop the Executive Office of the President, which oversees the agencies' activities on the president's behalf, assisting in the development and implementation of policy programs.

Like the merit and patronage systems, the executive leadership system has brought problems as well as improvements to the administration of government. The executive leadership concept, if carried too far, can threaten the balance between executive power and legislative power on which the U.S. constitutional system is based, and it can make the president's priorities, not fairness, the criterion by which provision of services is determined. Richard Nixon abused the system, for example, by ordering the OMB to impound (that is, fail to spend) more than $40 billion in appropriated funds of programs he disliked. (The courts ruled that Nixon's action was an unlawful infringement on Congress's constitutional authority over spending. To prevent a recurrence of the problem, Congress in 1974 passed legislation that gives the president the authority to withhold funds for only forty-five days unless Congress passes legislation to rescind the appropriation.)

Nevertheless, executive leadership through the president is a vital part of the effort to bring greater accountability and direction to the administration of government. The executive leadership principle was the basis for the creation of the Senior Executive Service (SES). Established by Congress at the urging of President Carter, the SES represents a compromise between two traditions: a president-led bureaucracy and an expert one. The SES consists of roughly eight thousand top-level career civil servants who receive higher salaries than their peers but who can be assigned, dismissed, or transferred by order of the president. Unlike regular presidential appointees, SES bureaucrats cannot be fired. If the president relieves them of their jobs, they have "fallback" rights to their former rank in the regular civil service. The SES gives the president greater access to and control over individuals who are already expert in the bureaucracy's work. However, the SES has at least one drawback: after years of work in the bureaucracy, some top-level bureaucrats have difficulty transferring their loyalty from an agency to the president.

The executive leadership system is not a panacea but, along with the patronage and merit systems, is a necessary component of any effective strategy for managing the modern federal bureaucracy.[18] The federal bureaucracy today embodies aspects of all three systems, a situation that reflects the tensions inherent in governmental administration. The bureaucracy is expected to carry out programs fairly, but it is also expected to respond to political forces and to principles of effective management. The first of these requirements is addressed primarily through the merit system, the second through the patronage system, and the third through the executive leadership system (see Table 16-2).

The Bureaucracy's Power Imperative

A common misperception is that the president, as the chief executive, has the sole claim on the bureaucracy's loyalty. In fact, each of the elected institutions has reason to claim proprietorship: the president as chief executive and Congress as the source of the authorization and funding of the bureaucracy's programs. Faced with a threat from either Congress or the presidency, agencies often find an ally in the other institution. One presidential appointee asked a congressional committee whether it had any problem with his plans to reduce one of his agency's programs. The committee chairman replied, "No, you have the problem, because if you touch that bureau I'll cut your job out of the budget."[19]

The U.S. system of separate institutions sharing power results in a natural tendency for each institution to guard its turf. In addition, the president and members of Congress differ in their constituencies and thus in the interests to which they are most responsive. For example, although the agricultural sector is just one of many concerns of the president, it is of vital interest to senators and representatives from farm states. Finally, because the president and Congress are elected separately, the White House and one or both houses of

TABLE 16-2 Strengths and Weaknesses of Major Systems for Managing the Bureaucracy

System	Strengths	Weaknesses
Patronage	Makes the bureaucracy more responsive to election outcomes by allowing the president to appoint some executive officials.	Gives executive authority to individuals chosen for their partisan loyalty rather than administrative or policy expertise; can favor interests that supported the president's election.
Merit	Provides for *competent* administration in that employees are hired on the basis of ability and allowed to remain on the job and thereby become proficient, and provides for *neutral* administration in that civil servants are not partisan appointees and are expected to work in an evenhanded way.	Can result in fragmented, unresponsive administration since career bureaucrats are secure in their jobs and tend to place the interests of their particular agency ahead of those of other agencies or the nation's interests as a whole.
Executive leadership	Provides for presidential leadership of the bureaucracy in order to make it more responsive and to coordinate and direct it (left alone, the bureaucracy tends toward fragmentation).	Can upset the balance between executive and legislative power and can make the president's priorities, not fairness or effective management, the basis for administrative action.

Congress may be in the hands of opposing parties. Since 1968, this source of executive-legislative conflict has been more often the rule than the exception.

If agencies are to operate successfully in this system, they must seek support where they can find it—if not from the president, then from Congress; if not today, then tomorrow. In other words, agencies must play politics.[20] Any agency that is content to sit idly by while new priorities for money and policy are determined is virtually certain to lose out to other agencies that are willing to fight for power.

THE AGENCY POINT OF VIEW

agency point of view The tendency of bureaucrats to place the interests of their agency ahead of other interests and ahead of the priorities sought by the president or Congress.

Administrators have little choice but to look out for their agency's interests, a perspective that is called the **agency point of view**.[21] This perspective comes naturally to most high-ranking civil servants. Their careers within the bureaucracy have taught them to do their part in making the organization effective. Many bureaucrats are also personally committed to their agency's objectives as a result of having spent years working on its programs. More than 80 percent of all top careerists reach their high-level positions by rising through the ranks of the same agency.[22] As one top administrator said when testifying before the House Appropriations Committee, "Mr. Chairman, you would not think it proper for me to be in charge of this work and not be enthusiastic about it . . . would you? I have been in it for thirty years, and I believe in it."[23]

Professionalism also cements agency loyalties. As public policy making has become more complex, high-level administrative positions have increasingly been filled by scientists, engineers, lawyers, educators, physicians, and other professionals. Most of them take jobs in an agency whose programs are consistent with their professional values.

Studies confirm that bureaucrats believe in the importance of their agency's work. One study found that social welfare administrators are three times as likely as other civil servants to believe that social welfare programs should be given a high budget priority.[24]

SOURCES OF BUREAUCRATIC POWER

In promoting their agency's interests, bureaucrats rely on their specialized knowledge, the support of interests that benefit from the programs they run, and the backing of the president and Congress.

The Power of Expertise

Most of the policy problems that the federal government confronts do not lend themselves to simple solutions. Whether the issue is space travel or hunger in America, expert knowledge is essential to the development of effective public policy. Much of this expertise is held by bureaucrats. They spend their careers working in a particular policy area, and many of them have had scientific, technical, or other specialized training.[25]

By comparison, elected officials are generalists. To some degree, members of Congress do specialize through their committee work, but they rarely have the time or inclination to acquire a commanding knowledge of a particular issue. The president's understanding of policy issues is even more general. Not surprisingly, the president and members of Congress regularly depend on the bureaucracy for policy advice and guidance.

Not all agencies acquire a great amount of leverage from their staffs' expert knowledge. Those that have an edge have highly specialized, professional staffs. For example, the expert judgments of the health scientists and physicians in the National Institutes of Health (NIH) are rarely challenged by elected officials. They may question the political assessments of these health professionals but are unlikely to question their scientific evaluations, which are sometimes decisive. For example, as much as some elected officials may have wanted to avoid the issues surrounding the emerging AIDS epidemic during the 1980s, they were eventually forced into action by the warnings of health scientists about the dire consequences of a do-nothing policy.

The power of expertise is conditioned by the extent to which an agency's employees share the same goals. In many agencies, such as the NIH, careerists with different professional backgrounds have similar values. In other agencies, professional infighting breaks down this cohesiveness and gives outsiders an opportunity to support the faction whose aims agree with their own. An example is the Federal Trade Commission (FTC), which is divided between its lawyers, who tend to emphasize issues that can be quickly and successfully litigated, and its economists, who tend to stress larger and more complicated issues that have broad implications for national commerce.[26]

HOW THE UNITED STATES COMPARES

EDUCATIONAL BACKGROUNDS OF BUREAUCRATS

To staff its bureaucracy, the U.S. government tends to hire persons with specialized educations to hold specialized jobs. This approach heightens the tendency of bureaucrats to take the agency point of view. By comparison, Great Britain tends to recruit its bureaucrats from the arts and humanities, on the assumption that general aptitude is the best qualification for detached professionalism. The continental European democracies also emphasize detached professionalism, but in the context of the supposedly impartial application of rules. As a consequence, high-ranking civil servants in Europe tend to have legal educations. The college majors of senior civil servants in the United States and other democracies reflect these tendencies.

College Major of Senior Civil Servants	Denmark	Germany	Great Britain	Italy	Netherlands	United States
Natural science/ engineering	16%	8%	26%	10%	25%	32%
Social science/ humanities/business	20	18	52	37	28	50
Law	60	63	3	53	45	18
Other	4	11	19	—	2	—
	100%	100%	100%	100%	100%	100%

From THE POLITICS OF BUREAUCRACY 4th ed. by B. Guy Peters. Copyright 1995 by Longman Publishers USA. Reprinted by permission of Addison-Wesley Educational Publishers Inc.

Nevertheless, all agencies acquire some power through their careerists' expertise. No matter how simple a policy issue may appear at first, it invariably involves more than meets the eye. A recognition that the United States has a trade deficit with Japan, for example, can be the premise for policy change, but this recognition does not begin to address such basic issues as the form that the new policy might take, its probable cost and effectiveness, and its connection to other trade issues. Among the officials most likely to understand these issues are the bureaucrats in the Commerce Department and the Federal Trade Commission.

The Power of Clientele Groups

clientele groups Special-interest groups that benefit directly from the activities of a particular bureaucratic agency and are therefore strong advocates of the agency.

Most agencies have **clientele groups,** which are special interests that benefit directly from an agency's programs. Clientele groups place pressure on Congress and the president to retain the programs from which they benefit.[27] A result is that agency programs, once started, are difficult to terminate. "Government activities," as public administration expert Herbert Kaufman says, "tend to go on indefinitely."[28]

The importance of clientele groups was evident in 1995 when House Speaker Newt Gingrich threatened to "zero out" funding for the Corporation for Public Broadcasting. The threat produced an immediate response (some of it orchestrated by public broadcasting stations) from audience members and

The popular children's program *Sesame Street* is produced through the Corporation for Public Broadcasting, a government agency that gains leverage in budgetary deliberations from its public support. The singer Garth Brooks is shown here with two muppets during his appearance on *Sesame Street*.

from groups such as the Childrens Television Workshop. They wrote, called, faxed, and cajoled members of Congress, saying that programs like *Sesame Street* and *All Things Considered* were irreplaceable by anything available from commercial broadcasting. Within a few weeks, Gingrich had relented somewhat, saying that a phase-out plan for ending the funding would be preferable to an abrupt cessation and that it might be prudent to retain funding for some activities, such as support of stations in rural areas not adequately served by commercial broadcasters.

In general, agencies lead and are led by the clientele groups that depend on the programs they administer.[29] Many agencies were created for the purpose of promoting particular interests in society. For example, the Department of Agriculture's career bureaucrats are dependable allies of farm interests year after year. The same cannot be said of the president, Congress as a whole, or either political party; they must balance farmers' demands against those of other interests.

The Power of Friends in High Places

Although members of Congress and the president sometimes appear to be at war with the bureaucracy, they need it as much as it needs them. An agency's resources—its programs, expertise, and group support—can assist elected officials in their efforts to achieve their goals. When George Bush came to the White House, he made the problem of drug-related crime a top priority, and he needed the help of Justice Department careerists to make his efforts successful. At a time when other agencies were feeling the pinch of a tight federal budget, the Justice Department's personnel increased by 20 percent during Bush's term of office.

Bureaucrats also seek favorable relations with members of Congress. Congressional support is vital because agencies' funding and programs are established through legislation. Agencies that offer benefits to major constituency interests are particularly likely to have close ties to Congress. In some policy areas, more or less permanent alliances—iron triangles—form among agencies, clientele groups, and congressional subcommittees. In other policy areas,

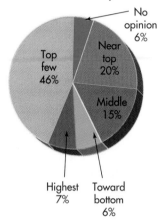

"In terms of the country's priorities, where would you rank 'cutting the size of the federal bureaucracy'?"

No opinion 6%

Near top 20%

Top few 46%

Middle 15%

Highest 7%

Toward bottom 6%

FIGURE 16-3 Public Confidence in the Bureaucracy
Americans generally have a low opinion of the federal bureaucracy even though by most indicators it is an effective organization of its type. *Source: Democratic Leadership Council, 1995.*

accountability The ability of the public to hold government officials responsible for their actions.

temporary issue networks form among bureaucrats, lobbyists, and members of Congress. As we saw in Chapters 10 and 13, these alliances enable agencies and interest groups to promote the programs they want and provide members of Congress with electoral support.

Bureaucratic Accountability

Bureaucratic politics raises the specter of a huge, permanent, and uncontrollable organization run by entrenched unelected officials. This image certainly characterizes the way that many Americans perceive the federal bureaucracy. Even though most Americans say that they have a favorable impression of their most recent personal experience with the bureaucracy (as, say, when a senior citizen applies for social security), they have an unfavorable impression of the bureaucracy as a whole (see Figure 16-3). This view is somewhat unfair—the effectiveness of the U.S. federal bureaucracy has been found in studies to compare favorably with that of other governmental bureaucracies at home and abroad[30]—but is nonetheless easy to understand. For one thing, the news media rarely cover the bureaucracy except when it makes a colossal mistake, fostering the impression that bureaucratic incompetence is widespread. In addition, the bureaucracy is a faceless institution that is largely beyond the citizens' direct control. When combined with Americans' traditional mistrust of concentrated political power, it is no surprise that they have qualms about the federal bureaucracy and want it more closely controlled.

Adapting the requirements of the bureaucracy to those of democracy has been a persistent challenge for public administration.[31] The issue is **accountability:** the capacity of the public to hold officials responsible for their actions. In the case of the bureaucracy, accountability works primarily through other institutions: the presidency, Congress, and the courts.

ACCOUNTABILITY THROUGH THE PRESIDENCY

The president can only broadly influence, not directly control, the bureaucracy. "We can outlast any president" is a maxim of bureaucratic politics. In recent years, with the emphasis on scaling down the bureaucracy, the saying seems more wishful than truthful. Nevertheless, each agency has its clientele and its congressional supporters, as well as statutory authority for its existence and activities. No president can unilaterally eliminate an agency or its funding and programs. Nor can the president be indifferent to the opinions of career civil servants—not without losing their support and expertise in developing and implementing presidential policy objectives.

To encourage the bureaucracy to cooperate, the president has important management tools that have developed out of the "executive leadership" concept discussed previously. These tools include reorganization, presidential appointees, and the executive budget.

Reorganization

The bureaucracy's extreme fragmentation—its hundreds of separate agencies—makes presidential coordination of its activities difficult. Agencies pursue independent, even contradictory paths, resulting in an undetermined amount of waste and duplication of effort. For example, more than one hundred units are responsible for different pieces of education policy.

All recent presidents have tried to streamline the bureaucracy and make it more accountable.[32] The most ambitious reorganization plan was Nixon's proposal to combine fifty domestic agencies into four large departments, which would have given him tighter control over domestic policy. Existing agencies fought Nixon's plan because it threatened their independence. Their clientele groups joined the opposition since they feared the loss of programs. Members of Congress rejected Nixon's plan because of the objections raised by various interests and also because they recognized that centralization would reduce their influence on the bureaucracy.

Presidents have frequently been able to make less sweeping changes in the bureaucracy's organization, such as reducing the autonomy or number of employees of particular agencies. These changes serve to upgrade or downgrade programs but ordinarily have not greatly improved presidential control of the bureaucracy.[33]

Presidential Appointments

Although there is almost no direct confrontation with a bureaucrat that a president cannot win, the president does not have time to deal personally with every troublesome careerist or make sure that the bureaucracy has complied with every presidential order. The president relies on political appointees in the agencies to ensure that directives are followed.

The power of presidential appointees is greater in those agencies where wide latitude exists in the making of decisions. Although the social security administration has a huge budget and gives monthly payments to more than forty million Americans, the eligibility of recipients is determined by relatively fixed rules. In contrast, most regulatory agencies have broad discretion over regulatory policy, and a change in leadership can have a substantial impact. For example, President Reagan's appointee to head the Federal Trade Commission, James Miller III, was a strong-willed economist who shared Reagan's belief that consumer protection policy had gone too far and was adversely affecting business interests. In Miller's first year as head of the FTC, the commission dropped one-fourth of its pending cases against business firms.[34] Overall, enforcement actions declined by about 50 percent during Miller's tenure compared with the previous period.

Presidential influence also works indirectly through its impact on career bureaucrats' willingness to pursue policies they prefer. A recent study by David Lazer of Harvard University found that bureaucrats tend to be more willing to seek support from top administration officials when they believe these officials share their policy views. When Clinton, a Democrat, succeeded Bush, a Republican, as president, there was a change in the frequency with which career bureaucrats initiated contact with the White House: those with liberal beliefs made contact more often while those with conservative beliefs made contact less often. Liberals were particularly likely to make contact when they disagreed with agency policy; their goal was to get White House support for a reversal of policy.[35]

However, as we noted in Chapter 14, there are limits to what a president can accomplish through appointments. High-level presidential appointees number in the hundreds, and their turnover rate is high: the average appointee remains in the administration for less than two years before moving on to other employment.[36] No president can keep track of all appointees, much less instruct them in detail on all intended policies. In addition, some presidential appointees will have a vested interest in the agencies they head. In choosing political appointees, the president is lobbied by groups that depend on agency programs. Rather than antagonize these groups, the president will accept their recommendations in some cases.

The Executive Budget

Faced with the difficulty of controlling the bureaucracy, presidents have come to rely heavily on their personal bureaucracy, the Executive Office of the President (EOP).

In terms of presidential management, the key unit within the EOP is the Office of Management and Budget (OMB). Funding, programs, and regulations are the mainstays of every agency, and the OMB has substantial influence on each of these areas. No agency can issue a major regulation without the OMB's verification that the regulation's benefits outweigh its costs, and no agency can propose legislation to Congress without the OMB's approval. However, the OMB's greatest influence over agencies derives from its budgetary role. At the start of the annual budget cycle, the OMB assigns each agency a budget limit in accord with the president's directives. The agency's tentative allocation requests are sent back to the OMB, which then conducts a final review of all requests before sending the full budget to Congress in the president's name.

In most cases, an agency's overall budget does not change much from year to year. This fact indicates that a significant portion of the bureaucracy's activities persist regardless of who sits in the White House or Congress.[37] It must be noted, however, that the bulk of federal spending is for programs such as social

The Old Executive Office Building is adjacent to the west wing of the White House. Its occupants are part of the Executive Office of the President (EOP) and serve as contacts between the president and agency bureaucrats.

security that, although enacted in the past, have the continuing support of the president, Congress, and the public.

ACCOUNTABILITY THROUGH CONGRESS

Congress has powerful means of influencing the bureaucracy. All agencies depend on Congress for their existence, authority, programs, and funding.

The most substantial control that Congress exerts on the bureaucracy is through its power to authorize and fund programs. Without authorization or funding, a program simply does not exist, regardless of the priority an agency claims it deserves. Congress can also void an administrative decision through legislation that prohibits it or mandates an alternative course of action. However, Congress lacks the institutional capacity to work out complex policies down to the last detail.[38] The bureaucracy would grind to a halt if it had to get congressional approval for all its policy decisions. Congress has no option in most cases but to give the bureaucracy a general heading and then let it proceed along that course.

Correcting Administrative Error: Legislative Oversight

Congress also exerts some control through its oversight function, which involves monitoring the bureaucracy's work to ensure compliance with legislative intent.[39] As we noted in Chapter 13, however, oversight is a difficult and relatively unrewarding task, and members of Congress ordinarily place less emphasis on oversight than on their other major duties. Only when an agency has clearly stepped out of line is Congress likely to take decisive corrective action by holding hearings to ask tough questions and to warn of legislative punishment.

A dramatic example is environmental regulation during Reagan's presidency. Regulatory activity, as was noted earlier in the chapter, dropped sharply when Reagan took office. Then in 1983, the news media disclosed that the Environmental Protection Agency (EPA) had privately arranged lenient settlements for firms that had committed serious violations of toxic-waste disposal regulations. The ensuing congressional investigation resulted in the resignation, dismissal, or conviction in court of more than a half-dozen top EPA officials. EPA director Anne Burford was cited for contempt of Congress for her refusal to cooperate with the investigation. The EPA's toxic-waste inspection level more than tripled soon thereafter, and when Congress restored EPA's budget, it rose again. Within two years, EPA's inspection rate was six times higher (from about 325 inspections a year to 2,000). In their study of this case, B. Dan Wood and Richard W. Waterman concluded: "Thus, for the EPA policy in which Congress was most directly involved, legislative influence was clearly manifest through the powers of oversight and appropriations."[40]

Congress has sometimes legislated its own authority to void bureaucratic decisions—a device called the *legislative veto*. When Congress authorized the Alaska oil pipeline, for example, it retained the authority to veto bureaucratic decisions about the pipeline's route. In 1983, however, the Supreme Court voided the use of a legislative veto as interference with the president's constitutional authority to execute the laws but limited its ruling to the law in question. During the same year, the Court affirmed two lower-court rulings that the legislative veto was unconstitutional. Whether the Supreme Court in some situations will rule differently remains to be tested by future cases, but Congress has from time to time continued to include the legislative veto in bills that presidents have signed into law.[41]

Because oversight is so difficult and unrewarding, Congress has shifted much of its oversight responsibility to the General Accounting Office (GAO). The GAO's primary function once was to keep track of the funds spent within the bureaucracy; now it also monitors the implementation of policies. The Congressional Budget Office (CBO) also does oversight studies. When the GAO or CBO uncovers a major problem with an agency's handling of a program, it notifies Congress, which can then take remedial action.

Restricting the Bureaucracy in Advance

Of course, an awareness by bureaucrats that misbehavior can trigger a response from Congress helps to keep them in line. Nevertheless, oversight cannot correct mistakes or abuses that have already occurred. Recognizing this limit on oversight, Congress has devised ways to constrain the bureaucracy *before* it acts. The simplest method is to draft laws that contain very specific provisions that limit bureaucrats' options when they implement policy. Another restrictive device is the "sunset law," which establishes a specific date when a law will expire unless it is reenacted by Congress. Advocates of sunset laws see them as a means to counter the bureaucracy's reluctance to give up programs that have outlived their usefulness. Since members of Congress usually want their policies to last far into the future, however, most legislation does not include a sunset provision.

ACCOUNTABILITY THROUGH THE COURTS

The judiciary's influence on agencies is less direct than that of the elected branches, but the courts, too, can and do act to ensure the bureaucracy's compliance with Congress's requirements. Legally, the bureaucracy derives its authority from acts of Congress, and an injured party can bring suit against an agency on the grounds that it has failed to carry out the law properly. Judges can then order an agency to change its application of the law.[42]

However, the courts have tended to support administrators if their actions seem at all consistent with the laws they are administering. The Supreme Court has held that agencies can choose rule-making procedures that meet the minimal threshold set down by Congress, that agencies can apply any reasonable interpretation of statutes unless Congress has specifically stated something to the contrary, and that agencies in many instances have wide discretion in deciding whether to enforce statutes.[43] These positions reflect the need for flexibility in administration. The bureaucracy and the courts would both grind to a halt if judges routinely chose to substitute their interpretations of the law for those of administrators. The judiciary cannot conduct a decision-by-decision oversight of the bureaucracy. Judges recognize that constraints on the bureaucracy must work mainly through the Congress and the president. The judiciary has promoted bureaucratic accountability primarily by encouraging administrators to act responsibly in their dealings with the public and by protecting individuals and groups from the bureaucracy's worst abuses.

Whistle-blowers Diane Klipfel and Mike Caseli of the Bureau of Alcohol, Tobacco, and Firearms (ATF) alleged that police officers assigned to ATF had stolen money from drug dealers. Soon thereafter, Klipfel and Caseli and their family were subject to threats, and action to fire the two was initiated. Although the Klipfel and Caseli case is an extreme one, whistle-blowers are frequently the target of retaliation from within their organization.

ACCOUNTABILITY WITHIN THE BUREAUCRACY ITSELF

A recognition of the difficulty of ensuring adequate accountability of the bureaucracy through the presidency, Congress, and the courts has led to the development of mechanisms of accountability within the bureaucracy itself. Two measures, whistle-blowing and demographic representativeness, are particularly noteworthy.

Whistle-Blowing

Although the bureaucratic corruption that is rampant in some countries is relatively uncommon in the United States, a certain amount of waste, fraud, and abuse is inevitable in a bureaucracy as big as that of the federal government. **Whistle-blowing,** the act of reporting instances of corruption or mismanagement by one's fellow bureaucrats, is a potentially effective internal check.[44] Whistle-blowing, however, has not been highly successful. A survey conducted by a Senate subcommittee indicated that most federal employees will not report instances of mismanagement because they fear reprisals from their superiors. Their fears are not groundless. For example, Alan Diehl, the U.S. Air Force's top civilian safety official, was assigned to a lesser position after releasing a report indicating that Air Force investigators had routinely misrepresented the causes of military air crashes in order to save the Air Force and its top officers the embarrassment that would have occurred if the actual causes had been revealed.[45]

To encourage federal employees to come forward when they see instances of mismanagement, Congress enacted the Whistle Blower Protection Act to protect them from retaliation. Federal law also provides whistle-blowers with financial rewards in some cases.

whistle-blowing An internal check on the bureaucracy whereby employees report instances of mismanagement that they observe.

Demographic Representativeness

Although the bureaucracy is an unrepresentative institution in the sense that its officials are not elected by the people, it can be representative in the demographic

TABLE 16-3   **Federal Job Rankings (GS) of Various Demographic Groups**   Women and minority group members are underrepresented in the top jobs of the federal bureaucracy but their representation has been increasing.

Grade Level*	WOMEN'S SHARE		BLACKS' SHARE		HISPANICS' SHARE	
	1976	*1997*	*1982*	*1997*	*1982*	*1997*
GS 1–4 (lowest ranks)	78%	69%	23%	28%	5%	8%
GS 5–8	60	69	19	25	4	7
GS 9–12	20	43	10	14	4	6
GS 13–15 (highest ranks)	5	27	5	8	2	4

*In general, the higher-numbered grades are managerial and professional positions, and the lower-numbered grades are clerical and manual labor positions.

SOURCE: Office of Workforce Information, 1998.

sense. If bureaucrats were a demographic microcosm of the general public, they presumably would treat the various groups and interests in society more fairly.[46] "A public service . . . which is broadly representative of all categories of the population," public administration scholar Frederick Mosher concludes, "may be thought of as satisfying Lincoln's prescription of government 'by the people' in the limited sense."[47]

At present, the bureaucracy is not demographically representative at its top levels (see Table 16-3). More than 60 percent of managerial and professional positions are held by white males. However, the employment status of women and, to a lesser extent, minorities has improved somewhat in recent years, and top officials in the bureaucracy include a greater proportion of women and minorities than is found in Congress or the judiciary. Moreover, if all levels of the federal bureaucracy are considered, it comes reasonably close to being representative of the nation's population.[48]

demographic representativeness
The idea that the bureaucracy will be more responsive to the public if its employees at all levels are demographically representative of the population as a whole.

Demographic representativeness is only a partial answer to the problem of bureaucratic accountability. A fully representative civil service would still be required to play agency politics. The careerists in, say, defense agencies and welfare agencies are not very different in their demographic backgrounds, but they differ markedly in their opinions about policy. Each group believes that the goals of its agency should take priority. The inevitability of agency politics is the most significant of all political facts about the U.S. federal bureaucracy.[49]

Reinventing Government

There have been numerous attempts during the twentieth century to enhance the bureaucracy's efficiency, responsiveness, and accountability. Another wave of this reform effort began in the 1990s, and it seeks to improve the administration of government by the reduction of its size, cost, and lines of authority.

This effort is based in part on the notion that the bureaucracy would be more effective and responsive if it were made smaller. In *Reinventing Government,*

David Osborne and Ted Gaebler argue that the bureaucracy of today was created in response to earlier problems, particularly those spawned by the Industrial Revolution and a rampant spoils system. They claim that the information age requires a different kind of administrative structure, one that is more flexible and less hierarchical. Instead of the provision of goods and services, the bureaucracy ought to be in the business of creating incentives that will encourage individuals to make their own way and ought to foster competition among and between agencies and private firms. This approach requires a more decentralized form of administration that is oriented toward consumers and results. Osborne and Gaebler would empower lower-level employees to make decisions that previously were made at the top of the bureaucracy.[50]

This concept informed the Clinton administration's National Performance Review and is embedded in some laws and administrative practices. OPM's relationship to federal agencies, described earlier in the chapter, is a case in point. Another example is the practice of making extensive use of private contractors rather than government employees for certain tasks. Yet another example is a recent law that requires agencies to monitor their performance by standards such as efficiency, responsiveness, and outcomes. These standards have long been considered gauges of administrative effectiveness but have often been overlooked as bureaucrats went about their customary ways of doing business. The law seeks to overcome this inertia by *requiring* agencies to actively monitor their performance.

The downsizing of the federal bureaucracy is also being driven by political forces. Chronic budget deficits in the 1970–95 period and the public's dissatisfaction with Washington helped create political momentum to reduce the scope of the federal government. The momentum intensified with the Republican takeover of Congress in 1995, but some results were already apparent. Federal employment, for example, had declined by one hundred thousand positions from its level when Clinton took office.[51]

The new era will be one of smaller government, not small government. There are limits to how far the federal government can be trimmed. Some activities can be delegated to states and localities, and others can be privatized, but many, if not most, of Washington's programs cannot be reassigned. National defense, social security, and Medicare are but three examples, and they alone account for the bulk of federal spending (see Chapters 19 and 20).

Some analysts question the logic and presumed consequences of the changes that are taking place. They have asked, for example, whether the principles of decentralized management and market-oriented programs are as sound as their advocates claim. The delegation of control to lower-level administrators weakens the hierarchical connection between elected and administrative officials. A reason for hierarchy was to ensure that decisions made at the bottom of the bureaucracy were faithful to the laws made by Congress. Free to act on their own, lower-level administrators, as they did under the spoils system, might favor certain people and interests over others.[52] There is also the issue of the identity of the "customers" in a market-oriented administration.[53] Who are the Security and Exchange Commission's customers—firms, brokerage houses, or shareholders? Will not some agencies inevitably favor their more powerful customers at the expense of the less powerful ones?

★ CRITICAL THINKING ★

WHAT'S YOUR OPINION?

Reinventing Government
In *Reinventing Government* (1992), David Osborne and Ted Gaebler argue that the bureaucracy should be less hierarchical. They would delegate power downward, allowing working-level federal employees to make decisions that were previously made at the top. The bureaucracy would be more flexible and more market oriented than in the past.

Other analysts contend that this idea rests on a faulty conception of government. They argue that lower-level employees should operate in a line-of-authority flowing from the top. Without this, the "faithful execution of the laws" is jeopardized. Working-level employees will make decisions that are inconsistent or at odds with the acts of Congress they are charged with implementing. The appropriateness of a market-centered government is also questioned. Are citizens equivalent to consumers, and if so, which consumers should be served when their interests conflict?

What is your view on this dispute? Are there particular activities of the federal government where Osborne and Gaebler's view is more appropriate? What criteria would you apply to whether an activity should be governed by the decentralized or the hierarchical model? How appropriate is the market-centered notion of government?

A second objection to the changes taking place is that government may be "hollowed out" in the sense that it may not have the financial and human resources to adequately perform the missions it retains.[54] Even many of those who are the strongest advocates of scaling down the federal government worry about this possibility in particular areas. For example, congressional Republicans, who have in most cases sought to reduce the scale of federal programs, have advocated increases in defense spending out of a belief that earlier cutbacks had reduced military readiness to an unacceptable level. Increased defense spending was also advocated by Republican nominee George W. Bush during the 2000 presidential campaign.

Thus, although the current wave of administrative reform is unique in its specific elements, it involves long-standing questions about the bureaucracy. How can it be made more responsive, and yet act fairly? How can it be made more efficient, and yet accomplish what Americans require of it? How can it be made more creative, and yet be held accountable? There are, as history makes clear, no easy or final answers to these questions.

www.mhhe.com/patterson5

Self-Quiz

Summary

Bureaucracy is a method of organizing people and work. It is based on the principles of hierarchical authority, job specialization, and formalized rules. As a form of organization, bureaucracy is the most efficient means of getting people to work together on tasks of great magnitude and complexity. It is also a form of organization that is prone to waste and rigidity, which is why efforts are being made to "reinvent" it.

The United States could not be governed without a large federal bureaucracy. The day-to-day work of the federal government, from mail delivery to provision of social security to international diplomacy, is done by the bureaucracy. Federal employees work in roughly four hundred major agencies, including cabinet departments, independent agencies, regulatory agencies, government corporations, and presidential commissions. Yet the bureaucracy is more than simply an administrative giant. Administrators exercise considerable discretion in their policy decisions. In the process of implementing policy, they make important policy and political choices.

Each agency of the federal government was created in response to political demands on national officials. Because of its origins in political demands, the administration of government is necessarily political. An inherent conflict results from two simultaneous but incompatible demands on the bureaucracy: that it respond to the preferences of partisan officials but also that it administer programs fairly and competently. These tensions are evident in the three concurrent personnel management systems under which the bureaucracy operates: patronage, merit, and executive leadership.

Administrators are actively engaged in politics and policymaking. The fragmentation of power and the pluralism of the American political system result in a policy process that is continually subject to conflict and contention. There is no clear policy or leadership mandate in the American system, and hence government agencies must compete for the power required to administer their programs effectively. Accordingly, civil servants tend to have an agency point of view: they seek to advance their agency's programs and to repel attempts by others to weaken their position. In promoting their agency, civil servants rely on their policy expertise, the backing of their clientele groups, and support from the president and Congress.

Administrators are not elected by the people they serve, yet they wield substantial independent power. Because of this, the bureaucracy's accountability is a central issue. The major checks on the bureaucracy are provided by the president, Congress, and the courts. The president has some power to reorganize the bureaucracy and the authority to appoint the political head of each agency. The president also has management tools (such as the executive budget) that can be used to limit administrators' discretion. Congress has influence on bureaucratic agencies through its authorization and funding powers and through various devices (including sunset laws and oversight hearings) that hold administrators accountable for their actions. The judiciary's role in ensuring the bureaucracy's accountability is smaller than that of the elected branches, but the courts do have the authority to force agencies to act in accordance with legislative intent, established procedures, and constitutionally guaranteed rights. Nevertheless, administrators are not fully accountable. They exercise substantial independent power, a situation that is not easily reconciled with democratic values.

Efforts are currently under way to scale down the federal bureaucracy. This reduction includes cuts in budgets, staff, and organizational units, and also involves changes in the way the bureaucracy does its work. This process is a response to political forces and also to new management theories.

Key Terms

accountability
agency point of view
bureaucracy
cabinet (executive) departments
clientele groups
demographic representativeness
executive leadership system
formalized rules
government corporations
hierarchical authority

independent agencies
job specialization
merit (civil service) system
neutral competence
patronage system
policy implementation
presidential commissions
regulatory agencies
spoils system
whistle-blowing

Suggested Readings

Aberbach, Joel D. *Keeping a Watchful Eye.* Washington, D.C.: Brookings Institution, 1990. A careful assessment of congressional oversight of the bureaucracy.

Brehm, John, and Scott Gates. *Working, Shirking, and Sabotage: Bureaucratic Response to a Democratic Public.* Ann Arbor: University of Michigan Press, 1996. A generally favorable assessment of the bureaucracy's responsiveness to the public it serves.

Cook, Brian J. *Bureaucracy and Self-Government: Reconsidering the Role of Public Administration in American Politics.* Baltimore, Md.: Johns Hopkins University Press, 1996. A thorough history of public administration in American politics.

Gore, Albert, Jr. *Creating a Government That Works Better and Costs Less: The Report of the National Performance Review.* Washington, D.C.: U.S. Superintendent of Documents, 1993. The report of Vice President Gore's task force on streamlining government.

Ingraham, Patricia, and David Rosenbloom. *The Promise and Paradox of Civil Service Reform.* Pittsburgh, Pa.: University of Pittsburgh Press, 1992. An insightful analysis of the civil service reform issue.

Kerwin, Cornelius M. *Rulemaking: How Government Agencies Write Law and Make Policy,* 2nd ed. Washington, D.C.: Congressional Quarterly Press, 1999. Suggests that the most important function that government agencies perform is rule making.

Kettl, Donald F., Patricia W. Ingraham, Ronald P. Sanders, and Constance Horner. *Civil Service Reform: Building a Government That Works.* Washington, D.C.: Brookings Institution Press, 1996. A careful analysis of government management.

Light, Paul C. *Thickening Government: Federal Hierarchy and the Diffusion of Accountability.* Washington, D.C.: Brookings Institution, 1995. An illuminating study of the impact of bureaucratic hierarchy on accountability.

Osborne, David, and Ted Gaebler. *Reinventing Government: How the Entrepreneurial Spirit Is Transforming the Public Sector.* New York: Addison-Wesley, 1992. The book that Washington policy makers regard as the guide to transforming the bureaucracy.

West, William F. *Controlling the Bureaucracy: Institutional Constraints in Theory and Practice.* Armonk, N.Y.: Sharpe, 1995. An assessment of bureaucratic control through administrative due process and presidential and congressional action.

Wood, B. Dan, and Richard W. Waterman. *Bureaucratic Dynamics: The Role of Bureaucracy in a Democracy.* Boulder, Colo.: Westview Press, 1994. A penetrating analysis of bureaucratic agencies and their power relationships with the president, Congress, and constituent groups.

CHAPTER 17

The Federal Judicial System: Applying the Law

★

It is emphatically the province and duty of the judicial department to say what the law is. Those who apply the rule to particular cases, must of necessity expound and interpret that rule. If two laws conflict with each other, the courts must decide on the operation of each.

—John Marshall[1]

★ ★ ★

Through its ruling in *Bush v. Gore*, the U.S. Supreme Court effectively ended the 2000 presidential election. At issue was whether the "under-votes" in Florida—ballots on which counting machines had detected no vote for president—would be tabulated by hand. Florida's top court had ordered a statewide manual recount, but the U.S. Supreme Court by a narrow 5 to 4 margin had issued a rare emergency order halting the action. Three days later, the Supreme Court's majority delivered its ruling, saying that the manual recount violated the Constitution's equal protection clause. Florida's high court had said that officials should base the hand count on the "intent of the voter." The Supreme Court held that this standard gave county officials in Florida too much leeway and violated the right of citizens to have their votes counted fairly and equally.

The ruling brought charges that the Supreme Court had acted politically rather than on any strict interpretation of the law. In issuing a halt to the recount, the Court had divided sharply along ideological lines. The majority consisted of its most conservative members, all of whom were Republican appointees: Chief Justice William Rehnquist and associate justices Sandra Day O'Connor, Anthony Kennedy, Antonin Scalia, and Clarence Thomas. In a dissenting opinion, Justice John Paul Stevens said: "Preventing the recount from being completed will inevitably cast a doubt upon the legitimacy of the election." Stevens argued that the Florida high court's decision had properly reflected "the basic principle, inherent in our Constitution and our democracy, that every legal vote should be counted."

Bush v. Gore was hardly the first time that the Supreme Court has been a center of controversy.[2] If liberals were angered by its 2000 election decision, conservatives were outraged, for example, by a series of abortion rulings that began with *Roe v. Wade* in 1973.[3] The *Roe* decision touched off a heated debate within the legal community. Some legalists supported the decision, arguing that the judiciary must act to protect basic rights, even ones, including abortion, that are not explicitly provided by the Constitution.[4] Other legalists claimed that the Court has overstepped its authority. From their perspective, the problem with the *Roe* decision was that a right of abortion is not supported by any specific constitutional guarantee and therefore should not be established by judicial fiat.[5]

These examples illustrate three key points about court decisions. First, the judiciary is an extremely important policymaking body. Some of its rulings are as consequential as nearly any law passed by Congress or executive action taken by the president. Second, the judiciary has considerable discretion in its rulings. The *Bush v. Gore* and *Roe v. Wade* decisions were not based on any literal reading of the law: the justices in each case invoked *their* interpretation of the Constitution's provisions for individual rights.

Third, the judiciary is a political as well as legal institution, as illustrated by the conflict surrounding recent Supreme Court nominations. Once a law is established, it is expected to be administered in an evenhanded way. But the law itself is a product of contending political forces, is developed through a political process, has political content, and is applied by political appointees.

This chapter describes the federal judiciary and the work of its judges and justices. Like the executive and legislative branches, the judiciary is an independent branch of the U.S. government, but unlike the two other branches, its top officials are not elected by the people. The judiciary is not a democratic institution, and its role is different from and, in some areas, more controversial than those of the executive and legislative branches. This chapter explores this issue in the process of discussing several main points:

★ *The federal judiciary includes the Supreme Court of the United States, which functions mainly as an appellate court; courts of appeals, which hear appeals; and district courts, which hold trials.* Each state has a court system of its own, which for the most part is independent of supervision by the federal courts.

★ *Judicial decisions are constrained by applicable constitutional law, statutory law, and precedent.* Nevertheless, political factors have a major influence on judicial appointments and decisions; judges are political officials as well as legal ones.

★ *The judiciary has become an increasingly powerful policymaking body in recent decades, which has raised the question of the judiciary's proper role in a democracy.* The philosophies of judicial restraint and judicial activism provide different answers to this question.

The Federal Judicial System

The writers of the Constitution were determined that the judiciary would be a separate branch of the federal government but, for practical reasons, did not spell out the full structure of the federal court system. The Constitution simply establishes the Supreme Court of the United States and grants Congress the authority to establish lower federal courts of its choosing.

Federal judges are nominated by the president, and if confirmed by the U.S. Senate, they are appointed by the president to the office. The Constitution states that judges "shall hold their offices during good behavior." However, the Constitution does not contain a precise definition of "good behavior," and no Supreme Court justice and only a very small number of lower-court judges have been removed from office through impeachment and conviction by Congress. In practice, federal judges and justices serve until they retire or die.

Unlike the offices of president, senator, and representative, the Constitution places no age, residency, or citizenship qualifications on federal judicial office. Nor does the Constitution require a judge to have legal training. Tradition alone dictates that federal judges have an educational or professional background in the law.

Demonstrators rally outside the U.S. Supreme Court building during hearings on the *Bush v. Gore* case which effectively brought the 2000 presidential election to an end. At times, the policy rulings of the judiciary are as significant as the decisions of the president or Congress.

THE SUPREME COURT OF THE UNITED STATES

The Supreme Court of the United States is the nation's highest court. The chief justice of the United States presides over the Supreme Court and, like the eight associate justices, is selected by the president and is subject to Senate confirmation. The chief justice has the same voting power as the other justices but has usually exercised additional influence because of the position's leadership role.

The Constitution grants the Supreme Court both original and appellate jurisdiction. A court's **jurisdiction** is its authority to hear cases of a particular type. **Original jurisdiction** is the authority to be the first court to hear a case. The Supreme Court's original jurisdiction embraces legal disputes involving foreign diplomats and those in which the opposing parties are state governments. The Court in its entire history has convened as a court of original jurisdiction only a few hundred times and has rarely done so in recent years.

The Supreme Court does its most significant work as an appellate court. **Appellate jurisdiction** is the authority to review cases that have already been heard in lower courts and are appealed to the higher court by the losing party; such courts are called appeals courts or appellate courts. The Supreme Court's appellate jurisdiction extends to cases arising under the Constitution, federal law and regulations, and treaties. The Court also hears appeals involving admiralty or maritime issues and legal controversies that cross state or national boundaries. Appellate courts, including the Supreme Court, do not retry cases; rather, they determine whether a trial court acted in accord with applicable law.

jurisdiction (of a court) A given court's authority to hear cases of a particular kind. Jurisdiction may be original or appellate.

original jurisdiction The authority of a given court to be the first court to hear a case.

appellate jurisdiction The authority of a given court to review cases that have already been tried in lower courts and are appealed to it by the losing party; such a court is called an appeals court or appellate court.

Selecting Cases

The primary function of the judiciary is to interpret the law in such a way that rules made in the past (for example, the Constitution or legislation) can be applied reasonably in the present. This function gives the courts—all courts—a role in policymaking. Antitrust legislation, for example, is designed to prevent uncompetitive business practices, but like all such legislation, it is not self-enforcing. It is up to the courts to decide whether and how these laws apply to the case at hand.

As the nation's highest court, the Supreme Court is particularly important in establishing legal precedents that guide lower courts. A *precedent* is a judicial decision that serves as a rule for settling subsequent cases of a similar nature. Lower courts are expected to follow precedent—that is, to resolve cases of a like nature in ways consistent with upper-court rulings. However, for reasons that will be explained later, they do not always do so.

The Supreme Court's ability to set legal precedent is strengthened by its nearly complete discretion in choosing the cases it will hear. The large majority of cases reach the Supreme Court through a **writ of *certiorari*** in which the losing party in a lower-court case explains in writing why its case should be ruled upon by the Court. Four of the nine justices must agree to accept a particular case before it is granted a writ. Each year roughly seven thousand parties apply for *certiorari*, but the Court accepts only about a hundred cases for a full hearing and signed ruling (see Figure 17-1). The Court issues another one hundred to two hundred *per curiam* (unsigned) decisions, which are made summarily without a hearing and simply state the facts of the case and the Court's decision. The Court is most likely to grant *certiorari* when the U.S. government through the solicitor general (the high-ranking Justice Department official who serves as the government's lawyer in Supreme Court cases) requests it.[6]

Case selection is a vital part of the Supreme Court's work. Through its review of applications for *certiorari*, the Court keeps abreast of legal controversies. Justice William Brennan noted that the *certiorari* process enables the Court to acquire a general idea of the compelling legal issues arising in lower courts and to address those that are most in need of immediate attention.[7] When the Court does accept a case, chances are that most of the justices disagree with the lower

writ of *certiorari* Permission granted by a higher court to allow a losing party in a legal case to bring the case before it for a ruling; when such a writ is requested of the U.S. Supreme Court, four of the Court's nine justices must agree to accept the case before it is granted *certiorari*.

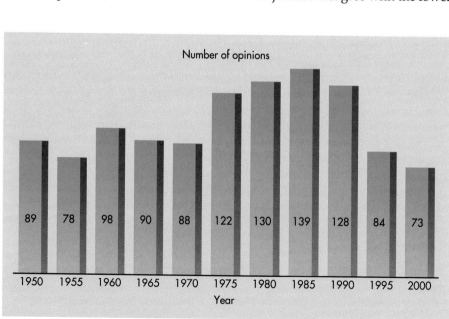

FIGURE 17-1   Supreme Court Opinions, 1950–2000
The number of signed Supreme Court opinions each term is relatively small. The Court has considerable control over the cases it selects and focuses on those that have broad legal significance.
Source: Supreme Court of the United States. The Court's term runs from October 1 to June 30; the year indicated is the closing year of the term.

Number of opinions

| 89 | 78 | 98 | 90 | 88 | 122 | 130 | 139 | 128 | 84 | 73 |

| 1950 | 1955 | 1960 | 1965 | 1970 | 1975 | 1980 | 1985 | 1990 | 1995 | 2000 |

Year

court's ruling. In recent years about three-fourths of the Supreme Court's decisions have reversed the judgments of lower courts.[8]

The Court seldom accepts a routine case, even if the justices believe that a lower court has erred. The Supreme Court's job is not to correct every mistake of other courts, but to resolve broad legal questions. As a result, the justices usually choose cases that involve substantial legal issues. This criterion is vague but essentially means that a case must center on an issue of significance not merely to the parties involved but to the nation. As a result, most of the cases heard by the Court raise major constitutional issues, or affect the lives of many Americans, or address issues that are being decided inconsistently by the lower courts, or are in conflict with a previous Supreme Court ruling.[9] The last of these situations is particularly likely to propel a case to the Supreme Court, which naturally takes a keen interest in lower-court judgments that depart from its rulings.

Deciding Cases

Once the Supreme Court accepts a case, it sets a date on which the attorneys for the two sides will present their oral arguments. Strict time limits, usually thirty minutes per side, are placed on these arguments, because each side has already submitted written arguments to the justices.

The open hearing is far less important than the **judicial conference** that follows, which is attended only by the nine justices. The conference's proceedings are kept strictly confidential. This secrecy allows the justices to speak freely and tentatively about a case. The chief justice presides over the conference and ordinarily speaks first.[10] The other justices then speak in order of their seniority

judicial conference A closed meeting of the justices of the U.S. Supreme Court to discuss and vote on the cases before them; the justices are not supposed to discuss conference proceedings with outsiders.

The Supreme Court building is located across from the Capitol in Washington, D.C. The courtroom, the justices' offices, and the conference room are on the first floor. Administrative staff offices and the Court's records and reference materials occupy the other floors.

(length of service on the Court). This arrangement enhances the senior members' ability to influence the discussion. After the discussion, the justices vote on the case; the least senior justice usually votes first and the chief justice votes last.

The chief justice is expected to provide leadership but has no power to compel the other justices to respond. Consequently, the chief justice's intellectual capacities, knowledge of the law, political awareness, and persuasiveness are significant aspects of the chief justice's leadership. Charles Evans Hughes is reputed to have been the most effective leader in the Court's history, although John Marshall is generally regarded as the greatest chief justice. The current chief justice, William Rehnquist, is widely viewed as a personally aloof but intellectually assertive leader.

Issuing Decisions and Opinions

After a case has been discussed and decided on in conference, the Court prepares and issues its ruling, which consists of a decision and one or more opinions. The **decision** indicates which party the Court supports and by how large a margin. The **opinion** explains the reasons behind the decision. The opinion is the most important part of a Supreme Court ruling because it informs others of the justices' interpretations of laws. When a majority of the justices agree on the legal basis of a decision, the result is a **majority opinion.** For example, in the landmark *Brown v. Board of Education of Topeka* (1954) opinion, the Court held that government-sponsored school segregation was unconstitutional because it violated the Fourteenth Amendment's guarantee that all Americans are entitled to equal protection under the laws. Enforced segregation of the public schools was therefore constitutionally impermissible. This opinion became the legal basis by which communities throughout the southern states were ordered by lower courts to end their policy of segregating students in their public schools by race.[11]

When part of the majority, the chief justice decides which of the justices will write the majority opinion. Otherwise, the senior justice in the majority determines the author. Chief justices have often given themselves the influential task of writing the majority opinion in important cases. John Marshall did so often: *Marbury v. Madison* (1802) and *McCulloch v. Maryland* (1819) were among the opinions he wrote.

The justice who writes the Court's majority opinion has an important and difficult job, since the other justices who voted with the majority must agree with the written opinion. Because the vote on a case is not considered final until the decision is made public, plenty of compromising and old-fashioned horse trading can take place during the writing stage. The majority opinion often goes through a series of drafts and is circulated among all nine justices. In *Brown v. Board of Education,* Justice Felix Frankfurter, the lone initial holdout, was persuaded to make the decision unanimous by the continued urgings of his colleagues and by their willingness to incorporate some of his concerns into the majority opinion.

In some cases there is no majority opinion because a majority of the justices agree on the decision but cannot agree on the legal basis for it. The result is a **plurality opinion,** which presents the view held by most of the justices who side with the winning party. Another type of opinion is a **concurring opinion,**

www.mhhe.com/patterson5

Simulation

decision   A vote of the Supreme Court in a particular case that indicates which party the justices side with and by how large a margin.

opinion (of a court)   A court's written explanation of its decision, which serves to inform others of the legal basis for the decision. Supreme Court opinions are expected to guide the decisions of other courts.

majority opinion   A Supreme Court opinion that results when a majority of the justices are in agreement on the legal basis of the decision.

plurality opinion   A court opinion that results when a majority of justices agree on a decision in a case but do not agree on the legal basis for the decision. In this instance, the legal position held by most of the justices on the winning side is called a plurality opinion.

concurring opinion   A separate opinion written by a Supreme Court justice who votes with the majority in the decision on a case but who disagrees with their reasoning.

which is a separate view written by a justice who votes with the majority but disagrees with its reasoning.

Justices on the losing side can write a **dissenting opinion** to explain their reasons for disagreeing with the majority position. Sometimes these dissenting views become a later Court's majority position. In a 1942 dissenting opinion, Justice Hugo Black wrote that defendants in state felony trials should have legal counsel, even if they could not afford to pay for it. Two decades later, in *Gideon v. Wainwright* (1963), the Court adopted this position.[12]

dissenting opinion The opinion of a justice in a Supreme Court case that explains the reasons for disagreeing with the majority's decision.

OTHER FEDERAL COURTS

There are more than one hundred federal courts but there is only one Supreme Court, and its position at the top of the country's judicial system gives the Supreme Court unparalleled importance. It is a mistake, however, to conclude that the Supreme Court is the only court of consequence. Judge Jerome Frank once wrote of the "upper-court myth," which is the view that appellate courts and in particular the Supreme Court make up the only truly significant judicial arena and that lower courts just dutifully follow the rulings handed down by the appellate level.[13] The reality is very different, as the following discussion will explain.

U.S. District Courts

The lowest federal courts are the district courts (see Figure 17-2). There are more than ninety federal district courts altogether—at least one in every state and as many as four in some states. District court judges, who number about eight hundred in all, are appointed by the president with the consent of the Senate. Federal cases usually originate in district courts, which are trial courts, where the parties argue their sides. District courts are the only courts in the federal system in which juries hear testimony. Most cases at this level are presented before a single judge.

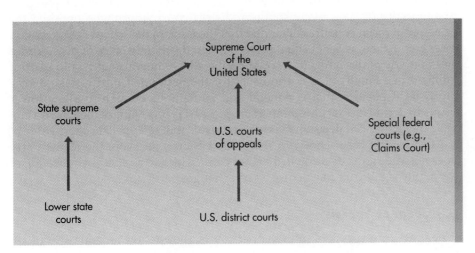

FIGURE 17-2 The Federal Judicial System
This simplified diagram shows the relationships among the various levels of federal courts and between state and federal courts. The losing party in a case can appeal a lower-court decision to the court at the next-highest level, as the arrows indicate. Decisions can normally be removed from state courts to federal courts only if they raise a constitutional question.

The Supreme Court is not the only federal court that "matters" in the American judicial system. Most federal cases originate in U.S. district courts, and most appealed cases are settled in U.S. courts of appeals, never reaching the Supreme Court. Shown here is testimony at a trial in district court, the only level in the federal system in which juries decide the outcome of cases.

Lower federal courts unquestionably rely on and follow Supreme Court decisions in their own rulings. The Supreme Court reiterated this requirement in a 1982 case, *Hutto v. Davis:* "Unless we wish anarchy to prevail within the federal judicial system, a precedent of this Court must be followed by the lower federal courts no matter how misguided the judges of those courts may think it to be."[14]

However, the idea that lower courts are guided strictly by Supreme Court rulings is part of the upper-court myth. District court judges may misunderstand the Supreme Court's position and deviate from it for that reason. In addition, the facts of a case before a district court are seldom identical to those of a case settled by the Supreme Court. The lower-court judge must decide whether a different legal principle must be invoked. In some cases, district court judges have willfully disregarded Supreme Court precedent, finding a basis for decision that allows them to reach a judgment they prefer. For example, after the Supreme Court declared in *Brown v. Board of Education* that racial segregation of public schools violated the Fourteenth Amendment's guarantee of equal protection under the law, many southern district court judges who opposed the principle of racial equality concluded that the issue in the school desegregation cases before them was not equal protection but the maintenance of public order and that school desegregation could not be allowed because it would disrupt public order. Finally, it is not unusual for the Supreme Court to take a very broad legal position that is general and ambiguous enough to allow lower courts to decide its exact meaning in practice. Trial-court judges then have a creative role in judicial decision making that rivals that of appellate court judges.

Most federal cases end with the district court's decision; the losing party does not appeal the decision to a higher court. This fact is another indication of the highly significant role of district court judges.

U.S. Courts of Appeals

When cases are appealed from district courts, they go to a federal court of appeals. These appellate courts make up the second level of the federal court system. Courts of appeals do not use juries. No new evidence is submitted in an appealed case; appellate courts base their decisions on a review of lower-court records. Appellate judges act as supervisors in the legal system, reviewing trial-court decisions and correcting what they consider to be legal errors. Facts (i.e., the circumstances of a case) found by district courts are presumed to be correct.

The United States has twelve general appeals courts, each of which serves a "circuit" that is comprised of between three and nine states, except the one that serves the District of Columbia only. There is also the U.S. Court of Appeals for the Federal Circuit, which specializes in appeals of cases involving patents and international trade. Between four and twenty-six judges sit on each court of appeals, but each case is usually heard by a panel of three judges. On rare occasions, all the judges of a court of appeals sit as a body (*en banc*) in order to resolve difficult controversies, typically ones that have resulted in conflicting decisions within the same circuit.

Courts of appeals offer the only real hope of reversal for many appellants, since the Supreme Court hears so few cases. Fewer than 1 percent of the cases heard by federal appeals courts are later reviewed by the Supreme Court. "Because the Supreme Court only handles several hundred cases a year," Sheldon Goldman points out, "the influence of lower courts is considerable. For most intents and purposes, the courts of appeals function as regional supreme courts for the nation. As a result, we're talking about some major policy makers."[15]

Special U.S. Courts

In addition to the Supreme Court, the courts of appeals, and the district courts, the federal judiciary includes a few specialty courts. Among them are the U.S. Claims Court, which hears cases in which the U.S. government is being sued for damages; the U.S. Court of International Trade, which handles cases involving appeals of U.S. Customs Office rulings; and the U.S. Court of Military Appeals, which hears appeals of military courts-martial. Some federal agencies and commissions also have adjudicative powers, and their decisions can be appealed to a federal court of appeals.

THE STATE COURTS IN THE FEDERAL SYSTEM

The American states are separate governments within the United States' federal system. Each state is protected in its sovereignty by the Tenth Amendment, and each state has its own court system. Like the federal courts, state court systems have trial courts at the bottom level and appellate courts at the top.

Each state decides for itself the structure of its courts and the method of judicial appointment. In some states, judges are appointed by the governor, but judgeships are *elective offices* in most states. The common form involves competitive elections of either a partisan or nonpartisan nature, although some states use a system called the *merit plan* (also called the "Missouri Plan" because Missouri was the first state to use it) under which the governor selects a judge from a short list of acceptable candidates provided by a judicial selection commission. After a year or more on the bench, the judge selected must be approved by the voters in order to serve a longer term. Thereafter, the judge must face a periodic (usually every six years) "retention election" in which voters decide whether he or she will continue in the office (see "States in the Nation").

★ STATES IN THE NATION

PRINCIPAL METHODS OF SELECTING JUDGES FOR STATES' HIGHEST COURT

The states rely on a variety of methods for selecting the judicial officers of their highest court, including the merit plan, partisan election, nonpartisan election, and political appointment. The states that appoint judges grant this power to the governor except in Virginia, Connecticut, and South Carolina, where the legislature makes the choice.

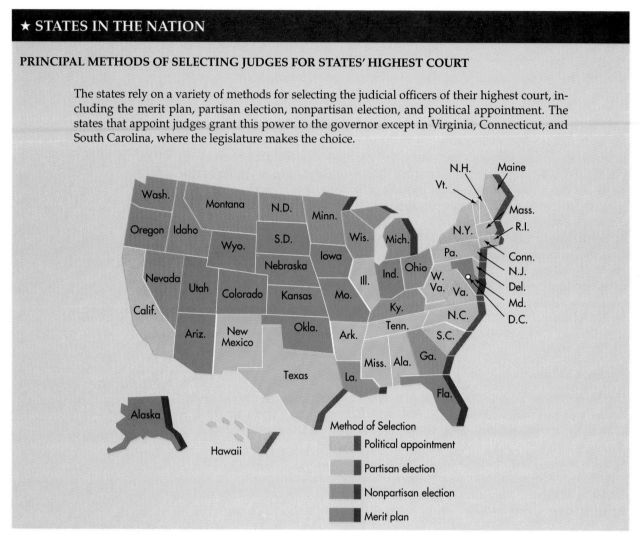

SOURCE: Council of State Governments.

Besides the upper-court myth, there exists a "federal court myth," which holds that the federal judiciary is the most significant part of the judicial system and that state courts play a subordinate role. This view is inaccurate as well. More than 95 percent of the nation's legal cases are decided in state courts. Most crimes (from shoplifting to murder) and most civil controversies (such as divorces and corporate disputes) are defined by state or local law. Moreover, nearly all cases that originate in state courts also end there. The federal courts never come into the picture because the case does not involve a federal issue.

In state criminal cases, after a person has been convicted and after all avenues of appeal in the state court system have been exhausted, the defendant can seek a writ of habeas corpus from a federal district court (see Chapter 4). The federal court often confines itself to the federal aspects of the matter, such as whether the defendant in a criminal case received the protections guaranteed

Members of the Supreme Court of the state of Texas stand at the bench in their courtroom. Upwards of 95 percent of the nation's legal cases are decided in the state court systems, an indicator of the federal-court myth.

by the U.S. Constitution. In addition, the federal court must accept the facts determined by the state court unless such findings are clearly in error. In short, legal and factual determinations of state courts can bind the federal courts—a clear contradiction of the federal court myth.

However, cases traditionally within the jurisdiction of the states can become federal cases through rulings of federal courts. In *Roe v. Wade* (1973), for example, the Supreme Court concluded that women had the right under the Constitution to choose an abortion, thus making abortion rights, which had been a state issue, also a federal one.[16] (This situation is called "diversity of citizenship" jurisdiction, meaning that both state and federal courts have some jurisdiction over the issue.)

Federal Court Appointees

The quiet setting of the courtroom, the dignity of its proceedings, and the lack of fanfare with which a court delivers its decisions give the impression that the judiciary is about as far removed from the world of politics as a governmental institution can possibly be. The reality is different. Federal judges and justices are political officials who exercise the authority of a separate and powerful branch of government. All federal jurists bring their political views with them to the courtroom and have regular opportunities to promote their political beliefs through the cases they decide. Accordingly, the process by which federal judges are appointed is a partisan one.

SELECTING SUPREME COURT JUSTICES AND FEDERAL JUDGES

The formal mechanism for appointments to the Supreme Court and the lower federal courts is the same: the president nominates and the Senate confirms or rejects. Beyond that basic similarity, however, there are significant differences.

Merit and Judicial Selection
Over the years the partisanship evident in court appointments has occasionally come under attack. In the early twentieth century, Progressive reformers persuaded some states to exclude their judgeships from party patronage positions. The Missouri Plan (described in the section of this chapter titled "The State Courts in the Federal System") is a more recent reflection of the belief that partisan loyalty should not play a deciding role in the filling of judicial offices. No such thoroughgoing reform has taken place at the federal level, although President Carter used selection panels to compile lists of five candidates to fill appellate court vacancies on the basis of merit.

The issue of merit in the selection of judges and justices is a complicated one because there is no consensus even on the issue of whether prior judicial experience is necessary. Justice Felix Frankfurter claimed that it was not.

What is your view? Should merit play a larger role in judicial appointments, or is it more important that judges be chosen on the basis of their policy views? What are the relative advantages of appointing "politicians" and "judges" to the Supreme Court?

Supreme Court Nominees

A Supreme Court appointment is a critical choice for a president.[17] The cases that come before the Court tend to be controversial and have far-reaching implications. And since the Court is a small body, each justice's vote can be crucial to the decisions it makes. Because most justices retain their positions for many years, presidents can influence judicial policy through their appointments long after they have left office. The careers of some Supreme Court justices provide dramatic testimony to the enduring effects of judicial appointments. Franklin D. Roosevelt appointed William O. Douglas to the Supreme Court in 1939, and for thirty years after Roosevelt's death in 1945, Douglas remained a strong liberal influence on the Court. John Marshall was appointed chief justice in 1801 by the second president, John Adams, and served until 1835, when the seventh president, Andrew Jackson, was in his second term.

Presidents have employed a variety of approaches in their efforts to select a Supreme Court nominee who will reflect their political philosophy. A president may choose to depend chiefly on his own counsel, ask the Justice Department for advice, or seek the views of interested parties who share his general philosophy. Nominees must also be acceptable to others. Every nominee is closely scrutinized by the legal community, interested groups, and the media; must undergo an extensive background check by the FBI; and then must gain the approval of a Senate majority.

Within the Senate, a key body is the Judiciary Committee, whose members have responsibility for conducting hearings on judicial nominees and recommending their confirmation or rejection by the full Senate. Nearly 20 percent of presidential nominees have been rejected by the Senate on grounds of judicial qualification, political views, personal ethics, or partisanship. Most of these rejections in the country's history occurred before 1900, and partisan politics was the main reason. Today a nominee with strong professional and ethical credentials is less likely to be blocked for partisan reasons alone. An exception was Robert Bork, whose 1987 nomination by President Reagan was rejected primarily because of strong opposition from Senate Democrats who disagreed with his judicial philosophy. Middle-of-the-road, noncontroversial nominees almost always are approved by the Senate. One such nominee, Ruth Bader Ginsburg, was confirmed by a 96-to-3 Senate vote in 1993.

Presidents often take into account the Senate's probable reaction when choosing a nominee. In selecting Ginsburg and Stephen Breyer as his first nominees, President Clinton eschewed the choice of more controversial judges who might have been closer to his own views on issues before the Court. In general, though, the burden of proof rests with the Senate. To avoid the charge of unprincipled partisanship, the Senate has unofficially accepted the premise that it must build an overwhelming case against confirmation before denying the president's nominee a seat on the nation's highest court. This approach was evident in 1991 during confirmation hearings on Republican President George Bush's nomination of Clarence Thomas. Although Thomas was charged with sexual harassment by Anita Hill, a former co-worker and a lawyer, the Democratic-controlled Senate was unable to obtain confirming evidence and narrowly approved Thomas for a seat on the Supreme Court.

The Justices of the U.S. Supreme Court pose for a photo. From left, they are: Clarence Thomas, Antonin Scalia, Sandra Day O'Connor, Anthony Kennedy, David Souter, Stephen Breyer, John Paul Stevens, Chief Justice William Rehnquist, and Ruth Bader Ginsburg.

Lower-Court Nominees

The president normally gives the deputy attorney general the task of screening potential nominees for lower-court judgeships.[18] **Senatorial courtesy** is also a consideration in these appointments: this tradition, which dates back to the 1840s, holds that a senator from the state in which a vacancy has arisen should be given a say in the nomination if the senator is of the same party as the president.[19] If not consulted, the senator involved can request that confirmation be denied, and other senators will normally grant the request as a "courtesy" to a fellow senator.[20] Not surprisingly, presidents have preferred to give senators a voice in judicial appointments.

Although the president does not become as personally involved in selecting lower-court nominees as in naming potential Supreme Court justices, lower-court appointments are collectively a significant factor in the impact of a president's administration. Recent presidents have appointed about two hundred judges each term.

senatorial courtesy The tradition that a U.S. senator from the state in which a federal judicial vacancy has arisen should have a say in the president's nomination of the new judge if the senator is of the same party as the president.

JUSTICES AND JUDGES AS POLITICAL OFFICIALS

Presidents generally manage to appoint jurists who have a similar political philosophy. Although Supreme Court justices are free to make their own decisions, their legal positions can usually be inferred from their prior activities. A study by the judicial scholar Robert Scigliano found that about three of every four appointees have behaved on the Supreme Court approximately as presidents could have expected.[21] Of course, a president has no guarantee that a nominee will fulfill his hopes. Justices Earl Warren and William Brennan proved more liberal than President Dwight D. Eisenhower would have liked. When he was asked whether he had made any mistakes as president, Eisenhower replied, "Yes, two, and they are both sitting on the Supreme Court."[22]

The Role of Partisanship

In nearly every instance, presidents have chosen members of their own party as Supreme Court nominees. Partisanship is also decisive in nominations to lower-court judgeships. More than 90 percent of recent district and appeals court nominees have been members of the president's own party.[23]

The fact that judges and justices are chosen through a partisan political process should not be interpreted to mean that they engage in blatant partisanship while on the bench. Judges and justices are officers of a separate branch and prize their judicial independence. All Republican appointees do not vote the same way on cases, nor do all Democrats. Nevertheless, the partisan backgrounds of judges are a significant influence on their decisions. A study of the voting records of appellate court judges, for example, found that Republican appointees tend to be more conservative than Democratic appointees in their civil rights and civil liberties decisions.[24] In Supreme Court cases, Democratic and Republican appointees have often been on opposite sides, although other divisions also occur.

Other Characteristics of Judicial Appointees

In recent years, increasing numbers of federal justices and judges have had prior judicial experience; the assumption is that such individuals are best qualified for appointment to the federal bench. Most recent appellate court appointees have been district or state judges or have worked in the office of the attorney general.[25] Elective office (particularly a seat in the U.S. Senate) was

President Dwight D. Eisenhower shakes hands with William Brennan in the Oval Office after selecting Brennan to be an associate justice of the Supreme Court. Eisenhower would later say that he made a mistake in appointing Brennan to the Court. Brennan's decisions were more liberal than Eisenhower had expected.

TABLE 17-1 Justices of the Supreme Court, 2000 Most recent appointees held an appellate court position before being nominated to the Supreme Court.

Justice	Year of Appointment	Nominating President	Position Before Appointment
William Rehnquist*	1971	Nixon	Assistant attorney general
John Paul Stevens	1975	Ford	Judge, U.S. Court of Appeals
Sandra Day O'Connor	1981	Reagan	Judge, Arizona Court of Appeals
Antonin Scalia	1986	Reagan	Judge, U.S. Court of Appeals
Anthony Kennedy	1988	Reagan	Judge, U.S. Court of Appeals
David Souter	1990	Bush	Judge, U.S. Court of Appeals
Clarence Thomas	1991	Bush	Judge, U.S. Court of Appeals
Ruth Bader Ginsburg	1993	Clinton	Judge, U.S. Court of Appeals
Stephen Breyer	1994	Clinton	Judge, U.S. Court of Appeals

*Appointed chief justice in 1986.

once a common route to the Supreme Court,[26] but now justices have typically held an appellate court judgeship before their appointment (see Table 17-1).

White males are greatly overrepresented on the federal bench, just as they dominate in Congress and at the top levels of the executive branch.[27] However, the number of women and minority-group judges increased substantially as a result of the appointments of President Clinton. Partisanship has been a significant factor in the appointment of women and minorities to the bench (see Table 17-2). Democratic presidents Carter and Clinton were more likely than Republican presidents Reagan and Bush to appoint such individuals, a reflection of the differences in the parties' coalitions (see Chapter 9).

TABLE 17-2 Background Characteristics of Presidents' Judicial Nominees The judicial nominees of recent presidents have differed in their gender and racial characteristics.

	JUDICIAL APPOINTEES OF:			
	Carter	Reagan	Bush	Clinton
Men	85%	92%	81%	69%
Women	15	8	19	31
Whites	79%	93%	88%	75%
African Americans	14	2	7	17
Hispanics	6	4	4	6
Asians	1	1	1	2

SOURCE: From People for the American Way. Reprinted by permission.

The Supreme Court itself is also demographically unrepresentative. Until 1916, when Louis D. Brandeis was appointed to the Court, no Jewish justice had ever served. At least one Catholic, but at most times only one, has been on the Court almost continuously for nearly a century. Thurgood Marshall in 1967 became the first black justice, and Sandra Day O'Connor in 1981 became the first woman. Antonin Scalia in 1986 became the Court's first justice of Italian descent. No person of Hispanic or Asian descent has ever been a member of the Court.

Judicial scholars disagree on the importance of the Court's demographic makeup. Henry J. Abraham dismisses concerns about it, claiming that the Court was never meant to be a representative body. In contrast, Sheldon Goldman asserts that the judiciary's sensitivity to society's diverse interests depends to a degree on the social backgrounds that the justices bring with them to the Court.[28]

The Nature of Judicial Decision Making

Federal judges and justices are political officials: they constitute one of three co-equal branches of the national government. Yet, unlike members of Congress or the president, judges serve in a legal institution and make their decisions in a legal context. As a consequence, their discretionary power is less than that of elected officials. Article III of the Constitution bars the federal judiciary from issuing decisions except on actual cases before it. This restriction prevents the courts from developing legal positions outside the context of the judicial process. As federal judge David Bazelon noted, a judge "can't wake up one morning and simply decide to give a helpful little push to a school system, a mental hospital, or the local housing agency."[29]

The most substantial restriction on the courts is the law itself. Although a president or Congress can make almost any decision that is politically acceptable, the judiciary must justify its decision in terms of existing provisions of the law.[30] When asked by a friend to "do justice," Oliver Wendell Holmes Jr. replied, "That is not my job. My job is to play the game according to the rules."[31] In playing according to the rules, judges engage in a creative legal process that requires them to identify the facts of the case, determine and sometimes formulate the relevant legal principles or rules, and then apply them to the case at hand.

THE CONSTRAINTS OF THE FACTS

facts (of a court case) The relevant circumstances of a legal dispute or offense as determined by a trial court. The facts of a case are crucial because they help determine which law or laws are applicable in the case.

A basic distinction in any legal case is between "the facts" and "the laws." The **facts** of a case, as determined by trial courts, are the relevant circumstances of a legal dispute or offense. In the case of a person accused of murder, for example, key facts would include evidence about the murder and whether the rights of the accused were respected by police in the course of their investigation. The facts of a case are crucial because they determine which law or laws are applicable to the case. The courts must respond to the facts of a dispute. This restriction is a very substantial one. A murder case cannot be used as an occasion to pronounce judgment on freedom of religion.

THE CONSTRAINTS OF THE LAW

In deciding cases, the judiciary is also constrained by existing laws. As distinct from the facts of a case, the **laws** of a case are the constitutional provisions, legislative statutes, or judicial precedents that apply to the situation. To use an obvious comparison, the laws governing a case of alleged murder differ from the laws that apply to an antitrust suit. When addressing a case, a court must determine which laws are relevant.

laws (of a court case) The constitutional provisions, legislative statutes, or judicial precedents that apply to a court case.

Interpretation of the Constitution

The Constitution is the nation's highest law, but it is a sparsely worded document and for that reason is open to interpretation. For example, the Fourth Amendment of the Constitution protects individuals against "unreasonable searches and seizures," but the meaning of "unreasonable" is not spelled out. Nevertheless, judges respect the Constitution's purpose and intent. The question for a judge is what the Framers had in mind by a particular provision. For example, in deciding whether wiretapping and other electronic means of surveillance are covered by the prohibition against unreasonable searches and seizures, the issue is what rights the amendment was designed to protect. Electronic surveillance was not invented until 150 years after the Fourth Amendment was ratified. But the Fourth Amendment was intended to protect individuals against the government's intrusion into their private lives. For this reason, the courts have concluded that government cannot indiscriminately tap a person's telephone.

Interpretation of Statutes

The power of the courts to decide whether a governmental institution has acted within its constitutional powers is called *judicial review* (see Chapter 2). Without this power, the judiciary would be unable to restrain a Congress or presidency that has gone out of control. Yet the process of judicial review pits a court's judgment against that of another institution and invokes the nation's highest law—the Constitution. The imposing nature of judicial review has led the judiciary, when possible, to prefer statutory rulings to constitutional ones.

As a practical matter, it is also true that most cases arising in the courts involve issues of statutory law rather than constitutional law. Statutory law includes legislation that has been enacted by Congress and administrative regulations that have been developed by the bureaucracy on the basis of statutory law. There are thousands upon thousands of such laws and regulations, and they are usually what is at issue in a court case. There is no constitutional provision at issue, for example, when a worker sues a company over a job-related injury or a person is arrested for using a color copy machine to create counterfeit currency.

When hearing a case involving statutory law or administrative regulation, judges often will try to determine whether the meaning of the statute or regulation can be determined by common sense (the "plain meaning rule"). The question for the judge is what the law or regulation was intended to protect (such as a particular issue of worker safety).

SOURCES OF LAW THAT CONSTRAIN THE DECISIONS OF THE FEDERAL JUDICIARY

U.S. Constitution: The federal courts are bound by the provisions of the U.S. Constitution. The sparseness of its wording, however, requires the Constitution to be applied in the light of present circumstances. Thus, judges are accorded some degree of discretion in their constitutional judgments.

Statutory law: The federal courts are constrained by statutes and by administrative regulations derived from the provisions of statutes. Most laws, however, are somewhat vague in their provisions and often have unanticipated applications. As a result, judges have some freedom in deciding cases based on statutes.

Precedent: Federal courts tend to follow precedent (or *stare decisis*), which is a legal principle developed in earlier court decisions. Because times change and not all cases have a clear precedent, judges have some discretion in their evaluation of the way earlier cases apply to a current case.

Sometimes the courts will study the legislative record to determine what Congress had in mind when enacting a statute. An example is the 1999 Supreme Court case that involved the 1990 Americans with Disabilities Act, which extends to the disabled the same employment and other protections enjoyed by other Americans. The Supreme Court ruled that two nearsighted sisters who had been denied jobs with United Airlines because of their eyesight were not covered by the act. In making this judgment, the Court noted that Congress in passing the act had calculated that roughly 40 million Americans with disabilities would be protected by it. But if nearsightedness and other easily correctable impairments were considered "disabilities," then over 150 million Americans would be considered "disabled." Therefore, said the Court, Congress could not have meant to include nearsighted people when passing the law.[32]

Interpretation of Precedent

precedent A judicial decision in a given case that serves as a rule of thumb for settling subsequent cases of a similar nature; courts are generally expected to follow precedent.

The U.S. legal system developed from the English common-law tradition, which includes the principle that a court's decision on a case should be consistent with previous judicial rulings. This principle is known as **precedent** and reflects the philosophy of *stare decisis* (Latin for "to stand by things that have been settled")—the doctrine that principles of law, once established, should be accepted as authoritative in all subsequent similar cases. Precedent is an important constraint on the courts. To persist in ignoring precedent would be to direct the law onto an unpredictable course, creating confusion and uncertainty among those who must make choices on the basis of their understanding of how the law has been applied in previous instances.

Political Influences on Judicial Decisions

Although judicial rulings are justified by reference to laws, judges nearly always have some degree of discretion in their decisions.[33] The Constitution is a sparsely worded document and must be adapted to new and changing situations. As a result, federal judges must interpret the Constitution in the context of the issue at hand. The judiciary also has no choice at times but to apply its own judgment to statutory law. Congress often cannot anticipate or reach agreement on all the specific applications of a legislative act and therefore uses general language to state the act's purpose. The judiciary must decide what this language means in the context of a specific case arising under the act. Precedent is even less precise as a guide to decision. Precedent is more a rule of thumb than a strict command; it must constantly be weighed against what Justice Oliver Wendell Holmes Jr. described as the "felt necessities of the time."

The Supreme Court's rulings in a 1998 case (*Faragher v. Boca Raton*) involving sexual harassment in the workplace illustrates the ambiguity that can exist in the written law. The Court developed its ruling in the context of the antidiscrimination provisions of the Civil Rights Act of 1964. The act itself, however, contains no description of, or even reference to, job-related sexual harassment. Nevertheless, the act does prohibit workplace discrimination, and the Court could not easily dismiss sexual harassment as an irrelevant form of job-related discrimination. In judging the case, however, the Court had no choice except to determine for itself which actions in the workplace are instances of harassment and which are not. In this sense, the Court was "making" law; it was deciding how legislation enacted by Congress applied to actions that Congress had not addressed when it wrote the legislation.[34] (The Court's ruling in the case is discussed in Chapter 5.)

In sum, judges have leeway in their decisions. As a consequence, their rulings reflect not only legal influences but political ones, which come from both outside and inside the judicial system.

"OUTSIDE" INFLUENCES ON COURT DECISIONS

The courts can make unpopular choices, but in the long run, their decisions must be seen as fair if they are to be obeyed. In other words, the judiciary cannot ignore the expectations of the general public, interest groups, and elected officials, particularly the president and members of Congress. The precise impact of these outside pressures cannot be measured, but judicial experts agree that the courts are affected by them.

The Force of Public Opinion

Judges are responsive to public opinion, although much less so than are elected officials. In some cases, the Court has tailored its rulings in an effort to gain public support or dampen public resistance. In the *Brown* case, for example, the justices, recognizing that school desegregation would be an explosive issue in the South, attempted to defuse the reaction by requiring only that desegregation take place "with all deliberate speed" rather than immediately or on a fixed timetable. The Supreme Court's apparent strategy has been to stay close enough to popular opinion to avoid seriously eroding public support for its decisions.[35]

The judiciary does not have to follow public opinion slavishly in order to keep its authoritative position. Only a few judicial decisions affect a large portion of the public directly, and most Americans do not want to endure the legal difficulties that might attend violation of the law. Moreover, the fact that

The judicial branch is increasingly an arena in which interest groups contend for influence. Many of these disputes have pitted environmental groups against economic interests. Shown here are demonstrators on the issue of whether the Maine Atlantic Salmon should be declared an endangered species and placed off limits to commercial fishing.

public opinion on controversial issues is always divided means that the courts will not stand alone no matter which side of such an issue their rulings favor. As an example, opinion polls indicate that Americans are sharply divided on the issue of a woman's right to obtain an abortion in the early months of pregnancy.

Lobbying the Courts

Interest groups use the courts to advance their policy goals. Although litigation is expensive (the cost of carrying a case all the way to the Supreme Court can exceed $500,000), it often costs less than lobbying Congress or the executive on a major issue. And obviously some interests, particularly those represented by persons who are in an unpopular or underprivileged minority, may have a better chance of success in a legal suit than with an elected institution.

The array of interests that use lawsuits as a policy tactic include traditional advocacy groups such as the American Civil Liberties Union (ACLU), which concentrates on human rights issues, and the National Association for the Advancement of Colored People (NAACP), which focuses on racial equality disputes. Newer controversies have also spawned their groups. The Alliance Defense Fund, the American Center for Law and Justice, the Becket Fund for Religious Liberty, the Christian Legal Society's Center for Law and Religious Freedom, the Rutherford Institute, and the Western Center for Law and Religious Freedom are a few of the litigant groups involved just in the area of religious rights and practices.

Lawsuits are only one way in which interest groups make their views known to the courts. They also participate in cases brought by others through *amicus curiae* ("friend of the court") briefs, which they file in support of one of the parties to the case.[36] Traditionally *amicus* briefs were brought primarily by liberal groups, but conservative groups also use them heavily because of a recognition that the courts are today more conservative than before. Overall, the number of *amicus* briefs has risen dramatically, both in the number of cases in which such briefs are filed and in the number of briefs filed in individual cases.

The Leverage of Public Officials

The influence of groups and the general public on the judiciary is also registered indirectly, through the elected branches of government. In response to public and group pressure, elected officials try to persuade the judiciary to hand down rulings favored by their constituents. Both Congress and the president have powerful means of influencing the federal judiciary.

Congress is constitutionally empowered to establish the Supreme Court's size and appellate jurisdiction, and Congress can rewrite legislation that it feels the judiciary has misinterpreted. Although Congress seldom punishes the judiciary directly, its members have often expressed displeasure with judicial action. In a 1998 Senate speech, the chair of the Judiciary Committee, Orrin Hatch (R-Utah), lashed out at judges who he claimed were "making laws instead of interpreting the law." Such judges, Hatch asserted, "should resign to run for public office—at least they would be accountable for their actions."[37] Other Republicans on the Judiciary Committee shared Hatch's view, and they delayed confirmation of a number of President Clinton's judiciary nominees on the grounds that they were unlikely to be "strict constructionists." (*Strict constructionism* holds that a judicial officer should apply a narrow interpretation of the laws, whereas *loose constructionism* holds that a judicial officer can apply an expansive interpretation.)

Presidents can also influence the federal courts through their judicial appointments. When Democrat Bill Clinton took office in 1992, more than a hundred federal judgeships were vacant. President Bush had expected to win reelection and had not moved quickly to fill vacancies as they arose. By the time it was apparent that Bush might lose the election, the Democrat-controlled Congress was able to delay action on the nominations. This delay enabled Clinton to fill the positions with loyal Democrats who could be expected to partially offset the influence of the Republican judges appointed during the previous twelve years by Presidents Reagan and Bush.

Although subject to the influence of elected institutions, the judiciary views certain positions as basic to individual rights rather than as matters of majority opinion. In such instances, the judiciary seldom lets the public or elected officials dictate its course of action. Despite continuing public support for school prayer (see Figure 17-3), for instance, the Supreme Court has not backed down from its basic position that prayer in the schools violates the First Amendment's establishment clause. The Court prizes its independence and its position as a coequal branch of government. The fact that judges are not popularly elected and that they hold their appointments indefinitely makes it possible for them to resist pressures from Congress and the president.

CURRENT CONTROVERSIES

SHOULD ALL THE FLORIDA BALLOTS HAVE BEEN COUNTED?

In *Colegrove v. Green* (1946), Justice Felix Frankfurter warned the Supreme Court about getting involved in election politics, saying that it "ought not to enter this political thicket." In 2000, the Court thrust itself into the thorniest political thicket of all—a presidential campaign. In *Bush v. Gore*, the Court by a narrow majority blocked a statewide manual recount of uncounted ballots in Florida, thereby settling the election in favor of Republican George W. Bush. His Democratic opponent, Al Gore, had argued that all the Florida votes—not just those that could be read by machine—should count. Bush supporters retorted that a manual recount would be inherently subjective and open to mischief. These opposing views also existed within the Supreme Court, as the following opinions show.

YES: [The Florida Supreme Court's] decisions were rooted in long established precedent. . . . [I]t relied on the sufficiency of the general "intent of the voter" standard articulated by the state legislature. . . . What must underlie . . . [the] assault on this procedure is an unstated lack of confidence in the impartiality and capacity of the state judges who would make the critical decisions if the vote count were to proceed. Otherwise, their position is wholly without merit.

—Justice John Paul Stevens's dissenting opinion

NO: [T]he standards for accepting or rejecting contested ballots might vary not only from county to county but indeed within a single county from one recount team to the next. . . . [I]t is obvious that the recount cannot be conducted in compliance with the requirements of equal protection and due process without substantial additional work. It would require not only the adoption (after opportunity for argument) of adequate statewide standards for determining what is a legal vote, and practicable procedures to implement them, but also orderly judicial review of any disputed matters that might arise.

—Supreme Court majority's opinion

"INSIDE" INFLUENCES: THE JUSTICES' OWN POLITICAL BELIEFS

The judiciary symbolizes John Adams's characterization of the U.S. political system as "a government of laws, and not of men." The characterization has value as myth, but as the judicial scholar John Schmidhauser notes, "laws are made, enforced, and interpreted by men."[38] As an inevitable result, the decisions of the courts bear the indelible imprint of judges' political beliefs.[39]

This influence is most evident in the Supreme Court. The justices are frequently divided in their opinions, and the divisions often reflect the justices' political backgrounds. During the 1999 Supreme Court term, for example, sixteen cases were decided by a 5 to 4 decision. In fourteen of those cases, Chief Justice William Rehnquist and justices Antonin Scalia and Clarence Thomas, all of whom are Republican appointees, were opposed by justices Stephen Breyer and Ruth Bader Ginsburg, the two Democratic appointees on the Court.[40]

The relationship between justices' personal beliefs and their decisions is not a simple one. Liberalism and conservatism are not the same among justices as among elected officials. Because justices are constrained by legal principles, their political differences, though not small or inconsequential, are seldom total. For example, the conservative-leaning Rehnquist Court has modified substantially the criminal justice rulings of the more liberal Warren Court of the 1960s but has not repudiated what is arguably the Warren Court's most important legacy in this area: the broad principle that the Constitution provides substantial protections for the accused in state trial proceedings. Moreover, the position of some justices depends on the type of issue in question.[41] For example, Justice Byron White, who was appointed by the Democratic president John F. Kennedy, proved to be fairly conservative on civil liberties issues, particularly the rights of the accused, but moderate on questions of governmental regulation of the economy.

Most Supreme Court justices hold relatively stable political views during their tenure. As a result, major shifts in the Supreme Court's position usually occur in conjunction with changes in its membership. When the Court in the 1980s moved away from the criminal justice rulings of the 1960s, it was because the more recently appointed justices believed that government should have more leeway in its efforts to fight crime. Shifts in the Court's direction are related to political trends. Justices are political appointees who are nominated in part because their legal positions seem to be compatible with those of the president.

Nevertheless, the Court's membership has its unpredictable aspects. The turnover of justices depends on retirement and death, which occur irregularly. Whether a president will be able to appoint several, one, or no justices is never certain. The Republican president Richard Nixon made four Supreme Court appointments during his six years in office, whereas the Democratic president Jimmy Carter made none during his four-year term.

Judicial Power and Democratic Government

The issue of judicial power is heightened by the fact that the courts are not a majoritarian institution. Federal judges are not elected and cannot be held directly accountable by the public for their decisions. The principle of self-government

FIGURE 17-3 Opinions on Prayer in Public Schools Despite public support for allowing daily prayer in schools, the Supreme Court has held that such prayer violates the First Amendment. *Source: Gallup/CNN/ USA Today, poll, 1999.*

No opinion 21%

Favor voluntary prayer 65%

Oppose 14%

The Supreme Court resists pressure from the public and from elected officials on some issues, such as school prayer, that it considers to be questions of individual rights rather than of majority opinion.

asserts that lawmaking majorities have the power to decide society's policies. Because the United States has a constitutional system that places checks on the will of the majority, however, there is obviously an important role in the system for a countermajoritarian institution such as the judiciary. Yet court decisions often reflect the political philosophy of the judges, who constitute a tiny political elite that wields significant power.[42] A critical question is how far judges, who are not elected, ought to go in substituting their policy judgments for those of officials who are elected by the people.

This power is most dramatically evident when a court declares unconstitutional a law enacted by Congress. Such acts of *judicial review* place the judgment of unelected judges over the decision of the people's elected representatives. The difficult process of amending the Constitution (needing two-thirds majorities in the House and Senate and approval by three-fourths of the states) makes such amendments an impracticable means of reversing the Supreme Court. In the nation's history, only four constitutional amendments (for example, the Sixteenth, which permits a federal income tax) have reversed Supreme Court decisions.

THE DEBATE OVER THE PROPER ROLE OF THE JUDICIARY

legitimacy (of judicial power)
The issue of the proper limits of judicial authority in a political system based in part on the principle of majority rule.

The question of judicial power centers on the basic issue of **legitimacy**—the proper authority of the judiciary in a political system based in part on the principle of majority rule. The judiciary's policymaking significance and discretion have been sources of controversy throughout the country's history, but the controversies have perhaps never been livelier than during recent decades. The power of judicial review, which was first asserted in 1803 in *Marbury v. Madison* (see Chapter 2), was applied sparingly for a century and a half but since then has been invoked frequently. Although the judiciary rarely reverses the decisions of elected officials in certain areas, such as foreign policy and economic regulation (see Chapter 3), it has not hesitated to do so in other areas, such as civil liberties and civil rights (see Chapters 4 and 5). The judiciary at times has acted almost legislatively by defining broad social policies, such as abortion, busing, affirmative action, church-state relations, and prison reform. In a recent year, for example, the prison systems in forty-two states were operating under court orders that mandated improvements in health care or overcrowding. School prayer is an older example. Until the Supreme Court in 1962 prohibited the reciting of prayer in public schools, the practice was governed by state legislatures and, in some cases, by local school districts. Through such actions the judiciary has restricted the policymaking authority of the states, has narrowed legislative discretion, and has made judicial action an effective alternative to election victory for certain interests.[43]

The judiciary has become more extensively involved in policymaking for many of the same reasons that Congress and the president have been thrust into new policy areas and become more deeply involved in old ones. Social and economic changes have required government to play a larger role in society, and this development has generated a seemingly endless series of new legal controversies.

Of course, the structure of the U.S. political system requires a relatively assertive judiciary. When the U.S. Constitution established the judiciary as a coequal branch of government, it broke from the English tradition whereby courts had an active role in defining private relationships (*private law*) but were not allowed to define governmental relationships or the relationship of individuals to government (*public law*). Under the U.S. constitutional system, the judiciary in general and the Supreme Court in particular were granted a major role in the sphere of public-law policymaking. The Supreme Court has the responsibility of interpreting the Constitution, overseeing federalism and the separation of powers, and defining individual rights (see "How the United States Compares").

Nevertheless, the scope of judicial action raises an important question. How far should the judiciary go in asserting its authority when that authority collides with or goes beyond the action of elected institutions? There are two general schools of thought on this question: those of judicial restraint and judicial activism. Although these terms are somewhat imprecise and often misused, they are helpful in efforts to clarify opposing philosophical positions on the Court's proper role.[44]

FIGURE 17-4 Public Confidence in the Supreme Court
Although the public's trust in the Supreme Court has declined somewhat in recent decades, the Supreme Court retains a high confidence level compared with other U.S. institutions. The public's support is essential to the Court's efforts to achieve compliance with its decisions. *Source: Harris Interactive poll, January 2000. Used by permission.*

The Doctrine of Judicial Restraint

The doctrine of **judicial restraint** holds that the judiciary should be highly respectful of precedent and should defer to the judgment of legislatures. The restraint doctrine emphasizes the consistency of law and rule through elected institutions. It holds that broad issues of the public good should be decided in nearly all cases by the majority through legislation enacted by elected officials. The judges' role is to discover the application of legislation and precedent to specific cases rather than to search for new principles that essentially change the meaning of the law.

Advocates of judicial restraint support their position with two major arguments. First, they contend that when the judiciary assumes policy functions that traditionally belong to elected institutions, it undermines the fundamental premise of self-government: the right of the majority to choose society's policies.[45] Second, judicial self-restraint is admired because it preserves the public support (see Figure 17-4) that is essential to the long-term authority of the courts.[46] The judiciary must be concerned with **compliance**—with whether its decisions will be respected and obeyed. If the judiciary thwarts the majority's desires, public confidence in its legitimacy can be endangered, and other officials may act to undermine judicial decisions.[47]

Advocates of judicial restraint acknowledge that established law is never so precise as to provide exact answers to every question raised by every case and requires some degree of judicial discretion. And in rare circumstances, decisive judicial action may be both appropriate and necessary, as in the historic *Brown v. Board of Education* decision (1954). Although the Constitution does not provide an explicit basis for school desegregation, government-supported racial discrimination violates the principle of equal justice under the law.[48] Louis Lusky is among the advocates of judicial restraint who argue that the broad moral language of the Fourteenth Amendment, which says that no state shall deny to any person the equal protection of its laws, was adequate justification for the Supreme Court to require state governments to end their policy of segregated public schools.[49]

judicial restraint The doctrine that the judiciary should be highly respectful of precedent and should defer to the judgment of legislatures. The doctrine claims that the job of judges is to work within the confines of laws set down by tradition and lawmaking majorities.

compliance The issue of whether judicial decisions will be respected and obeyed.

The Supreme Court in 1996 struck down an amendment to the Colorado constitution that would have barred civil rights protections for homosexuals. The ruling was criticized by some advocates of judicial restraint.

Yet many advocates of judicial restraint see no constitutional justification for many of the Supreme Court's civil rights decisions. In *Romer v. Evans* (1996), for example, the Court struck down an amendment to the Colorado constitution that was adopted by majority vote in a statewide referendum. The amendment had nullified existing civil rights protections for homosexuals in the state and had also barred the passage of new ones. In a blistering dissent, Justice Antonin Scalia said the Court's decision to invalidate the Colorado amendment was "an act not of judicial judgment but of political will." Scalia said that the statewide referendum was "the most democratic of procedures" and that the decision of Colorado voters should have been upheld.[50]

The Doctrine of Judicial Activism

In contrast to the judicial restraint position is the idea that the courts should take a generous view of judicial power and involve themselves extensively in interpreting and enlarging upon the law. Although advocates of this doctrine, which is known as **judicial activism,** acknowledge the principles of precedent and majority rule, they claim that the courts should not be overly deferential to existing legal principles or to the judgments of elected officials.

judicial activism   The doctrine that the courts should develop new legal principles when judges see a compelling need, even if this action places them in conflict with the policy decisions of elected officials.

Until recently, the doctrine of judicial activism was associated almost entirely with liberal activists who contend that courts should resort to general principles of fairness when existing law is insufficient. Liberal judicial activists argue, for example, that fairness for African American children requires that in some circumstances children should be bused to achieve school integration. In areas where social justice depends substantially on protection of the rights of the individual, the judiciary is said to have a responsibility to act positively and decisively.[51]

Liberal activists who emphasize the Court's obligation to protect civil rights and liberties find justification for their position in the U.S. Constitution's strong

HOW THE UNITED STATES COMPARES

JUDICIAL POWER

U.S. courts are highly political by comparison with the courts of most other democracies. First, U.S. courts operate within a common-law tradition, which makes judge-made law (through precedent) a part of the legal code. Many democracies have a civil-law tradition, in which nearly all law is defined by legislative statutes. Second, because U.S. courts operate in a constitutional system of divided power, they are required to rule on conflicts between state and nation or between the executive and legislative branches, which thrusts the judiciary into the middle of political conflicts. It should not be surprising, then, that federal judges and justices are appointed through an overtly political process in which partisan views and activities are major considerations. Many federal judges, particularly at the district level, have no significant prior judicial experience. In fact, the United States is one of the few countries that does not mandate formal training for judges.

The pattern is different in most European democracies. Judgeships there tend to be career positions. Individuals are appointed to the judiciary at an early age and then work their way up the judicial ladder largely on the basis of seniority. Partisan politics does not play a large role in appointment and promotion. By tradition,

European judges see their job as the strict interpretation of statutes, not the creative application of them.

The power of U.S. courts is nowhere more evident than in the exercise of judicial review—the voiding of a legislative or executive action on the grounds that it violates the Constitution. Judicial review had its origins in European experience and thought, but it was first formally applied in the United States when, in *Marbury v. Madison* (1803), the Supreme Court declared an act of Congress unconstitutional. Some democracies, including Great Britain, still do not allow broadscale judicial review, but most democracies now provide for it.

In the so-called American system of judicial review, all judges can evaluate the applicability of constitutional law to particular cases and can declare ordinary law invalid when it conflicts with constitutional law. By comparison, the so-called Austrian system restricts judicial review to a special constitutional court. Judges in other courts cannot declare a law void on the grounds that it is unconstitutional: they must apply ordinary law as it is written. In the Austrian system, moreover, constitutional decisions are often made in response to requests for judicial review by political officials (such as the chief executive).

moral language and several of its provisions.[52] They view the Constitution as designed chiefly to protect people from unreasonable governmental interference in their lives—a goal that can be accomplished only by a judiciary that is willing to stand up to the lawmaking majority whenever the latter tries to restrict individual choice. They see the Constitution as a charter for liberties, not as a set of narrow rules. An activist interprets the Sixth Amendment's right to counsel, for example, not just as the right of a defendant to hire counsel but as the right to have a competent lawyer even if the defendant cannot afford one. When the Sixth Amendment was enacted in the late eighteenth century, criminal trials were short and straightforward, and it was at least possible in some instances for poor people to defend themselves competently. But criminal law and procedures today are so complex that a defendant without legal counsel would be at a serious disadvantage. Moreover, society today can afford to provide poor defendants with legal assistance. By such reasoning, the judicial activist school would argue that the Supreme Court was acting properly when it ruled in *Gideon v. Wainwright* (1963) that state governments had to provide indigent defendants with counsel at public expense.[53]

The Supreme Court and Social Policy

As the Supreme Court has extended its reach into areas that were once dominated by Congress and the president, some analysts have questioned whether the Court has the capacity (as distinct from the authority) to devise workable policies in all these areas.

Donald Horowitz argues in *The Courts and Social Policy* that unlike members of Congress or executive officials, who usually start their policy deliberations from a general perspective, justices of the Supreme Court start with a particular case, which often involves unusual or extreme circumstances. Horowitz also notes that the Court acts on the basis of less complete information than does Congress, which often holds hearings, conducts research, and by other means considers a wide range of facts before deciding on policy. The basic function of courts is to resolve specific disputes, and admissible evidence is generally limited to material directly relevant to the case at hand.

How important are these limits on the Court's policymaking capacity? Why?

Judicial activism is not, however, confined to liberals. In the 1860s–1930s period, conservative activists on the Supreme Court struck down most legislative efforts to regulate economic activity (see Chapter 3). Judicial activism from the right recently became an issue again when the Court overturned several precedents in the area of the rights of the accused. In 1990, Chief Justice William Rehnquist, in a rare action, asked Congress to restrict the right of those convicted in state courts to file habeas corpus appeals in federal courts. Congress rejected the proposal, and in 1991 a majority on the Rehnquist Court took action on its own to achieve the goal. In one ruling, the Court held that an inmate could not obtain a federal appeal simply because his or her lawyer had made a procedural mistake during the trial in a state court. Chief Justice Rehnquist wrote that precedent is not "an inexorable command."[54]

Conservative activism is also evident in recent Supreme Court cases on the issue of federalism. Since the late 1930s, the Court had deferred to Congress on commerce policy, but it has recently struck down several commerce-related statutes (see Chapter 3). The Court's four most conservative justices (Rehnquist, Scalia, Thomas, and Kennedy), joined by Justice O'Connor, supported the major decisions, each of which was decided by a 5-to-4 margin. In one of these cases, *Kimel v. Florida Board of Regents* (2000), the Court ruled that Congress did not have the power to require states to comply with the federal age-discrimination law because age is not among the forms of discrimination expressly prohibited by the Fourteenth Amendment's equal protection clause. The various rulings reflected Chief Justice William Rehnquist's long-held goal of limiting Congress's authority over the states.[55] "[The Rehnquist Court] doesn't defer to government at any level," said Walter Dellinger, a former solicitor general. "The Court is confident it can come up with the right decisions, and it believes it is constitutionally charged with doing so."[56]

Arguably, conservative activism was never more evident than in the Supreme Court's *Bush v. Gore* (2000) decision. The five justices in the majority were the same justices who in previous decisions had upheld states' rights and had opposed expansive applications of the Fourteenth Amendment's equal protection clause. Yet they invoked the equal protection clause to block the statewide manual recount that had been ordered by Florida's high court because no uniform standard for counting the ballots existed. When the Court issued a rare stay order to stop the recount, Justice Antonin Scalia claimed that it was justified because the recount could cast doubt on the legitimacy of Bush's election. The fact was, Bush had not yet been officially elected. Some observers suggested that, if Bush had been trailing in the Florida vote, the Court's majority would have allowed the recount to continue. Justice John Paul Stevens, who thought the Florida high court had acted properly in ordering a manual count, basically accused his colleagues on the Supreme Court of devising a ruling based on their partisan desires rather than on the law. Stevens noted that different standards for casting and counting ballots were found throughout the United States. The Court's ruling in *Bush v. Gore*, said Stevens, "can only lend credence to the most cynical appraisal of the work of judges throughout the land."

Whether from the right or the left, judicial activism is characterized by a willingness to pit the judgment and power of the courts against the judgment and power of elected representatives or their administrative agents. To a degree, all judges are activists in the sense that their decisions are necessarily creative ones. The law as expressed through the Constitution, statutes, and precedent is not precise enough to provide an automatic answer to every court case. Judges and justices have no choice but to exercise judgment when the text of the law is inexact. And, to a degree, all judges are restrained in the sense that their decisions must have roots in the law. Judges cannot simply make any decision they might choose; they are confined by the facts of a case and the laws that might reasonably be applied to it. But judges and justices vary in the degree to which they are willing to contest the judgment of other political institutions and the degree to which they are willing to depart from the wording of the law. These differences separate the judicial activists from the practitioners of judicial restraint.

THE JUDICIARY'S PROPER ROLE: A QUESTION OF COMPETING VALUES

The dispute between advocates of judicial activism and advocates of judicial restraint is a philosophical one that involves opposing values. The debate is important because it addresses the normative question of what role the judiciary ought to play in American democracy. Should unelected judges involve themselves deeply in policy by adopting a broad conception of their power, or should they give wide discretion to elective institutions? Should judges defer to precedent, or should they be willing to change course, even at the risk of sending the law down uncharted paths? These questions cannot be answered simply on the basis of whether one personally agrees or disagrees with a particular judicial decision. The answer necessarily depends on a value judgment about the role of the judiciary in a governing system based on the often-conflicting concepts of majority rule and individual rights.

The United States is a constitutional democracy that recognizes both the power of the majority to rule and the claim of the minority to protection of its rights. The judiciary was not established as the nation's moral conscience and does not have a monopoly on the issue of minority interests and rights. Yet the judiciary was established as a coequal branch of government and was charged with the responsibility for protecting individual rights and minority interests. In short, the constitutional question of how far the courts should be allowed to go in substituting their judgment for that of elected institutions and established law is open to interpretation. The trade-off is significant on all issues: minority rights versus majority rule, states' rights versus federal power, legislative authority versus judicial authority. The question of whether judicial restraint or judicial activism is more desirable is one that every student of American government should ponder.

www.mhhe.com/patterson5

Self-Quiz

Summary

At the lowest level of the federal judicial system are the district courts, where most federal cases begin. Above them are the federal courts of appeals, which review cases appealed from the lower courts. The U.S. Supreme Court is the nation's highest court. Each state has its own court system, consisting of trial courts at the bottom and one or two appellate levels at the top. Cases originating in state courts ordinarily cannot be appealed to the federal courts unless a federal issue is involved, and then the federal

courts can choose to rule only on the federal aspects of the case. Federal judges at all levels are nominated by the president, and if confirmed by the Senate, they are appointed by the president to the office. Once on the federal bench, they serve until they die, retire, or are removed by impeachment and conviction.

The Supreme Court is unquestionably the most important court in the country. The legal principles it establishes are binding on lower courts, and its capacity to define the law is enhanced by the control it exercises over the cases it hears. However, it is inaccurate to assume that lower courts are inconsequential (the upper-court myth). Lower courts have considerable discretion, and the great majority of their decisions are not reviewed by a higher court. It is also inaccurate to assume that federal courts are far more significant than state courts (the federal court myth).

The courts have less discretionary authority than elected institutions. The judiciary's positions are constrained by the facts of a case and by the laws as defined through the Constitution, statutes and government regulations, and legal precedent. Yet existing legal guidelines are seldom so precise that judges have no choice in their decisions. As a result, political influences have a strong impact on the judiciary. It responds to national conditions, public opinion, interest groups, and elected officials, particularly the president and members of Congress. Another political influence on the judiciary is the personal beliefs of judges, who have individual preferences that are evident in the way they decide on issues that come before the courts. Not surprisingly, partisan politics plays a significant role in judicial appointments.

In recent decades, the Supreme Court has issued broad rulings on individual rights, some of which have required governments to take positive action on behalf of minority interests. As the Court has crossed into areas traditionally left to lawmaking majorities, the legitimacy of its policies has been questioned. Advocates of judicial restraint claim that the justices' personal values are inadequate justification for exceeding the proper judicial role. They argue that the Constitution entrusts broad issues of the public good to elective institutions and that judicial activism ultimately undermines public respect for the judiciary. Judicial activists counter that the courts were established as an independent branch and should not hesitate to promote new principles when they see a need, even if this action puts them into conflict with elected officials.

Key Terms

appellate jurisdiction
compliance
concurring opinion
decision
dissenting opinion
facts (of a court case)
judicial activism
judicial conference
judicial restraint
jurisdiction (of a court)

laws (of a court case)
legitimacy (of judicial power)
majority opinion
opinion (of a court)
original jurisdiction
plurality opinion
precedent
senatorial courtesy
writ of *certiorari*

Suggested Readings

Carp, Robert A. and Ronald Stidham. *The Federal Courts,* 3d ed. Washington, D.C.: Congressional Quarterly Press, 1998. A study of the federal judiciary system.

Epstein, Lee, and Jack Knight. *The Choices Justices Make.* Washington, D.C.: Congressional Quarterly Press, 1997. A critical analysis of Supreme Court decision making.

Hughes, John C. *The Federal Courts, Politics, and the Rule of Law.* New York: Longman, 1995. An analysis of the federal courts as a dynamic system.

Maltz, Earl M. *Rethinking Constitutional Law: Originalism, Interventionism, and the Politics of Judicial Review.* Lawrence: University Press of Kansas, 1994. A critical and timely analysis of constitutional interpretation in the modern age.

McKeever, Robert. *The United States Supreme Court: A Political and Legal Analysis.* New York: St. Martin's Press, 1997. A political and legal analysis of the United States Supreme Court.

O'Brien, David M. *Storm Center:* The Supreme Court in American Politics, 5th ed. New York: W. W. Norton, 2000. An analysis of the Supreme Court in the context of the controversy surrounding the role of the judiciary in the U.S. political system.

Perry, Michael J. *The Constitution in the Courts: Law or Politics?* New York: Oxford University Press, 1994. A sweeping assessment of the constitutional role of the Supreme Court by a proponent of judicial activism.

Salokar, Rebecca Mae. *The Solicitor General: The Politics of Law.* Philadelphia, Pa.: Temple University Press, 1992. A study of the important and increasingly political role of the nation's top trial lawyer.

Scalia, Antonin. *A Matter of Interpretation: Federal Courts and the Law.* Princeton, N.J.: Princeton University Press, 1997. A critical assessment of how the Supreme Court interprets law.

Schwartz, Bernard. *Decision: How the Supreme Court Decides Cases.* New York: Oxford University Press, 1996. A behind-the-scenes look at Supreme Court justices' decisions.

Segal, Jeffrey A., and Harold J. Spaeth. *The Supreme Court and the Attitudinal Model.* New York: Cambridge University Press, 1993. A provocative analysis that claims that justices' personal beliefs are the main determinant of Supreme Court decisions.

Slotnick, Elliot E., and Jennifer A. Segal. *Television News and the Supreme Court.* New York: Cambridge University Press, 1998. A study of television news and the Supreme Court.

Watson, George L., and John Alan Stookey. *Shaping America: The Politics of Supreme Court Appointments.* New York: Longman, 1995. An examination of the process by which Supreme Court justices are nominated and confirmed.

PART FOUR

Public Policy

★ ★ ★

olitics, said Harold Lasswell, is the struggle over "who gets what, when, and how." Americans differ in many of their interests, and they also disagree over policy. Yet they are often able to find common ground. The typical response when a policy problem arises is not only to fight over it but also to resolve it. This philosophy speaks volumes about the nature of American governance.

The three chapters in this section are designed mainly to address broad policy issue areas—the economy and environment (Chapter 18); welfare, education, and health (Chapter 19); and foreign and defense policy (Chapter 20).

There is a common pattern to policy action in these areas: it tends to be piecemeal and reactive. The nation's diversity and fragmented governing structure make it difficult for policymakers to deal with issues except in small parts and until they have reached the problem stage. This tendency increases the likelihood that major errors of policy will be avoided but also increases the chance that problems will be left to grow to the point where solutions are harder and more costly.

Regardless, a democratic nation's policies reflect the nature of its political system and its people. They indicate the way that a society has chosen to govern itself. ★

CHAPTER 18

Economic and Environmental Policy: Contributing to Prosperity

★

We the people of the United States, in order to . . .
insure domestic tranquility . . .

—Preamble, U.S. Constitution

★ ★ ★

The stock market had been on a dizzying ride upward. It had gained nearly 20 percent since the start of the year. Then, in early spring of 2000, investors got jittery. Signs of inflation were beginning to surface, the government was pursuing a hard line in its anti-trust suit with the software giant Microsoft, and the turnaround in the Asian economies looked shaky. The Dow Jones and Nasdaq indexes dropped sharply, knocking more than $2 trillion off the value of stocks. Would history repeat itself? Would the United States get swamped by another global economic depression like the one that followed the collapse of the stock market in 1929?

In fact, Wall Street and the rest of America reacted rather calmly to the market downturn in early 2000. There was continued volatility in the Dow Jones, but there was no panic. Among the reasons was the fact that substantial government programs were in place to stabilize and stimulate the U.S. economy. When the Great Depression struck, no such programs existed. Moreover, the response to the 1929 crash guaranteed that the economic crisis would worsen. Businesses cut back on production, investors fled the stock market, depositors withdrew their bank savings, and consumers slowed their spending. All these actions accelerated the downward spiral. In 2000, however, government programs were in place if need be to protect depositors' savings, to slow the drop in stock prices, and to steady the economy through adjustments in interest rates and spending programs.

This chapter examines the economic role of the government, focusing on its promotion and regulation of economic interests and its fiscal and monetary policies. Directly or indirectly, the federal government is a party to almost every economic transaction in which Americans engage. Although the private decisions of firms and individuals are the main force in the American economic system, these decisions are influenced by government policy. Washington seeks to maintain high productivity, employment, and purchasing power; regulates business practices that would otherwise harm the environment or result in economic inefficiencies and inequities; and promotes economic interests. The main ideas presented in this chapter are the following:

★ *Through regulation, the U.S. government imposes restraints on business activity that are designed to promote economic efficiency and equity.* This regulation is often the cause of political conflict, which is both ideological and group centered.

★ *Through regulatory and conservation policies, the U.S. government seeks to protect and preserve the environment from the effects of business firms and consumers.*

★ *Through promotion, the U.S. government helps private interests to achieve their economic goals.* Business in particular benefits from the government's promotional efforts, which take place largely in the context of group politics.

★ *Through its taxing and spending decisions (fiscal policy), the U.S. government seeks to maintain a level of economic supply and demand that will keep the economy prosperous.* The condition of the economy is generally the leading issue in American electoral politics and has a major influence on each party's success.

★ *Through its money-supply decisions (monetary policy), the U.S. government— through the "Fed"—seeks to maintain a level of inflation consistent with sustained controllable economic growth.*

Government as Regulator of the Economy

economy A system of production and consumption of goods and services that are allocated through exchange among producers and consumers.

laissez-faire doctrine A classic economic philosophy that holds that owners of business should be allowed to make their own production and distribution decisions without government regulation or control.

An **economy** is a system of production and consumption of goods and services, which are allocated through exchange. When a shopper chooses groceries at a store and pays money for them, that transaction is one of the million economic exchanges that make up the economy. In *The Wealth of Nations* (1776), Adam Smith presented the case for the **laissez-faire doctrine,** which holds that private individuals and firms should be left alone to make their own production and distribution decisions. Smith reasoned that when there is a demand for a good (that is, when people are willing and able to buy a good), private entrepreneurs will respond by producing the good and distributing it to places where demand exists. Smith argued that the desire for profit is the "invisible hand" that guides the system of demand and supply toward the greatest benefit for all.

Smith acknowledged that the doctrine of laissez-faire capitalism had a few limits. Certain areas of the economy, such as roadways and postal services, were natural monopolies and were better run by government than by private firms. In addition, by regulating banking, currency, and contracts, government could give stability to private transactions. Otherwise, Smith argued, the economy was best left in private hands.

In contrast, Karl Marx proposed a worker-controlled economy. In *Das Kapital* (*Capital,* 1867) Marx argued that a free market system is exploitative because producers, through their control of production and markets, can compel workers to labor at a wage below the value they add to production and can force consumers to pay higher prices for goods than are justified by the cost of production. To end the exploitation of labor, Marx proposed a collective economy. When the workers owned the means of production, the economy would operate in the interest of all people.

Marx and Smith represent the extremes of economic theory. No country in the world has an economy that conforms fully to either the laissez-faire or the collectivist model. All national economies today are of "mixed" form in that they contain elements of both private and public control. However, the world's economies vary greatly in their mix. The United States tends toward private ownership, whereas China tends toward collective ownership. In between, but closer to the American type of economy, are certain European countries whose governments, on behalf of their people, own and operate a number of key in-dustries, including steel, airlines, banking, and oil.

Although the U.S. government itself owns only a few businesses (such as Amtrak), it plays a substantial economic role through the **regulation** of pri-vately owned businesses. U.S. firms are not free to act as they please but must operate within production and distribution rules set by federal regulations. Regulatory policy is generally intended to promote either economic *efficiency* or *equity* (see Table 18-1).

regulation   A term that refers to government restrictions on the economic practices of private firms.

EFFICIENCY THROUGH GOVERNMENT INTERVENTION

Economic efficiency results when firms fulfill as many of society's needs as pos-sible while using as few of its resources as possible. **Efficiency** refers to the re-lationship of inputs (the labor and material that go into making a product or service) to outputs (the product or service itself). The greater the output for a given input, the more efficient the production process.

Adam Smith and other classical economists believed that the free market was the optimal means of achieving efficiency. Producers would try to use as few re-sources as possible in order to keep their prices low so that they could compete successfully for customers. Efficient producers would be able to underprice in-efficient ones, who would thereby be driven out of business.

efficiency   An economic principle that holds that firms should fulfill as many of society's needs as possible while using as few of its resources as possible. The greater the output (production) for a given input (for example, an hour of labor), the more efficient the process.

Preventing Restraint of Trade

The assumption that the market always determines price is flawed. The same incentive—the profit motive—that drives producers to respond to demand can drive them to corner the market on a good. If a producer gains a monopoly on a good or colludes with other producers to fix its price, consumers are forced to pay an artificially high price. Rather than selling at a low price in order to attract customers, the producer will charge as high a price as the market will bear.

Restraint of trade was prevalent in the United States in the late nineteenth century when large trusts came to dominate many areas of the economy,

TABLE 18-1   The Main Objectives of Regulatory Policy   The government intervenes in the economy to promote efficiency and equity.

Objective	Definition	Representative Actions by Government
Efficiency	Fulfillment of as many of society's needs as possible at the cost of as few of its resources as possible. The greater the output for a given input, the more efficient is the process.	Preventing restraint of trade; requiring producers to pay the costs of damage to the environment; reducing restrictions on business that cannot be justified on a cost-benefit basis.
Equity	When the outcome of an economic transaction is fair to each party.	Requiring firms to bargain in good faith with labor; protecting consumers in their purchases; protecting workers' safety and health.

In *The Wealth of Nations* (1776), Adam Smith provided a philosophical justification for a free market economy.

including the oil, steel, railroad, and sugar markets. Railroad companies, for example, had no competition on short routes and gouged their customers. In 1887, Congress took its first step toward regulating the trusts by enacting the Interstate Commerce Act. The legislation created the Interstate Commerce Commission (ICC), which was charged with regulating railroad practices and fares. Three years later, the Sherman Antitrust Act declared that any business combination or practice in restraint of trade was illegal. A probusiness Supreme Court made these legislative acts less effective than anticipated, and so the Mann-Elkins Act (1911) and the Clayton Act (1914) were passed to broaden the government's regulatory authority. The Federal Trade Commission (FTC) was established in 1914 to regulate trade practices.

Today the FTC is one of many federal agencies charged with regulating business competition. In a few cases, the government has prohibited mergers or required divestments in order to increase competition. In 1999, for example, the Federal Communications Commission (FCC) voided a proposed merger of Bell Atlantic and GTE, ruling that the companies had failed to show that the merger would not hurt consumers. In other cases, the government has pressured companies whose marketing practices threaten competition. An example is the Justice Department's recent suit against Microsoft for using its Windows Operating System to promote its Internet Explorer at the expense of other web browsers such as Netscape Navigator.

In most cases, however, the government tolerates business concentration, even permitting the merger of competing firms, such as Time Warner's merger with Turner Broadcasting in 1996. Although such mergers reduce competition, the government tolerates concentrated ownership in the oil, automobile, and other industries in which high capital costs make it difficult for smaller firms to compete successfully.[1] Government acceptance of corporate giants also reflects a realization that market competition no longer involves just domestic firms. For example, the "Big Three" U.S. automakers (General Motors, Ford, and Chrysler) face stiff competition from imports, particularly those from Japan and

Although corporate mergers decrease competition, the government has generally tolerated mergers in business sectors in which capital costs are high. Here, Steve Case (left) and Gerald Levin (right) announce the merger of America Online (AOL) and Time-Warner, which created the world's largest communication conglomerate.

Germany. The recent merger of Chrysler and Germany's Daimler-Benz is testimony to the increased globalization of market competition.

The U.S. government's general policy toward corporate giants that act in restraint of trade has been to penalize them financially. In 1993, a number of air carriers (including American, Delta, United, Northwest, and US Air) were found to have engaged in price fixing and were ordered to award hundreds of millions of dollars in certificates to travelers who could prove they had flown on these carriers during the period in question. More than four million individuals, organizations, and businesses filed claims.

Making Business Pay for Indirect Costs

Economic inefficiencies can result not only from restraint of trade but from the failure of businesses or consumers to pay the full costs of resources used in production. Classical economics assumes that market prices reflect all the costs of production, but this assumption is rarely warranted. Consider companies whose industrial wastes seep into nearby lakes and rivers. The price of these companies' products does not reflect the water pollution, and hence customers do not pay all the costs that society has incurred in the making of the products. Economists label such unpaid costs **externalities.**

Until the 1960s, the federal government did not require firms to pay such costs. The impetus to begin doing so came not only from lawmakers but also from the scientific community and environmental groups. The Clean Air Act of 1963 and the Water Quality Act of 1964 required industry to install antipollution devices to keep the discharge of air and water pollutants within specified limits. In 1970, Congress created the Environmental Protection Agency (EPA) to monitor compliance with federal regulations governing air and water quality and the disposal of toxic wastes. (Environmental policy is discussed more fully later in the chapter.)

externalities Burdens that society incurs when firms fail to pay the full costs of production. An example of an externality is the pollution that results when corporations dump industrial wastes into lakes and rivers.

Curbing Overregulation

Although government intervention is intended to increase economic efficiency, the effect can be the opposite. Government regulation raises the cost of doing business. Firms have to expend work hours to monitor and implement government regulations, which in some instances (for example, pollution control) also require companies to buy and install expensive equipment. These costs are efficient to the degree that they produce commensurate benefits. As a result of regulation, for example, worker safety has improved greatly (for example, in the past decade or so, workplace deaths and injuries have declined by more than 20 percent).

Yet if government places needless or excessive regulatory burdens on firms, they waste resources in the process of complying. The result is higher-priced goods that are more expensive for consumers and less competitive in the domestic and global markets (see "How the United States Compares"). In other words, too much regulation is a source of inefficiency. An example is a provision of the Safe Drinking Water Act that required communities to reduce contaminants in their water supply from the current level, whatever that level happened to be. In most communities, the effect was to improve the quality of the water supply. But in Anchorage, Alaska, the result was an absurd remedy.

HOW THE UNITED STATES COMPARES

GLOBAL ECONOMIC COMPETITIVENESS

The United States ranks second only to Singapore in global economic competitiveness, according to a survey by the World Economic Forum, a private economic research organization in Switzerland.

The ranking is based on eight different factors: institutional openness, internationalization, government, management, finance, infrastructure, science and technology, and labor. The United States is strong on its technology,

management, and finance. Its weakest point was the people factor, where it was downgraded on education programs and welfare services (for example, the United States, unlike other advanced industrialized countries, does not have government-provided health care).

The United States is ranked substantially higher than its major economic rivals, Japan and Germany. They trailed by a wide margin.

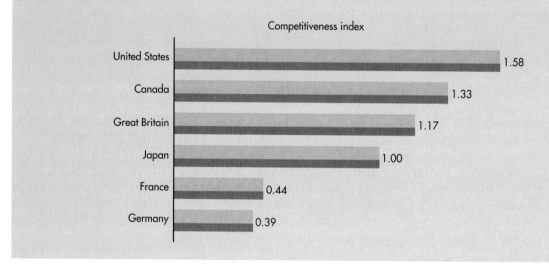

The city's water supply was so clean already that officials had to ask local fish-processing plants to dump their wastes into the sewer system so that Anchorage would have impurities to remove from its water.[2]

Situations of this kind have led to regulatory reform.[3] In 1995, Congress enacted legislation to tighten the regulatory process by requiring cost-benefit analysis and risk assessment (the severity of the problem) to be taken into account in certain regulatory decisions.

Deregulation

deregulation The rescinding of excessive government regulations for the purpose of improving economic efficiency.

Another response to regulatory excess is the policy of **deregulation**—the rescinding of regulations already in force for the purpose of improving efficiency. This process began in 1977 with passage of the Airlines Deregulation Act, which eliminated government-set airfares and, in some instances, government-mandated air routes. The change had the intended effect: airfares declined in price, and there was more competition between airlines on most routes. Congress followed airline deregulation with partial deregulation of the trucking, banking, energy, and communications industries, among others.

The free market principle has its limits, however, just as the regulatory principle can be carried too far. Deregulation has not been an unqualified success.[4] The savings and loan (S&L) industry is a prime example. S&Ls had been hit hard by the high inflation of the 1970s, and they hoped to restore their financial base through high-yield investments. Since existing regulations prevented them from pursuing riskier investments, the S&L industry successfully lobbied Congress for a change. When deregulation lifted restrictions on how S&Ls could invest depositors' savings, many of them began to engage in highly speculative ventures, such as commercial real estate. By 1989, the S&L industry was in crisis. Bad management, poor investments, and outright fraud had resulted in an industrywide loss of billions of dollars. In order to save what was left of the industry, President Bush and Congress developed a bailout plan that cost the taxpayers an estimated $100 billion.

The savings and loan crisis demonstrates that the issue of business regulation is not a simple question of whether or not to regulate. On the one hand, too much regulation can burden firms with bureaucratic red tape, costly implementation procedures, and limited options. On the other hand, too little regulation can give firms the leeway to exploit the public unfairly or recklessly. Either too little or too much regulation can result in economic inefficiency. The challenge for policymakers is to strike the proper balance between regulatory measures and free market mechanisms.

EQUITY THROUGH GOVERNMENT INTERVENTION

As we noted earlier, the government intervenes in the economy to bring equity as well as efficiency to the marketplace. **Equity** occurs when an economic transaction is fair to each party.[5] Whereas efficiency refers to the relationship of inputs to outputs, equity refers to *outcomes:* whether they are reasonable and mutually acceptable. A transaction can be considered fair if each party enters into it freely and is not unknowingly at a disadvantage (for example, if the seller knows a product is defective, equity requires that the buyer also know of the defect).

An early equity measure was the creation of the Food and Drug Administration (FDA) in 1907. Because consumers are often unable to tell whether foods and drugs are safe to use, the FDA works to keep adulterated foods and dangerous or ineffective drugs off the market. In the 1930s, financial reforms were among the equity measures enacted under the New Deal. The Securities and Exchange Act of 1934 and the Banking Act of 1934 were designed in part to protect investors and savers from dishonest or imprudent brokers and bankers. The New Deal also provided greater equity for organized labor, which previously had been in a weak position in its dealings with management. Under the terms of the 1935 National Labor Relations Act (also called the Wagner Act), employers could no longer refuse to negotiate pay and working conditions with employees' unions. The Fair Labor Standards Act of 1938 established minimum wages, maximum working hours, and constraints on the use of child labor.

The 1960s and 1970s produced the greatest number of equity reforms. From 1965 to 1977, ten federal agencies, such as the Consumer Product Safety Commission, were established to protect consumers, workers, and the public from harmful effects of business activity. Among the products declared to be unsafe in the 1960s and 1970s were the insecticide DDT, cigarettes, and leaded gasoline. The rule eliminating lead in gasoline, for example, has given society a

equity (in relation to economic policy)   The situation in which the outcome of an economic transaction is fair to each party. An outcome can usually be considered fair if each party enters into a transaction freely and is not knowingly at a disadvantage.

Shown here are demonstrators protesting the practices of Health Maintenance Organizations (HMOs). The central issue of business regulation is the proper balance of regulatory and free market mechanisms. Critics of HMOs say they are more interested in profits than in patients' health and that more regulation of their activities is warranted.

major benefit; the average level of lead in children's blood has decreased by 75 percent since the measure went into effect.[6]

THE POLITICS OF REGULATORY POLICY

Economic regulation has come in waves, as changes in national conditions have produced intermittent bursts of social consciousness.

The Reforms of the Progressive and New Deal Eras

The first wave of regulation came during the Progressive era, when reformers sought to break the power of the trusts by placing constraints on unfair business practices. The second wave came in the New Deal era, when reformers sought to stimulate economic recovery through regulatory policies that were designed as much to save business as to restrain it.

Although business fought Progressive and New Deal reforms, long-term opposition was lessened by the fact that most of the resulting regulation applied to a particular industry rather than to firms of all types. This pattern made it possible for an affected industry to gain influence with those officials who were responsible for regulating its activities. By cultivating close ties to the FCC, for example, the broadcast networks managed to obtain policies that protected their near monopoly on broadcasting and gave them high and sustained profits.[7] Although not all industries have had as much leverage with their regulators as broadcasting has, it is generally true that industries have not been greatly hampered by the older form of regulation and in many cases have substantially benefited from it.

The Era of New Social Regulation

The third wave of regulatory reform, in the 1960s and 1970s, differed from the Progressive and New Deal phases in both its policies and its politics. The third

The Environmental Protection Agency (EPA) is headquartered in this building in Washington, D.C. The EPA is a regulatory agency with a broad mandate and a director appointed and subject to removal by the president.

wave has been called the era of "new social regulation" because of the social goals it addressed in its three major policy areas: environmental protection, consumer protection, and worker safety.

Most of the regulatory agencies established during the third wave have much broader policy mandates than those created earlier. They have responsibility not for a single industry but for firms of all types, and their policy scope covers a wide range of activities. The EPA, for example, is charged with regulating environmental pollution of almost any kind by almost any firm. Unlike the older agencies that are run by a commission whose members serve for fixed terms, some of the newer agencies, including the EPA, are headed by a single director, who is appointed by the president with Senate approval and is subject to immediate removal by the president.

Because newer agencies such as the EPA have a wide-ranging clientele, no one firm or industry can easily influence agency policy to a great extent. There is also strong group competition in some of the newer regulatory spheres. For example, business lobbies must compete with environmental groups such as the Sierra Club and Greenpeace for influence with the EPA.[8] The firms regulated by the older agencies, in contrast, face no powerful competition in their lobbying activities. Broadcasters, for example, are largely unopposed in their efforts to influence the FCC. Although television viewers and radio listeners have a stake in FCC decisions, they are not well enough organized to petition it effectively.

In the case of both the newer and older regulatory agencies, a form of *pluralist* politics prevails, but the range of influential groups is broader in the case of the newer agencies. The newer agencies are also more affected by partisan politics. With their stronger commitment to business interests, Republican leaders have been less supportive of environmental, consumer, and worker interests than have Democratic leaders and have thus been less supportive of regulatory activity in these areas. When Republicans took control of Congress in 1995, for example, they wrote legislation restricting the scope of environmental regulation.

www.mhhe.com/patterson5

Graphic

Government as Protector of the Environment

Few changes in public opinion and policy during recent decades have been as dramatic as those relating to the environment. Most Americans today recycle some of their garbage, and nearly two-thirds say they are either an active environmentalist or sympathetic to environmental concerns (see Figure 18-1). In the 1960s, few Americans bothered to sort their trash and few could have answered a polling question that asked them whether they were an "environmentalist." The term was not commonly used, and people would not have understood its meaning.

The modern environmental movement gained impetus with the publication in 1962 of Rachel Carson's *The Silent Spring*.[9] Written at a time when the author was dying of breast cancer, *Silent Spring* revealed the threat of pesticides such as DDT to waterways and wildlife and challenged the notion that scientific progress was an unqualified benefit to society. Carson's appearance at a Senate hearing contributed to legislative action that produced the 1963 Clean Air Act and the 1965 Water Quality Act. It was the first time in the nation's history that the federal government had taken major steps to protect the nation's air, water, and ground from pollution. Today, this protection extends to nearly two hundred potentially harmful forms of emission.

CONSERVATIONISM: THE OLDER WAVE

Although government policy aimed at protecting the ambient environment is relatively new, the government has been involved in land conservation for more than a century. The first national park was created at Yellowstone in 1872 and, like the later ones, was established to preserve the nation's natural heritage for generations to come. The national park system serves more than one hundred million visitors each year and covers a total of eighty million acres, an area larger than every state except Alaska, Texas, California, and Montana.

The national parks are run by the National Park Service, an agency within the Department of Interior. Another agency, the U.S. Forest Service, which is located within the Department of Agriculture, manages the national forests,

FIGURE 18-1 Public Opinion on the Issue of Environmentalism Most Americans regard themselves as either active environmentalists or as sympathetic to environmental concerns. *Source: Wirthlin Worldwide survey, October 22–26, 1999.*

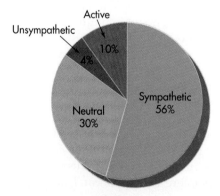

Active
Unsympathetic
10%
4%
Sympathetic 56%
Neutral 30%

"Do you think of yourself as an active environmentalist, or two, sympathetic to environmental concerns but not active, or three, neutral, or four, generally unsympathetic to environmental concerns?"

which cover an area more than twice the size of the national parks. They, too, have been preserved in part to protect the nation's natural heritage.

The nation's parks and forests, however, are subject to a "dual use" policy. They are nature preserves and recreation areas, but they are also rich in natural resources—minerals, forests, and grazing lands. The federal government sells permits to ranchers, timber companies, and mining firms that gives them the right to take some of these resources, a policy that can place their interests in conflict with those of conservationists.

A case in point is the spotted-owl controversy that erupted in the Pacific Northwest in the late 1980s. The spotted owl is an endangered species found in the region's virgin forests, which are also a mainstay of the region's timber industry. The issue of timber rights in the spotted owl's habitat pitted timber companies, loggers, and logging towns against conservationists in a bitter dispute that was waged through lawsuits, public demonstrations, and the lobbying of Congress and the White House. The timber interests eventually prevailed but did not get the extensive logging rights they were seeking.

Conservation groups have also found themselves directly in conflict with the federal government. One of the biggest disputes took place over the snail darter, a small fish whose only habitat would have been destroyed by a dam that the Tennessee Valley Authority was planning to build. Conservationists gained a victory when the Supreme Court ruled that the 1973 Endangered Species Act prohibited government from avoidable action that threatens the existence of endangered species.[10] Their victory was short-lived, however. Congress responded to the Court's decision by amending the Endangered Species Act to allow agencies to consider costs as well as benefits when deciding whether to proceed with development projects that conflict with conservation objectives.

Conservation groups employ sophisticated political strategies, relying on all forms of lobbying at all levels of government and often banding together to promote common issues. Their success has spawned a countercoalition of

The federal government's environmental efforts include programs designed to conserve nature through the protection of forests and other natural assets. Shown here is a scene from Yellowstone National Park.

economic interests that calls itself the "wise-use" movement and that promotes the claim that prudent use of natural resources is a wiser form of conservation than letting nature alone determine how land will evolve. "We've come to the conclusion that our policies provide for greater environmental protection," said Representative George P. Radanovich (R-Calif.), a congressional supporter of the coalition. "So our strategy has changed. The challenge has been how do we 'outgreen' the [conservationists]."[11] The wise-use coalition includes more than a thousand groups, many of which represent logging, ranching, and mining interests. When Secretary of the Interior Bruce Babbitt sought to raise grazing fees on federal lands in 1993, the coalition mobilized members of Congress from the western states and defeated the plan.

Some conservation groups work outside the realm of government action through initiatives designed to enlist private parties in the conservation effort. The Nature Conservancy is a prime example. Formed in the 1950s, it describes itself as "nature's real estate agency." Through land purchases, bequests, and trusteeships, the Nature Conservancy has acquired ownership or guardianship of nearly ten million acres in the United States. This land is kept in a wild state in order to preserve the habitat of imperiled species of plants and animals.

ENVIRONMENTALISM: THE NEWER WAVE

As previously indicated, the 1960s was the pivotal decade in the federal government's realization that Americans needed protection from the harmful effects of air, water, and ground pollutants. The period was capped by the first Earth Day. Held in the spring of 1970, it was the brainchild of Senator Gaylord Nelson (D-Wis.), who had devoted nearly ten years to finding ways to draw the public's attention to environmental issues. With the first Earth Day, Nelson succeeded to a degree not even he could have imagined: ten thousand grade schools and high schools, two thousand colleges, and one thousand communities participated in the event, which included public rallies and environmental cleanup efforts. Earth Day has been held every year since and is now a worldwide event.

The year 1970 also marked the creation of the Environmental Protection Agency. Within a few months, the EPA was issuing new regulations at such a

Environmental regulations restricting the level of automobile pollution have greatly improved air quality in America's cities.

rapid pace that business firms had difficulty keeping track of all the mandates, much less complying fully with them. They eventually found an ally in President Gerald Ford, who, in a 1975 speech to the National Federation of Industrial Business, claimed that business regulation was costing $150 billion annually, or $2,000 for every American family.[12] Although Ford's estimate exceeded that of economic analysts, his point was not lost on policy makers or the people. The economy was in a slump, and the costs of complying with the new regulations were impeding an economic recovery. Polls indicated a decline in public support for regulatory action.

Since then, environmental protection policy has not been greatly expanded but neither has it greatly contracted. The emphasis has been on administering and amending the laws put into effect in the 1960s and 1970s.

Environmental regulation has had a dramatic effect on air and water quality (see Figure 18-2). Pollution levels today are far below their levels of the 1960s when yellowish-gray fog ("smog") hung over cities like Los Angeles and New York; when bodies of water like the Potomac River and Lake Erie were open sewers; and when communities like the Love Canal neighborhood of Niagara Falls, New York, sat atop contaminated ground that slowly poisoned its occupants.

The positive impact of environmental policy has not eliminated the conflict surrounding it. An ongoing issue is how far government should go in the efforts to reduce pollution. When the Clinton administration in 1997 announced tougher standards for ozone and tiny airborne particles, majorities in the House and Senate opposed the initiative. They claimed that existing standards were sufficient and that the changes were supported by questionable scientific research. The main effect of the new standards, they said, would be to saddle business with millions of dollars in compliance costs. "The choice here is not

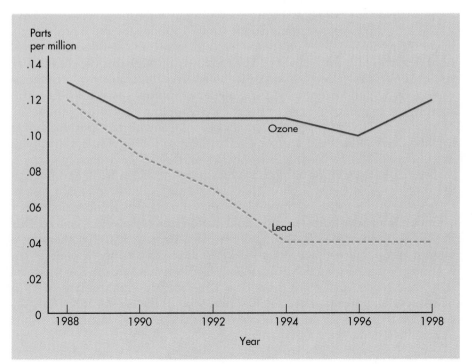

FIGURE 18-2   Indicators of Improvements in Air Quality
The quality of the air that Americans breathe has improved as a result of environmental regulation. *Source: Environmental Protection Agency, 2000.*

between clean air and dirty air," said Representative John Dingell (D-Mich.), an opponent of the new standards. "It is a choice between clean air and jobs."[13]

Not all environmental problems have improved so dramatically as air pollution. The disposal of solid-waste toxic substances has been a persistent problem. Although a federal "superfund" for the cleanup of toxic wastes was established by Congress in 1980, administrative delays, litigation, and technological problems have hindered progress in this area. The time required for the completion of the average cleanup of a toxic waste site has actually increased since the superfund was created.[14] The public has contributed to the slowdown. Communities and neighborhoods have fought nearly every attempt to locate toxic-waste disposal sites in their vicinity. Resistance has been so widespread that the phenomena has acquired a term of its own—NIMBY (Not in My Backyard).

Compliance with environmental regulations is obtained through monitoring devices, reporting requirements, on-site inspections, and fines for regulatory violations. Because it is difficult to uncover some forms of illegal pollution, the EPA has devised mechanisms designed to encourage voluntary compliance. One device is the EPA's negotiated regulation process, in which affected interests are brought together in advance of a proposed regulation in order to resolve their differences and secure binding agreements that can be written into the new regulation.

A more substantial innovation has been the use of "pollution credits." The Clean Air Act was amended in 1990 to allow firms to accumulate credits by achieving a lower level of pollution than is mandated by law. These credits can then be sold to firms that fail to reach required levels. Although this approach has enabled inefficient firms to avoid the steps necessary to reduce pollution, its principal effect has been to encourage other firms to reduce their pollution to lower-than-required levels and thus qualify for pollution credits, which can be sold to less-efficient firms at a hefty price. Overall pollution has been reduced to a level below that which would have been achieved without the marketplace incentive.

The program's success prompted the Clinton administration to propose it at the 1997 Global Warming Conference in Kyoto, Japan. The world's carbon emissions, President Clinton said, could be reduced "through the force of the market."[15] The Kyoto conference was called to address the problem of greenhouse gases, which could eventually cause air temperatures and sea levels to rise sharply, creating flooding and drought and disrupting agriculture production. The Kyoto conference accepted Clinton's proposal and also adopted technological and energy-efficiency measures as its formula for a gradual reduction in greenhouse gases. The Sierra Club was among the U.S. environmental groups that criticized the Clinton administration's proposal as too weak a response to the problem of global warming. They had wanted Clinton to back a carbon-fuels tax and an accelerated timetable for the reduction in carbon emissions.

Environmental groups are among the nation's most powerful lobbies. During the 1960s, environmental groups grew at a faster rate than any other type of interest group. Their membership increased threefold during the period[16] and continued to rise during the 1970s and 1980s before leveling off. The U.S. environmental lobby consists of more than 250 separate organizations, most of which specialize in a particular policy area. Most of the organizations are quite small, but there are several, including the Sierra Club, that have memberships that number in the hundreds of thousands.

The government has shifted some of the cost of cleaning up toxic waste dumps and other kinds of pollution from the general public to the firms that discharge the pollutants. The costs of environmental protection, and how the costs will be distributed, is a contentious political issue.

Government as Promoter of Economic Interests

The U.S. government has always made important contributions to the nation's economy. The Constitution was written in part to provide for a national government strong enough to promote a sound economy. The Constitution stipulated that the government was to regulate commerce, create a strong currency, develop uniform commercial standards, and provide a stable credit system. The fledgling government also immediately demonstrated its concern for economic interests. Congress in 1789 gave a boost to the nation's shipping industry by placing a tariff on imported goods carried by foreign ships. Since that first favor, the U.S. government has provided thousands of direct benefits to economic interests.

Chapters 13 and 16 described how congressional and bureaucratic politics results in the promotion of group interests. This section briefly examines a few illustrations of the scope of government's contribution to the *pluralistic* interests of business, labor, and agriculture.

PROMOTING BUSINESS

American business is not opposed to government regulation as such. It objects only to regulatory policies that are adverse to its interests. We have noted that, at various times and in differing ways, many federal regulatory agencies have served primarily the interests of the industries they are intended to regulate.

Loans and tax breaks are another way that government promotes business. Firms receive loan guarantees, direct loans, tax credits for capital investments, and tax deductions for capital depreciation. Over the past forty years, the burden of federal taxation has shifted dramatically, from corporations to individuals. A few decades ago, the revenues raised from taxes on corporate income were roughly the same as the revenues raised from taxes on individual income. Today, individual taxpayers carry the heavier burden by a more than 4-to-1 ratio. Some analysts do not regard the change as particularly significant, arguing that higher corporate taxes would be passed along to the public anyway in the form of higher prices for goods and services.

The most significant contribution that government makes to business is the traditional services it provides, such as education, transportation, and defense. Colleges and universities, which are funded primarily by governments, furnish business with most of its professional and technical work force and with much of the basic research that goes into product development. The nation's roadways, waterways, and airports are other public sector contributions without which business could not operate. In short, America's business has no bigger booster than government.

PROMOTING LABOR

Laissez-faire thinking dominated government's approach to labor well into the twentieth century. The governing principle, developed by the courts in the early nineteenth century, held that workers had limited rights of collective action. Union activity was regarded as interference with the natural supply of labor and the free setting of wages. The extent of hostility toward labor is evident in the use of federal troops during the late 1800s to break up strikes.

The 1930s brought significant changes. The key legislation was the National Labor Relations Act of 1935, which guaranteed workers the right to bargain collectively and prohibited business from discriminating against union employees and from unreasonably interfering with union activities. The Taft-Hartley Act of 1947 took away some of labor's gains, including compulsory union membership for workers whose workplace is unionized. Under the provisions of Taft-Hartley, each state can decide for itself whether all workers in work units that are unionized must become union members (union shop) or whether a worker can choose not to join the union (open shop). Despite these modifications, the National Labor Relations Act has remained a cornerstone of labor's power. The legislation not only required that business bargain with organized labor but also estab-

Striking janitors parade in Beverly Hills, California. Although government provides support for labor through a variety of policies, U.S. workers have less power and fewer rights than their European counterparts, a reflection of America's individualistic culture.

lished the National Labor Relations Board (NLRB), an independent regulatory commission that is empowered to enforce compliance with labor law by both business and labor. Government has also aided labor over the years by legislating minimum wages and maximum work hours, unemployment benefits, safer and more healthful working conditions, and nondiscriminatory hiring practices.

Although government support for labor extends beyond these examples, it is not nearly as extensive as its assistance to business. America's individualistic culture has hindered the formulation of public policies that are as favorable to labor as those in European countries.

PROMOTING AGRICULTURE

Until well into the twentieth century, most Americans still lived on farms and in small rural communities. Agriculture was America's dominant business and was assisted by government's land policies. The Homestead Act of 1862, for example, opened government-owned lands to settlement, creating spectacular "land rushes" by offering 160 free acres of government land to each family that staked a claim, built a house, and farmed the land for five years.

Farm programs today provide assistance to small farmers and large commercial enterprises (agribusinesses) and cost the federal government billions of dollars annually. One goal of this spending is to stabilize farmers' income, which can fluctuate greatly from one year to the next, depending on market and growing conditions. Flooding in 1998 from the El Niño weather pattern, for example, caused extensive crop damage in California. The federal government responded with millions of dollars in emergency assistance to afflicted farmers. Income stabilization policy, however, is not limited to emergency aid. There are a variety of federal programs in place that aim to stabilize farmers' income. Price support programs, for example, are designed to keep the prices of farm products relatively high even when the market is weak.

In 1996, Congress passed the Freedom to Farm Act. It trimmed the crop allocation and price subsidy programs that had previously characterized U.S. farm policy. The 1996 legislation was designed to let the market largely determine the prices that farmers would receive for their crops and to let farmers themselves decide on the crops they would plant. However, the program has a safety net—a floor price was set for commodities in case the market slumped (for example, the government guarantee for corn was set at roughly $1.90 a bushel). As it happened, crop prices fell sharply in 1998 and the prospect that they will soon rise is dim. Subsidy payments to American farmers totaled $18 billion in fiscal year 1999. Payments were even higher in fiscal year 2000—a severe drought led Congress to provide an additional $6 billion in emergency relief for stricken farmers. Most analysts believe that it will be many years before substantial federal assistance to farmers is a thing of the past.

Fiscal Policy: Government as Manager of Economy, I

Until the 1930s, the U.S. government adhered to the prevailing free market theory and made no attempt to maintain the stability of the economy as a whole. The economy was regarded as largely self-regulating. The economy was fairly prosperous, but it periodically experienced economic depression that resulted in widespread joblessness and financial loss.

The greatest economic catastrophe in the nation's history—the Great Depression of the 1930s—finally brought an end to traditional economics. Franklin D. Roosevelt's emergency spending and job programs, designed to stimulate the economy and put Americans back to work, heralded the change. Roosevelt's efforts to stimulate the economy were controversial at the time, but today government is expected to have ongoing policies that will maintain high economic production, employment, and growth and that will control prices and interest rates.

TAXING AND SPENDING POLICY

The government's efforts to maintain a stable economy are made mainly through its taxing and spending decisions, which together are referred to as its **fiscal policy** (see Table 18-2).

fiscal policy A tool of economic management by which government attempts to maintain a stable economy through its taxing and spending decisions.

The annual federal budget is the foundation of fiscal policy. George Washington wrote his budget on a single sheet of paper, but the federal budget today is thousands of pages long and takes eighteen months to prepare and enact. The budget is a massive policy statement that allocates federal expenditures among thousands of government programs and provides for the revenues—taxes, social insurance receipts, and borrowed funds—to pay for these expenditures (see Figure 18-3). From one perspective, the budget is the national government's allocation of costs and benefits. Every federal program benefits some interest, whether it be farmers who get price supports, defense firms that obtain military contracts, or retirees who receive monthly social security checks. Not surprisingly, the process of enacting the annual federal budget is a highly political one. Agencies and groups have an obvious stake in promoting their interests.

From another standpoint, that of fiscal policy, the budget is a device for stimulating or dampening economic growth. Changes in overall levels of spending and taxing are means of keeping the economy's normal ups and downs from becoming extreme.

Fiscal policy has its origins in the economic theories of John Maynard Keynes. In *The General Theory of Employment, Interest, and Money* (1936), Keynes noted that employers become overly cautious during a depression and will not expand production, even as wages drop. Challenging the traditional idea that government should draw back during depressions, Keynes claimed that severe economic downturns can be shortened only by increased government spending. Keynes said that government should engage in **deficit spending**—spending more than

deficit spending When the government spends more than it collects in taxes and other revenues.

TABLE 18-2   Fiscal Policy: A Summary   Taxing and spending levels can be adjusted in order to affect economic conditions.

Problem	Fiscal Policy Actions
Low productivity and high unemployment	Demand side: increase spending
	Supply side: cut business taxes
Excess production and high inflation	Decrease spending
	Increase taxes

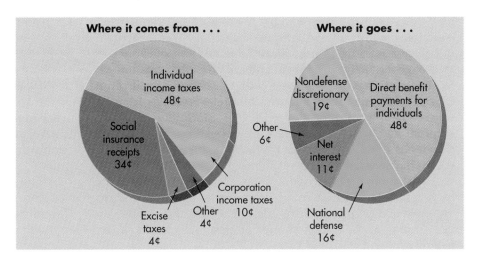

FIGURE 18-3   The Federal Budget Dollar, Fiscal Year 2001
Source: Office of Management and Budget.

it gets from taxes, which can be accomplished through the borrowing and printing of money. By placing additional money in the hands of consumers and investors, government can stimulate production, employment, and spending and thus promote recovery.[17]

According to Keynesian theory, the government's response should be commensurate with the severity of the problem. During an **economic depression**—an exceptionally steep and sustained downturn in the economy—the government should engage in massive new spending programs to hasten the recovery. During a less severe **economic recession,** new government spending should be less substantial.

Demand-Side Stimulation

Keynes's theory focused on government's efforts to stimulate consumer spending. This **demand-side economics** emphasizes the consumer "demand" component of the supply-demand equation. When the economy is sluggish, the government can increase its spending, thus placing more money in consumers' hands. With additional money to spend, consumers buy more goods and services. This increased demand, in turn, fosters production and employment. In this way, government spending contributes to economic recovery.

Although heightened spending is a tool that government can employ during a severe economic crisis, it is not a sensible response to every economic dip. Its application is affected by government's overall financial situation. In the early 1990s, for example, the U.S. economy was in its longest downturn since World War II, but policymakers chose not to boost federal spending temporarily as a means of blunting the recession. The reason was simple enough. During the previous two decades, there had been a **budget deficit**—each year, the federal government had spent more than it had received in tax and other revenues. The result was a huge **national debt,** which is the total cumulative amount that the U.S. government owes to creditors. By the early 1990s, the debt had reached $4 trillion, and an enormous amount of money was required each year merely to pay the interest on the national debt. Interest payments were larger than the entire federal budget as

economic depression   A very severe and sustained economic downturn. Depressions are rare in the United States: the last one was in the 1930s.

economic recession   A moderate but sustained downturn in the economy. Recessions are part of the economy's "normal" cycle of ups and downs.

demand-side economics   A form of fiscal policy that emphasizes "demand" (consumer spending). Government can use increased spending or tax cuts to place more money in consumers' hands and thereby increase demand.

budget deficit   When the government's expenditures for the year exceed its tax and other revenues.

national debt   The total cumulative amount that the U.S. government owes to creditors.

The economist John Maynard Keynes developed a theory of government spending and taxation that became the basis for government efforts to manage the economy through fiscal policy.

balanced budget When the government's tax and other revenues for the year are equal to or exceed its expenditures.

budget surplus When the government's tax and other revenues for the year exceed its expenditures.

recently as 1970 and were roughly the total of all federal income taxes paid by Americans who lived west of the Mississippi River. This drain on the government's resources made it politically difficult for policy makers to increase the level of government spending in order to boost the economy.

The situation is much different today. In 1998, for the first time since 1969, the U.S. government had a **balanced budget**—revenues from taxes for the year were equal to government expenditures. Since then, there has been a **budget surplus**—the federal government has received more in tax and other revenues than it has spent. The surplus was attributable to a surging U.S. economy that was in the midst of its longest period of sustained growth in the country's history. With more people working and with the stock market moving ever higher, tax revenues had increased and government welfare expenditures had declined. The rosy budget picture also reflected the fiscal discipline of the Clinton administration and the Republican Congress, which had slowed the growth in federal expenditures.

The economic turnaround has greatly changed the fiscal outlook (see Figure 18-4). The federal budget surplus exceeded $100 billion in 2000 and is projected to continue to grow for another decade. The bonanza has led policymakers to seek new spending programs and tax cuts, but it will also make it easier, when the economy recedes, as it inevitably will, for government to apply demand-side measures to hasten the economic recovery. An increase in federal spending is once again a tool that policy makers could employ during a recessionary period.

FIGURE 18-4 The Federal Budget Deficit/Surplus, 1975–2009
The Federal government ran a budget deficit until recently; it now has a budget surplus that is projected to last for many years. *Source: Office of Management and Budget.*

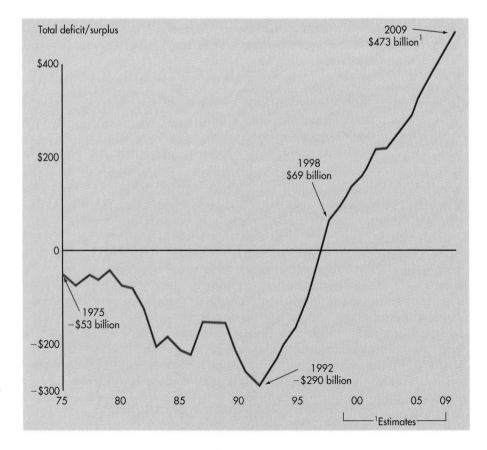

CURRENT CONTROVERSIES

SHOULD CONGRESS EXEMPT THE INTERNET FROM SALES TAXES?

The Internet Tax Freedom Act was passed in 1998 by Congress and placed a three-year moratorium on state and local taxes on e-commerce. It also barred the federal government from levying taxes on Internet commerce, declaring that the Internet should be a tariff-free zone. When Congress reconsidered the issue in 2000, there was a substantial division of opinion both within the institution and outside. Advocates of the exemption claimed that a sales tax would inhibit the growth of the Internet and of e-commerce. Opponents claimed that a tax-free Internet was unfair to the mail-order and walk-in retailers whose goods and services were subject to taxation. Critics also said that state and local government services would be adversely affected by the loss of sales tax revenues.

YES: The benefits which we, as a nation, have obtained as a result . . . of being the incubator, the developer, and now the provider in expertise in the area of the Internet, and the use of the Internet for commerce . . . are basically incalculable; the amount of new jobs which have been created; the number of people whose standard of living has been increased; the number of people who have been able to purchase goods at less of a price. . . . These benefits dramatically exceed any benefit which we would obtain by allowing a large number of different states or municipalities to start taxing the Internet for the purposes of expanding their local governments.

—Senator Judd Gregg (R-N.H.)

NO: Requiring online merchants to collect an existing sales tax does not create a new tax. Brick-and-mortar retailers are required—by law—to collect sales tax on all consumer goods purchased in their stores. [We favor] equal application of the sales tax on all commercial transactions. . . . Commerce on the Internet is growing at a phenomenal rate, increasing the potential for loss of major tax revenues. . . . According to the U.S. Census Bureau, more than 47.9 percent of state revenues come from sales tax. These revenues fund essential community needs such as schools, police, and transportation services. If sales tax is not collected on e-commerce transactions, state and local governments stand to lose more than $10 billion per year by the year 2003.

—E-Fairness

The importance of demand-side fiscal policy, however, cannot be measured only by its effect during economic downturns. Although the United States has had recessionary periods since the 1930s, none of these downturns has been anywhere near the severity of the Great Depression. One reason is that government spending is now at permanently high levels. Each month, for example, roughly forty million Americans receive a social security check from the government. In turn, they spend it on food, clothing, housing, entertainment, and other goods and services. They pump billions of dollars each month into the U.S. economy, which creates jobs and income for millions of other Americans. And social security is only one—albeit the largest—of the federal spending programs. Every day, the federal government spends about $4 billion, which is more than the typical large corporation pumps into the economy during an entire year. The U.S. economy thus has a constant demand-side stimulus: government spending on an ongoing and massive scale.

Supply-Side Stimulation

A fiscal policy alternative to demand-side stimulation is **supply-side economics,** which emphasizes the business (supply) component of the supply-demand

supply-side economics A form of fiscal policy that emphasizes "supply" (production). An example of supply-side economics would be a tax cut for business.

equation.[18] Supply-side theory was a cornerstone of President Reagan's economic program. He believed that economic growth would flow as easily from stimulation of the business sector as from stimulation of consumer demand. "Reaganomics" included substantial tax breaks for businesses and upper-income individuals.

Reagan contended that increased prosperity for wealthy Americans would "trickle down" to those at the bottom as production increased and more jobs were created. However, the benefits of the economic growth of the 1980s were confined largely to higher-income Americans. The real income of the poorest 20 percent of families dropped by more than 10 percent during the decade, while the real income of the richest 20 percent rose by roughly 30 percent. Meanwhile, taxes for the poorest 20 percent increased by 3 percent, while taxes for the highest 20 percent decreased by 5 percent.[19] The result was a widening of the "income gap" between America's poorer and richer families.

The Reagan administration also overestimated the stimulus effect of its tax-cuts policy. It had estimated that the increased tax revenues from increased business activity would soon offset the loss of revenue from reducing the tax rate. However, the loss from the tax cuts was much greater than the increased revenues from the economic growth that followed. A result was that the tax cuts contributed to the rising federal budget deficit.

Despite these discouraging aspects, Reagan's supply-side measures contributed to the economic growth in the mid-1980s and again in the 1990s. The Reagan tax cuts allowed business firms to spend more on capital investments and enabled higher-income Americans to place more money into the stock markets, which provided additional funds for business investment.

Supply-side economics was also evident in some economic policies of the 1990s. After the Republicans assumed control of Congress in 1995, for example, they reduced the **capital-gains tax,** which is the tax that individuals pay on gains in capital investments, such as property and stocks. A reduction in the capital-gains tax increases the incentive for individuals to invest their money in capital markets. Firms use this money to expand their operations and markets, thereby creating jobs and increasing the supply of goods, each of which can stimulate consumer demand, which contributes to economic growth.

capital-gains tax Tax that individuals pay on money gained from the sale of a capital asset, such as property or stocks.

Controlling Inflation

inflation A general increase in the average level of prices of goods and services.

High unemployment and low production are only two of the economic problems that government is called on to solve. Another is **inflation,** which is an increase in the average level of prices of goods and services. Before the late 1960s, inflation was a minor irritant: prices rose by less than 4 percent annually. But inflation rose sharply during the last years of the Vietnam War and remained high throughout the 1970s, reaching a postwar record rate of 13 percent in 1979. Since then, inflation has moderated considerably (see Figure 18-5) and concern about it has lessened.

To fight inflation, government can apply remedies opposite to those used to fight unemployment and low productivity. Inflation normally occurs when jobs are plentiful and people have extra money to spend. Demand is high in such periods, and prices are pulled up in what is known as "demand-pull" inflation. By reducing its spending or by raising personal income taxes, government takes

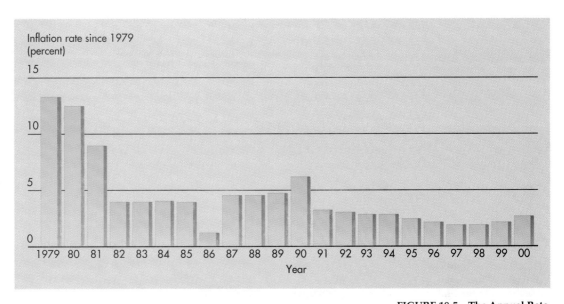

Inflation rate since 1979
(percent)

FIGURE 18-5 The Annual Rate of Inflation, 1979–2000
Price increases have declined in the last decade in comparison with the late 1970s. *Source: U.S. Department of Labor.*

money from consumers, thus reducing demand and dampening prices. (The main policy tool for addressing inflation is monetary policy, which is discussed later in the chapter.)

THE PROCESS AND POLITICS OF FISCAL POLICY

The president and Congress jointly determine fiscal policy, mainly through the annual budgetary process. The Constitution grants Congress the power to tax and spend, but the president, as chief executive, has a major role in shaping the budget. The president's veto power also provides him a strong tool when negotiating the budget with Congress. In reality, the budgetary process involves give-and-take between Congress and the president, as each tries to exert influence over the final budget.[20]

The Budgetary Process

The budgetary process is a very elaborate one, as could be expected when billions of dollars in federal spending are at issue. From beginning to end, the process lasts a year and a half (see Figure 18-6).

The budgetary process begins in the executive branch when the president, in consultation with the Office of Management and Budget (OMB), establishes general budget guidelines. The OMB is part of the Executive Office of the President (see Chapter 14) and takes its directives from the president. Hundreds of agencies and thousands of programs are covered by the budget, and the OMB uses the president's decisions to determine the instructions that will govern each agency's budget preparations. For example, each agency is assigned a budget ceiling within which it must work.

The agencies receive these instructions in the spring and then work through the summer to develop a detailed agency budget, taking into account their

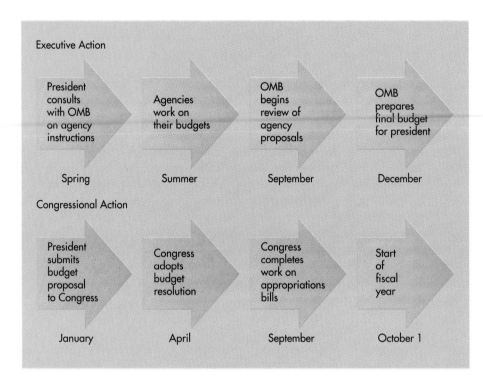

FIGURE 18-6 Federal Budgetary Process The budget begins with the president's instructions to the agencies and ends when Congress enacts the budget. The entire process spans about eighteen months.

existing programs and any new or proposed ones. These agency budgets then go to the OMB in September for a full review that invariably includes further consultation with each agency. The agency budgets are then finalized and combined into the full budget. Throughout, the OMB is in close touch with the White House to ensure that the budget items conform to the president's objectives.

The OMB usually acts to restrain the agencies since they naturally tend to want more resources while the OMB has the job of tailoring the budget to the president's priorities. In point of fact, however, the president does not have any real say over most of the budget. About two-thirds of the budget involves mandatory spending. The spending is authorized by current law, and the government must allocate and spend the money unless the law itself is rescinded, which is unlikely. Examples are social security and Medicare, which provide mandatory benefits to all individuals who apply and meet the eligibility criteria. The president does not have the authority to suspend or redefine these programs. Interest on the national debt is also part of the budget and here, too, the president has no real option. The federal government is obligated to pay interest on the money it has borrowed.

The OMB focuses on the third of the budget that involves discretionary spending, which includes such areas as defense, foreign aid, education, national parks, space exploration, public broadcasting, and highways. In reality, even a large part of this spending is not truly discretionary. No president would even consider slashing defense spending to almost nothing or closing the national parks, and even modest cuts in a discretionary program may encounter resistance in Congress.

The president, then, works on the margins of the budget, trying to push it in directions that are consistent with administration goals. The effort in many policy areas consists of a modest increase or decrease in spending compared with the previous year. There are also always a few areas where the president will attempt a more dramatic adjustment. During each year of his second term, for example, President Clinton asked for significant increases in education and health spending.

In January, the president transmits the full budget to Congress. This budget is only a proposal because Congress has the constitutional power to appropriate funds. In reviewing the president's proposed budget, Congress relies heavily on the Congressional Budget Office (CBO), which, as was discussed in Chapter 12, is the congressional equivalent to OMB. The CBO carefully studies the items in the budget and also subjects the budget's revenue estimates and projected program costs to its own analysis. If the CBO believes that an agency has misjudged the amount of money that is needed to meet its legislatively required programs, it will bring this information to the attention of the appropriate members of Congress. Similarly, if the CBO concludes that the OMB has miscalculated how much the government can be expected to receive in taxes and other revenues, this information will be noted.

The key congressional committees in the budgetary process are the budget and the appropriations committees. The House and Senate Budget Committees are responsible for drafting a "budget resolution," which includes projections on total spending, total revenues, and allocations between the mandatory and discretionary spending categories. These guidelines are then submitted to the full House and Senate for approval. The budget ceilings that are part of the resolution place a tentative limit on how much money will be allocated for each spending area.

The House Appropriations Committee through its subcommittees then takes on the primary task of reviewing the budget items, which includes hearings with each federal agency. There are thirteen such subcommittees, and each has responsibility for a substantive area, such as defense or agriculture. Agency budgets are invariably changed at this stage. A subcommittee may cut an agency's budget because it believes that the agency's work is not very important or that the agency has asked for more funds than it needs to carry out its programs. Or the subcommittee may decide to increase an agency's budget beyond what the president has requested. Whichever, each subcommittee leaves its own mark on each agency's budget. The subcommittees' recommendations are then submitted to the House Appropriations Committee for final review and submission to the full House for a vote. The Senate Appropriations Committee and its subcommittees conduct a similar process, but the Senate is a smaller body and its review of agency requests is normally less thorough. To some degree, the Senate committee and its subcommittees serve as "a court of appeals" for agencies that have had their budget requests reduced by the process in the House.

During Congress' work on the budget, the president's recommendations undergo varying degrees of change. The priorities of a majority in Congress are never exactly those of the president, even when they are of the same party. When they are of opposite parties, their priorities may differ greatly.

Budget Committee chairman Pete Domenici (R-N.M.) points to a chart during a Senate hearing. The Senate and House budget committees have responsibility for proposing how spending should be allocated across major policy areas.

www.mhhe.com/patterson5

Graphic

After the work of the appropriations committees is completed and has been approved by the full House and Senate, differences in the Senate and House versions of the appropriations bills are reconciled in conference committee (see Chapter 13). The legislation is then sent to the president for approval or veto. The threat of a presidential veto is often enough to persuade Congress to restore some of its cuts in the president's original proposals. In the end, the budget inevitably reflects both presidential and congressional priorities. Neither branch ever gets everything that it wants, but each branch always gets some of what it wants.

Once the budget has been passed by both the House and Senate and is signed by the president, it takes effect on October 1, which is the starting date of the federal government's fiscal year. If agreement on the budget has not been reached by October 1, temporary funding is required in order to maintain government operations. In late 1995, President Clinton and the Republican Congress deadlocked to such an extent on budgetary issues that they could not even agree on temporary funding. Their standoff twice forced a brief shutdown of nonessential government activities.

PARTISAN DIFFERENCES

Politics plays a significant part in the making of fiscal policy because Democrats and Republicans often disagree over its direction. The Democratic coalition has traditionally included the majority of lower-income and working-class Americans. Accordingly, the party's leaders are sensitive to rising unemployment because blue-collar workers are usually the first and most deeply affected. Democrats in Washington have usually responded to a sluggish economy with increased government spending, which offers direct help to the unemployed and stimulates demand. Virtually every increase in federal unemployment benefits during the past fifty years, for example, has been initiated by Democratic officeholders.

Republican leaders are more likely than Democrats to be concerned about inflation. It attacks the purchasing power of all Americans, including higher-income individuals who are less likely than lower-income persons to be affected by rising unemployment rates. Inflation also raises the cost of doing business, because firms must pay higher interest rates for the money they borrow. Since business and the middle class make up a significant chunk of its electoral base, the Republican party usually wants to hold government spending at a level where the inflationary effects are small. Thus, in response to the unusual combination of high inflation and high unemployment in the mid-1970s, Republican president Gerald Ford placed more emphasis on fighting inflation, whereas his Democratic successor, Jimmy Carter, concentrated initially on reducing unemployment. Each president would have preferred to hold down both unemployment and inflation if he could, but each attacked the problem that was of greater concern to his party's constituents.

Tax policy also has partisan dimensions. Democratic policymakers have typically sought tax policies that are more beneficial to working-class and lower-middle-class Americans. Democrats have favored a **graduated** (or progressive) **personal income tax,** in which the tax rate goes up substantially as income rises. Republicans have preferred to keep taxes on upper incomes at a relatively low level, contending that this policy encourages the savings and investment that foster economic growth. These differences were evident, for example, in the battle over the Taxpayer Refund and Relief Act of 1999, which President Clinton vetoed. The GOP-sponsored bill contained the largest tax cut since 1981; the chief beneficiaries would have been upper-income taxpayers. In the House of Representatives, 98 percent of Republicans and only 3 percent of Democrats supported the bill. In the Senate, 95 percent of Republicans and 11 percent of Democrats backed it.[21]

The difference between Republican and Democratic lawmakers can also be illustrated by their preference for demand-side or supply-side fiscal policies. The Democrats lean toward demand-side remedies, since government spending programs tend to be somewhat redistributive: they provide disproportionally more benefits to people in lower-income categories. Republicans have preferred supply-side remedies, which provide tax cuts for business and higher-income groups as a means of stimulating the economy.

graduated personal income tax
A tax on personal income in which the tax rate increases as income increases; in other words, the tax is higher for higher income levels.

Monetary Policy: Government as Manager of Economy, II

Fiscal policy is not the only instrument of economic management available to government; another is **monetary policy,** which is based on manipulation of the amount of money in circulation (see Table 18-3). Monetarists such as the economist Milton Friedman hold that control of the money supply is the key to sustaining a healthy economy. Too much money in circulation contributes to inflation because too many dollars are chasing too few goods, which drives up prices. Too little money in circulation results in a slackening economy and rising unemployment, because consumers lack the ready cash and easy credit required to push spending levels up. Monetarists believe in tightening or loosening the money supply as a way of slowing or invigorating the economy.

monetary policy A tool of economic management, available to government, based on manipulation of the amount of money in circulation.

★ STATES IN THE NATION

FEDERAL TAXING AND SPENDING

Federal spending and taxation are the basis of fiscal policy, which has an uneven effect on the states. Some states get a positive "balance of payments" in that their citizens pay less in taxes on average than they receive in federal spending. The biggest winner is New Mexico, which in 1998 had a positive balance of payments of $3,697 per person. Seventeen other states had a positive balance of $1,000 or more. In contrast, some states have a negative balance of payments; their citizens pay more in federal taxes than they get back through federal spending. Connecticut ($2,380) led this list in 1998. Eleven other states had a negative balance of $500 or more per capita. Most of the "winners" are in the South; most of the "losers" are in the Midwest and Northeast.

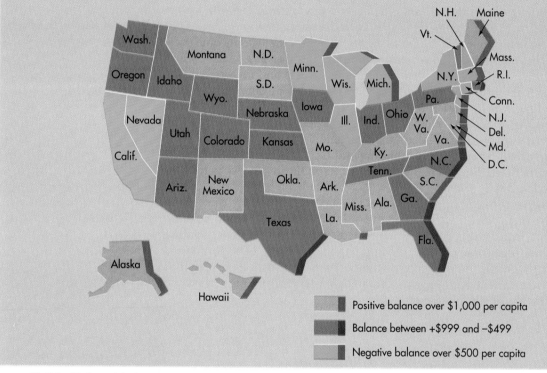

Positive balance over $1,000 per capita

Balance between +$999 and −$499

Negative balance over $500 per capita

SOURCE: *The Federal Budget and the States: Fiscal Year 1998*. Report of the Taubman Center for State and Local Government, John F. Kennedy School of Government, Harvard University, December 9, 1999, p. 20.

THE FED

Control over the money supply rests not with the president or Congress but with the Federal Reserve System (known as the "Fed"), which was created by the Federal Reserve Act of 1913. The Fed is directed by a board of governors whose seven members serve for fourteen years, except for the chair and vice-chair, who serve for four years. All members are appointed by the president with the approval of the Senate. The Fed regulates the activities of all national banks and those state banks that choose to become members of the Federal Reserve System—about six thousand banks in all.

TABLE 18-3   Monetary Policy: A Summary   The money supply can be adjusted in order to affect economic conditions.

Problem	Monetary Policy Action by Federal Reserve
Low productivity and high unemployment (require an increase in the money supply)	Buys securities
	Lowers interest rate on loans to member banks
	Lowers cash reserve that member banks must deposit in Federal Reserve System
Excess productivity and high inflation (require a decrease in the money supply)	Sells securities
	Raises interest rate on loans to member banks
	Raises cash reserve that member banks must deposit in Federal Reserve System

The Fed decides how much money to add or to subtract from the economy, seeking a balance that will permit steady growth without causing an unacceptable level of inflation. The most visible way that the Fed affects the money supply is by lowering or raising the interest rates charged on money borrowed from the Federal Reserve by its member banks. When the Fed raises the interest rate, banks also tend to raise the rate they charge for new loans, which discourages borrowing and thus reduces the amount of money entering the economy. Conversely, by lowering the interest rate, the Fed encourages firms and individuals to borrow from banks, which increases the money supply.

The Fed's interest-rate decisions are closely watched by the financial markets, political leaders, and the media. Any increase or decrease is a sign that the Fed has concluded that the economy is growing too quickly or too slowly.

The Fed also affects the money supply by selling and buying government securities in the open market. By offering securities at an attractive price, the Fed encourages investors to exchange their cash for securities, thus taking money out of the economy. On the other hand, when the Fed buys securities that people hold, it puts cash into their hands, thus expanding the money supply.

The third and final way the Fed affects the money supply is by raising or lowering the cash reserve that member banks are required to deposit with the Federal Reserve. This reserve is a proportion of each member's total deposits. By increasing the reserve rate, the Fed takes money from member banks and thus takes it out of circulation. When the Fed lowers the reserve rate, banks have more money available and can make more loans to consumers and investors.

Economists debate the relative effectiveness of monetary policy and fiscal policy, but monetary policy has one obvious advantage: it can be implemented more quickly. The Fed can adjust interest and reserve rates on short notice, thus providing the economy a psychological boost to go along with the financial effect of a change in the money supply. In contrast, changes in fiscal policy usually take much longer to implement; Congress is normally a slow-acting institution, and new taxing and spending programs ordinarily require a substantial preparation period before they can be put into effect.

The University of Chicago economist Milton Friedman became the leading proponent of monetary policy as a tool for managing the economy. Friedman was named "Economist of the Century" by *Time* magazine.

How Powerful Should the Fed Be?

To some observers, the Fed is the preferred vehicle for economic management. They say the Fed can help manage growth and inflation by manipulating interest rates. They claim that Congress and the president base decisions on political factors rather than the sound economic analysis employed by the Fed.

Other analysts contend that the Fed has gotten carried away with its power. They argue that economic theories are not as precise as the Fed assumes. The Fed's assumption that an unemployment rate below 6 percent is inflationary, for example, was regarded by some economists as mere guesswork, a judgment confirmed when the rate fell to 4 percent in the 1998–2000 period without triggering inflationary pressures. The argument against the Fed's role also stems from a belief that it is too beholden to the bankers and thus too willing to trade employment goals for inflationary objectives. Finally, there is the argument that macroeconomic decisions properly belong in the hands of the people's representatives, since these decisions affect everyone.

What is your position in this debate? Is the Fed too powerful?

THE POLITICS OF THE FED

The greater flexibility of monetary policy has positioned the Fed as the institution with primary policy responsibility for keeping the U.S. economy on a steady course. The Fed's power can easily be exaggerated. The U.S. economy is subject to a lot of influences, and the Fed's impact is relatively modest. Nevertheless, the Fed is a vital component of U.S. economic policy and has become increasingly so. Alan Greenspan, chair of the Federal Reserve System, has been described by the *Washington Post* as "The Man Who Really Runs America."[22] The recommendations of Greenspan carry the most weight in the board's decisions, and his public statements affect the financial markets. In 2000, Greenspan said that the stock market was overvalued and that the economy would be better off if it were lower. The Dow-Jones average plummeted several hundred points as Greenspan's statement spread through Wall Street.

The power of the Fed raises important questions. One is the issue of representation: Whose interests does the Fed serve—those of the public as a whole or those of the banking sector? The Fed is not a wholly impartial body. Although it makes decisions in the context of economic theories and projections, it is "the bankers' bank" and is protective of monied interests. The Fed is typically more concerned with rising inflation, which erodes the value of money, than with rising unemployment, which has its greatest impact on people at the bottom of the economic ladder. The Fed tends to hike interest rates when signs of rising inflation appear. Higher rates have the effect of slowing inflation but also slow job and income growth.

The Fed's defense of this practice is that inflation hurts everybody, a claim that is indisputable when inflation gets out of control, as it did in the late 1970s. The double-digit inflation during this period hurt nearly every aspect of the U.S. economy, and the recovery period was long and slow. Economists disagree, however, over the point at which inflation is overly high and thereby harmful to the economy as a whole. If inflation is too low, economic growth is curtailed, incomes stagnate, and unemployment rises, which can trigger an economic recession.

Elected officials have sometimes complained that the Fed is too protective of financial interests. In 1994, for example, the Fed embarked on a series of interest-rate hikes to contain growth. In defending the action, Greenspan argued that it was designed to head off an upward spiral of wages and prices. Yet the Fed acted before signs of inflation were clearly present in the economy, bringing criticism from congressional Democrats and Clinton administration officials, who claimed that the Fed was blunting the nation's economic recovery. Unemployment exceeded the 6 percent level, and the Fed's critics said that unseen inflationary pressures should not drive economic policy when millions of Americans were still looking for work. House Democratic leader Richard Gephardt complained that the Fed was placing the interests of bankers and financiers ahead of those of ordinary Americans.

A related issue is one of accountability: should the Fed, an unelected body, have so much power? Although appointed by the president, members of the Federal Reserve Board are not subject to removal. They serve for fixed terms and are relatively insulated from political pressures, including the changes that take place through elections. Moreover, the Fed announces its decisions after closed-door meetings, although it has implemented a policy of signaling beforehand the

Fed chairman Alan Greenspan testifies before a congressional committee. Greenspan has sometimes been called "the most powerful man in America."

policies it is likely to announce. Of course, the Fed, as a banking institution, has a vested interest in a healthy economy (too much inflation erodes banks' returns on loans, too much unemployment decreases demand for loans) and thus operates within its own system of checks and balances. Nevertheless, the restraints on the Fed are much weaker than are those on popularly elected institutions.

At the time the Fed was created in 1913, economists had not yet "invented" the theory of monetary policy, and the Fed had no role in the management of the nation's economy. If the Fed were being created today, it would likely have a different structure, although there is general agreement among policymakers that some degree of independence is desirable.

The Fed is a preeminent example of *elitist* politics at work. Congress at some future point may decide that an overly independent Fed can no longer be tolerated and may bring monetary policy more closely under the control of elected institutions. Whether this move happens may hinge on the Fed's willingness to exercise power sparingly and in the broad interests of society. (The economic policies of the federal government in the areas of social welfare and national security are discussed in the next two chapters.)

www.mhhe.com/patterson5

Self-Quiz

Summary

Although private enterprise is the main force in the American economic system, the federal government plays a significant role through its policies to regulate, promote, and stimulate the economy.

Regulatory policy is designed to achieve efficiency and equity, which require government to intervene, for example, to maintain competitive trade practices (an efficiency goal) and to protect vulnerable parties in economic transactions (an equity goal). Many of the regulatory decisions of the federal government, particularly those of older agencies, are made largely in the context of group politics. Business lobbies have an especially strong influence on

the regulatory policies that affect them. In general, newer regulatory agencies have policy responsibilities that are broader in scope and apply to a larger number of firms than those of the older agencies. As a result, the policy decisions of newer agencies are more often made in the context of party politics. Republican administrations are less vigorous in their regulation of business than are Democratic administrations.

Business is the major beneficiary of the federal government's efforts to promote economic interests. A large number of programs, including those to provide loans and research grants, are designed to assist businesses, which are also protected from failure through such measures as tariffs and favorable tax laws. Labor, for its part, gets government assistance through laws concerning such matters as worker safety, the minimum wage, and collective bargaining. Yet America's individualistic culture tends to put labor at a disadvantage, keeping it less powerful than business in its dealings with the government. Agriculture is another economic sector that depends substantially on government's help, particularly in the form of income stabilization programs, such as those that provide subsidies and price supports.

The U.S. government pursues policies that are designed to protect and conserve the environment. A few decades ago, the environment was not a policy priority. Today, there are many programs in this area, and the public has become an active participant in efforts to conserve resources and prevent exploitation of the environment.

Through its fiscal and monetary policies, Washington attempts to maintain a strong and stable economy—one that is characterized by high productivity, high employment, and low inflation. Fiscal policy is based on government decisions in regard to spending and taxing, which are aimed at either stimulating a weak economy or dampening an overheated (inflationary) economy. Fiscal policy is worked out through Congress and the president and is consequently responsive to political pressures. However, since it is difficult to raise taxes or cut programs, the government's ability to apply fiscal policy as an economic remedy is limited. Monetary policy is based on the money supply and works through the Federal Reserve System, which is headed by a board whose members hold office for fixed terms. The Fed is a relatively independent body, a fact that has given rise to questions as to whether it should have such a large role in national economic policy.

Key Terms

balanced budget
budget deficit
budget surplus
capital-gains tax
deficit spending
demand-side economics
deregulation
economic depression
economic recession
economy
efficiency

equity (in relation to economic policy)
externalities
fiscal policy
graduated personal income tax
inflation
laissez-faire doctrine
monetary policy
national debt
regulation
supply-side economics

Suggested Readings

Brown, Lester R., and Ed Ayres, eds. *The World Watch Reader on Global Environmental Issues.* New York: W. W. Norton, 1998. A compilation of environmental policy articles.

Friedman, Milton, and Walter Heller. *Monetary Versus Fiscal Policy.* New York: Norton, 1969. Opposing arguments by a leading monetarist and a leading Keynesian.

Fukuyama, Francis. *Trust: The Social Virtue and the Creation of Prosperity.* New York: Free Press, 1995. A claim that personal trust rather than public policy is the foundation of economic prosperity.

Gould, Kenneth A., Allan Schnaiberg, and Adam S. Weinberg. *Local Environmental Struggles: Citizen Activism in the Treadmill of Production.* New York: Cambridge University Press, 1996. An analysis through case studies of opportunities and constraints on environmental action in the United States.

Harris, Richard A., and Sidney M. Milkis. *The Politics of Regulatory Change: A Tale of Two Agencies,* 2d ed. New York: Oxford University Press, 1996. An analysis of the Reagan, Bush, and Clinton administrations' approaches to regulatory policy.

Kettl, Donald F. *Deficit Politics: Public Budgeting in Its Institutional and Historical Context.* New York: Macmillan, 1992. An analysis of budgetary politics that aims to explain why the United States suffers repeated annual deficits.

Schick, Allen with Felix Lostracco. *The Federal Budget: Politics, Policy, Process,* revised ed. Washington, D.C.: Brookings Institution Press, 2000. A forward look at the federal budget.

Shaiko, Ronald G. *Voices and Echoes for the Environment.* New York: Columbia University Press, 1999. The representation and communication of environmental groups.

Streeter, Thomas. *Selling the Air: A Critique of the Policy of Commercial Broadcasting in the United States.* Chicago: University of Chicago Press, 1996. An analysis of the impact of government regulation on the broadcasting market.

Wildavsky, Aaron. *The New Politics of the Budgetary Process,* 2d ed. New York: HarperCollins, 1992. An overview of the federal budgetary process, including new developments related to the deficit.

Young, H. Peyton. *Equity: In Theory and Practice.* Princeton, N.J.: Princeton University Press, 1995. A systematic assessment of what economic equity entails in theory and actual situations.

CHAPTER 19

Welfare and Education Policy: Providing for Personal Security and Need

★

We the people of the United States, in order to . . .
promote the general welfare . . .

—Preamble, U.S. Constitution

★ ★ ★

*I*t happened with unpredicted suddenness. In just five years, the number of people on the welfare rolls had plummeted by 48 percent nationwide. Caseloads had peaked in 1994 but now were down in every state. What was surprising was the size of the drop. The number of families on welfare had declined by more than 80 percent in Wisconsin, Idaho, and Wyoming, and by more than half in twenty-three other states. There were only three states—Hawaii, Rhode Island, and New Mexico—in which the drop was less than 20 percent (see "States in the Nation"). The trend defied what has been described as the welfare "reverse gravity" law: rolls that go up but do not come down.

Two factors were driving the change. One was the booming national economy. Unemployment had steadily declined, and as more Americans went into the work force, the demand for welfare decreased. The second factor was the 1996 welfare reform act, which had shortened welfare eligibility and required that able-bodied recipients find work or risk loss of all benefits. The question on policymakers' minds concerned the proportion of the decline that was attributable to the change in the welfare system. Representative Clay Shaw Jr. (R-Fla.), who sponsored the reform law, declared that it was the primary reason for the dramatic drop: "It shows the faith we had in [the legislation] was well placed." Senator Daniel Patrick Moynihan (D-N.Y.), who led the opposition to the bill, said; "It doesn't show anything yet." Moynihan claimed the real test would come when the economy turned downward, and he expressed doubt that the chronically unemployed would find jobs in that situation.[1]

These contrasting views typify views of social welfare policy. It's an area in which opposing philosophies of government collide. Many people, like Moynihan, believe the government must provide substantial and sustained assistance to those Americans who are less equipped to compete effectively in the marketplace. Others, like Shaw, believe that welfare payments, except to those who are unmistakably unfit to work, discourage personal effort and create welfare dependency.

Another source of conflict over welfare policy is the country's federal system of government. Welfare was traditionally a responsibility of state and local governments. Only since the 1930s has the federal government also played a significant role. Some welfare programs are jointly run by the federal and state governments. They are funded at different levels from one state to the next but operate within guidelines set down by the national government and are partly funded by Washington. The strictness of federal guidelines and the amount that the federal government should contribute to the programs have long been deeply contentious issues.

This chapter examines the social problems that federal welfare programs are designed to alleviate and describes how these programs operate. It also addresses public education policies. A goal of this chapter is to provide an informed basis for understanding issues of social welfare and education and to show why disagreements in these areas are so substantial. They involve hard choices that almost inevitably require trade-offs between federal and state power and between the values of individual self-reliance and egalitarian compassion. The main points of the chapter are these:

★ *Poverty is a large and persistent problem in America, deeply affecting about one in seven Americans, including many of the country's most vulnerable individuals— children, female-headed families, and minority group members.* Social welfare programs have been a major factor in reducing the extent of poverty in the United States.

★ *Welfare policy has been a partisan issue, with Democrats taking the lead on government programs to alleviate economic insecurity and Republicans acting to slow down or reverse these initiatives.* Major changes in social welfare have usually occurred in the context of majority support for the change.

★ *Social welfare programs are designed to reward and foster self-reliance or, when this is not possible, to provide benefits only to those individuals who are truly in need.* U.S. welfare policy is not based on the assumption that every citizen has a right to material security.

★ *Americans favor social insurance programs (such as social security) over public assistance programs (such as AFDC).* As a result, most social welfare expenditures are not targeted toward the nation's neediest citizens.

★ *A prevailing principle in the United States is equality of opportunity, which in terms of policy is most evident in the area of public education.* America invests heavily in its public schools and colleges.

Poverty in America: The Nature of the Problem

In the broadest sense, social welfare policy encompasses all efforts by government to improve the social conditions of any and all citizens. In a narrower sense, which is the way the term will be used in most of this chapter, social welfare policy refers to those efforts by government to help individuals avoid becoming burdens to society or, when that is not possible, to help individuals who cannot fully help themselves to meet their basic human needs, including food, clothing, and shelter.

THE POOR: WHO AND HOW MANY?

America's social welfare needs are substantial. Although Americans are far better off economically than most of the world's peoples, poverty is a significant and persistent problem in the United States. The government defines the **poverty line** as the annual cost of a thrifty food budget for an urban family of four, multiplied by three to include the cost of housing, clothing, and other

poverty line As defined by the federal government, the annual cost of a thrifty food budget for an urban family of four, multiplied by three to allow also for the cost of housing, clothes, and other expenses. Families below the poverty line are considered poor and are eligible for certain forms of public assistance.

★ STATES IN THE NATION

THE DECLINING NUMBER OF FAMILIES ON WELFARE

The welfare rolls in the United States peaked in March 1994. After that, the number of American families on welfare dropped precipitously, which analysts attributed to both the surge in the U.S. economy and the 1996 welfare reform bill that instituted new work rules. The decline in the welfare rolls was dramatic in all regions of the country. The biggest drop (89 percent) was in Wisconsin. The smallest (7 percent) was in Hawaii.

Decline in Welfare Recipients

- Less than 35%
- 35 – 49%
- 50 – 59%
- 60% or more

SOURCE: Department of Health and Human Services. Period of change is January 1993 to March 1999.

expenses. Families whose incomes fall below that line are officially considered poor. In 2000, the poverty line was set at an annual income of roughly $16,700 for a family of four. One in seven Americans, more than thirty-five million people, including nearly fifteen million children, live near or below the poverty line. If they could join hands, they would form a line that stretched from New York to Tokyo and back again.

Observers disagree on whether the official poverty line is a valid indicator of the true extent of poverty in the United States. Some benefit programs, such as social security for retirees, provide cash payments to recipients. Other programs provide **in-kind benefits,** which are cash equivalents such as food stamps. The purpose of in-kind benefits is to ensure that recipients use the support as

in-kind benefits Government benefits that are cash equivalents, such as food stamps or rent vouchers. This form of benefit ensures that recipients will use public assistance in a specified way.

Millions of Americans live in poverty. Many reside in inner-city areas, such as this street in Philadelphia. Because the suburbs are relatively untouched by the problem, many of their residents have no sense of the scale of poverty in America.

government intends—on groceries rather than on luxuries. In-kind government benefits are not included in the calculation of family income, which has led some observers to say that the official poverty line overestimates the number of poor people. If in-kind benefits were included, the proportion of the population living below the poverty line would drop about two percentage points.[2]

Other analysts say that the income level set by the government, regardless of how it is calculated, is set too low, that a family of four cannot live adequately on $16,700 a year. They would place the poverty line substantially higher. Arguments about the poverty line are not mere verbal battles. The U.S. government's official poverty line is used to determine eligibility for a number of welfare programs, including health care.

America's poor include individuals of all ages, races, religions, and regions, but poverty is substantially more prevalent among some groups. Children are one of the largest groups of poor Americans. They constitute nearly 40 percent of the total, and one in every five children live in poverty. Most poor children live in single-parent families, usually with the mother. In fact, as can be seen from Figure 19-1, a high proportion of Americans residing in families headed by divorced, separated, or unmarried women live below the poverty line. These

FIGURE 19-1 Percentage of Families Living in Poverty, by Family Composition and Race/Ethnicity
Poverty is far more prevalent among female-headed households and among African American and Hispanic households. *Source: U.S. Bureau of the Census, 2000.*

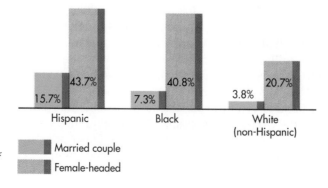

Hispanic: 15.7% (Married couple), 43.7% (Female-headed)
Black: 7.3% (Married couple), 40.8% (Female-headed)
White (non-Hispanic): 3.8% (Married couple), 20.7% (Female-headed)

Married couple
Female-headed

families are at a disadvantage because most women earn less than men for comparable work, especially in nonprofessional fields. Women without higher education or a special skill often cannot find a job that pays enough to justify the child care expenses they incur because of their work. In recent years, single-parent, female-headed families have been three times as likely as single-parent, male-headed families and seven times as likely as two-income families to fall below the poverty line. Poverty in America has increasingly become a women's problem, a situation referred to as "the feminization of poverty."

Poverty is also widespread among minority group members. About 10 percent of whites live below the official poverty line, compared with about 30 percent of African Americans and Hispanics.

Poverty is geographically concentrated. Although it is often portrayed as an urban problem, it is somewhat more prevalent in rural areas. About one in six rural residents—as compared with one in eight urban residents—live in families with incomes below the poverty line. The urban figure is misleading, however, in that the poverty rate is very high in inner-city areas, where minority group members are concentrated.[3] Suburbs are the safe haven from poverty. Because suburbanites are removed from it, many of them have no sense of the impoverished condition of what Michael Harrington called "the other America."[4]

The "invisibility" of poverty in America is evident in polls that show that most Americans substantially underestimate the number of poor in their country. There is certainly nothing in the daily lives of many Americans or what they see on television that would lead them to think that poverty rates are uncommonly high. Yet the United States has the highest level of poverty among the advanced industrialized nations, and its rate of child poverty is more than twice that of the average in comparable countries (see "How the United States Compares").

LIVING IN POVERTY: BY CHOICE OR CHANCE?

Many Americans hold to the idea that poverty is largely a matter of choice—that most low-income Americans are unwilling to make the effort to hold a responsible job and get ahead in life. In his book *Losing Ground*, Charles Murray argued that America has a permanent underclass of unproductive citizens who prefer to live on welfare and whose children receive little educational encouragement at home and grow up to be copies of their parents.[5] There are, indeed, such people in America. They likely number in the millions. They are the toughest challenge for policy makers because almost nothing about their lives equips them to escape from poverty and its attendant ills.

Yet most poor Americans are in their situation as a result of circumstance rather than of choice. A ten-year study of American families by a University of Michigan research team found that most of the poor are poor only for a while and that they are poor for temporary reasons—loss of a job, desertion by the father, and so on.[6] When the U.S. economy goes into a tailspin, the impact devastates many families. In the recessionary period of 1990–1992, more than four million Americans fell into poverty as a result of job loss.

It is also the case that holding a full-time job does not guarantee that a family will rise above the poverty line. A family of four with one employed adult who works forty hours a week at $6 an hour (which is roughly the minimum wage

Most people who are poor in America are victims of a temporary setback, such as job layoffs during an economic recession. Conversely, the number of Americans living below the poverty line shrinks substantially when the economy is prosperous and jobs are plentiful.

HOW THE UNITED STATES COMPARES

CHILDREN LIVING IN POVERTY

The United States has the highest child poverty rate among industrialized nations. One in five American children lives in poverty; in most other industrialized nations, fewer than one in ten do so.

One reason for the difference is that income in the United States is less evenly distributed. As a consequence, the United States has the highest percentage of both rich and poor children in the industrialized world. In addition, the United States spends less on government assistance for the poor. Without government help, for example, the child poverty rate in the United States and France would be about equal—25 percent. Through its governmental programs, France reduces the rate to less than 7 percent. Through its welfare programs, the United States cuts the rate only slightly.

Child poverty in the United States is made worse by the relatively large number of single-parent families, although Sweden, which has a similarly large number, has one of the world's lowest rates of child poverty.

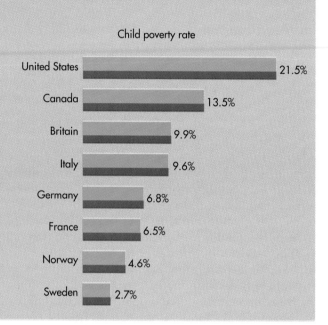

Child poverty rate

United States	21.5%
Canada	13.5%
Britain	9.9%
Italy	9.6%
Germany	6.8%
France	6.5%
Norway	4.6%
Sweden	2.7%

Adapted from Timothy Smeeding, "Doing Poorly: The Real Income of American Children in a Comparative Perspective," Luxembourg Income Study Working Paper No. 127 (Syracuse: Maxwell School of Citizenship and Public Affairs, 1995), reprinted in *The State of America's Children Yearbook* (Children's Defense Fund, 1996). Used by permission.

level) has an annual income of about $12,000, which is well below the poverty line. Millions of Americans—mostly household workers, service workers, unskilled laborers, and farm workers—are in this position. The U.S. Bureau of Labor Statistics estimates that roughly 7 percent of Americans who work full time do not earn enough to lift their family above the poverty line.[7]

The Politics and Policies of Social Welfare

Welfare policy has generally been debated along partisan lines, a reflection of differences in the coalitions and philosophies of the Republican and Democratic parties. With its ties to labor, the poor, and minorities, the Democratic party has initiated nearly all major federal welfare programs. The key House of Representatives vote on the Social Security Act of 1935, for example, found 85 percent of Democrats supporting it and 99 percent of Republicans against it.[8]

Republicans gradually came to accept the idea that the federal government has a role in social welfare but argued that the role should be kept as small as practicable. Thus, during the 1960s, Republican opposition to President Lyndon Johnson's Great Society was substantial. His programs included federal initiatives in health care, education, public housing, nutrition, and other areas traditionally dominated by state and local government.[9] The Great Society programs were enacted largely because they were supported by Johnson's fellow Democrats. More than 70 percent of congressional Republicans voted against the 1965 Medicare and Medicaid programs, which provide government-paid medical assistance for the elderly and the poor. In the 1980s, in the face of opposition from congressional Democrats, Republican President Reagan made social welfare spending the prime target of his effort to cut the domestic budget. Compared with the decade beginning in the late 1960s, when welfare spending per poor person nearly tripled, the 1980s saw a 20 percent decline in actual dollars spent on each welfare recipient. The 1996 welfare reform bill, which was designed to cut welfare costs and rolls, was passed largely with Republican votes: a majority of congressional Democrats opposed it.

Although the Republican and Democratic parties have been at odds on the issue of social welfare, they have also had reason to work together. Social welfare is an ongoing issue because it is a pressing problem that requires action. There are millions of Americans who need help from government if they are to meet their basic subsistence needs. This help has taken various forms—job training efforts, education initiatives, income redistribution measures, and individual-benefit policies.

www.mhhe.com/patterson5

Graphic

JOB TRAINING

The government's social welfare effort has included attempts to provide jobs and job training. Employment policy and welfare policy have been loosely linked since the Great Depression, when Franklin Roosevelt combined public jobs programs with social security legislation. At one point during the depression, a fifth of the nation's entire work force was employed in public jobs.

Americans strongly favor work over welfare as a means of public assistance. Work is believed to foster initiative and responsibility, while welfare is thought to create dependency and irresponsibility. In a Los Angeles *Times* poll, respondents were asked what action government should take to help the poor. Only 6 percent said that the government should provide money or services, whereas 20 percent preferred public works jobs and 72 percent favored job training.

The history of work and job training programs, however, is an uneven one. For example, an ambitious program that began in the early 1970s under Republican President Richard Nixon, and which at its peak provided employment for four million people, was terminated a decade later amid charges that it was too costly and had failed to place people in permanent jobs as opposed to subsidized temporary positions. Subsequent job-training programs were less ambitious and, if anything, even less successful in moving the unemployed into permanent jobs.

The picture changed when the Republican-controlled Congress passed the 1996 Welfare Reform Act. The historic bill ended a six-decade federal guarantee of cash assistance to needy families, replacing it with a system of cash grants to the states, which have responsibility for caring for welfare recipients and getting them into jobs. The legislation's goal is to reduce long-term welfare dependency by limiting the time that recipients can receive welfare and by providing the states with incentives to prepare recipients for work. States may not let recipients receive federal welfare assistance for more than five years (although a fifth of recipients can be exempted from this requirement), and within two years on welfare, a recipient must find work or face the loss of benefits. States receive federal funds with which to provide benefits, community service jobs, and job training, but unless they meet the program's goals (for example, half of their welfare recipients must be moved from welfare to work by the year 2002), they will have their federal assistance reduced. In other words, the welfare reform act includes incentives to encourage both states and welfare recipients to create situations that will lead to employment.

The long-term effectiveness of the new program is yet to be determined. The trend so far is cause for optimism. The number of Americans on welfare has declined sharply since the 1996 Welfare Reform Act was passed. Nevertheless, the economy was strong and growing when the law took effect, and new jobs were plentiful. The real test of the new program will come when the economy goes into a prolonged slump. Another test will be whether the states can train welfare recipients who are severely lacking in job skills. Most of the welfare recipients who have found employment since 1996 had enough skills that they required little or no job training. Those who have been hardest to place in jobs are the ones with the least education and fewest skills.[10]

EDUCATION INITIATIVES: HEAD START

The social welfare effort also includes special education programs, most notably Head Start. It provides preschool education for poor children in order to give them a better chance to succeed when they begin school. Head Start was established in the 1960s as part of President Lyndon Johnson's War on Poverty, which

President Clinton signs into law the 1996 welfare reform bill that ended the sixty-one-year-old federal guarantee of aid to the poor. The new legislation limits federal welfare assistance to a period of five years.

The Head Start education program is designed to give preschool children from poorer homes a better chance to succeed when they enter school. Shown here is a teacher reading to a Head Start class in Austin, Texas.

was designed to alleviate the problems of America's poor, such as malnutrition, job training, health care, and housing. Funding in some of these areas was cut sharply in the 1980s. Head Start's budget dropped to a level that allowed only 10 percent of eligible children to participate. As evidence mounted of poverty's devastating impact on children's development, President Bush and the Democratic Congress concluded that Head Start was the kind of social investment that the country could hardly afford not to make, and it became one of the few domestic programs to receive a substantial funding increase during the Bush administration. Additional funding was provided when Bill Clinton took office. Nevertheless, less than half of the eligible children are enrolled in Head Start, and many who complete the program do not sustain their advantage because their home situation provides no support for educational achievement.

INCOME AND TAX MEASURES

The income of the average American family exceeds $40,000, which, although below the average of several other countries, is substantial enough to provide a reasonable standard of living. Of course, the average income is just that—an average. It hides other averages—for example, the average white family's income is more than $15,000 higher than the average black family's income—and it hides wide disparities in the income of those individuals at the top and the bottom of the income ladder.

In fact, the United States has substantial income inequality (see Figure 19-2). The top 20 percent of Americans receive half of the total income, while the other 80 percent get the other half. The bottom 20 percent receive less than 5 percent of the total income, and most of them live in poverty. In contrast, Americans at

Share of all U.S. income

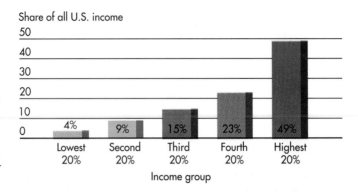

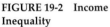

FIGURE 19-2   Income Inequality
The United States has the highest degree of income inequality of any industrialized democracy. U.S. citizens in the top fifth get nearly half of all income; those in the bottom fifth get less than one-twentieth of all income. *Source: U.S. Bureau of the Census, 2000.*

the top of the income ladder live very well. The upper 5 percent have about as much total yearly income as the bottom 50 percent. This 10-to-1 ratio is greater than that found in other industrialized democracies, and the gap between rich and poor in the United States has widened in recent decades.

Tax Rates

Income taxes in the United States have not been the instrument of redistribution that they are in other democracies. The top tax rate in the United States is 39.5 percent and does not apply until income reaches the $250,000 level. An upper tax rate of 50 percent or more is common in Europe, and there are fewer loopholes, such as the deduction of home mortgage interest, that provide tax breaks for the more well-to-do. In terms of the actual rate of taxes paid, middle-income and moderately high-income Americans are in about the same situation. The higher marginal tax rate on higher-income people is offset by their additional deductions and the existence of nonprogressive taxes such as the social security tax. (This tax is a flat rate that begins with the first dollar earned each year and stops completely after about $65,000 in earnings.)

The net result is that the *effective tax rate* (the actual percentage of income that is spent to pay taxes) of high-income and middle-income Americans is not greatly different. When social security and personal income taxes are combined, the average family's effective tax rate is about 25 percent. For families with an income of a million or more, the effective tax rate is only a few points higher.[11]

Although well-to-do Americans pay relatively low taxes, the fact that they make a lot of money means, in absolute terms, that they contribute a sizable share of tax revenues. The top 10 percent of taxpayers in terms of income pay about half of the personal income taxes received by the federal government. Some of this tax revenue is redistributed downward to lower-income groups through social welfare programs.

The Earned Income Tax Credit

The United States also has a policy designed to reallocate income directly to lower-income persons. This policy is the Earned Income Tax Credit (EITC). Low-income families with at least one child are eligible for EITC. About ten million American families receive EITC payments; the maximum payment to any one family is about $3,750. Eligibility for payment is determined when persons file their personal income taxes. Those with family incomes below a specified level receive the payment, which phases out as income rises.

Individual-Benefit Programs

EITC involves what is called a **transfer payment,** or a government benefit that is given directly to an individual. All spending to promote the general welfare is designed to help individuals, but much of it—such as federal funds for public school construction and hospital equipment—is not in the form of transfer payments. Many federal programs, however, do transfer benefits directly to individuals, such as social security payments to retired people. These individual-benefit programs are what most people have in mind when they speak of "social welfare."

Individual-benefit programs are designed to alleviate the personal hardships associated with such conditions as joblessness, poverty, and old age. Any individual who meets the established criteria of eligibility is entitled to the benefits afforded by these programs. For this reason, each of these programs is termed an **entitlement program.** In this sense, they have the same force in law as taxes. Just as individuals are required by law to pay taxes to government on the income they earn, individuals are entitled by law to receive government benefits for which they qualify. Because of this feature, spending on entitlement programs is difficult to control. Unlike programs that have a fixed budget, entitlement spending is determined by the number of eligible recipients. As they increase in number, entitlement spending increases, whether the money has been budgeted or not.

All told, individual-benefit programs are the major thrust of U.S. social welfare policy. The federal budget for such programs is roughly $900 billion, which is more money than is spent on all other government activity, including national defense.

At an earlier time in the nation's history, the federal government spent almost nothing on social welfare. Welfare policy was deemed to fall within the powers reserved to the states by the Tenth Amendment and to be adequately addressed by them, even though they did not offer substantial welfare services. Individuals were expected to fend for themselves, and when they were unable to do so, they were usually supported by relatives and friends. This approach reflected the idea of **negative government,** which holds that government governs best by staying out of people's lives, thus giving them as much freedom as possible to determine their own pursuits and encouraging them to become self-reliant.

The situation changed dramatically with the Great Depression. The unemployment level reached 25 percent, which prompted demands for help from the federal government. Franklin D. Roosevelt's New Deal brought economic relief in the form of public works jobs and welfare programs and helped change public attitudes about the federal government's welfare role.[12] Americans came to look favorably on Washington's help. This attitude reflected a faith in **positive government**—the idea that government intervention is necessary in order to enhance personal liberty and security when individuals are buffeted by economic and social forces beyond their control.

transfer payment A government benefit that is given directly to an individual, as in the case of social security payments to a retiree.

entitlement program Any of a number of individual benefit programs, such as social security, that require government to provide a designated benefit to any person who meets the legally defined criteria for eligibility.

negative government The philosophical belief that government governs best by staying out of people's lives, thus giving individuals as much freedom as possible to determine their own pursuits.

positive government The philosophical belief that government intervention is necessary in order to enhance personal liberty when individuals are buffeted by economic and social forces beyond their control.

Since the 1930s, the federal government's welfare role has increased immeasurably, and individuals now expect the federal government to provide benefits to ease the loss of income caused by retirement, disability, unemployment, and the like. Not all individual-benefit programs are alike, however, in their philosophy or level of public support. Individual-benefit programs fall into two general categories: *social insurance* and *public assistance.* Programs in the first category enjoy widespread public support and receive a higher level of funding; programs in the second category encounter substantial public opposition and receive a lower level of funding.

SOCIAL INSURANCE PROGRAMS

More than forty million Americans receive monthly benefits from social insurance programs—including social security, Medicare, unemployment insurance, and workers' compensation. The two major programs, social security and Medicare, cost the federal government more than $600 billion per year. Individuals who paid special payroll taxes when they were employed are eligible for benefits. This is why such programs are labeled **social insurance:** recipients get an insurance benefit under a program that they have helped fund. This self-financing feature of social insurance programs accounts for their strong public support.[13]

social insurance   Social welfare programs based on the "insurance" concept, so that individuals must pay into the program in order to be eligible to receive funds from it. An example is social security for retired people.

Social Security

The leading social insurance program is social security for retirees. The program began with passage of the Social Security Act of 1935 and is funded through payroll taxes on employees and employers (currently set at 6.2 percent). Franklin D. Roosevelt emphasized that retiring workers would receive an in-

For many elderly Americans, social security benefits make it possible to maintain a secure, independent retirement.

surance benefit that they had earned through their payroll taxes, not a handout from the government. Today, social security has Americans' full support. Social security is also one of the few welfare programs run entirely by the federal government. Washington collects the payroll taxes that fund the program and sends monthly checks directly to the more than thirty-five million social security recipients, who, on average, receive more than $750 a month.

Although many people believe that an individual's social security benefits are financed by his or her past contributions, they are actually funded largely through payroll taxes on the current work force. The typical social security recipient gets more money from the government than he or she has paid into the fund. Thus it is necessary to use contributions from the current work force to finance the program. The average recipient takes about ten years to recover his or her lifetime contributions plus interest, and receives "free" benefits from that time forward.

In the last year, several social security reform bills were introduced in Congress, and a major reform of the system will likely occur in the near future. Because of medical and other advances, Americans live longer than they once did, and a social security crisis will occur during the twenty-first century unless the current system is changed. Roughly 20 percent of the U.S. population will be age sixty-five or over in the year 2030, and there will not be enough workers by then to fund the payout to retirees without adjustments to the current program.

The reason why change is likely in the near future is that, the longer the delay, the more painful the solution—higher taxes and lower benefits. There are a number of ways of ensuring the solvency of social security, and there are proponents for nearly every possibility, from investing social security taxes in stocks to raising the income level on which social security taxes are levied. The plan most likely to be enacted is one that preserves social security as a safety net for the elderly poor while creating opportunities for taxpayers to get a greater return on a portion of their social security payments through investments in the stock market.

Unemployment Insurance

The 1935 Social Security Act provides for unemployment benefits for workers who have lost their jobs involuntarily. Unemployment insurance is a joint federal-state program. The federal government collects the payroll taxes that fund unemployment benefits, but states have the option of deciding whether the taxes will be paid by employers only or by both employees and employers (most states use the first option). Individual states also set the tax rate, conditions of eligibility, and benefit level, subject to minimum standards established by the federal government. Although unemployment benefits vary widely among states, they average about a third ($180 a week) of what an average worker makes while employed, and in most cases the benefits are terminated after twenty-six to thirty-nine weeks.

The unemployment program does not have the same high level of public support as social security. The situation reflects in part a common belief that the loss of a job, or the failure to find a new one right away, is somehow a personal failing. Unemployment statistics, however, suggest otherwise. For example, U.S. Bureau of Labor statistics indicate that, of those who lost their jobs in 1994,

only 16 percent had made the decision to quit working. The others became unemployed because of either a temporary layoff or the permanent elimination of
a job position.

Medicare

After World War II, most European democracies instituted systems of government-paid health care, and President Harry Truman, a Democrat, proposed a
similar program for Americans. The American Medical Association (AMA)
called Truman's plan "un-American," lobbied hard against it, and threatened
to mobilize local physicians to campaign against members of Congress who
supported "socialized medicine." Truman's proposal never came to a vote in
Congress. In 1961, President John F. Kennedy, also a Democrat, proposed a
health care program restricted to social security recipients, but the AMA, the
insurance industry, and conservative members of Congress succeeded in
blocking the plan.

The 1964 elections swept a tide of liberal Democrats into Congress, and the
result was Medicare. Enacted in 1965, the program provides medical assistance
to retirees and is funded primarily through payroll taxes (the current tax rate is
2.9 percent). Medicare, too, is based on the insurance principle, and therefore it
has gained nearly the same high level of public support as social security.

Medicare provides for care in a hospital or nursing home, but the recipient
pays part of the initial cost and pays most of the expenses after one hundred
days. Medicare does not cover all physicians' fees, but enrollees in the program
have the option of paying an insurance premium for fuller coverage of these
fees. Enrollees who cannot afford the additional premium can apply to have the
government pay it.

Like the social security program, the Medicare program is likely to undergo
a major reform in the near future. The rising cost of medical care and the growing number of elderly have combined to threaten the solvency of the Medicare
program; it is projected within a decade to run out of money unless new revenues and cost-cutting measures are devised. Among the options under consideration are increased payroll taxes, more cost-sharing by recipients, more use of
managed care options, and more substantial controls on government payments
to doctors and hospitals.

PUBLIC ASSISTANCE PROGRAMS

public assistance A term that
refers to social welfare programs
funded through general tax
revenues and available only to
the financially needy. Eligibility
for such a program is established
by a means test.

means test The requirement
that applicants for public
assistance must demonstrate they
are poor in order to be eligible for
the assistance.

Unlike social insurance programs, **public assistance** programs are funded
through general tax revenues and are available only to the financially needy. Eligibility for such entitlement programs is established by a **means test,** a demonstration that the applicant is poor enough to qualify for the benefit. In other
words, applicants for public assistance must prove that they are poor. Public assistance programs are commonly referred to as "welfare" and the recipients as
"welfare cases." Opinion polls show that public assistance programs have less
public support than do social insurance programs.

About twenty-five million Americans receive public assistance, typically
through programs established by the federal government, administered mainly
by the states, and funded jointly by the state and federal governments. Most

Supplemental Security Income (SSI) is a combined federal-state program that provides public assistance to blind and disabled people.

Americans have the mistaken impression that public assistance programs account for the lion's share of federal welfare spending. A poll found that Americans believe welfare programs are the second-largest federal program (foreign aid ranked first).[14] In fact, the federal government spends roughly two times as much on its two major social insurance programs, social security and Medicare, as it does on all public assistance programs combined.

Supplemental Security Income (SSI)

A major public assistance program is Supplemental Security Income (SSI), which originated as federal assistance to the blind and elderly poor as part of the Social Security Act of 1935. By the 1930s, most states had begun or were considering such programs. Although the federal legislation was designed to replace their efforts, the states have retained a measure of control over benefits and eligibility and are required to provide some of the funding. Because SSI recipients (who now include the disabled in addition to the blind and elderly poor) have obvious reasons for their inability to provide for themselves, this public assistance program is not widely criticized.

Aid to Needy Families

Perhaps the most controversial of the major public assistance programs was Aid for Families with Dependent Children (AFDC). Partly funded by the federal government but administered by the states, the AFDC program was created in the 1930s as survivors' insurance to assist children whose fathers had died prematurely. Relatively small and noncontroversial at inception, AFDC was the target of severe criticism by the 1970s. Although some attacks on it were based on false claims (for example, that most of the recipients were unwed teenage mothers when, in fact, less than 10 percent were in this category),[15] AFDC was widely unpopular because it was linked in people's minds to welfare dependency and irresponsibility. It was an entitlement program, which meant that any single parent (and, in some states, two parents) living in poverty could claim the benefit and keep it for as long as a dependent child was in the household. Some AFDC recipients were content to live indefinitely on this assistance, and in some cases, their children also grew to become AFDC recipients, thereby creating what was called "a vicious cycle of poverty." By 1995, AFDC was supporting fourteen million Americans at an annual cost of more than $15 billion.

In 1996, AFDC was terminated as part of the Welfare Reform Act. Funding for AFDC was replaced by the Temporary Assistance for Needy Families block grant (TANF), which gives each state an annual cash grant that is to be used to design its own program for assisting needy families and getting welfare recipients into jobs. These programs must operate within tight federal guidelines, including the following:

- Americans' eligibility for federal cash assistance is limited to no more than five years in their lifetime.
- Within two years, the head of most families on welfare will have to find work or risk the loss of benefits.
- Unmarried teenage mothers are qualified for welfare benefits only if they remain in school and live with a parent or legal guardian.
- Single mothers will lose a portion of their benefits if they refuse to cooperate in identifying the father of their children.

Although states are allowed to make some exceptions to some of the rules (for example, an unmarried teenage mother who faces sexual abuse at home is permitted to live elsewhere), the rules govern in most cases. States are also empowered in some areas to impose more restrictive rules. For example, a state can deny increased benefits to a mother who is already receiving assistance and has another child.

Within the limits, states can design a program of their choosing, and wide differences are expected. Even AFDC benefits varied widely, ranging from less than $300 in most southern and southwestern states to more than $450 in most northeastern and some midwestern states. Because the TANF grants that states will initially receive are roughly proportional to the amounts they were spending on AFDC, these regional differences are certain to persist. Perhaps the biggest challenge facing the states, in addition to ensuring that the poor do not wind up in the streets, is the development of welfare-to-work programs that actually do free families from welfare dependency.

The new welfare program is such a substantial departure from the past that the long-term picture is difficult to predict. Some observers believe it will have dire effects. The liberal Urban Institute estimates that within a decade the bill will push more than one million children into poverty as their family's eligibility for assistance expires. Other observers see it as the long-awaited answer to

Wisconsin Governor Tommy Thompson describes his state's welfare-to-work program at a Republican Governors Association meeting in Milwaukee. The Wisconsin initiative is often cited as a role model for the new welfare reform program that Congress enacted in 1996. Standing with Thompson are (from left to right) South Carolina Governor David Beasley, Michigan Governor John Engler, and Iowa Governor Terry Branstad.

welfare dependency. They point, for example, to the higher-than-anticipated decline in welfare recipients during the program's first years. The conservative Heritage Foundation concluded in a report that the new program's tough rules had succeeded in forcing able-bodied unemployed to find gainful work.[16]

Food Stamps

The food stamp program, which took its present form in 1961, is fully funded by the federal government. The program provides an *in-kind benefit*—not cash, but food stamps that can be spent only on grocery items.

Food stamps are available only to people who qualify on the basis of low income. The program is intended to improve the nutrition of poor families by enabling them to purchase qualified items, mainly foodstuffs, with food stamps. Some critics say that food stamps stigmatize their users by making it obvious to onlookers in the checkout line that they are "welfare cases." More prevalent criticisms are that the program is too costly and that too many undeserving people receive food stamps. The 1996 welfare reform bill restricts to three months in any three-year period the food-stamp eligibility of able-bodied adults with no children.

Subsidized Housing

Low-income persons are also eligible for subsidized housing. Most of the federal spending in this area is on housing vouchers rather than the construction of low-income housing units. Under the voucher system, the individual receives a monthly rent-payment voucher, which is given in lieu of cash to the landlord, who then hands the voucher over to the government in exchange for cash. The welfare recipient is given a voucher (an in-kind benefit) rather than cash in order to ensure that the funds are actually used to obtain housing. About five million households annually receive a federal housing subsidy.

★ CRITICAL THINKING ★

WHAT'S YOUR OPINION?

**What System of Health Care
Should America Have?**
There are two broad
approaches to medical care.
One, which exists throughout
Europe and in Canada, is a
national (government-based)
health system. The alternative
approach, which exists in the
United States, is based on the
private sector but also
includes public aspects.

The United States has the
most expensive health care
system in the world. It
absorbs 14 percent of the
gross national product (GNP).
The national health care
systems of western Europe
account for less than 10
percent of GNP. A national
health care system also
provides broader coverage;
everyone has access. In
contrast, more than thirty-five
million Americans are too
poor to buy their own health
insurance but are not poor
enough to qualify for public
insurance (Medicaid).

The advantages of a
private-centered health
system are its responsiveness
to eligible persons and its
level of services. In a national
health care system, there is
often a long wait to obtain
certain services, such as
elective surgery.

Which type of medical
system do you favor? Why?

The U.S. government spends much less on public housing than on tax breaks for homeowners, most of whom are middle- and upper-income Americans. Homeowners are allowed tax deductions for their mortgage interest payments and their local property tax payments. The total of these tax concessions is three times as much as is spent by the federal government on housing for low-income families.

Medicaid

When it enacted Medicare in 1965, Congress also established Medicaid, which provides health care for poor people who are already on welfare. It is considered a public assistance program, rather than a social insurance program like Medicare, because it is based on need and funded by general tax revenues. Roughly 60 percent of Medicaid funding is provided by the federal government and about 40 percent by the states. More than twenty million Americans receive Medicaid assistance.

Medicaid is controversial because of its costs. As health care costs have spiraled far ahead of the inflation rate, so have the costs of Medicaid. It absorbs more than half of all public assistance dollars spent by the U.S. government and has forced state and local governments to cut other services to meet the costs of their share. "It's killing us," was how one local official described the impact of Medicaid on his community's budget.[17]

As is true of other public assistance programs, Medicaid has been criticized for supposedly serving too many people who could take care of themselves if they tried harder. The idea is contradicted, ironically, by the situation faced by many working Americans. There are nearly forty million Americans who make too much money to qualify for Medicaid but who cannot afford health insurance. This situation encouraged presidential candidate Bill Bradley to propose during the 2000 Democratic nominating race that all Americans be provided health insurance, at government expense if necessary. His opponent, Al Gore, countered with a proposal to gradually expand health coverage with a long-term goal of universal coverage.

Education as Equality of Opportunity: The American Way

All democratic societies promote economic security, but they do so to different degrees. Economic security has a higher priority in European democracies than in the United States. European democracies have instituted such programs as government-paid health care for all citizens, compensation for all unemployed workers, and retirement benefits for all elderly citizens. As we have seen, the United States provides these benefits only to some citizens in each category. For example, not all elderly Americans are entitled to social security benefits. If they paid social security taxes for a long enough period when they were employed, they (including their spouses) receive benefits. Otherwise, they do not, even if they are in dire economic need.

Such policy differences between Europe and the United States stem from cultural and historical differences. Democracy developed in Europe in reaction to centuries of aristocratic rule, the inequities of which brought the issue of human equality to the forefront. When strong labor and socialist parties then emerged as a consequence of industrialization, European democracies initiated sweeping social welfare programs that brought about greater economic equality. In contrast, American democracy emerged out of a tradition of limited government that emphasized personal freedom. Equality was a lesser issue, and class consciousness was weak. No major labor or socialist party emerged in America during industrialization to represent the working class, and there was no persistent and strong demand for welfare policies that would bring about an economic leveling.

EQUALITY, INEQUALITY, AND PUBLIC OPINION

These differing legacies are evident today in the opinions of Americans and Europeans. When asked in a Gallup poll whether they placed a higher value on freedom or on equality, Americans chose freedom by 72 percent to 20 percent. Among Europeans, the margin was only 49 percent to 35 percent.[18] On the basis of his study of political values, Karl Lamb concluded that most Americans "cannot really imagine a society that would provide substantial material equality."[19]

Instead, Americans place their trust in the economic marketplace. They look upon jobs and the personal income that comes from work as the proper basis of economic security. Americans are disinclined to help the poor through welfare payments; they prefer that the poor be given training and education so that they can learn to help themselves. This attitude is consistent with Americans' preference for **equality of opportunity,** which is the idea that individuals should have an equal chance to succeed on their own. The concept embodies *equality* in its emphasis on giving everyone a fair chance to get ahead. Yet equality of opportunity also embodies *liberty* because it allows people to succeed or fail on their own as a result of what they do with their opportunities. The presumption is that people will end up differently—some rich, some poor. It is sometimes said that equality of opportunity offers individuals an equal chance to become unequal.

equality of opportunity The idea that all individuals should be given an equal chance to succeed on their own.

In practice, equality of opportunity works itself out primarily in the private sector, where Americans compete for jobs, promotions, and other advantages. However, a few public policies have the purpose of enhancing equality of opportunity. The most significant of these policies is public education.

America's broad-based system of public education stems from an amalgam of its egalitarian and individualistic beliefs. Leon Sampson, a nineteenth-century American socialist, noted the stark difference between the philosophy of public education in the United States and that in Europe. "The European ruling classes," he said, "were open in their contempt for the proletariat. But in the United States equality, and even classlessness, the creation of wealth for all and political liberty were extolled in the public schools." Sampson concluded that American schools embodied a unique conception of equality: everyone was being trained in much the same way so that each person would have the opportunity to succeed. "It is," he said, "a socialist conception of capitalism."[20]

PUBLIC EDUCATION: LEVELING THROUGH THE SCHOOLS

During the nation's first century, the question of a free education to all children divided the landed wealthy from the advocates of broad-based democracy. The wealthy feared that an educated public would challenge their power. The democrats wanted to provide more people with the foundation for economic advantage. The democrats won out. Public schools sprang up in nearly every community and were open free of charge to children who could attend.

Today, as was discussed in Chapter 1, the United States invests more heavily in public education at all levels than does any other country. The curriculum in American schools is also relatively standardized. Unlike those countries that divide children even at the grade school level into different tracks that lead ultimately to different occupations, the United States aims to educate children in much the same way. Of course, public education is not a uniform experience for American children. The quality of education depends significantly on the wealth of the community in which a child resides. The federal program that provides aid to poorer school districts does not appreciably alter the situation. In creating the program, members of Congress wrote the legislation broadly enough to enable schools in their constituencies to get some of the money. To receive federal assistance, a school district needs only ten poor students, which means that 93 percent of school districts qualify. Less than half of the money in the education aid program for poor children goes to schools in areas where poverty is widespread.[21]

Nevertheless, the United States through its public schools educates a broad segment of the population. Arguably, no country in the world has made an equivalent effort to give children, whatever their parents' background, an equal opportunity in life through education. This spending level on public elementary and secondary schools averages roughly $6,000 per pupil, compared with less than $3,000 per pupil in western Europe. America's commitment to broad-based education extends to college. The United States is far and away the world leader in terms of the proportion of adults receiving a college education.[22]

The nation's education system preserves both the myth and reality of the American dream. The belief that success can be had by anyone who works for it could not be sustained if the education system were tailored for a privileged elite. And educational attainment is related to personal success, at least as measured by annual incomes. In fact, the gap in income between those with and without a college education is now greater than at any time in the country's history.

In part because the public schools have such a large role in creating an equal opportunity society, they have been heavily criticized in recent years. Violence in the schools is a major parental concern. So too is the decline in student performance on standardized tests, such as the Scholastic Aptitude Test (SAT). American students are not even in the top ten internationally by their test scores in science or math.[23]

Disgruntled parents have demanded changes, and these demands have led some communities to allow parents to choose the public school their children will attend. Under this policy, the schools compete for students, and those that attract the most students are rewarded with the largest budgets. Americans say they favor such a policy by more than a 2-to-1 margin. Advocates of the policy contend that it compels school administrators and teachers to do a better job and gives students the option of rejecting a school that is performing poorly.[24] Opponents of the policy say that it creates a few well-funded schools and a lot of poorly funded ones, yielding no net gain in educational quality. Critics also claim that the policy discriminates against poor and minority group children, whose parents are less likely to be in a position to steer them toward the better schools.[25]

A more contentious issue is a "voucher system" that would allow parents to use tax dollars to send their children even to private or parochial schools (see Figure 19-3). The recipient school would receive a voucher redeemable from the government and the student would get a corresponding reduction in his or her tuition. In the 2000 presidential campaign, the Democrat Al Gore and the Republican George W. Bush took opposing positions on the issue. Gore claimed that vouchers would undermine the public schools while Bush argued that vouchers would hurt only those schools that were failing their students and would encourage such schools to improve.

The issue of school choice goes to the heart of the issue of equal opportunity. On the one hand, an elite-centered school system widens the gap between the country's richer and poorer groups. On the other hand, making students compete with one another for the best education can be justified in terms of the country's individualistic tradition.

THE FEDERAL ROLE IN EDUCATION: POLITICAL DIFFERENCES

Education has traditionally been a state and local responsibility. Most school policies—from length of the school year to teachers' qualifications—are set by state legislatures and local school boards. Over 90 percent of the funds spent on schools are provided through state and local tax revenues. Federal intervention in school policy has often been resisted by states and localities, as exemplified by their response to desegregation and busing directives (see Chapter 5). State and local governments have been less hesitant when it comes to federal education grants, but as indicated by the federal program that provides aid to poorer schools, it is difficult to get congressional support for grant programs targeted at the schools that are most in need. Few members of Congress are willing to support large appropriations for education that do not benefit their constituents, which has reduced Washington's contribution to a goal—quality education for every American child—that nearly every official endorses, at least in the abstract.

Indeed, it was not until 1965 that Congress enacted the first general federal aid to education legislation: the Higher Education Act and the Elementary and Secondary Education Act. The former became the foundation for Pell Grants, federal loans to college students, and federally subsidized college work-study programs. The latter provided funding for such items as school construction, textbooks, special education, and teacher training.

These acts were not the very first federal programs in the education area. A century earlier, for example, Congress had passed the Morrill Act, which provided states with free tracts of land if the land was used to establish colleges. America's great "land grant" universities are the consequence. The G.I. bill that was enacted after World War II and that enabled millions of service veterans to attend college was another. Yet a third was the National Defense Education Act of 1958, which provided loans and special institutes for students in science and related fields. But not until the 1965 legislation did the federal government assume a broader, ongoing role in public education.

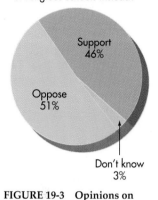

"In areas where schools are not improving, would you support or oppose the federal government giving parents money to send their children to private or religious schools instead?"

Support 46%

Oppose 51%

Don't know 3%

FIGURE 19-3   Opinions on School Vouchers
Americans are divided in their opinions on school vouchers even in cases where the public schools are performing poorly. *Source: Washington Post/ABC News, 2000.*

CURRENT CONTROVERSIES

SHOULD SCHOOL VOUCHERS BECOME NATIONAL POLICY?

As the demand for quality schools has increased, some parents have sought an answer in a "school voucher" system. Each student would be entitled to a taxpayer-provided voucher of a few thousand dollars, which could be applied to admission at a public, private, or religious school of the student's choice. Advocates claim that the voucher system would create competition for students that would enhance performance levels across the entire school system. Opponents say that the voucher system would undermine the public schools not only by decreasing their funding but also by drawing the better students away from public into private schools. They also say that the voucher system is little more than a middle-class subsidy since, even with a voucher, poorer families cannot afford the price of private school tuition.

YES: Modern day choice proposals are aimed at helping children who are most in need. In Milwaukee and Cleveland decades of failure and lost years of learning prompted the pilot programs. . . . Parents now know that they have a guarantee: either the school their child attends will work, or they will be given an opportunity to enroll their child in one of their choice that does work. . . . [Just as] important, however, is that these programs work to instill institutional incentives for school improvement and they consider every child's education an uncompromising priority. . . . Some opponents call the concept of choice radical. They say the best children will leave failing schools, leaving the worst behind. But aren't they really saying that they know schools are already failing? Aren't they really saying that they are worried about bricks and mortar, and not about children?
— The Center for Education Reform

NO: Although supporters have tried, over the years, to present vouchers as a good way to "reform" public education, vouchers are quite simply and plainly a way to use public money to send children to private schools. They're a scheme to siphon off money from public schools rather than help them improve. . . . A particularly dishonest argument that voucher advocates use in selling "parental choice" is that all parents should have the right to choose a good private school for their children—"the way President and Mrs. Clinton did for Chelsea." The people using this argument conveniently forget to point out that good private schools generally have many more applicants than places, so it's the schools—not the parents—who do the choosing. And of course they don't mention that parents can't choose what they can't afford. As one New York City parent said about a private school voucher she won in a lottery, "You're supposed to be poor to get the scholarship, but you have to be rich to use it."
— American Federation of Teachers

Since then, federal assistance to public schools and colleges has been an important part of their financing, albeit a small part relative to the overall amount that the nation spends on public education. Federal funds during the past two decades have been split almost equally between support for college and for public school education.

As education, particularly in the public schools, has become increasingly an issue of national debate, the pressures on Washington to play an even larger role have intensified. In 1989, George Bush declared he would be "the education president," saying that he would do more for education than any other president had done. Unlike his predecessor, Ronald Reagan, Bush did not threaten to abolish the Department of Education, which Congress had created in 1979. He urged it to coordinate federal education efforts and to help states and localities strengthen their programs. For himself, Bush took on the task of promoting school choice, urging states and localities to allow parents to make the decision about which school their children would attend.

The Supreme Court has held that American children are entitled to an "adequate" education but do not have a right to an "equal" education. America's public schools differ greatly in quality, primarily as a result of the differences in the wealth of the communities they serve. Some public schools are overcrowded and have few facilities and little equipment. Others are very well equipped and have spacious facilities and small class sizes.

Bill Clinton also made education a top issue of his presidency. Clinton rejected the idea of unrestricted school choice, arguing that it would weaken the nation's public schools and make them a repository of America's poorest and most difficult-to-educate children. But Clinton proposed standardized national testing as a means of evaluating schools' performance and advocated federal grants for the purpose of renovating the nation's most outmoded school buildings. Then, in 1998, Clinton persuaded reluctant congressional Republicans to accept, as part of a budget compromise, a multi-billion-dollar grant that would allow the nation's overcrowded schools to hire tens of thousands of new teachers. GOP lawmakers are less politically attuned to low-income constituents than are Democratic lawmakers and are philosophically less inclined toward federal solutions to public school problems. In 1995, for example, a majority of House Republicans supported an unsuccessful effort to abolish the Department of Education and to give states almost complete discretion in the use of federal grants for education. In other words, many of the partisan and philosophical differences that affect federal welfare policy also affect federal education policy.

Culture, Politics, and Social Welfare

Surveys have repeatedly indicated that a majority of Americans are convinced that most people on welfare could get along without it if they tried. Because public assistance programs have limited public support, there are constant political pressures to reduce welfare expenditures and to weed out undeserving recipients. The unwritten principle of social welfare in America, reflecting the country's individualistic culture, is that the individual must somehow earn any social welfare benefit or, barring that, demonstrate a convincing need for the benefit. The result is a welfare system that is both *inefficient*, in that much of the money spent on welfare never reaches the recipients, and *inequitable*, in that most of the money spent on social welfare never gets to the people who are most in need of help.

INEFFICIENCY: THE WELFARE WEB

The United States has by far the most intricate system of social welfare in the world. Scores of separate programs have been established to address different, often overlapping needs. A single individual in need of public assistance may qualify for many, none, or one of these programs, and the eligibility criteria are sometimes bizarre. Consider the case of Gary Myers of Springfield, Missouri, who declared bankruptcy because he could not afford to pay $1,400 in hospital bills that his family had incurred. Had Myers made exactly $4 less than his $509 monthly wage as a security guard, he would have qualified for government payment of his medical expenses. Because of the extra $4 Myers received nothing.[26]

Beyond the question of the equity of such rules is the question of their efficiency. The unwritten principle that the individual must somehow earn or deserve a particular benefit makes the U.S. welfare system highly labor intensive. Consider, for example, the 1996 welfare reform bill, which limits eligibility to families with incomes below a certain level and, in most instances, to families with a single parent living in the home. Because of this requirement, the eligibility of each applicant must be periodically checked by a caseworker (see Figure 19-4). This procedure makes such programs doubly expensive; in addition to payments to the recipients, there are the costs of paying caseworkers, supervisors, and support staffs as well as processing the extensive paperwork involved.

The administrative costs of welfare are substantially lower in Europe since eligibility is either universal, as in the case of health care, or less stringently defined. There have been proposals to adopt a Europeanlike system in the United States; President Nixon's attempt to establish a guaranteed annual income for every American family is an example. All these proposals have failed to win broad support, mainly because they run counter to Americans' belief in individualism. Thus, it is not surprising that the 1996 welfare bill created additional layers of welfare administration. Recipients' lifetime welfare histories will have to be maintained, and states will have to establish job placement and training programs that can move millions of people from welfare to work. Whether the change will be cost-effective will be determined by whether large numbers of welfare recipients actually find long-term employment. Whether the change fits the American way of welfare is more easily judged: it clearly does.

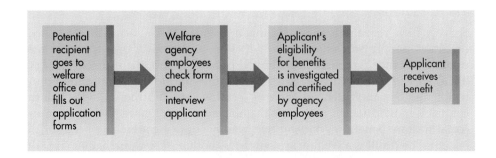

FIGURE 19-4   The Cumbersome Administrative Process by Which Welfare Recipients Get Their Benefits

One of the many ironies of U.S. social welfare policy is that tax deductions on home mortgages for the middle and upper classes are government subsidies, just as are rent vouchers for the poor, but only the latter are stigmatized as a government "handout."

INEQUITY: THE MIDDLE-CLASS ADVANTAGE

Most Americans hold to the traditional belief in individualism and self-reliance, which they generalize to other people.[27] Although Americans recognize a need for programs for the poor and disadvantaged, they tend to minimize both the number of such individuals and the extent of their need. The situation means that less advantaged Americans cannot count on a great deal of political support from other sectors of society. Even the much-heralded War on Poverty of the 1960s was less a war than a skirmish. Weak middle-class support for the effort, reports that the programs were poorly administered and were not reaching the target audience, and the fiscal pressures of the Vietnam conflict combined to undermine the antipoverty effort. Congressional appropriations for the War on Poverty programs never totaled as much as $2 billion in a given year.

Social security and Medicare are another story entirely. These two social insurance programs have broad public support even though together they cost the federal government more than twice what is spent on all major public assistance programs (see Figure 19-5). A reason for the difference in public funding

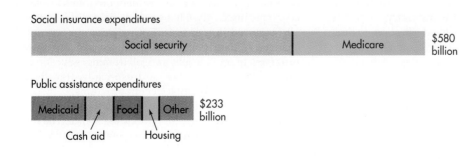

FIGURE 19-5 Federal Spending for Social Insurance and Public Assistance Programs Social insurance spending far exceeds public assistance spending. *Source: Office of Management and Budget, 1998.*

and approval for social security is that it benefits the majority. Most Americans are either actual or potential social security recipients. It is good politics for elected officials to appeal to the forty million retired Americans who get a monthly social security check.

Social security recipients feel entitled to their benefits by virtue of their payroll tax contributions. As indicated earlier, however, they receive far greater benefits than they have "earned" through their payroll taxes. So they are, in a sense, getting public assistance.

It is important to note, however, that the existence of social security substantially lessens the demand for other forms of public assistance. Social security keeps millions of Americans, mostly widows, out of poverty. About a fourth of social security recipients have no other significant source of income. Without social security, they would be completely dependent on public assistance programs.

Nevertheless, many social security recipients, while legally entitled to the benefits they receive, have no actual financial need for them. Only a third of social security recipients are in the lowest fifth of the population in income. Families in the top fifth of the income population receive more in federal social insurance benefits than is spent on family assistance, food stamps, and housing subsidies combined.

The contradictions and difficulties of social welfare in America come together in the contrasting cases of social insurance and public assistance. Although the latter is targeted toward the truly needy, it is less acceptable politically and culturally and receives much less funding. The situation testifies to the strength of traditional American values of individualism and self-reliance and to the power of money and votes. The social security program is a preeminent example of *majoritarian* politics at work.

www.mhhe.com/patterson5

Self-Quiz

Social welfare, as we have seen, is the arena in which many of the conflicts of the American political system come together: individualism versus equality, Congress versus the president, national authority versus local authority, public sector versus private sector, Republicans versus Democrats, poorer versus richer, social insurance versus public assistance. The politics of welfare is a politics of contradictory values and competing interests, which ensures that it will be a contentious issue for years to come.

Summary

The United States has a complex social welfare system of multiple programs addressing specific welfare needs. Each program applies only to those individuals who qualify for benefits by meeting the specific eligibility criteria. In general, these criteria are designed to reward and promote self-reliance or, when help is necessary, to ensure that laziness is not rewarded or fostered—in short, to limit benefits to those individuals who truly cannot help themselves. This approach to social welfare reflects Americans' traditional belief in individualism.

Poverty is a large and persistent problem in America. About one in seven people fall below the government-defined poverty line, and they include a disproportionate number of children, female-headed families, minority group members, and rural and inner-city dwellers. The ranks of the poor are increased by economic recessions and reduced through government welfare programs.

Welfare policy has been a partisan issue, with Democrats taking the lead on government programs to alleviate economic insecurity. Changes in social welfare have usually occurred in the context of majority support for the change. Welfare policy has been worked out through programs to provide jobs and job training, education programs, income measures, and especially, transfer payments through individual-benefit programs.

Individual-benefit programs fall into two broad categories: social insurance and public assistance. The former includes such programs as social security for retired workers and Medicare for the elderly. Social insurance programs are funded by payroll taxes on potential recipients, who thus, in a sense, earn the benefits they later receive. Because of this arrangement, social insurance programs have broad public support. Public assistance programs, in contrast, are funded by general tax revenues and are targeted toward needy individuals and families. These programs are not controversial in principle: most Americans believe that government should assist the truly needy. However, because of a widespread belief that most welfare recipients could get along without assistance if they tried, these programs do not have universal public support, are only modestly funded, and are politically vulnerable.

The balance between economic equality and individualism tilts more heavily toward individualism in the United States than in other advanced industrialized democracies. Entitlement to social security, for example, is not a universal right of the elderly in the United States, whereas it is elsewhere.

Compared to other democracies, however, the United States attempts to more equally educate its children, a policy consistent with its cultural emphasis on equality of opportunity. Education policy is traditionally a state and local responsibility, but the federal government's role has increased in response to demands for financial assistance to public schools and colleges.

Social welfare is a contentious issue. A major reason is that opposing sides disagree fundamentally on the nature of the problem. In one view, social welfare is too costly and assists too many people who could help themselves; another view holds that social welfare is not broad enough and that too many disadvantaged Americans live in poverty. In light of these irreconcilable differences, in combination with federalism and the widely shared view that welfare programs should target specific problems, the existing system of multiple programs, despite its administrative complexity and inefficiency, has been the only politically feasible alternative.

Key Terms

entitlement program
equality of opportunity
in-kind benefits
means test
negative government

positive government
poverty line
public assistance
social insurance
transfer payment

Suggested Readings

Chubb, John E., and Terry M. Moe. *Politics, Markets, and America's Schools*. Washington, D.C.: Brookings Institution, 1990. The authors recommend a new system of public education designed around parent-student choice and school competition.

Cook, Fay Lomax, and Edith J. Barrett. *Support for the American Welfare State: The Views of Congress and the Public*. New York: Columbia University Press, 1992. A thorough study of the views underlying welfare policy.

Gans, Herbert J. *The War against the Poor. The Underclass and Anti-Poverty Policy*. New York: Basic Books, 1996. A study of attitudes toward and policies affecting poverty.

Henig, Jeffrey R. *Rethinking School Choice: Limits of the Market Metaphor*. Princeton, N.J.: Princeton University Press, 1995. An argument against parental choice as the basis of public school enrollment.

Hochschild, Jennifer. *Facing Up to the American Dream: Race, Class, and the Soul of the Nation*. Princeton, N.J.: Princeton University Press, 1996. An analysis of how whites and African Americans view their own and each other's opportunities.

Longman, Phillip. *The Return of Thrift. How the Collapse of the Middle Class Welfare State Will Reawaken Values in America*. New York: Free Press, 1996. Examines the relationship between the growth of middle-class welfare programs and changing American values.

Melnick, R. Shep. *Between the Lines: Interpreting Welfare Rights*. Washington, D.C.: Brookings Institution, 1994. An analysis of the intricate relationship between social welfare legislation and its interpretation in the courts.

Murray, Charles. *Losing Ground: American Social Policy, 1950–1980*. New York: Basic Books, 1984. An unfavorable assessment of the U.S. welfare system.

Newman, Katherine S. *No Shame in My Game*. New York: Alfred A. Knopf and Russell Sage Foundation, 1999. A careful study of America's working poor.

Rich, Michael J. *Federal Policymaking and the Poor: National Goals, Local Choices, and Distributional Outcomes*. Princeton, N.J.: Princeton University Press, 1993. A study of the impact of a federal poverty program.

Wilson, William Julius. *When Work Disappears: The World of the New Urban Poor*. New York: Knopf, 1996. An important analysis of jobs and poverty in the inner city.

CHAPTER 20

Foreign and Defense Policy: Protecting the American Way

★

We the people of the United States, in order to . . .
provide for the common defense . . .

—Preamble, U.S. Constitution

★ ★ ★

*I*n 2000, the leaders of the world's most powerful industrial nations met for their seventh annual summit meeting. They discussed global economic stability, including a rebound in the Asian economies. They urged several lagging countries to get their banking systems in order. They also tackled issues thrust on them by recent events, including the change in leadership in Russia.

The G-7 summit meeting sharply dramatized the changing nature of world politics and the role of the United States in it. America's once bitter enemy, Russia, was a struggling nation, trying with only a small amount of success to shed its communist past. In fact, two of the countries at the summit, Germany and Japan, were closer to the position of rivals of the United States than was Russia. The rivalry, however, was economic in nature; Germany and Japan each had a trade surplus with the United States and were tough competitors in the global marketplace. Yet the focus of the summit was cooperation rather than competition. The underlying assumption was that the world's most powerful nations could all gain if they set aside their differences and worked together to promote economic growth and limit political instability.

As the G-7 summit illustrates, national security is an issue of economic vitality as well as of military strength. The primary goal of U.S. foreign policy is the preservation of the American state. This objective requires military readiness in order to protect the territorial integrity and international interests of the United States. But the American state also represents a society of more than 250 million people whose livelihood depends in significant part on the nation's position in the international economy.[1] Through participation in global policies that foster economic growth, the United States can secure the jobs and trade that are essential to the maintenance of a high standard of living.

The national security policies of the United States embrace an extraordinary array of activities—so many, in fact, that they could not possibly be addressed adequately in an entire book, much less a single chapter. There are some 160 countries in the world, and the United States has relations of one kind or another—military, diplomatic, economic—with all of them. This chapter narrows the subject by focusing on a few main ideas:

★ *Since World War II, the United States has acted in the role of world leader, which has substantially affected its military, diplomatic, and economic policies.*

★ *The policy machinery for foreign and defense affairs is dominated by the president and includes military, intelligence, diplomatic, and economic agencies and organizations.*

★ *The United States maintains a high degree of defense preparedness.* This readiness mandates a substantial level of defense spending and a worldwide deployment of U.S. conventional and strategic forces. A consequence of these requirements is a military-industrial complex that benefits from and is a cause of high levels of military spending.

★ *Changes in the international marketplace have led to increased economic interdependence among nations, which has had a marked influence on the United States' economy and on its security planning.* Increasingly, national security policy has been defined in economic terms rather than military terms.

The Roots of U.S. Foreign and Defense Policy

For nearly half a century, U.S. defense policy was defined by conflict with the Soviet Union. From the Berlin airlift in 1948 to the Vietnam escalation in 1965 to the Star Wars initiative in 1983, the United States seemed willing to pay any price to halt the spread of communism. Then, in the late 1980s, the Soviet empire suddenly and dramatically began to fall apart. In December 1991, the

Since the end of the Cold War, U.S. national security policy has increasingly been defined in the context of America's position in the global economy. Pictured here is the Seattle harbor, one of the nation's busiest ports. Of the 50 states, Washington is the most economically dependent on international trade.

Soviet Union itself ceased to exist. For decades, there had been two superpowers, the Soviet Union and the United States. Now there is only one.

With the end of the cold war, the United States is positioned to redefine its foreign and defense policies.[2] The country is still at the center of world politics, but its challenges have changed: they are less military and more economic.[3] A strong domestic base, more than a mighty military arsenal, has become the key to global success.

Although the age of superpower conflict is over, the changes in foreign and defense policy that lie ahead will take shape within a context defined by that era. Decisions made in the past carry into the future, both informing and channeling new ones.

THE UNITED STATES AS GLOBAL SUPERPOWER

Before World War II, the United States was an **isolationist** country, deliberately avoiding a large role in world affairs. A different America emerged from the war. It had more land, sea, and air power than any other country in the world, a huge military-industrial base, and several hundred overseas military bases. The United States had become an **internationalist** country, deeply involved in the affairs of other nations.

isolationism The view that the country should deliberately avoid a large role in world affairs and, instead, concentrate on domestic concerns.

internationalism The view that the country should involve itself deeply in world affairs.

U.S. national security policy after World War II was built on a concern with the power and intentions of the Soviet Union.[4] At the Yalta Conference in 1945, U.S. president Franklin Roosevelt and Soviet leader Josef Stalin had agreed that Eastern European nations were entitled to self-determination within a Soviet zone of influence, but Stalin breached the agreement. After the war, Soviet occupation forces assisted the communist parties in Eastern Europe in capturing state power, usually by coercive means. In the words of Britain's wartime prime minister, Winston Churchill, an "iron curtain" had fallen across Europe.

Great Britain's Winston Churchill, America's Franklin D. Roosevelt, and the Soviet Union's Josef Stalin meet at Yalta in 1945 to discuss the order of the postwar world.

The Doctrine of Containment

The Soviet Union's aggressive action led U.S. policymakers to assess Soviet aims. Particularly noteworthy was the evaluation of George Kennan, a U.S. diplomat and expert on Soviet affairs. Kennan concluded that invasions from the West in World Wars I and II had made the Soviet Union (which had lost twenty-five million lives in World War II, compared with U.S. losses of five hundred thousand) almost paranoid in its concern for regional security. Although Kennan believed that the USSR would someday mature into a responsible world power, he contended that it was an immediate threat to neighboring countries. He counseled a policy of "long-term, patient but firm, and vigilant containment."[5] Kennan's analysis contributed to the formulation of the doctrine of **containment,** which was based on the idea that the Soviet Union was an aggressor nation that had to be stopped from achieving its territorial ambitions.

Harry S Truman, who became president after Roosevelt's death in 1945, rejected Kennan's view that the USSR was motivated by a concern for *regional* security. Truman saw the Soviet Union as an aggressive ideological foe that was bent on *global* domination and that could be stopped only by the forceful use of U.S. power. Truman's view was based on assumptions derived from territorial concessions made to Germany's Adolf Hitler by Britain and France at a conference in Munich in 1938; rather than appeasing Hitler, these concessions convinced him that Germany could bully its way to further gains. The idea that appeasement only encourages further aggression was the *lesson of Munich,* and it became the dominant view of U.S. policymakers in the postwar period.

containment A doctrine, developed after World War II, based on assumptions that the Soviet Union was an aggressor nation and that only a determined United States could block Soviet territorial ambitions.

The Cold War

Developments in the late 1940s embroiled the United States in a **cold war** with the Soviet Union. The term refers to the fact that the two countries were not

cold war The lengthy period after World War II when the United States and the USSR were not engaged in actual combat (a "hot war") but were nonetheless locked in a state of deep-seated hostility.

Cold war propaganda, like this poster warning Americans of the danger of Soviet-backed communist encroachment in the Philippines in the late 1940s, contributed to a climate of opinion in the United States that led to public support of efforts to contain Soviet power.

directly engaged in actual combat (a "hot war") but were locked into a deep-seated hostility that lasted forty-five years. From the United States' perspective, the cold war was an extension of containment policy and included support for governments threatened by communist takeovers. In China, the Nationalist government had the support of the United States, but it was defeated in 1949 by the Soviet-supplied communist forces of Mao Zedong. In June 1950, when the Soviet-backed North Koreans invaded South Korea, President Truman immediately committed U.S. troops to the conflict, which ended in stalemate and the loss of thirty-five thousand American lives.

THE LIMITS OF AMERICAN POWER: THE VIETNAM WAR

For the United States, a major turning point in foreign policy was the Vietnam War. It was the most costly application of the containment doctrine: fifty-eight thousand American soldiers lost their lives.[6]

Vietnam was part of France's colonial empire until the French army was defeated in 1954 by guerrilla forces led by Ho Chi Minh, a nationalist with communist sympathies. The Geneva conference that ended the war resulted in a partitioning of Vietnam: the northern region was placed under Ho Chi Minh's leadership and the southern region under anti-communist leaders. The United States provided economic assistance to South Vietnam, anticipating that its government would quickly develop the public support that would enable it to prevail in a Vietnam unification election that was scheduled for 1956. When it became apparent that Ho Chi Minh would easily win the election, the United States helped to get it canceled and began to increase its military assistance to the South Vietnamese army. By the time of President John F. Kennedy's assassination in 1963, the United States had about seventeen thousand military advisers in South Vietnam. Lyndon Johnson sharply escalated the war in 1965 by committing U.S. combat units to the conflict. By the late 1960s, 550,000 Americans were fighting in South Vietnam.

U.S. forces in Vietnam were technically superior in combat to the communist fighters, but they were fighting an enemy they could not easily identify in a society they did not fully understand.[7] Vietnam was a guerrilla war, with no front lines and few set battles. As the conflict dragged on, American public opinion, most visibly among the young, turned against the war, which contributed to President Johnson's decision not to run for reelection in 1968. Public opinion forced Richard Nixon, who became president in 1969, to aim not for victory but for a gradual disengagement. U.S. combat troops left Vietnam in 1973, and two years later, North Vietnamese forces concluded their takeover of the country.

Détente

America's defeat in Vietnam forced U.S. policymakers to reconsider the country's international role. The *lesson of Vietnam* was that there were limits to the country's ability to assert its will in the world. Nixon claimed that the United States could no longer act as the "Lone Ranger" for the free world and sought to reduce tensions with communist countries.[8] The new philosophy was reflected by the Helsinki Accords of 1971, in which the United States accepted the territorial boundaries of Eastern Europe. Then Nixon took a historic journey to the People's Republic of China in 1972, the first official contact with that country since the communists took power in 1949.

Another indication of a change in policy was the Strategic Arms Limitation Talks (SALT), which began in 1969. The SALT talks presumed that the United States and the Soviet Union each had an interest in retaining enough nuclear weapons to deter the other from an attack but that neither side had an interest in mutual destruction. Along with the lowering of east-west trade barriers, these efforts marked the start of a new era of communication and cooperation, or **détente** (a French word meaning "a relaxing"), between the United States and the Soviet Union.[9]

détente A French word meaning "a relaxing" and used to refer to an era of improved relations between the United States and the Soviet Union that began in the early 1970s.

Disintegration of the "Evil Empire"

Although the period of détente during the 1970s marked a major shift in U.S.-Soviet relations, it did not last. The Soviet invasion of Afghanistan in 1979 convinced U.S. leaders that the USSR was still bent on expansion and threatened Western interests in the oil-rich Middle East. Ronald Reagan, elected president in 1980, called for a renewed hard line toward the Soviet Union, which he described as the "evil empire."

U.S. policymakers did not fully realize it at the time, but the Soviet Union was collapsing under its heavy defense expenditures, isolation from Western technology and markets, and inefficient centralized command economy. In March 1985, Mikhail Gorbachev became the Soviet leader and proclaimed a need to restructure Soviet society, an initiative known as *perestroika*. He also ordered the withdrawal of Soviet troops from Afghanistan (which had become his country's Vietnam) and sought to reduce tensions with the United States.

Gorbachev's efforts came too late to save the Soviet Union. In 1989, the withdrawal of Soviet troops from Eastern Europe accelerated a prodemocracy movement that was already under way in the region. Poland initiated major reforms. Hungary dismantled the "iron curtain" that had blocked free travel to Austria. Then, in November, the Berlin Wall between East and West Germany—the most visible symbol of the separation of East and West—came down. On December 8, 1991, the leaders of the Russian, Belarus, and Ukrainian republics declared that the Soviet Union no longer existed.

A NEW WORLD ORDER

The end of the cold war prompted President George Bush to call for a "new world order." His formulation abandoned the assumption that world affairs are a zero-sum game, in which for one nation to gain something, another nation has to lose. Bush contended that nations can move forward together. The concept emphasized **multilateralism**—the idea that major nations should act together in response to problems and crises.[10]

multilateralism The situation in which nations act together in response to problems and crises.

Multilateralism characterized the U.S. response to Iraq's invasion of Kuwait in August 1990. President Bush worked through the United Nations, which demanded the unconditional withdrawal of Iraqi forces and imposed a trade embargo on Iraqi oil. The military force arrayed against Iraq was also nominally a UN force, although it was led by a U.S. commander and consisted mostly of U.S. troops. Several countries, including Germany and Japan, supported the effort with money instead of troops.

The Gulf operation was successful from a strictly military perspective. Despite the size and combat readiness of Iraq's army, the shooting war ended quickly, prompting President Bush to claim that the United States had "kicked the Vietnam syndrome [the legacy of America's defeat in Vietnam] once and for all." But the outcome of the Gulf War was much less successful from another perspective. Bush's decision to stop the war short of a march on Baghdad left Saddam Hussein in power, and he responded by repressing ethnic and religious minorities in Iraq and by defying UN directives that called for the destruction of Iraq's weapons of mass destruction. The United States has been forced to conduct periodic air strikes on Iraqi installations, which have helped contain Hussein but have not dislodged him from power.

Multilateralism has also been applied in the Balkans. In 1992, the Bosnian Serbs, supported by the Serb-dominated Yugoslav government, attacked Muslims and Croats in Bosnia. Forced evacuations and mass executions were part of the Serbs' effort to rid areas of Bosnia of rival ethnic and religious groups. Finally, in 1995, after UN economic sanctions and limited air strikes had failed to deter Serb aggression, planes of the United States and its Western allies undertook a bombing campaign that led to U.S.-negotiated peace talks (the Dayton Accords). The talks brought an end to hostilities and the deployment to Bosnia of sixty thousand peacekeeping troops (including twenty thousand from the United States). Whether this action will result in lasting peace in Bosnia is yet to be determined; the peacekeeping force, which was scheduled to remain in Bosnia for two years, is still there, serving as a buffer between the contending parties.

War in the Balkans flared again in 1999, after the Yugoslav Serbs began a campaign of "ethnic cleansing" in the Serbian province of Kosovo, which had a population that was 90 percent ethnic Albanian. After failed attempts at a negotiated settlement, planes from the NATO countries (North Atlantic Treaty Organization, discussed later in this chapter) attacked Serbia. (Yugoslavia is a federation that includes Serbia and Montenegro.) The mountainous terrain made air power less effective than it had been in the Iraqi desert, and the Serb army and militia units intensified their campaign against the ethnic Albanians, which created a refugee problem on a scale not seen in Europe since World War II. The refugees fled into neighboring Macedonia and Albania, which lacked the resources to handle the influx. The conflict also increased tensions between Russia and the West; Russia is a traditional ally of the Serbs and vehemently opposed the NATO action. The war with Serbia threatened to destabilize the entire region, and some foreign policy analysts concluded that NATO's military intervention had worsened an already bleak situation. Others argued that "Operation Allied Force" (as the NATO operation was officially labeled) was the only option left to Western leaders. Serbian President Slobodan Milosevic had blatantly pursued his campaign of ethnic cleansing, even in the face of Western economic sanctions and the threat of indictment by an international war crimes tribunal. After weeks of intensive bombing, Milosevic pulled his troops out of Kosovo. Ethnic Albanians moved back in, and despite the presence of UN peacekeeping troops, commenced revenge attacks on some of the Serbs who remained.

As these examples indicate, multilateralism has been only somewhat successful as a strategy for resolving international conflicts. With the deployment of enough resources, the world's major powers can intervene with some success in many parts of the developing world. However, these interventions are not always popular at home and offer no guarantee of long-term success. Regional and internal conflicts typically stem from enduring ethnic, religious, factional, or national hatreds or from chronic problems such as famine, overcrowding, or government corruption. Even if these hatreds or problems can be momentarily eased, they are often too deep-seated to be permanently resolved.

The Process of Foreign and Military Policymaking

National security is unlike other areas of government policy because it rests on relations with powers outside rather than within a country. Nations have sovereignty within their recognized territory; each nation is the ultimate governing authority over this territory and the people within it. In reality, the world is not composed of equal sovereign states. Some are more powerful than others, and the strong sometimes bully the weak. Nevertheless, there is no international body that is recognized by all nations as the final (sovereign) authority on disputes between them.

As a result, the chief instruments of national security policy—diplomacy, military force, economic exchange, and intelligence gathering—differ from those of domestic policy.

THE POLICYMAKING INSTRUMENTS

Diplomacy is the process of negotiation between countries. In most cases, nations prefer to settle their differences by talking rather than by fighting. By definition, acts of diplomacy involve negotiations between two (*bilateral*) or more (*multilateral*) nations.

Military power is a second instrument of foreign policy, and it can be used *unilaterally*—that is, by a single nation acting alone. Most countries use military power as a defensive measure; they maintain forces, or enter into military alliances with other countries, in order to protect themselves from potential aggressors. Throughout the history of nations, however, there have always been a few countries that use military force more actively. The United States is such a nation. In the nineteenth century, it used force to take territory from the Indian tribes and from Mexico and Spain. Although the United States has not pursued territorial goals since then, it has otherwise made frequent use of its military power. Recent examples include the unilateral invasions of Grenada in 1983, Panama in 1989, and Haiti in 1994; the multilateral war against Iraq in 1991; and the bombing of Bosnian Serbs in 1995 and Yugoslav Serbs in 1999.

Economic exchange is a third instrument of world politics. This aspect of international relations usually takes one of two forms—trade or assistance. Trade among nations is the more important form. Nearly all countries aspire to a strong trading position so as to have access to outside products and markets for their products. Some countries, however, are so weak economically that they require assistance from more prosperous countries. This assistance is typically designed to help both the weaker and stronger partners.

A fourth instrument of world politics is intelligence gathering, which is the process of monitoring other countries' activities. For many reasons, but primarily because all nations pursue their individual self-interest, each nation keeps a watchful eye on the others.

THE POLICYMAKING MACHINERY

In the case of the United States, the lead actor in the application of these instruments of foreign policy is the president. As we indicated in Chapters 14 and 15 and will discuss later in this chapter, the president shares power and responsibility for foreign and military policy with Congress, but the president has the stronger claim to leadership because of his constitutional roles as commander in chief, chief diplomat, and chief executive. For example, although President Clinton discussed his plans for invading Haiti with congressional leaders, he said the military operation would proceed even if they opposed it.

The president has an executive agency, the National Security Council (NSC), that provides advice on foreign and military issues. The NSC is chaired by the president and includes the vice president and the secretaries of state and defense as full members, and the director of the Central Intelligence Agency (CIA) and the chair of the Joint Chiefs of Staff as advisory members. Since State, Defense, and the CIA often have conflicting and self-centered views of national security, the NSC acts to keep the president in charge by providing a broader perspective. The NSC's staff of experts is directed by the president's national security adviser, who, with an office in the White House and access to defense, diplomatic, and intelligence sources, has become influential in the formulation of U.S. policy.

The complexity of international politics makes it impossible for any individual or government agency to direct U.S. policy single-handedly. Moreover, as a world power, the United States relies on outside institutions, such as the United Nations, to pursue some of its policy objectives. The key organizational units in

In a ceremony symbolizing America's role as world leader, President Clinton brings Palestinian leader Yasser Arafat (left) and Israeli prime minister Benjamin Netanyahu together for a historic handshake after the signing of an interim Mideast peace accord in 1998. King Hussein of Jordan (second from left and now deceased) looks on. Arafat and Netanyahu reached agreement during lengthy talks mediated by Clinton and held at Wye Plantation, Maryland.

the foreign policy area can be categorized according to their primary functions—defense, intelligence, diplomacy, and trade.

Defense Organizations

The Department of Defense (DOD), which has roughly 1.3 million uniformed personnel and seven hundred thousand civilian employees, is responsible for the military security of the United States (see Figure 20-1). DOD was created in 1947 when the three military services—the Army, Navy, and Air Force—were placed under the secretary of defense. Each service has its own secretary, but they report to the defense secretary, who represents all the services in relations with Congress and the president. Each service naturally regards its mission and budget as more important than those of the other services. The defense secretary helps reduce the adverse effects of these interservice rivalries.

The secretary of defense is always an important policymaker, but the influence of recent secretaries has varied widely, depending on the secretary's personality and the president's inclinations. Bush's defense secretary, Dick Cheney,

FIGURE 20-1   Department of Defense (DOD)
The DOD consists of the three uniformed services (Army, Navy, Air Force), the Joint Chiefs of Staff, and various commands and agencies. *Source: Department of Defense, 2000.*

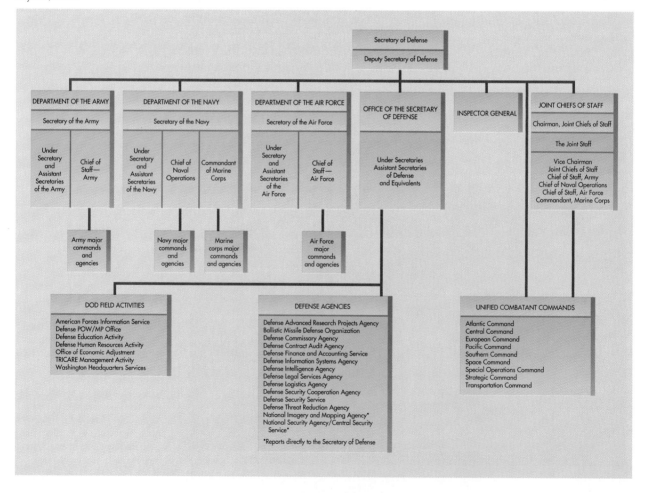

played a major and highly visible role, for example, in the planning of the Persian Gulf conflict.

The president also receives military advice from the Joint Chiefs of Staff (JCS). The JCS includes a chair, a vice chair, and a member from each of the uniformed services—the Army, Navy, Air Force, and Marine Corps. The JCS helps shape military strategy and evaluates the military's personnel and weapons needs. Whenever the members of the JCS disagree, the chair's view prevails. During the Persian Gulf War, General Colin Powell, the first African American to serve as JCS chair, was deeply involved in strategic decision making, including a controversial recommendation that President Bush halt the fighting before all major Iraqi combat units were destroyed.

Of the country's military alliances, the North Atlantic Treaty Organization (NATO) is the most important. NATO was created as a "forward defense" against the a possible Soviet invasion of Western Europe. The NATO forces, which include troops of the United States, Canada, and most Western European countries, conduct joint military exercises and engage in joint strategic and tactical military planning. After the demise of the Soviet Union, NATO was restructured as a smaller, more flexible force that might deal with new risks, such as international terrorism and ethnic rivalries. NATO's attack on Serbia in 1999 was the first ever military campaign for the alliance.

In 1997, NATO expanded its membership to include three countries of Eastern Europe, a change Russia opposed. Poland, Hungary, and the Czech Republic were once part of the Soviet military alliance (the Warsaw Pact countries), and Russia views NATO expansion as a threat to its interests. NATO leaders see an expanded European alliance as the best guarantee of lasting peace on the continent. (In 1999, European nations decided to create their own collective military force; the long-term implications for NATO are unclear.)

Intelligence Organizations

Foreign and military policy requires a high state of knowledge about what is happening in the world. Responsibility for the gathering of such information falls on specialized federal agencies, including the Central Intelligence Agency (CIA); the National Security Agency, which specializes in electronic communications analysis; and separate intelligence agencies within the Departments of State and Defense.[11] The federal government spends a vast amount annually on intelligence activities: $25 billion is roughly the figure for 2001.

With the decline of the Soviet threat, intelligence agencies have made increased efforts to stop international drug trafficking and terrorism. These efforts are a deterrent but cannot prevent all such activities. The U.S. embassies in Kenya and Tanzania, for example, had no advance warning when terrorist bombs blew them apart in 1998, killing several hundred people, including a dozen Americans.

Diplomatic Organizations

The U.S. Department of State conducts most of the country's day-to-day business with foreign countries through its embassies, headed by U.S. ambassadors. The department's traditional duties include negotiating political agreements with other nations, protecting U.S. citizens and interests abroad, promoting U.S.

Madeleine Albright is the first woman to serve as secretary of state. Her policy authority, like that of other federal executives, derives from acts of Congress and from the president's constitutional powers.

economic interests, gathering foreign intelligence, and representing the United States abroad. For all its activities and prominence, the State Department is relatively small. Only about twenty-five thousand people—foreign service officers, policy analysts, administrators, and others—work in State. Some observers regard the State Department as tradition-bound and less central to foreign policy decision making than its reputation seems to suggest.

The secretary of state is often described as second in importance only to the president within the executive branch in the determination of national security policy. Whether the secretary, in fact, has this level of influence depends on the president's willingness to rely heavily on the secretary. Madeleine Albright, secretary of state under Clinton, took a leading role in foreign policy, including the effort to negotiate a comprehensive peace settlement in the Middle East.

American's diplomatic efforts also take place through international organizations, such as the Organization of American States (OAS) and the United Nations. The UN was established after the Second World War by the victorious allies.[12] Its security council, which included the United States, France, Britain, the Soviet Union, and the Republic of China, was to be an instrument of multilateral policymaking; the world's strongest powers would work together for global harmony and prosperity. When the United States and Soviet Union entered into the cold war, all hope of such cooperation vanished.

The breakdown of the Soviet bloc in 1989 renewed the possibility that the world's great powers could work together to achieve common goals. The first major opportunity came in the Persian Gulf conflict of 1990–91, when the United States led a UN force that first blocked Iraqi forces and then attacked them. Some analysts believe that the UN may finally be able to play the large role in international affairs that was envisioned for it when it was chartered. International terrorism, ethnic conflict, and drug trafficking are among the problems that the UN has recently addressed.

Other analysts believe the United Nations is basically unsuited to the role of global arbiter on a large scale. UN operations are normally effective only to the degree that member nations are in agreement on a course of action and have the resolve to implement it fully. This agreement and resolve are often lacking because nations have conflicting objectives. Moreover, the realities of politics

Since the end of the cold war, the United Nations has played an increasingly large role in international politics. Shown here is a court session at The Hague, Netherlands, where a UN war crimes tribunal is investigating those accused of genocide, murder, torture, and rape in Bosnia and Kosovo.

require national leaders to be more responsive to domestic public opinion than to the views of the international community. The killing of U.S. troops in Somalia turned American public opinion against the country's participation in the UN operation there, and President Clinton responded by withdrawing U.S. forces.

Although the United States was the leader in the formation of the United Nations, U.S. politicians have had divided opinions of the organization. Critics say the United States pays an unfair share of the UN's costs and argue that U.S. troops should only serve under the direct command of U.S. officers.

Economic Organizations

The shift in emphasis in global affairs from military forces to economic markets has brought to the fore a new set of government agencies, those representing economic sectors. The Agriculture, Commerce, Labor, and Treasury Departments are playing increasingly important roles in foreign affairs. In addition, some specialty agencies, such as the Federal Trade Commission and the Export-Import Bank of the United States, are involved in international trade and finance.

The United States also works through major international organizations that promote goals, such as economic development and free trade, that are consistent with U.S. policy objectives. The newest of these international organizations is the World Trade Organization (WTO), which was created in 1995 and is the formal institution through which most nations negotiate general rules of international trade. The WTO also adjudicates disagreements over the meaning of these rules. In 1998, for example, U.S.-based Kodak films lost a dispute with the Japanese film company Fuji. Kodak had charged that Fuji was involved in unfair marketing practices, which prevented Kodak from gaining a significant share of film sales in Japan. The WTO sided with Fuji's argument that its sales volume was a result of the quality of its film and customer preference.

The World Bank and the International Monetary Fund (IMF) are older institutions. Created at the 1944 Bretton Woods Conference by the United States and Great Britain, they are designed to assist developing countries. The World Bank makes long-term loans to poor countries for capital investment projects, such as the construction of dams, power plants, highways, and factories, that will promote economic growth. In contrast, the IMF makes short-term loans so that countries experiencing temporary problems will not collapse economically or resort to ruinous practices, such as the imposition of high tariffs. In 1997 and 1998, for example, the IMF made multi-billion-dollar loans to Korea, Thailand, and other Asian countries whose economies had gone into a tailspin from poor investment practices and currency devaluation.

The Military Dimension of National Security Policy

The dissolution of the Soviet Union brought about the first significant scaling back of U.S. defense spending since the end of the Vietnam War (see Figure 20-2). Nevertheless, the United States spends far more on defense, in both relative and absolute terms, than its allies do. On a per capita basis, U.S. military spending is more than twice that of other members of the NATO alliance (see "How the United States Compares"). The U.S. defense budget is second to none in the world, but so is the military power it buys. During the Gulf War, the Iraqi army, fourth largest in the world, was no match for the United States' superior military equipment and technology. The war lasted about six weeks, with fewer than 200 U.S. casualties, but left an estimated 50,000 to 100,000 Iraqi dead.

DEFENSE CAPABILITY

The United States owes its status as the world's only superpower in part to the strength of its conventional forces. The U.S. Navy has a dozen aircraft carriers, nearly one hundred attack submarines, and hundreds of other fighting and supply ships. The U.S. Air Force has thousands of high-performance aircraft. The U.S. Army has more than five hundred thousand troops on active duty, and

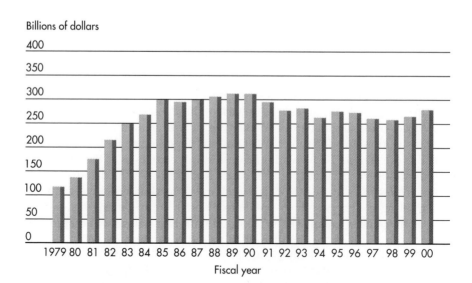

FIGURE 20-2 Defense Expenditures
Spending on national defense rose sharply during the early 1980s. It has since declined, largely because of the federal budget deficit and the end of the cold war. *Source: Office of Management and Budget.*

HOW THE UNITED STATES COMPARES

THE BURDEN OF MILITARY SPENDING

The United States bears a disproportionate share of the defense costs of the NATO alliance. The U.S. military establishment is huge and is deployed all over the world, and the taxpayers spend more than $250 billion per year to maintain it. These expenditures directly account for roughly 5 percent of the U.S. gross national product (GNP). By comparison, defense spending by Germany, Italy, and Canada accounts for 3 percent or less of their GNPs. The percentages for Britain and France are higher but not as high as for the United States. Japan, which is not part of NATO, spends only 1 percent of its GNP on defense. Japan's small military force is confined by World War II peace agreements to the country's islands and the adjoining waters.

The United States has pressured its allies to carry a larger share of the defense burden, but these countries have resisted, contending that the cost would be too high and that their security would not be substantially improved. A partial exception to this situation was the Persian Gulf War. U.S. troops and equipment accounted for the bulk of the military strength arrayed against Iraq, but the financial cost of the war effort was borne by other countries. Germany, Japan, Saudi Arabia, and Kuwait were among the countries that helped fund the war. In fact, other countries gave the United States $20 billion more than it spent on the war.

The chart below indicates the approximate per capita level of defense spending in the United States and countries with which it is closely aligned.

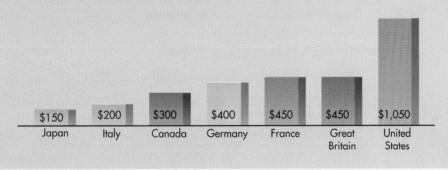

$150	$200	$300	$400	$450	$450	$1,050
Japan	Italy	Canada	Germany	France	Great Britain	United States

SOURCE: OECD and Defense Department statistics.

they are amply supported by tanks, artillery pieces, armored personnel carriers, and attack helicopters.

The capability of U.S. conventional forces rests substantially on the advanced state of their weaponry. The computer has revolutionized weapons systems, and the United States has been the world leader in this development. In the Gulf War, Iraq's Soviet-built tanks were virtual deathtraps when pitted against U.S. precision-guided bombs and missiles. Iraq's air defenses were overwhelmed by the U.S. Air Force's F-117 Stealth attack planes, which are virtually undetectable by radar. To maintain this technological superiority, the Pentagon is already at work on the next generation of weaponry. It will include weapons that are not only "smart" (precision-guided) but "brilliant" (able on their own to seek and identify enemy targets). An example is a long-range missile under development that will search out and destroy armored vehicles up to two hundred miles away. Such weaponry could make tanks as obsolete as the horse cavalry they replaced. According to observers, no other nation is anywhere close to the United States in the testing and production of advanced weapon systems.[13]

Assessments of military power have traditionally been based on the number of planes, tanks, and other weapons a nation possessed, and how those numbers compared with those of potential adversaries. But, increasingly, these assessments must also account for the ability of a nation to connect these weapons to information. Surveillance devices (such as satellites), high-speed computers, and sophisticated software give military commanders the ability to gather, process, and disseminate information about tactical and strategic situations and thus to direct the use of available weaponry in the most efficient and effective way. The United States has a substantial lead in this area and will retain it for years to come.

Even though there is a "revolution in military power," older weapons systems are still a part of the American arsenal. The nuclear weapons that starkly defined the nation's cold war with the Soviet Union are an example. During the cold war, the United States followed a policy of **deterrence,** which included a nuclear arsenal capable of destroying the Soviet Union many times over. Deterrence was based on the notion that the Soviet Union would be deterred from launching a nuclear attack by the knowledge that, even if it destroyed the United States, it too would be obliterated.

deterrence The idea that nuclear war can be discouraged if each side in a conflict has the capacity to destroy the other with nuclear weapons.

THE USES OF MILITARY POWER

U.S. military forces have been trained for or called upon for six types of military action.

Unlimited Nuclear Warfare

The idea of an all-out nuclear war was always too horrible to imagine, but the fear of nuclear holocaust has diminished since the cold war ended. The United States and Russia have reduced their nuclear arsenals and have created monitoring systems that are designed to reduce the possibility that either side could launch a surprise attack. Nevertheless, both sides retain their capacity for a full-scale nuclear war. America's nuclear weapons are deployed in what is called the "nuclear triad," which refers to the three ways in which these weapons can be launched—by land-based missiles, submarine-based missiles, and bombers. The triad provides a "second-strike capability"—the ability to absorb a first-strike nuclear attack and survive with enough nuclear power for massive retaliation (second strike).

Limited Nuclear Warfare

Some experts believe that, while the risk of an all-out nuclear attack on the United States has diminished, the possibility that a single nuclear weapon might be used against the United States may have increased. A major concern arising from the breakup of the Soviet Union has been control of its nuclear weapons, strategic and tactical. In addition, terrorist groups and "outlaw" regimes, such as Iraq, are a threat because the technology and materials that are required to build nuclear weapons are more widely accessible than ever before. Accordingly, the United States, Russia, and other nuclear powers are cooperating to reduce the spread of nuclear weapons. One goal of the Persian Gulf conflict was the destruction of Iraq's nuclear program.

Unlimited Conventional Warfare

The end of the cold war has also reduced the prospect of an unlimited conventional war. A great part of U.S. military preparedness and strategy in the past half century was based on the scenario of an invasion of Western Europe by the Soviet Union and its allies. Even if the cold war should begin anew, Russia or any other part of the former Soviet Union would require years to build its military capacity to the point where it could pose a credible threat to the west. Since the end of the cold war, U.S. policy has aimed to prevent a resurgence of aggressive Russian nationalism. Through economic and other forms of encouragement, the United States and other industrialized nations have sought to assist Russia in a transition toward a more open and democratic political system.

Limited Conventional Warfare

Recent conflicts in the Gulf and the Balkans have demonstrated that the United States has the military capacity to punish a well-armed foe. These conflicts have not demonstrated, however, that limited conventional wars routinely produce satisfactory results over the longer term. The reason is simple enough. If a political problem can be easily resolved, there is almost never a reason to apply military force. Diplomatic, economic, and other forms of intervention are normally sufficient to achieve a resolution. Limited conventional warfare comes into play when other methods fail—that is, when the division between the contending parties is too deep to be resolved peacefully or when an aggressor is unrelenting. However, military force is unlikely to correct the problem that triggered the military response. Thus, in the Persian Gulf and Kosovo, military intervention by the United States punished the aggressor party but did not settle the underlying dispute.

Before the 1970s, limited conventional warfare was seen as an instrument of containment policy. Since then, some analysts have questioned whether the United States has a coherent strategy for the limited use of its military power. They argue that U.S. intervention has been sporadic and restricted by a determination to avoid casualties, which results in a reliance on air power even in those situations where military objectives would require the full use of ground forces. They cite the continuing threat that Iraq poses in the Gulf region and that Serbs pose in the Balkans as evidence of the lack of a coherent strategy.

U.S. policymakers have defended the tendency to rely on air power by saying that the American public, since Vietnam, has been unwilling to support military operations that would incur high casualties and that, in any event, the strategic goal did not include total victory. Said a Bush administration official about the Gulf War: "The President was not prepared to pay the political price that increased American casualties would have involved or to take responsibility for putting Iraq back together after an unconditional surrender or to

In the jungle warfare of Vietnam, American soldiers had difficulty finding the enemy and adapting to guerrilla tactics.

figure out how to contain the power of Iran and Syria once the Iraqi regime was destroyed."[14]

Counterinsurgency

insurgency   A type of military conflict in which irregular soldiers rise up against an established regime.

The Vietnam conflict was an **insurgency,** an uprising by irregular forces against an established government. In most Third World countries, insurgencies originate in the grievances of people who are struggling against the monopoly of economic and political power by a ruling elite. In the past, the insurgents often received support in the form of military equipment from the Soviet Union. Most insurgencies were therefore seen by the United States as a threat to its political and economic interests.

U.S. involvement in Third World insurgencies dropped sharply after Vietnam and diminished even further with the end of the cold war. Neither the American public nor U.S. officials have wanted to involve the nation deeply in such wars, although more limited activities, such as the training and equipping of foreign troops, are a part of U.S. defense policy.

Police-Type Action

With the end of the cold war, U.S. policymakers began to pay closer attention to other global problems, including drug trafficking, political instability, population movement, and terrorism. The U.S. military has become increasingly involved with these problems. U.S. peacekeeping missions in Somalia, the Balkans, and Haiti are examples, as is the use of U.S. military advisers in drug-interdiction operations in Latin America. U.S. military personnel have also been used to stop boat people from Cuba, Haiti, and other Caribbean islands from entering the United States illegally.

U.S. military commanders have been reluctant to expand their mission to include police-type actions, such as immigration control, that traditionally have been a civilian responsibility. But given the high cost of keeping a large defense

Pictured here is a U.S. attack helicopter. America's military power rests substantially on the advanced state of its weaponry.

force, the absence of a highly visible and dangerous enemy such as the former Soviet Union, and the increase in the types of problems that require police-type action, it is likely that the pressure to use U.S. troops in unconventional ways will continue.

THE POLITICS OF NATIONAL DEFENSE

All Americans would agree that the physical security of the United States is of paramount concern. The consensus breaks down, however, on specific issues. The Vietnam conflict created deep and lasting divisions of opinion over the proper uses of America's military capacity. In contrast, U.S. policy in the Persian Gulf crisis had majority support from start to end.

Public Opinion and Elite Conflict

Defense policy is a mix of *majoritarian* and *elite* politics. On issues of broad national concern, majority opinion is a vital component.[15] It was public opinion, for example, that ultimately forced U.S. policymakers to withdraw American troops from Vietnam and Somalia.

Debates over foreign and defense policy, however, typically take place among political elites.[16] Most citizens are not interested enough to contribute significantly to most of these debates. Few Americans, for example, can name even half the countries in Africa, much less speak knowledgeably about their politics. This situation gives officials and foreign policy specialists wide latitude in determining policy.

The Military-Industrial Complex

Political disputes over defense policy are more than honest differences of opinion among people. They also involve billions of dollars in jobs and contracts.[17] In fiscal year 2000, the U.S. defense budget exceeded $250 billion, or roughly 5 percent of the gross national product. A high level of defense spending has been justified by reference to the nation's security needs. However, an alternative explanation for high defense spending points to the demands of the U.S. armed services and defense firms. In his 1961 farewell address, President Dwight D. Eisenhower warned against the "unwarranted influence" and "misplaced power" of what he termed "the military-industrial complex."[18]

military-industrial complex
The three components (the military establishment, the industries that manufacture weapons, and the members of Congress from states and districts that depend heavily on the arms industry) that mutually benefit from a high level of defense spending.

The **military-industrial complex** has three components: the military establishment, the industries that manufacture weapons, and the members of Congress from states and districts that depend heavily on the arms industry. The military-industrial complex is not, as is sometimes suggested, a well-coordinated, unified network of interests engaged in a conspiracy to keep the United States on a wartime footing. Rather, it is an aggregation of interests that benefit from a high level of defense spending, regardless of whether these expenditures can be justified from the standpoint of national security.

Many U.S. firms could not flourish without military contracts, and some could not survive at all, for they produce only military equipment. These firms obviously do not act only out of patriotism; they are profit-making organizations whose business includes the aggressive marketing of weapons. They often get a receptive response from members of Congress from states and districts that depend heavily on defense contracts. The economic impact of even a single weapon system can be substantial. The B-1 bomber, for example, was built with the help of 5,200 subcontractors located in forty-eight states and in all but a handful of congressional districts. "This geographic spread gives all sections of the country an important stake in the airplane," one assessment of the B-1 concluded.[19] Without doubt, some proportion of U.S. defense spending reflects the workings of the military-industrial complex rather than the requirements of national security. The problem is that no one knows exactly what this proportion is, and the estimates vary widely.

www.mhhe.com/patterson5

Graphic

Defense firms have been hurt by recent cutbacks in U.S. military spending, and they have turned to export sales. Nine of the world's ten largest arms-making companies are American firms, and they currently control about two-thirds of the world's arms sales.[20]

The Economic Dimension of National Security Policy

Economic considerations are a vital component of national security policy. In the simplest sense, economic strength is a prerequisite of military strength: a powerful defense establishment can only be maintained by a country that is economically well off. In a broader and more important sense, economic prosperity enables a people to "secure" their way of life. As President Eisenhower said, it is folly to weaken at home what one is trying to strengthen abroad.

The cold war sometimes hid the essential truth of this observation. Global power, in addition to being a means by which nations achieved other goals, became an end in itself. The Soviet Union paid the highest price. In the end, its status as a military superpower was achieved at the expense of economic growth and development and ultimately led to its collapse.[21] The United States may also have paid a stiff price. In a widely read book, *The Rise and Fall of the Great*

Powers, Paul Kennedy concluded that the United States had succumbed to "imperial overstretch" by straining its resources to maintain its superpower status and, in the process, had weakened its domestic economic base.[22]

A CHANGING WORLD ECONOMY

However, some aspects of U.S. superpower policy had clear economic benefits. The sharpest example is the European Recovery Plan, better known as the Marshall Plan. Proposed in 1947 and named after one of its chief architects, the widely respected General George Marshall, it is perhaps the boldest and most successful U.S. foreign policy initiative of the twentieth century. It called for $3 billion in immediate aid for the postwar rebuilding of Europe, with an additional $10 billion or so to follow. The Marshall Plan was unprecedented both in its scope (today, the equivalent cost would be more than $100 billion) and in its implications—for the first time, the United States had committed itself to a continuing major role in European affairs. Through the Marshall Plan, the countries of Western Europe regained economic and political stability in a relatively short time.

Apart from enabling the countries of Western Europe to better confront the perceived Soviet military and political threat, the Marshall Plan was also designed to meet the economic needs of the United States. Wartime production had lifted the country out of the Great Depression, but the end of the war in 1945 brought a recession and renewed fears of hard times. A rejuvenated Western Europe furnished a market for U.S. goods. In effect, Western Europe became a junior partner within a system of global trade that worked to the advantage of the United States.

Since then, major changes have taken place in the world economy. Germany and Japan have become economic rivals of the United States. Trade between these countries results in a deficit for the United States, particularly in the case of trade with Japan. The United States imports billions more annually in goods and services from Japan than it exports to that country. In addition, Western Europe, including Germany, has become a less-receptive market for U.S. goods. European countries are now each other's best customers, trading among themselves through the European Union (EU).

In economic terms, the world can best be described as tripolar—in other words, economic power is concentrated in three centers. One center is the United States, which produces roughly 20 percent of the world's goods and services. Another center is Japan, which accounts for 10 percent of the world's economy; China and its fast-growing economy can also be located in this center. The third and largest economic center, with more than 25 percent of the world's gross product, is the EU, which includes Belgium, Denmark, France, Germany, Great Britain, Greece, Ireland, Italy, Luxembourg, the Netherlands, Portugal, Spain, Sweden, Finland, and Austria.

By a few indicators, the United States is the weakest of the three economic centers: it has, for example, the worst trade imbalance. In other ways, however, the United States is the strongest of the three economic powers. Its economy is more well-rounded. Like the EU and Japan, the United States has a strong industrial base, but unlike Japan, it also has a strong agricultural sector, and unlike both Japan and the EU, it has abundant natural resources. Its vast fertile plains have made it the world's leading agricultural producer. The United

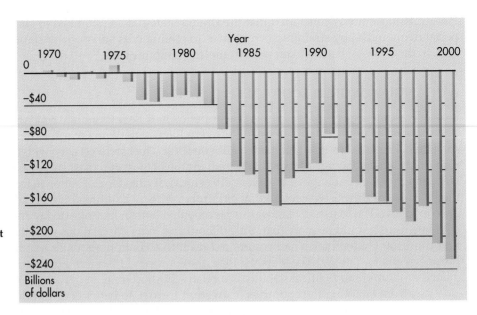

FIGURE 20-3   The Trade Deficit Not since 1975 has the United States had a trade surplus; the deficit reached a record level in 2000. *Source: U.S. Bureau of Census, Trade Data Services, 2000.*

States ranks among the top three countries worldwide in production of wheat, corn, potatoes, peanuts, cotton, eggs, cattle, and pigs. As for natural resources, the United States ranks among the top five nations in copper, uranium, lead, sulfur, zinc, coal, gold, iron ore, natural gas, silver, and magnesium.[23]

As we discussed in Chapter 18, the United States also ranks highest in the world in terms of its global economic competitiveness. This ranking was assigned by the Switzerland-based Institute for Management Development, which bases its competitiveness surveys on countries' capacity to generate wealth. The United States owes its position to such factors as the strength of its domestic economy and its technical know-how.[24]

This competitive advantage has been evident since the early 1990s. As Asia and parts of Europe has struggled with slow growth rates, the United States has enjoyed high employment and steady economic growth without the accelerated inflation that normally accompanies such a period. The gloomy economic projections of Paul Kennedy and others in the late 1980s have proven wrong, and other countries have increasingly looked to the United States, and particularly its high-flying technology sector, for policy and market innovations that could spark their own economic expansion.

www.mhhe.com/patterson5

Graphic

One area where the United States has struggled is its balance of trade. In terms of total goods and services, the United States is the world's leading exporting nation. U.S. firms export roughly $1 trillion in goods and services each year. The problem is that imports to the United States are even greater. The effect is a substantial trade deficit. The United States has not had a trade surplus in any year since 1975 and recently has had annual deficits of $150 billion or more (see Figure 20-3).

AMERICAN GOALS IN THE GLOBAL ECONOMY

The United States depends on other countries for raw materials, finished goods, and capital to meet Americans' production and consumption demands. Meeting

Microsoft's Bill Gates speaks to an audience about his firm's international scope. Global trade opportunities for American business firms have become an increasingly important objective of U.S. foreign policy.

this objective requires the United States to have influence on world markets. The broad goals of the United States in the world economy include:

• Sustaining a stable and open system of trade that will promote prosperity at home
• Maintaining access to energy and other resources that are vital to the regular functioning of the U.S. economy
• Keeping the widening gap between the rich and poor countries from destabilizing the world's economy[25]

Global trade has also been linked with other U.S. objectives, including the strengthening of human rights and the spread of democracy. It is generally assumed that a market-based economy promotes the social, economic, and political development that fosters individualism and a demand for freedom of expression and travel. Yet there is the question of whether the United States should develop close trading relations with countries that have poor human rights records.

Global Trade

Since the end of the cold war, U.S. foreign policy has centered on the global economy. International commerce is not only more competitive than in the past; it is more important. Nations' economies are increasingly interconnected as a result of the transportation and communication revolution. Because of it, **multinational corporations** (firms with major operations in more than one country) now find it easy to manage worldwide operations. From a headquarters in New York, a firm has no difficulty directing a production facility in Thailand that is filling orders for markets in Europe and South America. Money, goods, and services now flow freely and quickly across national borders, and large firms increasingly think about markets in global rather than national terms. And as firms have adjusted their behavior, nations have also had to adjust. U.S. presidents once went abroad primarily to strengthen security alliances. Presidents

multinational corporations
Business firms with major operations in more than one country.

economic globalization The increased interdependence of nations' economies. The change is a result of technological, transportation, and communication advances that have enabled firms to deploy their resources across the globe.

Bush and Clinton traveled primarily for the purpose of strengthening trade relations and negotiating international economic agreements.

Economic globalization is a term that describes the increased interdependence of nations' economies. This development is both an opportunity and a threat to U.S. economic interests. The opportunity rests with the possibility of increased demand abroad for U.S. goods and services as a result of open trade with other countries and economic growth within these countries. The threat lies in the fact that foreign firms also compete in the global marketplace and may use their competitive advantages, such as cheaper labor, to outposition U.S. firms. In addition, as nations' economies become more interdependent, instability in one market can spread quickly to others, causing a broad decline in the global economy.

The effect of interdependency was evident in the summer of 1998 when the U.S. stock market dropped sharply in response to adverse economic developments in Asia and Latin America. The economic downturn in these regions also affected the U.S. balance of trade. As their economies slowed, their demand for goods declined, and U.S. exports declined accordingly. In addition, as the value of currency in these regions dropped, U.S. firms had to compete at home with foreign goods that were suddenly lower in price. The net effect was a record trade deficit in 1998 of $180 billion.

Not surprisingly, global economic stability has been a high priority for U.S. officials. Working unilaterally and through international organizations such as the World Bank and IMF, the U.S. government has provided financial and other assistance when economic instability occurs elsewhere in the world. The United States has also pressured other nations to reform their economic policies to meet the demands of a global marketplace. Banking reforms in Japan, Thailand, and Indonesia are examples of the type of changes the United States has sought. New international financial institutions that would be tailored to the demands of the new global economy have also been part of the U.S. policy agenda.

If U.S. policymakers are generally in agreement on the need for stable international markets, they are divided over a second issue: free trade. Although the principle of free trade is widely embraced as a linchpin of the global economy, it is a contentious issue in specific contexts. In simple terms, the opposing sides on trade issues can be described as the protectionism and the free-trade positions. **Protectionism** emphasizes the immediate interests of domestic producers and includes measures designed to enable them to compete successfully in the domestic market with foreign competitors. For some protectionists, the issue is simply a matter of defending domestic firms against the actions of their foreign competitors. For others, the issue is one of "fair trade." They become protectionist in those instances where foreign firms have an unfair competitive advantage, as, for example, when they are subsidized by their government, which allows them to market their goods at an artificially low price.

protectionism The view that the immediate interests of domestic producers should have a higher priority (through, for example, protective tariffs) than should free trade between nations.

The Congress is a center of protectionist sentiment in the United States. Many members of Congress are determined to protect locally operating firms that are adversely affected by foreign competitors. In fact, most Americans believe that free trade results in a loss of jobs to low-wage countries. But there is a paradoxical aspect to this opinion; most Americans also say that they favor free trade mechanisms as long as the process is fair to all sides (see Figure 20-4).

free trade The view that the long-term economic interests of all countries are advanced when tariffs and other trade barriers are kept to a minimum.

The **free trade** position assumes that the long-term economic interests of all countries are advanced when tariffs and other trade barriers are kept to a

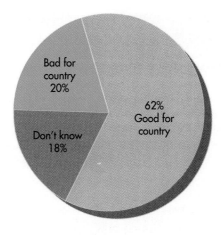

FIGURE 20-4   Opinions on World Trade Organization Most Americans believe U.S. participation in the World Trade Organization is good for the country, although they worry that free trade results in lost jobs and lower wages for American workers. *Source: From Pew Research Center for the People & the Press, April–May, 2000. Used by permission.*

minimum. Most free-trade advocates couple their advocacy with fair-trade demands, but they are committed philosophically and in practice to the idea that free trade fuels economic growth and results in a net gain for U.S. business.

The political leadership on free trade has usually come from the White House, although it is fair to say that most members of Congress, except on vital interests affecting their constituencies, support the principle of global free trade. But presidents have been stronger advocates of free trade as a result of their tendency to take a national view of issues. All recent presidents have embraced the notion that free trade promotes growth and produces a net gain for U.S. firms and workers. And since their political fortunes tend to rise and fall with the overall strength of the nation's economy, presidents have typically pursued free-trade policies. In the 2000 presidential election, both of the major-party nominees were free-trade advocates, ensuring that the pattern will carry into the new administration.

Opposing views on global trade clashed in 1993 over the issue of the North American Free Trade Agreement (NAFTA), which aims to create an EU-type market among the United States, Canada, and Mexico. Opponents of the agreement, who included organized labor, most environmental groups, and a majority of the Democrats in Congress, argued that it would result in the loss of countless jobs to Mexico. Its proponents, who included President Clinton, most large U.S. corporations, and most congressional Republicans, contended that the agreement would boost the economies of all three countries and was necessary if the United States was to maintain a leading position in global trade. The measure obtained majority support in Congress, but only after side agreements were worked out to protect some American producers from the adverse effects of open trade in North America.

In 1997, NAFTA was once again a focus of debate in Congress, but this time in the context of a proposal to extend the president's fast-track trade negotiation authority. This authority allows the president to negotiate trade agreements with other countries, which are then submitted to Congress for an up or down vote. Congress can defeat but cannot amend such agreements. Labor, environmental groups, and a majority of Democrats in Congress opposed the extension, saying that trade agreements routinely fail to protect workers and the environment and that Congress ought to retain authority to amend any agreement

★ STATES IN THE NATION

FOREIGN EXPORTS AND STATE ECONOMIES

The states differ considerably in the extent to which their economies depend on foreign exports. The state of Washington, with its aerospace, fishing, and logging industries and proximity to Canada and Asia, is the leading exporter. Trade with foreign countries accounts for 22 percent of the state's economy. Louisiana (16 percent), Alaska (11 percent), and Vermont (11 percent) are the only other states whose exports exceed 10 percent of the total state economy.

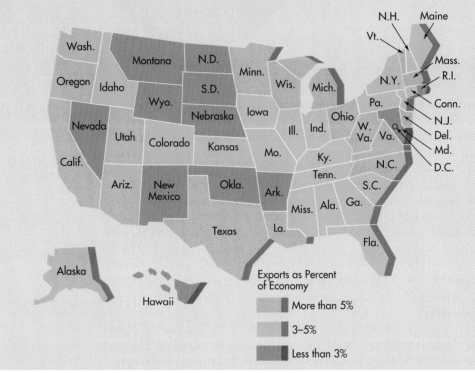

Exports as Percent of Economy

- More than 5%
- 3–5%
- Less than 3%

SOURCE: U.S. Bureau of the Census.

negotiated by the president. They argued that NAFTA had been an environmental and employment nightmare; for example, recently constructed factories on the Mexican side of the border were dumping tons of pollutants into the Rio Grande. This time, the opponents of free trade prevailed; the proposal to extend the president's fast-track authority was defeated.

In general, however, momentum is on the side of free-trade advocates. A prime example is the General Agreement on Tariffs and Trade (GATT), which received congressional approval in 1994 and was also ratified by most other countries. GATT established rules aimed at creating a nearly global free market: the rules lower worldwide tariffs by a third, strengthen protection of intellectual property (such as patents and copyrights), and create panels that will arbitrate trade disputes and establish standards in areas such as the environment, securities, and worker safety. This multilateral trading system is coordinated by the World Trade Organization (WTO), which was established in 1995 as the successor to GATT. The WTO's member nations (roughly 130 in number) have basically committed themselves to an open trade policy buttressed by regulations that are designed to ensure fair play among the participants.

The WTO, however, is certain to be the target of intense criticism. Some Americans oppose, in principle, any international organization with the power to set policy that is binding on the United States. The WTO will be no different in this respect than the UN has been. The WTO will also be subject to more precise forms of pressure, as was evident when mass protests disrupted the 1999 WTO Conference in Seattle. To gain support among member nations, the WTO has focused on trade barriers and has shied from issues that are more contentious, such as a country's labor laws. The Seattle protests, which drew international activists as well as ones from the United States, were aimed at forcing the WTO to take environmental and labor practices (for example, child labor) into account in its trade agreements. It is generally conceded that the Seattle protests were but one round in what is sure to be a protracted struggle over the shape of global trade policy.

Access to Natural Resources

Although the United States is rich in natural resources, it is not self-sufficient. The major deficiency is oil; domestic production provides for only about half the nation's use.

Outside the United States, most of the world's oil is found in the Middle East, Latin America, and Russia. Access to this oil has occurred mainly through the marketplace, but U.S. military force has also been instrumental. In the Middle East, for example, U.S. oil companies controlled one-tenth of Middle Eastern oil reserves before World War II began. Just twenty years later, they controlled six-tenths.[26] This change was in part the result of the ability of U.S. firms after the war to furnish the capital to reopen oil fields damaged by the conflict and to open new fields. The United States also gained leverage through its support of reactionary regimes in Iran and other Middle Eastern countries, which responded by giving U.S. firms a larger role in their oil production.

The 1990–91 war in the Persian Gulf is a more recent example of how U.S. military force has served the nation's resource needs. Iraq's invasion of oil-rich Kuwait threatened western supplies, and its defeat quelled the threat.

In general, however, military power has increasingly become a less-effective means of preserving economic leverage. Economic interdependence has made military intervention mostly counterproductive. For example, when Iranian fundamentalists took over the U.S. embassy in Teheran in 1979, one of the reasons the United States refrained from attacking Iran's oil fields was that the action would have substantially reduced the Middle East's oil-producing capacity.

Relations with the Developing World

Political instability in the less developed countries, as in the case of Iraq's invasion of Kuwait, is disruptive to world markets. Less developed countries also offer marketplace opportunities. In order to progress, they need to acquire the

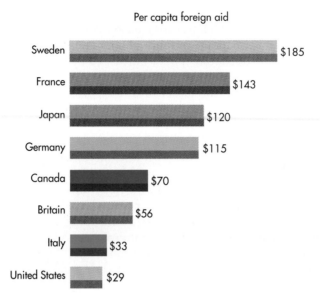

Per capita foreign aid

Sweden — $185
France — $143
Japan — $120
Germany — $115
Canada — $70
Britain — $56
Italy — $33
United States — $29

FIGURE 20-5   Per Capita Assistance to Developing Countries
The United States ranks relatively high (though not the highest) in terms of total amount spent on foreign aid to developing countries but ranks low in terms of per capita expenditures. *Source: OECD (Organization for Economic Cooperation and Development), 1998.*

goods and services that more industrialized countries can provide. To foster this demand, the United States and the other industrialized countries provide developmental assistance to poorer countries. These contributions include direct foreign aid and also indirect assistance through international organizations such as the IMF and the World Bank. Since World War II, the United States has been far and away the leading source of aid to the developing countries of the world. The United States is still a major contributor but is now far down the list in terms of its per capita annual contributions (see Figure 20-5). The primary recipient of U.S. foreign aid is Israel, which gets more than a third of the total.

Foreign aid is a prime target of politicians. Upon being named chair of the Senate Foreign Relations Committee, Jesse Helms (R-N.C.) said he would trim millions in aid "going down foreign ratholes."[27] Many Americans share the view that the United States ought not to be funding discretionary programs abroad when there are pressing needs at home. The unpopularity of foreign aid is also a consequence of the public's exaggerated notion of how much the United States spends in this area. In a 1994 poll that asked respondents to name the largest federal programs, foreign aid was at the top of the list (27 percent said it was the most expensive federal program). In fact, foreign aid is near the bottom, accounting for less than 1 percent of the total federal budget.[28]

Foreign aid accounts for only some of the funds that flow from the United States to developing countries: private investment is another source. U.S. firms invest more heavily abroad than do firms from any other country. In 1998, U.S. multinational corporations invested roughly $50 billion abroad. Foreign investment by U.S.-based multinationals works to America's advantage in at least two important ways. First, it sends a flow of overseas profits back to the United States, which strengthens the country's financial base. Second, it makes other nations dependent on the prosperity of the United States; their economies are linked to U.S. businesses.[29]

Economic development and foreign aid were the focus of President Clinton's 1998 trip to sub-Saharan Africa, the first such trip by an American president. In

American foreign policy has always been an amalgam of ideals and hard realities. During his 1998 trip to China, the first such presidential visit since the Tiananmen Square massacre of prodemocracy demonstrators nearly a decade earlier, President Clinton spoke of the importance of democracy and personal freedom while also working to strengthen economic and diplomatic ties between the United States and China.

Johannesburg, South Africa, Clinton said that while economic development was the long-term goal, it was not a substitute for short-term assistance. "Trade cannot replace aid when there is still so much poverty," the president said.[30] During the cold war, the United States had been willing to back almost any type of regime in Africa as long as it was aligned against the Soviet Union. Since then, the United States has had a different view of Africa, much as its view of Asia, Eastern Europe, and South America has changed. The emphasis has been on economic trade, human rights, and democratic institutions. These objectives, more clearly now than at any time since World War I, are the foundation of U.S. foreign policy.

Some critics suggest that the United States has placed too much emphasis on trade issues and not enough on issues of human rights and democracy. Trade with China, in particular, has been a point of contention. The Chinese government's brutal crackdown on prodemocracy demonstrators in Beijing's Tiananmen Square in 1989 and subsequent treatment of political dissidents led some U.S. policymakers and activists to conclude that China's trade with the United States should be contingent on a dramatic improvement in its human rights record. And in fact, the United States has pressured China and other countries to improve their human rights policies. But the pressure in most instances has stopped at the point where trade relations would be jeopardized.

When President Clinton announced that he would make an official visit to China in 1998, he was pressured to cancel it by many human-rights groups and some members of Congress. To go, they argued, would be perceived as tacit acceptance of the Chinese government's treatment of its political dissidents. Objections to the proposed trip intensified when it was learned that Chinese leaders insisted that Clinton be met in Tiananmen Square, the traditional welcoming point for foreign leaders but also the site of the massacre of prodemocracy student dissidents nearly a decade earlier.

Clinton did not cancel his trip. While there, he engaged in a debate on individual rights with Chinese President Jiang Zemin that was broadcast live throughout the country, the first time any such broadcast had been permitted in

CURRENT CONTROVERSIES

SHOULD CHINA'S HUMAN RIGHTS POLICIES BE A CONDITION FOR TRADE?

America's role in the world has been defined not only by the realities of global politics but also by its political values. After the two world wars, for example, the United States advocated the democratic form of government as a path toward a more peaceful world. A more recent issue is whether U.S. trade relations should be contingent on countries' human rights records. Trade with China is the prime case. China is a relatively closed society with a weak human rights record, and yet it is also a huge potential marketplace. Some officials have argued that the U.S. should restrict trade with China until it improves its human rights policies. Others have argued that China's market is too big to ignore and that normalized trade relations are the surest way to encourage change within China.

YES: Since 1949, Communist China has operated one of the most brutal and repressive regimes the world has ever known. . . . It has killed millions of its own citizens, outlawed religion, obliterated freedom of the press, and fought against the United States in Korea and Indochina . . . [Its] policies on the political dissidents, religious freedom, and population control are abhorrent. The State Department report on China's human rights practices illustrates an appalling picture. It provides example after example of torture, forced confessions, suppression of basic human rights, denial of due process, and, worst of all, forced abortion and sterilization. Is this a government to which the United States of America should give most-favored-nation status? I don't think so.

—U.S. Senator Bob Smith (R-N.H.)

NO: China is the largest country in the world. . . . We can't close our eyes to China. I am not saying we should accept what China is doing. . . . [But] there is an old saying in life that if you stick your finger in somebody's eye and you treat somebody like the enemy, guess what. They are going to be an enemy . . . All Presidents . . . and all Congresses that have looked at this issue have reached the same conclusion—that normal trade relations with China will create the foundation for a much greater probability that we are going to achieve the success we want with various other issues that we have with China.

—U.S. Senator Max Baucus (D-Mont.)

China. Most analysts concluded that Clinton's visit had improved the prospects of political reform in China. The president himself talked about the importance of constructive engagement, arguing that China was too big to ignore and that America's political and economic goals were better served by working with China than by punishing it. He also argued that China's economic development would foster aspirations that would lead to free expression and democratic elections. However, Clinton's trip did not change everyone's mind about how China should be handled. House majority whip Tom DeLay (R-Texas) said that Chinese leaders "respect strength and persistence, and the president was found wanting."[31]

Nevertheless, as indicated by the strong support for trade with China expressed in 2000 by the major-party presidential nominees, George W. Bush and Al Gore, there is broad bipartisan support for the notion that the surest way to promote democracy and freedom in the developing world is to promote free market economies. Congress acted on this assumption when it voted in 2000 to normalize trade with China on a continuing basis.

THE POLITICS OF GLOBAL ECONOMIC POLICY

The global economy has changed a great deal since America's halcyon days in the period immediately following World War II. It is greatly more competitive and less responsive to military power.

The United States depends more heavily than in the past on the strength of its own economy to forge a favorable position in world trade. This situation has caused U.S. corporations in recent years to launch cost-cutting measures in order to make their products more competitive in the global market.[32] The changes have also led U.S. policymakers to alter their approaches to business regulation, public education, and many other policies that affect the country's competitive position. Another indicator of a new approach is the emphasis that the United States has placed on the WTO, whose member nations are committed to lowering trade barriers so as to promote the type of world trading system that can benefit all participating countries.

Public opinion in recent years has consistently supported the idea that the United States should turn its attention away from military priorities toward economic ones. This opinion seems to reflect the lesson that American elites and officials have drawn from international experiences during the last half-century, particularly during the past decade or so. The consensus is broad enough to suggest that economic priorities will continue to be a driving factor in American foreign policy.

www.mhhe.com/patterson5

Self-Quiz

Summary

From 1945 to 1990, U.S. foreign and defense policies were dominated by a concern with the Soviet Union. During most of this period, the United States pursued a policy of containment based on the premise that the Soviet Union was an aggressor nation bent on global conquest. Containment policy led the United States into wars in Korea and Vietnam and to maintain a large defense establishment. U.S. military forces are deployed around the globe, and the nation has a large nuclear arsenal. The end of the cold war, however, made some of this weaponry and much of the traditional military strategy less relevant to maintaining America's security. A redefinition of the military's role in meeting the nation's security needs is taking place.

With the end of the cold war, the United States adopted a new approach to foreign affairs, which President George Bush labeled as a "new world order." This approach proposes that nations work together toward common goals and includes efforts to address global problems such as drug trafficking and environmental pollution. The Persian Gulf War and the Kosovo conflict are notable examples of the multilateralism that is a characteristic of the new world order.

Increasingly, national security is being defined in economic terms. After World War II, the United States helped establish a global trading system within which it was the leading partner. The nation's international economic position, however, gradually weakened, owing to domestic problems and to the emergence of strong competitors, particularly Japan and Germany. In recent years, a revitalized economic sector has restored America's prominence in global markets and is increasingly the driving force in U.S. foreign policy.

The chief instruments of national security policy are diplomacy, military force, economic exchange, and intelligence gathering. These are exercised through specialized agencies of the U.S. government, such as the Departments of State and Defense, which are largely responsive to presidential leadership. Increasingly, national security policy has also relied on international organizations such as the UN and WTO, which are responsive to the global concerns of major nations.

Key Terms

cold war
containment

détente
deterrence

economic globalization
free trade
insurgency
internationalism
isolationism

military-industrial complex
multilateralism
multinational corporations
protectionism

Suggested Readings

Barnet, Richard J., and John Cavanagh. *Global Dreams: Imperial Corporations and the New World Order.* New York: Simon & Schuster, 1994. Argues that the key players in today's world are large multinational corporations.

Dumbrell, John. *American Foreign Policy: Carter to Clinton.* New York: St. Martin's Press, 1996. A thorough history of United States foreign policy since the Vietnam War.

Greider, William. *One World, Ready or Not: The Manic Logic of Global Capitalism.* New York: Simon & Schuster, 1997. A critical analysis of the global economy and its effect on Americans' lives.

Holsti, Ole. *Public Opinion and American Foreign Policy.* Ann Arbor: University of Michigan Press, 1996. An analysis that concludes public opinion has had a significant and positive impact on U.S. foreign policy.

Johnson, Loch K. *Secret Agencies: U.S. Intelligence Agencies in a Hostile World.* New Haven, Conn.: Yale University Press, 1996. A nuanced assessment of the record of U.S. intelligence agencies.

Karnow, Stanley. *Vietnam: A History.* New York: Penguin, 1983. A thorough history of American involvement in Vietnam.

Kenen, Peter B., ed. *Understanding Interdependence: The Macroeconomics of the Open Economy.* Princeton, N.J.: Princeton University Press, 1995. A survey of the organization and workings of the international monetary system.

Kirshner, Jonathan. *Currency and Coercion: The Political Economy of International Monetary Power.* Princeton, N.J.: Princeton University Press, 1997. A study of how states use currency and coercion to advance their security.

Lindsay, James M. *Congress and the Politics of U.S. Foreign Policy.* Baltimore, Md.: Johns Hopkins University Press, 1994. An analysis of Congress's increasingly assertive role in foreign policy.

Nye, Joseph. *Bound to Lead: The Changing Nature of United States Power.* New York: Basic Books, 1990. An analysis of the U.S. role in world affairs in the aftermath of the cold war.

Ohmae, Kenichi. *The End of the Nation State: The Rise of Regional Economies.* New York: Free Press, 1995. An analysis of the impact of economic change on national sovereignty.

PART FIVE

State and Local Governments

★ ★ ★

*A*ll politics is local," said Tip O'Neill, the legendary Speaker of the U.S. House of Representatives. O'Neill was referring to the powerful influence that local interests have on Washington policymakers, but he could have been talking about the American experience more broadly. From the earliest days of the Republic, Americans have embraced the notion of local control of government. To be sure, Americans have periodically looked to Washington for answers to their policy problems and have gradually entrusted federal officials with a larger share of governing responsibility. But states and localities remain vital centers of policy and politics, and they continue to offer citizens the most direct forms of popular political participation.

The chapter in this section examines state and local governments. It explores their constitutional foundation, their governing institutions, their provisions for popular participation, their politics, and their programs and policies.

Every society makes provisions for forms of local and regional government, but few countries do so more thoroughly than the United States. It has about 80,000 different local and regional governments. The chapter that follows will describe what they are, what they do, and how they impact on American life. ★

CHAPTER 21

State and Local Politics: Maintaining Our Differences

★

*The powers not delegated to the United States
by the Constitution, nor prohibited by it to the States,
are reserved for the States . . .*

—Tenth Amendment

★　★　★

The Supreme Court in *Reno v. Condon* (2000) upheld a federal law that prohibited states from selling their computer files of information acquired from drivers' license applicants. Some states had been making millions from the sale of the databases to mass marketing and other firms. When citizens objected to the practice, Congress responded with the 1994 Drivers Privacy Protection Act. The state of South Carolina brought suit, claiming that Congress lacked the authority to tell the states what they could do with their databases. The Supreme Court ruled against South Carolina, saying that the law simply "regulates the states as owners of databases," an action permissible under Congress's constitutional power to regulate commerce. "[The] sale or release [of databases] into the interstate stream of business is sufficient to support Congressional regulation."[1]

One day earlier, however, the Supreme Court in *Kimel v. Florida Board of Regents* (2000) ruled that the states were not bound by the Federal Age Discrimination Act. The legislation was passed in 1967 and later amended to include state government employees, who were granted the power to sue in federal courts in cases of alleged age discrimination in the workplace. In 1995, a group of faculty members and librarians at Florida State University brought suit, charging that the state's wage policy violated the federal act. The State of Florida, in turn, claimed that the law infringed in its authority as a sovereign government. The Supreme Court ruled in Florida's favor, saying that the law "is not 'appropriate legislation' under . . . the Fourteenth Amendment." The Court said that age discrimination is not inherently unconstitutional and thus Congress lacked the authority to require state governments to apply a federal age-discrimination law.[2]

These cases reflect both the dynamic and contentious nature of American federalism. The U.S. political system, as was described in detail in Chapter 3 and discussed elsewhere in this text, divides power between a national government and the separate states.

During the more than two centuries that the United States has existed, there has been a gradual expansion of national power and a corresponding reduction in state-to-state differences. Yet the states and their creations, the local governments, continue to be vitally important centers of politics and policies. In fact, in terms of their day-to-day impact on Americans' lives, they are far more significant than the government in Washington. The roads that Americans drive on, the schools they attend, the laws they obey, and much more, are defined principally by state and local action rather than by federal action. In fact, contrary to what many Americans might believe, states and localities have nearly five times as many employees as the federal government does (see Figure 21-1).

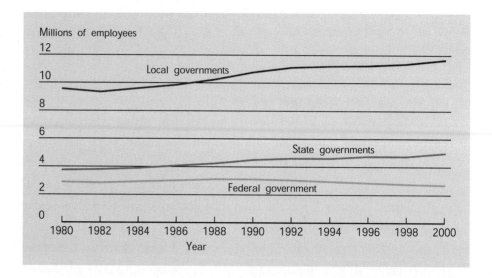

FIGURE 21-1 Employees of the Federal, State, and Local Governments
Levels of employment in state and local governments have increased in recent years, whereas the number of federal government employees has remained fairly constant. *Source: U.S. Bureau of the Census, 2000.*

The purpose of this chapter is to describe more fully the American states and the localities within them. The great number of state and local governments, and the variety they exhibit, hinder any easy summary of what they are all about. Yet there are some general patterns, and it is these patterns on which this chapter concentrates. It includes a comparison of the states, which will indicate major factors behind some of the differences in their politics and policies. The main points of discussion in this chapter are the following:

★ *All states apply the constitutional principle of separation of powers, but the states otherwise differ from one another, and from the federal government, in the way in which they structure their governments.* The use of elections as a means of choosing officials of all types, including judges and lesser executives (for example, state treasurer), is widespread.

★ *Local governments are not sovereign; they are chartered by their state government, which sets the limits of their power.* Of the units of local government (county, municipality, township, school district, and special district), the basic unit is the municipality. A municipality may be governed in one of four ways—the strong mayor–council, weak mayor–council, commission, or city manager system.

★ *States and localities have primary responsibility for most of the policies, such as public education, that directly touch Americans' daily lives.* The nature of these policies is affected by the wealth of the state or locality and also by its political culture, party system, and group system.

The Structure of the State Government

The Constitution of the United States contains provisions that forbid the states from interfering with the lawful exercise of national authority, and the states are required by the Constitution to provide their residents with a "republican" (that is, representative) form of government. In addition, the "supremacy clause" of the Constitution requires the states to comply with legitimate national laws while the "full faith and credit" provision requires them to respect the laws of other states (for example, a contract issued by one state is legally binding in other states).

Nevertheless, the Constitution was intended primarily to define national power and national institutions and does not say very much about the states or their powers. In fact, the Framers of the Constitution did not believe it was necessary to define the powers of the states. They held that the Constitution implied that the states held all legitimate governing powers not granted to the national government. This situation was unsettling to states'-rights advocates, who insisted on a constitutional amendment—the Tenth—which reserves for the states those powers not delegated to the national government (see Chapter 3).

The Tenth Amendment is part of the Bill of the Rights, whose provisions for individual rights initially applied only to action by the federal government. It was not until the twentieth century that the Bill of Rights was extended to include action by state and local governments (see Chapters 4 and 5). The Fourteenth Amendment was the basis for the change. It prohibits a state from depriving any person of "life, liberty, or property, without due process of law" or from denying any person within its jurisdiction the "equal protection of the laws."

THE STATE CONSTITUTIONS

Each state's constitution is its supreme law, except where valid national law applies. In each state, the constitution establishes executive, legislative, and judicial branches and defines the lawful powers of each one. The concept of checks and balances—the notion that each branch will act as a curb on the power of the others—is embedded in each of the state constitutions. Each of them also includes a bill of rights.

Although the state constitutions in these respects resemble the Constitution of the United States, they have distinctive features. On average they are roughly four times the length of the U.S. Constitution. Vermont is the only state whose constitution is shorter than the nation's. Until it was replaced in 1974, Louisiana's constitution was by far the longest and most detailed. At 250,000 words, it was nearly thirty times the length of the U.S. Constitution. The longest state constitution still in effect today is Alabama's, which has approximately 175,000 words and more than five hundred amendments.

The length of state constitutions reflects the significant issues they address, such as the lawful powers and forms of local governments, the tax authority of both the state and local governments, and the executive agencies of the state government. However, the state constitutions contain many provisions that more properly belong in statutes than in a constitution. Enterprising state legislators have often preferred to embed their favorite policies in constitutional amendments, which are harder to change than ordinary laws are. For example, many of the state constitutions include benefits for special-interest groups, such as veterans, farmers, and businesses. Minnesota's constitution was amended in the early 1970s to permit the state to give each Vietnam veteran from the state a $600 bonus. California's constitution is filled with all sorts of tax provisions, which, among other things, limit the types and amount of taxation.

Most constitutional scholars would agree that the length of state constitutions is a drawback. As was indicated in Chapter 2, the U.S. Constitution is a

The U.S. Constitution in its emphasis on a separation of executive, legislative, and judicial power has been a model for state constitutions. The U.S. Capitol Building has also served as a model for the states. Shown here is the capitol building of the state of Texas. It is located in Austin.

sparsely worded document, which has enabled succeeding generations to adapt it to their changing needs. Not so with many of the state constitutions. They are often so loaded down with narrow and detailed provisions that they deny policy makers the flexibility to respond effectively to change. The constitutional provisions that bestow benefits on interest groups, for example, do more than confer a special status on a particular group; they also bind the subsequent decisions of policy makers.

The length of state constitutions reflects in part the relative ease with which they can be amended. Unlike amendments to the U.S. Constitution, which require a two-thirds majority in the House and Senate and then ratification by three-fourths of the state legislatures, a state constitution can be amended by legislative action combined with voter ratification. The typical process is a two-thirds vote of approval in each chamber of the state legislature and ratification by a simple majority of voters in the next election. Delaware is the only state where voter ratification is not required; however, two consecutive sessions of the Delaware legislature must approve an amendment for it to be ratified. More than forty states also provide for amendment by a **state constitutional convention,** and more than two hundred such conventions have been held. Finally, a third of the states permit amendment through a **constitutional initiative.** By obtaining the signatures of a certain number of registered voters, a citizen or group can petition to place a proposed amendment on the ballot at the next election. If it gets majority support, it becomes part of the constitution. In 1996, for example, California voters approved Proposition 209, which bans in the state any public employment, education, or contracting program that is based on race, ethnicity, or sex. California leads the nation in terms of the number of constitutional initiatives proposed and enacted. California's constitution has roughly five hundred amendments, many of which were added through the initiative process.

state constitutional convention A state convention convened to amend the state constitution or draft a new one.

constitutional initiative The process by which a citizen or group can petition to place a proposed amendment on the ballot at the next election by obtaining the signatures of a certain number of registered voters, and if the amendment gets majority support, it becomes part of the constitution.

BRANCHES OF GOVERNMENT

All states make use of the principle of checks and balances that underpins the national government (see Chapter 2). There is nothing in the Constitution of the United States that would prohibit a state from adopting a parliamentary form of government, but no state has tried it. The executive, legislative, and judiciary in each state are separate branches that share power. Each branch thus serves as a check on the power of the others.

The Executive Branch

Most states wrote their first constitutions during periods when mistrust of executive authority was high. Consequently, they provided for relatively weak governors. The model still applies in some states, especially in the South and in New England. Texas's governor, for example, has only modest formal powers. The governor can propose legislation, but by tradition, the Texas House and Senate leaders set the legislative agenda without including the governor in their deliberations. In 1999, Texas governor George W. Bush did persuade the Texas legislature to cut taxes, but House and Senate leaders responded only after forcing him to accept many provisions that he opposed.[3]

Roughly half the states impose a two-term limit on their governors. Virginia, Mississippi, and Kentucky restrict the governor to a single term. In nearly all states, the governor's term of office is four years, but New Hampshire and Vermont confine it to two years.

Although the governorship is not a very powerful office in most states, governors have gained power in recent decades as a result of an increase in the size and complexity of government. The initiation of the state budget now resides with the governor rather than the legislature in nearly every state. And every state now grants the governor the power to veto legislative acts. There was a time when a number of states denied their governors this power. North Carolina was the last to change; it amended its constitution in 1996 to give the governor the veto power. In forty-three states, the governor also has a line-item veto, which enables the governor to reject a part of an appropriations bill without voiding the whole act.

Governors have the power to appoint the heads of agencies and commissions. This power has become increasingly important as state agencies have assumed broader policy responsibilities. In most states, governors also have the power to reorganize the executive branch (for example, the merging of two agencies), subject to the legislature's veto. The extent of such powers, however, varies from state to state. The political scientist Thad Boyle has systematically evaluated the institutional powers of the states' governors and concluded that the office is "very strong" in nine states (including Ohio, Pennsylvania, and Tennessee), "strong" in twenty-one states (including Arizona, Kentucky, and Michigan), "moderate" in seventeen states (including California, Florida, and Texas), and "weak" in three states (Vermont, North Carolina, and South Carolina).[4]

Regardless of formal powers, however, the governor is often the most visible and widely known politician in the state. This position provides a bully pulpit that allows the governor to assume a leadership role on policy issues. This role has increased in importance as policy control has "devolved" from Washington to the states in recent years (see Chapter 3). Wisconsin's Tommy Thompson, for example, is among the governors who took the lead in promoting the recent changes in the nation's welfare policies (see Chapter 19).

In 1998, Jesse "The Body" Ventura, a former professional wrestler who had not previously held a prominent public office, was elected Minnesota's governor. He is an exception. Most governors have previously held other public office, such as state lieutenant governor, state attorney general, big-city mayor, or state legislator. To gain the governor's post, they have typically had first to win their party's primary. However, there are a few states where nomination is gained through a party convention.

HOW THE UNITED STATES COMPARES

STATE POWER IN A FEDERAL SYSTEM

Federalism involves the division of sovereign authority between a national government and area (state) governments. As was discussed in Chapter 3, the first federal system of government in world history was established in the United States in 1787. The American states already existed, and the only realistic alternative for the writers of the Constitution was a form of government that protected the states' integrity and authority.

Other nations of the period had unitary systems (sovereignty invested solely in the national government), and most nations today still have that system. However, the federal system has been adopted in some countries, including Canada and Germany.

Federal systems, however, are not the same everywhere. They differ primarily in the degree of autonomy granted to the subnational (state) governments. The United States allocates an extraordinary level of authority to the state governments. They have more discretionary authority and more far-reaching power than is typically the case in a federal system, a reflection of the American tradition of local control and of Americans' long-standing suspicion of centralized power.

The American states and their local units, for example, have a degree of control over education policy that is nearly unmatched. The federal government provides some of the funding for public schools and has imposed anti-discrimination requirements on these institutions. However, the states and localities decide nearly all aspects of education policy. They set the school calendar, course requirements, achievement standards, teacher qualifications, and so on. There are no national education standards that states and localities are required to meet.

Campaigns for governor, like those for the U.S. Senate, have become increasingly expensive. In a large state like New York or Texas, spending in the governor's campaign can easily top $20 million. Spending in California's 1998 race exceeded $50 million; Gray Davis, the winner, spent $34 million.

The governor is the state's chief executive but, in many states, is not the sole elected executive official. In most states, the voters also choose one or more of the following executives: lieutenant governor, attorney general, secretary of state, state treasurer, education commissioner, agriculture commissioner, and public utilities commissioner. The governor is the chief executive but shares executive power with other officials, who have separate electoral bases and who may be of the opposite party. In only three states, Maine, New Hampshire, and New Jersey, is the governor, like the president at the national level, the sole elected executive official.

The direct election of multiple executive officials has roots in early Americans' distrust of executive power and also in the Jacksonian and Progressive eras, when accountability to the people through the vote was a prevailing philosophy. The multiple executive system weakens the governor's control of the executive branch. At times, even the governor's control of his own office can be at risk. In California, the lieutenant governor is elected separately from the governor and becomes acting governor when the governor travels outside the state's borders. When Jerry Brown was California's governor, the state's lieutenant governor, Mike Curb, was from the opposite party, and Brown would sometimes cancel, delay, or shorten a trip outside the state in order to prevent the lieutenant governor from taking action while he was away. On one of Brown's trips, Curb lifted the state's pollution control regulations. Upon his return, Brown issued an executive order reinstating them.[5]

Of the executive officials other than governor, the most powerful is the attorney general, who is elected to the post in forty-three states. The attorney general is the state's chief legal officer and sets priorities for legal action. An attorney general might decide, for example, to concentrate the state's legal resources on environmental protection or investigations of alleged political corruption. The office of attorney general has often been a stepping stone to a governorship or a seat in the U.S. Senate.

The Legislature

Like Congress, state legislatures have within their authority the most impressive array of constitutional powers that a democracy can bestow. The legislatures make the laws, appropriate the money, define the structure of the executive and the judiciary, oversee the operations of the other branches, and represent the people.

With one exception, the state legislatures are **bicameral**—that is, they have two chambers. The upper house in every state is called the senate. State senates average about forty members, who serve four-year terms in most states. The lower house is always the larger one. Lower houses average about 100 members, who are elected to two-year terms in most states. In nearly all states, the lower chamber is called either the house or the general assembly. Nebraska is the only state with a unicameral (one-house) legislature. It is called, simply enough, the Nebraska Unicameral Legislature.

bicameral legislatures A legislature having two chambers.

The state legislatures are organized and operate in ways similar to Congress (see Chapter 12). Their leadership is provided by party leaders chosen by each chamber's members, but most of the legislative work and executive oversight is carried out in committees. Unlike Congress, however, there are some states where legislative bills can be submitted for consideration directly by executive officials. In Congress, only the members themselves have the power to submit bills, although the bills are sometimes drafted in the executive branch.

Like Congress, the state legislatures could not manage their workload if they lacked committees to which tasks were delegated. More than fifty thousand bills are enacted into law each year by state legislatures—an average of more than one thousand bills for each state.

The distribution of power within state legislatures varies widely. Some legislatures are extraordinarily democratic in the sense that power is widely disbursed, and the job of the leaders is primarily to organize the members' work. In other states, power is concentrated in the top leadership, and other members, especially relative newcomers, are expected to follow their lead. In New York State, the annual budget is determined through bargaining among three top officials—the senate majority leader, the speaker of the assembly, and the governor. They negotiate until a final "deal" is reached, which the legislature as a whole is then expected to enact in its entirety.

For a long period, state legislatures were synonymous with malapportionment. Cities were grossly underrepresented because rural legislators, who had controlled the state legislatures since the days when the United States was a farming nation, refused to reapportion them. Vermont was the extreme case. From 1793 to the 1960s, its legislative distribution did not change. In the state's lower house, each village, town, or city had one representative, regardless of

Shown here is the senate chamber of the New York legislature. Except for Nebraska, all states have a two-chamber legislature.

population. Thus, the city of Burlington had exactly the same voting power as the smallest village in the state. Not surprisingly, the policy needs of America's cities were neglected by state legislatures, while the interests of farmers and rural communities were quite well served.

The situation changed abruptly in the early 1960s when the Supreme Court of the United States declared that state legislatures must represent people rather than communities or areas. The "one person, one vote" method of apportioning state legislatures immediately gave a larger share of legislative seats to populated urban areas—although, ironically, the cities never got their full due. By the time the Supreme Court outlawed malapportionment in the 1960s, so many people had moved out of the central cities that the suburbs gained the most advantage from reapportionment. The suburbs, like the rural areas, are more conservative and more Republican than the cities; thus, there has never been a time when the concerns of cities have dominated the actions of state legislatures.

Until the past few decades, most of the state legislatures were relatively unimposing institutions. They were in session only for short periods each year, were deficient in staff and information resources, and were vulnerable to powerful lobbying groups. Beginning in the 1960s, however, they began to meet for longer periods and to expand their staffs. Legislators' pay also increased significantly at this time. The increase was substantial enough in a few states, such as New York and California, to create professional legislators—individuals whose chief occupation is an elective position within a state legislature. New York's legislators are paid more than $60,000 a year in salary. Many of them also hold party or committee leadership positions, for which they receive supplementary allowances.

Most analysts have welcomed the change toward more professional state legislatures. The Advisory Commission on Intergovernmental Relations, an agency established by Congress, noted in one of its reports: "Today's state legislatures are more functional, accountable, independent, and representative, and are equipped with greater information handling capacity than their predecessors."[6]

Some states have resisted the tendency toward longer sessions, larger staffs, and higher salaries. New Hampshire, Rhode Island, Alabama, Nebraska, and West Virginia are among the states that pay their legislators $10,000 a year or less. A recent development that could partly restore the "citizen legislature" is *term limitations,* or legal restrictions on the number of years that elected officials can remain in office. The term-limit movement has been based on the public's dissatisfaction with government, a belief that "professional" politicians are part of the problem, and a sense that an answer to the problem is to replace them with "amateurs" who are more closely connected to the people they serve (see Figure 21-2). Voters in Oklahoma were the first to act on this belief, deciding by a 2-to-l margin in 1990 to limit state legislators to twelve years of service. California and Colorado voters followed suit in the same year, and about half the states now have term limits for at least some offices.

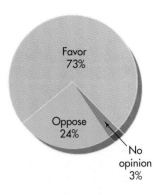

FIGURE 21-2 The Public's View of Term Limitations Most Americans favor term limits for elected officials. *Source: Gallup Poll, March 1999.*

The Courts

As a consequence of America's federal system, each state has its separate court system. Like the federal system, the state systems have trial courts at the bottom level and appellate courts at the top. About two-thirds of the states have two appellate levels, and the other third have only a single appellate court (the state's supreme court). Most of the less-populated states have determined that they do not need a second appellate level. Those with a second appellate level have created it primarily to relieve the heavy caseload that would otherwise fall on the top court.

The states vary in the way they organize and label their courts. Most of the states have district courts and a supreme court, but the states tend also to give some lower courts specialized titles and jurisdictions. Family courts, for example, settle such issues as divorce and child-custody disputes, and probate courts handle the disposition of the estates of people who have died. Below such specialized trial courts are less-formal trial courts, such as magistrate courts and justice of the peace courts. They handle a variety of minor cases, such as traffic infractions, and usually do not use a jury. Jury trial is not a constitutional requirement of the states, nor do they have to follow the federal tradition of a twelve-member jury or of a unanimous verdict when a jury is used.

States vary in their methods of selecting judges. In about a fourth of the states, judges are appointed by the governor, but in most states, judgeships are elective offices. Several states use the Missouri Plan (so called because Missouri was the first state to use it), under which a judicial selection commission provides a short list of acceptable candidates from which the governor selects one. After a trial period of a year or more, the judge selected must be approved by the electorate in a yes-no vote in order to serve a longer term.

State courts are undeniably important. As we indicated in Chapter 17, there is a federal court myth that holds that the federal courts are the more significant component of the American judicial system. In fact, the state judiciary is the locus of most court action. Upward of 95 percent of the nation's legal cases are decided in state courts (or local courts, which are agents of the states). Moreover, nearly all cases that originate in state courts also end there; the federal courts never enter the picture. Of course, one federal court—the U.S. Supreme Court—

is a silent partner of the state and local courts, requiring them to act within minimum standards of justice (for example, the prohibition of forced confessions).

The workload on the state court system is enormous. State courts handle more than 100 million cases annually, and though many of these cases involve minor infractions, more than ten million have potentially serious consequences for at least one party in the case, including imprisonment, financial deprivation, or personal loss, as in the case of a parent who loses a child custody dispute.

The application of justice in the state court systems is relatively uneven. To say that the state courts are riddled with incompetence and favoritism would be unfair to the many skilled and conscientious jurists who work within them. But it is not unfair to say that the state courts do not have enough resources to handle adequately the staggering load of cases thrust on them. Long delays are commonplace, which places pressure on these systems to reduce the caseload through plea bargains and other mechanisms that increase the likelihood of arbitrary outcomes. Many judges, particularly those who operate in the lower courts, are poorly informed about the laws they are asked to apply. And a few are downright incompetent, having acquired their positions simply because they had political connections or the name recognition to win a judicial election.

Most states have made efforts in recent decades to raise the performance level of their court systems. Administrative and legal procedures have been changed, for example, to expedite the handling of cases. In the past, the pursuit of justice in many state courts was slow and procedurally arbitrary. There are still delays and procedural injustices, but they are less prevalent today as a result of federally imposed standards and state-initiated reforms, such as those that require law enforcement officials to dismiss a case unless it is presented to a judge or grand jury within a specified period of time. States have also established disciplinary boards to identify and remove or reprimand incompetent or biased judges.

CITIZENS, PARTIES, AND ELECTIONS

When the Framers wrote the U.S. Constitution, they allowed for only minimal popular participation. The House of Representatives was the only popularly elected institution and the only one with a short term of office, two years. The democratic spirit of the Revolution of 1776 was more apparent at the state level. Every state but South Carolina held an annual legislative election, and several states chose their governors through annual election by the people.

Today, the states hold elections less frequently, but they have stayed ahead of the federal government in their emphasis on elections as a means of popular influence and control. As was noted previously, most states elect their treasurer, attorney general, and secretary of state by popular ballot. Many states also choose their judges by direct election. No federal judges are chosen by this means.

Citizens as Legislators

initiative The process by which citizens can place legislative measures on the ballot through signature petitions, and if the measure receives a majority vote, it becomes law.

State voters also get the opportunity to vote directly on issues of policy. In all states except Delaware, amendments to the state constitution require the approval of the electorate. In addition, more than a third of the states give popular majorities the power of the **initiative,** which allows citizens through signature petitions to place legislative measures on the ballot. If such a measure receives a majority vote, it becomes law, just as if it had been enacted by the state's legislature. A related measure is the **referendum,** which permits the legislature to submit proposals to the voters for approval or rejection. The initiative and referendum were introduced around 1900 as Progressive reforms. The Progressives also sought to protect the public from wayward state and local officials through the **recall,** in which citizens can petition for the removal from office of an elected official before the scheduled completion of his or her term. The state of Arizona would probably have recalled its governor, Evan Mecham, in 1987 had he not been impeached by the state legislature before the recall process could be completed.

Of these mechanisms, the initiative has been the most important. Increasingly, it has become an instrument of group politics.[7] The average citizen does not have the time or money to organize a statewide petition drive. Many groups do, and they have increasingly recognized that the initiative is an alternative to the traditional method of lobbying the state legislature. Not only are their chances of success often greater, but they also get the opportunity to decide exactly how the measure will be worded. Once the initiative is placed on the ballot, a group can use its resources to mount a statewide advertising campaign to urge its passage. An irony is that the initiative was devised by the Progressives to protect citizens against the hold that powerful interests had acquired over state legislatures. The initiative was to be a means by which citizens could bypass the legislature and thus overcome the power of entrenched interests. Oregon is among the states where restrictions on the use of the initiative by organized interests is under debate. It is even conceivable that some states may choose in the future to abolish the initiative.

Voter Registration and Turnout

Although the states have been electoral innovators, their history also includes attempts to restrict access to the ballot. The clearest example is that of southern states after the Civil War. The Fifteenth Amendment was ratified in 1870, prohibiting states from using race as the basis for denial of suffrage. Southern states responded with a number of devices that were designed to keep African Americans from voting. Through poll taxes, the grandfather clause, whites-only primary elections, and rigged literacy tests as a qualification for registration to vote, blacks in many areas of the South were effectively disenfranchised.[8]

Action by the national government was necessary to bring a halt to state efforts to disenfranchise large groups of voters (see Chapter 5). Major steps included a Supreme Court decision outlawing whites-only primaries, a constitutional amendment barring poll taxes, and the Voting Rights Act of 1965, which forbids discrimination in voting and registration. However, the legacy of a century of state-supported efforts to keep blacks and poor whites from voting in the South is still evident. The region has the lowest voter turnout rate in the country. By comparison, states like Minnesota, Wisconsin, and Idaho, which have pioneered methods such as election-day registration that are designed to encourage voting, are among the leaders in voter turnout.

The decline in voter turnout in presidential and congressional elections in recent decades (see Chapter 7) has also been characteristic of state elections. The

referendum The process through which the legislature may submit proposals to the voters for approval or rejection.

recall The process by which citizens can petition for the removal from office of an elected official before the scheduled completion of his or her term.

★ CRITICAL THINKING ★

WHAT'S YOUR OPINION?

The Initiative
The initiative would seem to epitomize citizen power. Through petition, citizens can place an initiative on the state ballot, and if approved by a majority of voters, it becomes law, just as if it had been passed by the state legislature. It is an imposing task, however, to circulate the statewide petition that is required to place an initiative on the ballot. A large number of signatures are required, and they are subject to verification. Organized groups have found the initiative a convenient tool for achieving their legislative goals without having to work through the legislature. They have the resources to organize a successful petition drive and then to campaign for the initiative's approval by voters. Some analysts, including the *Washington Post*'s David Broder, have concluded that the initiative process is broken and that states should either restrict or eliminate it. Others contend that the initiative remains a powerful tool that the public can use when it feels that state officials are out of touch. What's your opinion?

Elections are a hallmark of American government at all levels. Over the course of an average year, citizens in many locations could easily vote in three or four different elections. In most states, citizens can also vote directly on issues of public policy through the referendum or initiative.

average turnout in gubernatorial elections that do not coincide with a presidential election, for example, is less than 40 percent—a drop of several percentage points since the early 1960s.

The Structure of the Local Governments

If the significance of a level of government was determined strictly on the basis of numbers, the local level would win handily. The United States has one national government and fifty state governments, but it has more than eighty thousand local governments, which include counties, municipalities, school districts, and special districts, such as water, sewage, and conservation districts.

Local governments, however, do not have sovereignty—that is, they do not have final authority within their governing spheres. Their authority drives from that of the state within which they are located. The general principle that describes the relationship between state power and localities is called **Dillon's rule.** It holds that local governments are creatures of their states, which in theory even have the power to abolish them. The rule derives its name from the judge, John F. Dillon, who propounded it in a nineteenth-century treatise on municipal governments. These governments, he wrote, possess only those powers that are "expressly granted" them by their state or are "necessarily . . . implied in or incident to" these powers.[9]

Dillon's rule The term used to describe relations between state and local government; it holds that local governments are creatures of the state, which in theory even has the power to abolish them.

The most important aspect of Dillon's rule is that local governments must act within constraints placed on them by the state. The state's reach extends even to the issue of whether a local unit of government will provide a particular service. The state of Wisconsin, for example, requires each of its cities to have a solid-waste disposal facility.

States differ markedly in the degree of freedom they grant their local units. The states that grant the highest degree of autonomy to local units, and those that grant the least, are found in all regions of the country. For example, Oregon, North Carolina, and Connecticut rank high on local autonomy, while Idaho, Mississippi, and Massachusetts rank low.

charter The chief instrument by which a state governs its local units; it spells out in detail what a local government can and cannot do.

The chief instrument by which a state governs its local units is the **charter.** No local government can exist without a charter, which is issued by the state and defines the limits within which a local unit must operate. By tradition, local charters are restrictive. They spell out in considerable detail what a local government can and cannot do. A typical charter, for example, specifies the types and limits of taxation that a local government may impose on its residents. The charters of some types of local government include a grant of lawmaking power. These governments can issue **ordinances,** which are local laws. A locality might, for example, pass an ordinance requiring dog owners to leash their pet or an ordinance specifying a curfew for teenagers.

There are limits to a state's ability to control its local units. A state government does not have the time, the money, or the staff to make all the decisions concerning its many local units. Nor can a state expect the same restrictions to work equally well for all local units. A charter that is suited to a city of a million inhabitants would probably not be suited to a village of several hundred people. Accordingly, all states give their local units some discretionary authority and make allowance for differences among them. In most cases, the charters for cities are different from those for towns, which in turn differ from those for villages.

Home rule is a device that is designed to give local governments more leeway in their policies. It developed out of a protest movement that sought to free local government from meddlesome interference by the states. Its guiding principle was the so-called **Cooley's rule,** articulated in an 1871 ruling by Michigan judge Thomas Cooley who boldly declared that cities should be self-governing.[10] Home rule was first tried in 1875 in Missouri, and it allows a local government to design and amend its own charter, subject to the laws and constitution of the state and also subject to veto by the state.

The long-term trend in the states has been toward home rule and other means of grating localities a larger measure of independence. It is partly a philosophical issue: Americans are accustomed to a substantial degree of local autonomy and expect their state governments to refrain from interfering too deeply in local affairs. It is also a practical issue: states lack the capacity to make the everyday decisions of their local governments.

Local government is the source of most public employment. Compared with fewer than three million federal workers and four million state employees, more than ten million people work in local government. They are one of the most heavily unionized groups in the country. Schoolteachers are represented through the American Federation of Teachers (AFT) and the National Education Association (NEA), and other local public employees are represented through such unions as the International Association of Fire Fighters (IAFF) and the American Federation of State, County, and Municipal Employees (AFSCME). These unions have more than three million members, and they have been quite successful in obtaining better working conditions and job benefits for their members.

ordinance A law issued by a local government under authority granted by the state government.

home rule A device designed to give local governments more leeway in their policies; it allows a local government to design and amend its own charter, subject to the laws and constitution of the state and also subject to veto by the state.

Cooley's rule The term used to describe the idea that cities should be self-governing, articulated in an 1871 ruling by Michigan judge Thomas Cooley.

TYPES OF LOCAL GOVERNMENT

There is wide variation within and among states in the structure and responsibilities of local government. A full description of the various types could fill several books. The purpose of the following sections is to highlight some of the major types.

County Government

The oldest form of local government in the United States is the county, and it remains a top local governing unit in rural areas and in those few states, such as

New York, where the county has broad responsibility for providing government services. The county is governed through an elected county commission (which, in some states, is called a county legislature or board of supervisors). In most states, there are also elected county sheriffs and county attorneys, and a few states have elected chief county executives.

Counties are subdivisions of a state. They blanket the state in the sense that it is divided completely into county units. The shape and number of these county units, however, varies markedly. Texas is divided into 254 counties. Alaska is larger in area but has only 16 county units. In most states, the county functions as an administrative subdivision of the state. The county's responsibility is to carry out programs, such as highway maintenance or welfare services, that are established by the state. Some analysts believe that the county will increase in importance in upcoming years because of the prominence of issues such as waste disposal that cannot be addressed adequately at the municipal level but require a regional response.

County government illustrates the variation that exists in local governmental structures. Two states, Louisiana and Alaska, call their counties by another name (parishes in Louisiana, boroughs in Alaska). Moreover, the role of the county is not always the same even within a particular state. The county is typically a more visible unit of government in rural areas (where, for example, the county sheriff is often the most widely known public official) than in urban areas (where, for example, residents may not even know where their county officials are located). Also, counties vary greatly in population. They range from some urban counties with more than a million inhabitants to some rural counties with only a few thousand residents. The largest is Los Angeles County in California, which has a population of roughly eight million.

Municipal Government

In most parts of the United States, the major unit of local government is the municipality, which can be a city, town, or village. Municipalities exist partly to carry out activities of the state government, but they exist primarily to serve the self-governing needs of their residents. Most Americans depend on their municipal governments for law enforcement, water, and sanitation services.

Municipalities are legal entities that operate under a charter granted by the state. As indicated previously, a charter defines the limits within which a local governing unit must operate. Over the years, and consistent with the philosophy of local autonomy, municipal charters have become less restrictive. Moreover, rather than drafting separate charters for each municipality, states have developed more general charters that apply to all municipalities within a category (such as "small city" or "medium-sized city," as defined by population). Of course, some municipalities are in a class by themselves and require a specific charter. New York City, for example, has taxing and other powers not granted to other municipalities in New York State.

strong mayor–council system
Most common form of municipal government, consisting of the mayor as chief executive and the local council as the legislative body, in which the mayor has veto power and a prescribed responsibility for budgetary and other policy actions.

The traditional and most common form of municipal government is the mayor-council system, which includes the mayor as the chief executive and the local council as the legislative body (see Table 21-1). The mayor-council system takes two forms. The more common form is the **strong mayor–council system,** in which the mayor has veto power and a prescribed responsibility for budgetary and other policy actions. The mayor, rather than the council, is

TABLE 21-1 Common Forms of Municipal Government

Strong Mayor–Council System

An elected mayor has veto power over an elected council and has substantial authority over the budget and other policies.

Weak Mayor–Council System

An elected mayor does not have veto power and is generally weak relative to the elected council.

Commission System

Executive and legislative power is vested in an elected commission whose members each have a specified policy role, such as police commissioner.

City Manager System

An appointed chief executive administers programs and can be fired by the elected council.

---

the more powerful policy maker. The alternative is the **weak mayor–council system,** in which the mayor's policymaking powers are less substantial than the council's. The mayor has no power to veto the council's actions and often has no formal role in such activities as budget making.

A different type of municipal government entirely is the **commission system.** This form invests executive and legislative authority in a commission, with each commissioner serving as a member of the local council but also having a specified executive role, such as police commissioner or public works commissioner. The commission system has lost considerable favor in recent decades. Its major weakness is that it has no chief executive with the power and responsibility to set the local government's overall direction. There are now only about 100 U.S. communities that employ this governing system. St. Petersburg, Florida, is one of the few cities of any size that still has the commission system.

A final type of municipal government is the **city manager system,** which was pioneered in Ohio during the Progressive era as a reaction against inefficiency and partisan corruption in many of the nation's cities. The system entrusts the executive role to a professionally trained manager, who is chosen, and can be fired, by the city council. This arrangement ensures that the manager will be at least somewhat responsive to political and popular pressures. Most city managers have specialized university training in the operation of municipal government. The typical form of this education is the master of public administration (MPA), which includes courses in areas such as public finance, budgeting, and organization. However, city managers are usually "outsiders" who did not grow up in the community they administer and who typically lack the political support that is necessary to exert strong leadership. Most of the larger cities that installed the city manager system have since reverted to the mayor-council system, but the city manager form is the most common type of government in smaller cities. California is among the states where the city manager system has been widely adopted.

A local chief executive, whether a mayor or city manager, is, above all, an administrator whose main responsibility is to oversee the work of the component units of local government—the police, fire, sanitation, and other departments. Increasingly, local chief executives are also expected to provide economic leadership by fostering a business climate that will keep old firms in the community

weak mayor–council system Form of municipal government in which the mayor's policymaking powers are less substantial than the council's; the mayor has no power to veto the council's actions and often has no formal role in such activities as budget making.

commission system Form of municipal government that invests executive and legislative authority in a commission, with each commissioner serving as a member of the local council but also having a specified executive role, such as police commissioner or public works commissioner.

city manager system Form of municipal government that entrusts the executive role to a professionally trained manager, who is chosen, and can be fired, by the city council.

★ STATES IN THE NATION

PER-PUPIL SPENDING ON PUBLIC ELEMENTARY AND SECONDARY SCHOOLS

Each state spends more per pupil on public schools than does the typical country in Western Europe. However, the states vary substantially in their school expenditures. The state of Utah spends the least—less than $4,000 per pupil each year. Alaska spends the most—nearly $10,000 per pupil each year.

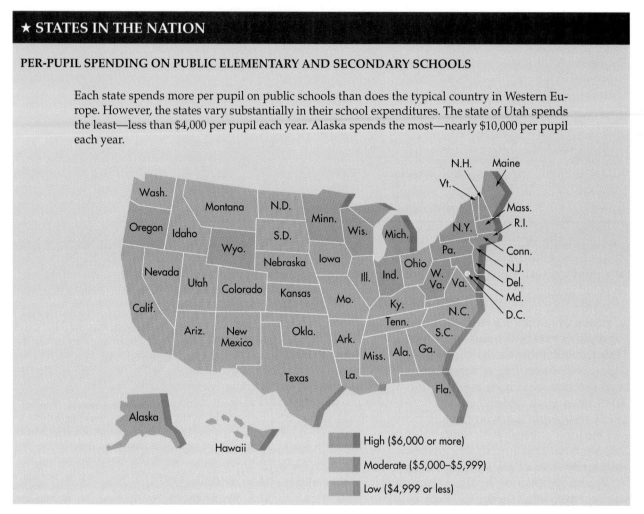

High ($6,000 or more)

Moderate ($5,000–$5,999)

Low ($4,999 or less)

SOURCE: National Education Association, 1996.

and attract new ones. In many cities, including Baltimore, San Antonio, and Minneapolis, mayors have played key roles in the revitalization of downtown areas. Of course, not all chief executives accomplish much, or even get the opportunity. In smaller towns and villages particularly, the position of mayor is often more honorary than active; it is a part-time position held by a trusted member of the community.

Towns and Townships

The word *town* is used in reference to a municipality that is smaller than a city and larger than a village. In most areas of New England, however, a town more often refers to a governing unit that functions as both a municipality and a county. In these areas, the county is often nothing more than a geographical entity, since the town encompasses both one or more communities and their contiguous rural areas. The town has responsibility for both community streets and rural roads as well as other local services. The fabled town meetings that once governed New England towns still exist, but they now seldom attract many people, and the towns are effectively governed by a town council of elected officials, who, in the larger towns, usually entrust day-to-day operations to a full-time town manager.

In several Midwestern states, and a few states elsewhere, townships are an important governing unit. They are subunits of counties and, in rural areas particularly, have key policy responsibilities, including roadways and other public services. They resemble New England towns in that they were created as geographic units and vary widely in their population density. Thus, they are unlike municipalities where, for the most part, residents live closely together. Townships also differ from municipalities in that, as subunits of the county, they are not empowered to enact local ordinances. They carry out county policy; they do not make policy of their own.

School Districts

The tradition of local public schools is deeply embedded in the American political experience. Unlike Europe, where private schools and national educational standards have historically been more important, the United States has emphasized public education and local control. This control is exercised through local school boards. In a few places, the school board is subordinate to the municipal government, but elsewhere it is an independent body. School policy is established by the local board rather than by the local mayor or council. The chief executive of the local public school system is a specially trained professional, the superintendent of schools. The superintendent is hired, and can be fired, by the local board.

Some states have recently authorized charter schools as an alternative to traditional public schools. Such schools are granted a charter (much as local governments have a charter) within which they must operate. Charter schools have greater freedom than do other public schools in selecting their admission, curriculum, and other policies.

Special Districts and Metropolitan Government

Another form of municipal government, and one of increasing importance, is the special district. As society has become more complex and interdependent, a need has arisen for local governing institutions that are responsive to the resulting policy needs. Special districts that deal with such policy areas as water supply, soil conservation, and waste disposal are an answer. These districts also provide an answer to the problem of coordinating the efforts of independent municipal governments. Issues such as pollution control are not easily addressed within a single community. Special districts bring municipalities together; the typical form of governance of these districts is a board that includes a member from each municipality within the district's boundaries. The day-to-day operations of these districts, however, are typically entrusted to trained administrators, who often have specialized educations, such as the waste-management engineers who oversee municipal sewage systems.

Members of the Metro Dade police departments say the Pledge of Allegiance during a public ceremony. Miami and surrounding communities in south Florida have a metropolitan government. It provides police, sanitation, and other services to the area's residents. In most U.S. metropolitan areas, such services are provided by each community separately.

metropolitan government
Form of local government created when local governments join together and assign it responsibility for a range of activities so as to reduce the waste and duplication that results when every locality in a densely populated area has its own police force, its own sanitation department, and so on.

Special districts ordinarily have responsibility for a specific policy activity, such as solid-waste management or soil conservation. In some urban areas, however, local governments have joined to create a **metropolitan government** that is given responsibility for a broader range of activities. An example is the Dade County (Florida) Metropolitan Government, which includes Miami and surrounding communities. Each community is represented on the Dade County Commission, which has responsibility for providing most of the local services. A metropolitan government is designed to reduce the waste and duplication that results when every locality in a densely populated area has its own police force, its own sanitation department, its own planning board, and so on. Although a metropolitan government is more efficient, the tradition of strong local autonomy makes it an unappealing option to many Americans.

LOCAL ELECTIONS AND PARTICIPATION

The principle of elective office dominates local government. In addition to an elected mayor, most communities have an elected town or city council. The office of county commissioner is also an elective office throughout the country. Except in a few eastern states, local officials are chosen in nonpartisan elections. No party labels appear on the ballot.

Perhaps no local institution symbolizes the nature of American democracy better than the public schools. School board members are elected and, in many communities, the voters even have the opportunity to approve or reject school budgets and bonding proposals. In contrast, school officials in European countries are typically appointed to their positions, and school budgets are set primarily by national governments.

Voting in local elections is subject to state registration laws. However, as we saw in Chapter 7, many local governments have tried to weaken the link between their level of government and the state and national levels by scheduling local elections for odd-numbered years rather than the even-numbered ones during which all federal and most state elections are held. A predictable effect of this scheduling is that voter turnout is somewhat lower at each level than would be the case if national, state, and local elections were held simultaneously. The average turnout in local elections in most states is very low—30 percent or less. Turnout figures can be deceptive. There are countless instances of extraordinary turnout in local elections when a contentious issue is on the ballot. School bonding issues, for example, often produce a high turnout, and increasingly have pitted families with children in the public schools against the growing number of elderly Americans who, on the whole, are less supportive of school spending proposals.[11]

Local elections embody many of the conflicts that are found, in one form or another, throughout U.S. politics. Many communities, for example, use at-large (community-wide) districts to elect members of the local council. The justification for the approach is the notion that at-large council members will act on behalf of the whole community and not sections of it, as might be the case if they were elected from separate districts within the community. However, at-large districts tend to result in the election of council members who are demographically similar to the majority of voters. Black and Hispanic candidates have fared poorly in these systems, which has created pressures to change at-large districts to separate-district systems.

Elections, however, are only one form of citizen influence on local government. Although the opportunities for ordinary citizens to direct state and national officials are confined mostly to periodic elections, there are additional opportunities available in local settings. As we saw in Chapter 7, group participation is relatively high in the United States, and many groups are involved in community-oriented activities. A few cities, including St. Paul, Minnesota, have even delegated authority to neighborhood councils that may have responsibility, for example, for creating and operating community centers or playgrounds.

The news media are also influential in local politics. Local newspapers and television stations sometimes take the lead in highlighting local issues and exposing inept or unethical officials. In any case, most local officials are wary of antagonizing the local media. On the state level, the media are less powerful since a state's boundaries rarely coincide with a news organization's market. Thus, state officials and policy actions receive less scrutiny from the press.

It would be a mistake to conclude, however, that local officials are highly responsive to local residents as a whole. Studies have found that in some locations officials are primarily attentive to the community's economic and social elite. They constitute a local power structure that, even more than public officials themselves, decides community policies.[12]

State and Local Finance

The federal government raises more tax revenues than do all fifty states and the thousands of local governments combined. Although states and localities have a substantial tax base, they are in an inherently competitive situation. People and businesses faced with state or local tax increases can move to another state or locality where taxes are lower. Between the 1960s and 1980s, there was a substantial movement of business firms from the northeast and midwest to the south and southwest. These firms were lured by the cheaper labor and lower energy costs of the sunbelt and also by the lower tax rates of southern states.

Local governments are also in a relatively weak tax position. They compete with one another for the jobs and income that business firms represent. Every sizable city in the United States offers tax breaks or other incentives to companies that might relocate there. The predatory nature of the competition makes it difficult for any locality to raise its tax rate substantially and virtually forces them to give tax breaks to firms that could well afford to pay.

A community may even find that it has to pay a business to remain in the community. An obvious example, but not the only one, is the sports franchise that threatens to move its team unless the host city builds an expensive new stadium or arena. Minneapolis, Boston, and Miami are among the cities that decided it was in the community's interest to comply with such a demand. Los Angeles is among those that refused the demand and lost a professional sports team as a result.

States and localities are denied a form of taxation available to the federal government—tariffs. Congress has the power to levy taxes on goods shipped to the United States from abroad. The U.S. Constitution prohibits states from placing a duty on goods that cross their borders since such action would disrupt interstate commerce.

SOURCES OF REVENUE

The major sources of state revenue are sales taxes, personal income taxes, corporate income taxes, and user fees, such as motor vehicle licenses (see Figure 21-3). There are, however, substantial variations in the taxing policies of the states. A few states have no personal income tax. South Dakota is one of these states. It also has no corporate income tax. Not surprisingly, South Dakota has one of the lowest levels of public services in the nation. Its neighboring state of Minnesota, for example, spends substantially more per capita on public education than does South Dakota.

Income Taxes

Although a few states do not levy an income tax, it is still a major revenue source, accounting for roughly 40 percent of all state tax revenue. The competitive nature of state tax policy, however, serves to hold down income tax rates. The highest

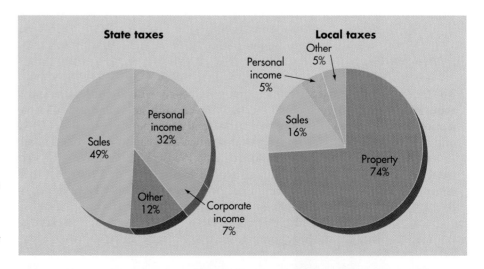

FIGURE 21-3   Sources of State and Local Government Revenue States rely on sales and personal income taxes for most of their revenues. Localities depend heavily on property taxes. *Source: U.S. Bureau of Census, 2000.*

marginal rate on personal income on federal tax returns is 39.5 percent. The highest ordinary rate at the state level is less than 10 percent and, in most states, is roughly 5 percent. A few localities—New York City, among them—raise revenue through income taxes. These taxes enable a local government to collect revenue from individuals who work in the community and use its services in the process, but who live elsewhere, usually a nearby suburb.

Sales Tax

The **general sales tax** is the chief source of revenue for the states, accounting for about half of all taxes they raise. The sales tax is a flat-rate tax on consumer goods and thereby places a relatively heavy burden on lower-income persons, who spend a higher proportion of their income on such goods than do upper-income persons. The regressive nature of the sales tax has been a source of criticism, and some states exempt food and medicine from the sales tax in order to relieve somewhat the burden it places on lower-income people. Nevertheless, the sales tax is a reliable method of raising large sums of money, and the states have increasingly used it to obtain their revenues.

In many states, local governments also obtain revenue from the sales tax, and in some states, the local share varies by location. In New York, for example, the state's sales tax is four cents on the dollar while the local tax varies from two cents to four cents. Another form of sales tax is the **excise tax,** which is applied only to selected items, such as gasoline and jewelry. It is sometimes called the "sin tax" because liquor and cigarettes are among the items included.

Lotteries and Fees

Although sales and income taxes account for the very large share of state revenues, they are not the only significant revenue sources. Lotteries, for example, account for a small but rising percentage of revenue. They were banned by Congress as a form of illegal gambling until a few decades ago, but today, more than two-thirds of the states run a lottery. The major complaint today about state lotteries is that many of the regular players are low-income Americans who cannot afford to play but who dream of striking it rich. In their lottery advertising, states play up this dream but rarely mention that the odds of winning the biggest jackpots are roughly those of being hit, not once but twice, by lightning. States also do not publicize the fact that they retain more than half the money spent to purchase lottery tickets.

License and user fees are a fourth source of state revenue. The most important are the license fees that states charge for vehicle registration and drivers' licenses. But there are also, for example, license fees charged to doctors and lawyers that allow them to practice in a state and liquor license fees charged to stores and restaurants that sell or dispense liquor. A few states also derive substantial revenue from severance taxes that are imposed on those who extract natural resources, such as oil, coal, or bauxite, from the state's soil.

Property Taxes

As Figure 21-3 indicates, local governments rely primarily on the property tax for their revenues. This form of taxation accounts for three-fourths of all revenues

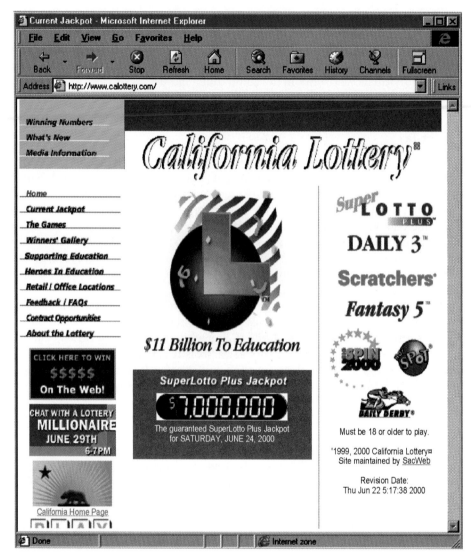

States are in an inherently competitive situation with regard to taxation. A state cannot raise taxes very high without losing firms and residents to a state where taxes are lower. This situation has led states to develop alternative sources of revenue. One of the most common is a state lottery. The payout to lottery winners and vendors is typically about half the amount taken in; the rest goes to the state government.

raised directly by local government, but it has drawbacks. It is paid, for example, in a lump sum, which heightens taxpayers' awareness of its cost and leads them to resist any increase. Few actions are more likely to result in the defeat of a local official in the next election than a steep increase in property taxes. Accordingly, localities have turned increasingly to sales taxes (shared with the state and collected with the state's permission) and local income taxes (collected with the state's permission). The revenues from these sources increase automatically when the economy expands, thus providing localities with increased revenues without a raise in the tax rate.

Government Grants

States and localities also depend on revenues provided by other governments. More than 15 percent of state revenues are provided by federal grants-in-aid

The state of Hawaii is one of many states that depend heavily on federal spending for their economic vitality. Shown here is a scene from the naval base at Pearl Harbor.

programs, while local governments get about 30 percent of their revenues from the state and 5 percent from Washington. States and localities could not easily manage without these grants, but the money has a drawback not attached to their other revenues—it comes with strings attached. As we saw in Chapter 3, grants are provided for specific uses only.

The states and localities also benefit from federal spending. The states of the south and west, particularly, owe many of their jobs to federal programs. In Hawaii, for example, thirty thousand active U.S. military personnel are stationed at bases that include Pearl Harbor (Navy), Schofield Barracks (Army), and Hickam Field (Air Force).

Federal grants-in-aid and other federal policies tend to reduce the importance of state-to-state differences in wealth as a factor in state and local policies. Federal assistance is targeted disproportionately for less affluent states and communities. In addition, many federal programs require matching grants and uniform standards of participating states. However, the leveling effect of this federal policy is not very great, and states differ enormously in their economic wealth. The level of public services in all areas—education, welfare, health, and so on—is higher in wealthier states. In comparison with the five poorest states (Mississippi, West Virginia, Utah, Arkansas, and South Carolina), the five wealthiest states (Connecticut, New Jersey, Alaska, Massachusetts, and New York) spend over $1,000 per pupil more on public education each year.

Borrowing

A final source of revenue is borrowing. States and localities issue bonds for purchase by investors. Although borrowing is sometimes necessary, state and local government try to hold it to a minimum since the funds at some point will have to be repaid, with interest.

THE UPS AND DOWNS OF STATE AND LOCAL FINANCE

Some analysts have concluded that economics, not politics, is the chief determinant of a state's public policies. Whether that observation is literally true, there is no question that the wealth of a state has a great influence on its policies. In the mid-1980s, the states were beneficiaries of a sharp upturn in the national

CURRENT CONTROVERSIES

DO THE REVENUES GENERATED BY GAMBLING OUTWEIGH THE COSTS?

States and localities are in an inherently competitive position with regard to raising revenues. People and firms faced with state or local tax increases can move to another state or locality where taxes are lower. Accordingly, states and localities have looked for revenue sources, such as license fees, that seem somewhat less onerous than income or sales taxes. In recent decades, gambling in one form or another has become a prime source of direct and indirect new revenues. Most states today conduct lotteries, with the revenues going either into a general fund or for a special purpose, such as the public schools. A few states, such as New Jersey, have also legalized casino gambling. At one time, Nevada was the only state with legalized gambling. The trend toward legalized gambling is heralded by some as a net benefit in terms of jobs and tax revenues. Others claim that the long-term costs of gambling far outweigh its short-term benefits.

YES: The gaming industry is helping the economy grow by creating jobs, paying taxes, and providing economic stability to hundreds of communities across the United States. Today the industry directly and indirectly employs more than one million people, from card dealers, construction workers, and carpet makers to ranchers, dancers, and cooks. In 1995, the casino gaming industry alone reported $25 billion in total revenues (double the revenues from 1990). . . . While gaming opponents may offer vague economic theories about gaming revenues, the facts show empirically that when gaming-entertainment is introduced into a region, it creates jobs and generates tax revenues.

—American Gaming Association

NO: Gambling costs far more than it benefits. Studies show that for every dollar gambling produces for a regional economy, three dollars are lost because of the economic and social costs of gambling. When government legalizes more gambling, taxpayers lose—whether they gamble or not. Gambling cannibalizes local businesses. A hundred dollars spent in a slot machine is a hundred dollars that is not spent in a local restaurant, theatre, or retail store. . . . Gambling victimizes the poor. The poorest citizens spend the largest percentage of their incomes on gambling. Those who can afford it the least gamble the most.

—National Coalition Against Legalized Gambling

economy. As corporate and personal incomes rose, so did the tax revenues flowing into the state treasuries. Policy initiatives flowed from the states, which seemed especially adept at combining programs designed to stimulate economic development with programs designed to tighten fiscal responsibility.

Innovative governors were leaders of the change. Their experimental economic and social programs, from technological development to welfare reform, were widely publicized.[13] An example was the so-called Massachusetts Miracle. In Boston and the surrounding area, dozens of high-technology firms sprang up almost overnight, creating unprecedented prosperity for the state. Its governor, Michael Dukakis, was given much of the credit for the economic boom. He was voted the nation's most effective governor by the other governors, which contributed to the political reputation that helped him gain the Democratic party's 1988 presidential nomination.

By 1990, however, many of the states were in trouble. More than half had budget deficits and faced the prospect of service cuts and tax increases. Many states faced serious long-term economic problems in the form of declining industries and strong foreign competitors. All the states had no choice but to cut back on either their plans or their programs; they had no money for significant new initiatives.

This situation also encouraged states to develop new approaches in areas such as health and welfare policy. Led once again by innovative governors, such as Wisconsin's Tommy Thompson, the states devised programs that were more efficient and in many instances more effective than the previous ones.[14] By 1995, the state capitals had clearly eclipsed Washington as a source of policy ideas. This realization encouraged Congress to shift additional policy responsibilities to the states through, for example, the expanded use of block grants (see Chapter 3).

As the national economy grew rapidly after 1995, the states once again were in a strong financial position. An increase in tax revenues from heightened business activity and personal income enabled them to spend more in areas such as education and highway construction. States also used their surplus revenues to cut taxes, reduce outstanding debt, and build up cash reserves as a hedge against the next economic downswing.

This pattern of boom and bust results because the states and localities, unlike the federal government, have only a limited capacity to borrow money. The U.S. Constitution denies them the authority to print their own currency, which means, in hard times, that they have little choice but to cut back their services.

State and Local Policy

Through the Tenth Amendment, the states possess what is sometimes called the **police power**, a term that refers to the broad power of government to regulate the health, safety, and morals of the citizenry. Possession of this power has meant that the American states carry out many of the policy responsibilities that in other countries are dealt with at the national level. Law enforcement, public education, public health, and roads are among the policy areas that in America are defined largely by the state and local governments.

police power A term that refers to the broad power of government to regulate the health, safety, and morals of the citizenry.

Although the policies enacted by Congress get more attention from the press, the acts of state legislatures have more influence on the day-to-day lives of most Americans. For example, most crimes are defined by state law, most criminal acts are investigated by authorities operating under state law, most trials take place under state law, and most prisoners are held in penitentiaries and jails that operate under laws enacted by state legislatures.

POLICY PRIORITIES

One way to see how the states use their power is to rank policy areas by level of spending (see Figure 21-4). The top spending category for the states is public education, followed by public welfare, health and hospitals, and highways. These four areas are by far the most significant components of state spending. There is a large dropoff in spending between the fourth category, highways, and the fifth one, police.

The policy priorities of local governments are less easily described (see Figure 21-4). Some local units, such as school boards, operate in only one policy area. Municipalities vary in size from the largest cities to the smallest villages, and their policies differ accordingly. Despite such differences, a few patterns to local spending are discernible. Far and away the biggest expense for

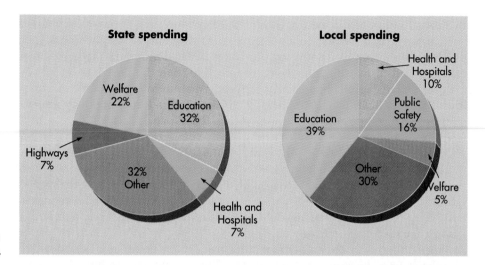

FIGURE 21-4   Spending Priorities of State and Local Governments
Education is the major spending category for both state and local governments. *Source: U.S. Bureau of Census, 2000 (state), 1999 (local).*

local governments is public education; it accounts for about 40 percent of all spending at the local level. Public safety (police, fire, corrections) ranks second at roughly 15 percent, with health and hospitals in third place with about 10 percent. Welfare and roads are the leading areas among the other spending categories.

PUBLIC POLICY PATTERNS

A brief description of some of the policy activities of state and local governments, and where they get the money to pay for these activities, will provide a broader perspective on the role of states and localities in the American system.

Education

Public education, including primary schools, secondary schools, and colleges and universities, accounts for the largest share of combined state and local spending, about a third of the total. Education spending by state and local governments dwarfs that of the federal government—more than 90 percent to less than 10 percent. Even higher education is mainly a state and local responsibility, which means that the greatest share of the country's investment in the technical research and personnel that underpin the economy is provided by subnational governments. They also make the key substantive policy decisions in the education area, from curriculum to performance standards to length of schooling.

Of the many issues affecting public education in the states, two stand out in recent years. One is the disparity in spending among school districts, which, in most instances, reflects differences in communities' wealth. Suburban schools, for example, are typically better funded and have better facilities than the inner-city schools in the same metropolitan area. Should such differences be allowed? In a 1973 Texas case, the Supreme Court concluded that a state has no obligation to provide students with an equal education: its obligation is "to provide an 'adequate' education for all children."[15] Nevertheless, state financial contributions to local schools are typically designed to help poorer districts more than wealthier ones. This tendency, however, does not begin to offset the disparity in the quality of schools between a state's poorest communities and its richest ones.

In recent years, pressures have intensified to reduce disparities in school spending. In 1998, New Jersey's highest court settled a years-long battle over school funding by ordering Governor Christine Todd Whitman to develop a plan to equalize spending in the state's public schools. Courts in about twenty states have ruled against inequitable school financing systems, although they have not gone as far as New Jersey's top court in ordering an equalization plan.[16]

Another major education issue is the quality of American schools (see Chapter 19). U.S. students do poorly on standardized tests in comparison with students of other advanced industrialized nations. Twelfth-grade American students are not even among the top ten in physics, math, or any other subject where cross-national comparisons can reliably be made. This situation has contributed to debates over merit pay for teachers, national tests for all U.S. students, and parent-student choice of schools. Some analysts claim that American public schools are simply not providing the quality of education found in other Western democracies and that alternative approaches must be found. Other analysts say the schools are not the problem, or at least not the major problem. They say that both the diversity of American society and the absence of a strong intellectual tradition limit the schools' ability to educate students at the highest level.

Welfare Assistance

The most expensive social welfare program in the United States is entirely a national one—social security for retirees. However, the states are vitally involved in the provision of most welfare services, particularly public assistance programs for the needy (see Chapter 19). Programs such as TANF, Medicaid, and food stamps operate within federal guidelines, but the states have discretionary authority over benefit and eligibility levels. These programs are funded jointly by the state and national governments and are administered primarily by the state governments. They have the local offices that are necessary for administering need-based welfare programs, which, as we noted in Chapter 19, require regular contacts between caseworkers and welfare recipients.

Welfare programs account for about 15 percent of all state and local spending. This spending and the American tradition of self-reliance make welfare a contentious political issue. The states have devised various ways of holding down spending. In response to the rapid increase in Medicaid costs, for example, the state of Oregon conducted a systematic study of medical procedures in order to identify, and make ineligible for Medicaid reimbursement, those procedures that physicians apply electively. Medicaid, however, is sure to remain a central issue. It is a joint federal-state program, but the high costs of medical care have made Medicaid the single largest item in state budgets. Health care costs are certain to rise in the future. Just as certain is the continuing need of poorer Americans for medical care. At some point, these fiscal and medical realities are sure to collide.

With passage of the 1996 Welfare Reform Act, the states assumed the primary responsibility for welfare and employment policy.

The high cost and controversial nature of welfare assistance were major factors underlying the 1996 welfare reform act (see Chapter 19). The legislation increases the states' ability to define eligibility for welfare benefits and assigns them responsibility for training welfare recipients to enter the work force.

Because the number of welfare recipients has declined sharply in nearly every state since passage of the 1996 act, welfare is a less pressing issue today. Analysts are divided, however, on how well the new system will work when the country suffers its next economic recession. If the welfare rolls swell and the number of ineligible but needy families rises dramatically, the ensuing conflict could exceed even many of the past battles.

Health and Hospitals

Nearly 10 percent of state and local expenditures are in the health and hospitals policy area. All states and many localities operate public hospitals, and most of the laws and regulations affecting medical practices are established by state governments. In addition, states and localities have public health programs such as immunization campaigns, mobile x-ray units, and health inspections of motels and restaurants.

Highways

Until the 1950s, the roadways of America were built almost entirely with state and local funds. The interstate highway system was begun in the 1950s and was funded largely by the national government. Today, Washington provides about a third of the total spending on highways, and states and localities contribute the rest. State and local governments set most policies governing use of highways, including traffic infractions and shipping methods. Highway spending accounts for about 5 percent of state and local expenditures.

Police and Prisons

Some democracies have a national police force, but the United States does not. It has local and state police forces. They enforce state laws and local ordinances, which collectively govern most aspects of crime and punishment. The state police include the highway patrol, game wardens, prison guards, and liquor control officers, and they are generally well trained and highly professional. Local police are less specialized, are more uneven in their training and professionalism, and are required to do most of the "dirty" work of law enforcement—crime control and the maintenance of public order. Roughly 8 percent of state and local spending is for police-related activities.

States and localities in recent years have invested heavily in prisons and other correctional facilities. As was indicated in Chapter 4, the United States on a per capita basis is rivaled only by Russia in the number of its people who are imprisoned. The large prison population in the United States reflects a policy of lengthened and mandatory sentencing that developed in the past decade largely because of escalating drug-related crime. Many prisoners are in jail for possession or purchase of relatively small quantities of illegal drugs. As the fiscal and human costs of this policy have increased, some state and local officials have questioned its wisdom and have sought alternatives, including giving judges more discretion in the sentencing of nonviolent first offenders.

The Environment

The environment is a relatively small part of state and local budgets, but money alone is not a reliable indicator of policy effort in the environmental area, since much of it works through regulatory activities that impose costs on firms and consumers.

Most states and localities were complacent about environmental protection until the federal government in the 1960s and 1970s greatly broadened the scope of its activities. Today, states and localities are active participants in the effort to protect the environment. For example, they routinely require environmental impact statements for major development projects and have acted to protect their land and water resources from pollutants. In addition, conservation through the preservation of parks, natural resources, and wildlife has increasingly been a focus of state policy. New York, for example, has taken steps to purchase and otherwise protect tens of thousands of acres of undeveloped land in its Adirondack Mountains.

Sewage and garbage disposal is a special problem for local governments. As environmental standards have increased, it has become an increasingly costly activity, ranking only behind schools, roadways, and public safety as an expenditure category for cities. It has also become increasingly contentious because neighborhoods nearly always resist the nearby placement of a new sewage treatment place, garbage incinerator, or landfill. Public resistance has forced many communities into costly solutions such as the shipping of garbage to distant landfills, which, because of the cost, also displeases residents.

THE POLITICS OF STATE AND LOCAL POLICY

The general economic conditions of a state, as was mentioned previously, has a substantial impact on its policies. Richer states are simply in a stronger position

The environment has become an important issue of state and local politics as a result of the public's growing awareness of the damage caused by pollution. Here, a bucket of oysters is dumped into New York harbor as part of an effort to restock oyster beds destroyed by contaminated wastes.

to provide more and better services than poorer states are. West Virginia with its per capita income of $19,362 can hardly be expected to have schools, hospitals, roadways, and other facilities that match those of Washington state with a per capita income of $27,961.

Wealth alone, however, cannot fully explain state-to-state difference. Public policies also reflect variations in states' policies and culture, as the following discussion will indicate.

Political Culture

Although Americans, as was indicated in Chapter 1, share a common political heritage that is built around principles such as liberty, equality, and self-government, distinctive regional subcultures persist. These subcultures, as the political scientist Daniel Elazar has noted, reflect differences in ethnic settlement patterns, historical episodes, economic conditions, partisan competition, and other influences.[17]

The states in the northern tier of the nation have what Elazar describes as a **moralistic subculture.** This subculture is characterized by an emphasis on "good government" (the public interest), "clean government" (honesty), and "civic government" (public participation). The states that share this subculture

moralistic subculture
American subculture characterized by an emphasis on the public interest, honesty, and public participation; typical of states in the northern tier of the nation.

were populated primarily by northern Europeans, including the English, Germans, and Scandinavians. Minnesota is an example of a moralistic state. Minnesota has one of the highest rates of voter turnout in the country and one of the lowest rates of political corruption. Political competition in this subculture tends to focus on issues rather than personalities, and activist government is accepted. Taxes are relatively high, but so is the level of public services. States in this region spend more heavily than other states in areas such as public education, and their students tend to score higher on standardized tests than do students in other regions. The region also has some of the best public universities in the nation.

The middle part of the United States, from Massachusetts to Maryland and then westward through Illinois and Missouri to southwestern states such as Arizona, is described by Elazar as having an **individualistic subculture.** This subculture is oriented toward private life and economic gain, and politics is largely an extension of this perspective. Political conflict is rough-and-tumble, political power is closely guarded, and public policy is often narrowly applied. Illinois is an example of an individualistic state and is renowned for the battles between the city of Chicago and the downstate area for political control and policy advantage. Compared with states that have a moralistic subculture, those with an individualistic subculture tend to spend less per capita on public services. They place greater emphasis on self-sufficiency and are generally less willing to use political power to reduce economic and social inequality.

individualistic subculture American subculture oriented toward private life and economic gain, with politics largely an extension of this perspective; characterizing middle, western, and southwestern states.

A **traditionalistic subculture,** in Elazar's terms, typifies the states of the old Confederacy and a few states bordering on it, such as West Virginia. This subculture reflects the stratified, plantation society out of which it grew: it is conservative in its focus and elitist in its leadership. The politics of a traditionalistic state is likely to be dominated by a small number of prominent leaders, many of whom have gained power through family ties. Government is likely to be a topic of considerable interest in a traditionalistic state, but not because government is activist. In fact, traditionalists prefer a government that reinforces the existing power structure. Until recent decades, when the influence of suburban Washington brought political change to Virginia, it epitomized the traditionalistic subculture. For years, Virginia politics was controlled by elite families, such as the Byrds, who aimed to preserve the racial, social, and economic hierarchy that had defined Virginia society since the colonial period.

traditionalistic subculture American subculture reflecting the stratified society out of which it grew, which is conservative in its focus and elitist in its leadership; typifies states of the old Confederacy and those on its borders.

These subcultures do not coincide exactly with state borders, and elements of each subculture are found in every region of the country. Other subcultures also exist. The South, for example, has a populist heritage that runs counter to its dominant traditionalist subculture. Several of the South's best-known politicians, including Alabama's George Wallace and Louisiana's Huey Long, rose to prominence by attacking entrenched power structures in their own states. Nevertheless, Elazar's typology illustrates the important point that the American states are politically diverse. They operate within the framework of a common federal government and a larger political culture, but they have distinctive features that make and mold their politics and policies.

Party Competition

The states vary significantly in their support for one major party or the other. Where the Republicans are stronger, as in the mountain states, taxes and the level of public services tend to be lower. Where Democrats are stronger, as in the northeast, the reverse situation tends to hold.

The intensity of party competition has a somewhat less obvious, but no less important, relationship to public policy. In states where party competition is weak, politics tends to be somewhat exclusive: a sizable share of the population, usually the poorest groups, will be more or less ignored by government. The dominant party has gained control without the help of these groups, and the minority party could not gain control even with their help. In other words, neither party has a strong incentive to seek their vote. The classic case of a neglected public was the black community in the South in the period before the modern civil rights movement of the 1950s and 1960s. African Americans were politically powerless. Neither the white Democrats who ran the South nor the white Republicans who offered token opposition had a real interest in bringing black people into their coalition.

Where party competition is more intense, any sizable group in a state is likely to receive the attention of one party or the other and thus to be in a position to influence public policy. In the modern South, which is increasingly competitive between the parties, black voters are a growing force and have tipped the balance in some elections. They are also more likely than at any time in the past to have policy influence.

The state party systems have become more competitive by some indicators and less competitive by others. Compared with the 1960s, there are fewer states today in which one party has 60 percent or more of the legislators. However, the number of state legislative races in which the incumbent has no or only token opposition has increased.[18] Faced with a well-funded and popular incumbent, the opposing party has increasingly conceded the election. The professionalization of state legislatures has had an effect similar to the professionalization of Congress: legislators have used their positions to solidify public support and dominate campaign contributions, which in turn have discouraged election challengers.

Group Competition

Interest-group systems can be looked at in a similar way. In those states where interest groups are many in number and somewhat evenly balanced in their political resources, public policy tends to serve a broad range of interests. An example is the state of New York, which has many competing factions, including, for example, business and labor, the upstate and downstate areas, and environmentalists and developers. Almost any legislation that makes it through the New York state legislature requires negotiation among numerous groups.

In states where a particular group or interest is dominant, however, government tends to serve that group or interest above all others. A classic example was the Anaconda Copper Company in Montana, which, during the period that it accounted for nearly all the state's mining and manufacturing, nearly ran the state. A more recent example is the influence of the Church of Jesus Christ of Latter-day Saints in Utah. The large share of the state's residents are Mormons, and a policy alternative that is actively opposed by the church has almost no chance of becoming law. Thus, the church for years opposed the sale of hard liquor in Utah, and such sales were prohibited by law. The law was changed recently, but only after Mormon leaders agreed not to oppose the change, which

Utah is a state where political alternatives are substantially shaped by a dominant interest. Policy proposals that are actively opposed by the Church of Jesus Christ of Latter-day Saints have almost no chance of becoming law. Shown here is a winter picture with holiday lights of the Mormon Temple in Salt Lake City.

was prompted by the state's desire to improve its ability to attract tourists and conventions.

Utah with its Mormon population is one of the most distinctive states in the union, but every state has its special characteristics. California is no more like Mississippi than Mississippi is like Rhode Island. Yet, as we have seen, the American states also have many aspects in common. The differences and similarities among the states are testimony to the enduring nature of the American governing experiment. The states are different enough to provide their residents with a special identity and a special political experience; yet they are alike enough to allow the triumph of the national union that the Framers so keenly envisioned two hundred years ago.

The Great Balancing Act: Localism in a Large Nation

The structure of U.S. government—federalism and localism—was established when the nation was founded two centuries ago. The seven million Americans of the time lived closer together, and yet farther apart, than Americans of today. They were crowded along the eastern seaboard, but travel from Savannah in the south to Boston in the north could take weeks. Communication was equally slow: news traveled no faster than the people could carry it. The United States today has 275 million people spread across a continent, reaching even into Alaska and Hawaii. Yet communication is instantaneous, and an airplane can span the distance between Boston to Los Angeles in a few hours.

Is the constitutional structure that was created two hundred years ago suited to modern needs? It is a question that scholars and policymakers sometimes ask. Yet none have concluded that the nation would be better off without its three relatively distinctive levels of government. They accept the essential wisdom of James Madison's argument on the strength of "a compound republic."[19]

The arguments today are confined to issues of the relative balance of power among the three levels. And if conservatives are more inclined than liberals to stress localism, each side embraces the alternative position when doing so furthers its policy goals.

Accordingly, the relative balance among the levels has shifted from time to time. Throughout most of the twentieth century, power shifted upward toward the federal government as society became ever more complex and interdependent. The demand for greater efficiency and equality could only be met through a stronger national response. The U.S. economy had to be transformed into a national economy, and demands for equal treatment by disadvantaged Americans had to be addressed nationally if they were to be met.

In more recent years, there has been a flow of power back to the states and localities. The trend can be explained in part by the discovery that national solutions to certain policy problems are less effective than their original advocates envisioned. It is also attributable to Americans' respect for local differences and their willingness to experiment with new approaches. The federal social welfare programs that were established in the 1960s were not failures—they did succeed in lifting millions of Americans out of poverty. But they were also not unbridled successes—they fostered welfare dependency and fueled taxpayer resentment. The welfare reform legislation enacted in 1996 sought a new balance, one that would preserve a safety net for low-income Americans yet encourage the able-bodied among them to enter the work force. Few analysts believe that the act is the final answer to Americans' welfare needs. But it is the current answer and will remain so until an emerging problem generates political pressure for something different. Whether that "something" will enlarge or diminish the federal, state, or local role cannot be predicted. The response will depend on the nature of the problem and the political outlook of the moment. As the historian Daniel Boorstin observed, pragmatism rather than orthodoxy is the defining characteristic of American politics.[20]

If anything, this pragmatism will be even more evident in the years to come. Americans will become more, not less, interdependent as a result of expected changes in communication, computer technology, and the global economy. An effect of interdependency, as we saw in Chapter 3, is an increase in the demands on government at all levels. The examples are countless. The environment, for instance, was barely an issue until the cumulative impact of economic development virtually forced Americans to take notice. Once they did, they turned to all levels of government for answers. As the national, state, and local governments responded, it became apparent to officials at each level that effective solutions would require cooperation between them. There is no reason to believe that the great domestic policy issues of the twenty-first century will require a different type of response.

The writers of the U.S. Constitution could not possibly have envisioned life in twenty-first-century America. Theirs was a world of horse-drawn carriages and candlelight, not a world of jet airplanes and computers.[21] But they did envision a governing system flexible enough to respond to changing needs during changing times. The persistence of this system across more than two centuries is testimony to their vision and to the willingness of succeeding generations of Americans to find a combination of national, state, and local authority that could meet their governing needs.

www.mhhe.com/patterson5

Self-Quiz

Summary

Although developments in the twentieth century have narrowed the differences among the American states, they, and the localities that govern under their authority, remain distinctive and vital systems of government.

All states apply the constitutional principle of separate branches sharing power, but the structure of the state governments differs in some respects from that of the federal government. An example is the more widespread use of elections at the state level. Most states elect by popular vote their judges and a number of executives, including an attorney general and treasurer in addition to a governor. Through the initiative or the referendum, nearly all states also allow their residents to vote directly on issues of policy.

Local governments are chartered by the state. They are not sovereign governments, but most states have chosen to grant local units a considerable level of policymaking discretion. Local governments include counties, municipalities, school districts, and special districts. Of these, the independent school district is the most distinctively American institution, but the municipality is the primary governing unit. Municipalities are governed by one of four types of systems: the strong mayor–council system,

the weak mayor–council system, the commission system, or the city manager system.

The states and localities have primary responsibility for most of the public policies that directly touch Americans' daily lives. For example, the major share of legislation devoted to public education and about 90 percent of the funding for it are provided by the states and localities. Public welfare, public health, roads, and police are other policy areas dominated by these subnational governments. They do not, however, have the amount of revenue that is available to the federal government. Competition between them holds down their taxing capacity. Their policies are also conditioned by the wealth of the state or locality, and by the structure of its party and interest group systems.

Key Terms

bicameral legislature
charter
city manager system
commission system
constitutional initiative
Cooley's rule
Dillon's rule
home rule
individualistic subculture
initiative

metropolitan government
moralistic subculture
ordinance
police power
recall
referendum
state constitutional convention
strong mayor–council system
traditionalistic subculture
weak mayor–council system

Suggested Readings

Broder, David. *Democracy Derailed.* San Diego: Harcourt, 2000. An analysis of how powerful groups have captured the initiative process.

Ehrenhalt, Alan. *Democracy in the Mirror.* Washington, D.C.: Congressional Quarterly, 1998. A look at grassroots politics in America.

Hedge, David. *Governance and the Changing American States.* Boulder, Colo.: Westview Press, 1998. An analysis of how political change is affecting the states.

Hero, Rodney. *Faces of Inequality.* New York: Oxford University Press, 2000. An assessment of how states' politics and policies are shaped by their racial and ethnic composition.

Hill, Kim Quaile, and Kenneth R. Mladenka. *Democratic Governance in American States and Cities,* 2d ed. Belmont, Calif.: Wadsworth Publishing, 1996. An overview of state and local government in the United States.

Hunter, Kenneth G. *Interest Groups and State Economic Development Policies.* Westport, Conn.: Praeger, 1999. A look at the influence of groups in state policy decisions.

Morehouse, Sarah McCally. *The Governor as Party Leader.* Ann Arbor: University of Michigan Press, 1998. An examination of how governors campaign and govern.

Rosenthal, Alan. *The Decline of Representative Government.* Washington, D.C.: Congressional Quarterly Press, 1998. A critical assessment of trends in state legislative governing and electing.

Tarr, G. Alan. *Understanding State Constitutions.* Princeton, N.J.: Princeton University Press, 1998. A thorough assessment of state constitutions and how they differ from the U.S. Constitution.

Appendixes

THE DECLARATION OF INDEPENDENCE

In Congress, July 4, 1776

THE UNANIMOUS DECLARATION
OF THE THIRTEEN UNITED
STATES OF AMERICA

When, in the course of human events, it becomes necessary for one people to dissolve the political bands which have connected them with another, and to assume, among the powers of the earth, the separate and equal station to which the laws of nature and of nature's God entitle them, a decent respect to the opinions of mankind requires that they should declare the causes which impel them to the separation.

We hold these truths to be self-evident, that all men are created equal; that they are endowed by their Creator with certain unalienable rights; that among these, are life, liberty, and the pursuit of happiness. That, to secure these rights, governments are instituted among men, deriving their just powers from the consent of the governed; that, whenever any form of government becomes destructive of these ends, it is the right of the people to alter or to abolish it, and to institute a new government, laying its foundation on such principles, and organizing its powers in such form, as to them shall seem most likely to effect their safety and happiness. Prudence, indeed, will dictate that governments long established, should not be changed for light and transient causes; and, accordingly, all experience hath shown, that mankind are more disposed to suffer, while evils are sufferable, than to right themselves by abolishing the forms to which they are accustomed. But, when a long train of abuses and usurpations, pursuing invariably the same object, evinces a design to reduce them under absolute despotism, it is their right, it is their duty, to throw off such government and to provide new guards for their future security. Such has been the patient sufferance of these colonies, and such is now the necessity which constrains them to alter their former systems of government. The history of the present King of Great Britain is a history of repeated injuries and usurpations, all having, in direct object, the establishment of an absolute tyranny over these States. To prove this, let facts be submitted to a candid world:

He has refused his assent to laws the most wholesome and necessary for the public good.

He has forbidden his governors to pass laws of immediate and pressing importance, unless suspended in their operation till his assent should be obtained; and, when so suspended, he has utterly neglected to attend to them.

He has refused to pass other laws for the accommodation of large districts of people, unless those people would relinquish the right of representation in the legislature; a right inestimable to them, and formidable to tyrants only.

He has called together legislative bodies at places unusual, uncomfortable, and distant from the depository of their public records, for the sole purpose of fatiguing them into compliance with his measures.

He has dissolved representative houses repeatedly for opposing, with manly firmness, his invasions on the rights of the people.

He has refused, for a long time after such dissolutions, to cause others to be elected; whereby the legislative powers, incapable of annihilation, have returned to the people at large for their exercise; the state remaining, in the meantime, exposed to all the danger of invasion from without, and convulsions within.

He has endeavored to prevent the population of these States; for that purpose, obstructing the laws for naturalization of foreigners, refusing to pass others to encourage their migration hither, and raising the conditions of new appropriations of lands.

He has obstructed the administration of justice, by refusing his assent to laws for establishing judiciary powers.

He has made judges dependent on his will alone, for the tenure of their offices, and the amount and payment of their salaries.

He has erected a multitude of new offices, and sent hither swarms of officers to harass our people, and eat out their substance.

He has kept among us, in time of peace, standing armies, without the consent of our legislatures.

He has affected to render the military independent of, and superior to, the civil power.

He has combined, with others, to subject us to a jurisdiction foreign to our Constitution, and unacknowledged by our laws; giving his assent to their acts of pretended legislation:

For quartering large bodies of armed troops among us:

For protecting them by a mock trial, from punishment, for any murders which they should commit on the inhabitants of these States:

For cutting off our trade with all parts of the world:

For imposing taxes on us without our consent:

For depriving us, in many cases, of the benefit of trial by jury:

For transporting us beyond seas to be tried for pretended offences:

For abolishing the free system of English laws in a neighboring province, establishing therein an arbitrary government, and enlarging its boundaries, so as to render it at once an example and fit instrument for introducing the same absolute rule into these colonies:

For taking away our charters, abolishing our most valuable laws, and altering, fundamentally, the powers of our governments:

For suspending our own legislatures, and declaring themselves invested with power to legislate for us in all cases whatsoever.

He has abdicated government here, by declaring us out of his protection, and waging war against us.

He has plundered our seas, ravaged our coasts, burnt our towns, and destroyed the lives of our people.

He is, at this time, transporting large armies of foreign mercenaries to complete the works of death, desolation, and tyranny, already begun, with circumstances of cruelty and perfidy scarcely paralleled in the most barbarous ages, and totally unworthy of the head of a civilized nation.

He has constrained our fellow citizens, taken captive on the high seas, to bear arms against their country, to become the executioners of their friends, and brethren, or to fall themselves by their hands.

He has excited domestic insurrections amongst us, and has endeavored to bring on the inhabitants of our frontiers, the merciless Indian savages, whose known rule of warfare is an undistinguished destruction of all ages, sexes, and conditions.

In every stage of these oppressions, we have petitioned for redress, in the most humble terms; our repeated petitions have been answered only by repeated injury. A prince, whose character is thus marked by every act which may define a tyrant, is unfit to be the ruler of a free people.

Nor have we been wanting in attention to our British brethren. We have warned them, from time to time, of attempts made by their legislature to extend an unwarrantable jurisdiction over us. We have reminded them of the circumstances of our emigration and settlement here. We have appealed to their native justice and magnanimity, and we have conjured them, by the ties of our common kindred, to disavow these usurpations, which would inevitably interrupt our connections and correspondence. They, too, have been deaf to the voice of justice and of consanguinity. We must, therefore, acquiesce in the necessity which denounces our separation, and hold them as we hold the rest of mankind, enemies in war, in peace, friends.

We, therefore, the representatives of the United States of America, in general Congress assembled, appealing to the Supreme Judge of the world for the rectitude of our intentions, do, in the name, and by the authority of the good people of these colonies, solemnly publish and declare, that these united colonies are, and of right ought to be, free and independent states: that they are absolved from all allegiance to the British Crown, and that all political connection between them and the state of Great

Britain is, and ought to be, totally dissolved; and that, as free and independent states, they have full power to levy war, conclude peace, contract alliances, establish commerce, and to do all other acts and things which independent states may of right do. And, for the support of this declaration, with a firm reliance on the protection of Divine Providence, we mutually pledge to each other our lives, our fortunes, and our sacred honor.

The foregoing Declaration was, by order of Congress, engrossed, and signed by the following members:

JOHN HANCOCK

New Hampshire
Josiah Bartlett
William Whipple
Matthew Thornton

Massachusetts Bay
Samuel Adams
John Adams
Robert Treat Paine
Elbridge Gerry

Rhode Island
Stephen Hopkins
William Ellery

Connecticut
Roger Sherman
Samuel Huntington
William Williams
Oliver Wolcott

New York
William Floyd
Philip Livingston
Francis Lewis
Lewis Morris

New Jersey
Richard Stockton
John Witherspoon
Francis Hopkinson
John Hart
Abraham Clark

Pennsylvania
Robert Morris
Benjamin Rush
Benjamin Franklin
John Morton
George Clymer
James Smith
George Taylor
James Wilson
George Ross

Delaware
Caesar Rodney
George Reed
Thomas M'Kean

Maryland
Samuel Chase
William Paca
Thomas Stone
Charles Carroll, of Carrollton

Virginia
George Wythe
Richard Henry Lee
Thomas Jefferson
Benjamin Harrison
Thomas Nelson, Jr.
Francis Lightfoot Lee
Carter Braxton

North Carolina
William Hooper
Joseph Hewes
John Penn

South Carolina
Edward Rutledge
Thomas Heyward, Jr.
Thomas Lynch, Jr.
Arthur Middleton

Georgia
Button Gwinnett
Lyman Hall
George Walton

Resolved, That copies of the Declaration be sent to the several assemblies, conventions, and committees, or councils of safety, and to the several commanding officers of the continental troops; that it be proclaimed in each of the United States, at the head of the army.

THE CONSTITUTION OF THE UNITED STATES OF AMERICA[1]

We the People of the United States, in Order to form a more perfect Union, establish Justice, insure domestic Tranquility, provide for the common defence, promote the general Welfare, and secure the Blessings of Liberty to ourselves and our Posterity, do ordain and establish this CONSTITUTION for the United States of America.

Article I

SECTION 1

All legislative Powers herein granted shall be vested in a Congress of the United States, which shall consist of a Senate and House of Representatives.

SECTION 2

The House of Representatives shall be composed of Members chosen every second Year by the People of the several States, and the Electors in each State shall have the Qualifications requisite for Electors of the most numerous Branch of the State Legislature.

No Person shall be a Representative who shall not have attained to the Age of twenty-five Years, and been seven Years a Citizen of the United States, and who shall not, when elected, be an Inhabitant of that State in which he shall be chosen.

[Representatives and direct Taxes[2] shall be apportioned among the several States which may be included within this Union, according to their respective Numbers, which shall be determined by adding to the whole Number of free Persons, including those bound to Service for a Term of Years, and excluding Indians not taxed, three fifths of all other Persons.][3] The actual Enumeration shall be made within three Years after the first Meeting of the Congress of the United States, and within every subsequent Term of ten Years, in such Manner as they shall by Law direct. The Number of Representatives shall not exceed one for every thirty Thousand, but each State shall have at Least one Representative; and until such enumeration shall be made, the State of New Hampshire shall be entitled to chuse three, Massachusetts eight, Rhode-Island and Providence Plantations one, Connecticut five, New York six, New Jersey four, Pennsylvania eight, Delaware one, Maryland six, Virginia ten, North Carolina five, South Carolina five, and Georgia three.

When vacancies happen in the Representation from any State, the Executive Authority thereof shall issue Writs of Election to fill such Vacancies.

The House of Representatives shall chuse their Speaker and other Officers; and shall have the sole Power of Impeachment.

SECTION 3

The Senate of the United States shall be composed of two Senators from each State, chosen by the Legislature thereof, for six Years; and each Senator shall have one Vote.

---

1. This version, which follows the original Constitution in capitalization and spelling, was published by the United States Department of the Interior, Office of Education, in 1935.

2. Altered by the Sixteenth Amendment.

3. Negated by the Fourteenth Amendment.

Immediately after they shall be assembled in Consequence of the first Election, they shall be divided as equally as may be into three Classes. The Seats of the Senators of the first Class shall be vacated at the Expiration of the second Year, of the second Class at the Expiration of the fourth Year, and of the third Class at the Expiration of the sixth Year, so that one-third may be chosen every second Year; and if Vacancies happen by Resignation, or otherwise, during the Recess of the Legislature of any State, the Executive thereof may make temporary Appointments until the next Meeting of the Legislature, which shall then fill such Vacancies.

No Person shall be a Senator who shall not have attained to the Age of thirty Years, and been nine Years a Citizen of the United States, and who shall not, when elected, be an Inhabitant of that State for which he shall be chosen.

The Vice President of the United States shall be President of the Senate, but shall have no vote, unless they be equally divided.

The Senate shall chuse their other Officers, and also a President pro tempore, in the absence of the Vice President, or when he shall exercise the Office of President of the United States.

The Senate shall have the sole Power to try all Impeachments. When sitting for that purpose they shall be on Oath or Affirmation. When the President of the United States is tried, the Chief Justice shall preside: And no person shall be convicted without the Concurrence of two thirds of the Members present.

Judgment in Cases of Impeachment shall not extend further than to removal from Office, and disqualification to hold and enjoy any Office of honor, Trust, or Profit under the United States: but the Party convicted shall nevertheless be liable and subject to Indictment, Trial, Judgment and Punishment, according to Law.

SECTION 4

The Times, Place and Manner of holding Elections for Senators and Representatives, shall be prescribed in each State by the Legislature thereof; but the Congress may at any time by Law make or alter such Regulations, except as to the Places of Chusing Senators.

The Congress shall assemble at least once in every Year, and such Meeting shall be on the first Monday in December, unless they shall by Law appoint a different Day.

SECTION 5

Each House shall be the Judge of the Elections, Returns and Qualifications of its own Members, and a Majority of each shall constitute a Quorum to do Business; but a smaller number may adjourn from day to day, and may be authorized to compel the Attendance of absent Members, in such Manner, and under such Penalties, as each House may provide.

Each House may determine the Rules of its Proceedings, punish its Members for disorderly Behaviour, and, with the Concurrence of two thirds, expel a Member.

Each House shall keep a Journal of its Proceedings, and from time to time publish the same, excepting such Parts as may in their Judgment require Secrecy; and the Yeas and Nays of the Members of either House on any question shall, at the Desire of one fifth of those Present, be entered on the Journal.

Neither House, during the Session of Congress, shall, without the Consent of the other, adjourn for more than three days, nor to any other Place than that in which the two Houses shall be sitting.

SECTION 6

The Senators and Representatives shall receive a Compensation for their Services, to be ascertained by Law, and paid out of the Treasury of the United States. They shall in all Cases, except Treason, Felony, and Breach of the Peace, be privileged from Arrest during their Attendance at the Session of their respective Houses, and in going to and returning from the same; and for any Speech or Debate in either House, they shall not be questioned in any other Place.

No Senator or Representative shall, during the Time for which he was elected, be appointed to any civil Office under the Authority of the United States, which shall have been created, or the Emoluments whereof shall have been increased, during such time; and no Person holding any Office under the United States shall be a Member of either House during his continuance in Office.

SECTION 7

All Bills for raising Revenue shall originate in the House of Representatives; but the Senate may propose or concur with Amendments as on other bills.

Every Bill which shall have passed the House of Representatives and the Senate, shall, before it becomes a Law, be presented to the President of the United States; if he approve he shall sign it, but if not he shall return it, with his Objections, to that House in which it shall have originated, who shall enter the Objections at large on their Journal, and proceed to reconsider it. If after such Reconsideration two thirds of that House shall agree to pass the bill, it shall be sent, together with the objections, to the other House, by which it shall likewise be reconsidered, and if approved by two thirds of that House, it shall become a Law. But in all such Cases the Votes of both Houses shall be determined by Yeas and Nays, and the Names of the Persons voting for and against the Bill shall be entered on the Journal of each House respectively. If any Bill shall not be returned by the President within ten Days (Sundays excepted) after it shall have been presented to him, the Same shall be a Law, in like Manner as if he had signed it, unless the Congress by their Adjournment prevent its Return, in which Case it shall not be a Law.

Every Order, Resolution, or Vote to which the Concurrence of the Senate and House of Representatives may be necessary (except on a question of Adjournment) shall be presented to the President of the United States; and before the Same shall take Effect, shall be approved by him, or being disapproved by him, shall be repassed by two thirds of the Senate and House of Representatives, according to the Rules and Limitations prescribed in the Case of a Bill.

SECTION 8

The Congress shall have Power To lay and collect Taxes, Duties, Imposts and Excises, to pay the Debts and provide for the common Defence and general Welfare of the United States; but all Duties, Imposts and Excises shall be uniform throughout the United States;

To borrow money on the credit of the United States;

To regulate Commerce with foreign Nations, and among the several States, and with the Indian Tribes;

To establish a uniform rule of Naturalization, and uniform Laws on the subject of Bankruptcies throughout the United States;

To coin Money, regulate the Value thereof, and of foreign Coin, and fix the Standard of Weights and Measures;

To provide for the Punishment of counterfeiting the Securities and current Coin of the United States;

To establish Post Offices and post Roads;

To promote the Progress of Science and useful Arts, by securing for limited Times to Authors and Inventors the exclusive Right to their respective Writings and Discoveries;

To constitute Tribunals inferior to the Supreme Court;

To define and punish Piracies and Felonies committed on the high Seas, and Offenses against the Law of Nations;

To declare War, grant Letters of Marque and Reprisal, and make Rules concerning Captures on Land and Water;

To raise and support Armies, but no Appropriation of Money to that Use shall be for a longer Term than two Years;

To provide and maintain a Navy;

To make Rules for the Government and Regulation of the land and naval forces;

To provide for calling forth the Militia to execute the Laws of the Union, suppress Insurrections and repel Invasions;

To provide for organizing, arming, and disciplining the Militia, and for governing such Part of them as may be employed in the Service of the United States, reserving to the States respectively, the Appointment of the Officers, and the Authority of training the Militia according to the discipline prescribed by Congress;

To exercise exclusive Legislation in all Cases whatsoever, over such District (not exceeding ten Miles square) as may, by Cession of particular

States, and the acceptance of Congress, become the Seat of the Government of the United States, and to exercise like Authority over all Places purchased by the Consent of the Legislature of the State in which the Same shall be, for the Erection of Forts, Magazines, Arsenals, Dock-yards, and other needful Buildings;—And

To make all Laws which shall be necessary and proper for carrying into Execution the foregoing Powers, and all other Powers vested by this Constitution in the Government of the United States, or in any Department or Officer thereof.

SECTION 9

The Migration or Importation of such Persons as any of the States now existing shall think proper to admit, shall not be prohibited by the Congress prior to the Year one thousand eight hundred and eight, but a tax or duty may be imposed on such Importation, not exceeding ten dollars for each Person.

The privilege of the Writ of Habeas Corpus shall not be suspended, unless when in Cases of Rebellion or Invasion the public Safety may require it.

No bill of Attainder or ex post facto Law shall be passed.

No capitation, or other direct, Tax shall be laid unless in Proportion to the Census or Enumeration herein before directed to be taken.

No Tax or Duty shall be laid on Articles exported from any State.

No Preference shall be given by any Regulation of Commerce or Revenue to the Ports of one State over those of another: nor shall Vessels bound to, or from, one State, be obliged to enter, clear, or pay Duties in another.

No Money shall be drawn from the Treasury, but in Consequence of Appropriations made by Law; and a regular Statement and Account of the Receipts and Expenditures of all public Money shall be published from time to time.

No Title of Nobility shall be granted by the United States: And no Person holding any Office of Profit or Trust under them, shall, without the Consent of the Congress, accept of any present, Emolument, Office, or Title, of any kind whatever, from any King, Prince, or foreign State.

SECTION 10

No State shall enter into any Treaty, Alliance, or Confederation; grant Letters of Marque and Reprisal; coin Money; emit Bills of Credit; make any Thing but gold and silver Coin a Tender in Payment of Debts; pass any Bill of Attainder, ex post facto Law, or Law impairing the Obligation of Contracts, or grant any Title of Nobility.

No State shall, without the Consent of the Congress, lay any Imposts or Duties on Imports or Exports, except what may be absolutely necessary for executing its inspection Laws; and the net Produce of all Duties and Imposts, laid by any State on Imports or Exports, shall be for the use of the Treasury of the United States; and all such Laws shall be subject to the Revision and Control of the Congress.

No state shall, without the Consent of Congress, lay any duty of Tonnage, keep Troops, or Ships of War in time of Peace, enter into any Agreement or Compact with another State, or with a foreign Power, or engage in War, unless actually invaded, or in such imminent Danger as will not admit of delay.

Article II

SECTION 1

The executive Power shall be vested in a President of the United States of America. He shall hold his Office during the Term of four years, and, together with the Vice President, chosen for the same Term, be elected, as follows:

Each State shall appoint, in such Manner as the Legislature thereof may direct, a Number of Electors, equal to the whole Number of Senators and Representatives to which the State may be entitled in the Congress: but no Senator or Representative, or Person holding an Office of Trust or Profit under the United States, shall be appointed an Elector.

[The Electors shall meet in their respective States, and vote by Ballot for two persons, of whom one at least shall not be an Inhabitant of the same State with themselves. And they shall make a List of all the Persons voted for, and of the Number of Votes for each; which List they shall sign and certify, and transmit sealed to the Seat of the Government of the United States, directed to the President of the

Senate. The President of the Senate shall, in the Presence of the Senate and House of Representatives, open all the Certificates, and the Votes shall then be counted. The Person having the greatest Number of Votes shall be the President, if such Number be a Majority of the whole Number of Electors appointed; and if there be more than one who have such Majority, and have an equal Number of Votes, then the House of Representatives shall immediately chuse by Ballot one of them for President; and if no Person have a Majority, then from the five highest on the List the said House shall in like Manner chuse the President. But in chusing the President, the Votes shall be taken by States, the Representation from each State having one Vote; a quorum for this Purpose shall consist of a Member or Members from two-thirds of the States, and a Majority of all the States shall be necessary to a Choice. In every Case, after the Choice of the President, the Person having the greatest Number of Votes of the Electors shall be the Vice President. But if there should remain two or more who have equal votes, the Senate shall chuse from them by Ballot the Vice President.]⁴

The Congress may determine the Time of chusing the Electors, and the Day on which they shall give their Votes; which Day shall be the same throughout the United States.

No person except a natural-born Citizen, or a Citizen of the United States, at the time of the Adoption of this Constitution, shall be eligible to the Office of President; neither shall any Person be eligible to that Office who shall not have attained to the Age of thirty-five years, and been fourteen Years a Resident within the United States.

In Case of the Removal of the President from Office, or of his Death, Resignation, or Inability to discharge the Powers and Duties of the said Office, the same shall devolve on the Vice President, and the Congress may by Law provide for the Case of Removal, Death, Resignation, or Inability, both of the President and Vice President, declaring what Officer shall then act as President, and such Officer shall act accordingly, until the disability be removed, or a President shall be elected.

The President shall, at stated Times, receive for his Services a Compensation, which shall neither be increased nor diminished during the Period for which he shall have been elected, and he shall not receive within that Period any other Emolument from the United States, or any of them.

Before he enter on the execution of his Office, he shall take the following Oath or Affirmation:—"I do solemnly swear (or affirm) that I will faithfully execute the Office of President of the United States, and will, to the best of my Ability, preserve, protect, and defend the Constitution of the United States."

SECTION 2

The President shall be Commander in Chief of the Army and Navy of the United States, and of the Militia of the several States, when called into the actual Service of the United States; he may require the Opinion, in writing, of the principal Officer in each of the executive Departments, upon any subject relating to the Duties of their respective Offices, and he shall have Power to Grant Reprieves and Pardons for Offenses against the United States, except in Cases of Impeachment.

He shall have Power, by and with the Advice and Consent of the Senate, to make Treaties, provided two-thirds of the Senators present concur; and he shall nominate, and by and with the Advice and Consent of the Senate, shall appoint Ambassadors, other public Ministers and Consuls, Judges of the supreme Court, and all other Officers of the United States, whose Appointments are not herein otherwise provided for, and which shall be established by Law: but the Congress may by Law vest the Appointment of such inferior Officers, as they think proper, in the President alone, in the Courts of Law, or in the Heads of Departments.

The President shall have Power to fill up all Vacancies that may happen during the Recess of the Senate, by granting Commissions which shall expire at the End of their next Session.

SECTION 3

He shall from time to time give to the Congress Information of the State of the Union, and recommend to their Consideration such Measures as he shall judge necessary and expedient; he may, on

4. Revised by the Twelfth Amendment.

extraordinary occasions, convene both Houses, or either of them, and in Case of Disagreement between them, with respect to the Time of Adjournment, he may adjourn them to such Time as he shall think proper; he shall receive Ambassadors and other public Ministers; he shall take care that the Laws be faithfully executed, and shall Commission all the Officers of the United States.

SECTION 4

The President, Vice President and all civil Officers of the United States, shall be removed from Office on Impeachment for, and Conviction of, Treason, Bribery, or other high Crimes and Misdemeanors.

Article III

SECTION 1

The judicial Power of the United States, shall be vested in one supreme Court, and in such inferior Courts as the Congress may from time to time ordain and establish. The Judges, both of the supreme and inferior Courts, shall hold their Offices during good Behaviour, and shall, at stated Times, receive for their Services, a Compensation, which shall not be diminished during their Continuance in Office.

SECTION 2

The judicial Power shall extend to all Cases, in Law and Equity, arising under this Constitution, the Laws of the United States, and Treaties made, or which shall be made, under their Authority;—to all Cases affecting ambassadors, other public ministers and consuls;—to all cases of admiralty and maritime Jurisdiction;—to Controversies to which the United States shall be a Party;—to Controversies between two or more states;—between a State and Citizens of another State;[5]—between Citizens of different States—between Citizens of the same State claiming Lands under Grants of different States, and

5. Qualified by the Eleventh Amendment.

between a State, or the Citizens thereof, and foreign States, Citizens, or Subjects.

In all Cases affecting Ambassadors, other public Ministers and Consuls, and those in which a State shall be Party, the supreme Court shall have original Jurisdiction. In all the other Cases before mentioned, the supreme Court shall have appellate Jurisdiction, both as to Law and Fact, with such Exceptions, and under such Regulations as the Congress shall make.

The trial of all Crimes, except in Cases of Impeachment, shall be by Jury; and such Trial shall be held in the State where the said Crimes shall have been committed; but when not committed within any State, the Trial shall be at such Place or Places as the Congress may by Law have directed.

SECTION 3

Treason against the United States, shall consist only in levying War against them, or in adhering to their Enemies, giving them Aid and Comfort. No Person shall be convicted of Treason unless on the Testimony of two Witnesses to the same overt Act, or on Confession in open Court.

The Congress shall have power to declare the Punishment of Treason, but no Attainder of Treason shall work Corruption of Blood, or Forfeiture except during the Life of the Person attainted.

Article IV

SECTION 1

Full Faith and Credit shall be given in each State to the public Acts, Records, and judicial Proceedings of every other State. And the Congress may by general Laws prescribe the Manner in which such Acts, Records and Proceedings shall be proved, and the Effect thereof.

SECTION 2

The Citizens of each State shall be entitled to all Privileges and Immunities of Citizens in the several States.

A Person charged in any State with Treason, Felony, or other Crime, who shall flee from Justice, and be found in another State, shall on demand of the executive Authority of the State from which he fled, be delivered up, to be removed to the State having Jurisdiction of the crime.

No Person held to Service or Labour in one State, under the Laws thereof, escaping into another, shall, in Consequence of any Law or Regulation therein, be discharged from such Service or Labour, but shall be delivered up on Claim of the Party to whom such Service or Labour may be due.

SECTION 3

New States may be admitted by the Congress into this Union; but no new State shall be formed or erected within the Jurisdiction of any other State; nor any State be formed by the Junction of two or more States, or parts of States, without the Consent of the Legislatures of the States concerned as well as of the Congress.

The Congress shall have Power to dispose of and make all needful Rules and Regulations respecting the Territory or other Property belonging to the United States; and nothing in this Constitution shall be so construed as to Prejudice any Claims of the United States, or of any particular State.

SECTION 4

The United States shall guarantee to every State in this Union a Republican Form of Government, and shall protect each of them against Invasion; and on Application of the Legislature, or of the Executive (when the Legislature cannot be convened) against domestic Violence.

Article V

The Congress, whenever two-thirds of both Houses shall deem it necessary, shall propose Amendments to this Constitution, or, on the Application of the Legislatures of two-thirds of the several States, shall call a Convention for proposing Amendments, which, in either Case, shall be valid to all Intents and Purposes, as part of this Constitution, when ratified by the Legislatures of three-fourths of the several States, or by Conventions in three-fourths thereof, as the one or the other Mode of Ratification may be proposed by the Congress; Provided that no

Amendment which may be made prior to the Year One thousand eight hundred and eight shall in any Manner affect the first and fourth Clauses in the Ninth Section of the first Article; and that no State, without its Consent, shall be deprived of its equal Suffrage in the Senate.

Article VI

All Debts contracted and Engagements entered into, before the Adoption of this Constitution, shall be as valid against the United States under this Constitution, as under the Confederation.

This Constitution, and the Laws of the United States which shall be made in Pursuance thereof; and all Treaties made, or which shall be made, under the Authority of the United States, shall be the supreme Law of the Land; and the Judges in every State shall be bound thereby, any Thing in the Constitution or Laws of any State to the Contrary notwithstanding.

The Senators and Representatives before mentioned, and the Members of the several State Legislatures, and all executive and judicial Officers, both of the United States and of the several States, shall be bound by Oath or Affirmation to support this Constitution; but no religious Tests shall ever be required as a qualification to any Office or public Trust under the United States.

Article VII

The Ratification of the Conventions of nine States shall be sufficient for the Establishment of this Constitution between the States so ratifying the same.

Done in Convention by the Unanimous Consent of the States present the Seventeenth Day of September in the Year of our Lord one thousand seven hundred and Eighty seven, and of the Independence of the United States of America the Twelfth. In Witness whereof We have hereunto subscribed our Names.[6]

---

6. These are the full names of the signers, which in some cases are not the signatures on the document.

George Washington
President and deputy from Virginia

New Hampshire
John Langdon
Nicholas Gilman

Massachusetts
Nathaniel Gorham
Rufus King

Connecticut
William Samuel Johnson
Roger Sherman

New York
Alexander Hamilton

New Jersey
William Livingston
David Brearley
William Paterson
Jonathan Dayton

Pennsylvania
Benjamin Franklin
Thomas Mifflin
Robert Morris
George Clymer
Thomas FitzSimmons
Jared Ingersoll
James Wilson
Gouverneur Morris

Delaware
George Read
Gunning Bedford, Jr.
John Dickinson
Richard Bassett
Jacob Broom

Maryland
James McHenry
Daniel of St. Thomas Jenifer
Daniel Carroll

Virginia
John Blair
James Madison, Jr.

North Carolina
William Blount
Richard Dobbs Spaight
Hugh Williamson

South Carolina
John Rutledge
Charles Cotesworth Pinckney
Charles Pinckney
Pierce Butler

Georgia
William Few
Abraham Baldwin

Articles in Addition to, and Amendment of, the Constitution of the United States of America, Proposed by Congress, and Ratified by the Legislatures of the Several States, Pursuant to the Fifth Article of the Original Constitution[7]

Amendment I

Congress shall make no law respecting an establishment of religion, or prohibiting the free exercise thereof; or abridging the freedom of speech, or of the press; or the right of the people peaceably to assemble, and to petition the Government for a redress of grievances.

Amendment II

A well regulated Militia, being necessary to the security of a free State, the right of the people to keep and bear Arms shall not be infringed.

Amendment III

No Soldier shall, in time of peace, be quartered in any house, without the consent of the Owner, nor in time of war, but in a manner to be prescribed by law.

Amendment IV

The right of the people to be secure in their persons, houses, papers, and effects, against unreasonable searches and seizures, shall not be violated, and no Warrants shall issue, but upon probable cause, supported by Oath or affirmation, and particularly

7. This heading appears only in the joint resolution submitting the first ten amendments, which are collectively known as the Bill of Rights. They were ratified on December 15, 1791.

describing the place to be searched, and the persons or things to be seized.

Amendment V

No person shall be held to answer for a capital or otherwise infamous crime, unless on a presentment or indictment of a Grand Jury, except in cases arising in the land or naval forces, or in the Militia, when in actual service in time of War or public danger; nor shall any person be subject for the same offence to be twice put in jeopardy of life or limb; nor shall be compelled in any criminal case to be a witness against himself, nor be deprived of life, liberty, or property, without due process of law; nor shall private property be taken for public use, without just compensation.

Amendment VI

In all criminal prosecutions, the accused shall enjoy the right to a speedy and public trial, by an impartial jury of the State and district wherein the crime shall have been committed, which district shall have been previously ascertained by law, and to be informed of the nature and cause of the accusation; to be confronted with the witnesses against him; to have compulsory process for obtaining witnesses in his favour, and to have the Assistance of Counsel for his defence.

Amendment VII

In suits at common law, where the value in controversy shall exceed twenty dollars, the right of trial by jury shall be preserved, and no fact tried by a jury, shall be otherwise reexamined in any Court of the United States, than according to the rules of the common law.

Amendment VIII

Excessive bail shall not be required, nor excessive fines imposed, nor cruel and unusual punishments inflicted.

Amendment IX

The enumeration of the Constitution, of certain rights, shall not be construed to deny or disparage others retained by the people.

Amendment X

The powers not delegated to the United States by the Constitution, nor prohibited by it to the States, are reserved to the States respectively, or to the people.

Amendment XI [1798]

The Judicial power of the United States shall not be construed to extend to any suit in law or equity, commenced or prosecuted against one of the United States by Citizens of another State, or by Citizens or Subjects of any Foreign State.

Amendment XII [1804]

The Electors shall meet in their respective States and vote by ballot for President and Vice-President, one of whom, at least, shall not be an inhabitant of the same State with themselves; they shall name in their ballots the person voted for as President, and in distinct ballots the person voted for as Vice-President, and they shall make distinct lists of all persons voted for as President, and of all persons voted for as Vice-President, and of the number of votes for each, which lists they shall sign and certify, and transmit sealed to the seat of the government of the United States, directed to the President of the Senate;—The President of the Senate shall, in the presence of the Senate and House of Representatives, open all the certificates and the votes shall then be counted;—The person having the greatest number of votes for President, shall be the President, if such number be a majority of the whole number of Electors appointed; and if no person have such majority, then from the persons having the highest numbers not exceeding three on the list of those voted for as President, the House of Representatives shall choose immediately, by ballot, the President. But in choosing the President, the votes shall be taken by states, the representation from each state having one vote; a quorum for this purpose shall consist of a member or members from two-thirds of the states, and a majority of all the states shall be necessary to a choice. And if the House of Representatives shall not choose a President whenever the right of choice shall devolve upon them, before the fourth day of March next following, then the Vice-President shall act as President, as in the case of the death or other constitutional disability of the President.—The person having the greatest number of votes as Vice-President, shall be the Vice-President, if such number be a majority of the whole number of Electors appointed, and if no person have a majority, then from the two highest numbers on the list, the Senate shall choose the Vice-President; a quorum for the purpose shall consist of two-thirds of the whole number of Senators, and majority of the whole number shall be necessary to a choice. But no person constitutionally ineligible to the office of President shall be eligible to that of Vice-President of the United States.

Amendment XIII [1865]

SECTION 1

Neither slavery nor involuntary servitude, except as a punishment for crime whereof the party shall have been duly convicted, shall exist within the United States, or any place subject to their jurisdiction.

SECTION 2

Congress shall have power to enforce this article by appropriate legislation.

Amendment XIV [1868]

SECTION 1

All persons born or naturalized in the United States, and subject to the jurisdiction thereof, are citizens of the United States and of the State wherein they reside. No State shall abridge the privileges or immunities of citizens of the United States; nor shall any State deprive any person of life, liberty, or property, without due process of law; nor deny to any person within its jurisdiction the equal protection of the laws.

SECTION 2

Representatives shall be apportioned among the several States according to their respective numbers, counting the whole number of persons in each State, excluding Indians not taxed. But when the right to vote at any election for the choice of electors for President and Vice-President of the United States, Representatives in Congress, the Executive and Judicial officers of a State, or the members of the Legislature thereof, is denied to any of the male inhabitants of such State, being twenty-one years of age, and citizens of the United States, or in any way abridged, except for participation in rebellion, or other crime, the basis of representation therein shall be reduced in the proportion which the number of such male citizens shall bear to the whole number of male citizens twenty-one years of age in such State.

SECTION 3

No person shall be a Senator or Representative in Congress, or elector of President and Vice-President, or hold any office, civil or military, under the United States, or under any State, who, having previously taken an oath, as a member of Congress, or as an officer of the United States, or as a member of any State legislature, or as an executive or judicial officer of any State, to support the Constitution of the United States, shall have engaged in insurrection or rebellion against the same, or given aid or comfort to the enemies thereof. But Congress may by a vote of two-thirds of each House, remove such disability.

SECTION 4

The validity of the public debt of the United States, authorized by law, including debts incurred for payment of pensions and bounties for services in suppressing insurrection or rebellion, shall not be questioned. But neither the United States nor any State shall assume or pay any debts or obligation incurred in aid of insurrection or rebellion against the

United States, or any claim for the loss or emancipation of any slave; but all such debts, obligations, and claims shall be held illegal and void.

SECTION 5

The Congress shall have the power to enforce, by appropriate legislation, the provisions of this article.

Amendment XV [1870]

SECTION 1

The right of citizens of the United States to vote shall not be denied or abridged by the United States or by any State on account of race, color, or previous condition of servitude—

SECTION 2

The Congress shall have power to enforce this article by appropriate legislation.

Amendment XVI [1913]

The Congress shall have power to lay and collect taxes on incomes, from whatever source derived, without apportionment among the several States, and without regard to any census or enumeration.

Amendment XVII [1913]

The Senate of the United States shall be composed of two Senators from each State, elected by the people thereof, for six years; and each Senator shall have one vote. The electors in each State shall have the qualifications requisite for electors of the most numerous branch of the State legislatures.

When vacancies happen in the representation of any State in the Senate, the executive authority of such State shall issue writs of election to fill such vacancies: *Provided*, That the legislature of any State may empower the executive thereof to make temporary appointments until the people fill the vacancies by election as the legislature may direct.

This amendment shall not be so construed as to affect the election or term of any Senator chosen before it becomes valid as part of the Constitution.

Amendment XVIII [1919]

SECTION 1

After one year from the ratification of this article the manufacture, sale, or transportation of intoxicating liquors within, the importation thereof into, or the exportation thereof from the United States and all territory subject to the jurisdiction thereof for beverage purposes is hereby prohibited.

SECTION 2

The Congress and the several States shall have concurrent power to enforce this article by appropriate legislation.

SECTION 3

This article shall be inoperative unless it shall have been ratified as an amendment to the Constitution by the legislatures of the several States, as provided in the Constitution, within seven years from the date of the submission hereof to the States by the Congress.

Amendment XIX [1920]

The right of citizens of the United States to vote shall not be denied or abridged by the United States or by any State on account of sex.

Congress shall have power to enforce this article by appropriate legislation.

Amendment XX [1933]

SECTION 1

The terms of the President and Vice-President shall end at noon on the 20th day of January, and the terms of Senators and Representatives at noon on the 3d day of January, of the years in which such terms would have ended if this article had not been ratified; and the terms of their successors shall then begin.

SECTION 2

The Congress shall assemble at least once in every year, and such meeting shall begin at noon on the 3d day of January, unless they shall by law appoint a different day.

SECTION 3

If, at the time fixed for the beginning of the term of the President, the President elect shall have died, the Vice-President elect shall become President. If a President shall not have been chosen before the time fixed for the beginning of his term or if the President elect shall have failed to qualify, then the Vice-President elect shall act as President until a President shall have qualified; and the Congress may by law provide for the case wherein neither a President elect nor a Vice-President elect shall have qualified, declaring who shall then act as President, or the manner in which one who is to act shall be selected, and such person shall act accordingly until a President or Vice-President shall have qualified.

SECTION 4

The Congress may by law provide for the case of the death of any of the persons from whom the House of Representatives may choose a President whenever the right of choice shall have devolved upon them, and for the case of the death of any of the persons from whom the Senate may choose a Vice-President whenever the right of choice shall have devolved upon them.

SECTION 5

Sections 1 and 2 shall take effect on the 15th day of October following the ratification of this article.

SECTION 6

This article shall be inoperative unless it shall have been ratified as an amendment to the Constitution by the legislatures of three-fourths of the several States within seven years from the date of its submission.

Amendment XXI [1933]

SECTION 1

The eighteenth article of amendment to the Constitution of the United States is hereby repealed.

SECTION 2

The transportation or importation into any State, Territory, or possession of the United States for delivery or use therein of intoxicating liquors, in violation of the laws thereof, is hereby prohibited.

SECTION 3

This article shall be inoperative unless it shall have been ratified as an amendment to the Constitution by conventions in the several States, as provided in the Constitution, within seven years from the date of the submission hereof to the States by the Congress.

Amendment XXII [1951]

No person shall be elected to the office of the President more than twice, and no person who has held the office of President, or acted as President, for more than two years of a term to which some other person was elected President shall be elected to the office of the President more than once.

But this Article shall not apply to any person holding the office of President when this Article was proposed by the Congress, and shall not prevent any person who may be holding the office of President, or acting as President, during the term within which this Article becomes operative from holding the office of President or acting as President during the remainder of such term.

This article shall be inoperative unless it shall have been ratified as an amendment to the Constitution by the legislatures of three-fourths of the several states within seven years from the date of its submission to the states by the Congress.

Amendment XXIII [1961]

SECTION 1

The District constituting the seat of Government of the United States shall appoint in such manner as the Congress may direct:

A number of electors of President and Vice-President equal to the whole number of Senators and Representatives in Congress to which the District would be entitled if it were a State, but in no event more than the least populous State; they shall be in addition to those appointed by the States, but they shall be considered, for the purposes of the election of President and Vice-President, to be electors appointed by a State; and they shall meet in the District and perform such duties as provided by the twelfth article of amendment.

SECTION 2

The Congress shall have power to enforce this article by appropriate legislation.

Amendment XXIV [1964]

SECTION 1

The right of citizens of the United States to vote in any primary or other election for President or Vice President, for electors for President or Vice President, or for Senator or Representative in Congress, shall not be denied or abridged by the United States or any state by reason of failure to pay any poll tax or other tax.

SECTION 2

The Congress shall have the power to enforce this article by appropriate legislation.

Amendment XXV [1967]

SECTION 1

In case of the removal of the President from office or of his death or resignation, the Vice President shall become President.

SECTION 2

Whenever there is a vacancy in the office of the Vice President, the President shall nominate a Vice President who shall take office upon confirmation by a majority vote of both Houses of Congress.

SECTION 3

Whenever the President transmits to the President Pro Tempore of the Senate and the Speaker of the House of Representatives his written declaration that he is unable to discharge the powers and duties of his office, and until he transmits to them a written declaration to the contrary, such powers and duties shall be discharged by the Vice President as Acting President.

SECTION 4

Whenever the Vice President and a majority of either the principal officers of the executive departments or of such other body as Congress may by law provide, transmit to the President Pro Tempore of the Senate and the Speaker of the House of Representatives their written declaration that the President is unable to discharge the powers and duties of his office, the Vice President shall immediately assume the powers and duties of the office as Acting President.

Thereafter, when the President transmits to the President Pro Tempore of the Senate and the Speaker of the House of Representatives his written declaration that no inability exists, he shall resume the powers and duties of his office unless the Vice President and a majority of either the principal officers of the executive departments or of such other body as Congress may by law provide, transmit within four days to the President Pro Tempore of the Senate and the Speaker of the House of Representatives their written declaration that the President is unable to discharge the powers and duties of his office. Thereupon Congress shall decide the issue, assembling within forty-eight hours for that purpose if not in session. If the Congress, within twenty-one days after receipt of the latter written declaration, or, if Congress is not in session, within twenty-one days after Congress is required to assemble, determines by two-thirds vote of both Houses that the President is unable to discharge the powers and duties of his office, the Vice President shall continue to discharge the same as Acting President; otherwise, the President shall resume the powers and duties of his office.

Amendment XXVI [1971]

SECTION 1

The right of citizens of the United States, who are eighteen years of age or older, to vote shall not be denied or abridged by the United States or by any State on account of age.

SECTION 2

The Congress shall have the power to enforce this article by appropriate legislation.

Amendment XXVII [1992]

No law varying the compensation for the service of Senators and Representatives shall take effect until an election of Representatives shall have intervened.

FEDERALIST NO. 10
(JAMES MADISON)

Among the numerous advantages promised by a well-constructed Union, none deserves to be more accurately developed than its tendency to break and control the violence of faction. The friend of popular governments never finds himself so much alarmed for their character and fate as when he contemplates their propensity to this dangerous vice. He will not fail, therefore, to set a due value on any plan which, without violating the principles to which he is attached, provides a proper cure for it. The instability, injustice, and confusion introduced into the public councils have, in truth, been the mortal diseases under which popular governments have everywhere perished, as they continue to be the favorite and fruitful topics from which the adversaries to liberty derive their most specious declamations. The valuable improvements made by the American constitutions on the popular models, both ancient and modern, cannot certainly be too much admired; but it would be an unwarrantable partiality to contend that they have as effectually obviated the danger on this side, as was wished and expected. Complaints are everywhere heard from our most considerate and virtuous citizens, equally the friends of public and private faith and of public and personal liberty, that our governments are too unstable, that the public good is disregarded in the conflicts of rival parties, and that measures are too often decided, not according to the rules of justice and the rights of the minor party, but by the superior force of an interested and overbearing majority. However anxiously we may wish that these complaints had no foundation, the evidence of known facts will not permit us to deny that they are in some degree true. It will be found, indeed, on a candid review of our situation, that some of the distresses under which we labor have been erroneously charged on the operation of our governments; but it will be found, at the same time, that other causes will not alone account for many of our heaviest misfortunes; and, particularly, for that prevailing and increasing distrust of public engagements and alarm for private rights which are echoed from one end of the continent to the other. There must be chiefly, if not wholly, effects of the unsteadiness and injustice with which a factious spirit has tainted our public administration.

By a faction I understand a number of citizens, whether amounting to a majority or minority of the whole, who are united and actuated by some common impulse of passion, or of interest, adverse to the rights of other citizens, or to the permanent and aggregate interests of the community.

There are two methods of curing the mischiefs of faction: the one, by removing its causes; the other, by controlling its effects.

There are again two methods of removing the causes of faction: the one, by destroying the liberty which is essential to its existence; the other, by giving to every citizen the same opinions, the same passions, and the same interests.

It could never be more truly said than of the first remedy that it was worse than the disease. Liberty is to faction what air is to fire, an ailment without which it instantly expires. But it could not be a less folly to abolish liberty, which is essential to political life, because it nourishes faction than it would be to wish the annihilation of air, which is essential to animal life, because it imparts to fire its destructive agency.

The second expedient is as impracticable as the first would be unwise. As long as the reason of man continues fallible, and he is at liberty to exercise it, different opinions will be formed. As long as the connection subsists between his reason and his self-love, his opinions and his passions will have a reciprocal influence on each other; and the former will be objects to which the latter will attach themselves. The diversity in the faculties of men, from which the rights of property originate, is not less an insuperable obstacle to a uniformity of interest. The protection of these faculties is the first object of government. From the protection of different and unequal faculties of acquiring property, the possession of different degrees and kinds of property immediately results; and from the influence of these on the sentiments and views of the respective proprietors ensues a division of the society into different interests and parties.

The latent causes of faction are thus sown in the nature of man; and we see them everywhere brought into different degrees of activity, according to the different circumstances of civil society. A zeal for different opinions concerning religion, concerning government, and many other points, as well of speculation as of practice; an attachment to different leaders ambitiously contending for preeminence and power; or to persons of other descriptions whose fortunes have been interesting to the human passions, have, in turn, divided mankind into parties, inflamed them with mutual animosity, and rendered them much more disposed to vex and oppress each other than to co-operate for their common good. So strong is this propensity of mankind to fall into mutual animosities that where no substantial occasion presents itself the most frivolous and fanciful distinctions have been sufficient to kindle their unfriendly passions and excite their most violent conflicts. But the most common and durable source of factions has been the various and unequal distribution of property. Those who hold and those who are without property have ever formed distinct interests in society. Those who are creditors, and those who are debtors, fall under a like discrimination. A landed interest, a manufacturing interest, a mercantile interest, a moneyed interest, with many lesser interests, grow up of necessity in civilized nations, and divide them into different classes, actuated by different sentiments and views. The regulation of these various and interfering interests forms the principal task of modern legislation and involves the spirit of party and faction in the necessary and ordinary operations of government.

No man is allowed to be a judge in his own cause, because his interest would certainly bias his judgment, and, not improbably, corrupt his integrity. With equal, nay with greater reason, a body of men are unfit to be both judges and parties at the same time; yet what are many of the most important acts of legislation but so many judicial determinations, not indeed concerning the rights of single persons, but concerning the rights of large bodies of citizens? And what are the different classes of legislators but advocates and parties to the causes which they determine? Is a law proposed concerning private debts? It is a question to which the creditors are parties on one side and the debtors on the other. Justice ought to hold the balance between them. Yet the parties are, and must be, themselves the judges; and the most numerous party, or in other words, the most powerful faction must be expected to prevail. Shall domestic manufacturers be encouraged, and in what degree, by restrictions on foreign manufacturers? [These] are questions which would be differently decided by the landed and the manufacturing classes, and probably by neither with a sole regard to justice and the public good. The apportionment of taxes on the various descriptions of property is an act which seems to require the most exact impartiality; yet there is, perhaps, no legislative act in which greater opportunity and temptation are given to a predominant party to trample on the rules of justice. Every shilling with which they overburden the inferior number is a shilling saved to their own pockets.

It is in vain to say that enlightened statesmen will be able to adjust these clashing interests and render them all subservient to the public good. Enlightened statesmen will not always be at the helm. Nor, in many cases, can such an adjustment be made at all without taking into view indirect and remote considerations, which will rarely prevail over the immediate interest which one party may find in disregarding the rights of another or the good of the whole.

The inference to which we are brought is that the *causes* of faction cannot be removed and that relief is only to be sought in the means of controlling its *effects*.

If a faction consists of less than a majority, relief is supplied by the republican principle, which enables the majority to defeat its sinister views by regular vote. It may clog the administration, it may convulse the society; but it will be unable to execute and mask its violence under the forms of the Constitution. When a majority is included in a faction, the form of popular government, on the other hand, enables it to sacrifice to its ruling passion or interest both the public good and the rights of other citizens. To secure the public good and private rights against the danger of such a faction, and at the same time to preserve the spirit and the form of popular government, is then the great object to which our inquiries are directed. Let me add that it is the great desideratum by which alone this form of government can be rescued from the opprobrium under which it has so long labored and be recommended to the esteem and adoption of mankind.

By what means is this object attainable? Evidently by one of two only. Either the existence of the same passion or interest in a majority at the same time must be prevented, or the majority, having such coexistent passion or interest, must be rendered, by their number and local situation, unable to concert and carry into effect schemes of oppression. If the impulse and the opportunity be suffered to coincide, we well know that neither moral nor religious motives can be relied on as an adequate control. They are not found to be such on the injustice and violence of individuals, and lose their efficacy in proportion to the number combined together, that is, in proportion as their efficacy becomes needful.

From this view of the subject it may be concluded that a pure democracy, by which I mean a society consisting of a small number of citizens, who assemble and administer the government in person, can admit of no cure for the mischiefs of faction. A common passion or interest will, in almost every case, be felt by a majority of the whole, a communication and concert results from the form of government itself; and there is nothing to check the inducements to sacrifice the weaker party or an obnoxious individual. Hence it is that such democracies have ever been spectacles of turbulence and contention; have ever been found incompatible with personal security or the rights of property; and have in general been as short in their lives as they have been violent in their deaths. Theoretic politicians, who have patronized this species of government, have erroneously supposed that by reducing mankind to a perfect equality in their political rights, they would at the same time be perfectly equalized and assimilated in their possessions, their opinions, and their passions.

A republic, by which I mean a government in which the scheme of representation takes place, opens a different prospect and promises the cure for which we are seeking. Let us examine the points in which it varies from pure democracy, and we shall comprehend both the nature of the cure and the efficacy which it must derive from the Union.

The two great points of difference between a democracy and a republic are: first, the delegation of the government, in the latter, to a small number of citizens elected by the rest; secondly, the greater number of citizens and greater sphere of country over which the latter may be extended.

The effect of the first difference is, on the one hand, to refine and enlarge the public views by passing them through the medium of a chosen body of citizens, whose wisdom may best discern the true interest of their country and whose patriotism and love of justice will be least likely to sacrifice it to temporary or partial considerations. Under such a regulation it may well happen that the public voice, pronounced by the representatives of the people, will be more consonant to the public good than if pronounced by the people themselves, convened for the purpose. On the other hand, the effect may be inverted. Men of factious tempers, of local prejudices, or of sinister designs, may, by intrigue, by corruption, or by other means, first obtain the suffrages, and then betray the interests of the people. The question resulting is, whether small or extensive republics are most favorable to the election of proper guardians of the public weal; and it is clearly decided in favor of the latter by two obvious considerations.

In the first place it is to be remarked that however small the republic may be the representatives must be raised to a certain number in order to guard against the cabals of a few; and that however large it may be they must be limited to a certain number in order to guard against the confusion of a multitude. Hence, the number of representatives in the two cases not being in proportion to that of the constituents, and being proportionally greatest in the small republic, it follows that if the proportion of fit characters be not less in the large than in the small republic, the former will present a greater option, and consequently a greater probability of a fit choice.

In the next place, as each representative will be chosen by a greater number of citizens in the large than in the small republic, it will be more difficult for unworthy candidates to practice with success the vicious arts by which elections are too often carried; and the suffrages of the people being more free, will be more likely to center on men who possess the most attractive merit and the most diffusive and established characters.

It must be confessed that in this, as in most other cases, there is a mean, on both sides of which inconveniencies will be found to lie. By enlarging too much the number of electors, you render the representative too little acquainted with all their local circumstances and lesser interests; as by reducing it too much, you render him unduly attached to these, and too little fit to comprehend and pursue great and national objects. The federal Constitution forms a happy combination in this respect; the great and aggregate interests being referred to the national, the local and particular to the State legislatures.

The other point of difference is the greater number of citizens and extent of territory which may be brought within the compass of republican than of democratic government; and it is this circumstance principally which renders factious combinations less to be dreaded in the former than in the latter. The smaller the society, the fewer probably will be the distinct parties and interests composing it; the fewer the distinct parties and interests, the more frequently will a majority be found of the same party; and the smaller the number of individuals composing a majority, and the smaller the compass within which they are placed, the more easily will they concert and execute their plans of oppression. Extend the sphere and you take in a greater variety of parties and interests; you make it less probable that a majority of the whole will have a common motive to invade the rights of other citizens; or if such a common motive exists, it will be more difficult for all who feel it to discover their own strength and to act in unison with each other. Besides other impediments, it may be remarked that, where there is a consciousness of unjust or dishonorable purposes, communication is always checked by distrust in proportion to the number whose concurrence is necessary.

Hence, it clearly appears that the same advantage which a republic has over a democracy in controlling the effects of faction is enjoyed by a large over a small republic—is enjoyed by the Union over the States composing it. Does this advantage consist in the substitution of representatives whose enlightened views and virtuous sentiments render them superior to local prejudices and to schemes of injustice? It will not be denied that the representation of the Union will be most likely to possess these requisite endowments. Does it consist in the greater security afforded by a greater variety of parties, against the event of any one party being able to outnumber and oppress the rest? In an equal degree does the increased variety of parties comprised within the Union increase this security. Does it, in fine, consist in the greater obstacles opposed to the concert and accomplishment of the secret wishes of an unjust and interested majority? Here again the extent of the Union gives it the most palpable advantage.

The influence of factious leaders may kindle a flame within their particular States but will be unable to spread a general conflagration through the other States. A religious sect may degenerate into a political faction in a part of the Confederacy; but the variety of sects dispersed over the entire face of it must secure the national councils against any danger from that source. A rage for paper money, for an abolition of debts, for an equal division of property, or for any other improper or wicked project, will be less apt to pervade the whole body of the Union than a particular member of it, in the same proportion as such a malady is more likely to taint a particular county or district than an entire State.

In the extent and proper structure of the Union, therefore, we behold a republican remedy for the diseases most incident to republican government. And according to the degree of pleasure and pride we feel in being republicans ought to be our zeal in cherishing the spirit and supporting the character of federalists.

FEDERALIST NO. 51
(JAMES MADISON)

To what expedient, then, shall we finally resort, for maintaining in practice the necessary partition of power among the several departments as laid down in the Constitution? The only answer that can be given is that as all these exterior provisions are found to be inadequate, the defect must be supplied, by so contriving the interior structure of the government as that its several constituent parts may, by their mutual relations, be the means of keeping each other in their proper places. Without presuming to undertake a full development of this important idea I will hazard few general observations which may perhaps place it in a clearer light, and enable us to form a more correct judgment of the principles and structure of the government planned by the convention.

In order to lay a due foundation for that separate and distinct exercise of the different powers of government, which to a certain extent is admitted on all hands to be essential to the preservation of liberty, it is evident that each department should have a will of its own; and consequently should be so constituted that the members of each should have as little agency as possible in the appointment of the members of the others. Were this principle rigorously adhered to, it would require that all the appointments for the supreme executive, legislative, and judiciary magistracies should be drawn from the same fountain of authority, the people, through channels having no communication whatever with one another. Perhaps such a plan of constructing the several departments would be less difficult in practice than it may be in contemplation appear. Some difficulties, however, and some additional expense would attend the execution of it. Some deviations, therefore, from the principle must be admitted. In the constitution of the judiciary department in particular, it might be inexpedient to insist rigorously on the principle; first, because peculiar qualifications being essential in the members, the primary consideration ought to be to select that mode of choice which best secures these qualifications; second, because the permanent tenure by which the appointments are held in that department must soon destroy all sense of dependence on the authority conferring them.

It is equally evident that the members of each department should be as little dependent as possible on those of the others for the emoluments annexed to their offices. Were the executive magistrate, or the judges, not independent of the legislature in this particular, their independence in every other would be merely nominal.

But the great security against a gradual concentration of the several powers in the same department consists in giving to those who administer each department the necessary constitutional means and personal motives to resist encroachments of the others. The provision for defense must in this, as in all other cases, be made commensurate to the danger of attack. Ambition must be made to counteract ambition. The interest of the man must be connected with the constitutional rights of the place. It may be a reflection on human nature that such devices should be necessary to control the abuses of government. But what is government itself but the greatest of all reflections on human nature? If men were angels no government would be necessary. If angels were to govern men, neither external nor internal controls on government would be necessary. In framing a government which is to be administered by men over men, the great difficulty lies in this: you must first enable the government to control the governed; and in the next place oblige it to control itself. A dependence on the people is, no doubt, the primary control on the government; but experience has taught mankind the necessity of auxiliary precautions.

This policy of supplying, by opposite and rival interests, the defect of better motives, might be traced through the whole system of human affairs, private as well as public. We see it particularly displayed in all the subordinate distributions of power, where the constant aim is to divide and arrange the several offices in such a manner as that each may be a check on the other—that the private interest of every individual may be a sentinel over the public rights. These inventions of prudence cannot be less requisite in the distribution of the supreme powers of the State.

But it is not possible to give to each department an equal power of self-defense. In republican government, the legislative authority necessarily predominates. The remedy for this inconveniency is to divide the legislature into different branches; and to render them, by different modes of election and different principles of action, as little connected with each other as the nature of their common functions and their common dependence on the society will admit. It may even be necessary to guard against dangerous encroachments by still further precautions. As the weight of the legislative authority requires that it should be thus divided, the weakness of the executive may require, on the other hand, that it should be fortified. An absolute negative on the legislature appears, at first view, to be the natural defense with which the executive magistrate should be armed. But perhaps it would be neither altogether safe nor alone sufficient. On ordinary occasions it might not be exerted with the requisite firmness, and on extraordinary occasions it might be perfidiously abused. May not this defect of an absolute negative be supplied by some qualified connection between this weaker department and the weaker branch of the stronger department, by which the latter may be led to support the constitutional rights of the former, without being too much detached from the rights of its own department?

If the principles on which these observations are founded be just, as I persuade myself they are, and they be applied as a criterion to the several State constitutions, and to the federal Constitution, it will be found that if the latter does not perfectly correspond with them, the former are infinitely less able to bear such a test.

There are, moreover, two considerations particularly applicable to the federal system of America, which place that system in a very interesting point of view.

First. In a single republic, all the power surrendered by the people is submitted to the administration of a single government; and the usurpations are guarded against by a division of the government into distinct and separate departments. In the compound republic of America, the power surrendered by the people is first divided between two distinct governments, and then the portion allotted to each subdivided among distinct and separate departments. Hence a double security arises to the rights of the people. The different governments will control each other, at the same time that each will be controlled by itself.

Second. It is of great importance in a republic not only to guard against the society against the oppression of its rulers, but to guard one part of the society against the injustice of the other part. Different interests necessarily exist in different classes of citizens. If a majority be united by a common interest, the rights of the minority will be insecure. There are but two methods of providing against this evil: the one by creating a will in the community independent of the majority—that is, of the society itself; the other, by comprehending in the society so many separate descriptions of citizens as will render an unjust combination of a majority of the whole very improbable, if not impracticable. The first method prevails in all governments possessing an hereditary or self-appointed authority. This, at best, is but a precarious security; because a power independent of the society may as well espouse the unjust views of the major as the rightful interests of the minor party, and may possibly be turned against both parties. The second method will be exemplified in the federal republic of the United States. Whilst all authority in it will be derived from and dependent on the society, the society itself will be broken into so many parts, interests and classes of citizens, that the rights of individuals, or of the minority, will be in little danger from interested combinations of the majority. In a free government the security for civil rights must be the same as that for religious rights. It consists in the one case in the multiplicity of interests, and in the other in the multiplicity of sects. The degree of security in both cases will depend on the number of interests and sects; and this may be presumed to depend on the extent of country and number of people comprehended under the same government. This view of the subject must particularly recommend a proper federal system to all the sincere and considerate friends of republican government, since it shows that in exact proportion as the territory of the Union may be formed into more circumscribed Confederacies, or States, oppressive combinations of a majority will be facilitated; the best security, under the republican forms, for the rights of every class of citizen, will be diminished; and consequently the stability and independence of some member of the government, the only other security, must be proportionately increased. Justice is the end of government. It is the end of civil society. It ever has been and ever will be pursued until it be obtained, or until liberty be lost in the pursuit. In a society under the forms of which the stronger faction can readily unite and oppress the weaker, anarchy may as truly be said to reign as in a state of nature, where the weaker individual is not secured against the violence of the stronger; and as, in the latter state, even the stronger individuals are prompted, by the uncertainty of their condition, to submit to a government which may protect the weak as well as themselves; so, in the former state, will the more powerful factions or parties be gradu-

ally induced, by a like motive, to wish for a government which will protect all parties, the weaker as well as the more powerful. It can be little doubted that if the State of Rhode Island was separated from the Confederacy and left to itself, the insecurity of rights under the popular form of government within such narrow limits would be displayed by such reiterated oppressions of factious majorities that some power altogether independent of the people would soon be called for by the voice of the very factions whose misrule had proved the necessity of it. In the extended republic of the United States, and among the great variety of interests, parties, and sects which it embraces, a coalition of a majority of the whole society could seldom take place on any other principles than those of justice and the general good; whilst there being thus less danger to a minor from the will of a major party, there must be less pretext, also, to provide for the security of the former, by introducing into the government a will not dependent on the latter, or, in other words, a will independent of the society itself. It is no less certain than it is important, notwithstanding the contrary opinions which have been entertained, that the larger the society, provided it lie within a practicable sphere, the more duly capable it will be of self-government. And happily for the *republican cause*, the practicable sphere may be carried to a very great extent by a judicious modification and mixture of the federal principle.

GLOSSARY

accountability The ability of the public to hold government officials responsible for their actions.

affirmative action A term that refers to programs designed to ensure that women, minorities, and other traditionally disadvantaged groups have full and equal opportunities in employment, education, and other areas of life.

age-cohort tendency The tendency for a significant break in the pattern of political socialization to occur among younger citizens, usually as the result of a major event or development that disrupts preexisting beliefs.

agency point of view The tendency of bureaucrats to place the interests of their agency ahead of other interests and ahead of the priorities sought by the president or Congress.

agenda setting The power of the media through news coverage to focus the public's attention and concern on particular events, problems, issues, personalities, and so on.

agents of socialization Those agents, such as the family and the media, that have significant impact on citizens' political socialization.

air wars A term that refers to the fact that modern campaigns are often a battle of opposing televised advertising campaigns.

alienation A feeling of personal powerlessness that includes the notion that government does not care about the opinions of people like oneself.

Anti-Federalists A term used to describe opponents of the Constitution during the debate over ratification.

apathy A feeling of personal noninterest or unconcern with politics.

appellate jurisdiction The authority of a given court to review cases that have already been tried in lower courts and are appealed to it by the losing party; such a court is called an appeals court or appellate court. (See also **original jurisdiction.**)

authority The recognized right of an individual or institution to exercise power. (See also **power.**)

balanced budget When the government's tax revenues for the year are equal to or exceed its expenditures.

bicameral legislature A legislature having two chambers.

bill A proposed law (legislative act) within Congress or another legislature. (See also **law.**)

Bill of Rights The first ten amendments to the Constitution. They include such rights as freedom of speech and trial by jury.

block grants Federal grants-in-aid that permit state and local officials to decide how the money will be spent within a general area, such as education or health. (See also **categorical grants.**)

budget deficit When the government's expenditures for the year exceed its tax revenues.

budget surplus When the government's tax and other revenues for the year exceed its expenditures.

bureaucracy A system of organization and control based on the principles of hierarchical authority, job specialization, and formalized rules. (See also **formalized rules; hierarchical authority; job specialization.**)

cabinet A group consisting of the heads of the (cabinet) executive departments, who are appointed by the president, subject to confirmation by the Senate. The cabinet was once the main advisory body to the president but no longer plays this role. (See also **cabinet departments.**)

cabinet (executive) departments The major administrative organizations within the federal executive bureaucracy, each of which is headed by a secretary (cabinet officer) and has responsibility for a major function of the federal government, such as defense, agriculture, or justice. (See also **cabinet; independent agencies.**)

candidate-centered politics Election campaigns and other political processes in which candidates, not political parties, have most of the initiative and influence. (See also **party-centered politics.**)

capital-gains tax Tax that individuals pay on money gained from the sale of a capital asset, such as property or stocks.

capitalism An economic system based on the idea that government should interfere with economic transactions as little as possible. Free enterprise and self-reliance are the collective and individual principles that underpin capitalism.

categorical grants Federal grants-in-aid to states and localities that can be used only for designated projects. (See also **block grants.**)

charter The chief instrument by which a state governs its local units; it spells out in detail what a local government can and cannot do.

checks and balances The elaborate system of divided spheres of authority provided by the U.S. Constitution as a means of controlling the power of government. The separation of powers among the branches of the national government, federalism, and the different methods of selecting national officers are all part of this system.

citizens' (noneconomic) groups Organized interests formed by individuals drawn together by opportunities to promote a cause in which they believe but that does not provide them significant individual economic benefits. (See also **economic groups; interest group.**)

city manager system Form of municipal government that entrusts the executive role to a professionally trained manager, who is chosen, and can be fired, by the city council.

civic duty The belief of an individual that civic and political participation is a responsibility of citizenship.

civil liberties The fundamental individual rights of a free society, such as freedom of speech and the right to a jury trial, which in the United States are protected by the Bill of Rights.

civil rights (equal rights) The right of every person to equal protection under the laws and equal access to society's opportunities and public facilities.

civil service system See **merit system.**

clear-and-present-danger test A test devised by the Supreme Court in 1919 to define the limits of free speech in the context of national security. According to the test, government cannot abridge political expression unless it presents a clear and present danger to the nation's security.

clientele groups Special-interest groups that benefit directly from the activities of a particular bureaucratic agency and are therefore strong advocates of the agency.

cloture A parliamentary maneuver that, if a three-fifths majority votes for it, limits Senate debate to thirty hours and has the effect of defeating a filibuster. (See also **filibuster.**)

cold war The lengthy period after World War II when the United States and the USSR were not engaged in actual combat (a "hot war") but were nonetheless locked in a state of deep-seated hostility.

collective (public) goods Benefits that are offered by groups (usually citizens' groups) as an incentive for membership but that are nondivisible (e.g., a clean environment) and therefore are available to nonmembers as well as members of the particular group. (See also **free-rider problem; private goods.**)

commerce clause The clause of the Constitution (Article I, Section 8) that empowers the federal government to regulate commerce among the states and with other nations.

commission system Form of municipal government that invests executive and legislative authority in a commission, with each commissioner serving as a member of the local council but also having a specified executive role, such as police commissioner or public works commissioner.

common-carrier role The media's function as an open channel through which political leaders can communicate with the public. (See also **public representative role; signaler role; watchdog role.**)

comparable worth The idea that women should get pay equal to men for work that is of similar difficulty and responsibility and that requires similar levels of education and training.

compliance The issue of whether a court's decisions will be respected and obeyed.

concurring opinion A separate opinion written by a Supreme Court justice who votes with the majority in the decision on a case but who disagrees with their reasoning. (See also **dissenting opinion; majority opinion; plurality opinion.**)

confederacy A governmental system in which sovereignty is vested entirely in subnational (state) governments. (See also **federalism; unitary system.**)

conference committee A temporary committee that is formed to bargain over the differences in the House and Senate versions of a bill. The committee's members are usually appointed from the House and Senate standing committees that originally worked on the bill.

conservatives Those who emphasize the marketplace as the means of distributing economic benefits but look to government to uphold traditional social values. (See also **liberals; libertarians; populists.**)

constituency The individuals who live within the geographical area represented by an elected official. More narrowly, the body of citizens eligible to vote for a particular representative.

constitution The fundamental law that defines how a government will legitimately operate.

constitutional democracy A government that is democratic in its provisions for majority influence through elections and constitutional in its provisions for minority rights and rule by law.

constitutional initiative The process by which a citizen or group can petition to place a proposed amendment on the ballot at the next election by obtaining the signatures of a certain number of registered voters, and if the amendment gets majority support, it becomes part of the constitution.

constitutionalism The idea that there are definable limits on the rightful power of a government over its citizens.

containment A doctrine, developed after World War II, based on the assumptions that the Soviet Union was an aggressor nation and that only a determined United States could block Soviet territorial ambitions.

Cooley's rule The term used to describe the idea that cities should be self-governing, articulated in an 1871 ruling by Michigan judge Thomas Cooley.

cooperative federalism The situation in which the national, state, and local levels work together to solve problems.

---

de facto discrimination Discrimination on the basis of race, sex, religion, ethnicity, and the like that results from social, economic, and cultural biases and conditions. (See also **de jure discrimination.**)

de jure discrimination Discrimination on the basis of race, sex, religion, ethnicity, and the like that results from a law. (See also **de facto discrimination.**)

dealignment A situation in which voters' partisan loyalties have been substantially and permanently weakened. (See also **party identification; realignment.**)

decision A vote of the Supreme Court in a particular case that indicates which party the justices side with and by how large a margin.

deficit spending When the government spends more than it collects in taxes and other revenues.

delegates Elected representatives whose obligation is to act in accordance with the expressed wishes of the people whom they represent. (See also **trustees.**)

demand-side economics A form of fiscal policy that emphasizes "demand" (consumer spending). Government can use increased spending or tax cuts to place more money in consumers' hands and thereby increase demand. (See also **fiscal policy; supply-side economics.**)

democracy A form of government in which the people govern, either directly or through elected representatives.

demographic representativeness The idea that the bureaucracy will be more responsive to the public if its employees at all levels are demographically representative of the population as a whole.

denials of power A constitutional means of limiting governmental action by listing those powers that government is expressly prohibited from using.

deregulation The rescinding of excessive government regulations for the purpose of improving economic efficiency.

descriptive reporting The style of reporting that aims to describe *what* is taking place or has occurred.

détente A French word meaning "a relaxing" and used to refer to an era of improved relations between the United States and the Soviet Union that began in the early 1970s.

deterrence The idea that nuclear war can be discouraged if each side in a conflict has the capacity to destroy the other with nuclear weapons.

devolution The passing down of authority from the national government to states and localities.

Dillon's rule The term used to describe relations between state and local government; it holds that local governments are creatures of the State, which in theory even has the power to abolish them.

direct primary See **primary election.**

dissenting opinion The opinion of a justice in a Supreme Court case that explains the reasons for disagreeing with the majority's decision. (See also **concurring opinion; majority opinion; plurality opinion.**)

diversity The principle that individual differences should be respected, are a legitimate basis of self-interest, and are a source of strength for the American nation.

dual federalism A doctrine based on the idea that a precise separation of national power and state power is both possible and desirable.

due process clause (of the Fourteenth Amendment) The clause of the Constitution that has been used by the judiciary to apply the Bill of Rights to the action of state government.

economic depression A very severe and sustained economic downturn. Depressions are rare in the United States: the last one was in the 1930s.

economic globalization The increased interdependence of nations' economies. The change is a result of technological, transportation, and communication advances that have enabled firms to deploy their resources across the globe.

economic groups Interest groups that are organized primarily for economic reasons but that engage in political activity in order to seek favorable policies from government. (See also **citizens' groups; interest group.**)

economic recession A moderate but sustained downturn in the economy. Recessions are part of the economy's "normal" cycle of ups and downs.

economy A system of production and consumption of goods and services that are allocated through exchange among producers and consumers.

efficiency An economic principle that holds that firms should fulfill as many of society's needs as possible while using as few of its resources as possible. The greater the output (production) for a given input (for example, an hour of labor), the more efficient the process.

elastic clause See **"necessary and proper" clause.**

electoral college An unofficial term that refers to the electors who cast the states' electoral votes.

electoral mastery A strong base of popular support that frees a congressional incumbent from constant worry over reelection.

electoral votes The method of voting that is used to choose the U.S. president. Each state has the same number of electoral votes as it has members in Congress (House and Senate combined). By tradition, electoral voting is tied to a state's popular voting; thus, the presidential candidate with the most popular votes overall has usually also had the most electoral votes.

elitism The view that the United States is essentially run by a tiny elite (composed of wealthy or well-connected individuals) who control public policy through both direct and indirect means.

entitlement program Any of a number of individual benefit programs, such as social security, that require government to provide a designated benefit to any person who meets the legally defined criteria for eligibility.

enumerated (expressed) powers The seventeen powers granted to the national government under Article I, Section 8 of the Constitution. These powers include taxation and the regulation of commerce as well as the authority to provide for the national defense.

equal protection clause A clause of the Fourteenth Amendment that forbids any state to deny equal protection of the laws to any individual within its jurisdiction.

equal rights See **civil rights.**

equality The principle that all individuals have moral worth and are entitled to fair treatment under the law.

equality of opportunity The idea that all individuals should be given an equal chance to succeed on their own.

equality of result The objective of policies intended to reduce or eliminate the effects of discrimination so that members of traditionally disadvantaged groups will have the same benefits of society as do members of advantaged groups.

equity (in relation to economic policy) The situation in which the outcome of an economic transaction is fair to each party. An outcome can usually be considered fair if each party enters into a transaction freely and is not knowingly at a disadvantage.

establishment clause The First Amendment provision that government may not favor one religion over another or favor religion over no religion, and that prohibits Congress from passing laws respecting the establishment of religion.

exclusionary rule The legal principle that government is prohibited from using in trials evidence that was obtained by unconstitutional means (for example, illegal search and seizure).

executive departments See **cabinet departments.**

executive leadership system An approach to managing the bureaucracy that is based on presidential leadership and presidential management tools, such as the president's annual budget proposal. (See also **merit system; patronage system.**)

expressed powers See **enumerated powers.**

externalities Burdens that society incurs when firms fail to pay the full cost of resources used in production. An example of an externality is the pollution that results when corporations dump industrial wastes into lakes and rivers.

---

facts (of a court case) The relevant circumstances of a legal dispute or offense as determined by a trial court. The facts of a case are crucial because they help determine which law or laws are applicable in the case.

federalism A governmental system in which authority is divided between two sovereign levels of government: national and regional. (See also **confederacy; unitary system.**)

Federalists A term used to describe supporters of the Constitution during the debate over ratification.

filibuster A procedural tactic in the U.S. Senate whereby a minority of legislators prevents a bill from coming to a vote by holding the floor and talking until the majority gives in and the bill is withdrawn from consideration. (See also **cloture.**)

fiscal federalism A term that refers to the expenditure of federal funds on programs run in part through states and localities.

fiscal policy A tool of economic management by which government attempts to maintain a stable economy through its taxing and spending decisions. (See also **demand-side economics; monetary policy; supply-side economics.**)

formalized rules A basic principle of bureaucracy that refers to the standardized procedures and established regulations by which a bureaucracy conducts its operations. (See also **bureaucracy.**)

free-exercise clause A First Amendment provision that prohibits the government from interfering with the practice of religion or prohibiting the free exercise of religion.

free-rider problem The situation in which the benefits offered by a group to its members are also available to nonmembers. The incentive to join the group and to promote its cause is reduced because nonmembers (free riders) receive the benefits (e.g., a cleaner environment) without having to pay any of the group's costs. (See also **collective goods.**)

free trade The view that the long-term economic interests of all countries are advanced when tariffs and other trade barriers are kept to a minimum. (See also **protectionism.**)

freedom of expression Americans' freedom to communicate their views, the foundation of which is the First Amendment rights of freedom of conscience, speech, press, assembly, and petition.

---

gender gap The tendency of women and men to differ in their political attitudes and voting preferences.

government The institutions, processes, and rules that facilitate control of a particular area and its inhabitants.

government corporations Bodies, such as the U.S. Postal Service and Amtrak, that are similar to private corporations in that they charge for their services, but different in that they receive federal funding to help defray expenses. Their directors are appointed by the president with Senate approval.

graduated personal income tax A tax on personal income in which the tax rate increases as income increases; in other words, the tax is higher for higher income levels.

grants-in-aid Federal cash payments to states and localities for programs they administer.

grants of power The method of limiting the U.S. government by confining its scope of authority to those powers expressly granted in the Constitution.

grassroots lobbying A form of lobbying designed to persuade officials that a group's policy position has strong constituent support.

grassroots party A political party organized at the level of the voters and dependent on their support for its strength.

Great Compromise The agreement of the constitutional convention to create a two-chamber Congress with the House apportioned by population and the Senate apportioned equally by state.

---

hard money Campaign funds given directly to candidates to spend as they choose.

hierarchical authority A basic principle of bureaucracy that refers to the chain of command within an organization whereby officials and units have control over those below them. (See also **bureaucracy.**)

hired guns The professional consultants who run campaigns for high office.

home rule A device designed to give local governments more leeway in their policies; it allows a local government to design and amend its own charter, subject to the laws and constitution of the state and also subject to veto by the state.

honeymoon period The president's first months in office, a time when Congress, the press, and the public are more inclined than usual to support presidential initiatives.

ideology A consistent pattern of opinion on particular issues that stems from a core belief or set of beliefs.

Imminent Lawless Action Test A legal test that says government cannot lawfully suppress advocacy that promotes lawless action unless such advocacy is aimed at producing, and is likely to produce, imminent lawless action.

implied powers The federal government's constitutional authority (through the "necessary and proper" clause) to take action that is not expressly authorized by the Constitution but that supports actions that are so authorized. (See also **"necessary and proper" clause.**)

in-kind benefits Government benefits that are cash equivalents, such as food stamps or rent vouchers. This form of benefit ensures that recipients will use public assistance in a specified way.

inalienable (natural) rights Those rights that persons theoretically possessed in the state of nature, prior to the formation of governments. These rights, including those of life, liberty, and property, are considered inherent and as such are inalienable. Since government is established by people, government has the responsibility to preserve these rights.

independent agencies Bureaucratic agencies that are similar to cabinet departments but usually have a narrower area of responsibility. Each such agency is headed by a presidential appointee who is not a cabinet member. An example is the National Aeronautics and Space Administration. (See also **cabinet departments.**)

individual goods See **private goods.**

individualism A philosophical belief that stresses the values of hard work and self-reliance and holds that the individual should be left to succeed or fail on his or her own.

individualistic subculture American subculture oriented toward private life and economic gain,

with politics largely an extension of this perspective; characterizing middle, western, and southwestern states.

inflation A general increase in the average level of prices of goods and services.

initiative The process by which citizens can place legislative measures on the ballot through signature petitions, and if the measure receives a majority vote, it becomes law.

inside lobbying Direct communication between organized interests and policymakers, which is based on the assumed value of close ("inside") contacts with policymakers.

insurgency A type of military conflict in which irregular soldiers rise up against an established regime.

interest group A set of individuals who are organized to promote a shared political interest. (See also **citizens' groups; economic groups.**)

interest-group liberalism The tendency of public officials to support the policy demands of self-interested groups (as opposed to judging policy demands according to whether or not they serve a larger conception of "the public interest").

intermediate-scrutiny test A test applied by courts to laws that attempt a gender classification. In effect, the test eliminates gender as a legal classification unless it serves an important objective and is substantially related to the objective's achievement.

internationalism The view that the country should involve itself deeply in world affairs. (See also **isolationism.**)

interpretive reporting The style of reporting that aims to explain *why* something is taking place or has occurred.

iron triangle A small and informal but relatively stable group of well-positioned legislators, executives, and lobbyists who seek to promote policies beneficial to a particular interest. (See also **issue network.**)

isolationism The view that the country should deliberately avoid a large role in world affairs and, instead, concentrate on domestic concerns. (See also **internationalism**.)

issue network An informal network of public officials and lobbyists who have a common interest and expertise in a given area and who are brought together temporarily by a proposed policy in that area. (See also **iron triangle**.)

---

job specialization A basic principle of bureaucracy that holds that the responsibilities of each job position should be explicitly defined and that a precise division of labor within the organization should be maintained. (See also **bureaucracy**.)

judicial activism The doctrine that the courts should develop new legal principles when judges see a compelling need, even if this action places them in conflict with the policy decisions of elected officials. (See also **judicial restraint**.)

judicial conference A closed meeting of the justices of the U.S. Supreme Court to discuss and vote on the cases before them; the justices are not supposed to discuss conference proceedings with outsiders.

judicial restraint The doctrine that the judiciary should be highly respectful of precedent and should defer to the judgment of legislatures. The doctrine claims that the job of judges is to work within the confines of laws set down by tradition and lawmaking majorities. (See also **judicial activism**.)

judicial review The power of courts to decide whether a governmental institution has acted within its constitutional powers and, if not, to declare its action null and void.

jurisdiction (of a congressional committee) The policy area in which a particular congressional committee is authorized to act.

jurisdiction (of a court) A given court's authority to hear cases of a particular kind. Jurisdiction may be original or appellate.

---

laissez-faire doctrine A classic economic philosophy that holds that

owners of businesses should be allowed to make their own production and distribution decisions without government regulation or control.

law (as enacted by Congress) A legislative proposal, or bill, that is passed by both the House and Senate and is either signed or not vetoed by the president. (See also **bill**.)

lawmaking function The authority (of a legislature) to make the laws necessary to carry out the government's powers. (See also **oversight function; representation function**.)

laws (of a court case) The constitutional provisions, legislative statutes, or judicial precedents that apply to a court case.

legitimacy (of election) The idea that the selection of officeholders should be based on the will of the people as reflected through their votes.

legitimacy (of judicial power) The issue of the proper limits of judicial authority in a political system based in part on the principle of majority rule.

libel Publication of material that falsely damages a person's reputation.

liberals Those who favor activist government as an instrument of economic security and redistribution but reject the notion that government should favor a particular set of social values. (See also **conservatives; libertarians; populists**.)

libertarians Those who oppose government as an instrument of traditional values and of economic security. (See also **conservatives; liberals; populists**.)

liberty The principle that the people should be free to act and think as they choose, provided they do not infringe unreasonably on others' freedom.

limited government A government that is subject to strict limits on its lawful uses of powers and hence on its ability to deprive people of their liberty.

lobbying The process by which interest-group members or lobbyists

attempt to influence public policy through contacts with public officials.

logrolling The trading of votes between legislators so that each gets what he or she most wants.

---

majoritarianism The idea that the majority prevails not only in elections but also in determining policy.

majority opinion A Supreme Court opinion that results when a majority of the justices is in agreement on the legal basis of the decision. (See also **concurring opinion; dissenting opinion; plurality opinion**.)

material incentive An economic or other tangible benefit that is used to attract group members.

means test The requirement that applicants for public assistance must demonstrate they are poor in order to be eligible for the assistance. (See also **public assistance**.)

merit (civil service) system An approach to managing the bureaucracy whereby people are appointed to government positions on the basis of either competitive examinations or special qualifications, such as professional training. (See also **executive leadership system; patronage system**.)

metropolitan government Form of local government created when local governments join together and assign it responsibility for a range of activities so as to reduce the waste and duplication that results when every locality in a densely populated area has its own police force, its own sanitation department, and so on.

military-industrial complex The three components (the military establishment, the industries that manufacture weapons, and the members of Congress from states and districts that depend heavily on the arms industry) that mutually benefit from a high level of defense spending.

momentum A strong showing by a candidate in early presidential nominating contests, which leads to a buildup of public support for the candidate.

monetary policy A tool of economic management, available to government, based on manipulation of the amount of money in circulation. (See also **fiscal policy.**)

money chase A term used to describe the fact that U.S. campaigns are very expensive and that candidates must spend a great amount of time raising funds in order to compete successfully.

moralistic subculture American subculture characterized by an emphasis on the public interest, honesty, and public participation; typical of states in the northern tier of the nation.

multilateralism The situation in which nations act together in response to problems and crises.

multinational corporations Business firms with major operations in more than one country.

multiparty system A system in which three or more political parties have the capacity to gain control of government separately or in coalition.

---

national debt The total cumulative amount that the U.S. government owes to creditors.

natural rights See **inalienable rights.**

"necessary and proper" clause (elastic clause) The authority granted Congress in Article I, Section 8 of the Constitution "to make all laws which shall be necessary and proper" for the implementation of its enumerated powers. (See also **implied powers.**)

negative government The philosophical belief that government governs best by staying out of people's lives, thus giving individuals as much freedom as possible to determine their own pursuits. (See also **positive government.**)

neutral competence The administrative objective of a merit-based bureaucracy. Such a bureaucracy should be "competent" in the sense that its employees are hired and retained on the basis of their expertise and "neutral" in the sense that

it operates by objective standards rather than partisan ones.

New Jersey (small-state) Plan A constitutional proposal for a strengthened Congress but one in which each state would have a single vote, thus granting a small state the same legislative power as a larger state.

news The news media's version of reality, usually with an emphasis on timely, dramatic, and compelling events and developments.

news media See **press.**

nomination The designation of a particular individual to run as a political party's candidate (its "nominee") in the general election.

noneconomic groups See **citizens' groups.**

North-South Compromise The agreement over economic and slavery issues that enabled northern and southern states to settle differences that threatened to defeat the effort to draft a new constitution.

---

objective journalism A model of news reporting that is based on the communication of "facts" rather than opinions and that is "fair" in that it presents all sides of partisan debate. (See also **partisan press.**)

open party caucuses Meetings at which a party's candidates for nomination are voted on and that are open to all the party's rank-and-file voters who want to attend.

open-seat election An election in which there is no incumbent in the race.

opinion (of a court) A court's written explanation of its decision, which serves to inform others of the legal basis for the decision. Supreme Court opinions are expected to guide the decisions of other courts. (See also **concurring opinion; dissenting opinion; majority opinion; plurality opinion.**)

ordinance A law issued by a local government under authority granted by the state government.

original jurisdiction The authority of a given court to be the first court to hear a case. (See also **appellate jurisdiction.**)

outside lobbying A form of lobbying in which an interest group seeks to use public pressure as a means of influencing officials.

oversight function A supervisory activity of Congress that centers on its constitutional responsibility to see that the executive carries out the laws faithfully and spends appropriations properly. (See also **lawmaking function; representation function.**)

---

packaging (of a candidate) A term of modern campaigning that refers to the process of recasting a candidate's record into an appealing image.

partisan press Newspapers and other communication media that openly support a political party and whose news in significant part follows the party line. (See also **objective journalism.**)

party caucus A group that consists of a party's members in the House or Senate and that serves to elect the party's leadership, set policy goals, and determine party strategy.

party-centered politics Election campaigns and other political processes in which political parties, not individual candidates, hold most of the initiative and influence. (See also **candidate-centered politics.**)

party coalition The groups and interests that support a political party.

party competition A process in which conflict over society's goals is transformed by political parties into electoral competition in which the winner gains the power to govern.

party discipline The willingness of a party's House or Senate members to act together as a cohesive group and thus exert collective control over legislative action.

party identification The personal sense of loyalty that an individual may feel toward a particular political party. (See also **dealignment; realignment.**)

party leaders Members of the House and Senate who are chosen by the

Democratic or Republican caucus in each chamber to represent the party's interests in that chamber and who give some central direction to the chamber's deliberations.

party organizations The party organizational units at national, state, and local levels; their influence has decreased over time because of many factors. (See also **candidate-centered politics; party-centered politics; primary election.**)

party realignment An election or set of elections in which the electorate responds strongly to an extraordinarily powerful issue that has disrupted the established political order. A realignment has a lasting impact on public policy, popular support for the parties, and the composition of the party coalitions.

patronage system An approach to managing the bureaucracy whereby people are appointed to important government positions as a reward for political services they have rendered and because of their partisan loyalty. (See also **executive leadership system; merit system; spoils system.**)

pluralism A theory of American politics that holds that society's interests are substantially represented through the activities of groups.

plurality opinion A court opinion that results when a majority of justices agrees on a decision in a case but does not agree on the legal basis for the decision. In this instance, the legal position held by most of the justices on the winning side is called a plurality opinion. (See also **concurring opinion; dissenting opinion; majority opinion.**)

police power A term that refers to the broad power of government to regulate the health, safety, and morals of the citizenry.

policy Generally, any broad course of governmental action; more narrowly, a specific government program or initiative.

policy implementation The primary function of the bureaucracy; it refers to the process of carrying out

the authoritative decisions of Congress, the president, and the courts.

political action committee (PAC) The organization through which an interest group raises and distributes funds for election purposes. By law, the funds must be raised through voluntary contributions.

political culture The characteristic and deep-seated beliefs of a particular people.

political movements See **social movements.**

political participation A sharing in activities designed to influence public policy and leadership, such as voting, joining political parties and interest groups, writing to elected officials, demonstrating for political causes, and giving money to political candidates.

political party An ongoing coalition of interests joined together to try to get their candidates for public office elected under a common label.

political socialization The learning process by which people acquire their political opinions, beliefs, and values.

political system The various components of American government constitute a political system. The parts are separate, but they connect with each other, affecting how each performs.

politics The process through which society makes its governing decisions.

population In a public opinion poll, the people (for example, the citizens of a nation) whose opinions are being estimated through interviews with a sample of these people.

populists Those who favor activist government as a means of promoting both economic security and traditional values. (See also **conservatives; liberals; libertarians.**)

pork barrel projects Legislative acts whose tangible benefits are targeted at a particular legislator's constituency.

positive government The philosophical belief that government intervention is necessary in order to enhance

personal liberty when individuals are buffeted by economic and social forces beyond their control. (See also **negative government.**)

poverty line As defined by the federal government, the annual cost of a thrifty food budget for an urban family of four, multiplied by three to allow also for the cost of housing, clothes, and other expenses. Families below the poverty line are considered poor and are eligible for certain forms of public assistance.

power The ability of persons or institutions to control policy. (See also **authority.**)

precedent A judicial decision in a given case that serves as a rule of thumb for settling subsequent cases of a similar nature; courts are generally expected to follow precedent.

presidential approval rating A measure of the degree to which the public approves or disapproves of the president's performance in office.

presidential commissions Organizations within the bureaucracy that are headed by commissioners appointed by the president. An example is the Commission on Civil Rights.

press (news media) Those print and broadcast organizations that are in the news-reporting business.

primacy tendency The tendency for early learning to become deeply embedded in one's mind.

primary election A form of election in which voters choose a party's nominees for public office. In most states, eligibility to vote in a primary election is limited to voters who designated themselves as party members when they registered to vote. A primary is direct when it results directly in the choice of a nominee; it is indirect (as in the case of presidential primaries) when it results in the selection of delegates who then choose the nominee.

prior restraint Government prohibition of speech or publication before the fact, which is presumed by the courts to be unconstitutional unless the justification for it is overwhelming.

private (individual) goods Benefits that a group (most often an economic group) can grant directly and exclusively to the individual members of the group. (See also **collective goods.**)

probability sample A sample for a poll in which each individual in the population has a known probability of being selected randomly for inclusion in the sample. (See also **public opinion poll.**)

procedural due process The constitutional requirement that government must follow proper legal procedures before a person can be legitimately punished for an alleged offense.

proportional representation A form of representation in which seats in the legislature are allocated proportionally according to each political party's share of the popular vote. This system enables smaller parties to compete successfully for seats. (See also **single-member districts.**)

prospective voting A form of electoral judgment in which voters choose the candidate whose policy promises most closely match their own preferences. (See also **retrospective voting.**)

protectionism The view that the immediate interests of domestic producers should have a higher priority (through, for example, protective tariffs) than should free trade between nations. (See also **free trade.**)

public assistance A term that refers to social welfare programs funded through general tax revenues and available only to the financially needy. Eligibility for such a program is established by a means test. (See also **means test; social insurance.**)

public goods See **collective goods.**

public opinion Those opinions held by ordinary citizens that they express openly.

public opinion poll A device for measuring public opinion whereby a relatively small number of individuals (the sample) is interviewed for the purpose of estimating the opinions of a whole community (the population). (See also **probability sample.**)

public representative role A role whereby the media attempt to act as the public's representatives. (See also **common-carrier role; signaler role; watchdog role.**)

purposive incentive An incentive to group participation based on the cause (purpose) that the group seeks to promote.

realignment See **party realignment.**

reapportionment The reallocation of House seats among states after each census as a result of population changes.

reasonable-basis test A test applied by courts to laws that treat individuals unequally. Such a law may be deemed unconstitutional if its purpose is held to be "reasonably" related to a legitimate government interest.

recall The process by which citizens can petition for the removal from office of an elected official before the scheduled completion of his or her term.

redistricting The process of altering election districts in order to make them as nearly equal in population as possible. Redistricting takes place every ten years, after each population census.

referendum The process through which the legislature may submit proposals to the voters for approval or rejection.

registration The practice of placing citizens' names on an official list of voters before they are eligible to exercise their right to vote.

regulation Government restrictions on the economic practices of private firms.

regulatory agencies Administrative units, such as the Federal Communications Commission and the Environmental Protection Agency, that have responsibility for the monitoring and regulation of ongoing economic activities.

representation function The responsibility of a legislature to represent various interests in society. (See also **lawmaking function; oversight function.**)

representative democracy A system in which the people participate in the decision-making process of government not directly but indirectly, through the election of officials to represent their interests.

republic Historically, the form of government in which representative officials met to decide on policy issues. These representatives were expected to serve the public interest but were not subject to the people's immediate control. Today, the term *republic* is used interchangeably with *democracy.*

reserved powers The powers granted to the states under the Tenth Amendment to the Constitution.

retrospective voting A form of electoral judgment in which voters support the incumbent candidate or party when their policies are judged to have succeeded and oppose the candidate or party when their policies are judged to have failed. (See also **prospective voting.**)

rider An amendment to a bill that deals with an issue unrelated to the content of the bill. Riders are permitted in the Senate but not in the House.

sample In a public opinion poll, the relatively small number of individuals interviewed for the purpose of estimating the opinions of an entire population. (See also **public opinion poll.**)

sampling error A measure of the accuracy of a public opinion poll. It is mainly a function of sample size and is usually expressed in percentage terms. (See also **probability sample.**)

selective incorporation The absorption of certain provisions of the Bill of Rights (for example, freedom of speech) into the Fourteenth Amendment so that these rights are protected from infringement by the states.

self-government The principle that the people are the ultimate source and proper beneficiary of governing authority; in practice, a government based on majority rule.

senatorial courtesy The tradition that a U.S. senator from the state in which a federal judicial vacancy has arisen should have a say in the president's nomination of the new judge if the senator is of the same party as the president.

seniority A member of Congress's consecutive years of service on a particular committee.

separated institutions sharing power The principle that, as a way to limit government, its powers should be divided among separate branches, each of which also shares in the power of the others as a means of checking and balancing them. The result is that no one branch can exercise power decisively without the support or acquiescence of the others.

separation of powers The division of the powers of government among separate institutions or branches.

service relationship The situation where party organizations assist candidates for office but have no power to require them to accept or campaign on the party's main policy positions.

service strategy Use of personal staff by members of Congress to perform services for constituents in order to gain their support in future elections.

signaler role The accepted responsibility of the media to alert the public to important developments as soon as possible after they happen or are discovered. (See also **common-carrier role; public representative role; watchdog role.**)

single-issue politics The situation in which separate groups are organized around nearly every conceivable policy issue and press their demands and influence to the utmost.

single-member districts The form of representation in which only the candidate who gets the most votes in a district wins office. (See also **proportional representation.**)

slander Spoken words that falsely damage a person's reputation.

social capital The sum of face-to-face interactions among citizens in a society.

social insurance Social welfare programs based on the "insurance" concept, so that individuals must pay into the program in order to be eligible to receive funds from it. An example is social security for retired people. (See also **public assistance.**)

social (political) movements Active and sustained efforts to achieve social and political change by groups of people who feel that government has not been properly responsive to their concerns.

soft money Campaign contributions that are not subject to legal limits and are given to parties rather than directly to candidates.

sovereignty The ultimate authority to govern within a certain geographical area.

split-ticket voting The pattern of voting in which the individual voter in a given election casts a ballot for one or more candidates of each major party. (See also **straight-ticket voting.**)

spoils system The practice of granting public office to individuals in return for political favors they have rendered. (See also **patronage system.**)

standing committee A permanent congressional committee with responsibility for a particular area of public policy. An example is the Senate Foreign Relations Committee.

state constitutional convention A state convention convened to amend the state constitution or draft a new one.

stewardship theory A theory that argues for a strong, assertive presidential role, with presidential authority limited only at points specifically prohibited by law. (See also **Whig theory.**)

straight-ticket voting The pattern of voting in which the individual voter in a given election supports only candidates of one party. (See also **split-ticket voting.**)

strict-scrutiny test A test applied by courts to laws that attempt a racial or ethnic classification. In effect, the strict-scrutiny test eliminates race or ethnicity as legal classification when it places minority group members at a disadvantage. (See also **suspect classifications.**)

strong mayor–council system Most common form of municipal government, consisting of the mayor as chief executive and the local council as the legislative body, in which the mayor has veto power and a prescribed responsibility for budgetary and other policy actions.

structuring tendency The tendency of earlier political learning to structure (influence) later learning.

suffrage The right to vote.

sunset laws Legislative acts that have a specific expiration date unless reenacted.

supply-side economics A form of fiscal policy that emphasizes "supply" (production). An example of supply-side economics would be a tax cut for business. (See also **demand-side economics; fiscal policy.**)

supremacy clause Article VI of the Constitution, which makes national law supreme over state law when the national government is acting within its constitutional limits.

suspect classifications Legal classifications, such as race and national origin, that have invidious discrimination as their purpose and are therefore unconstitutional. (See also **strict-scrutiny test.**)

symbolic speech Action (for example, the waving or burning of a flag) for the purpose of expressing a political opinion.

traditionalistic subculture American subculture reflecting the stratified society out of which it grew, which is conservative in its focus and elitist in its leadership; typifies states of the old Confederacy and those on its borders.

transfer payment A government benefit that is given directly to an individual, as in the case of social security payments to a retiree.

trustees Elected representatives whose obligation is to act in accordance with their own consciences as to what policies are in the best interests of the public. (See also **delegates**.)

two-party system A system in which only two political parties have a real chance of acquiring control of the government.

tyranny of the majority The potential of a majority to monopolize power for its own gain and to the detriment of minority rights and interests.

---

unitary system A governmental system in which the national government alone has sovereign (ultimate) authority. (See also **confederacy; federalism**.)

unit rule The rule that grants all of a state's electoral votes to the candidate who receives most of the popular votes in the state.

unity The principle that Americans are one people who form an indivisible union.

---

veto A veto occurs when the president refuses to sign a bill, thereby keeping it from becoming law unless Congress overrides the veto.

Virginia (large-state) Plan A constitutional proposal for a strong Congress with two chambers, both of which would be based on numerical representation, thus granting more power to the larger states.

voter turnout The proportion of persons of voting age that actually votes in a given election.

---

watchdog role The accepted responsibility of the media to protect the public from deceitful, careless, incompetent, and corrupt officials by standing ready to expose any official who violates accepted legal, ethical, or performance standards. (See also **common-carrier role; public representative role; signaler role**.)

weak mayor–council system Form of municipal government in which the mayor's policymaking powers

are less substantial than the council's; the mayor has no power to veto the council's actions and often has no formal role in such activities as budget making.

Whig theory A theory that prevailed in the nineteenth century and held that the presidency was a limited or restrained office whose occupant was confined to expressly granted constitutional authority. (See also **stewardship theory**.)

whistle-blowing An internal check on the bureaucracy whereby individual bureaucrats report instances of mismanagement that they observe.

writ of *certiorari* Permission granted by a higher court to allow a losing party in a legal case to bring the case before it for a ruling; when such a writ is requested of the U.S. Supreme Court, four of the Court's nine justices must agree to accept the case before it is granted *certiorari*.

NOTES

Chapter 1

[1]Alexis de Tocqueville, *Democracy in America (1835–1840)*, ed. J. P. Mayer and A. P. Kerr (Garden City, N.Y.: Doubleday/Anchor, 1969), 640.

[2]Clinton Rossiter, *Conservativism in America* (New York: Vintage, 1962), 67.

[3]James Bryce, *The American Commonwealth*, vol. 2 (1900; reprint, New York: Macmillan, 1960), 247–54.

[4]Theodore H. White, "The American Idea," *New York Times Magazine*, July 6, 1986, 12.

[5]Ralph Barton Perry, *Puritanism and Democracy* (New York: Vanguard, 1944), 124–25; see also Peter D. Salins, *Assimilation, American Style* (New York: Basic Books, 1996); Philip L. Fetzer, *The Ethnic Moment* (Armonk, N.Y.: M. E. Sharpe Publishers, 1996); Ronald Schmidt, *Language Policy and Identity Politics in the United States* (Philadelphia: Temple University Press, 2000); Debra DeLaet, *U.S. Immigration Policy in the Age of Rights* (Westport, Conn.: Praeger Publishers, 2000).

[6]See John Harmon McElroy, *American Beliefs: What Keeps a Big Country and a Diverse People United* (Chicago: I. R. Dee, 1999).

[7]Tocqueville, *Democracy in America*, 310.

[8]See Douglas Muzzio and Richard Behn, "Thinking About Welfare," *The Public Perspective*, February/March 1995, 35–38; Stanley Feldman and John Zaller, "The Political Culture of Ambivalence: Ideological Responses to the Welfare State," *American Journal of Political Science* 36 (1992): 268–307.

[9]See Claude Lévi-Strauss, *Structural Anthropology* (Chicago: University of Chicago Press, 1983); Clifford Geertz, *Myth, Symbol, and Culture* (New York: Norton, 1974); Anne Norton, *Republic of Signs* (Chicago: University of Chicago Press, 1993).

[10]U.S. Census Bureau and Department of Justice figures.

[11]Quoted in Ralph Volney Harlow, *The Growth of the United States*, vol. 2 (New York: Henry Holt, 1943), 497.

[12]Harold D. Lasswell, *Politics: Who Gets What, When, How* (New York: McGraw-Hill, 1938).

[13]Theodore Lowi and Benjamin Ginsberg, *American Government: Freedom and Power* (New York: Norton, 1990), 8.

[14]Harold D. Lasswell and Abraham Kaplan, *Power and Society* (New Haven, Conn.: Yale University Press, 1950), 75–77.

[15]*Federalist* No. 47.

[16]See Charles H. McIlwain, *Constitutionalism: Ancient and Modern* (Ithaca, N.Y.: Cornell University Press, 1983).

[17]Tocqueville, *Democracy in America*, ch. 6.

[18]Benjamin I. Page and Robert Shapiro, "Effects of Public Opinion on Policy," *American Political Science Review* 77 (March 1983): 178; see also Urie Bronfenbrenner, Peter McClelland, Stephen Leci, Phyllis Moen, and Elaine Wethington, *The State of Americans* (New York: Free Press, 1996).

[19]See Robert Dahl, *On Democracy* (New Haven, Conn.: Yale University Press, 1998).

[20]C. Wright Mills, *The Power Elite* (New York: Oxford University Press, 1965).

[21]G. William Domhoff, *Who Rules America? Power and Politics in the Year 2000* (Mountain View, Calif.: Mayfield Publishing, 1998).

[22]Roberto Michels, *Political Parties* (1911; reprint, New York: Collier, 1962).

[23]David Easton, *The Political System* (New York: Knopf, 1965), 97.

[24]E. E. Schattschneider, *Two Hundred Million Americans in Search of a Government* (New York: Holt, Rinehart & Winston, 1969), 42.

Chapter 2

[1]Quoted in Charles S. Hyneman, "Republican Government in America," in George J. Graham Jr. and Scarlett G. Graham, eds., *Founding Principles of American Government*, rev. ed. (Chatham, N.J.: Chatham House, 1984), 19.

[2]Tape of White House Conversation, March 22, 1973.

[3]John Locke, *The Two Treatises of Government*, ed. Thomas I. Cook (New York: Hafner, 1947), 159–86, 228–47.

[4]Winthrop D. Jordan and Leon F. Litwack, *The United States*, 6th ed. (Englewood Cliffs, N.J.: Prentice-Hall, 1987), 72–74.

[5]George Bancroft, *History of the Formation of the Constitution of the United States of America*, 3d ed., vol. 1 (New York: D. Appleton, 1883), 166.

[6]Catherine Drinker Bowen, *Miracle at Philadelphia* (Boston: Little, Brown, 1986), 10.

[7]Alfred H. Kelly, Winifred A. Harbison, and Herman Belz, *The American Constitution*, 7th ed. (New York: Norton, 1991), 122.

[8]See, for example, Winthrop D. Jordan, et al., *The United States*, 6th ed. (Englewood Cliffs, N.J.: Prentice-Hall, 1987), 142–45.

[9]Max Weber, "Politics as a Vocation," in Hans H. Gerth and C. Wright Mills, eds., *From Max Weber: Essays in Sociology* (New York: Oxford University Press, 1958), 78.

[10]Gaillard Hunt, ed., *The Writings of James Madison* (New York: Putnam, 1904), 274.

[11]*Federalist* No. 47.

[12]See *Federalist* Nos. 47 and 48.

[13]Richard Neustadt, *Presidential Power* (New York: Macmillan, 1986), 33.

[14]Henry J. Abraham, *The Judicial Process*, 6th ed. (New York: Oxford University Press, 1993), 320–22.

[15]*Marbury v. Madison*, 1 Cranch 137 (1803).

[16]Martin Diamond, *The Founding of the Democratic Republic* (Itasca, Ill.: Peacock, 1981), 62–71; see also Daniel Levin, *Representing Popular Sovereignty* (Albany: State University of New York Press, 1999).

[17]*Federalist* No. 10.

[18]Leslie F. Goldstein, "Judicial Review and Democratic Theory: Guardian Democracy vs. Representative Democracy," *Western Political Quarterly* 40 (1987): 391–412.

[19]Richard Henry Lee, "Letters from the Federal Farmer," in Forrest McDonald, ed., *Empire and Nation* (Englewood Cliffs, N.J.: Prentice-Hall, 1962), 103–17.

[20]Benjamin Ginsberg, *The Consequences of Consent* (New York: Random House, 1982), 22.

[21]Dahl, *Pluralist Democracy*, 92.

[22]This interpretation is taken from Walter Lippmann, *Public Opinion* (New York: Free Press, 1965), 178–79; for a general discussion of the uncertain meaning of the Constitution, see Lawrence H. Tribe and Michael C. Dorf, *On Reading the Constitution* (Cambridge, Mass.: Harvard University Press, 1991).

[23]Charles S. Beard, *An Economic Interpretation of the Constitution* (1913; reprint, New York, Macmillan, 1941).

Chapter 3

[1]Woodrow Wilson, *Constitutional Government in the United States* (New York: Columbia University Press, 1908), 173.

[2]Thomas E. Patterson, *The 1996 Election and Other Recent Developments* (New York: McGraw-Hill, 1997), 29.

[3]See Vincent Ostrom, *The Meaning of American Federalism* (San Francisco: Institute for Contemporary Studies, 1991).

[4]*Federalist* No. 2.

[5]*Federalist* No. 45.

[6]*McCulloch v. Maryland*, 4 Wheaton 316 (1819).

[7]*Gibbons v. Ogden*, 22 Wheaton 1 (1824).

[8]Oliver Wendell Holmes Jr., *Collected Legal Papers* (New York: Harcourt, Brace, 1920), 295–96.

[9]John C. Calhoun, *The Works of John C. Calhoun* (New York: Russell & Russell, 1968).

[10]See *Cooley v. Board of Wardens of the Port of Philadelphia*, 53 Howard 299 (1851).

[11]*Dred Scott v. Sanford*, 19 Howard 393 (1857).

[12]*U.S. v. Cruikshank*, 92 U.S. 452 (1876).

[13]Edward S. Corwin, *The Constitution and What It Means Today*, 12th ed. (Princeton, N.J.: Princeton University Press, 1958), 248.

[14]*Slaughter-House Cases*, 16 Wallace 36 (1873).

[15]*Civil Rights Cases*, 109 U.S. 3 (1883).

[16]*Plessy v. Ferguson*, 163 U.S. 537 (1896).

[17]*Santa Clara County v. Southern Pacific Railroad Co.*, 118 U.S. 394 (1886).

[18]*U.S. v. E. C. Knight Co.*, 156 U.S. 1 (1895).

[19]*Hammer v. Dagenhart*, 247 U.S. 251 (1918).

[20]*Lochner v. New York*, 198 U.S. 25 (1905).

[21]Kelly, Harbison, and Belz, *The American Constitution*, 529.

[22]James E. Anderson, *The Emergence of the Modern Regulatory State* (Washington, D.C.: Public Affairs Press, 1962), 2–3.

[23]*Schechter Poultry Co. v. United States*, 295 U.S. 495 (1935).

[24]*NLRB v. Jones and Laughlin Steel*, 301 U.S. 1 (1937).

[25]*American Power and Light v. Securities and Exchange Commission*, 329 U.S. 90 (1946); see also Richard A. Maidment, *The Judicial Response to the New Deal* (New York: Manchester University Press, 1992).

[26]Louis Fisher, *American Constitutional Law* (New York: McGraw-Hill, 1990), 384.

[27]Richard A. Maidment, *The Judicial Response to the New Deal: The U.S. Supreme Court and Economic Regulation* (New York: Manchester University Press, 1992).

[28]*Heart of Atlanta Motel v. United States*, 379 U.S. 241 (1964).

[29]*Brown v. Board of Education*, 347 U.S. 483 (1954).

[30]*Miranda v. Arizona*, 384 U.S. 436 (1966).

[31]See Thomas Anton, *American Federalism and Public Policy* (Philadelphia: Temple University Press, 1989).

[32]Morton Grodzins, *The American System: A New View of Government in the United States* (Chicago: Rand McNally, 1966).

[33]Rosella Levaggi, *Fiscal Federalism and Grants-in-Aid* (Brookfield, Vt.: Avebury, 1991).

[34]See David L. Shapiro, *Federalism: A Dialogue* (Evanston, Ill.: Northwestern University Press, 1995). See also Douglas D. Rose, "National and Local Forces in State Politics," *American Political Science Review* 67 (December 1973): 1162–73.

[35]Richard Nathan and Fred Doolittle, *Reagan and the States* (Princeton, N.J.: Princeton University Press, 1987); Timothy J. Conlan, *New Federalism* (Washington, D.C.: Brookings Institution, 1988).

[36]*Garcia v. San Antonio Authority*, 469 U.S. 528 (1985).

[37]*United States v. Lopez*, 514 U.S. 549 (1995).

[38]*Printz v. United States*, 117 S. Ct. 2157 (1997).

[39]*Kimel v. Florida Board of Regents*, No. 98-791 (2000).

[40]*Reno v. Condon*, No. 98-1464 (2000).

[41]Andrew W. Dobelstein, *Politics, Economics, and Public Welfare* (Englewood Cliffs, N.J.: Prentice-Hall, 1980), 5.

[42]Survey for the Times Mirror Center for the People and the Press by Princeton Survey Research Associates, July 12–27, 1994.

[43]Daniel J. Boorstin, *The Americans: The Democratic Experience* (New York: Vintage Books, 1974); see also David Walker, *The Rebirth of Federalism* (Chatham, N.J.: Chatham House Publishers, 2000).

Chapter 4

[1]Julian P. Boyd, ed., *The Papers of Thomas Jefferson*, vol. 12 (Princeton, N.J.: Princeton University Press, 1955), 440.

[2]*Anderson v. Creighton*, 483 U.S. 635 (1987).

[3]*Bose Corp. v. Consumers Union of the United States*, 466 U.S. 485 (1984).

[4]*Schenck v. Pro-Choice Network*, No. 95-106 (1997).

[5]*Schenck v. United States*, 249 U.S. 47 (1919).

[6]*Dennis v. United States*, 341 U.S. 494 (1951).

[7]See, for example, *Yates v. United States*, 354 U.S. 298 (1957); *Noto v. United States*, 367 U.S. 290 (1961); *Scales v. United States*, 367 U.S. 203 (1961).

[8]*United States v. Carolene Products Co.*, 304 U.S. 144 (1938).

[9]*United States v. O'Brien*, 391 U.S. 367 (1968).

[10]*United States v. Eichman*, 496 U.S. 310 (1990).

[11]*Texas v. Johnson*, 109 S. Ct. 2544 (1989).

[12]*Buckley v. Valeo*, 424 U.S. 1 (1976).

[13]*Buckley v. American Constitutional Law Foundation*, No. 97-930 (1999).

[14]*New York Times Co. v. United States*, 403 U.S. 713 (1971).

[15]*Nebraska Press Assn. v. Stuart*, 427 U.S. 539 (1976).

[16]*Barron v. Baltimore*, 7 Peters 243 (1833).

[17]*Gitlow v. New York*, 268 U.S. 652 (1925).

[18]*Fiske v. Kansas*, 274 U.S. 30 (1927) (speech); *Near v. Minnesota*, 283 U.S. 697 (1931) (press); *Cantwell v. Connecticut*, 310 U.S. 296 (1940) (religion); and *DeFonge v. Oregon*, 299 U.S. 253 (1937) (assembly and petition).

[19]*Near v. Minnesota.*

[20]*Brandenburg v. Ohio*, 395 U.S. 444 (1969).

[21]*R.A.V. v. St. Paul*, No. 90-7675 (1992).

[22]*Wisconsin v. Mitchell*, No. 92-515 (1993).

[23]*National Socialist Party v. Skokie*, 432 U.S. 43 (1977).

[24]*Forsyth County v. Nationalist Movement*, No. 91-538 (1992).

[25]*New York Times Co. v. Sullivan*, 376 U.S. 254 (1964).

[26]*Milkovich v. Lorain Journal*, 497 U.S. 1 (1990); see also *Masson v. The New Yorker*, No. 89-1799 (1991).

[27]*National Endowment for the Arts v. Finley*, No. 97-371 (1998).

[28]*Roth v. U.S.*, 354 U.S. 476 (1957).

[29]*Miller v. California*, 413 U.S. 15 (1973).

[30]*Barnes v. Glen Theatre*, No. 90-26 (1991).

[31]*Stanley v. Georgia*, 394 U.S. 557 (1969).

[32]*Osborne v. Ohio*, 495 U.S. 103 (1990).

[33]*Denver Area Consortium v. Federal Communications Commission*, No. 95-124 (1996).

[34]*Reno v. American Civil Liberties Union*, No. 96-511 (1997).

[35]See Michael J. Perry, *Religion in Politics* (New York: Oxford University Press, 1997).

[36]*Board of Regents v. Allen*, 392 U.S. 236 (1968).

[37]*Lemon v. Kurtzman*, 403 U.S. 602 (1971).

[38]Ibid.

[39]*Mitchell v. Helms*, No. 98-1648 (2000).

[40]*Engel v. Vitale*, 370 U.S. 421 (1962).

[41]*Abington School District v. Schempp*, 374 U.S. 203 (1963).

[42]*Wallace v. Jaffree*, 472 U.S. 38 (1985).

[43]*Santa Fe Independent School District v. Does*, No. 99-62 (2000).

[44]*Goldman v. Weinberger*, 475 U.S. 503 (1986).

[45]*City of Boerne v. Flores*, No. 95-2074 (1997).

[46]*Wisconsin v. Yoder*, 406 U.S. 295 (1972); see also *Church of the Lukumi Babalu Aye v. City of Hialeah*, No. 91-948 (1993).

[47]*Edwards v. Aguillard*, 487 U.S. 578 (1987).

[48]*Griswold v. Connecticut*, 381 U.S. 479 (1965).

[49]*Roe v. Wade*, 401 U.S. 113 (1973).

[50]*Webster v. Reproductive Health Services*, 492 U.S. 490 (1989); see also *Rust v. Sullivan*, No. 89-1391 (1991).

[51]*Planned Parenthood v. Casey*, No. 91-744 (1992).

[52]*Bowers v. Hardwick*, 478 U.S. 186 (1986).

[53]*Vacco v. Quill*, 117 S.C. 36 (1996); *Washington v. Glucksberg*, No. 96-110 (1997).

[54]*McNabb v. United States*, 318 U.S. 332 (1943).

[55]*Powell v. Alabama*, 287 U.S. 45 (1932).

[56]*Palko v. Connecticut*, 302 U.S. 319 (1937).

[57]*Mapp v. Ohio*, 367 U.S. 643 (1961).

[58]*Gideon v. Wainwright*, 372 U.S. 335 (1963).

[59]*Malloy v. Hogan*, 378 U.S. 1 (1964).

[60]*Miranda v. Arizona*, 384 U.S. 436 (1966); see also *Escobedo v. Illinois*, 378 U.S. 478 (1964).

[61]*Pointer v. Texas*, 380 U.S. 400 (1965).

[62]*Klopfer v. North Carolina*, 386 U.S. 213 (1967).

[63]*Duncan v. Louisiana*, 391 U.S. 145 (1968).

[64]*Benton v. Maryland*, 395 U.S. 784 (1969).

[65]*Weeks v. United States*, 232 U.S. 383 (1914).

[66]*Nix v. Williams*, 467 U.S. 431 (1984); see also *United States v. Leon*, 468 U.S. 897 (1984).

[67]*Michigan v. Sitz*, No. 88-1897 (1990).

[68]*Knowles v. Iowa*, No. 97-7597 (1999).

[69]*Wyoming v. Houghton*, No. 98-184 (1999).

[70]*Ohio v. Robinette*, No. 95-981 (1997).

[71]*Whren v. United States*, 517 U.S. 806 (1996).

[72]*Chicago v. Morales*, No. 97-1121 (1999).

[73]*Richards v. Wisconsin*, No. 96-5955 (1997).

[74]*Wilson v. Layne*, No. 98-83 (1999).

[75]*Townsend v. Sain*, 372 U.S. 293 (1963).

[76]*Keeney v. Tamaya-Reyes*, No. 90-1859 (1992); see also *Coleman v. Thompson*, No. 89-7662 (1991).

[77]*Brecht v. Abrahamson*, No. 91-7358 (1993); see also *McCleskey v. Zant*, No. 89-7024 (1991).

[78]*Felker v. Turpin*, No. 95-8836 (1996); but see *Stewart v. Martinez-Villareal*, No. 97-300 (1998).

[79]*Williams v. Taylor*, No. 99-6615 (2000).

[80]See *Batson v. Kentucky*, 476 U.S. 79 (1986); *Edmonson v. Leesville Concrete Company*, No. 89-7743 (1991); *Powers v. Ohio*, 499 U.S. 400 (1991).

[81]*Minnick v. Mississippi*, 498 U.S. 146 (1991).

[82]*Jaffee v. Redmond*, No. 95-266 (1994).

[83]Kurt Heine, "Philadelphia Cops Beat One of Their Own," *Syracuse Herald-American*, January 15, 1995, A13.

[84]*Wilson v. Seiter*, No. 89-7376 (1991).

[85]*Harmelin v. Michigan*, No. 89-7272 (1991).

[86]See Alpheus T. Mason, *The Supreme Court: Palladium of Freedom* (Ann Arbor: University of Michigan Press, 1962); see also Henry J. Abraham, *Freedom and the Court* (New York: Oxford University Press, 1998).

Chapter 5

[1]Speech of Martin Luther King Jr. in Washington, D.C., August 2, 1963.

[2]*Washington Post* wire story, May 14, 1991.

[3]Reported on *CBS Evening News*, January 16, 1989.

[4]Robert Nisbet, "Public Opinion Versus Popular Opinion," *Public Interest* 41 (1975): 171.

[5]See, for example, John R. Howard, *The Shifting Wind* (Albany: State University of New York Press, 1999).

[6]The classic analysis of this system of legalized segregation is C. Vann Woodward, *The Strange Career of Jim Crow*, 3d rev. ed. (New York: Oxford University Press, 1974).

[7]*Plessy v. Ferguson*, 163 U.S. 537 (1896).

[8]See, for example, *Missouri ex rel. Gaines v. Canada*, 305 U.S. 57 (1938).

[9]*Brown v. Board of Education of Topeka,* 347 U.S. 483 (1954).

[10]See Francis M. Wilhoit, *The Politics of Massive Resistance* (New York: Braziller, 1973).

[11]See David J. Garrow, *Protest at Selma: Martin Luther King and the Voting Rights Act of 1965* (New Haven, Conn.: Yale University Press, 1978).

[12]See Steven A. Shull, *The President and Civil Rights Policy: Leadership and Change* (Westport, Conn.: Greenwood, 1989).

[13]See Sar Levitan, William Johnson, and Robert Taggert, *Still a Dream* (Cambridge, Mass.: Harvard University Press, 1975).

[14]See Derrick Bell, *And We Are Not Saved: The Elusive Quest for Racial Justice* (New York: Basic Books, 1987); Robert C. Smith and Richard S. Hzer, *Race, Class, and Culture* (Albany: State University of New York Press, 1992).

[15]See Keith Reeves, *Voting Hopes or Fears?* (New York: Oxford University Press, 1997).

[16]See Glenna Matthews, *The Rise of Public Women* (New York: Oxford University Press, 1994).

[17]*Tinker v. Colwell,* 193 U.S. 473 (1904).

[18]For a history of the women's voting rights movement, see Eleanor Flexner, *Century of Struggle,* rev. ed. (Cambridge, Mass.: Harvard University Press, 1975).

[19]See Ellen Carol DuBois, *Feminism and Suffrage: The Emergence of an Independent Women's Movement in America, 1848–1869* (Ithaca, N.Y.: Cornell University Press, 1978).

[20]See Jane Mansbridge, *Why We Lost the ERA* (Chicago: University of Chicago Press, 1986).

[21]See Kathleen Hall Jamieson, *Beyond the Double Bind* (New York: Oxford University Press, 1995).

[22]Linda Witt, Karen M. Paget, and Glenna Matthews, *Running as a Woman* (New York: Free Press, 1994).

[23]Mary Lou Kendrigan, *Political Equality in a Democratic Society: Women in the United States* (Westport, Conn.: Greenwood, 1984); Timothy Bledsoe and Mary Herring, "Victims of Circumstance: Women in Pursuit of Political Office," *American Political Science Review* 84 (1990): 213–24.

[24]*County of Washington v. Gunther,* No. 80-429 (1981).

[25]See, however, Sara M. Evans and Barbara Nelson, *Wage Justice* (Chicago: University of Chicago Press, 1989).

[26]*Faragher v. City of Boca Raton,* No. 97-282 (1998); *Burlington Industries v. Ellerth,* No. 97-569 (1998).

[27]*Davis v. Monroe County,* No. 97-843 (1999); *United States v. Morrison et al,* No. 99-5 (2000).

[28]See Joane Nagel, *American Indian Ethnic Renewal* (New York: Oxford University Press, 1996).

[29]See Rudulfo O. de la Garza, Louis DeSipio, F. Chris Garcia, John Garcia, and Angelo Falcon, *Latino Voices* (Boulder, Colo.: Westview Press, 1992).

[30]*De Canas v. Bica,* 424 U.S. 351 (1976).

[31]Nancy Gibbs, "Keep Out, You Tired, You Poor . . . ," *Time,* October 3, 1994, 46–47.

[32]James Truslow Adams, *The March of Democracy,* vol. 4 (New York: Scribner's, 1933), 284–85.

[33]*Lau v. Nichols,* 414 U.S. 563 (1974).

[34]*Cedar Rapids v. Garrett F.,* No. 96-1793 (1999).

[35]*Sutton v. United Air Lines,* No. 97-1943 (1999); *Murphy v. United Parcel Service,* No. 97-1992 (1999).

[36]*Boy Scouts of America v. Dale,* No. 99-699 (2000).

[37]*Romer v. Evans,* 517 U.S. 620 (1996).

[38]*Craig v. Boren,* 429 U.S. 190 (1976).

[39]*Rostker v. Goldberg,* 453 U.S. 57 (1980).

[40]*United States v. Virginia,* No. 94-1941 (1996).

[41]Survey by Federal Financial Institutions Examination Council, 1998.

[42]U.S. Conference of Mayors Report, 1998.

[43]See J. Morgan Kousser, *The Shaping of Southern Politics: Suffrage Restriction and the Establishment of the One-Party South, 1880–1910* (New Haven, Conn.: Yale University Press, 1974).

[44]V. O. Key Jr., *Southern Politics* (New York: Knopf, 1949), 495.

[45]*Smith v. Allwright,* 321 U.S. 649 (1944).

[46]See Bernard Grofman, Lisa Handley, and Richard Niemi, *Minority Representation and the Quest for Voting Equality* (New York: Cambridge University Press, 1992); David Lublin, *The Paradox of Representation* (Princeton, N.J.: Princeton University Press, 1997).

[47]*Bush v. Verg,* No. 94-805 (1996); *Shaw v. Hunt,* No. 94-923 (1996); *Muller v. Johnson,* No. 94-631 (1995).

[48]*Hunt v. Cromartie,* No. 98-85 (1999).

[49]See Terry Eastland, *Ending Affirmative Action* (New York: Basic Books, 1997); but see also Barbara A. Bergmann, *In Defense of Affirmative Action* (New York: Basic Books, 1997).

[50]*University of California Regents v. Bakke,* 438 U.S. 265 (1978).

[51]*Steelworkers v. Weber,* 443 U.S. 193 (1979); *Fullilove v. Klutnick,* 448 U.S. 448 (1980).

[52]*Local No. 28, Sheet Metal Workers v. Equal Employment Opportunity Commission,* 478 U.S. 421 (1986); see also *Local No. 93, International Association of Firefighters v. Cleveland,* 478 U.S. 501 (1986); *Firefighters v. Stotts,* 459 U.S. 969 (1984); *Wygant v. Jackson,* 476 U.S. 238 (1986).

[53]See *Wards Cove Packing v. Antonio,* 490 U.S. 642 (1989).

[54]*Adarand v. Pena,* No. 94-310 (1995).

[55]Jodi Wilgoren, "New Law in Texas Preserves Racial Mix in State's Colleges," *The New York Times,* November 24, 1999, A1.

[56]*Swann v. Charlotte-Mecklenburg County Board of Education,* 402 U.S. 1 (1971).

[57]See Jennifer Hochschild, *The New American Dilemma* (New Haven, Conn.: Yale University Press, 1984); Michael W. Giles and Thomas G. Walker, "Judicial Policy-Making and Southern School Segregation," *Journal of Politics* 37 (1975): 936.

[58]*Washington v. Seattle School District,* 458 U.S. 457 (1982).

[59]Christopher Jencks and Meredith Phillips, eds., *The Black-White Test Score Gap* (Washington, D.C.: Brookings Institution Press, 1998).

[60]Quoted in Megan Twohey, "Desegregation Is Dead," *National Journal* 31, no. 38 (September 18, 1999), 2614.

[61]*Board of Education of Oklahoma City v. Dowell,* 498 U.S. 237 (1991).

[62]*Missouri v. Jenkins,* 515 U.S. 70 (1995).

[63]*Sheff v. O'Neill,* No. 95-2071 (1996).

[64]Quoted in Twohey, "Desegregation Is Dead." See also David J. Armor, *Forced Justice: School Desegregation and the Law* (New York: Oxford University Press, 1995).

[65]Linda Darling-Hammond, "Black America: Progress and Prospects," Brookings Institution, 1998.

[66]Quoted in Twohey, "Desegregation Is Dead."

[67]Gunnar Myrdal, *An American Dilemma: The Negro Problem and Modern Democracy* (New York: Harper, 1944).

Chapter 6

[1]V. O. Key Jr., *Public Opinion and American Democracy* (New York: Knopf, 1961), 8.

[2]Elisabeth Noelle-Neumann, *The Spiral of Silence,* 2d ed. (Chicago: University of Chicago Press, 1993), ch. 1.

[3]See Benjamin I. Page and Robert Shapiro, *The Rational Public* (Chicago: University of Chicago Press, 1992), 285–88.

[4]Noelle-Neumann, *The Spiral of Silence,* 285–88.

[5]Robert Nisbet, "Public Opinion Versus Popular Opinion," *Public Interest* 41 (1975): 167.

[6]Ibid.

[7]*Federalist* No. 10.

[8]George Gallup, "Polls and the Political Process—Past, Present, and Future," *Public Opinion Quarterly* 40 (Winter 1965): 547–48.

[9]Michael X. Delli Carpini and Scott Keeter, *What Americans Know About Politics and Why It Matters* (New Haven, Conn.: Yale University Press, 1996).

[10]Survey of students of the eight Ivy League schools by Luntz & Weber Research and Strategic Services, for the University of Pennsylvania's Ivy League Study, November 13–December 1, 1992.

[11]Sidney Verba and Norman H. Nie, *Participation in America: Political Democracy and Social Equality* (New York: Harper & Row, 1972), 281–84.

[12]Debra J. Saunders, "Poll Shows America in Deep Dumbo," *The San Francisco Chronicle,* April 23, 1993, A30.

[13]David W. Moore and Frank Newport, "Misreading the Public: The Case of the Holocaust Poll," *The Public Perspective,* March/April 1994, 28–29.

[14]James Bryce, *The American Commonwealth,* vol. 2 (New York: Macmillan, 1900), 247–54.

[15]Steven A. Peterson, *Political Behavior: Patterns in Everyday Life* (Newbury Park, Calif.: Sage Publications, 1990), 28–29.

[16]Ibid.

[17]See James E. Combs, *Polpop 2: Politics and Popular Culture in America* (Bowling Green, Ohio: Bowling Green University Press, 1991).

[18]M. Kent Jennings and Richard G. Niemi, *Generations and Politics* (Princeton, N.J.: Princeton University Press, 1981); David Easton and Jack Dennis, *Children in the Political System* (New York: McGraw-Hill, 1969).

[19]Kent Tedin, "The Influence of Parents on the Political Attitudes of Adolescents," *American Political Science Review* 68 (December 1974): 1579–92; M. Kent Jennings and Richard G. Niemi, *The Political Character of Adolescence* (Princeton, N.J.: Princeton University Press, 1974).

[20]See Robert D. Hess and Judith V. Torney, *The Development of Political Attitudes in Children* (Chicago: Aldine, 1967), 219; Orit Ichilov, *Political Socialization, Citizenship Education, and Democracy* (New York: Teachers College Press, 1990).

[21]Noelle-Neumann, *The Spiral of Silence.*

[22]See Shanto Iyengar, *Is Anyone Responsible? How Television Frames Political Issues* (Chicago: University of Chicago Press, 1991); Shanto Iyengar and Donald Kinder, *News That Matters: Television and American Opinion* (Chicago: University of Chicago Press, 1987); Marion Just et al., *Crosstalk* (Chicago: University of Chicago Press, 1996).

[23]See John R. Zaller, *The Nature and Origins of Mass Opinion* (New York: Cambridge University Press, 1992).

[24]See E. J. Dionne, *Why Americans Hate Politics* (New York: Simon & Schuster, 1992); E. J. Dionne, *They Only Look Dead* (New York: Simon & Schuster, 1996); David Frum, *What's Right?* (New York: Basic Books, 1996).

[25]John L. Sullivan, James E. Pierson, and George E. Marcus, "Ideological Constraint in the Mass Public," *American Journal of Political Science* 22 (May 1978): 233–49.

[26]CNN/USA Today poll conducted by the Gallup Organization, 1997.

[27]Philip Converse, "The Nature of Belief Systems in Mass Publics," in David Apter, ed., *Ideology and Discontent* (New York: Free Press, 1965), 206.

[28]"The Gender Story," *The Public Perspective,* August/September 1996, 1–33; Sue Tolleson Rinehart, *Gender Consciousness and Politics* (New York: Routledge, 1992).

[29]Susan A. MacManus, *Young v. Old: Generational Combat in the Twenty-first Century* (Boulder, Colo.: Westview Press, 1996).

[30]See Angus Campbell, Philip Converse, Warren Miller, and Donald Stokes, *The American Voter* (New York: Wiley, 1960), chs. 3 and 4.

[31]Martin P. Wattenberg, *The Decline of American Political Parties, 1952–1984* (Cambridge, Mass.: Harvard University Press, 1990).

[32]See E. E. Schattschneider, *The Semisovereign People* (New York: Holt, Rinehart & Winston, 1980), ch. 8.

[33]See Domhoff, *The Power Elite and the State.*

[34]Benjamin I. Page and Robert Y. Shapiro, "Effects of Public Opinion on Policy," *American Political Science Review* 77 (March 1983): 178.

[35]See Benjamin Ginsberg, *The Consequences of Consent* (New York: Random House, 1982); but also see Samuel L. Popkin, *The Reasoning Voter: Communication and Persuasion in Presidential Campaigns* (Chicago: University of Chicago Press, 1991).

[36]See Paul Brace and Barbara Hinckley, *Follow the Leader: Opinion Polls and Modern Presidents* (New York: Basic Books, 1992).

Chapter 7

[1]Walter Lippmann, *Public Opinion* (New York: Free Press, 1965), 36.

[2]Sidney Verba, Kay Schlozman, and Henry Brady, *Voice and Equality* (Cambridge, Mass.: Harvard University Press, 1995); see also Steven J. Rosenstone and John Mark Hansen, *Mobilization, Participation, and Democracy in America* (New York: Macmillan, 1993).

[3]Quoted in Ralph Volney Harlow, *The Growth of the United States* (New York: Henry Holt, 1943), 312.

[4]See William H. Flanigan and Nancy Zingale, *The Political Behavior of the American Electorate,* 9th ed. (Washington, D.C.: Congressional Quarterly Press, 1998), 24–26.

[5]Example from Gus Tyler, "One Cheer for the Democrats," *New Leader,* November 3, 1986, 6.

[6]Turnout figures provided by Washington, D.C., embassies of the respective countries, 2000.

[7]See Stanley Kelley Jr., Richard E. Ayres, and William G. Bowen, "Registration and Voting: Putting First Things First," *American Political Science Review* 61 (June 1967): 359–79.

[8]Ivor Crewe, "Electoral Participation," in David Butler, Howard R. Penniman, and Austin Ranney, eds., *Democracy at the Polls* (Washington, D.C.: American Enterprise Institute, 1981), 249.

[9]Vanishing Voter Project, Joan Shorenstein Center on Press, Politics, and Public Policy, Harvard University, May 2000.

[10]Benjamin Ginsberg, *The Consequences of Consent* (New York: Random House, 1982), 49.

[11]Crewe, "Electoral Participation," 251–53.

[12]Malcom Jewell and David Olson, *American State Politics and Elections* (Homewood, Ill.: Irwin Press, 1978), 50.

[13]A. Karnig and B. Walter, "Municipal Elections," in *Municipal Yearbook, 1977* (Washington, D.C.: International City Management Assn., 1977).

[14]Richard Boyd, "Decline of U.S. Voter Turnout," *American Politics Quarterly* 9 (April 1981): 142.

[15]Austin Ranney, "Candidate Selection," in Butler, Penniman, and Ranney, *Democracy at the Polls*, 88.

[16]Ruy A. Teixeira, *The Disappearing American Voter* (Washington, D.C.: Brookings Institution, 1992).

[17]Crewe, "Electoral Participation," 251–53.

[18]G. Bingham Powell, "Voting Turnout in Thirty Democracies," in Richard Rose, ed., *Electoral Participation: A Comparative Analysis* (Beverly Hills, Calif.: Sage, 1980), 6.

[19]M. Margaret Conway, Gertrude A. Steuernagel, and David Ahern, *Women and Political Participation: Cultural Change in the Political Arena* (Washington, D.C.: Congressional Quarterly Press, 1997).

[20]See Joseph Nye, David King, and Philip Zelikow, *Why People Don't Trust Government* (Cambridge, Mass.: Harvard University Press, 1997).

[21]See, for example, Norman H. Nie, G. Bingham Powell, and Kenneth Prewitt, "Social Structure and Political Participation," *American Political Science Review* 63 (September 1969).

[22]Nye, King, and Zelikow, *Why People Don't Trust Government*.

[23]John M. Strate, Charles J. Parrish, Charles D. Elder, and Coit Ford III, "Life Span Civic Development and Voting Participation," *American Political Science Review* 83 (June 1989): 443–65.

[24]M. Margaret Conway, *Political Participation in the United States*, 2d ed. (Washington, D.C.: Congressional Quarterly Press, 1991), 23–25.

[25]Verba, Schlozman, and Brady, *Voice and Equality*.

[26]Vanishing Voter Project.

[27]Sidney Verba and Norman Nie, *Participation in America* (New York: Harper & Row, 1972), 340.

[28]Mark Kesselman and Joel Kreiger, *European Politics in Transition* (Lexington, Mass.: Heath, 1987), 87.

[29]But see Jeffrey Stonecash, *Class and Party in American Politics* (Boulder, Colo.: Westview Press, 2000).

[30]Seymour Martin Lipset, *Political Man* (Garden City, N.Y.: Doubleday/Anchor, 1963), 194.

[31]U.S. Bureau of the Census, 2000.

[32]Michael Delli Carpini and Scott Keeter, *What Americans Know About Politics* (New Haven, Conn.: Yale University Press, 1996).

[33]Thomas E. Patterson, *The Mass Media Election* (New York: Praeger, 1980), chs. 7–10.

[34]Gallup Reports, 1936–2000.

[35]V. O. Key Jr., *The Responsible Electorate* (Cambridge, Mass.: Belknap Press of Harvard University Press, 1966), ch. 1.

[36]Verba, Schlozman, and Brady, *Voice and Equality*.

[37]Joseph Schumpeter, *Capitalism, Socialism, and Democracy* (New York: Harper Torchbooks, 1950), 269.

[38]W. Russell Neuman, *The Paradox of Mass Politics* (Cambridge, Mass.: Harvard University Press, 1986), 176.

[39]Samuel H. Barnes et al., eds., *Political Action* (Beverly Hills, Calif.: Sage, 1979), 541–42.

[40]Russell J. Dalton, *Citizen Politics in Western Democracies*, 3d ed. (Chatham, N.J.: Chatham House, 1996), 43.

[41]Robert Putnam, *Bowling Alone* (New York: Simon & Schuster, 2000).

[42]For example, interest group membership has risen.

[43]Robert Putnam, *Making Democracy Work* (Princeton, N.J.: Princeton University Press, 1994).

[44]Survey of Pew Center for People and the Press, 1990.

[45]Verba and Nie, *Participation in America*, 131.

[46]Neuman, *The Paradox of Mass Politics*, 99.

[47]See Benjamin Ginsberg, *The Consequences of Consent* (New York: Random House, 1982), ch. 2.

[48]See Laura R. Woliver, *From Outrage to Action* (Urbana: University of Illinois Press, 1993).

[49]Lee Bruce Stokes, "New Players in the Trade Game," *National Journal*, December 18, 1999, 3630.

[50]Dalton, *Citizen Politics in Western Democracies*, 38.

[51]Ibid., 68.

[52]Ronald Inglehart, "Post-Materialism in an Environment of Insecurity," *American Political Science Review* 75 (1981): 880–900; Edward N. Mueller and Mitchell A. Seligson, "Inequality and Insurgency," *American Political Science Review* 81 (1987): 425–51.

[53]William Watts and Lloyd A. Free, eds., *The State of the Nation* (New York: University Books, Potomac Associates, 1967), 97.

[54]Harry Holloway with John George, *Public Opinion*, 2d ed. (New York: St. Martin's Press, 1986), 157.

[55]Robert E. Lane, "Market Justice, Political Justice," *American Political Science Review* 80 (1986): 383; see also Jennifer Nedelsky, *Private Property and the Limits of American Constitutionalism* (New York: Oxford University Press, 1990).

[56]Walter Dean Burnham, "The Class Gap," *The New Republic*, May 9, 1988, 30; see also Stephen Earl Bennett and David Resnick, "The Implications of Nonvoting for Democracy in the United States," *American Journal of Political Science* 34 (August 1990): 771–802.

[57]See Verba and Nie, *Participation in America*, 332; V. O. Key Jr., *Southern Politics* (New York: Vintage Books, 1949), 527.

Chapter 8

[1]E. E. Schattschneider, *Party Government* (New York: Rinehart, 1942), 1.

[2]See John Aldrich, *Why Parties? The Origin and Transformation of Political Parties in America* (Chicago: University of Chicago Press, 1995).

[3]Vanishing Voter Project, Harvard University, April 2000.

[4]L. Sandy Maisel, *Parties and Elections in America*, 2d ed. (New York: McGraw-Hill, 1993), 27.

[5]Aldrich, *Why Parties?*

[6]See Richard P. McCormick, *The Second American Party System: Party Formation in the Jacksonian Era* (Chapel Hill: University of North Carolina Press, 1966).

[7]Tocqueville, *Democracy in America (1835–1840)*, 60.

[8]See Aldrich, *Why Parties?* 151.

[9]See Kristi Andersen, *The Creation of a Democratic Majority, 1928–1936* (Chicago: University of Chicago Press, 1979).

[10]See Kevin Phillips, *The Emerging Republican Majority* (New Rochelle, N.Y.: Arlington House, 1969).

[11]William H. Flanigan and Nancy Zingale, *Political Behavior of the American Electorate*, 9th ed. (Washington, D.C.: Congressional Quarterly Press, 1998), 58–63.

[12]Frederick G. Dutton, *Changing Sources of Power* (New York: McGraw-Hill, 1971), ch. 6.

[13]See Dionne, *Why Americans Hate Politics*.

[14]The classic account of the relationship of electoral and party systems is Maurice Duverger, *Political Parties* (New York: Wiley, 1954), bk. II, ch. 1; see also Arend Lijphardt, *Electoral Systems and Party Systems* (New York: Oxford University Press, 1994).

[15]Steven J. Rosenstone, Roy L. Behr, and Edward H. Lazarus, *Third Parties in America*, 2d ed. (Princeton, N.J.: Princeton University Press, 1996).

[16]Ibid.

[17]Walter Dean Burnham, *Critical Elections and the Mainsprings of American Politics* (New York: Norton, 1970), 27.

[18]See Lawrence Goodwyn, *The Populist Movement* (New York: Oxford University Press, 1978).

[19]Nancy Gibbs and Michael Duffy, "Fall of the House of Newt," *Time*, November 16, 1998, 47.

[20]Gerald M. Pomper, *Passions and Interests: Political Party Concepts of American Democracy* (Lawrence: University Press of Kansas, 1992), ch. 1.

[21]Jeffrey Stonecash, *Class and Party in American Politics* (Boulder, Colo.: Westview Press, 2000).

[22]Schattschneider, *The Semisovereign People*, 140.

[23]See Domhoff, *Who Rules America Now?* 117–29.

[24]Pomper, *Passions and Interests*, ch. 6.

[25]See Kelly D. Patterson, *Political Parties and the Maintenance of Liberal Democracy* (New York: Columbia University Press, 1996).

Chapter 9

[1]Frank J. Sorauf, *Party Politics in America*, 5th ed. (Boston: Little, Brown, 1984), 61.

[2]See Alan Ehrenhalt, *The United States of Ambition* (New York: Times Books, 1991).

[3]James W. Davis, *National Conventions in an Age of Party Reform* (Westport, Conn.: Greenwood Press, 1983), 4.

[4]Samuel J. Eldersveld, *Political Parties in American Society* (New York: Basic Books, 1982), 96–97.

[5]See Joseph Schlesinger, *Political Parties and the Winning of Office* (Ann Arbor: University of Michigan Press, 1991).

[6]See Paul S. Herrnson, *Party Campaigning in the '80s* (Cambridge, Mass.: Harvard University Press, 1988). John Aldrich, *Why Parties? The Original Transformation of Political Parties in America* (Chicago: University of Chicago Press, 1995).

[7]See Sarah McCally Morehouse, "Money Versus Party Effort," *American Journal of Political Science* 34 (1990): 706–724.

[8]James L. Gibson, Cornelius Cotter, John Bibby, and Robert Huckshorn, "Assessing Party Organizational Strength," *American Journal of Political Science* 27 (May 1983): 200.

[9]Joseph Napolitan, *The Election Game and How to Win It* (New York: Doubleday, 1972).

[10]David B. Magleby and Candice J. Nelson, *The Money Chase: Congressional Campaign Finance Reform* (Washington, D.C.: Brookings Institution, 1990).

[11]John F. Bibby, *Politics, Parties, and Elections in America*, 3d ed. (Chicago: Nelson-Hall, 1996), 205.

[12]Federal Elections Commission data, 2000.

[13]Michael W. Traugott and Paul J. Lavrakas, *The Voters' Guide to Election Polls* (Chatham, N.J.: Chatham House, 1996).

[14]Kiku Adatto, "Sound Bite Democracy," Joan Shoronstein Center on the Press, Politics, and Public Policy, Research Paper R-2, Harvard University, Cambridge, Mass., June 1990.

[15]Darrell M. West, *Air Wars: Television Advertising in Election Campaigns, 1952–1992*, 2d ed. (Washington, D.C.: Congressional Quarterly Press, 1997), 140–46.

[16]Ibid.

[17]Stephen Ansolabehere and Shanto Iyengar, *Going Negative* (New York: Free Press, 1995), ch. 5.

[18]West, *Air Wars*, 12.

[19]Ibid., 143.

[20]Thomas E. Patterson, *Out of Order* (New York: Vintage, 1994), ch. 2.

[21]Associated Press Wire, "Candidates Try E-mail Route to Election: Presidential Hopefuls All Using Web Sites," November 26, 1999.

[22]See James P. Pfiffner, *The Modern Presidency* (New York: St. Martin's Press, 1994), ch. 6.

[23]See Larry Sabato and Glenn Simpson, *Dirty Little Secrets* (New York: Times Books, 1996).

[24]See Anthony King, *Running Scared: The Victory of Campaigning over Governing in the United States* (New York: Free Press, 1997).

Chapter 10

[1]Schattschneider, *The Semisovereign People*, 35.

[2]Quoted in Norman J. Ornstein and Shirley Elder, *Interest Groups, Lobbying, and Policymaking* (Washington, D.C.: Congressional Quarterly Press, 1978), 11.

[3]Tocqueville, *Democracy in America*, bk. II, ch. 4.

[4]E. Pendleton Herring, *Group Representation Before Congress* (Washington, D.C.: Brookings Institution, 1929), 78.

[5]Mancur Olson, *The Logic of Collective Action*, rev. ed. (Cambridge, Mass.: Harvard University Press, 1971), 147.

[6]See Jack L. Walker, *Mobilizing Interest Groups in America* (Ann Arbor: University of Michigan Press, 1991).

[7]See Lawrence Rothenberg, *Linking Citizens to Government: Interest Group Politics at Common Cause* (New York: Cambridge University Press, 1992).

[8]Mancur Olson, *The Logic of Collective Action* (Cambridge, Mass.: Harvard University Press, 1965), 64.

[9]Christopher J. Bosso, "The Color of Money: Environmental Groups and the Pathologies of Fund Raising," in Allan J. Cigler and Burdett Loomis, *Interest Group Politics*, 4th ed. (Washington, D.C.: Congressional Quarterly Press, 1995), 101–3.

[10]Schlozman and Tierney, *Organized Interests*, 54; see also Ronald J. Hrebenar and Ruth K. Scott, *Interest Group Politics in America* (Englewood Cliffs, N.J.: Prentice-Hall, 1990), 167.

[11]See Beverly A. Cigler, "Not Just Another Special Interest: Intergovernmental Representation," in Cigler and Loomis, *Interest Group Politics*, 4th ed., 131–53.

[12]Schattschneider, *The Semisovereign People*, 20–46.

[13]See Paul S. Herrnson, Ronald G. Shaiko, and Clyde Wilcox, eds. *The Interest Group Connection* (Chatham, N.J.: Chatham House Publishers, 1998).

[14]Ornstein and Elder, *Interest Groups, Lobbying, and Policymaking*, 82–86.

[15]See John Mark Hansen, *Gaining Access* (Chicago: Chicago University Press, 1991).

[16]Ornstein and Elder, *Interest Groups, Lobbying, and Policymaking*, 70.

[17]Quoted in ibid., 77.

[18]See Marver Bernstein, *Regulating Business by Independent Commission* (Princeton, N.J.: Princeton University Press, 1955).

[19]Paul J. Quirk, *Industry Influence in Federal Regulatory Agencies* (Princeton, N.J.: Princeton University Press, 1981).

[20]John E. Chubb, *Interest Groups and the Bureaucracy: The Politics of Energy* (Stanford, Calif.: Stanford University Press, 1983), 200–201.

[21]Charles T. Goodsell, *The Case for Bureaucracy*, 3rd ed. (Chatham, N.J.: Chatham House, 1994), 55–60.

[22]Lee Epstein and C. K. Rowland, "Interest Groups in the Courts," *American Political Science Review* 85 (1991): 205–17.

[23]See Hansen, *Gaining Access*; but, see William P. Browne, *Cultivating Congress* (Lawrence: University of Kansas Press, 1995).

[24]Hugh Heclo, "Issue Networks and the Executive Establishment," in Anthony King, ed., *The New American Political System* (Washington, D.C.: American Enterprise Institute, 1978), 87–124.

[25]Ornstein and Elder, *Interest Groups, Lobbying, and Policymaking*, 88–93.

[26]Ernest Wittenberg and Elisabeth Wittenberg, *How to Win in Washington* (Cambridge, Mass.: Blackwell, 1989), 81.

[27]Quoted in Mark Green, "Political PAC-Man," *The New Republic*, December 13, 1982, 20; see also Frank J. Sorauf, *Inside Campaign Finance* (New Haven, Conn.: Yale University Press, 1992).

[28]Quoted in Larry Sabato, *PAC Power: Inside the World of Political Action Committees* (New York: Norton, 1984), 72.

[29]Federal Elections Commission, 2000.

[30]"Tobacco Industry Courts the Hill with Compromise, Conciliation," *Congressional Quarterly Weekly Report: Guide to American Government* (Washington, D.C.: Congressional Quarterly Press, 1998), 51–57.

[31]See Michael J. Malbin, "Of Mountains and Molehills," in Michael J. Malbin, *Parties, Interest Groups, and Campaign Finance Laws* (Washington, D.C.: American Enterprise Institute, 1981), 157–77.

[32]See Dan Clawson, Alan Neustadtl, and Denise Scott, *Money Talks* (New York: Basic Books, 1992); Thomas L. Gatz, *Improper Influence* (Ann Arbor: University of Michigan Press, 1996).

[33]V. O. Key Jr., *Public Opinion and American Democracy* (New York: Knopf, 1961), 428.

[34]See Robert Dahl, *Who Governs?* (New Haven, Conn.: Yale University Press, 1961).

[35]Walker, *Mobilizing Interest Groups in America*, 112.

[36]Theodore J. Lowi, *The End of Liberalism: The Second Republic of the United States* (New York: Norton, 1979).

[37]See William Domhoff, *The Power Elite and the State* (New York: Aldine de Gruyter, 1990).

[38]See Rothenberg, *Linking Citizens to Government*.

[39]Benjamin Ginsberg, *The Consequences of Consent* (New York: Random House, 1982), 214.

[40]Jonathan Rauch, *Demosclerosis: The Silent Killer of American Government* (New York: Times Books, 1994).

Chapter 11

[1]Theodore H. White, *The Making of the President, 1972* (New York: Bantam Books, 1973), 327.

[2]See Richard Davis, *The Press and American Politics*, 2d ed. (Upper Saddle River, N.J.: Prentice Hall, 1996), 24–27.

[3]Comment at the annual meeting of the American Association of Political Consultants, Washington, D.C., 1977.

[4]Thomas Jefferson to Colonel Edward Carrington, January 16, 1787.

[5]Frank Luther Mott, *American Journalism, a History: 1690–1960* (New York: Macmillan, 1962), 114–15.

[6]Culver H. Smith, *The Press, Politics, and Patronage* (Athens: University of Georgia Press, 1977), 163–68.

[7]Doris A. Graber, *Mass Media and American Politics*, 5th ed. (Washington, D.C.: Congressional Quarterly Press, 1997), 36; Mark Wahlgren Summers, *The Press Gang* (Chapel Hill: University of North Carolina Press, 1994).

[8]See Michael Schudson, *Discovering the News* (New York: Basic Books, 1978).

[9]Mott, *American Journalism*, 122–23, 220–27.

[10]Quoted in Smith, *The Press, Politics, and Patronage*, 241.

[11]Commission on Freedom of the Press, *A Free and Responsible Press* (Chicago: University of Chicago Press, 1974), 62–63.

[12]Mott, *American Journalism*, 220–27, 241, 243.

[13]Edwin Emery, *The Press and America: An Interpretive History of the Mass Media* (Englewood Cliffs, N.J.: Prentice-Hall, 1977), 350.

[14]Quoted in Mott, *American Journalism*, 529.

[15]See Dean Alger, *The Media and Politics*, 2d ed. (Belmont, Calif.: Wadsworth, 1996), 122–23.

[16]Quoted in David Halberstam, *The Powers That Be* (New York: Knopf, 1979), 208–9.

[17]Leo Bogart, *The Age of Television* (New York: Unger, 1956), 213.

[18]Theodore H. White, *America in Search of Itself: The Making of the President, 1956–1980* (New York: Harper & Row, 1982), 172–73.

[19]Quoted in Michael Robinson and Margaret Sheehan, *Over the Wire and on TV* (New York: Russell Sage Foundation, 1983), 226.

[20]William Cole, ed. *The Most of A.J. Liebling* (New York: Simon, 1963), 7.

[21]Figures from *Standard Rate and Data Service and Electronic Media*, various dates.

[22]Ibid.

[23]Graber, *Mass Media and American Politics*, 36.

[24]See Ben Bagdikian, *The Media Monopoly*, 5th ed. (Boston: Beacon, 1997).

[25]Edward J. Epstein, *News from Nowhere: Television and the News* (New York: Random House, 1973), 37.

[26]Timothy Crouse, *The Boys on the Bus* (New York: Ballantine, 1973), 20.

[27]White, *The Making of the President, 1972*, 346–48.

[28]Quoted in Kathleen Hall Jamieson and Karlyn Kohrs Campbell, *The Interplay of Influence*, 3d ed. (Belmont, Calif.: Wadsworth, 1992), 18.

[29]See John Chancellor and Walter R. Mears, *The News Business* (New York: Harper & Row, 1983).

[30]David L. Paletz and Robert M. Entman, *Media Power Politics* (New York: Free Press, 1981), 16.

[31]James David Barber, "Characters in the Campaign: The Literary Problem," in James David Barber, ed., *Race for the Presidency* (Englewood Cliffs, N.J.: Prentice-Hall, 1978), 114–15.

[32]See Timothy E. Cook, *Governing with the News* (Chicago: University of Chicago Press, 1997); Bartholomew Sparrow, *Uncertain Guardians* (Baltimore: Johns Hopkins University Press, 1999).

[33]Dean Alger, *Megamedia* (Lanham, Md.: Rowman & Littlefield, 1998).

[34]Ibid., 13–14.

[35]Study for Committee of Concerned Journalists, 1998.

[36]Walter Lippmann, *Public Opinion* (1922; New York: Free Press, 1965), 214.

[37]See Kenneth T. Walsh, *Feeding the Beast* (New York: Free Press, 1996).

[38]Donald Shaw and Maxwell McCombs, *The Emergence of American Political Issues: The Agenda-Setting Function of the Press* (St. Paul, Minn.: West Publishing, 1977).

[39]See, for example, F. Cook, T. Tyler, E. Goetz, M. Gordon, D. Protess, D. Leff, and H. Molotch, "Media and Agenda Setting: Effects on the Public, Interest Group Leaders, Policy Makers, and Policy," *Public Opinion Quarterly* 47 (1983): 16–35.

[40]Bernard C. Cohen, *The Press and Foreign Policy* (Princeton, N.J.: Princeton University Press, 1963), 13.

[41]"1993—The Year in Review," *Media Monitor*, January/February 1994, 2.

[42]See John Anthony Maltese, *Spin Control* (Chapel Hill: University of North Carolina Press, 1994); Howard Kurtz, *Spin Cycle* (New York: Free Press, 1998).

[43]Kiku Adatto, "Sound Bite Democracy," Joan Shorenstein Center on the Press, Politics, and Public Policy, Research Paper R-2, Harvard University, Cambridge, Mass., June 1990.

[44]See James Fallows, *Breaking the News* (New York: Pantheon, 1996).

[45]Patterson, *Out of Order*, ch. 3.

[46]Thomas E. Patterson, "Bad News, Bad Governance," ANNALS 546 (July 1996): 97–108.

[47]Data from Center for Media and Public Affairs, Washington, D.C., 1996.

[48]Doreen Carvajal, "For News Media, Some Introspection," *The New York Times*, April 5, 1998, 28.

[49]Quoted in Max Kampelman, "The Power of the Press," *Policy Review* 6 (1978): 19.

[50]Ibid.

[51]James Reston, "End of the Tunnel," *The New York Times*, April 30, 1975, 41.

[52]Quoted in Epstein, *News from Nowhere*, ix.

[53]"Internal Affairs: TV News Coverage of the White House Sex Scandals." *Media Monitor*, Center for Media and Public Affairs, Washington, D.C., March/April 1998.

[54]Lippmann, *Public Opinion*, 221.

[55]Bill Kovach and Tom Rosensteil, *Warp Speed* (New York: The Century Foundation Press, 1999).

Chapter 12

[1]David R. Mayhew, *Congress: The Electoral Connection* (New Haven, Conn.: Yale University Press, 1974), 49.

[2]See Jonathan S. Krasno, *Challenges, Competition, and Reelection* (New Haven, Conn.: Yale University Press, 1995).

[3]Lawrence C. Dodd, "A Theory of Congressional Cycles," in Gerald Wright, Leroy Rieselbach, and Lawrence C. Dodd, *Congress and Policy Change* (New York: Agathon, 1986).

[4]Bruce Cain, John Ferejohn, and Morris P. Fiorina, *The Personal Vote* (Cambridge, Mass.: Harvard University Press, 1987).

[5]Richard Fenno Jr., *Home Style: House Members in Their District* (Boston: Little, Brown, 1970), 101.

[6]For the opposing views, see Morris P. Fiorina, *Congress: Keystone of the Washington Establishment*, 2d ed. (New Haven, Conn.: Yale University Press, 1989), ch. 7; John R. Johannes, *To Serve the People* (Lincoln: University of Nebraska Press, 1984), ch. 8.

[7]"Congressional Facts and Figures," *The National Journal*, September 3, 1994, 2038.

[8]Paul S. Herrnson, *Congressional Elections: Campaigning at Home and in Washington* (Washington, D.C.: Congressional Quarterly Press, 1995).

[9]Federal Elections Commission, 2000.

[10]Jennifer Babson and Kelly St. John, "Momentum Helps GOP Collect Record Amounts from PACs," *Congressional Quarterly Weekly Report*, December 3, 1994, 3456.

[11]See Gary C. Jacobson, *The Politics of Congressional Elections*, 4th ed. (New York: Longman, 1997).

[12]Barbara Hinckley, *Congressional Elections* (Washington, D.C.: Congressional Quarterly Press, 1981), 29.

[13]Quoted in "A Tale of Myths and Measures: Who Is Truly Vulnerable?" *Congressional Quarterly Weekly Report*, December 4, 1993, 7; see also Dennis F. Thompson, *Ethics in Congress* (Washington, D.C.: Brookings Institution Press, 1995).

[14]James E. Campbell, *The Presidential Pulse of Congressional Elections* (Lexington: University Press of Kentucky, 1993).

[15]Linda L. Fowler and Robert D. McClure, *Political Ambition* (New Haven, Conn.: Yale University Press, 1989).

[16]Keith R. Poole and Howard Rosenthal, "Patterns of Congressional Voting," *American Journal of Political Science*, 35 (February 1991): 228.

[17]See Linda L. Fowler, *Candidates, Congress, and the American Democracy* (Ann Arbor: University of Michigan Press, 1994).

[18]*Congressional Quarterly Weekly Report*, various dates.

[19]Linda Witt, Karen M. Paget, and Glenna Matthews, *Running as a Woman: Gender and Power in American Politics* (New York: Free Press, 1993); see also Sue Thomas, *How Women Legislate* (New York: Oxford University Press, 1994).

[20]Ronald M. Peters Jr., *The American Speakership* (Baltimore, Md.: Johns Hopkins University Press, 1990).

[21]See Barbara Sinclair, *Legislators, Leaders, and Lawmaking* (Baltimore, Md.: Johns Hopkins University Press, 1995).

[22]See David W. Rohde, *Parties and Leaders in the Postreform House* (Chicago: University of Chicago Press, 1991).

[23]Fred R. Harris, *Deadlock or Decision: The U.S. Senate and the Rise of National Politics* (New York: Oxford University Press, 1993), 182.

[24]CBS News, February 27, 1987.

[25]Roger H. Davidson and Walter J. Oleszek, *Congress and Its Members* (Washington, D.C.: Congressional Quarterly Press, 1981), 185.

[26]Quoted in Frank H. Mackamar, *Understanding Congressional Leadership: The State of the Art* (Pekin, Ill.: Dickson Center, 1981), 9.

[27]Steven S. Smith, *The American Congress* (Boston: Houghton Mifflin, 1995), 152.

[28]See, for example, Donald Matthews, *U.S. Senators and Their World* (Chapel Hill: University of North Carolina Press, 1960).

[29]See Barbara Sinclair, *Transformation of the U.S. Senate* (Baltimore, Md.: Johns Hopkins University Press, 1989).

[30]See Sinclair, *Legislators, Leaders, and Lawmaking.*

[31]Jonathan D. Salant, "New Chairman Swing to Right; Freshmen Get Choice Posts," *Congressional Quarterly Weekly Report,* December 10, 1994, 3493.

[32]See Richard L. Hall and C. Lawrence Evans, "The Power of Subcommittees," *Journal of Politics* (May 1990): 335–55.

[33]See Gerald S. Strom, *The Logic of Lawmaking* (Baltimore, Md.: Johns Hopkins University Press, 1990).

[34]See Steven S. Smith and Christopher J. Deering, *Committees in Congress,* 2d ed. (Washington, D.C.: Congressional Quarterly Press, 1990), 125–65.

[35]David C. King, *Turf Wars: How Congressional Committees Claim Jurisdiction* (Chicago: University of Chicago Press, 1997).

[36]Smith, *The American Congress,* 189–98.

[37]See Stephen E. Frantzich and Steven E. Schier, *Congress: Games and Strategies* (Dubuque, Iowa: Brown & Benchmark, 1995), 127.

Chapter 13

[1]Roger H. Davidson and Walter J. Oleszek, *Congress and Its Members,* 2d ed. (Washington, D.C.: Congressional Quarterly Press, 1985), 7.

[2]Ibid.

[3]Randall B. Ripley, *Congress: Process and Policy,* 4th ed. (New York: Norton, 1988), 76.

[4]See Robert Spitzer, *President and Congress* (New York: McGraw-Hill 1993).

[5]Barbara Sinclair, *Unorthodox Lawmaking: New Legislative Processes in the U.S. Congress* (Washington, D.C.: Congressional Quarterly Press, 1997).

[6]See Timothy J. Conlan, Margaret T. Wrightson, and David R. Beam, *Taxing Choices: The Politics of Tax Reform* (Washington, D.C.: Congressional Quarterly Press, 1990).

[7]Arthur Maass, *Congress and the Common Good* (New York: Basic Books, 1983), 14.

[8]See Paul C. Light, *The President's Agenda,* rev. ed. (Baltimore, Md.: Johns Hopkins University Press, 1991).

[9]Hugh Heclo, "Introduction: The Presidential Illusion," in Hugh Heclo and Lester M. Salamon, eds., *The Illusion of Presidential Government* (Boulder, Colo.: Westview Press, 1981), 1–2.

[10]Quoted in Ripley, *Congress: Process and Policy,* 326.

[11]See Timothy E. Cook, *Governing with the News* (Chicago: University of Chicago Press, 1997).

[12]See Gerald S. Strom, *The Logic of Lawmaking* (Baltimore, Md.: Johns Hopkins University Press, 1990).

[13]Smith, *The American Congress,* 210–12.

[14]Barbara Hinckley, *Less Than Meets the Eye* (Washington, D.C.: Congressional Quarterly Press, 1997).

[15]See Herrnson, *Congressional Elections.*

[16]See Cain, Ferejohn, and Fiorina, *The Personal Vote.*

[17]Steven S. Smith and Christopher J. Deering, *Committees in Congress,* 3d ed. (Washington, D.C.: Congressional Quarterly Press, 1997), 74.

[18]Keith Krehbiel, "Are Congressional Committees Composed of Preference Outliers?" *American Political Science Review* 84 (1990): 149–64; Richard L. Hall and Bernard Grofman, "The Committee Assignment Process and the Conditional Nature of Committee Bias," *American Political Science Review* 84 (1990): 1149–66.

[19]See John R. Wright, "Contributions, Lobbying, and Committee Voting in the U.S. House of Representatives," *American Political Science Review* 84 (1990): 417–38.

[20]Richard L. Hall and Frank W. Wayman, "Buying Time: Moneyed Interests and the Mobilization of Bias in Congressional Committees," *American Political Science Review* 84 (1990): 797–820.

[21]Joel A. Aberbach, *Keeping a Watchful Eye* (Washington, D.C.: Brookings Institution, 1990); William T. Gormley, *Taming the Bureaucracy* (Princeton, N.J.: Princeton University Press, 1989).

[22]Davidson and Oleszek, *Congress and Its Members,* 2d ed., 7.

Chapter 14

[1]Woodrow Wilson, *Constitutional Government in the United States* (New York: Columbia University Press, 1908), 67.

[2]Jules Witcover, *Marathon: In Pursuit of the Presidency* (New York: New American Library, 1978).

[3]James W. Davis, *The American Presidency* (New York: Harper & Row, 1987), 13.

[4]See Barry M. Blechman and Stephen S. Kaplan, *Force Without War* (Washington, D.C.: Brookings Institution, 1978).

[5]Edward S. Corwin, *The President: Office and Powers, 1787–1957* (New York: New York University Press, 1959), 180–81.

[6]*United States* v. *Belmont,* 57 U.S. 758 (1937).

[7]Robert DiClerico, *The American President,* 4th ed. (Englewood Cliffs, N.J.: Prentice-Hall, 1995), 47.

[8]Quoted in Wilfred E. Binkley, *President and Congress,* 3d ed. (New York: Vintage, 1962), 142.

[9]Theodore Roosevelt, *An Autobiography* (New York: Scribner's, 1931), 383.

[10]George C. Edwards and Stephen J. Wayne, *Presidential Leadership,* 3d ed. (New York: St. Martin's Press, 1994), 6–7.

[11]See Richard M. Pious, *The American Presidency* (New York: Basic Books, 1979), 83.

[12]Robert J. Spitzer, *President and Congress* (New York: McGraw-Hill, 1993), 35–37.

[13]Raymond Tatalovich and Byron W. Daynes, *Presidential Power in the United States* (Monterey, Calif.: Brooks/Cole, 1984), 322–23.

[14]*Korematsu v. United States,* 323 U.S. 214 (1944); *Ex parte Endo,* 323 U.S. 283 (1944).

[15]Harry S Truman, *1946–1952: Years of Trial and Hope* (New York: Signet, 1956), 535.

[16]James Bryce, *The American Commonwealth* (New York: Commonwealth Edition, 1908), 230.

[17]See Richard Rose, *The Postmodern President,* 2d ed. (Chatham, N.J.: Chatham House, 1991).

[18]Quoted in Arthur M. Schlesinger Jr., *The Coming of the New Deal* (Boston: Houghton Mifflin, 1958), 13.

[19]Heclo, "Introduction: The Presidential Illusion," 6.

[20]James W. Ceaser, *Presidential Selection: Theory and Development* (Princeton, N.J.: Princeton University Press, 1979); see also John Haskell, *Fundamentally Flawed* (Lanham, Md.: Rowman & Littlefield, 1996).

[21]See Noble E. Cunningham Jr., "Presidential Leadership, Political Parties, and the Congressional Caucus, 1800–1824," in Patricia Bonami, James MacGregor Burns, and Austin Ranney, eds., *The American Constitutional System Under Strong and Weak Parties* (New York: Praeger, 1981), 1–20.

[22]Patterson, *Out of Order.*

[23]William Flanigan and Nancy Zingale, *Political Behavior of the American Electorate,* 9th ed. (Washington, D.C.: Congressional Quarterly Press, 1998), 163–64.

[24]Ibid., 189.

[25]Myron A. Levine, *Presidential Campaigns and Elections* (Itasca, Ill.: Peacock, 1995), 30.

[26]Sidney Kraus, ed., *The Great Debates* (Bloomington: Indiana University Press, 1962), 190.

[27]Kathleen Hall Jamieson, *Packaging the Presidency,* 3d ed. (New York: Oxford University Press, 1996).

[28]Patterson, *Out of Order.*

[29]Stephen Ansolabehere and Shanto Iyengar, *Going Negative: How Attack Ads Shrink and Polarize the Electorate* (New York: Free Press, 1995).

[30]See James P. Pfiffner, 2d ed., *The Strategic Presidency: Hitting the Ground Running* (Chicago: Dorsey Press, 1996).

[31]Davis, *The American Presidency,* 296.

[32]Richard P. Nathan, *The Administrative Presidency* (New York: Wiley, 1983), 36; see also John P. Burke, *The Institutionalized Presidency* (Baltimore, Md.: Johns Hopkins University Press, 1992); Thomas Weko, *The Politicizing Presidency* (Lawrence: University Press of Kansas, 1995).

[33]Davis, *The American Presidency,* 240; see also Bradley Patterson, *The Ring of Power* (New York: Basic Books, 1988), 90–91.

[34]Quoted in Stephen J. Wayne, *Road to the White House, 1992* (New York: St. Martin's Press, 1992), 143; see also Timothy Welch, ed., *At the President's Side* (Columbia: University of Missouri Press, 1997).

[35]See Shirley Anne Warshaw, *Powersharing: White House—Cabinet Relations in the Modern Presidency* (Albany: State University of New York Press, 1995).

[36]See Jeffrey E. Cohen, *The Politics of the United States Cabinet* (Pittsburgh: University of Pittsburgh Press, 1988).

[37]James Pfiffner, *The Modern Presidency* (New York: St. Martin's Press, 1994), 91–96.

[38]Quoted in James MacGregor Burns, "Our Super-Government—Can We Control It?" *The New York Times,* April 24, 1949, 32.

[39]See Paul C. Light, *Thickening Government: Federal Hierarchy and the Diffusion of Accountability* (Washington, D.C.: Brookings Institution, 1995).

[40]Pfiffner, *The Modern Presidency,* 117–22.

[41]Richard T. Johnson, *Managing the White House* (New York: Harper & Row, 1974), 238.

[42]See Charles E. Walcott and Karen M. Hult, *Governing the White House* (Lawrence: University of Kansas Press, 1995).

Chapter 15

[1]Heclo, "Introduction: The Presidential Illusion," 2.

[2]Arthur M. Schlesinger Jr., *The Imperial Presidency* (Boston: Houghton Mifflin, 1989).

[3]See Thomas Franck, ed., *The Tethered Presidency* (New York: New York University Press, 1981); Richard M. Pious, *The American Presidency* (New York: Basic Books, 1979); Harold M. Barger, *The Impossible Presidency* (Glenview, Ill.: Scott, Foresman, 1984).

[4]See Grant McConnell, *The Modern Presidency* (New York: St. Martin's Press, 1967).

[5]Charles O. Jones, *The Presidency in a Separated System* (Washington, D.C.: Brookings Institution, 1994).

[6]*Congressional Quarterly Weekly Report,* various dates.

[7]Erwin Hargrove, *The Power of the Modern Presidency* (New York: Knopf, 1974).

[8]"The Honeymoon That Wasn't," *Media Monitor,* September/October 1993, 2.

[9]James P. Pfiffner, *The Strategic Presidency: Hitting the Ground Running,* 2d ed. (Chicago: Dorsey Press, 1996), 45.

[10]Aaron Wildavsky, "The Two Presidencies," *Transaction,* December 1966, 7.

[11]Pfiffner, *The Modern Presidency,* ch. 6.

[12]Thomas P. (Tip) O'Neill, with William Novak, *Man of the House: The Life and Political Memoirs of Speaker Tip O'Neill* (New York: Random House, 1987), 297.

[13]Fred I. Greenstein, ed., *Leadership in the Modern Presidency* (Cambridge, Mass.: Harvard University Press, 1988), ch. 10.

[14]Richard E. Neustadt, *Presidential Power and the Modern Presidents* (New York: Free Press, 1990), 71–72; see also Robert J. Spitzer, *The Presidential Veto: Touchstone of the American Presidency* (Albany: State University of New York Press, 1988).

[15]*Clinton v. City of New York,* 97-1374 (1997).

[16]Neustadt, *Presidential Power,* 33.

[17]Ibid., 33.

[18]*Congressional Quarterly Weekly Reports,* various dates.

[19]Harvey G. Zeidenstein, "Presidents' Popularity and Their Wins and Losses on Major Issues: Does One Have a Greater Influence over the Other?" *Presidential Studies Quarterly,* Spring 1985, 287–300; see also Richard Brody, *Assessing the President* (Stanford, Calif.: Stanford University Press, 1991).

[20]Paul Brace and Barbara Hinckley, *Follow the Leader* (New York: Basic Books, 1992); Jeffrey E. Cohen, *Presidential Responsiveness and Public Policymaking* (Ann Arbor: University of Michigan Press, 1997).

[21]Gallup Polls, November 2–5, 1979, and November 30–December 3, 1979.

[22]Godfrey Hodgson, *All Things to All Men* (New York: Simon & Schuster, 1980), 239.

[23]See John Anthony Maltese, *Spin Control* (Chapel Hill: University of North Carolina Press, 1994).

[24]"They're No Friends of Bill," *Media Monitor* 8, no. 4 (July/ August 1994): 1.

[25]Samuel Kernell, *Going Public: New Strategies of Presidential Leadership*, 3d ed., (Washington, D.C.: Congressional Quarterly Press, 1997), 1.

[26]Jeffrey Tulis, *The Rhetorical Presidency* (Princeton, N.J.: Princeton University Press, 1987); see also Craig Allen Smith, *The White House Speaks* (Westport, Conn.: Greenwood, 1994).

[27]Mary E. Stuckey, *The President as Interpreter-in-Chief* (Chatham, N.J.: Chatham House, 1991).

[28]Craig Allen Smith, *The White House Speaks* (Westport, Conn.: Greenwood, 1994).

[29]Guy Gugliotta and Thomas Edsall, "Laurels and Lingering Doubts," *Washington Post*, July 4, 1998, A1.

[30]Richard Stengel and Eric Pooley, "Masters of the Message," *Time*, November 18, 1996, 78–96.

[31]Remarks by Mike McCurry at Harvard University's Kennedy School of Government, February 10, 1998.

[32]Heclo, "Introduction: The Presidential Illusion," 2.

[33]Theodore J. Lowi, *The "Personal" Presidency: Power Invested, Promise Unfulfilled* (Ithaca, N.Y.: Cornell University Press, 1985).

Chapter 16

[1]Norman Thomas, *Rule 9: Politics, Administration, and Civil Rights* (New York: Random House, 1966), 6.

[2]Quoted in Albert Gore Jr., *From Red Tape to Results: Creating a Government That Works Better and Costs Less* (Washington, D.C.: U.S. Superintendent of Documents, 1993), 1.

[3]James P. Pfiffner, "The National Performance Review in Perspective," working paper 94-4, Institute of Public Policy, George Mason University, 1994, 2.

[4]Ibid., 12.

[5]Max Weber, *Economy and Society,* trans. Guenther Roth and Claus Wittich (New York: Bedminster Press, 1968), 23.

[6]See John J. DiIulio, ed., *Deregulating the Public Service* (Washington, D.C.: Brookings Institution, 1994).

[7]*Rutan v. Republican Party of Illinois*, 497 U.S. 62 (1990).

[8]See Cornelius M. Kerwin, *Rulemaking* (Washington, D.C.: Congressional Quarterly Press, 1994).

[9]Michael Lipsky, *Street-Level Bureaucracy* (New York: Russell Sage Foundation, 1980); see also George Serra, "Citizen-Initiated Contact and Satisfaction with Bureaucracy," *Journal of Public Administration* 5 (April 1995): 175–88.

[10]Paul Van Riper, *History of the United States Civil Service* (Evanston, Ill.: Peterson, 1958), 36.

[11]Jay M. Shafritz, *Personnel Management in Government* (New York: Marcel Dekker, 1981), 9–13; Herbert Kaufman, "Emerging Conflicts in the Doctrine of Public Administration," *American Political Science Review* 50 (December 1956): 1060.

[12]James Q. Wilson, "The Rise of the Bureaucratic State," *Public Interest* 41 (Fall 1975): 77–103.

[13]U.S. Bureau of the Census, *Historical Statistics of the United States: Colonial Times to 1970*, pt. 2 (Washington, D.C.: U.S. Government Printing Office, 1975), 1102.

[14]David H. Rosenbloom, *Federal Service and the Constitution* (Ithaca, N.Y.: Cornell University Press, 1971), 83.

[15]For insights on this and other civil service mechanisms, see Patricia Ingraham and David Rosenbloom, *The Promise and Paradox of Civil Service Reform* (Pittsburgh: University of Pittsburgh Press, 1992); Donald F. Kettl, Patricia W. Ingraham, Ronald P. Sanders, and Constance Horner, *Civil Service Reform* (Washington, D.C.: Brookings Institution Press, 1996).

[16]Kaufman, "Emerging Conflicts in the Doctrine of Public Administration," 1060.

[17]Ibid., 1062.

[18]See Richard W. Waterman, *Presidential Influence and the Administrative State* (Knoxville: University of Tennessee Press, 1989).

[19]Quoted in Hugh Heclo, *A Government of Strangers* (Washington, D.C.: Brookings Institution, 1977), 225.

[20]Norton E. Long, "Power and Administration," *Public Administration Review* 10 (Autumn 1949): 269.

[21]See Herbert Kaufman, *The Administrative Behavior of Federal Bureaucrats* (Washington, D.C.: Brookings Institution, 1981), 4.

[22]See Heclo, *A Government of Strangers*, 117–18.

[23]Quoted in Aaron Wildavsky, *The Politics of the Budgetary Process*, 4th ed. (Boston: Little, Brown, 1984), 19.

[24]Joel D. Aberbach and Bert A. Rockman, "Clashing Beliefs Within the Executive Branch," *American Political Science Review* 70 (June 1976): 461.

[25]See B. Dan Wood and Richard W. Waterman, *Bureaucratic Dynamics* (Boulder, Colo.: Westview Press, 1994).

[26]Kenneth J. Meier, *Regulation* (New York: St. Martin's Press, 1985), 164.

[27]See John Brehm and Scott Gates, *Working, Shirking, and Sabotage* (Ann Arbor: University of Michigan Press, 1996).

[28]Herbert Kaufman, *Are Government Organizations Immortal?* (Washington, D.C.: Brookings Institution, 1976), 76.

[29]Long, "Power and Administration," 269; see also John Mark Hansen, *Gaining Access* (Chicago: University of Chicago Press, 1991).

[30]See B. Guy Peters, *The Politics of Bureaucracy*, 4th ed. (New York: Longman, 1995).

[31]See Martin Laffin, "Reinventing the Federal Government," in Christopher Peele, Christopher J. Bailey, Bruce Cain, and B. Guy Peters, eds., *Developments in American Politics 2* (Chatham, N.J.: Chatham House, 1995), 172–76.

[32]See Paul Light, *Thickening Government* (Washington, D.C.: Brookings Institution, 1995).

[33]James G. March and Johan P. Olson, "Organizing Political Life: What Administrative Reorganization Tells Us About Government," *American Political Science Review* 77 (June 1983): 281–96.

[34]Meier, *Regulation*, 110–11.

[35]David M. J. Lazer, "Regulatory Review: Presidential Control Through Selective Communication and Institutionalized Conflict," unpublished paper, 1997.

[36]See Heclo, *A Government of Strangers*.

[37]See William F. West, *Controlling the Bureaucracy* (Armonk, N.Y.: Sharp, 1995).

[38]See Donald Kettl, *Deficit Politics* (New York: Macmillan, 1992).

[39]See Joel D. Aberbach, *Keeping a Watchful Eye* (Washington, D.C.: Brookings Institution, 1990).

[40]B. Dan Wood and Richard W. Waterman, "Political Control of the Bureaucracy," *American Political Science Review* 85 (September 1991): 820–21; see also Cathy Marie Johnson, *The Dynamics of Conflict Between Bureaucrats and Legislators* (Armonk, N.Y.: Sharpe, 1992).

[41]Louis Fisher, *American Constitutional Law* (New York: McGraw-Hill, 1990), 280–81.

[42]David Rosenbloom, "The Evolution of the Administrative State, and Transformations of Administrative Law," in David Rosenbloom and Richard Schwartz, eds., *Handbook of Regulation and Administrative Law* (New York: Marcel Dekker, 1994), 3–36.

[43]See *Vermont Yankee Nuclear Power Corp. v. National Resources Defense Council, Inc.*, 435 U.S. 519 (1978); *Chevron v. National Resources Defense Council*, 467 U.S. 837 (1984); *Heckler v. Chaney*, 470 U.S. 821 (1985); but see, *FDA v. Brown & Williamson Tobacco Co.* (2000).

[44]Roberta Ann Johnson and Michael E. Kraft, "Bureaucratic Whistleblowing and Policy Change," *Western Political Quarterly* 43 (December 1990): 849–74.

[45]"Way, Way Off in the Wild Blue Yonder," *Time*, May 29, 1995, 32–33.

[46]See Brian J. Cook, *Bureaucracy and Self-Government* (Baltimore, Md.: Johns Hopkins University Press, 1996).

[47]Frederick C. Mosher, *Democracy and the Public Service*, 2d ed. (New York: Oxford University Press, 1982), 13.

[48]Office of Workforce Information, 1998.

[49]See Wood and Waterman, *Bureaucratic Dynamics*.

[50]David Osborne and Ted Gaebler, *Reinventing Government: How the Entrepreneurial Spirit Is Transforming the Public Sector* (New York: Addison-Wesley, 1992); see also Michael Barzelay and Babak J. Armajani, *Breaking Through Bureaucracy* (Berkeley: University of California Press, 1992); Robert D. Behn, *Leadership Counts* (Cambridge, Mass.: Harvard University Press, 1991).

[51]Pfiffner, "The National Performance Review in Perspective," 7.

[52]Ronald C. Moe, "The 'Reinventing Government' Exercise: Misinterpreting the Problem, Misjudging the Results," *Public Administration Review* (March/April 1994): 125–36.

[53]Tom Shoop, "From Citizens to Customers," *Government Executive* (May 1994): 27–30.

[54]See Mark Goldstein, *America's Hollow Government: How Washington Has Failed the People* (Homewood, Ill.: Business One Irwin, 1992); but see also James Pinkerton, *What Comes Next?* (New York: Hyperion, 1995).

Chapter 17

[1]*Marbury v. Madison*, 1 Cranch 137 (1803).

[2]*Planned Parenthood v. Casey*, No. 91-744 (1992).

[3]*Roe v. Wade*, 401 U.S. 113 (1973).

[4]See Michael J. Perry, *The Constitution and the Courts* (New York: Oxford University Press, 1994).

[5]Raoul Berger, *Government by Judiciary: The Transformation of the Fourteenth Amendment* (Cambridge, Mass.: Harvard University Press, 1977).

[6]Rebecca Mae Salokar, *The Solicitor General: The Politics of Law* (Philadelphia: Temple University Press, 1992); see also Cornell W. Clayton, *The Politics of Justice: The Attorney General and the Making of Legal Policy* (Armonk, N.Y.: Sharpe, 1992).

[7]D. Marie Provine, *Case Selection in the United States Supreme Court* (Chicago: University of Chicago Press, 1980), 62–63; see also H. W. Perry, *Deciding to Decide* (Cambridge, Mass.: Harvard University Press, 1991).

[8]Henry Glick, *Courts, Politics, and Justice,* 3d ed. (New York: McGraw-Hill, 1993), 214.

[9]See Bernard Schwartz, *Decision: How the Supreme Court Decides Cases* (New York: Oxford University Press, 1996).

[10]Lawrence Baum, *The Supreme Court*, 4th ed. (Washington, D.C.: Congressional Quarterly Press, 1996), 117.

[11]*Brown v. Board of Education of Topeka*, 347 U.S. 483 (1954).

[12]*Gideon v. Wainwright*, 372 U.S. 335 (1963).

[13]From a letter to the author by Frank Schwartz of Beaver College. This section reflects substantially Professor Schwartz's recommendations to the author, as does the later section that addresses the federal court myth. See also Robert A. Carp, *The Federal Courts*, 3d ed. (Washington, D.C.: Congressional Quarterly Press, 1998).

[14]*Hutto v. Davis*, 370 U.S. 256 (1982).

[15]Quoted in Howard Brownstein, "With or Without Supreme Court Changes, Reagan Will Reshape the Federal Court," *National Journal*, December 8, 1984, 2238.

[16]*Roe v. Wade*, 401 U.S. 113 (1973).

[17]See George L. Watson and John Alan Stookey, *Shaping America: The Politics of Supreme Court Appointments* (New York: Longman, 1995).

[18]See Carp, *The Federal Courts*.

[19]Stephen L. Wasby, *The Supreme Court in the Federal Judicial System*, 4th ed. (Chicago: Nelson-Hall, 1993), 75.

[20]Henry J. Abraham, *The Judicial Process*, 7th ed. (New York: Oxford University Press, 1998), 24–26.

[21]Robert Scigliano, *The Supreme Court and the Presidency* (New York: Free Press, 1971), 146; see also David Savage, *Turning Right: The Making of the Rehnquist Supreme Court* (New York: Wiley, 1992).

[22]Quoted in Baum, *The Supreme Court*, 37.

[23]See John C. Hughes, *The Federal Courts, Politics, and the Rule of Law* (New York: Longman, 1995).

[24]John Gottschall, "Reagan's Appointments to the U.S. Courts of Appeals," 70 *Judicature* 48 (1986): 54.

[25]Carp, *The Federal Courts*.

[26]Joseph B. Harris, *The Advice and Consent of the Senate* (Berkeley: University of California Press, 1953), 313.

[27]People for the American Way data, 1998.

[28]Henry J. Abraham, "The Judicial Function Under the Constitution," *News for Teachers of Political Science* 41 (Spring 1984): 14; Sheldon Goldman, "Should There Be Affirmative Action for the Judiciary?" *Judicature* 62 (May 1979): 494.

[29]Quoted in Louis Fisher, *American Constitutional Law* (New York: McGraw-Hill, 1990), 5.

[30]Baum, *The Supreme Court*, 117.

[31]Quoted in Charles P. Curtis, *Law and Large as Life* (New York: Simon & Schuster, 1959), 156–57.

[32]*Sutton v. United Air Lines*, No. 97-1943 (1999).

[33]See Lee Epstein and Jack Knight, *The Choices Justices Make* (New York: Longman, 1995).

[34]*Faragher v. City of Boca Raton*, No. 97-282 (1998).

[35]Wasby, *The Supreme Court in the Federal Judicial System*, 53.

[36]See Lee Epstein, *Conservatives in Court* (Knoxville: University of Tennessee Press, 1985), 80–88.

[37]Linda Greenhouse, "Sure Justices Legislate," *The New York Times*, July 5, 1998, 4-1.

[38]John Schmidhauser, *The Supreme Court* (New York: Holt, Rinehart & Winston, 1964), 6.

[39]Jeffrey A. Segal and Harold J. Spaeth, *The Supreme Court and the Attitudinal Model* (New York: Cambridge University Press, 1993).

[40]Linda Greenhouse, "The Justices Decide," *The New York Times*, June 27, 1999, Sect. 4, p. 1.

[41]See Schwartz, *Decision: How the Supreme Court Decides Cases*.

[42]David M. O'Brien, *Storm Center: The Supreme Court in American Politics*, 4th ed. (New York: Norton, 1996), 14–15.

[43]Ibid., 59–61.

[44]Some of the references cited in the following sections are taken from Abraham, "The Judicial Function," 12–14; see also Harry H. Wellington, *Interpreting the Constitution* (New Haven, Conn.: Yale University Press, 1990).

[45]Abraham, "The Judicial Function," 14.

[46]Alexander M. Bickel, *The Supreme Court and the Idea of Progress* (New Haven, Conn.: Yale University Press, 1978), 173–81.

[47]See Antonin Scalia, *A Matter of Interpretation* (Princeton, N.J.: Princeton University Press, 1997).

[48]Louis Lusky, *By What Right? A Commentary on the Supreme Court's Power to Revise the Constitution* (Charlottesville, Va.: Michie, 1975), 214–16.

[49]Ibid.

[50]*Romer v. Evans*, No. 94-1039 (1996).

[51]Abraham, "The Judicial Function," 13.

[52]See Larry W. Yackle, *Reclaiming the Federal Courts* (Cambridge, Mass.: Harvard University Press, 1994).

[53]*Gideon v. Wainwright*, 372 U.S. 335 (1963). Case example and argument are from Richard A. Posner, "What Am I? A Potted Plant?" *The New Republic*, September 28, 1987, 25.

[54]"Good for the Left, Now Good for the Right," *Newsweek*, July 8, 1991, 22.

[55]Linda Greenhouse, "The Justices Decide Who's in Charge," *The New York Times*, June 27, 1999.

[56]Quoted in ibid.

Chapter 18

The section titled "Efficiency Through Government Intervention" relies substantially on Alan Stone, *Regulation and Its Alternatives* (Washington, D.C.: Congressional Quarterly Press, 1982).

[1]See Marc Allen Eisner, *Regulatory Politics in Transition* (Baltimore: Johns Hopkins University Press, 1993).

[2]Paul Portney, "Beware of the Killer Clauses Inside the GOP's 'Contract,' " *The Washington Post National Weekly Edition*, January 23–29, 1995, 21.

[3]See Richard A. Harris and Sidney M. Milkis, *The Politics of Regulatory Change* (New York: Oxford University Press, 1996).

[4]See Larry N. Gerston, Cynthia Fraleigh, and Robert Schwab, *The Deregulated Society* (Pacific Grove, Calif.: Brooks/Cole, 1988); Donald F. Kettl, "The Savings and Loan Bailout: The Mismatch Between the Headlines and the Issues," *PS: Political Science and Politics* 23 (September 1991): 441–47.

[5]H. Peyton Young, *Equity: In Theory and Practice* (Princeton, N.J.: Princeton University Press, 1995).

[6]Molly Ivins, "GOP Job Bill Is Truly Bad," *Syracuse Post-Standard*, February 15, 1995, A10.

[7]See Thomas Streeter, *Selling the Air* (Chicago: University of Chicago Press, 1996).

[8]See Kenneth Gould, Allan Schnaiberg, and Adam Weinberg, *Local Environmental Struggles* (New York: Cambridge University Press, 1996).

[9]Rachel Carson, *The Silent Spring* (Boston: Houghton Mifflin, 1962).

[10]*Tennessee Valley Authority (TVA) v. Hill*, 437 U.S. 153 (1978).

[11]"Westerners Adjust Their Sights and Take Home Some Wins," *Congressional Quarterly Weekly Report, Spring 1998* (Washington, D.C.: Congressional Quarterly Press, 1998), 67.

[12]*U.S. News & World Report*, June 30, 1975, 25.

[13]"Hill Foes of New Clean Air Rules Unite Behind Moratorium Bill," *Congressional Quarterly Weekly Report, Spring 1998* (Washington, D.C.: Congressional Quarterly Press, 1998), 61.

[14]"Congress Prepares New Assault on Troubled Superfund Sites," *Congressional Quarterly Weekly Report, Spring 1998* (Washington, D.C.: Congressional Quarterly Press, 1998), 94–99.

[15]"Clinton Radio Address," January 31, 1998.

[16]Carol S. Greenwald, *Group Power* (New York: Praeger, 1977), 181.

[17]See Robert Lekachman, *The Age of Keynes* (New York: Random House, 1966).

[18]See Bruce Bartlett, *Reaganomics: Supply-Side Economics* (Westport, Conn.: Arlington House, 1981); Kenneth Hoover and Raymond Plant, *Conservative Capitalism in Britain and the United States* (New York: Routledge, 1989).

[19]House Ways and Means Committee data, 1991.

[20]Aaron Wildavsky, *The New Politics of the Budgetary Process* (New York: Harper-Collins, 1992); Allen Schick, *The Federal Budget* (Washington, D.C.: Brookings Institution Press, 1995).

[21]Richard W. Stevenson, "Tax Cut Goes to Clinton," *The New York Times*, September 16, 1999, A22.

[22]Steven Pearlstein, "The Man Who Really Runs America," *The Washington Post National Weekly Edition*, February 6–12, 1995, 23.

Chapter 19

[1]Jason DeParle, "Welfare Reform, One Year Later," *Syracuse Herald American*, January 4, 1998, D1.

[2]Sar Levitan, *Programs in Aid of the Poor*, 6th ed. (Baltimore, Md.: Johns Hopkins University Press, 1990), 36–37; Michael J. Rich, *Federal Policymaking and the Poor* (Princeton, N.J.: Princeton University Press, 1993).

[3]William Julius Wilson, *The Truly Disadvantaged: The Inner City, the Underclass, and Public Policy* (Chicago: University of Chicago Press, 1987).

[4]Michael Harrington, *The Other America: Poverty in the United States* (New York: Macmillan, 1962); see also Sheldon H.

Danziger, Gary D. Sandefur, and Daniel H. Weinberg, eds., *Confronting Poverty* (Cambridge, Mass.: Harvard University Press, 1994).

[5]Charles Murray, *Losing Ground: American Social Policy, 1950–1980* (New York: Basic Books, 1984).

[6]*Five Thousand American Families* (Ann Arbor: University of Michigan Institute for Social Research, 1977); also see William Julius Wilson, *When Work Disappears* (New York: Knopf, 1996).

[7]See Katherine S. Newman, *No Shame in My Game* (New York: Alfred A. Knopf and Russell Sage Foundation, 1999), 41.

[8]Everett Carll Ladd, *American Political Parties* (New York: Norton, 1970), 205.

[9]See Rich, *Federal Policymaking and the Poor*.

[10]DeParle, "Welfare Reform One Year Later," D4.

[11]Kevin Phillips, *Boiling Point* (New York: Random House, 1993), 109–11.

[12]V. O. Key Jr., *The Responsible Electorate* (Cambridge, Mass.: Belknap Press of Harvard University, 1966), 43.

[13]Fay Lomax Cook and Edith J. Barrett, *Support for the American Welfare State* (New York: Columbia University Press, 1992).

[14]Hobart Rowan, "The Budget: Fact and Fiction," *The Washington Post National Weekly Edition*, January 16–22, 1995, 5.

[15]"Welfare: Myths, Reality," Knight-Ridder News Service story, *Syracuse Post-Standard*, December 5, 1994, A1, A6.

[16]Judith Havemann, "Tough Steps Credited for Welfare Dip," *Washington Post*, May 10, 1999, A2.

[17]Quoted in Malcolm Gladwell, "The Medicaid Muddle," *The Washington Post National Weekly Edition*, January 16–22, 1995, 31.

[18]Herbert McClosky and John Zaller, *American Ethos: Public Attitudes Toward Capitalism and Democracy* (Cambridge, Mass.: Harvard University Press, 1984), 18.

[19]Karl A. Lamb, *As Orange Goes: Twelve California Families and the Future of American Politics* (New York: Norton, 1974), 178.

[20]Quoted in Michael Harrington, *Socialism* (New York: Bantam, 1973), 142.

[21]Constance Johnson and Penny Loeb, "Stupid Spending Tricks," *U.S. News & World Report*, July 18, 1994, 26.

[22]Based on Organization for Economic Co-Operation and Development (OECD) data, 2000.

[23]Laurel Shaper Walters, "World Educators Compare Notes," *Christian Science Monitor*, September 7, 1994, 8.

[24]See John E. Chubb and Terry M. Moe, *Politics, Markets, and America's Schools* (Washington, D.C.: Brookings Institution, 1990).

[25]See Jeffrey R. Henig, *Rethinking School Choice* (Princeton, N.J.: Princeton University Press, 1995).

[26]Matt Clark, "Forgotten Patients," *Newsweek*, August 22, 1988, 52.

[27]Cook and Barrett, *Support for the American Welfare State*.

Chapter 20

[1]See Peter B. Kenen, ed., *Understanding Interdependence: The Macroeconomics of the Open Economy* (Princeton, N.J.: Princeton University Press, 1995).

[2]John Dumbrell, *American Foreign Policy* (New York: St. Martin's Press, 1996).

[3]American Assembly Report (cosponsored by the Council on Foreign Relations), *Rethinking America's Security* (New York: Harriman, 1991), 8.

[4]For an overview of Soviet policy, see Alvin Z. Rubenstein, *Soviet Foreign Policy Since World War II*, 4th ed. (New York: Harper-Collins, 1992); for an assessment of U.S. policy, see Robert Dallek, *The American Style of Foreign Policy* (New York: Oxford University Press, 1990).

[5]Mr. X. (George Kennan), "The Sources of Soviet Conduct," *Foreign Affairs* 25 (July 1947): 566–82.

[6]See Stanley Karnow, *Vietnam: A History* (New York: Penguin, 1983).

[7]David M. Barrett, *Uncertain Warriors: Lyndon Johnson and His Vietnam Advisors* (Lawrence: University Press of Kansas, 1993).

[8]Charles Kegley and Eugene Wittkopf, *American Foreign Policy*, 2d ed. (New York: St. Martin's Press, 1982), 48.

[9]See Keith L. Nelson, *The Making of Détente* (Baltimore, Md.: Johns Hopkins University Press, 1995).

[10]For a general view of America's new world role, see Kenneth A. Oye, Robert J. Lieber, and Donald Rothchild, *Eagle in a New World: American Grand Strategy in the Post–Cold War Era* (New York: HarperCollins, 1992).

[11]Loch K. Johnson, *Secret Agencies* (New Haven, Conn.: Yale University Press, 1996).

[12]Adam Roberts and Benedict Kingsbury, *United Nations, Divided World*, 2d ed. (New York: Oxford University Press, 1993).

[13]John Barry, "The Battle over Warfare," *Newsweek*, December 5, 1994, 27–28.

[14]Richard J. Barnet, "Reflections: The Disorders of Peace," *The New Yorker*, January 20, 1992, 61.

[15]Ole Holsti, *Public Opinion and American Foreign Policy* (Ann Arbor: University of Michigan Press, 1996).

[16]See James M. Lindsay, *Congress and the Politics of U.S. Foreign Policy* (Baltimore, Md.: Johns Hopkins University Press, 1994); William Conrad Gibbons, *The U.S. Government and the Vietnam War* (Washington, D.C.: U.S. Government Printing Office, 1994).

[17]Murray L. Weidenbaum, *Small Wars, Big Defense* (New York: Oxford University Press, 1992).

[18]Quoted in Steve Rosen, *Testing Theories of the Military-Industrial Complex* (Lexington, Mass.: Lexington Books, 1973), 1.

[19]"The B-1: A Flight Through Adversity," *Los Angeles Times*, reprinted in *Syracuse Post-Standard*, July 29, 1983, A7.

[20]"Merchants Go Great Guns After Cold War," *The Wall Street Journal*, January 28, 1994, A6.

[21]See Elie Abel, *The Shattered Bloc: Beyond the Upheaval in Eastern Europe* (Boston: Houghton Mifflin, 1990).

[22]Paul Kennedy, *The Rise and Fall of the Great Powers* (New York: Random House, 1988); for an alternative view, see Joseph Nye, *Bound to Lead: The Changing Nature of American Power* (New York: Basic Books, 1990).

[23]U.S. government data, various agencies, 2000.

[24]*The World Competitiveness Yearbook* (Luasanne, Switzerland: International Institute for Management Development, 1999).

[25]American Assembly Report, *Rethinking America's Security*, 9; see also Robert O. Keohane, Joseph S. Nye, and Stanley Hoffmann, eds., *After the Cold War* (Cambridge, Mass.: Harvard University Press, 1993).

[26]Harry Magdoff, *The Age of Imperialism: The Economics of U.S. Foreign Policy* (New York: Monthly Review Press, 1969), 43.

[27]Tom Masland, "Going Down the Aid 'Rathole'?" *Newsweek*, December 5, 1994, 39.

[28]Hobart Rowen, "The Budget: Fact and Fiction," *The Washington Post National Weekly Edition*, January 16–22, 1995, 5.

[29]See Jonathan Kirshner, *Currency and Coercion* (Princeton, N.J.: Princeton University Press, 1997).

[30]Associated Press, "Clinton Remembers Those Who Fought Apartheid," *Syracuse Herald American*, March 29, 1998, A5.

[31]John F. Harris, "Jiang Earns Clinton's High Praise," *Washington Post*, July 4, 1998, A1.

[32]See Richard J. Barnet and John Cavanagh, *Global Dreams* (New York: Simon & Schuster, 1994).

Chapter 21

[1]*Reno v. Condon*, No. 98-1464 (2000).

[2]*Kimel v. Florida Board of Regents*, No. 98-791 (2000).

[3]Paul Burka, "What a Texas Record Can't Tell," *The New York Times*, April 28, 2000, A23.

[4]Thad Beyle, "Governors: The Middlemen and Women in Our Political System," in Virginia Gray and Herbert Jacobs, *Politics in the American States: A Comparative Analysis* (Washington, D.C.: Congressional Quarterly Press, 1996), 237.

[5]Amy Pyle, "California and the West," *Los Angeles Times*, October 24, 1999, A30.

[6]Advisory Commission on Intergovernmental Relations (ACIR), *The Question of State Government Capability* (Washington, D.C.: ACIR, 1985), 123.

[7]David Broder, *Democracy Derailed* (San Diego: Harcourt, 2000).

[8]V. O. Key Jr., *Southern Politics* (New York: Knopf, 1949), 495.

[9]John F. Dillon, *Commentaries on the Law of Municipal Corporations*, 5th ed. (Boston: Little, Brown, 1911), vol. 1, sec. 237.

[10]*People v. Hurlbut*, 24 Michigan 44 (1871).

[11]Susan MacManus, *Young v. Old: Generational Combat in the Twenty-first Century* (Boulder, Colo.: Westview Press, 1996).

[12]See, for example, Robert Dahl, *Pluralist Democracy in the United States* (Chicago: Rand McNally, 1967).

[13]David Osborne, *Laboratories of Democracy: A New Breed of Governor Creates Models for National Growth* (Cambridge, Mass.: Harvard Business School, 1988).

[14]Tommy Thompson, *Power to the People: An American State at Work* (New York: HarperCollins, 1996).

[15]*San Antonio Independent School District v. Rodriquez*, 411 U.S. 1 (1973).

[16]Abby Goodnough, "Major Court Challenge on How State Allocates School Funds," *The New York Times*, October 12, 1999, B1.

[17]Daniel Elazar, *American Federalism: A View from the States*, 2d ed. (New York: Crowell, 1972).

[18]Thomas R. Dye, *Politics in States and Communities*, 8th ed. (Englewood Cliffs, N.J.: Prentice Hall, 1994), 162.

[19]*Federalist* No. 10.

[20]Daniel J. Boorstin, *The Americans: The Democratic Experience* (New York: Vintage Books, 1974).

[21]Lawrence Grossman, *The Electronic Republic* (New York: Viking, 1995).

TEXT AND LINE ART CREDITS

Figure 1-3: Opinions about the source of personal success. Used by permission of the Pew Research Center for the People and the Press.

Table 1-1: Telling the American story to children. Used by permission of the Survey of American Political Culture, James Davison Hunter and Carol Bowman, Directors, University of Virginia

Box 1-3: How the U.S. compares. Used by permission of the Pew Research Center for the People and the Press.

Box 2-11: Direct democracy. Copyright 1998 The Council of State Governments. Reprinted with permission from *Book of the States*.

Figure 4-1: Opinions on the abortion issue. Time/CNN poll.

Figure 4-2: Opinions on police searches.

Box 4-4: Incarceration rates by country. From: CRIME AND PUNISHMENT IN AMERICA by Elliott Currie, c. 1998 by Elliot Curie. Reprinted by permission of Henry Holt and Company, LLC.

Table 5-1: From *Latino National Political Survey*, reported in Rudolfo O. de la Garza, Angelo Falcon, F. Chris Garcia, and John A. Garcia., "Hispanic Americans in the mainstream of U.S. Politics," *The Public Perspective*, July/August 1992, p. 19. C. The Roper Center for Public Opinion Research, University of Connecticut, Storrs, CT. Used by permission.

Figure 5-7: Opinions on affirmative action. The New York Times, December 14, 1997, Section 1, page 1, column 4. C. 1997 The New York Times Company.

Figure 6-1: Opinions on taxing and spending. Used by permission of National Opinion Research Center, University of Chicago.

Figure 6-4: Gallup Poll News Service, March 17-19, 2000. Used with permission.

Table 7-1: Opinions and obligations of citizens. Used by permission of the Survey of American Political Culture, James Davison Hunter and Carol Bowman, Directors, University of Virginia.

Figure 7-2: The perceived effect of electing a Republican or Democratic president. Used by permission of the Shorenstein Center Poll for the Vanishing Voter Project.

Figure 7-5: The game centered nature of election news. From OUT OF ORDER by Thomas E. Patterson. Copyright c. 1993 by Thomas E. Patterson. Reprinted by permission of Alfred A. Knopf, a Division of Random House Inc.

Figure 7-6: Conventional participation in 3 countries. From Helmut I. Anheier, Lester M. Salamon, and Edith Archambault, "Participating Citizens: U.S.-Europe Comparisons in Volunteer Action," *The Public Perspective*, March/April 1994. C. The Roper Center for Public Opinion Research, University of Connecticut, Storrs, CT. Used by permission.

Table 7-2: Opinions about peace demonstrations. Used by permission of the Gallup Organization.

Figure 9-2: Organization chart. Used by permission of the Republican National Committee.

Figure 9-4: Public confidence in congress. Used by permission of The Gallup Organization.

Figure 11-1: *Gallup Poll Monthly*, August 1994. Used by permission of The Gallup Organization.

Figure 11-2: Percentage of Americans who said crime was . . . *Gallup Poll Monthly*, August 1994. Used by permission of The Gallup Organization.

Figure 11-3: The shrinking sound bite. Adapted in part from Daniel C. Hallin, "Sound Bite News: Television Coverage of Elections 1968-1988," *Journal of Communication*, 42 (Spring 1992), p. 6; and in part from Center for Media and Public Affairs.

Figure 11-4: Gallup Poll News Service, February 1999. Used with permission.

Figure 11-5: The public's view of the press's skepticism. From The Pew Research Center for the People and the Press, February 25, 1999. Used by permission.

Figure 13-3: Percentage of roll-call votes. *CQ Congressional Monitor*, by permission of Congressional Quarterly Inc.

Box 13-4: National legislators' good influence or bad? Used by permission of the Pew Research Center for the People and the Press.

Box 13-5: Used by permission of the Pew Research Center for the People and the Press.

Table 15-1: Republished with permission of CQ Press, from *Congressional Quarterly Weekly Report*, January 7, 1989; permission conveyed through Copyright Clearance Center, Inc.

Figure 15-1: Republished with permission of CQ Press, from *Congressional Quarterly Weekly Report*, December 11, 1999; permission conveyed through Copyright Clearance Center, Inc.

Box 16-4: Educational backgrounds of bureaucrats. From THE POLITICS OF BUREAUCRACY 4th ed. by B. Guy Peters. Copyright 1995 by Longman Publishers USA. Re-

PHOTO CREDITS

Part Openers: American Icons, EyeWire, Inc.

Chapter 1

Opener: © Michael Evans/Sygma; **p. 7:** © Joseph Sohm/Stock Boston; **p. 11:** © Newhouse News Service; **p. 13:** © Culver Pictures; **p. 14:** © Walter Hodges/Stone; **p. 18:** © Bob Daemmrich/The Image Works; **p. 19:** © Christopher Bissell/Stone; **p. 22:** © John Neubauer/PhotoEdit; **p. 24:** © Ron Edmonds/AP Wide World Photos.

Chapter 2

Opener: © Dale E. Boyer/Photo Researchers; **p. 30:** © Wells/Archive Photos; **p. 32:** © Corbis-Bettmann; **p. 34:** © Corbis-Bettmann; **p. 35:** Library of Congress; **p. 36:** © Corbis-Bettmann; **p. 38:** © The Granger Collection; **p. 40:** © Bequest of the Honorable James Bowdoin III/Bowdoin College Museum of Art, Brunswick, Maine; **p. 43:** © The Granger Collection; **p. 47 top:** The White House Historical Association/ Photo by the National Geographic Society; **p. 47 bottom:** © Stock Montage; **p. 48:** © Rick Maiman/Corbis/Sygma; **p. 50:** © The Granger Collection

Chapter 3

Opener: © Bettmann/Corbis; **p. 61:** © Archive Photos; **p. 64:** The Granger Collection; **PH 3-4:** © Collection of The New York Historical Society, Neg. #6242; **p. 65:** © The New York Historical Society; **p. 68:** © The Granger Collection; **p. 69:** Library of Congress; **p. 70 top:** © Corbis-Bettmann; **p. 70 bottom:** Library of Congress; **p. 72:** © Corbis-Bettmann; **p. 73:** Library of Congress; **p. 74:** © AP/ Wide World Photos; **p. 77:** © David Adame/AP/Wide World Photos; **p. 83:** © AP/Wide World Photos; **p. 85:** © David Burnett/Contact Press Images

Chapter 4

Opener: © Clark Jones/Impact Visuals; **p. 92:** © Robert Brenner/PhotoEdit; **p. 92:** © UPI/Corbis-Bettmann; **p. 94:** © Bob Daugherty/AP/Wide World Photos; **p. 99:** © Jonathon Elderfield/Liaison Agency; **p. 100:** © Bonnie Kamin/PhotoEdit; **p. 102:** © Donna Binder/Impact Visuals; **p. 104:** © Greg Gibson/AP/Wide World Photos; **p. 106:** © Marilyn K. Yee/NYT Pictures; **p. 113:** © Liaison Agency; **p. 110:** © Alan Klehr/Stone

Chapter 5

Opener: © Flip Schulke/Black Star; **p. 122:** © Charles Moore/Black Star; **p. 125:** © Jacques Chenet/Woodfin Camp & Assoc.; **p. 128:** © Chip Henderson/Stone; **p. 130:** © Antonio Ribeiro/Liaison Agency; **p. 133:** © Tony Freeman/PhotoEdit; **p. 134:** Frank Siteman/Stock Boston/PNI; **p. 137:** © Will & Deni McIntyre/Photo Researchers; **p. 141:** © Bob Daemmrich/Corbis/Sygma; **p. 143:** © Jay Malin/Impact Visuals; **p. 146:** © Kim Kulish/Saba; **p. 147:** © Karim-Shamsi-Basha/Saba

Chapter 6

Opener: © Bob Daemmrich/Stock Boston; **p. 156:** © Stoddart/Katz/Saba; **p. 157:** © Joel Stettenheim/Saba; **p. 163:** © Corbis-Bettmann; **p. 169:** © Charles Gupton/The Stock Market; **p. 170:** © Reuters/Win McNamee/Archive Photos; **p. 175:** ©Theodore Vogal/Rapho/Photo Researchers; **p. 180:** © Reuters/Mike Segar/Archive Photos

Chapter 7

Opener: © Bob Daemmrich/The Image Works; **p. 186:** © Culver Pictures; **p. 192:** © Jonathon Nourok/Stone; **p. 196:** © Reuters Newsmedia Inc./Corbis; **p. 198:** © Paul Warner/AP/Wide World Photos; **p. 201:** © Michael Newman/PhotoEdit; **p. 204:** © Lara Jo Regan/Gamma Liaison; **p. 206:** © UPI/Corbis-Bettmann; **p. 209:** © Loren Callahan/Liaison Agency

Chapter 8

Opener: © Reuters Newsmedia Inc./Corbis; **p. 214:** © AFP/Corbis; **p. 218:** Library of Congress; **p. 219:** © UPI/Corbis-Bettmann; **p. 221:** © AFP/Corbis; **p. 225:** © I.P.O.L. (International Pictures On Line), NYC; **p. 227:** Library of Congress; **p. 228:** © Eric Miller/Liaison Agency; **p. 232:** © Terry Ashe/Gamma Liaison

Chapter 9

Opener: © Kevin Larkin/AP/Wide World Photos; **p. 238:** © Allan Tannenbaum/Corbis/Sygma; **p. 240:** Culver Pictures; **p. 242:** © Porter Gifford/Liaison Agency; **p. 243:** © Stock Montage; **p. 246:** © Beth A. Keiser/AP/Wide World Photos; **p. 249:** © Joe Marquette/AP/Wide World Photos **p. 256 left:** Democratic National Committee; **p. 256 right:** The following image has been reproduced with the express permission of the Republican National Committee/Republican National Committee; **p. 257:** © Damian Dovarganes/AP/Wide World Photos; **p. 252:** © Spencer Tiery/AP/Wide World Photos

Chapter 10

Opener: © Tom McCarthy/PhotoEdit; **p. 262:** © Felicia Martinez/PhotoEdit; **p. 267:** Library of Congress; **p. 268:** © William Thomas Cain/AP/Wide World Photos; **p. 270:** © Fred Chartrand/AP/Wide World Photos; **p. 271:** © AFP/Corbis; **p. 274:** © Rick Reinhard/Impact Visuals; **p. 276:** © Stephen Ferry/Gamma Liaison; **p. 279:** © Frederic Neema/Corbis/Sygma; **p. 280:** © Dennis Cook/AP/Wide World Photos; **p. 281:** © AP/Wide World Photos; **p. 285 top:** © George W. Gardner/Stock Boston; **p. 285 bottom:** © The New York Historical Society; **p. 288:** © David Barber/ PhotoEdit; **p. 289:** © Johnson/Gamma Liaison

Chapter 11

Opener: © Michael Schwarz/The Image Works; **p. 294:** © Allan Tannenbaum/Corbis/Sygma; **p. 297:** Stock Montage; **p. 299:** Brown Brothers; **p. 301 left:** House of Representatives; **p. 301 right:** US Senate; **p. 302:** © Mark Richards/PhotoEdit; **p. 304:** © Patrick Robert/Sygma; **p. 309:** © Les Stone/Corbis/Sygma; **p. 312:** © Reuters Newsmedia Inc./Corbis; **p. 315:** © Dirck Halstead/Gamma Liaison; **p. 316:** © Arnold Sachs/CNP/Archive Photos

Chapter 12

Opener: © Larry Gus/Corbis/Sygma; **p. 322:** © AP/Wide World Photos; **p. 325:** © Vanessa Vick/Photo Researchers; **p. 328:** © Don Heupel/AP/Wide World Photos; **p. 331 top:** © J.B. Forbes/AP/Wide World Photos; **p. 331 bottom:** © Corbis-Bettmann; **p. 336:** © Win. McNamee/Archive Photos; **p. 343:** © AP/Wide World Photos; **p. 345:** U.S. General Accounting Office

Chapter 13

Opener: © Dennis Brack/Black Star/PNI; **p. 353:** © AP/Wide World Photos; **p. 354:** © F. Lee Corkran/Corbis/Sygma; **p. 358:** © Reuters/Corbis-Bettmann; **p. 359:** © AP/Wide World Photos; **p. 360:** © Jonathon Nouron/PhotoEdit; **p. 361:** © John Van Hasselt/Corbis/Sygma; **p. 370:** © US Senate/AP/Wide World Photos

Chapter 14

Opener: © Reuters Newsmedia Inc./Corbis; **p. 376:** © AP/Wide World Photos; **p. 379:** © Corbis-Bettmann; **p. 381:** © UPI/Corbis-Bettmann; **p. 386:** © AP/Wide World Photos; **p. 388:** © AFP/Corbis; **p. 394:** © AP/Wide World Photos; **p. 398:** © AP/Wide World Photos; **p. 399:** © AP/Wide World Photos

Chapter 15

Opener: © Wally McNamee/Corbis/Sygma; **p. 410:** © Rene Burri/Magnum; **p. 414:** © UPI/Corbis-Bettmann; **p. 415:** © Bruce Hoertel/Gamma Liaison; **p. 424:** © Alain Mingam/Gamma Liaison; **p. 425:** © Diana Walker/Gamma Liaison; **p. 426:** Archive Photos

Chapter 16

Opener: © Bob Daemmrich/Stock Boston; **p. 430:** © NASA/Liaison Agency; **p. 436:** © Bernard Routrit/Woodfin; **p. 437:** © Charles Steiner/Sygma; **p. 438:** © Paul Chesley/Stone; **p. 441:** © Corbis-Bettmann; **p. 447:** © Don Perdue/Gamma Liaison; **p. 450:** © Wally McNamee/Woodfin Camp & Assoc.; **p. 453:** © Steve Liss/Gamma Liaison

Chapter 17

Opener: © Wally McNamee/Woodfin Camp & Assoc.; **p. 461:** © AP/Wide World Photos; **p. 463:** © Dennis Brack/Black Star; **p. 466:** © Billy E. Barnes/Stock Boston; **p. 469:** © Bob Daemmrich/The Image Works; **p. 471** © Ken Heinen/AP/Wide World Photos; **p. 472:** © AP/Wide World Photos; **p. 478:** © Michael C. York/AP/Wide World Photos; **p. 481:** © Bryce Flynn; **p. 484:** © Karl Gehring/Gamma Liaison; **p. 486:** © Dennis MacDonald/PhotoEdit

Chapter 18

Opener: © Jean Pierre Laffont/Sygma; **p. 495:** © National Portrait Gallery, London; **p. 496:** © Craig Hondrog/Liaison Agency; **p. 500:** © Reed Saxon/AP/Wide World Photos; **p. 501:** © Michael Newman/PhotoEdit; **p. 503:** © John M. Roberts/The Stock Market; **p. 504:** © Jim Pickerell/Stock Boston; **p. 507:** © Fred Ward/Black Star; **p. 508:** © Damian Dovarganes/AP/Wide World Photos; **p. 512:** © Hulton-Deutsch Collection/Corbis; **p. 518:** © AP/Wide World Photos; **p. 521:** © Bill Nation/Corbis/Sygma; **p. 523:** © Karin Cooper/Liaison Agency

Chapter 19

Opener: © John Henley/The Stock Market; **p. 530:** © Joseph Nettis/Stone; **p. 531:** © Michael Newman/PhotoEdit; **p. 534:** © Stephen Jaffe/Reuters/Archive Photos; **P19-05:** © Bob Daemmrich/Stock Boston; **p. 538:** © William Johnson/Stock Boston; **p. 591:** © Dana Fineman/Corbis/Sygma; **p. 543:** © Morry Gash/AP/Wide World Photos; **p. 549 left:** © Bob Daemmrich/The Image Works; **p. 549 right:** © David Young-Wolff/PhotoEdit; **p. 551 left:** © Sally Weigand/Index Stock Imagery; **p. 551 right:** © Glenn Kulbako/Index Stock Imagery

Chapter 20

Opener: © Win. McNamee/Reuters/Archive Photos; **p. 556:** © Vince Streano/Stone; **p. 557:** Courtesy of the U.S. Army; **p. 558:** Library of Congress; **p. 563:** © Dirck Halstead/Liaison

Agency; **p. 566:** © Jaffe/Gamma Liaison; **p. 567:** © Raphael Gaillarde/Gamma Liaison; **p. 572:** © UPI/Corbis-Bettmann; **p. 573:** © Sam Sargent/Liaison Agency; **p. 577:** © Najlah Feanny/Saba; **p. 583:** © Scott Applewhite/AP/Wide World Photos

Chapter 21

Opener: © Jonathon Elderfield/Liaison Agency; **p. 592:** © Larry Kolvoord/The Image Works; **p. 596:** © Sandra Baker/Liaison Agency; **p. 600:** © Jonathon Elderfield/Gamma Liaison; **p. 606:** © Lynne Sladky/AP/Wide World Photos; **p. 610:** Reprinted with permission of California State Lottery; **p. 611:** © Gerd Ludwig/Woodfin Camp & Assoc.; **p. 616:** © Andy Sacks/Stone; **p. 618:** © Mike Derer/AP/Wide World Photos; **p. 621:** © Gamma Liaison

AUTHOR INDEX

The single entries (e.g., 455) refer to text pages. The double entries refer to notes (e.g., 20–29 is a reference note to note 29 in Chapter 20). The notes follow the appendixes.

SUBJECT INDEX